Michael J. Wooldridge
Nicholas R. Jennings (Eds.)

Intelligent Agents

ECAI-94 Workshop on Agent Theories,
Architectures, and Languages
Amsterdam, The Netherlands
August 8-9, 1994
Proceedings

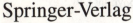

Springer-Verlag

Berlin Heidelberg New York
London Paris Tokyo
Hong Kong Barcelona
Budapest

Series Editors

Jaime G. Carbonell
School of Computer Science
Carnegie Mellon University
Pittsburgh, PA 15213-3891, USA

Jörg Siekmann
University of Saarland
German Research Center for Artificial Intelligence (DFKI)
Stuhlsatzenhausweg 3, D-66123 Saarbrücken, Germany

Volume Editors

Michael J. Wooldridge
Department of Computing, Manchester Metropolitan University
Chester Street, Manchester M1 5GD, United Kingdom

Nicholas R. Jennings
Department of Electronic Engineering, Queen Mary and Westfield College
University of London
Mile End Road, London E1 4NS, United Kingdom

CR Subject Classification (1991): I.2, D.2

ISBN 3-540-58855-8 Springer-Verlag Berlin Heidelberg New York

CIP data applied for

© Springer-Verlag Berlin Heidelberg 1995
Printed in Germany

Typesetting: Camera ready by author
SPIN: 10479243   45/3140-543210 - Printed on acid-free paper

Lecture Notes in Artificial Intelligence 890

Subseries of Lecture Notes in Computer Science
Edited by J. G. Carbonell and J. Siekmann

Lecture Notes in Computer Science

Edited by G. Goos, J. Hartmanis and J. van Leeuwen

Preface

This volume contains revised versions of twenty-four papers that were first presented at the 1994 workshop on Agent Theories, Architectures, and Languages. This workshop was held during the ECAI-94 conference in Amsterdam, the Netherlands, in August 1994. The aim of the workshop was to provide an arena in which researchers working in all areas related to the theoretical and practical aspects of agent synthesis could further extend their understanding and expertise by meeting and exchanging ideas, techniques and results with researchers working in related areas.

The workshop call for papers was divided into three themes:

- THEORIES.
  How do the various components of an agent's cognitive makeup conspire to produce rational behaviour? What is the relationship between these components? What formalisms are appropriate for expressing aspects of agent theory? Do we need logic-based formalisms? If not, is another type of mathematical framework appropriate?
- ARCHITECTURES.
  What structure should an artificial intelligent agent have? Is reactive behaviour enough? Or do we need deliberation as well? How can we integrate reactive and deliberative components cleanly? What is the relationship between an agent theory and architecture? How are we to reason about reactive systems?
- LANGUAGES.
  What are the right primitives for programming an intelligent agent? How are these primitives related to the theory of an agent, or its architecture? Can we realistically hope to execute agent specifications in complex, perhaps multi-modal languages? Should we aim for simple agents, with limited internal complexity, or for agents with complex reasoning abilities?

The articles contained in this volume address each of these aspects of agent technology. It is our belief that the articles are characteristic of the high-quality work being carried out in this area throughout the three continents they represent.

In order to assist the novice reader, and to put the articles in context, the organisers have prepared a survey article, which introduces the main issues in the theory and practice of intelligent agents. This article also includes a glossary of the most important terms used in this new area, an annotated list of some key systems, and an extensive bibliography. An index to the volume is also provided, to facilitate easy reference.

It is our hope that you will find all the articles in this volume both interesting and useful, and that they will act as a stimulus to all researchers working or hoping to work in this fascinating and increasingly significant area.

Mike Wooldridge
Nick Jennings

Workshop Organisation

Organising Committee

Michael Wooldridge (Manchester Metropolitan University, UK)
Nicholas R. Jennings (Queen Mary & Westfield College, UK)

Program Committee

Phil Cohen   (Oregon Graduate Institute of Science & Technology, USA)
Michael Fisher   (Manchester Metropolitan University, UK)
Piotr Gmytrasiewicz (University of Texas at Arlington, USA)
Hans Haugeneder   (Siemens AG, Germany)
Sarit Kraus   (Bar Ilan University, Israel)
Anand Rao   (Australian AI Institute, Australia)
Yoav Shoham   (Stanford University, USA)
Munindar Singh   (Microelectronics and Computer Technology Corporation, USA)

Additional Reviewers

John Bell
Stefan Bussmann
Afsaneh Haddadi
Daniel Mack

Acknowledgements

We are grateful to the ECAI-94 organisers for supporting this workshop, and in particular to Jan Treur and Frances Brazier for their assistance throughout. Thanks also to everyone who attended the workshop and made it such a success.

Contents

Agent Theories, Architectures, and Languages: A Survey

Michael Wooldridge

Department of Computing
Manchester Metropolitan University
Chester Street, Manchester M1 5GD
United Kingdom
M.Wooldridge@doc.mmu.ac.uk

Nicholas R. Jennings

Department of Electronic Engineering
Queen Mary & Westfield College
Mile End Road, London E1 4NS
United Kingdom
N.R.Jennings@qmw.ac.uk

Abstract. The concept of an *agent* has become important in both Artificial Intelligence (AI) and mainstream computer science. In this article, we present a survey of what we perceive to be the most important theoretical and practical issues associated with the design and construction of intelligent agents. The article also includes a short review of current and potential applications of agent technology, and closes with a glossary of key terms, an annotated list of systems, and a detailed bibliography. Pointers to further reading are provided throughout.

1 Introduction

One way of defining AI is by saying that it is the subfield of computer science which aims to construct agents that exhibit aspects of intelligent behaviour. The notion of an 'agent' is thus central to AI. It is perhaps surprising, therefore, that although architectures for intelligent agents have been studied in AI since the inception of the field, the area did not become a major research topic until the late 1980s. Since then, however, there has been an intense flowering of interest in the subject: agents are now widely discussed by researchers in mainstream computer science, as well as those working in data communications, concurrent systems research, robotics, and user interface design. Researchers from both industry and academia are now taking agent technology seriously. Our aim in this article is to survey what we perceive to be the most important issues in the design and construction of intelligent agents. We begin our article, in the following sub-section, with a discussion on the question of exactly what an agent *is*.

1.1 What *is* an Agent?

Carl Hewitt recently remarked[1] that the question *what is an agent?* is embarrassing for the agent-based computing community in just the same way that the question *what is intelligence?* is embarrassing for the mainstream AI community. The problem is that although the term is widely used, by many people working in closely related areas, it

---

[1] At the thirteenth international workshop on distributed AI.

defies attempts to produce a single universally accepted definition. This need not necessarily be a problem: after all, if many people are successfully developing interesting and useful applications, then it hardly matters that they do not agree on potentially trivial terminological details. However, there is also the danger that unless the issue is discussed, 'agent' might become a 'noise' term, subject to both abuse and misuse, to the potential confusion of the research community. It is for this reason that we briefly consider the question.

We distinguish two general usages of the term 'agent': the first is weak, and relatively uncontentious; the second is stronger, and potentially more contentious.

A Weak Notion of Agency: Perhaps the most general way in which the term agent is used is to denote a hardware or (more usually) software-based computer system that enjoys the following properties:

- *autonomy*: agents operate without the direct intervention of humans or others, and have some kind of control over their actions and internal state;
- *social ability*: agents interact with other agents (and possibly humans) via some kind of *agent-communication language* [67];
- *reactivity*: agents perceive their environment, (which may be the physical world, a user via a graphical user interface, a collection of other agents, the INTERNET, or perhaps all of these combined), and respond in a timely fashion to changes that occur in it;
- *pro-activeness*: agents do not simply act in response to their environment, they are able to exhibit goal-directed behaviour by *taking the initiative*.

A simple way of conceptualising an agent is thus as a kind of UNIX-like software process, that exhibits the properties listed above.

A Stronger Notion of Agency: For some researchers — particularly those working in AI — the term 'agent' has a stronger and more specific meaning than that sketched out above. These researchers generally mean an agent to be a computer system that, in addition to having the properties identified above, is either conceptualised or implemented using concepts that are more usually applied to humans. For example, it is quite common in AI to characterise an agent using *mentalistic* notions, such as knowledge, belief, intention, and obligation [176]. Some AI researchers have gone further, and considered *emotional* agents [14, 13]. (Lest the reader suppose that this is just pointless anthropomorphism, it should be noted that there are good arguments in favour of designing and building agents in terms of human-like mental states — see section 2.)

Other Attributes of Agency: Various other attributes are sometimes discussed in the context of agency. For example: *mobility* is the ability of an agent to move around an electronic network [204]; *veracity* is the assumption that an agent will not knowingly communicate false information [64, pp159–164]; *benevolence* is the assumption that agents do not have conflicting goals, and that every agent will therefore always try to do what is asked of it [160, p91]; and *rationality* is (crudely) the assumption that an agent will act in order to achieve its goals, and will not act in such a way as to prevent its goals being achieved — at least insofar as its beliefs permit [64, pp49–54]. (A discussion of various different attributes of agency, along with an attempt to formally define them, appears in [78].)

1.2   The Structure of this Article

Now that we have at least a preliminary understanding of what an agent is, we can embark on a more detailed look at their properties, and how we might go about constructing them. For convenience, we identify three key issues, and structure our survey around these (cf. [169, p1]):

- *Agent theories* are essentially *specifications*. Agent theorists address such questions as: How are we to conceptualise agents? What properties should agents have, and how are we to formally represent and reason about these properties?
- *Agent architectures* represent the move from specification to implementation. Those working in the area of agent architectures address such questions as: How are we to construct computer systems that satisfy the properties specified by agent theorists? What software and/or hardware structures are appropriate? What is an appropriate separation of concerns?
- *Agent languages* are programming languages that may embody the various principles proposed by theorists. Those working in the area of agent languages address such questions as: How are we to program agents? What are the right primitives for this task? How are we to effectively compile or execute agent programs?

The issue of agent theories is discussed in the section 2. In section 3, we discuss architectures, and in section 4, we discuss agent languages. A brief discussion of applications appears in section 5, and some concluding remarks appear in section 6. Appendix A provides a glossary of key terms, and an annotated list of key systems appears in Appendix B.

Finally, a note on the scope of the article. It is important to realise that we are writing very much from the point of view of AI, and the material we have chosen to review reflects this. Also, the article is *not* a review of Distributed AI, although the material we discuss arguably falls under this banner. We have deliberately avoided discussing topics that are the domain of classical DAI (such as cooperation protocols, cooperative problem solving, and so on); for reviews of this area, see [17, pp1–56] and [30].

2   Agent Theories

In the preceding section, we gave an informal overview of the notion of agency. In this section, we turn our attention to the *theory* of such agents, and in particular, to *formal* theories. We regard an agent theory as a specification for an agent; agent theorists develop formalisms for representing the properties of agents, and using these formalisms, try to develop theories that capture desirable properies of agents. Our starting point is the notion of an agent as an entity 'which appears to be the subject of beliefs, desires, etc.' [169, p1]. The philosopher Dennett has coined the term *intentional system* to denote such systems.

2.1   Agents as Intentional Systems

When explaining human activity, it is often useful to make statements such as the following:

> Janine took her umbrella because she *believed* it was going to rain.
> Michael worked hard because he *wanted* to possess a PhD.

These statements make use of a *folk psychology*, by which human behaviour is predicted and explained through the attribution of *attitudes*, such as believing and wanting (as in the above examples), hoping, fearing, and so on. This folk psychology is well established: most people reading the above statements would say they found their meaning entirely clear, and would not give them a second glance.

The attitudes employed in such folk psychological descriptions are called the *intentional* notions. The philosopher Daniel Dennett has coined the term *intentional system* to describe entities 'whose behaviour can be predicted by the method of attributing belief, desires and rational acumen' [44, p49]. Dennett identifies different 'grades' of intentional system:

> 'A *first-order* intentional system has beliefs and desires (etc.) but no beliefs and desires *about* beliefs and desires. ... A *second-order* intentional system is more sophisticated; it has beliefs and desires (and no doubt other intentional states) about beliefs and desires (and other intentional states) — both those of others and its own'. [44, p243]

One can carry on this hierarchy of intentionality as far as required. What objects can be described by this *intentional stance*? As it turns out, more or less anything can. In his doctoral thesis, Seel showed that even very simple, automata-like objects can be consistently ascribed intentional descriptions [169]; similar work by Rosenschein and Kaelbling, (albeit with a different motivation), arrived at a similar conclusion [162]. And yet intentional stance descriptions of very simple systems, (such as, for example, a light switch), seem infantile. Why is this? The answer seems to be that while the intentional stance description is perfectly consistent with the observed behaviour of a light switch, and is internally consistent,

> '... it does not *buy us anything*, since we essentially understand the mechanism sufficiently to have a simpler, mechanistic description of its behaviour'. [175, p6]

Put crudely, the more we know about a system, the less we need to rely on animistic, intentional explanations of its behaviour. However, with very complex systems, even if a complete, accurate picture of the system's architecture and working *is* available, a mechanistic, *design stance* explanation of its behaviour may not be practicable. The intentional notions are thus *abstraction tools*, which provide us with a convenient and familiar way of describing, explaining, and predicting the behaviour of complex systems.

So, an agent is a system that is most conveniently described by the intentional stance; one whose simplest consistent description requires the intentional stance. Before proceeding, it is worth considering exactly which attitudes are appropriate for representing agents. For the purposes of this survey, the two most important categories are *information attitudes* and *pro-attitudes*:

$$
\text{information attitudes} \left\{ \begin{array}{l} \text{belief} \\ \text{knowledge} \end{array} \right. \qquad \text{pro-attitudes} \left\{ \begin{array}{l} \text{desire} \\ \text{intention} \\ \text{obligation} \\ \text{commitment} \\ \text{choice} \\ \dots \end{array} \right.
$$

Thus, information attitudes are related to the information that an agent has about the world it occupies, whereas pro-attitudes are those that in some way guide the agent's actions. Precisely which *combination* of attitudes is most appropriate to characterise an agent is, as we shall see later, an issue of some debate. However, it seems reasonable to suggest that an agent must be represented in terms of at least one information attitude, and at least one pro-attitude. Note that pro- and information attitudes are closely linked, as a rational agent will make choices and form intentions, etc., on the basis of the information it has about the world. Much work in agent theory is concerned with sorting out exactly what the relationship between the different attitudes is.

2.2 Representing Intentional Notions

Suppose one wishes to reason about intentional notions in a logical framework. Consider the following statement (after [68, pp210–211]):

Janine believes Cronos is the father of Zeus. (1)

A naive attempt to translate (1) into first-order logic might result in the following:

Bel(Janine, Father(Zeus, Cronos)) (2)

Unfortunately, this naive translation does not work, for two reasons. The first is syntactic: the second argument to the *Bel* predicate is a *formula* of first-order logic, and is not, therefore, a term. So (2) is not a well-formed formula of classical first-order logic. The second problem is semantic, and is potentially more serious. The constants *Zeus* and *Jupiter*, by any reasonable interpretation, denote the same individual: the supreme deity of the classical world. It is therefore acceptable to write, in first-order logic:

(Zeus = Jupiter). (3)

Given (2) and (3), the standard rules of first-order logic would allow the derivation of the following:

Bel(Janine, Father(Jupiter, Cronos)) (4)

But intuition rejects this derivation as invalid: believing that the father of Zeus is Cronos is *not* the same as believing that the father of Jupiter is Cronos. So what is the problem? Why does first-order logic fail here? The problem is that the intentional notions — such as belief and desire — are *referentially opaque*, in that they set up *opaque contexts*, in which the standard substitution rules of first-order logic do not apply. Clearly, classical logics are not suitable in their standard form for reasoning about intentional notions: alternative formalisms are required.

The number of basic techniques used for alternative formalisms is quite small. Recall, from the discussion above, that there are two problems to be addressed in developing a logical formalism for intentional notions: a syntactic one, and a semantic one. It follows that any formalism can be characterized in terms of two independent attributes: its *language of formulation*, and its *semantic model* [111, p83].

There are two fundamental approaches to the syntactic problem. The first is to use a *modal* language, which contains non-truth-functional *modal operators*, which are applied to formulae. An alternative approach involves the use of a *meta-language*: a many-sorted first-order language containing terms that denote formulae of some other *object-language*. Intentional notions can be represented using a meta-language predicate, and given whatever axiomatization is deemed appropriate.

As with the syntactic problem, there are two basic approaches to the semantic problem. The first, best-known, and probably most widely used approach is to adopt a *possible worlds* semantics, where an agent's beliefs, knowledge, goals, and so on, are characterized as a set of so-called *possible worlds*, with an *accessibility relation* holding between them. Possible worlds semantics have an associated *correspondence theory* that makes them an attractive mathematical tool to work with [32]. However, they also have many associated difficulties, notably the well-known *logical omniscience* problem, which implies that agents are perfect reasoners. A number of variations on the possible-worlds theme have been proposed, in an attempt to retain the correspondence theory, but without logical omniscience. The commonest alternative to the possible worlds model for belief is to use a *sentential*, or *interpreted symbolic structures* approach. In this scheme, beliefs are viewed as symbolic formulae explicitly represented in a data structure associated with an agent [111].

2.3 Possible Worlds Semantics

The possible worlds model for logics of knowledge and belief was originally proposed by Hintikka [96], and is now most commonly formulated in a normal modal logic using the techniques developed by Kripke [115][2]. Hintikka's insight was to see that an agent's beliefs could be characterized as a set of *possible worlds*, in the following way. Consider an agent playing a card game such as poker[3]. In this game, the more one knows about the cards possessed by one's opponents, the better one is able to play. And yet complete knowledge of an opponent's cards is generally impossible, (if one excludes cheating).

---

[2] In Hintikka's original work, he used a technique based on 'model sets', which is equivalent to Kripke's formalism, though less elegant. See [98, pp351–352] for a comparison and discussion of the two techniques.

[3] This example was adapted from [86].

The ability to play poker well thus depends, at least in part, on the ability to deduce what cards are held by an opponent, given the limited information available. Now suppose our agent possessed the ace of spades. Assuming the agent's sensory equipment was functioning normally, it would be rational of her to believe that she possessed this card. Now suppose she were to try to deduce what cards were held by her opponents. This could be done by first calculating all the various different ways that the cards in the pack could possibly have been distributed among the various players. (This is not being proposed as an actual card playing strategy, but for illustration!) For argument's sake, suppose that each possible configuration is described on a separate piece of paper. Once the process was complete, our agent can then begin to systematically eliminate from this large pile of paper all those configurations which are *not possible, given what she knows*. For example, any configuration in which she did not possess the ace of spades could be rejected immediately as impossible. Call each piece of paper remaining after this process a *world*. Each world represents one state of affairs considered possible, given what she knows. Hintikka coined the term *epistemic alternatives* to describe the worlds possible given one's beliefs. Something true in *all* our agent's epistemic alternatives could be said to be believed by the agent. For example, it will be true in all our agent's epistemic alternatives that she has the ace of spades.

On a first reading, this seems a peculiarly roundabout way of characterizing belief, but it has two advantages. First, it remains neutral on the subject of the cognitive structure of agents. It certainly doesn't posit any internalized collection of possible worlds. It is just a convenient way of characterizing belief. Second, the mathematical theory associated with the formalization of possible worlds is extremely appealing [32].

Unfortunately, these *normal modal* formulations of belief and knowledge have some serious disadvantages. Chief among these is the so-called *logical omniscience* problem. Crudely, this problem is that such logics predict that agents believe all the logical cosequences of their beliefs. Clearly, this prediction is unreasonable for any resource bounded agent — and all real systems are resource bounded. Agents generally believe *some* of the logical consequences of their beliefs; they do not believe all the logically possible ones [111].

2.4 Alternatives to the Possible Worlds Model

As a result of the difficulties with logical omniscience, many researchers have attempted to develop alternative formalisms for representing belief.

Levesque — belief and awareness: In a 1984 paper, Levesque proposed a solution to the logical omniscience problem that involves making a distinction between *explicit* and *implicit* belief [118]. Crudely, the idea is that an agent has a relatively small set of explicit beliefs, and a very much larger (infinite) set of implicit beliefs, which includes the logical consequences of the explicit beliefs. A number of objections have been raised to Levesque's model [157, p135]: first, it does not allow quantification — this drawback has been rectified by Lakemeyer [116]; second, it does not seem to allow for nested beliefs; third, the notion of a situation, which underlies Levesque's logic is, if anything, more mysterious than the notion of a world in possible worlds; and fourth, under certain circumstances, Levesque's proposal still makes unrealistic predictions about agent's reasoning capabilities.

In an effort to recover from this last negative result, Fagin and Halpern have developed a 'logic of general awareness', based on a similar idea to Levesque's but with a very much simpler semantics [55]. However, this proposal has itself been criticised by some [112].

Konolige — the deduction model: A more radical approach to modelling resource bounded believers was proposed by Konolige [111]. His *deduction model of belief* is, in essence, a direct attempt to model the 'beliefs' of symbolic AI systems. Konolige observed that a typical knowledge-based system has two key components: a database of symbolically represented 'beliefs', (which may take the form of rules, frames, semantic nets, or, more generally, formulae in some logical language), and some logically incomplete inference mechanism. A belief logic was then developed, with the semantics to belief connectives given in terms of these structures: an agent believes ϕ if ϕ can be derived from its base beliefs using its deduction mechanism. Konolige went on to examine the properties of the deduction model at some length, and developed a variety of proof methods for his logics, including resolution and tableau systems [66]. The deduction model is undoubtedly simple; however, as a direct model of the belief systems of AI agents, it has much to commend it.

2.5   Meta-languages and syntactic modalities:

A meta-language is one in which it is possible to represent the properties of another language. A first-order meta-language is a first-order logic, with the standard predicates, quantifiers, terms, and so on, whose domain contains formulae of some other language, called the *object* language. Using a meta-language, it is possible to represent a relationship between a meta-language term denoting an agent, and an object language term denoting some formula. For example, the meta-language formula $Bel(Janine, \ulcorner Father(Zeus, Cronos) \urcorner)$ might be used to represent the example (1) that we saw earlier. The quote marks, $\ulcorner ... \urcorner$, are used to indicate that their contents are a meta-language term denoting the corresponding object-language formula.

Unfortunately, meta-language formalisms have their own package of problems, not the least of which is that they tend to fall prey to inconsistency [132, 190]. However, there have been some fairly successful meta-language formalisms, including those by Konolige [110], Haas [82], Morgenstern [134], and Davies [41]. Some results on retrieving consistency appeared in the late 1980s [145, 146, 45, 191].

2.6   Pro-attitudes: Goals and Desires

An obvious approach to developing a logic of goals or desires is to adapt possible worlds semantics — see, e.g., [36, 209]. In this view, each goal-accessible world represents one way the world might be if the agent's goals were realised. However, this approach falls prey to the *side effect* problem, in that it predicts that agents have a goal of the logical consequences of their goals (cf. the logical omniscience problem, discussed above).

This is not a desirable property: one might have a goal of going to the dentist, with the necessary consequence of suffering pain, without having a goal of suffering pain. The problem is discussed, (in the context of intentions), in [19]. The basic possible worlds model has been adapted by some researchers in an attempt to overcome this problem [195]. Other, related semantics for goals have been proposed [48, 109, 152].

2.7 Theories of Agency

All of the formalisms considered so far have focussed on just one aspect of agency. However, it is to be expected that a realistic agent theory will be represented in a logical framework that *combines* these various components. Additionally, we expect an agent logic to be capable of representing the *dynamic* aspects of agency. A complete agent theory, expressed in a logic with these properties, must define how the attributes of agency are related. For example, it will need to show how an agent's information and pro-attitudes are related; how an agent's cognitive state changes over time; how the environment affects an agent's cognitive state; and how an agent's information and pro-attitudes lead it to perform actions. Giving a good account of these relationships is the most significant problem faced by agent theorists.

An all-embracing agent theory is some time off, and yet significant steps have been taken towards it. In the following subsections, we briefly review some of this work.

Moore — knowledge and action: Moore was in many ways a pioneer of the use of logics for capturing aspects of agency [133]. His main concern was the study of *knowledge pre-conditions for actions* — the question of what an agent needs to know in order to be able to perform some action. He formalised a model of *ability* in a logic containing a modality for knowledge, and a dynamic logic-like apparatus for modelling action (cf. [89]). This formalism allowed for the possibility of an agent having incomplete information about how to achieve some goal, and performing actions in order to find out how to achieve it. Critiques of the formalism (and attempts to improve on it) may be found in [134, 117].

Cohen and Levesque — intention: One of the best-known and most influential contributions to the area of agent theory is due to Cohen and Levesque [36]. Their formalism was originally used to develop a theory of intention (as in 'I intend to…'), which the authors required as a pre-requisite for a theory of speech acts [37]. However, the logic has subsequently proved to be so useful for reasoning about agents that it has been used in an analysis of conflict and cooperation in multi-agent dialogue [64, 63], as well as several studies in the theoretical foundations of cooperative problem solving [119, 100, 26, 28]. A critique of Cohen and Levesque's theory of intention may be found in [180].

Rao and Georgeff — belief, desire, intention architectures: As we observed earlier, there is no clear consensus in either the AI or philosophy communities about precisely which combination of information and pro-attitudes are best suited to characterising rational agents. In the work of Cohen and Levesque, described above, just two basic attitudes were used: beliefs and goals. Further attitudes, such as intention, were defined in terms of these. In related work, Rao and Georgeff have developed a logical framework for agent theory based on three primitive modalities: beliefs, desires, and intentions [152, 151, 155]. Their formalism is based on a branching model of time, (cf. [51]), in which belief-, desire- and intention-accessible worlds are themselves branching time structures. In other work, they also consider the potential for adding (social) plans to their formalism [154, 108].

Singh: A quite different approach to modelling agents was taken by Singh, who has developed an interesting family of logics for representing intentions, beliefs, knowledge, know-how, and communication in a branching-time framework [177, 178, 182, 179]; these articles are collected and expanded in [181]. Singh's formalism is extremely rich, and considerable effort has been devoted to establishing its properties. However, its complexity prevents a detailed discussion here.

Werner: In an extensive sequence of papers, Werner has laid the foundations of a general model of agency, which draws upon work in economics, game theory, situated automata theory, situation semantics, and philosophy [200, 201, 202, 203]. At the time of writing, however, the properties of this model have not been investigated in depth.

Wooldridge — modelling multi-agent systems: For his 1992 doctoral thesis, Wooldridge developed a family of logics for representing the properties of multi-agent systems [208, 211]. Unlike the approaches cited above, Wooldridge's aim was not to develop a general framework for agent theory. Rather, he hoped to construct formalisms that might be used in the specification and verification of realistic multi-agent systems. To this end, he developed a simple, and in some sense generic model of multi-agent systems, and showed how the histories traced out in the execution of such a system could be used as the semantic foundation for a family of both linear and branching time temporal belief logics. He then gave examples of how these logics could be used in the specification and verification of protocols for cooperative action.

2.8 Social Aspects

Formalisms for representing communication in agent theory have tended to be based on *speech act theory*, as originated by Austin [8], and further developed by Searle [168] and others [38, 36]. Briefly, the key axiom of speech act theory is that communicative utterances are *actions*, in just the sense that physical actions are. They are performed by a speaker with the intention of bringing about a desired change in the world: typically, the speaker intends to bring about some particular mental state in a listener. Speech acts may *fail* in the same way that physical actions may fail: a listener generally has control over her mental state, and cannot be guaranteed to react in the way that the speaker intends.

Although not directly based on work in speech acts, (and arguably more to do with architectures than theories), we shall here mention work on *agent communication languages* [67]. The best known work on agent communication languages is that by the ARPA knowledge sharing effort [144]. This work has been largely devoted to developing two related languages: the knowledge query and manipulation language (KQML) and the knowledge interchange format (KIF). KQML provides the agent designer with a standard syntax for messages, and a number of *performatives* that define the *force* of a message. Example performatives include *tell*, *perform*, and *reply*; the inspiration for these message types comes largely from speech act theory. KIF provides a syntax for message *content* — KIF is essentially the first-order predicate calculus, recast in a LISP-like syntax.

2.9 Comments and Further Reading

For a detailed discussion of intentionality and the intentional stance, see [43, 44]. A number of papers on AI treatments of agency may be found in [5]. For an introduction to modal logic, see [32]; a slightly older, though more wide ranging introduction, may be found in [98]. As for the use of modal logics to model knowledge and belief, see [87], which includes complexity results and proof procedures. Related work on modelling knowledge has been done by the distributed systems community, who give the worlds in possible worlds semantics a precise interpretation; for an introduction and further references, see [86, 56]. Overviews of formalisms for modelling belief and knowledge may be found in [85, 111, 156, 208]. A variant on the possible worlds framework, called the *recursive modelling method*, is described in [75]; a deep theory of belief may be found in [121]. *Situation semantics*, developed in the early 1980s and recently the subject of renewed interest, represent a fundamentally new approach to modelling the world and cognitive systems [12, 46]. However, situation semantics are not (yet) in the mainstream of (D)AI, and it is not obvious what impact the paradigm will ultimately have.

Logics which integrate time with mental states are discussed in [114, 88, 212]; the last of these presents a tableau-based proof method for a temporal belief logic. Two other important references for temporal aspects are [173, 174]. Thomas has developed some logics for representing agent theories as part of her framework for agent programming languages; see [189, 187] and section 4. For an introduction to temporal logics and related topics, see [76, 50]. A non-formal discussion of intention may be found in [18], or more briefly [19]. Further work on modelling intention may be found in [80, 165, 77, 113]. Related work, focussing less on single-agent attitudes, and more on social aspects, is [101, 209, 213].

Finally, although we have not discussed formalisms for reasoning about action here, we suggested above that an agent logic would need to incorporate some mechanism for representing agent's actions. Our reason for avoiding the topic is simply that the field is so big, it deserves a whole review in its own right. Good starting points for AI treatments of action are [4, 5, 6]. Other treatments of action in agent logics are based on formalisms borrowed from mainstream computer science, notably dynamic logic (originally developed to reason about computer programs) [89]. The logic of *seeing to it that* has been discussed in the formal philosophy literature, but has yet to impact on (D)AI [16, 147, 15, 170].

3   Agent Architectures

Until now, this article has been concerned with agent theory — the construction of formalisms for reasoning about agents, and the properties of agents expressed in such formalisms. Our aim in this section is to shift the emphasis from theory to practice. We consider the issues surrounding the construction of computer systems that satisfy the properties specified by agent theorists. This is the area of *agent architectures*. The classical approach to building agents is to view them as a particular type of knowledge-based system. This paradigm is known as *symbolic AI*: we begin our review of architectures with a look at this paradigm, and the assumptions that underpin it.

3.1   Classical Approaches: Deliberative Architectures

The foundation upon which the symbolic AI paradigm rests is the *physical-symbol system hypothesis*, formulated by Newell and Simon [141]. A physical symbol system is defined to be a physically realizable set of physical entities (symbols) that can be combined to form structures, and which is capable of running processes that operate on those symbols according to symbolically coded sets of instructions. The physical-symbol system hypothesis then says that such a system is capable of general intelligent action.

It is a short step from the notion of a physical symbol system to McCarthy's dream of a *sentential processing automaton*, or *deliberative agent*. (The term 'deliberative agent' seems to have derived from Genesereth's use of the term 'deliberate agent' to mean a specific type of symbolic architecture [68, pp325–327].) We define a deliberative agent or agent architecture to be one that contains an explicitly represented, symbolic model of the world, and in which decisions (for example about what actions to perform) are made via logical (or at least pseudo-logical) reasoning, based on pattern matching and symbolic manipulation. The idea of deliberative agents based on purely logical reasoning is highly seductive: to get an agent to realise some theory of agency one might naively suppose that it is enough to simply give it logical representation of this theory and 'get it to *do a bit of theorem proving*' [172, section 3.2].

This approach, theoretically attractive though it is, seems very hard to achieve in practice. The underlying problem seems to be the difficulty of theorem proving in even very simple logics, but more generally, the computational complexity of symbol manipulation in general: recall that first-order logic is not even *decidable*, and modal extensions to it (including representations of belief, desire, time, and so on) tend to be *highly* undecidable. Even if one rejects a purely logical approach, one still finds that some key problems (such as planning — see below) appear to be intractable. It is because of these problems that some researchers have looked to alternative techniques for building agents; such alternatives are discussed in section 3.2. First, however, we consider efforts made within the symbolic AI community to construct agents.

Planning agents: Since the early 1970s, the AI planning community has been closely concerned with the design of artificial agents; in fact, it seems reasonable to claim that most innovations in agent design have come from this community. Planning is essentially automatic programming: the design of a course of action that, when executed, will result in the achievement of some desired goal. Within the symbolic AI community, it has long been assumed that some form of AI planning system will be a central component of any artificial agent.

Perhaps the best-know early planning system was STRIPS [59]. This system takes a symbolic descripion of both the world and a desired goal state, and a set of action descriptions, which characterise the pre- and post-conditions associated with various actions. It then attempts to find a sequence of actions that will achieve the goal, by using a simple means-ends analysis, which essentially involves matching the post-conditions of actions against the desired goal. The STRIPS planning algorithm was very simple, and proved to be ineffective on problems of even moderate complexity. Much effort was subsequently devoted to developing more effective techniques. Two major innovations were *hierarchical* and *non-linear* planning [163, 164]. However, in the mid 1980s, Chapman established some theoretical results which indicate that even such refined techniques will ultimately turn out to be unusable in any time-constrained system [31]. These results have had a profound influence on subsequent AI planning research; perhaps more than any other, they have caused some researchers to question the whole symbolic AI paradigm, and have thus led to the work on alternative approaches that we discuss in section 3.2.

In spite of these difficulties, various attempts have been made to construct agents whose primary component is a planner. For example: the Integrated Planning, Execution and Monitoring (IPEM) system is based on a sophisticated non-linear planner [7]; Wood's AUTODRIVE system has planning agents operating in a highly dynamic environment (a traffic simulation) [207]; Etzioni has built 'softbots' that can plan and act in a UNIX environment [53]; and finally, Cohen's PHEONIX system includes planner-based agents that operate in the domain of simulated forest fire management [35].

Bratman, Israel and Pollack — IRMA: In section 2, we saw that some researchers have considered frameworks for agent theory based on beliefs, desires, and intentions [152]. Some researchers have also developed agent architectures based on these attitudes. One example is the *Intelligent Resource-bounded Machine Architecture* (IRMA) [20]. This architecture has four key symbolic data structures: a plan library, and explicit representations of beliefs, desires, and intentions. Additionally, the architecture has: a reasoner, for reasoning about the world; a means-ends analyser, for determining which plans might be used to achieve the agent's intentions; an *opportunity analyser*, which monitors the environment in order to determine further options for the agent; a *filtering process*; and a *deliberation process*. The filtering process is responsible for determining the subset of the agent's potential courses of action that have the property of being consistent with the agent's current intentions. The choice between competing options is made by the deliberation process. The IRMA architecture has been evaluated in an experimental scenario known as the *Tileworld* [150].

Vere and Bickmore — HOMER: An interesting experiment in the design of intelligent agents was conducted by Vere and Bickmore [193]. They argued that the enabling technologies for intelligent agents are sufficiently developed to be able to construct a prototype autonomous agent, with linguistic ability, planning and acting capabilities, and so on. They developed such an agent, and christened it HOMER. This agent is a simulated robot submarine, which exists in a two-dimensional 'Seaworld', about which it has only partial knowledge. HOMER takes instructions from a user in a limited subset of English with about an 800 word vocabulary; instructions can contain moderately sophisticated temporal references. HOMER can plan how to achieve its instructions, (which typically relate to collecting and moving items around the Seaworld), and can then execute its plans, modifying them as required during execution. The agent has a limited *episodic memory*, and using this, is able to answer questions about its past experiences.

Jennings — GRATE*: GRATE* is a layered architecture in which the behaviour of an agent is guided by the mental attitudes of beliefs, desires, intentions, and joint intentions [102]. Agents are divided into two distinct parts: a domain level system and a cooperation and control layer. The former solves problems for the organisation; be it in the domain of industrial control, finance or transportation. The latter is a meta-level controller which operates on the domain level system with the aim of ensuring that the agent's domain level activities are coordinated with those of others within the community. The cooperation layer is composed of three generic modules: a control module which interfaces to the domain level system, a situation assessment module and a cooperation module. The assessment and cooperation modules provide an implementation of a model of joint responsibility [100], which specifies how agents should act both locally and towards other agents whilst engaged in cooperative problem solving. The performance of a GRATE* community has been evaluated against agents which only have individual intentions, and agents which behave in a selfish manner, in the domain of electricity transportation management. A significant improvment was noted when the situation became complex and dynamic [103].

3.2 Alternative Approaches: Reactive Architectures

As we observed above, there are many unsolved (some would say insoluble) problems associated with symbolic AI. These problems have led some researchers to question the viability of the whole paradigm, and to the development of what are generally know as *reactive* architectures. For our purposes, we shall define a reactive architecture to be one that does not include any kind of central symbolic world model, and does not use complex symbolic reasoning.

Brooks — behaviour languages: Possibly the most vocal critic of the symbolic AI notion of agency has been Rodney Brooks, a researcher at MIT who apparently became frustrated by AI approaches to building control mechanisms for autonomous mobile robots. In a 1985 paper, he outlined an alternative architecture for building agents, the so called *subsumption architecture* [21]. A subsumption architecture is a hierarchy of task-accomplishing *behaviours*. Each behaviour 'competes' with others to exercise control over the robot. Lower layers represent more primitive kinds of be-haviour, (such as avoiding obstacles), and have precedence over layers further up the hierarchy. It should be stressed that the resulting systems are, in terms of the amount of computation they need to do, *extremely* simple, with no explicit reasoning, or even pattern matching, of the kind found in symbolic AI systems. But despite this simpli-city, Brooks has demonstrated the robots doing tasks that would be impressive if they were accomplished by symbolic AI systems. Similar work has been reported by Steels, who described simulations of 'Mars explorer' systems, containing a large number of subsumption-architecture agents, that can achieve near-optimal performance in certain tasks [186].

Agre and Chapman — PENGI: Agre observed that most everyday activity is 'routine' in the sense that it requires little — if any — new abstract reasoning. Most tasks, once learned, can be accomplished in a routine way, with little variation. Agre proposed that an efficient agent architecture could be based on the idea of 'running arguments'. Crudely, the idea is that as most decisions are routine, they can be encoded into a low-level structure (such as a digital circuit), which only needs periodic updating, perhaps to handle new kinds of problems. His approach was illustrated with the celebrated PENGI system [3]. PENGI is a simulated computer game, with the central character controlled using a scheme such as that outlined above.

Rosenschein and Kaelbling — situated automata: Another sophisticated approach is that of Rosenschein and Kaelbling [161, 162, 107, 106]. In their *situated automata* paradigm, an agent is specified in declarative terms. This specification is then compiled down to a digital machine, which satisfies the declarative specification. This digital machine can operate in a provably time-bounded fashion; it does not do any symbol manipulation, and in fact no symbolic expressions are represented in the machine at all. The situated automata paradigm has attracted much interest, as it appears to combine the best elements of both reactive and symbolic, declarative systems. However, at the time of writing, the theoretical limitations of the approach are not well understood; there are similarities with the automatic synthesis of programs from temporal logic specifications, a complex area of much ongoing work in mainstream computer science (see the comments in [50]).

Maes — Agent Network Architecture: Pattie Maes has developed an agent architec-ture in which an agent is defined as a set of *competence modules* [122, 124, 125]. These modules loosely resemble the behaviours of Brooks' subsumption architecture (above). There are some similarities between the agent network architecture and neural network architectures. Perhaps the key difference is that it is difficult to say what the meaning of a node in a neural net is; it only has a meaning in the context of the net itself. As competence modules are defined in declarative terms, however, it is very much easier to say what their meaning is.

3.3 Hybrid Architectures

Many researchers have suggested that neither a completely deliberative nor completely reactive approach is suitable for building agents. They have argued the case for *hybrid* systems, which attempt to marry classical and alternative approaches.

Georgeff and Lansky — PRS: One of the best-known agent architectures is the *Procedural Reasoning System* (PRS), developed by Georgeff and Lansky [73]. Like IRMA, (see above), the PRS is a belief-desire-intention architecture, which includes a plan library, as well as explicit symbolic representations of beliefs, desires, and intentions. Beliefs are facts, either about the external world or the system's internal state, and are expressed in classical first-order logic. Desires are represented as *system behaviours* (rather than as static representations of goal states). A PRS plan library contains a set of partially-elaborated plans, called *knowledge areas* (KAs), each of which is associated with an *invocation condition*. This condition determines when the KA is to be *activated*. KAs may be activated in a goal-driven or data-driven fashion; KAs may also be *reactive*, allowing the PRS to respond rapidly to changes in its environment. The set of currently active KAs in a system represent its *intentions*. These various data structures are manipulated by a *system interpreter*, which is responsible for updating beliefs, invoking KAs, and executing actions. The PRS has been evaluated in a simulation of maintenance procedures for the space shuttle, as well as other domains [71].

Ferguson — TOURINGMACHINES: For his 1992 Doctoral thesis, Ferguson developed the TOURINGMACHINES hybrid agent architecture [58, 57]. The architecture consists of *perception* and *action* subsystems, which interface directly with the agent's environment, and three *control layers*, embedded in a *control framework*, which mediates between the layers. Each layer is an independent, activity-producing, concurrently executing process.

The *reactive layer* generates potential courses of action in response to events that happen too quickly for other layers to deal with. The *planning layer* constructs plans and selects actions to execute in order to achieve the agent's goals. The *modelling layer* contains symbolic representations of the cognitive state of other entities in the agent's environment. These models are manipulated in order to identify and resolve *goal conflicts* — situations where an agent can no longer achieve its goals, as a result of unexpected interference. The three layers are able to communicate with each other (via message passing), and are embedded in a control framework. The purpose of this framework is to mediate between the layers, and in particular, to deal with conflicting action proposals from the different layers.

Burmeister et al. — COSY: The COSY architecture is a hybrid BDI-architecture that includes elements of both the PRS and IRMA, and was developed specifically for a multi-agent testbed called DASEDIS [24, 83]. The architecture has five main components: (i) sensors; (ii) actuators; (iii) communications; (iv) cognition; and (v) intention. The key component is cognition, which is responsible for mediating between the intentions of the agent and its beliefs about the world, and choosing an appropriate action to perform.

Within the cognition component is a knowledge base containing the agent's beliefs, and three procedural components: a *script execution* component, a *protocol execution* component, and a *reasoning, deciding, and reacting* component. A script is very much like a script in Schank's original sense: it is a stereotypical recipe or plan for achieving a goal. Protocols are stereotypical dialogues representing cooperation frameworks such as the contract net [184]. The reasoning, deciding, and reacting component is perhaps the key component in COSY. It is made up of a number of other subsystems, and is structured rather like the PRS and IRMA (see above). An *agenda* is maintained, that contains a number of active scripts. These scripts may be invoked in a goal-driven fashion (to satisfy one of the agent's intentions), or a data-driven fashion (in response to the agent's current situation). A *filter* component chooses between competing scripts for execution.

Müller *et al.* — INTERRAP: INTERRAP, like Ferguson's TOURINGMACHINES, is a layered architecture, with each successive layer representing a higher level of abstraction than the one below it [139, 140, 138]. In INTERRAP, these layers are further subdivided into two vertical layers: one containing layers of knowledge bases, the other containing various control components, that interact with the knowledge bases at their level. At the lowest level is the *world interface* control component, and the corresponding *world model* knowledge base. The world interface component, as its name suggests, manages the interface between the agent and its environment, and thus deals with acting, communicating, and perception.

Above the world interface component is the *behaviour-based* component. The purpose of this component is to implement and control the basic reactive capability of the agent. Above the behaviour-based component in INTERRAP is the *plan-based component*. The highest layer in INTERRAP is the *cooperation component*.

3.4 Comments and Further Reading

Most introductory textbooks on AI discuss the physical symbol system hypothesis; a good recent example of such a text is [74]. A detailed discussion of the way that this hypothesis has affected thinking in symbolic AI is provided in [172]. There are many objections to the symbolic AI paradigm, in addition to those we have outlined above. Again, introductory textbooks provide the stock criticisms and replies.

There is a wealth of material on planning and planning agents. See [70] for an overview of the state of the art in planning (as it was in 1987), [5] for a thorough collection of papers on planning, (many of the papers cited above are included), and [205] for a detailed description of SIPE, a sophisticated planning system used in a real-world application (the control of a brewery!) Another important collection of planning papers is [72]. The book by Dean and Wellman and the book by Allen *et al.* contain much useful related material [42, 6]. There is now a regular international conference on planning; the proceedings of the first were published as [93].

The collection of papers edited by Maes [123] contains many interesting papers on alternatives to the symbolic AI paradigm. Kaelbling [105] presents a clear discussion of the issues associated with developing resource-bounded rational agents, and proposes an agent architecture somewhat similar to that developed by Brooks. A proposal by Nilsson for *teleo reactive programs* — goal directed programs that nevertheless respond to their environment — is described in [142]. The proposal draws heavily on the situated automata paradigm; other work based on this paradigm is described in [175, 109]. Schoppers has proposed compiling plans in advance, using traditional planning techniques, in order to develop *universal plans*, which are essentially decision trees that can be used to efficiently determine an appropriate action in any situation [166]. Another proposal for building 'reactive planners' involves the use of *reactive action packages* [60].

Other hybrid architectures are described in [47, 9, 25, 29, 131].

4 Agent Languages

By an *agent language*, we mean a system that allows one to program hardware or software computer systems in terms of some of the concepts developed by agent theorists. At the very least, we expect such a language to include some structure corresponding to an agent. However, we might also expect to see some other attributes of agency (beliefs, goals, or other mentalistic notions) used to program agents.

Concurrent Object Languages: Concurrent object languages are in many respects the ancestors of agent languages. The notion of a self-contained, concurrently executing object, with some internal state that is not directly accessible to the outside world, and responding to messages from other such objects, is very close to the concept of an agent as we have defined it. The earliest concurrent object framework was Hewitt's Actor model [95, 1]; another well-known example is the ABCL system [215]. For a discussion on the relationship between agents and concurrent object programming, see [65].

Shoham — agent-oriented programming: Yoav Shoham has proposed a 'new programming paradigm, based on a societal view of computation' [175, p4],[176]. The key idea that informs this *agent-oriented programming* (AOP) paradigm is that of directly programming agents in terms of the mentalistic, intentional notions that agent theorists have developed to represent the properties of agents. The motivation behind such a proposal is that, as we observed in section 2, humans use the intentional stance as an *abstraction* mechanism for representing the properties of complex systems. In the same way that we use the intentional stance to describe humans, it might be useful to use the intentional stance to program machines.

Shoham proposes that a fully developed AOP system will have three components:

- a logical system for defining the mental state of agents;
- an interpreted programming language for programming agents;
- an 'agentification' process, for compiling agent programs into low-level executable systems.

At the time of writing, Shoham has only published results on the first two components. (In [175, p12] he wrote that 'the third is still somewhat mysterious to me', though later in the paper he indicated that he was thinking along the lines of Rosenschein and Kaelbling's situated automata paradigm [162].) Shoham's first attempt at an AOP language was the AGENT0 system. The logical component of this system is a quantified multimodal logic, allowing direct reference to time. No semantics are given, but the logic appears to be based on [189]. The logic contains three modalities: belief, commitment and ability.

Corresponding to the logic is the AGENT0 programming language. In this language, an agent is specified in terms of a set of capabilities (things the agent can do), a set of initial beliefs and commitments, and a set of *commitment rules*. The key component, which determines how the agent acts, is the commitment rule set. Each commitment rule contains a *message condition*, a *mental condition*, and an action. In order to determine whether such a rule fires, the message condition is matched against the messages the agent has received; the mental condition is matched against the beliefs of the agent. If the rule fires, then the agent becomes committed to the action. Actions may be *private*, corresponding to an internally executed subroutine, or *communicative*, i.e., sending messages. Messages are constrained to be one of three types: 'requests' or 'unrequests' to perform or refrain from actions, and 'inform' messages, which pass on information — Shoham indicates that he took his inspiration for these message types from speech act theory [168, 38]. Request and unrequest messages typically result in the agent's commitments being modified; inform messages result in a change to the agent's beliefs.

Thomas — PLACA: AGENT0 was only ever intended as a prototype, to illustrate the principles of AOP. A more refined implementation was developed by Thomas, for her 1993 doctoral thesis [187]. Her Planning Communicating Agents (PLACA) language was intended to address one severe drawback to AGENT0: the inability of agents to plan, and communicate requests for action via high-level goals.

Fisher — Concurrent METATEM: One drawback with both AGENT0 and PLACA is that the relationship between the logic and interpreted programming language is only loosely defined: in neither case can the programming language be said to truly *execute* the associated logic. The Concurrent METATEM language developed by Fisher can make a stronger claim in this respect [62]. A Concurrent METATEM system contains a number of concurrently executing agents, each of which is able to communicate with its peers via asynchronous broadcast message passing. Each agent is programmed by giving it a temporal logic specification of the behaviour that it is intended the agent should exhibit. An agent's specification is executed directly to generate its behaviour. Execution of the agent program corresponds to iteratively building a logical model for the temporal agent specification. It is possible to prove that the procedure used to execute an agent specification is correct, in that if it is possible to satisfy the specification, then the agent will do so [11].

The IMAGINE Project — APRIL and MAIL: APRIL [128] and MAIL [92] are two languages for developing multi-agent applications that were developed as part of the ES-

PRIT project IMAGINE [90]. The two languages are intended to fulfill quite different roles. APRIL was designed to provide the core features required to realise most agent architectures and systems. Thus APRIL provides facilities for multi-tasking (via processes, which are treated as first-class objects, and a UNIX-like *fork* facility), communication (with powerful message-passing facilities supporting network-transparent agent-to-agent links); and pattern matching and symbolic processing capabilities. The generality of APRIL comes at the expense of powerful abstractions — an APRIL system builder must implement an agent or system architecture from scratch using APRIL's primitives. In contrast, the MAIL language provides a rich collection of pre-defined abstractions, including plans and multi-agent plans. APRIL was originally envisaged as the implementation language for MAIL. The MAIL system has been used to implement several prototype multi-agent systems, including an urban traffic management scenario [91].

General Magic, Inc. — TELESCRIPT: TELESCRIPT is a language-based environment for constructing agent societies that has been developed by General Magic, Inc.: it is perhaps the first commercial agent language [204].

TELESCRIPT technology is the name given by General Magic to a family of concepts and techniques they have developed to underpin their products. There are two key concepts in TELESCRIPT technology: *places* and *agents*. Places are virtual locations that are occupied by agents. Agents are the providers and consumers of goods in the *electronic marketplace* applications that TELESCRIPT was developed to support. Agents are software processes, and are mobile: they are able to move from one place to another, in which case their program and state are encoded and transmitted across a network to another place, where execution recommences. Agents are able to communicate with one-another: if they occupy different places, then they can connect across a network, in much the standard way; if they occupy the same location, then they can *meet* one another.

Connah and Wavish — ABLE: A group of researchers at Philips research labs in the UK have developed an *Agent Behaviour Language*, (ABLE), in which agents are programmed in terms of simple, rule-like *licences* [39, 196]. Licences may include some representation of time (though the language is not based on any kind of temporal logic): they loosely resemble behaviours in the subsumption architecture (see above). ABLE can be compiled down to a simple digital machine, realised in the 'C' programming language. The idea is similar to situated automata, though there appears to be no equivalent theoretical foundation. The result of the compilation process is a very fast implementation, which has reportedly been used to control a Compact Disk-Interactive (CD-I) application. ABLE has recently been extended to a version called Real-Time ABLE (RTA) [197].

4.1 Comments and Further Reading

A recent collection of papers on concurrent object systems is [2]. Various languages have been proposed that marry aspects of object-based systems with aspects of Shoham's agent-oriented proposal. Two examples are AGENTSPEAK and DAISY. AGENT-SPEAK is loosely based on the PRS agent architecture, and incorporates aspects of concurrent-object technology [198]. In contrast, DAISY is based on the concurrent-object language CUBL ([148]), and incorporates aspects of the agent-oriented proposal [149].

Other languages of interest include OZ [94] and IC PROLOG II [33]. The latter, as its name suggests, is an extension of PROLOG, which includes multiple-threads, high-level communication primitives, and some object-oriented features.

5 Applications

Although this article is not intended primarily as an applications review, it is nevertheless worth pointing at some current and potential applications of agent technology.

Cooperative problem solving and distributed AI: Although DAI encompasses most of the issues we have discussed in this article, it should be stressed that the classical emphasis in DAI has been on *macro* phenomona (the *social* level), rather than the *micro* phenomena (the *agent* level) that we have been concerned with in this article. DAI thus looks at such issues as how a group of agents can be made to cooperate in order to efficiently solve problems, and how the activities of such a group can be efficiently coordinated. DAI researchers have applied agent technology in a variety of areas. Example applications include power systems management [206, 192], air-traffic control [185], particle accelerator control [104], intelligent document retrieval [137], patient care [97], telecommunications network management [199], spacecraft control [167], computer integrated manufacturing [143], concurrent engineering [40], transportation management [61], job shop scheduling [136], and steel coil processing control [135]. The classic reference to DAI is [17], which includes both a comprehensive review article and a collection of significant papers from the field; a more recent review article is [30].

Interface agents: An *interface agent* is an agent that acts as a kind of intelligent assistant to a user with respect to some computer application [127, p71]. Much work on interface agents is being done by the computer supported cooperative work (CSCW) community; see [10, 79] for more details.

Information agents and cooperative information systems: An *information agent* is an agent that has access to at least one, and potentially many information sources, and is able to collate and manipulate information obtained from these sources in order to answer queries posed by users and other information agents. A number of studies have been made of information agents, including a theoretical study of how agents are able to incorporate information from different sources [120, 81], as well a prototype system called IRA (information retrieval agent) that is able to search for loosely specified articles from a range of document repositories [194]. Another important system in this area is called Carnot [99], which allows pre-existing and heterogenous database systems to work together to answer queries that are outside the scope of any of the individual databases.

Believable agents: A *believable agent* is one that 'provide[s] the illusion of life, thus permitting ... [an] audience's suspension of disbelief' [13, p122]. Such agents have obvious potential in computer games and virtual cinema environments. The Oz group at CMU have investigated various architectures for believable agents [14], and have developed at least one prototype implementation of their ideas [13].

6 Concluding Remarks

This article has reviewed the main concepts and issues associated with the theory and practice of intelligent agents. It has drawn together a very wide range of material, and has hopefully provided an insight into what an agent is, how the notion of an agent can be formalised, how appropriate agent architectures can be designed and implemented, how agents can be programmed, and the types of applications for which agent-based solutions have been proposed. The subject matter of this review is important because it is increasingly felt, both within academia and industry, that intelligent agents will be a key technology as computing systems become ever more distributed, interconnected, and open. In such environments, the ability of agents to autonomously plan and pursue their actions and goals, to cooperate, coordinate, and negotiate with others, and to respond flexibly and intelligently to dynamic and unpredictable situations will lead to significant improvements in the quality and sophistication of the software systems that can be conceived and implemented, and the application areas and problems which can be addressed.

Appendix A: Glossary of Key Terms

In this section, we present a glossary of the key terms that have been introduced in our survey.

ACL Agent communication language — a common language used by AGENTS for communicating with one another [67]. KQML and KIF form the best-known ACL [144].

ACTOR A pioneering concurrent object concept developed by Carl Hewitt at MIT, for which the best early reference is [95]. A good reference is [1], which (on page 131) defines an actor as 'A computational agent which has a mail address and a behaviour. Actors communicate by message-passing and carry out their actions concurrently.'

AGENT We distinguish two usages. The most general usage is to mean an AUTONOMOUS, self-contained, REACTIVE, PRO-ACTIVE computer system, typically with a central locus of control, that is able to communicate with other AGENTS via some ACL. A more specific usage is to mean a computer system that is either conceptualised or implemented in terms of concepts more usually applied to humans (such as beliefs, desires, and intentions). See also -BOT and INTENTIONAL SYSTEM.

AGENTIFICATION The process of taking a neutral application, and converting it into an agent (perhaps by embedding it in an 'agent wrapper') [67].

AGENT LANGUAGE A programming language that embodies some (possibly weak) notion of agency. Examples include AGENT0 [176] and TELESCRIPT [204].

AGENT-ORIENTED PROGRAMMING An approach to building AGENTS, which proposes programming them in terms of mentalistic notions such as belief, desire, and intention [176]. See also AGENT and INTENTIONAL SYSTEM.

ANTICIPATORY See PREDICTIVE.

ARCHITECTURE A particular methodology for building AGENTS; typically includes definitions of software data structures and operations on these structures.

AUTONOMY The assumption that, although we generally intend AGENTS to act on our behalf, they nevertheless act without direct human or other intervention, and have some kind of control over their internal state [27].

BDI ARCHITECTURE An ARCHITECTURE containing explicit representations of beliefs, desires, and intentions [153]. Beliefs are generally regarded as the information an agent has about its environment, which may be false; desires are those things that the AGENT would like to see achieved — desires need not be consistent, and we do not expect an AGENT to act on *all* its desires — and finally, intentions are those things the AGENT is either committed to doing (intending *to*) or committed to bringing about (intending *that*).

BELIEVABLE AGENT An AGENT, typically represented in a computer game or some kind of virtual environment, that acts in such a way as to cause a user/participant to suspend disbelief, in much the same way that an actor in a film can cause an audience to suspend disbelief [14].

BENEVOLENCE Crudely, the assumption that AGENTS will try to help one-another whenever they are asked [159].

BLACKBOARD ARCHITECTURE A kind of ARCHITECTURE in which a collection of *knowledge sources* communicate by writing on a globally accessible data structure known as the blackboard [52].

-BOT Another term for AGENT, usually one implemented in software. Hence softbot = software robot [54], knowbot = knowledge-based robot, and so on.

COGNITIVE STATE The internal state of an INTENTIONAL SYSTEM; typically the collection of beliefs, desires, intentions, etc., that characterise the AGENT at some instant.

COMMITMENT RULE A type of rule used in Shoham's AGENT0 system, that commits an AGENT to perform an action [176]. See also MENTAL CHANGE RULE and PLACA.

CONATIVE Crudely, to do with desire. Hence conative logic = a logic of desire.

COOPERATION PROTOCOL A concept from distributed AI; a protocol that defines how a group of AGENTS are to work together to achieve some goal. The best known example is the contract net [184].

DELIBERATIVE ARCHITECTURE An ARCHITECTURE that relies on explicit, internally held symbolic models and symbol manipulation (cf. [68, Chapter 13]).

DEONTIC To do with duty or obligation. Hence deontic logic = a logic of obligation.

DOXASTIC To do with belief. Hence doxastic logic = a logic of belief.

DYNAMIC LOGIC A program logic [89], sometimes adapted to reason about agent's actions (cf. [36]).

EPISTEMIC To do with knowledge. Hence epistemic logic = a logic of knowledge.

HYBRID ARCHITECTURE An ARCHITECTURE that attempts to marry the techniques of symbolic AI with with those of alternative approaches to agency. Examples include the PRS [73], TOURINGMACHINES [57], COSY [24, 83], and INTERRAP [139].

INFORMATION AGENT An AGENT that is able to answer queries from a user or other AGENT by collating and manipulating information from different (typically network-based) sources [120].

INFORMATION ATTITUDE A type of attitude that an AGENT has towards a proposition that relates to the information it has. Thus an AGENT may *believe* a proposition to be true of the world (and may be wrong in its belief), or it may *know* a proposition (in which case it is correct). See also DOXASTIC and EPISTEMIC.

INTENTIONAL SYSTEM A system whose behaviour can be predicted or explained by attributing to it attitudes such as belief, desire, and intention, together with some degree of RATIONALITY [44]. See also AGENT, AGENT-ORIENTED PROGRAMMING, and COGNITIVE STATE.

INTERFACE AGENT An interface AGENT is a computer program 'that [employs] artificial intelligence techniques in order to provide assistance to a user dealing with a particular application' [127, p71].

LAYERED ARCHITECTURE An ARCHITECTURE that is structured into a number of layers, each of which typically represents an increased level of abstraction from the layer beneath it. Examples include TOURINGMACHINES [57] and INTERRAP [139].

LOGICAL OMNISCIENCE The undesirable property that some EPISTEMIC (DOXASTIC) logics have, that predicts that AGENTS know (believe) all the logical consequences of their knowledge (beliefs). See the discussion in [111].

MENTAL CHANGE RULE A rule that defines how an AGENT is to update its MENTAL STATE from one cycle to the next. See also COMMITMENT RULE, AGENT0 [176], and PLACA [187, 188].

MENTAL STATE See COGNITIVE STATE.

META-LANGUAGE A language in which it is possible to represent the properties of another language, called the *object language*. Meta-languages have been used to formalise notions such as belief; see, e.g., [110].

MOBILITY The ability of an AGENT to move around a network, as typified by the TELESCRIPT language [204].

MODAL LOGIC The logic of necessity and possibility; the techniques of modal logic have been used to formalise mentalistic notions such as belief, desire, and so on, as well as temporal aspects. A good reference is [32].

OBCP Object-based concurrent programming. See, e.g., the ABCL system [215].

PERSONAL DIGITAL ASSISTANT (PDA) An AGENT that collaborates with the user to achieve the user's tasks. Rather than just acting in response to the user's instructions, a PDA learns the user's way of working, and begins to take the initiative by proposing courses of action. See [126, 127, 129] for example systems and discussions.

PLAN A representation of a course of actions that, when executed, will lead to the achievement of some goal [5]. Plans may involve more than one AGENT, in which case they are joint plans — see, e.g., [154].

PREDICTIVE Able to make predictions about the future, and in particular, able to predict the effect of actions (cf. [78, 49]).

PRO-ACTIVE Capable of taking the initiative; not driven solely by events, but capable of generating goals and acting RATIONALLY to achieve them.

PRO-ATTITUDE Crudely, an attitude that an AGENT has towards a proposition that makes it more likely that the AGENT will act to make the proposition true. Example pro-attitudes include goals and desires. See also BDI ARCHITECTURE.

RATIONALITY Crudely, the assumption that an AGENT will try to achieve its goals, and will not knowingly act to prevent its goals being achieved [64, pp49–54].

REACTIVE Capable of maintaining an ongoing interaction with the environment, and responding *in a timely fashion* to changes that occur in it. Note that the term is now widely used to mean a system that includes no symbolic representation or reasoning: such an AGENT does not reflect on the long-term effects of its actions, and does not consider the coordination of activity with other agents. Thus, a REACTIVE AGENT will always respond in a timely fashion to external stimulus. See also REACTIVE ARCHITECTURE and REFLEXIVE, and contrast with DELIBERATIVE.

REACTIVE ARCHITECTURE An ARCHITECTURE that does not employ any kind of central symbolic world model, such as those typically used in 'knowledge-based' AI, and does not use any kind of symbolic reasoning in order to make decisions. Examples include the BEHAVIOUR LANGUAGE [23], ABLE [197], and PENGI [3].

REFLEXIVE Behaves in a stimulus-response fashion, without employing any kind of DELIBERATION (cf. [78]). The term REACTIVE is often used in this sense.

SITUATED AUTOMATA Crudely, an approach in which an agent is specified in declarative terms, and this specification is is compiled down to an automata-like machine that realises the specification [106]. See also RULER [162] and GAPPS [107].

SOFTWARE AGENT Not just an AGENT implemented in software, but one that senses and acts in a software environment such as UNIX [53].

SPEECH ACT THEORY A pragmatic theory of communication, originated by Austin [8] and further developed by Searle [168] and others [38, 37]. The key axiom of speech act theory is that communicative utterances are *actions* performed by a speaker with the intention of bringing about some change in a hearer's mental state. See also ACL, KQML, and KIF.

SUBSUMPTION ARCHITECTURE See BEHAVIOUR LANGUAGE [23].

VERACITY Crudely, the assumption that an AGENT will not knowingly communicate false information.

Appendix B: Annotated List of Systems

In this section, we present an annotated list of relevant systems; for the most part, these systems were cited in the main review text. Note that we have deliberately *not* mentioned systems that we feel are better identified simply as Distributed AI systems. For this reason, you will find no mention of influential DAI systems such as Lesser's DVMT, Lenat's BEING's, and so on. A list of such systems is presented in [17, pp41–42].

ABCL An ACTOR-like language developed at Tokyo [215].

ABLE The AGENT behaviour language — a REACTIVE AGENT LANGUAGE [196], further developed into real-time able (RTA) [197]. Developed by Philips at Redhill.

ACT/*n* ACTOR languages developed at MIT [1].

AGENT0 A prototype AGENT-ORIENTED language, developed at Stanford [176].

AGENT-K A PROLOG implementation of AGENT0 [176] that uses KQML-based message passing. (No formal reference available at the time of writing.)

AGENTSPEAK An AGENT-ORIENTED language with some concurrent-object features, developed in Melbourne [198].

APRIL The Agent Process Interaction Language [128] — a language for building AGENT applications that supports multi-tasking, network transparent message-passing, and symbolic processing. Developed at Imperial College, as part of the ESPRIT project IMAGINE [90]. Used to implement MAIL [92].

ARCHON An ESPRIT project that resulted in some of the first installed AGENT-based systems; application domains include power systems management and particle accelerator control [206]. ARCHON allows both purpose-built and legacy systems to be incorporated into a cooperating community.

BEHAVIOUR LANGUAGE A language for programming AGENTS in terms of task-accomplishing 'behaviours', arranged into a *subsumption hierarchy* [21, 23, 22]. Developed at MIT.

CAP A scheduling assistant AGENT, that learns its user's preferences from experience [130].

COACH A teaching AGENT that learns about its user and adapts to meet their needs [171].

CONCURRENT METATEM An AGENT LANGUAGE in which AGENTS are programmed by giving them a temporal logic specification of the behaviour that it is intended they should exhibit; AGENTS directly execute their specification in order to generate their behaviour [62]. Developed in Manchester.

COSY A HYBRID BDI ARCHITECTURE, somewhat similar to the PRS [73] and IRMA [20], developed by Daimler Benz in Berlin [24, 83].

CUBL A OBJECT-BASED CONCURRENT PROGRAMMING language [148].

DAISY A prototype AGENT LANGUAGE [149], built on top of CUBL [148].

DA-SOC A testbed for distributed automation experiments, based on AGENT-ORIENTED principles [84].

DASEDIS A DAI testbed, built over the COSY ARCHITECTURE [24, 83].

GAPPS Goals as parallel program specifications — a program for generating the action part of an agent in the SITUATED AUTOMATA paradigm [107]. See also RULER [162].

GRATE* A DELIBERATIVE ARCHITECTURE based on partly formalised models of intention and joint intention [102].

INTERRAP A HYBRID, LAYERED ARCHITECTURE developed at DFKI in Saarbrücken [139], somewhat similar to TOURINGMACHINES [57].

IRMA The Intelligent Resource-bounded Machine Architecture [20]. An influential architecture for DELIBERATIVE agents.

KAOS Knowledgeable agent-oriented system [69] — a prototype AGENT-ORIENTED system, implemented in Smalltalk.

KIDSIM A 'kids simulation' AGENT for programming symbolic simulations, without using a programming language [183].

KIF Not strictly speaking a system, the knowledge interchange format is part of a forthcoming standard ACL, that deals with message content [144, 67]. Similar to first-order logic, cast in a LISP-like syntax. See also KQML.

KQML The knowledge query and manipulation language is, like KIF, not really a system, but part of a forthcoming standard ACL [144, 67]. KQML deals with the performatives that define the *force* of a message; these performatives are loosely inspired by SPEECH ACT THEORY. Example performatives include *ask* and *reply*.

M A software assistant to support collaborative human work, realised as a set of co-operating AGENTS [158].

MAIL A high-level language for multi-AGENT applications, implemented over APRIL [128]; includes as primitive such notions as PLANS and joint plans. Developed as part of the ESPRIT project IMAGINE [90].

MAXIMS An email manager AGENT [126, p35]. Developed at MIT.

MYWORLD An AGENT-ORIENTED testbed for distributed artificial intelligence [214], partly formalised in [210]. Developed in Manchester.

NEWT A news filtering AGENT [126, pp38–39]. Developed at MIT.

OAA The open AGENT architecture — a BLACKBOARD ARCHITECTURE, integrating a variety of different application AGENTS [34]. Developed at SRI/Stanford.

OZ Two usages: (i) a concurrent constraint language for multi-AGENT systems developed at DFKI Saarbrücken [94], and (ii) a project at Carnegie-Mellon University, aimed at developing BELIEVABLE AGENTS [14].

PACT The Palo Alto Collaborative Testbed — experiments in how one might integrate pre-existing software systems using agent technology, KQML, and KIF [144, p779–780].

PENGI A simulated computer game, with the main character controlled by a novel REACTIVE ARCHITECTURE [3]. Developed at MIT.

PHOENIX A HYBRID ARCHITECTURE, evaluated in the domain of simulated forest fire management [35].

PLACA An AGENT-ORIENTED language [187, 188], building on AGENT0 [176]. Developed at Stanford.

PRS The Procedural Reasoning System — an influential HYBRID ARCHITECTURE [73], applied in a variety of domains (such as fault diagnosis on the space shuttle). Developed largely by the Australian AI Institute at Melbourne.

RINGO A music recommendation assistant (!) [126, p40]. Developed at MIT.

RODNEY A planner-based UNIX softbot (software robot) [53]. Developed at the University of Washington. See also -BOT.

RULER A program for generating the perception part of an agent in the SITUATED AUTOMATA paradigm [162].

SITACT A compiler that takes as its input a set of plans, and from them generates a set of situation-action rules (cf. BEHAVIOUR LANGUAGE) that realise the plans [47].

S-R-K MODEL The skill-rule-knowledge LAYERED ARCHITECTURE [29], somewhat similar to TOURINGMACHINES [57] and INTERRAP [139].

TELESCRIPT A commercial development environment for AGENT-based applications, developed by General Magic [204].
TOURINGMACHINES A HYBRID, LAYERED ARCHITECTURE, evaluated in the domain of automated guided vehicle control [58, 57]. See also INTERRAP [139].
WILL A HYBRID ARCHITECTURE, developed at Amsterdam [131].

Acknowledgements

A considerably more detailed version of this article is available on request from the authors. The 'theories' section of the article was adapted from the first author's 1992 PhD thesis [208], and as such this work was supported by the EPSRC of the UK (formerly SERC). We are grateful to the people that read and commented on earlier drafts of this article, and in particular to those that attended the 1994 workshop on Agent Theories, Architectures, and Languages. A special vote of thanks also to Johannes Stein and Susanne Kalenka, who pointed out a number of errors and omissions in earlier versions of the glossary and systems list. It goes without saying that any errors or omissions that remain are the responsibility of the authors.

References

1. G. Agha. *ACTORS: A Model of Concurrent Computation in Distributed Systems*. The MIT Press, 1986.
2. G. Agha, P. Wegner, and A. Yonezawa, editors. *Research Directions in Concurrent Object-Oriented Programming*. The MIT Press, 1993.
3. P. Agre and D. Chapman. PENGI: An implementation of a theory of activity. In *Proceedings of the Sixth National Conference on Artificial Intelligence (AAAI-87)*, pages 268–272, Seattle, WA, 1987.
4. J. F. Allen. Towards a general theory of action and time. *Artificial Intelligence*, 23(2):123–154, 1984.
5. J. F. Allen, J. Hendler, and A. Tate, editors. *Readings in Planning*. Morgan Kaufmann, 1990.
6. J. F. Allen, H. Kautz, R. Pelavin, and J. Tenenberg. *Reasoning About Plans*. Morgan Kaufmann, 1991.
7. J. Ambros-Ingerson and S. Steel. Integrating planning, execution and monitoring. In *Proceedings of the Seventh National Conference on Artificial Intelligence (AAAI-88)*, pages 83–88, St. Paul, MN, 1988.
8. J. L. Austin. *How to Do Things With Words*. Oxford University Press, 1962.
9. R. Aylett and D. Eustace. Multiple cooperating robots — combining planning and behaviours. In S. M. Deen, editor, *Proceedings of the 1993 Workshop on Cooperating Knowledge Based Systems (CKBS-93)*, pages 3–11. DAKE Centre, University of Keele, UK, 1994.
10. R. M. Baecker, editor. *Readings in Groupware and Computer-Supported Cooperative Work*. Morgan Kaufmann, 1993.
11. H. Barringer, M. Fisher, D. Gabbay, G. Gough, and R. Owens. METATEM: A framework for programming in temporal logic. In *REX Workshop on Stepwise Refinement of Distributed Systems: Models, Formalisms, Correctness (LNCS Volume 430)*, pages 94–129. Springer-Verlag, June 1989.

12. J. Barwise and J. Perry. *Situations and Attitudes*. The MIT Press, 1983.

13. J. Bates. The role of emotion in believable agents. *Communications of the ACM*, 37(7):122–125, July 1994.

14. J. Bates, A. Bryan Loyall, and W. Scott Reilly. An architecture for action, emotion, and social behaviour. Technical Report CMU–CS–92–144, School of Computer Science, Carnegie-Mellon University, Pittsburgh, PA, May 1992.

15. N. Belnap. Backwards and forwards in the modal logic of agency. *Philosophy and Phenomenological Research*, LI(4):777–807, December 1991.

16. N. Belnap and M. Perloff. Seeing to it that: a canonical form for agentives. *Theoria*, 54:175–199, 1988.

17. A. H. Bond and L. Gasser, editors. *Readings in Distributed Artificial Intelligence*. Morgan Kaufmann, 1988.

18. M. E. Bratman. *Intentions, Plans, and Practical Reason*. Harvard University Press: Cambridge, MA, 1987.

19. M. E. Bratman. What is intention? In P. R. Cohen, J. L. Morgan, and M. E. Pollack, editors, *Intentions in Communication*, pages 15–32. The MIT Press, 1990.

20. M. E. Bratman, D. J. Israel, and M. E. Pollack. Plans and resource-bounded practical reasoning. *Computational Intelligence*, 4:349–355, 1988.

21. R. A. Brooks. A robust layered control system for a mobile robot. *IEEE Journal of Robotics and Automation*, 2(1):14–23, 1986.

22. R. A. Brooks. Intelligence without reason. In *Proceedings of the Twelfth International Joint Conference on Artificial Intelligence (IJCAI-91)*, pages 569–595, Sydney, Australia, 1991.

23. R. A. Brooks. Intelligence without representation. *Artificial Intelligence*, 47:139–159, 1991.

24. B. Burmeister and K. Sundermeyer. Cooperative problem solving guided by intentions and perception. In E. Werner and Y. Demazeau, editors, *Decentralized AI 3 — Proceedings of the Third European Workshop on Modelling Autonomous Agents and Multi-Agent Worlds (MAAMAW-91)*, pages 77–92. Elsevier Science Publishers B.V., 1992.

25. S. Bussmann and Y. Demazeau. An agent model combining reactive and cognitive capabilities. In *Proceedings of the IEEE International Conference on Intelligent Robots and Systems (IROS-94)*, Munich, Germany, September 1994.

26. C. Castelfranchi. Social power. In Y. Demazeau and J.-P. Müller, editors, *Decentralized AI — Proceedings of the First European Workshop on Modelling Autonomous Agents in Multi-Agent Worlds (MAAMAW-89)*, pages 49–62. Elsevier Science Publishers B.V., 1990.

27. C. Castelfranchi. Guarantees for autonomy in cognitive agent architecture. In M. Wooldridge and N. R. Jennings, editors, *Intelligent Agents — Proceedings of the 1994 Workshop on Agent Theories, Architectures, and Languages*, 1995. (In this volume).

28. C. Castelfranchi, M. Miceli, and A. Cesta. Dependence relations among autonomous agents. In E. Werner and Y. Demazeau, editors, *Decentralized AI 3 — Proceedings of the Third European Workshop on Modelling Autonomous Agents and Multi-Agent Worlds (MAAMAW-91)*, pages 215–231. Elsevier Science Publishers B.V., 1992.

29. B. Chaib-draa and P. Levesque. Hierarchical models and communication in multi-agent environments. In *Proceedings of the Sixth European Workshop on Modelling Autonomous Agents and Multi-Agent Worlds (MAAMAW-94)*, pages 119–134, Odense, Denmark, August 1994.

30. B. Chaib-draa, B. Moulin, R. Mandiau, and P. Millot. Trends in distributed artificial intelligence. *Artificial Intelligence Review*, 6:35–66, 1992.

31. D. Chapman. Planning for conjunctive goals. *Artificial Intelligence*, 32:333–378, 1987.

32. B. Chellas. *Modal Logic: An Introduction*. Cambridge University Press, 1980.

33. D. Chu. I.C. PROLOG II: A language for implementing multi-agent systems. In S. M. Deen, editor, *Proceedings of the 1992 Workshop on Cooperating Knowledge Based Systems (CKBS-92)*, pages 61–74. DAKE Centre, University of Keele, UK, 1993.

34. P. R. Cohen and A. Cheyer. An open agent architecture. In O. Etzioni, editor, *Software Agents — Papers from the 1994 Spring Symposium (Technical Report SS–94–03)*, pages 1–8. AAAI Press, March 1994.

35. P. R. Cohen, M. L. Greenberg, D. M. Hart, and A. E. Howe. Trial by fire: Understanding the design requirements for agents in complex environments. *AI Magazine*, 10(3):32–48, 1989.

36. P. R. Cohen and H. J. Levesque. Intention is choice with commitment. *Artificial Intelligence*, 42:213–261, 1990.

37. P. R. Cohen and H. J. Levesque. Rational interaction as the basis for communication. In P. R. Cohen, J. Morgan, and M. E. Pollack, editors, *Intentions in Communication*, pages 221–256. The MIT Press, 1990.

38. P. R. Cohen and C. R. Perrault. Elements of a plan based theory of speech acts. *Cognitive Science*, 3:177–212, 1979.

39. D. Connah and P. Wavish. An experiment in cooperation. In Y. Demazeau and J.-P. Müller, editors, *Decentralized AI — Proceedings of the First European Workshop on Modelling Autonomous Agents in Multi-Agent Worlds (MAAMAW-89)*, pages 197–214. Elsevier Science Publishers B.V., 1990.

40. M. R. Cutkosky, R. S. Engelmore, R. E. Fikes, M . R. Genesereth, T. Gruber, W. S. Mark, J. M. Tenenbaum, and J. C. Weber. PACT: An experiment in integrating concurrent engineering systems. *IEEE Computer*, 26(1):28–37, 1993.

41. N. J. Davies. *Truth, Modality, and Action*. PhD thesis, Department of Computer Science, University of Essex, Colchester, UK, March 1993.

42. T. L. Dean and M. P. Wellman. *Planning and Control*. Morgan Kaufmann, 1991.

43. D. C. Dennett. *Brainstorms*. The MIT Press, 1978.

44. D. C. Dennett. *The Intentional Stance*. The MIT Press, 1987.

45. J. des Rivieres and H. J. Levesque. The consistency of syntactical treatments of knowledge. In J. Y. Halpern, editor, *Proceedings of the 1986 Conference on Theoretical Aspects of Reasoning About Knowledge*, pages 115–130. Morgan Kaufmann, 1986.

46. K. Devlin. *Logic and Information*. Cambridge University Press, 1991.

47. J. Downs and H. Reichgelt. Integrating classical and reactive planning within an architecture for autonomous agents. In J. Hertzberg, editor, *European Workshop on Planning (LNAI Volume 522)*, pages 13–26, 1991.

48. J. Doyle, Y. Shoham, and M. P. Wellman. A logic of relative desire. In Z. W. Ras and M. Zemankova, editors, *Methodologies for Intelligent Systems — Sixth International Symposium, ISMIS-91 (LNAI Volume 542)*. Springer-Verlag, October 1991.

49. B. Ekdahl, E. Astor, and P. Davidsson. Towards anticipatory agents. In M. Wooldridge and N. R. Jennings, editors, *Intelligent Agents — Proceedings of the 1994 Workshop on Agent Theories, Architectures, and Languages*, 1995. (In this volume).

50. E. A. Emerson. Temporal and modal logic. In J. van Leeuwen, editor, *Handbook of Theoretical Computer Science*, pages 996–1072. Elsevier Science Publishers B.V., 1990.

51. E. A. Emerson and J. Y. Halpern. 'Sometimes' and 'not never' revisited: on branching time versus linear time temporal logic. *Journal of the ACM*, 33(1):151–178, 1986.

52. R. Engelmore and T. Morgan, editors. *Blackboard Systems*. Addison-Wesley, 1988.

53. O. Etzioni, N. Lesh, and R. Segal. Building softbots for UNIX. In O. Etzioni, editor, *Software Agents — Papers from the 1994 Spring Symposium (Technical Report SS–94–03)*, pages 9–16. AAAI Press, March 1994.

54. O. Etzioni and D. Weld. A softbot-based interface to the internet. *Communications of the ACM*, 37(7):72–76, July 1994.

55. R. Fagin and J. Y. Halpern. Belief, awareness, and limited reasoning. In *Proceedings of the Ninth International Joint Conference on Artificial Intelligence (IJCAI-85)*, pages 480–490, Los Angeles, CA, 1985.

56. R. Fagin, J. Y. Halpern, and M. Y. Vardi. What can machines know? on the properties of knowledge in distributed systems. *Journal of the ACM*, 39(2):328–376, 1992.

57. I. A. Ferguson. *TouringMachines: An Architecture for Dynamic, Rational, Mobile Agents*. PhD thesis, Clare Hall, University of Cambridge, UK, November 1992. (Also available as Technical Report No. 273, University of Cambridge Computer Laboratory).

58. I. A. Ferguson. Towards an architecture for adaptive, rational, mobile agents. In E. Werner and Y. Demazeau, editors, *Decentralized AI 3 — Proceedings of the Third European Workshop on Modelling Autonomous Agents and Multi-Agent Worlds (MAAMAW-91)*, pages 249–262. Elsevier Science Publishers B.V., 1992.

59. R. E. Fikes and N. Nilsson. STRIPS: A new approach to the application of theorem proving to problem solving. *Artificial Intelligence*, 5(2):189–208, 1971.

60. J. A. Firby. An investigation into reactive planning in complex domains. In *Proceedings of the Tenth International Joint Conference on Artificial Intelligence (IJCAI-87)*, pages 202–206, Milan, Italy, 1987.

61. K. Fisher, N. Kuhn, H. J. Müller, J. P. Müller, and M. Pischel. Sophisticated and distributed: The transportation domain. In *Proceedings of the Fifth European Workshop on Modelling Autonomous Agents and Multi-Agent Worlds (MAAMAW-93)*, Neuchatel, Switzerland, 1993.

62. M. Fisher. A survey of Concurrent METATEM — the language and its applications. In D. M. Gabbay and H. J. Ohlbach, editors, *Temporal Logic — Proceedings of the First International Conference (LNAI Volume 827)*, pages 480–505. Springer-Verlag, July 1994.

63. J. R. Galliers. A strategic framework for multi-agent cooperative dialogue. In *Proceedings of the Eighth European Conference on Artificial Intelligence (ECAI-88)*, pages 415–420, Munich, Federal Republic of Germany, 1988.

64. J. R. Galliers. *A Theoretical Framework for Computer Models of Cooperative Dialogue, Acknowledging Multi-Agent Conflict*. PhD thesis, Open University, UK, 1988.

65. L. Gasser and J. P. Briot. Object-based concurrent programming and DAI. In *Distributed Artificial Intelligence: Theory and Praxis*, pages 81–108. Kluwer Academic Publishers, 1992.

66. C. Geissler and K. Konolige. A resolution method for quantified modal logics of knowledge and belief. In J. Y. Halpern, editor, *Proceedings of the 1986 Conference on Theoretical Aspects of Reasoning About Knowledge*, pages 309–324. Morgan Kaufmann, 1986.

67. M. R. Genesereth and S. P. Ketchpel. Software agents. *Communications of the ACM*, 37(7):48–53, July 1994.

68. M. R. Genesereth and N. Nilsson. *Logical Foundations of Artificial Intelligence*. Morgan Kaufmann, 1987.

69. N. J. George, R. J. Jasper, M. R. LaFever, K. M. Morrison, D. B. Rosenthal, S. R. Tockey, J. D. Woolley, J. M. Bradshaw, G. A. Boy, and P. D. Holm. KAoS: A knowledgeable agent-oriented system. In O. Etzioni, editor, *Software Agents — Papers from the 1994 Spring Symposium (Technical Report SS–94–03)*, pages 24–30. AAAI Press, March 1994.

70. M. P. Georgeff. Planning. *Annual Review of Computer Science*, 2:359–400, 1987.

71. M. P. Georgeff and F. F. Ingrand. Decision-making in an embedded reasoning system. In *Proceedings of the Eleventh International Joint Conference on Artificial Intelligence (IJCAI-89)*, pages 972–978, Detroit, MI, 1989.

72. M. P. Georgeff and A. L. Lansky, editors. *Reasoning About Actions & Plans — Proceedings of the 1986 Workshop*. Morgan Kaufmann, 1986.

73. M. P. Georgeff and A. L. Lansky. Reactive reasoning and planning. In *Proceedings of the Sixth National Conference on Artificial Intelligence (AAAI-87)*, pages 677–682, Seattle, WA, 1987.

74. M. Ginsberg. *Essentials of Artificial Intelligence*. Morgan Kaufmann, 1993.

75. P. Gmytrasiewicz and E. H. Durfee. Elements of a utilitarian theory of knowledge and action. In *Proceedings of the Thirteenth International Joint Conference on Artificial Intelligence (IJCAI-93)*, pages 396–402, Chambéry, France, 1993.

76. R. Goldblatt. *Logics of Time and Computation*. Centre for the Study of Language and Information — Lecture Notes Series, 1987. (Distributed by Chicago University Press).

77. R. P. Goldman and R. R. Lang. Intentions in time. Technical Report TUTR 93–101, Tulane University, January 1991.

78. R. Goodwin. Formalizing properties of agents. Technical Report CMU–CS–93–159, School of Computer Science, Carnegie-Mellon University, Pittsburgh, PA, May 1993.

79. I. Greif. Desktop agents in group-enabled products. *Communications of the ACM*, 37(7):100–105, July 1994.

80. B. J. Grosz and C. L. Sidner. Plans for discourse. In P. R. Cohen, J. Morgan, and M. E. Pollack, editors, *Intentions in Communication*, pages 417–444. The MIT Press, 1990.

81. T. R. Gruber. The role of common ontology in achieving sharable, reusable knowledge bases. In R. Fikes and E. Sandewall, editors, *Proceedings of Knowledge Representation and Reasoning (KR&R-91)*. Morgan Kaufmann, April 1991.

82. A. Haas. A syntactic theory of belief and knowledge. *Artificial Intelligence*, 28(3):245–292, 1986.

83. A. Haddadi. A hybrid architecture for multi-agent systems. In S. M. Deen, editor, *Proceedings of the 1993 Workshop on Cooperating Knowledge Based Systems (CKBS-93)*, pages 13–26, DAKE Centre, University of Keele, UK, 1994.

84. S. Hägg, F. Ygge, R. Gustavsson, and H. Ottosson. DA-SoC: A testbed for modelling distributed automation applications using agent-oriented programming. In *Proceedings of the Sixth European Workshop on Modelling Autonomous Agents and Multi-Agent Worlds (MAAMAW-94)*, pages 39–51, August 1994.

85. J. Y. Halpern. Reasoning about knowledge: An overview. In J. Y. Halpern, editor, *Proceedings of the 1986 Conference on Theoretical Aspects of Reasoning About Knowledge*, pages 1–18. Morgan Kaufmann, 1986.

86. J. Y. Halpern. Using reasoning about knowledge to analyze distributed systems. *Annual Review of Computer Science*, 2:37–68, 1987.

87. J. Y. Halpern and Y. Moses. A guide to completeness and complexity for modal logics of knowledge and belief. *Artificial Intelligence*, 54:319–379, 1992.

88. J. Y. Halpern and M. Y. Vardi. The complexity of reasoning about knowledge and time. I. Lower bounds. *Journal of Computer and System Sciences*, 38:195–237, 1989.

89. D. Harel. Dynamic logic. In D. Gabbay and F. Guenther, editors, *Handbook of Philosophical Logic Volume II — Extensions of Classical Logic*, pages 497–604. D. Reidel Publishing Company, 1984. (Synthese library Volume 164).

90. H. Haugeneder. IMAGINE final project report. 1994.

91. H. Haugeneder and D. Steiner. A multi-agent approach to cooperation in urban traffic. In S. M. Deen, editor, *Proceedings of the 1993 Workshop on Cooperating Knowledge Based Systems (CKBS-93)*, pages 83–98. DAKE Centre, University of Keele, UK, 1994.

92. H. Haugeneder, D. Steiner, and F. G. McCabe. IMAGINE: A framework for building multi-agent systems. In S. M. Deen, editor, *Proceedings of the 1994 International Working*

Conference on Cooperating Knowledge Based Systems (CKBS-94), DAKE Centre, University of Keele, UK, June 1994.

93. J. Hendler, editor. *Artificial Intelligence Planning: Proceedings of the First International Conference*. Morgan Kaufmann, 1992.

94. M. Henz, G. Smolka, and J. Wuertz. Oz — a programming language for multi-agent systems. In *Proceedings of the Thirteenth International Joint Conference on Artificial Intelligence (IJCAI-93)*, pages 404–409, Chambéry, France, 1993.

95. C. Hewitt. Viewing control structures as patterns of passing messages. *Artificial Intelligence*, 8(3):323–364, 1977.

96. J. Hintikka. *Knowledge and Belief*. Cornell University Press: Ithaca, NY, 1962.

97. J. Huang, N. R. Jennings, and J. Fox. An agent architecture for distributed medical care. In M. Wooldridge and N. R. Jennings, editors, *Intelligent Agents — Proceedings of the 1994 Workshop on Agent Theories, Architectures, and Languages*, 1995. (In this volume).

98. G. E. Hughes and M. J. Cresswell. *Introduction to Modal Logic*. Methuen and Co., Ltd., 1968.

99. M. N. Huhns, N. Jacobs, T. Ksiezyk, W. M. Shen, M. P. Singh, and P. E. Cannata. Integrating enterprise information models in Carnot. In *Proceedings of the International Conference on Intelligent and Cooperative Information Systems*, pages 32–42, Rotterdam, The Netherlands, 1992.

100. N. R. Jennings. On being responsible. In E. Werner and Y. Demazeau, editors, *Decentralized AI 3 — Proceedings of the Third European Workshop on Modelling Autonomous Agents and Multi-Agent Worlds (MAAMAW-91)*, pages 93–102. Elsevier Science Publishers B.V., 1992.

101. N. R. Jennings. Commitments and conventions: The foundation of coordination in multi-agent systems. *Knowledge Engineering Review*, 8(3):223–250, 1993.

102. N. R. Jennings. Specification and implementation of a belief desire joint-intention architecture for collaborative problem solving. *Journal of Intelligent and Cooperative Information Systems*, 2(3):289–318, 1993.

103. N. R. Jennings. Controlling cooperative problem solving in industrial multi-agent systems using joint intentions. *Artificial Intelligence*, 74(2), 1995. (To appear).

104. N. R. Jennings, L. Z. Varga, R. P. Aarnts, J. Fuchs, and P. Skarek. Transforming standalone expert systems into a community of cooperating agents. *International Journal of Engineering Applications of Artificial Intelligence*, 6(4):317–331, 1993.

105. L. P. Kaelbling. An architecture for intelligent reactive systems. In M. P. Georgeff and A. L. Lansky, editors, *Reasoning About Actions & Plans — Proceedings of the 1986 Workshop*, pages 395–410. Morgan Kaufmann, 1986.

106. L. P. Kaelbling. A situated automata approach to the design of embedded agents. *SIGART Bulletin*, 2(4):85–88, 1991.

107. L. P. Kaelbling and S. J. Rosenschein. Action and planning in embedded agents. In P. Maes, editor, *Designing Autonomous Agents*, pages 35–48. The MIT Press, 1990.

108. D. Kinny, M. Ljungberg, A. S. Rao, E. Sonenberg, G. Tidhar, and E. Werner. Planned team activity. In C. Castelfranchi and E. Werner, editors, *Artificial Social Systems — Selected Papers from the Fourth European Workshop on Modelling Autonomous Agents and Multi-Agent Worlds, MAAMAW-92 (LNAI Volume 830)*, pages 226–256. Springer-Verlag, 1992.

109. G. Kiss and H. Reichgelt. Towards a semantics of desires. In E. Werner and Y. Demazeau, editors, *Decentralized AI 3 — Proceedings of the Third European Workshop on Modelling Autonomous Agents and Multi-Agent Worlds (MAAMAW-91)*, pages 115–128. Elsevier Science Publishers B.V., 1992.

34

110. K. Konolige. A first-order formalization of knowledge and action for a multi-agent planning system. In J. E. Hayes, D. Michie, and Y. Pao, editors, *Machine Intelligence 10*, pages 41–72. Ellis Horwood, 1982.

111. K. Konolige. *A Deduction Model of Belief*. Pitman/Morgan Kaufmann, 1986.

112. K. Konolige. What awareness isn't: A sentential view of implicit and explicit belief (position paper). In J. Y. Halpern, editor, *Proceedings of the 1986 Conference on Theoretical Aspects of Reasoning About Knowledge*, pages 241–250. Morgan Kaufmann, 1986.

113. K. Konolige and M. E. Pollack. A representationalist theory of intention. In *Proceedings of the Thirteenth International Joint Conference on Artificial Intelligence (IJCAI-93)*, pages 390–395, Chambéry, France, 1993.

114. S. Kraus and D. Lehmann. Knowledge, belief and time. *Theoretical Computer Science*, 58:155–174, 1988.

115. S. Kripke. Semantical analysis of modal logic. *Zeitschrift für Mathematische Logik und Grundlagen der Mathematik*, 9:67–96, 1963.

116. G. Lakemeyer. A computationally attractive first-order logic of belief. In *JELIA-90: Proceedings of the European Workshop on Logics in AI (LNAI Volume 478)*, pages 333–347. Springer-Verlag, 1991.

117. Y. Lespérance. A formal account of self knowledge and action. In *Proceedings of the Eleventh International Joint Conference on Artificial Intelligence (IJCAI-89)*, pages 868–874, Detroit, MI, 1989.

118. H. J. Levesque. A logic of implicit and explicit belief. In *Proceedings of the Fourth National Conference on Artificial Intelligence (AAAI-84)*, pages 198–202, Austin, TX, 1984.

119. H. J. Levesque, P. R. Cohen, and J. H. T. Nunes. On acting together. In *Proceedings of the Eighth National Conference on Artificial Intelligence (AAAI-90)*, pages 94–99, Boston, MA, 1990.

120. A. Y. Levy, Y. Sagiv, and D. Srivastava. Towards efficient information gathering agents. In O. Etzioni, editor, *Software Agents — Papers from the 1994 Spring Symposium (Technical Report SS–94–03)*, pages 64–70. AAAI Press, March 1994.

121. D. Mack. A new formal model of belief. In *Proceedings of the Eleventh European Conference on Artificial Intelligence (ECAI-94)*, pages 573–577, Amsterdam, The Netherlands, 1994.

122. P. Maes. The dynamics of action selection. In *Proceedings of the Eleventh International Joint Conference on Artificial Intelligence (IJCAI-89)*, pages 991–997, Detroit, MI, 1989.

123. P. Maes, editor. *Designing Autonomous Agents*. The MIT Press, 1990.

124. P. Maes. Situated agents can have goals. In P. Maes, editor, *Designing Autonomous Agents*, pages 49–70. The MIT Press, 1990.

125. P. Maes. The agent network architecture (ANA). *SIGART Bulletin*, 2(4):115–120, 1991.

126. P. Maes. Agents that reduce work and information overload. *Communications of the ACM*, 37(7):31–40, July 1994.

127. P. Maes. Social interface agents: Acquiring competence by learning from users and other agents. In O. Etzioni, editor, *Software Agents — Papers from the 1994 Spring Symposium (Technical Report SS–94–03)*, pages 71–78. AAAI Press, March 1994.

128. F. G. McCabe and K. L. Clark. April — agent process interaction language. In M. Wooldridge and N. R. Jennings, editors, *Intelligent Agents — Proceedings of the 1994 Workshop on Agent Theories, Architectures, and Languages*, 1995. (In this volume).

129. S. L. McGregor. Prescient agents. In D. Coleman, editor, *Proceedings of Groupware-92*, pages 228–230, 1992.

130. T. Mitchell, R. Caruana, D. Freitag, J. McDermott, and D. Zabowski. Experience with a learning personal assistant. *Communications of the ACM*, 37(7):81–91, July 1994.

131. D. Moffat and N. Frijda. Where there's a will there's an agent. In M. Wooldridge and N. R. Jennings, editors, *Intelligent Agents — Proceedings of the 1994 Workshop on Agent Theories, Architectures, and Languages*, 1995. (In this volume).

132. R. Montague. Syntactical treatments of modality, with corollaries on reflexion principles and finite axiomatizations. *Acta Philosophica Fennica*, 16:153–167, 1963.

133. R. C. Moore. A formal theory of knowledge and action. In J. F. Allen, J. Hendler, and A. Tate, editors, *Readings in Planning*, pages 480–519. Morgan Kaufmann, 1990.

134. L. Morgenstern. Knowledge preconditions for actions and plans. In *Proceedings of the Tenth International Joint Conference on Artificial Intelligence (IJCAI-87)*, pages 867–874, Milan, Italy, 1987.

135. K. Mori, H. Torikoshi, K. Nakai, K. Mori, and T. Masuda. Computer control system for iron and steel plants. *Hitachi Review*, 37(4):251–258, 1988.

136. R. E. Morley and C. Schelberg. An analysis of a plant-specific dynamic scheduler. In *Proceedings of the NSF Workshop on Dynamic Scheduling*, Cocoa Beach, Florida, 1993.

137. U. Mukhopadhyay, L. Stephens, and M. Huhns. An intelligent system for document retrieval in distributed office environments. *Journal of the American Society for Information Science*, 37:123–135, 1986.

138. J. P. Müller. A conceptual model of agent interaction. In S. M. Deen, editor, *Draft proceedings of the Second International Working Conference on Cooperating Knowledge Based Systems (CKBS-94)*, pages 389–404, DAKE Centre, University of Keele, UK, June 1994.

139. J. P. Müller and M. Pischel. Modelling interacting agents in dynamic environments. In *Proceedings of the Eleventh European Conference on Artificial Intelligence (ECAI-94)*, pages 709–713, Amsterdam, The Netherlands, 1994.

140. J. P. Müller, M. Pischel, and M. Thiel. Modelling reactive behaviour in vertically layered agent architectures. In M. Wooldridge and N. R. Jennings, editors, *Intelligent Agents — Proceedings of the 1994 Workshop on Agent Theories, Architectures, and Languages*, 1995. (In this volume).

141. A. Newell and H. A. Simon. Computer science as empirical enquiry. *Communications of the ACM*, 19:113–126, 1976.

142. N. J. Nilsson. Towards agent programs with circuit semantics. Technical Report STAN–CS–92–1412, Computer Science Department, Stanford University, Stanford, CA 94305, January 1992.

143. H. V. D. Parunak. Applications of distributed artificial intelligence in industry. In G. M. P. O'Hare and N. R. Jennings, editors, *Foundations of Distributed AI*. John Wiley & Sons, 1995. (To appear).

144. R. S. Patil, R. E. Fikes, P. F. Patel-Schneider, D. McKay, T. Finin, T. Gruber, and R. Neches. The DARPA knowledge sharing effort: Progress report. In C. Rich, W. Swartout, and B. Nebel, editors, *Proceedings of Knowledge Representation and Reasoning (KR&R-92)*, pages 777–788, 1992.

145. D. Perlis. Languages with self reference I: Foundations. *Artificial Intelligence*, 25:301–322, 1985.

146. D. Perlis. Languages with self reference II: Knowledge, belief, and modality. *Artificial Intelligence*, 34:179–212, 1988.

147. M. Perloff. *STIT* and the language of agency. *Synthese*, 86:379–408, 1991.

148. A. Poggi. Agents and resources management with CUBL. In *Proceedings of HICSS-94*, pages 112–121, Maui, HI, 1994.

149. A. Poggi. DAISY: An object-oriented system for distributed artificial intelligence. In M. Wooldridge and N. R. Jennings, editors, *Intelligent Agents — Proceedings of the 1994 Workshop on Agent Theories, Architectures, and Languages*, 1995. (In this volume).

150. M. E. Pollack and M. Ringuette. Introducing the Tileworld: Experimentally evaluating agent architectures. In *Proceedings of the Eighth National Conference on Artificial Intelligence (AAAI-90)*, pages 183–189, Boston, MA, 1990.

151. A. S. Rao and M. P. Georgeff. Asymmetry thesis and side-effect problems in linear time and branching time intention logics. In *Proceedings of the Twelfth International Joint Conference on Artificial Intelligence (IJCAI-91)*, pages 498–504, Sydney, Australia, 1991.

152. A. S. Rao and M. P. Georgeff. Modeling rational agents within a BDI-architecture. In R. Fikes and E. Sandewall, editors, *Proceedings of Knowledge Representation and Reasoning (KR&R-91)*, pages 473–484. Morgan Kaufmann, April 1991.

153. A. S. Rao and M. P. Georgeff. An abstract architecture for rational agents. In C. Rich, W. Swartout, and B. Nebel, editors, *Proceedings of Knowledge Representation and Reasoning (KR&R-92)*, pages 439–449, 1992.

154. A. S. Rao and M. P. Georgeff. Social plans: Preliminary report. In E. Werner and Y. Demazeau, editors, *Decentralized AI 3 — Proceedings of the Third European Workshop on Modelling Autonomous Agents and Multi-Agent Worlds (MAAMAW-91)*, pages 57–76. Elsevier Science Publishers B.V., 1992.

155. A. S. Rao and M. P. Georgeff. A model-theoretic approach to the verification of situated reasoning systems. In *Proceedings of the Thirteenth International Joint Conference on Artificial Intelligence (IJCAI-93)*, pages 318–324, Chambéry, France, 1993.

156. H. Reichgelt. A comparison of first-order and modal logics of time. In P. Jackson, H. Reichgelt, and F. van Harmelen, editors, *Logic Based Knowledge Representation*, pages 143–176. The MIT Press, 1989.

157. H. Reichgelt. Logics for reasoning about knowledge and belief. *Knowledge Engineering Review*, 4(2):119–139, 1989.

158. D. Riecken. M: An architecture of integrated agents. *Communications of the ACM*, 37(7):107–116, July 1994.

159. J. S. Rosenschein. *Rational Interaction: Cooperation Among Intelligent Agents*. PhD thesis, Computer Science Department, Stanford University, Stanford, CA 94305, 1985.

160. J. S. Rosenschein and M. R. Genesereth. Deals among rational agents. In *Proceedings of the Ninth International Joint Conference on Artificial Intelligence (IJCAI-85)*, pages 91–99, Los Angeles, CA, 1985.

161. S. Rosenschein. Formal theories of knowledge in AI and robotics. *New Generation Computing*, pages 345–357, 1985.

162. S. Rosenschein and L. P. Kaelbling. The synthesis of digital machines with provable epistemic properties. In J. Y. Halpern, editor, *Proceedings of the 1986 Conference on Theoretical Aspects of Reasoning About Knowledge*, pages 83–98. Morgan Kaufmann, 1986.

163. E. Sacerdoti. Planning in a hierarchy of abstraction spaces. *Artificial Intelligence*, 5:115–135, 1974.

164. E. Sacerdoti. The non-linear nature of plans. In *Proceedings of the Fourth International Joint Conference on Artificial Intelligence (IJCAI-75)*, pages 206–214, Stanford, CA, 1975.

165. M. D. Sadek. A study in the logic of intention. In C. Rich, W. Swartout, and B. Nebel, editors, *Proceedings of Knowledge Representation and Reasoning (KR&R-92)*, pages 462–473, 1992.

166. M. J. Schoppers. Universal plans for reactive robots in unpredictable environments. In *Proceedings of the Tenth International Joint Conference on Artificial Intelligence (IJCAI-87)*, pages 1039–1046, Milan, Italy, 1987.

167. U. M. Schwuttke and A. G. Quan. Enhancing performance of cooperating agents in real-time diagnostic systems. In *Proceedings of the Thirteenth International Joint Conference on Artificial Intelligence (IJCAI-93)*, pages 332–337, Chambéry, France, 1993.

168. J. R. Searle. *Speech Acts: An Essay in the Philosophy of Language*. Cambridge University Press, 1969.

169. N. Seel. *Agent Theories and Architectures*. PhD thesis, Surrey University, Guildford, UK, 1989.

170. K. Segerberg. Bringing it about. *Journal of Philosophical Logic*, 18:327–347, 1989.

171. T. Selker. Coach: A teaching agent that learns. *Communications of the ACM*, 37(7):92–99, July 1994.

172. N. Shardlow. Action and agency in cognitive science. Master's thesis, Department of Psychlogy, University of Manchester, Oxford Rd., Manchester M13 9PL, UK, 1990.

173. Y. Shoham. *Reasoning About Change: Time and Causation from the Standpoint of Artificial Intelligence*. The MIT Press, 1988.

174. Y. Shoham. Time for action: on the relation between time, knowledge and action. In *Proceedings of the Eleventh International Joint Conference on Artificial Intelligence (IJCAI-89)*, pages 954–959, Detroit, MI, 1989.

175. Y. Shoham. Agent-oriented programming. Technical Report STAN–CS–1335–90, Computer Science Department, Stanford University, Stanford, CA 94305, 1990.

176. Y. Shoham. Agent-oriented programming. *Artificial Intelligence*, 60(1):51–92, 1993.

177. M. P. Singh. Towards a theory of situated know-how. In *Proceedings of the Ninth European Conference on Artificial Intelligence (ECAI-90)*, pages 604–609, Stockholm, Sweden, 1990.

178. M. P. Singh. Group ability and structure. In Y. Demazeau and J.-P. Müller, editors, *Decentralized AI 2 — Proceedings of the Second European Workshop on Modelling Autonomous Agents and Multi-Agent Worlds (MAAMAW-90)*, pages 127–146. Elsevier Science Publishers B.V., 1991.

179. M. P. Singh. Towards a formal theory of communication for multi-agent systems. In *Proceedings of the Twelfth International Joint Conference on Artificial Intelligence (IJCAI-91)*, pages 69–74, Sydney, Australia, 1991.

180. M. P. Singh. A critical examination of the Cohen-Levesque theory of intention. In *Proceedings of the Tenth European Conference on Artificial Intelligence (ECAI-92)*, pages 364–368, Vienna, Austria, 1992.

181. M. P. Singh. *Multiagent Systems: A Theoretical Framework for Intentions, Know-How, and Communications (LNAI Volume 799)*. Springer-Verlag, 1994.

182. M. P. Singh and N. M. Asher. Towards a formal theory of intentions. In *Logics in AI — Proceedings of the European Workshop JELIA-90 (LNAI Volume 478)*, pages 472–486. Springer-Verlag, 1991.

183. D. C. Smith, A. Cypher, and J. Spohrer. KIDSIM: Programming agents without a programming language. *Communications of the ACM*, 37(7):55–67, July 1994.

184. R. G. Smith. *A Framework for Distributed Problem Solving*. UMI Research Press, 1980.

185. R. Steeb, S. Cammarata, F. A. Hayes-Roth, P. W. Thorndyke, and R. B. Wesson. Distributed intelligence for air fleet control. In A. H. Bond and L. Gasser, editors, *Readings in Distributed Artificial Intelligence*, pages 90–101. Morgan Kaufmann, 1988.

186. L. Steels. Cooperation between distributed agents through self organization. In Y. Demazeau and J.-P. Müller, editors, *Decentralized AI — Proceedings of the First European Workshop on Modelling Autonomous Agents in Multi-Agent Worlds (MAAMAW-89)*, pages 175–196. Elsevier Science Publishers B.V., 1990.

187. S. R. Thomas. *PLACA, an Agent Oriented Programming Language*. PhD thesis, Computer Science Department, Stanford University, Stanford, CA 94305, August 1993. (Available as technical report STAN–CS–93–1487).

188. S. R. Thomas. The PLACA agent programming language. In M. Wooldridge and N. R. Jennings, editors, *Intelligent Agents — Proceedings of the 1994 Workshop on Agent Theories, Architectures, and Languages*, 1995. (In this volume).

189. S. R. Thomas, Y. Shoham, A. Schwartz, and S. Kraus. Preliminary thoughts on an agent description language. *International Journal of Intelligent Systems*, 6:497–508, 1991.

190. R. Thomason. A note on syntactical treatments of modality. *Synthese*, 44:391–395, 1980.

191. R. Turner. *Truth and Modality for Knowledge Representation*. Pitman, 1990.

192. L. Z. Varga, N. R. Jennings, and D. Cockburn. Integrating intelligent systems into a co-operating community for electricity distribution management. *International Journal of Expert Systems with Applications*, 7(4), 1994.

193. S. Vere and T. Bickmore. A basic agent. *Computational Intelligence*, 6:41–60, 1990.

194. E. M. Voorhees. Software agents for information retrieval. In O. Etzioni, editor, *Software Agents — Papers from the 1994 Spring Symposium (Technical Report SS–94–03)*, pages 126–129. AAAI Press, March 1994.

195. J. Wainer. Yet another semantics of goals and goal priorities. In *Proceedings of the Eleventh European Conference on Artificial Intelligence (ECAI-94)*, pages 269–273, Amsterdam, The Netherlands, 1994.

196. P. Wavish. Exploiting emergent behaviour in multi-agent systems. In E. Werner and Y. Demazeau, editors, *Decentralized AI 3 — Proceedings of the Third European Workshop on Modelling Autonomous Agents and Multi-Agent Worlds (MAAMAW-91)*, pages 297–310. Elsevier Science Publishers B.V., 1992.

197. P. Wavish and M. Graham. Roles, skills, and behaviour: a situated action approach to organising systems of interacting agents. In M. Wooldridge and N. R. Jennings, editors, *Intelligent Agents — Proceedings of the 1994 Workshop on Agent Theories, Architectures, and Languages*, 1995. (In this volume).

198. D. Weerasooriya, A. Rao, and K. Ramamohanarao. Design of a concurrent agent-oriented language. In M. Wooldridge and N. R. Jennings, editors, *Intelligent Agents — Proceedings of the 1994 Workshop on Agent Theories, Architectures, and Languages*, 1995. (In this volume).

199. R. Weihmayer and H. Velthuijsen. Application of distributed AI and cooperative problem solving to telecommunications. In J. Liebowitz and D. Prereau, editors, *AI Approaches to Telecommunications and Network Management*. IOS Press, 1994.

200. E. Werner. Toward a theory of communication and cooperation for multiagent planning. In M. Y. Vardi, editor, *Proceedings of the Second Conference on Theoretical Aspects of Reasoning About Knowledge*, pages 129–144. Morgan Kaufmann, 1988.

201. E. Werner. Cooperating agents: A unified theory of communication and social structure. In L. Gasser and M. Huhns, editors, *Distributed Artificial Intelligence Volume II*, pages 3–36. Pitman/Morgan Kaufmann, 1989.

202. E. Werner. What can agents do together: A semantics of co-operative ability. In *Proceedings of the Ninth European Conference on Artificial Intelligence (ECAI-90)*, pages 694–701, Stockholm, Sweden, 1990.

203. E. Werner. A unified view of information, intention and ability. In Y. Demazeau and J.-P. Müller, editors, *Decentralized AI 2 — Proceedings of the Second European Workshop on Modelling Autonomous Agents and Multi-Agent Worlds (MAAMAW-90)*, pages 109–126. Elsevier Science Publishers B.V., 1991.

204. J. E. White. Telescript technology: The foundation for the electronic marketplace. White paper, General Magic, Inc., 2465 Latham Street, Mountain View, CA 94040, 1994.

205. D. Wilkins. *Practical Planning: Extending the Classical AI Planning Paradigm*. Morgan Kaufmann, 1988.

206. T. Wittig, editor. *ARCHON: An Architecture for Multi-Agent Systems*. Ellis Horwood, 1992.

207. S. Wood. *Planning and Decision Making in Dynamic Domains*. Ellis Horwood, 1993.

208. M. Wooldridge. *The Logical Modelling of Computational Multi-Agent Systems*. PhD thesis, Department of Computation, UMIST, Manchester, UK, October 1992. (Also available as Technical Report MMU–DOC–94–01, Department of Computing, Manchester Metropolitan University, Chester St., Manchester, UK).

209. M. Wooldridge. Coherent social action. In *Proceedings of the Eleventh European Conference on Artificial Intelligence (ECAI-94)*, pages 279–283, Amsterdam, The Netherlands, 1994.

210. M. Wooldridge. This is MYWORLD: The logic of an agent-oriented testbed for DAI. In M. Wooldridge and N. R. Jennings, editors, *Pre-proceedings of the 1994 Workshop on Agent Theories, Architectures, and Languages*, pages 147–163, Amsterdam, The Netherlands, August 1994.

211. M. Wooldridge and M. Fisher. A first-order branching time logic of multi-agent systems. In *Proceedings of the Tenth European Conference on Artificial Intelligence (ECAI-92)*, pages 234–238, Vienna, Austria, 1992.

212. M. Wooldridge and M. Fisher. A decision procedure for a temporal belief logic. In D. M. Gabbay and H. J. Ohlbach, editors, *Temporal Logic — Proceedings of the First International Conference (LNAI Volume 827)*, pages 317–331. Springer-Verlag, July 1994.

213. M. Wooldridge and N. R. Jennings. Formalizing the cooperative problem solving process. In *Proceedings of the Thirteenth International Workshop on Distributed Artificial Intelligence (IWDAI-94)*, pages 403–417, Lake Quinalt, WA, July 1994.

214. M. Wooldridge and D. Vandekerckhove. MYWORLD: An agent-oriented testbed for distributed artificial intelligence. In S. M. Deen, editor, *Proceedings of the 1993 Workshop on Cooperating Knowledge Based Systems (CKBS-93)*, pages 263–274. DAKE Centre, University of Keele, UK, 1994.

215. A. Yonezawa, editor. *ABCL — An Object-Oriented Concurrent System*. The MIT Press, 1990.

Changing Attitudes

John Bell

Applied Logic Group, Computer Science Department,
Queen Mary and Westfield College, University of London,
London E1_4NS, e-mail: jb@dcs.qmw.ac.uk

Abstract. This paper brings together ideas from work on commonsense causal reasoning and work on formalising attitudes, such as beliefs, desires, intentions and obligations, to provide the basis of a theory of changing attitudes. It takes the view that rational agents do not change their attitudes without reason, and aims to represent such changes in *teleological theories*. The infrastructure of these theories contain persistence rules which state that agents attitudes persist unless they have reason to change them. Theories giving the agents' reasons for changing their attitudes build on these. This leads to a discussion of rationality in resource-bounded agents and the paper concludes by outlining an AI-planning theory of rational agency.

1 Introduction

Much work has been done on the formal analysis of attitudes like belief, intention and obligation; for example [13, 19, 20]. Much work has also been done on the application of nonmonotonic logic to the problems of reasoning about change; for example [11]. This paper brings together ideas from both fields to sketch a theory of changing attitudes. It takes the view that rational agents do not change their attitudes without reason, and aims to represent such changes in *teleological theories*. The infrastructure of teleological theories consists of persistence rules which state that agents attitudes persist unless they have reason to change them. Theories giving the agents' reasons for changing their attitudes build on these. This leads to a discussion of rationality in resource-bounded agents and the paper concludes by outlining an AI-planning theory of rational agency.

2 Time, Events and Actions

Our language CA is a many-sorted first-order modal language with explicit reference to time points and intervals. It will be introduced informally as required. A formal account is given in the appendix.

2.1 Time

CA contains sentences such as On(A,L)(3) which states that block A is on location L at time point 3. Time is taken to be composed of points and, for simplicity, is assumed to be discrete and linear; that is, time is assumed to be isomorphic to the integers. Temporal intervals are defined as pairs (binary multi-sets) of points. Thus the sentence

On(A,L)([1,8]) states that block A is on location L for the interval lasting from time point 1 to time point 8, or, equivalently, from time point 8 to time point 1. Intervals of the form [t,t] can equally be written as time points. For interval i, i+1 is the interval which *increments* i; that is, i is the interval obtained by extending i by a time point. Thus if i is [1,3] then i+1 is [1,4], and if i is [3,3] then i+1 is [4,4]. Tense operators can be defined if required, and examples are given in the appendix.

A novel feature of CA is the modal operator Aff. Intuitively a sentence $\phi(i)$ is affected at an interval i if its truth value changes at i+1. Formally, for model M, world w in M and variable assignment g

M,w,g $\models$ Aff($\phi(i)$)(i) $\qquad$ iff $\qquad$ either M,w,g $\models$ $\phi(i)$ and M,w,g $\not\models$ $\phi(i+1)$,

$\qquad\qquad\qquad\qquad\qquad\qquad\qquad$ or M,w,g $\not\models$ $\phi(i)$ and M,w,g $\models$ $\phi(i+1)$

We thus have the axiom (schema) $\mathcal{A}$ and, consequently, the persistence rule (schema) $\mathcal{P}$.

$$Aff(\phi)(i) \equiv \neg(\phi(i) \equiv \phi(i+1)) \qquad\qquad\qquad (\mathcal{A})$$
$$\phi(i) \wedge \neg Aff(\phi)(i) \supset \phi(i+1) \qquad\qquad\qquad (\mathcal{P})$$

Note that we are using conventional abbreviations; thus enclosing universal quantification is omitted and $\varphi \wedge \psi \supset \chi$ abbreviates $(\varphi \wedge \psi) \supset \chi$. Also, as in natural language, multiple occurrences of the same interval term may be eliminated when the result is ambiguous. Thus Aff($\phi(i)$)(i) is abbreviated to Aff(ϕ)(i). The convention is that missing interval terms are the same as immediately enclosing ones. Note that φ, ψ and χ are used as meta-variables for formulas, while ϕ is used as a meta-variable for an incomplete sub-formula which can be completed by adjoining a temporal index.

2.2 Events

Primitive event types are combined with intervals to form event tokens. For example, Occurs(Pickup(A))(1) states that a (token of a) pickup-A (type) event occurs at time 1. Note that more than one (distinct) event (token) may occur simultaneously. Complex events are defined in the appendix.

2.3 Actions

A sentence of the form Agent(a,e)(i) states that a is a, possibly unintentional, agent of event e at interval i. Thus

Does(a,e)(i) $=_{df}$ Occurs(e)(i) $\wedge$ Agent(a,e)(i)

Intentional action is discussed in Section 5. Compound actions are discussed in the appendix.

3 Beliefs

Intuitively, Bel(a,φ)(i) means that agent a believes φ at interval i. The formal semantics are a natural extension of the traditional Hintikka possible-worlds semantics [22]. In a model M, for each world w agent a and interval i there is an associated possible-worlds frame $(\mathcal{W}_{(Bel,a,i,w)}, \mathcal{R}_{(Bel,a,i,w)})$ which is centered at w; that is, $\mathcal{W}_{(Bel,a,i,w)}$ is a set of possible worlds which contains w, and $\mathcal{R}_{(Bel,a,i,w)}$ is a binary relation on $\mathcal{W}_{(Bel,a,i,w)}$ which is such that $(w,w') \in \mathcal{R}_{(Bel,a,i,w)}$ for every $w' \neq w$ in $\mathcal{W}_{(Bel,a,i,w)}$. If $(w,w') \in \mathcal{R}_{(Bel,a,i,w)}$ then w' is a doxastic alternative for a at i in w; that is, in w at i, a considers that w' is indistinguishable from (the actual world) w. The semantic clause for Bel sentences is then a straightforward extension of the familiar one:

$$M,w,g \models Bel(a,\varphi)(i) \quad \text{iff} \quad M, w',g \models \varphi \text{ for all } (w,w') \in \mathcal{R}_{(Bel,a,i,w)}$$

As our static logic of beliefs we provisionally choose $\mathcal{KD}45_{\mathcal{B}}$; that is, the $\mathcal{KD}45$ axioms and rules [12] with the indexed Bel operator; for example, the negative introspection axiom becomes

$$\neg Bel(a,\varphi)(i) \supset Bel(a,\neg Bel(a,\varphi))(i) \tag{$\mathcal{E}_{\mathcal{B}}$}$$

Consequently the usual conditions are imposed on the accessibility relation.

Condition Each $\mathcal{R}_{(Bel,a,i,w)}$ is serial, transitive and Euclidean.

The static logic can be extended by including notions such as knowledge, common belief and distributed belief [15, 19]. It can also be refined; for example, the logical omniscience problem can be circumvented by distinguishing between explicit and implicit beliefs on the basis of awareness [14]. However, the prime concern here is with the dynamics of belief.

3.1 The Belief in Persistence

The first persistence rule for beliefs, the belief in persistence, can now be stated. If agent a believes that ϕ is true at i and a does not believe that ϕ is affected at i, then a should believe that ϕ continues to be the case at i+1. We therefore have

$$Bel(a,\phi)(i) \wedge \neg Bel(a,Aff(\phi))(i) \supset Bel(a,\phi)(i+1) \tag{$\mathcal{BP}$}$$

For example, suppose that Stan believes that gun G is loaded for the interval [1,2], (1), and that Stan does not believe that an event occurs which affects G's being loaded during this interval, (2). Then, by $\mathcal{BP}$, Stan believes that G is loaded for the interval [1,3], (3).

Bel(Stan, Loaded(G))([1,2])   (1)
$\neg$Bel(Stan, Aff(Loaded(G)))([1,2])   (2)
Bel(Stan, Loaded(G))([1,3])   (3)

Rules like $\mathcal{BP}$ are intended to be interpreted like Shoham's causal rules [28]; that is, they are intended to be used from left to right only, to reason "forwards in time" from the antecedent to the consequent. Typically also, we want to be able to infer the second premise of these rules nonmonotonically; for example, we want to be able to infer (2) if its negation cannot be inferred. This interpretation is enforced by restricting attention to the *preferred* models of theories containing such rules, those in which the beliefs of agents are minimised chronologically. For intervals i and i' we write i $<_e$ i' if i' ends after i, that is max(i) < max(i'), i $=_e$ i' if i ends as late as i' and i $\leq_e$ i' if i ends no later than i'.

Definition Let op be a modal operator and M and M' be models of $\mathcal{CA}$ which satisfy any additional conditions that may have been imposed. Then M is op-preferred to M', written M $<_{op}$ M', if M and M' differ at most on the interpretation of op and there exists an interval i such that

- M' $\models$ op(a,φ)(i') if M $\models$ op(a,φ)(i') for any a, φ and i' $\leq_e$ i, and
- M'$\models$ op(a,φ)(i) and M $\not\models$ op(a,φ)(i) for some a and φ

M is an op-preferred model if there is no model M' such that M' $<_{op}$ M. M is an op-preferred model of a theory Θ if M is a model of Θ and there is no model M' of Θ such that M' $<_{op}$ M.

So for the belief fragment of $\mathcal{CA}$ we are interested in Bel-preferred models of theories.

So much for what agents should believe about continuity. What should they believe about change? Here it is a matter of supplying an appropriate theory. For example, suppose that we have the move operator defined in (4)-(6). Let B1 and B2 be distinct blocks and L1 and L2 be distinct locations, (7). Suppose further that we have two agents, Stan and Ollie. At time 1 Stan believes that B1 is on L1 and that L2 is clear, while Ollie believes that B2 is on L2 while L1 is clear, (8)-(9). Stan wishes to clear L1 by moving B1 to L2 and Ollie wishes to clear L2 by moving B2 to L1. They both believe the facts about the move operator, (10). They thus knowingly perform the appropriate move operations, (11)-(12). As a result at time 2 in (Bel)-preferred models Stan correctly believes that B1 is on L2 but incorrectly believes that L1 is clear, (13), and Ollie is similarly confused, (14).

$$(On(b,loc1) \wedge Clear(loc2) \wedge Occurs(Move(b,loc1,loc2)))(t) \supset On(b,loc2)(t+1) \quad (4)$$
$$(On(b,loc1) \wedge loc1 \neq loc2 \supset \neg On(b,loc2))(t) \quad (5)$$
$$(Clear(loc) \equiv \neg \exists bOn(b,loc))(t) \quad (6)$$
$$(B1 \neq B2 \wedge L1 \neq L2)(t) \quad (7)$$
$$Bel(Stan,On(B1,L1) \wedge Clear(L2))(1) \quad (8)$$
$$Bel(Ollie,On(B2,L2) \wedge Clear(L1))(1) \quad (9)$$
$$Bel(Stan, (4) \wedge (5) \wedge (6) \wedge (7))(t) \wedge Bel(Ollie, (4) \wedge (5) \wedge (6) \wedge (7))(t) \quad (10)$$
$$Bel(Stan,Does(Stan,Move(B1,L1,L2)))(1) \wedge Does(Stan,Move(B1,L1,L2))(1) \quad (11)$$
$$Bel(Ollie,Does(Ollie,Move(B2,L2,L1)))(1) \wedge Does(Ollie,Move(B2,L2,L1))(1) \quad (12)$$
$$Bel(Stan, (On(B1,L2) \wedge Clear(L1)))(2) \wedge On(B2,L1)(2) \quad (13)$$
$$Bel(Ollie, (On(B2,L1) \wedge Clear(L2)))(2) \wedge On(B1,L2)(2) \quad (14)$$

We thus have a solution to the doxastic version of the frame problem, the problem of effectively formalising agents' beliefs about inertia, which, as some of the consequences of actions are inferred, avoids the doxastic version of the ramification problem; see for example [4].

3.2   The Persistence of Memory

We now consider memories; that is, beliefs about the past and present. Note that as an instance of $\mathcal{P}$ we have

$$\text{Bel}(a,\phi)(i) \land \neg\text{Aff}(\text{Bel}(a,\phi))(i) \supset \text{Bel}(a,\phi)(i+1) \tag{15}$$

But this just says that a's beliefs, like any other facts about the world, persist until they are affected. More interestingly, agents may change their beliefs about the past in the light of new evidence. However, agents should keep those beliefs about the past and present that they have no reason to change

$$(i' \leq_e i) \land \text{Bel}(a,\phi(i'))(i) \land \neg\text{Bel}(a,\text{Aff}(\text{Bel}(a,\phi(i'))))(i) \supset \text{Bel}(a,\phi(i'))(i+1) \tag{$\mathcal{PM}$}$$

For example, if Stan believes at time 2 that block B1 was on L1 at time 1, (16), and Stan has no reason to doubt this belief at time 2, (17), then, by $\mathcal{PM}$, Stan continues to believe it at time 3, (18).

$$\text{Bel}(\text{Stan},\text{On}(\text{B1},\text{L1})(1))(2) \tag{16}$$
$$\neg\text{Bel}(\text{Stan}, \text{Aff}(\text{Bel}(\text{Stan}, \text{On}(\text{B1},\text{L1})(1))))(2) \tag{17}$$
$$\text{Bel}(\text{Stan}, \text{On}(\text{B1},\text{L1})(1))(3) \tag{18}$$

An agent's beliefs about the past can change. For example, Stan may come to believe at time 4 that B1 was on L2 at time 1, (19), and so, given (20), we have (21).

$$\text{Bel}(\text{Stan}, \text{On}(\text{B1},\text{L2})(1))(4) \tag{19}$$
$$\text{Bel}(\text{Stan}, (5) \land (7))(t))(t) \tag{20}$$
$$\text{Bel}(\text{Stan}, \neg\text{On}(\text{B1},\text{L1})(1))(4) \tag{21}$$

3.3   The Persistence of Expectation

Similarly, an agent can have expectations about the future which can rationally be held until there is evidence to the contrary

$$(i <_e i') \land \text{Bel}(a,\phi(i'))(i) \land \neg\text{Bel}(a,\text{Aff}(\text{Bel}(a,\phi(i'))))(i) \supset \text{Bel}(a,\phi(i'))(i+1) \tag{$\mathcal{PE}$}$$

3.4   The Persistence of Belief

Combining $\mathcal{PM}$ and $\mathcal{PE}$ gives the general case

$$\text{Bel}(a,\phi(i'))(i) \land \neg\text{Bel}(a,\text{Aff}(\text{Bel}(a,\phi(i'))))(i) \supset \text{Bel}(a,\phi(i'))(i+1) \tag{$\mathcal{PB}$}$$

Question (Shoham): If at time 1 Stan believes that Ollie will believe φ at time 2, (22), and at time 2 Stan believes that Ollie did not believe φ at time 1, (23), what should Stan believe about Ollie's beliefs about φ at time 3? Answer: (24).

$$\text{Bel}(\text{Stan}, \text{Bel}(\text{Ollie},\varphi)(2))(1) \tag{22}$$
$$\text{Bel}(\text{Stan}, \neg\text{Bel}(\text{Ollie},\varphi)(1))(2) \tag{23}$$
$$\text{Bel}(\text{Stan}, \text{Bel}(\text{Ollie},\varphi)(3))(3) \land \text{Bel}(\text{Stan}, \neg\text{Bel}(\text{Ollie},\varphi)(1))(3) \tag{24}$$

From (22) we obtain Bel(Stan,Bel(Ollie,φ)(2))(2) by $\mathcal{PE}$, and then Bel(Stan, Bel(Ollie,φ)(3))(3) by $\mathcal{BP}$. From (23) we obtain Bel(Stan,¬Bel(Ollie, φ)(1))(3) by $\mathcal{PM}$.

Proposition The logic $\mathcal{KD45}_\mathcal{B} + \mathcal{A} + \mathcal{BP} + \mathcal{PB}$ is consistent.

4 Desires

Intuitively Des(a,φ)(i) means that agent a desires φ at interval i. The semantic clause for Des, and for each modal operator discussed in later sections, is analogous to that for Bel. Desires are the primary motivators of action. However desires need not be rational; an agent may have conflicting and even unrealisable desires. Consequently we take $\mathcal{K}_\mathcal{D}$ as the basis of our provisional static logic of desires and add the constraint $\mathcal{D1}$ which reflects the fact that desires can only be present-directed or future-directed.

$$\text{Des}(a,\phi(i'))(i) \supset i \leq_e i' \qquad\qquad (\mathcal{D1})$$

For the dynamic logic, we have persistence rules analogous to those for beliefs : the desire for persistence and the persistence of desire

$$\text{Des}(a,\phi)(i) \wedge \neg\text{Des}(a,\text{Aff}(\phi))(i) \supset \text{Des}(a,\phi)(i+1) \quad (\mathcal{DP})$$
$$\text{Des}(a,\phi(i'))(i) \wedge \neg\text{Des}(a,\text{Aff}(\text{Des}(a,\phi(i'))))(i) \supset \text{Des}(a,\phi(i'))(i+1) \qquad (\mathcal{PD})$$

As desires can arise from beliefs, we should apply the belief rules before the desire rules. This leads to the following generalisation.

Definition Let $op_1,...,op_n$ be modal operators and M and M' be models of $\mathcal{CA}$ which satisfy any additional conditions that may have been imposed. M is $(op_1,...,op_n)$-preferred to M', written M $<_{(op_1,...,opn)}$ M', if M and M' are $(op_1,...,op_{n-1})$-preferred models and M $<_{(opn)}$ M'; where M $<_{(op)}$ M' iff M $<_{op}$ M', and M is an $(op_1,...,op_{n-1})$-preferred model if there is no model M' such that M' $<_{(op_1,...,opn-1)}$ M. M is an $(op_1,...,op_n)$-preferred model of a theory Θ if M is a model of Θ and there is no model M' of Θ such that M' $<_{(op1,...,opn)}$ M.

We are thus interested in the (Bel,Des)-preferred models of belief-desire theories.
    Goals can be defined to be desires which the agent believes are realisable

$$\text{Goal}(a,\varphi)(i) =_{df} \text{Des}(a,\varphi)(i) \wedge \text{Bel}(a,\exists a',e,i'(\text{Does}(a',e)(i') \supset \varphi))$$

5 Intentions

Intuitively Int(a,φ)(i) means that agent a intends φ at interval i. As Anscombe points out [3], we use the concept of intention to characterise both our actions and our minds. We begin with the idea that intentions are, at least, rational desires. Thus an agent's intentions are consistent subset of its goals, $I_\mathcal{D}$, $I1$. Also, if an agent has an intention then it should believe that it has that intention, $I2$.

$$\text{Int}(a,\varphi)(i) \supset \neg \text{Int}(a,\neg\varphi)(i) \qquad\qquad (I_D)$$
$$\text{Int}(a,\varphi)(i) \supset \text{Goal}(a,\varphi)(i) \qquad\qquad (I1)$$
$$\text{Int}(a,\varphi)(i) \supset \text{Bel}(a,\text{Int}(a,\varphi))(i) \qquad\qquad (I2)$$

Condition Each $\mathcal{R}_{(\text{Int},a,i,w)}$ is serial.

Like desires, intentions can be present-directed or future-directed. They can be further subdivided into action-directed intentions, intentions involving the performance of some action, and end-directed intentions, intentions involving the bringing about of some state of affairs by performing some action.

Present-directed intentions characterise actions as done intentionally and with a certain intention. For example [27], an agent in London walking in direction d may equally be described as trying to get to Hyde Park and trying to get closer to Patagonia. What distinguishes the two actions is the agent's intention in action. Present-action-directed intentions require that the action takes place.

$$\text{Int}(a,\text{Does}(a,e))(i) \supset \text{Does}(a,e)(i) \qquad\qquad (I3)$$

Future-directed intentions, involve an intention to act in a certain way in the future. If an agent has a future-directed intention, the agent should believe that it is realisable and desire that it is so, and this follows from $I1$. The provisional static logic of intentions is thus $\mathcal{KD}_I + I1\text{-}I3$.

5.1 Intentional Persistence

The rule of intentional persistence states that present-directed intentions persist by default.

$$\text{Int}(a,\phi)(i) \land \neg\text{Int}(a,\text{Aff}(\phi))(i) \supset \text{Int}(a,\phi)(i+1) \qquad\qquad (IP)$$

For example, if Stan is walking intentionally at [1,2], (25), we want to use IP to conclude by default that he continues to do so at [1,3], (26).

$$\text{Int}(\text{Stan},\text{Does}(\text{Stan},\text{Walk}))([1,2]) \qquad\qquad (25)$$
$$\text{Int}(\text{Stan},\text{Does}(\text{Stan},\text{Walk}))([1,3]) \qquad\qquad (26)$$

Intentions depend on beliefs and may depend directly or indirectly on desires. This suggests that the intended interpretations of belief-desire-intention theories are the (Bel,Des,Int)-preferred models of such theories.

5.2 The Persistence of Intention

Bratman [9, 10] argues that future-directed intentions play a central role in our everyday practical reasoning, both individual and social. Intentions for the future involve an important kind of commitment to action. This stability, or persistence, of future intentions is important for at least two reasons. "First, we are not frictionless deliberators. Deliberation is a process that takes time and uses other resources, so there are obvious limits to the extent of deliberation at the time of action. By settling on future-directed intentions we allow present reasoning to shape future conduct, thereby extending the influence of Reason in our lives. Second, we have pressing needs for co-ordination, both intra-personal and social; and future-directed intentions play a crucial role in our efforts at achieving such co-ordination." [10, p.2].

Influenced by Bratman's informal theory, Cohen and Levesque [13] base their formal theory of future-directed intention on the notion of commitment. They introduce a Goal operator and go on to define intention as a kind of persistent goal. Goals may be thought of as consistent desires (modulo the unfortunate realism condition which has the consequence that all beliefs are goals [13] p. 234). An achievement goal (A-Goal) is a goal that the agent believes is not currently true. A persistent goal (P-Goal) is then defined to be an A-goal which the agent will not relinquish until the agent believes either that the goal has been achieved, or that it is no longer possible for the agent to achieve it. As Cohen and Levesque point out, this leads to fanaticism; once an agent has adopted a P-Goal the agent will not be deterred no matter how irrational it is to continue pursuing it. Consequently they give an extended definition of P-Goal which has a parameter allowing the specification of an agent's reasons for adopting the goal. The agent may then additionally abandon a P-Goal when one of these reasons for pursuing it no longer holds. In their example, an agent believes that it is going to rain and consequently decides to buy an umbrella. However, before the goal is achieved the weather clears up. The agent's reason for adopting the goal no longer holds, so the agent may abandon the goal. The problem with this proposal is that the agent's commitment persists as long as its reasons for adopting the goal do; no matter how unreasonable it is to continue to pursue it. For example, suppose that the agent has decided to buy an umbrella because it believes that it is going to rain, and suppose that the weather does not clear up. The agent then discovers that it has no money. The goal is still possible and the reason for adopting it still holds, but achieving it means stealing from a little old lady. The little old lady is not prepared to give up her money without a fight, but it is still possible for the agent to achieve the goal by killing her … . Problems such as this can be avoided by additionally allowing the goal to be dropped if any of a series of disqualifying conditions holds. However, this proposal is subject to the ramification problem : as the complexity of the domain increases it rapidly becomes impractical, or impossible, to *stipulate* these conditions in advance; see, for example [4].

There are similar problems with commitment in Rao and Georgeff's [26] account of intention. They introduce three commitment strategies. A *blind agent* maintains its intentions until it believes that it has actually achieved them. Clearly this is even worse that the fanatical commitment involved in P-Goals. A *single-minded agent* maintains its intentions as long as it believes that they are still realisable. This corresponds to the fanatical commitment in Cohen and Levesque's theory. While an *open-minded agent* is one which maintains its intention as long as it is still one of its goals. This avoids the problem of fanaticism, but at the cost of persistence. Nothing now distinguishes a goal from a fleeting sometime-achievable desire.

A better solution allows agents to *reason* about their intentions, and to abandon them when it is no longer rational to continue holding them. For example, when the agent discovers that it has no money it should give up the intention to buy an umbrella. However, agents are not continually reasoning about and revising their intentions; to do so would, defeat the purpose of future intentions, as they would no longer provide a means of overcoming resource-boundedness and of achieving co-operation. Thus reconsideration should be the exception, not the rule. This default persistence of intention can be achieved by means of the following rule.

$$\text{Int}(a,\phi(i'))(i) \ \wedge \ \neg\text{Int}(a,\text{Aff}(\text{Int}(a,\phi(i'))))(i) \supset \ \text{Int}(a,\phi(i'))(i+1) \qquad (\mathcal{PI})$$

When combined with *I3*, *PI* has the desired consequence that future intentions normally lead to action. For example, given that at time 1 Stan has the future intention to pickup A at time 3, (27), we can use *PI* to conclude, in (Int)-preferred models of the theory, that his intention persists until time 3, (28), and thus, by *I3*, that he carries out his intention (29).

$$\text{Int}(\text{Stan},\text{Does}(\text{Stan},\text{Pickup}(A))(3))(1) \qquad (27)$$
$$\text{Int}(\text{Stan},\text{Does}(\text{Stan},\text{Pickup}(A))(3))(3) \qquad (28)$$
$$\text{Does}(\text{Stan},\text{Pickup}(A))(3) \qquad (29)$$

6 Obligations

Intuitively $\text{Obl}(a,\phi)(i)$ means that ϕ is an obligation of a's at i. For simplicity no conditions are imposed on the accessibility relations and so our provisional static logic of obligations is $\mathcal{K}_O$ [20] together with *O1* (the Obl-analogue of *D1*). Once again, this needs to be refined and extended. For example, adding the axiom $\neg\text{Obl}(a,\varphi \wedge \neg\varphi)(i)$ rules out impossible obligations, however it also rules out moral dilemmas; that is, sentences of the form $\text{Obl}(a,\varphi)(i) \wedge \text{Obl}(a,\neg\varphi)(i)$. One solution might be to adopt a logic of local obligation analogous to Fagin and Halpern's logic of local belief [14], alternatively we could introduce imperatives [30].

As the basis of the dynamic theory, we again want rules which specify the default persistence of obligations.

$$\text{Obl}(a,\phi)(i) \wedge \neg\text{Obl}(a,\text{Aff}(\phi))(i) \supset \text{Obl}(a,\phi)(i+1) \quad (\mathcal{OP})$$
$$\text{Obl}(a,\phi(i'))(i) \wedge \neg\text{Obl}(a,\text{Aff}(\text{Obl}(a,\phi(i'))))(i) \supset \text{Obl}(a,\phi(i'))(i+1) \qquad (\mathcal{PO})$$

These rules provide a natural way of representing the distinction between prima facie and actual obligations, [2] pp. 658-9. At time t an obligation may arise to act at some future time t'. However this obligation may be *overruled* by a stronger and conflicting one arising in the meantime. In this case, the former obligation is said to be a *prima facie* obligation, an obligation which holds other things being equal, whereas the second *actual* obligation is unconditional. For example [2], at time 1 John promises to marry Suzy at time 7, (30). However, at time 6 he learns that his mother in Australia is dying, and so is obliged to visit her immediately, (31). This forces him to break his promise to Suzy, (32). In (Obl)-preferred models of the theory the prima facie obligation persists, by *PO*, until it is overruled by the actual obligation at time 6, (33)-(34).

$$\text{Obl}(\text{John},\text{Does}(\text{John},\text{Marry}(\text{Suzy}))(7))(1) \qquad (30)$$
$$\text{Obl}(\text{John},\text{Does}(\text{John},\text{Goto}(\text{Australia})))(6) \qquad (31)$$
$$\text{Obl}(\text{John},\text{Does}(\text{John},\text{Goto}(\text{Australia})))(6) \supset$$
$$\text{Obl}(\text{John},\text{Aff}(\text{Obl},\text{Does}(\text{John},\text{Marry}(\text{Suzy}))(7)))(6) \qquad (32)$$
$$\text{Obl}(\text{John},\text{Does}(\text{John},\text{Marry}(\text{Suzy}))(7))(6) \qquad (33)$$
$$\neg\text{Obl}(\text{John},\text{Does}(\text{John},\text{Marry}(\text{Suzy})))(7) \qquad (34)$$

In theories involving beliefs, desires, intentions and obligations, it seems reasonable to consider the (Bel,Des,Obl,Int)-preferred models, as obligations may lead to the adopting or dropping of intentions.

7 Rationality

We have outlined a framework in which attitudes persist by default. In so doing we have provided solutions to mentalistic versions of the frame problem (the $\mathcal{BP}$, $\mathcal{DP}$, IP, and $\mathcal{OP}$ rules) without invoking the corresponding versions of the ramification problem. In the formalisation of commonsense causal reasoning this is an appropriate place to stop. However, in the case of mental attitudes we need to go further. First we need default rules (such as, $\mathcal{PB}$, $\mathcal{PD}$, $\mathcal{PI}$, and $\mathcal{PO}$) in which the agent's attitudes persist by default, but can be changed by introspection. For example, in the case of intentions we have formalised the persistence of an agent's future intentions by default ($\mathcal{PI}$) and opened the way for the agent to *reason* about its intentions and to abandon them if it becomes irrational to continue holding them. We also need to specify appropriate teleological theories in which agents give up attitudes when it becomes unreasonable to hold them. For example, we need to fomalise the process by which the agent decides that its intention has become irrational.

A natural move at this stage is to introduce a rationality operator. Intuitively, Rat(a,φ)(i) means that φ is rational given a's mental state at i. Thus, Rat(a,Bel(a,φ))(i) states that a's belief that φ is true at i is rational given a's mental state at i, Rat(a,Int(a,φ))(i) states that φ is a rational intention of a's given a's mental state at i, and Rat(a,Does(a,e))(i) states that a's action e is rational given a's mental state at i. Then an agent might abandon an attitude (or action) if it reasons that it is no longer rational to hold (or do) it. For example, $\mathcal{PB}$ and $\mathcal{PI}$ might be replaced by

$$\text{Bel}(a,\phi(i'))(i) \;\wedge\; \neg\text{Bel}(a,\neg\text{Rat}(a, \text{Bel}(a,\phi(i'))))(i) \supset \text{Bel}(a,\phi(i'))(i{+}1) \qquad (\mathcal{PB}')$$
$$\text{Int}(a,\phi(i'))(i) \;\wedge\; \neg\text{Bel}(a,\neg\text{Rat}(a, \text{Int}(a,\phi(i'))))(i) \supset \text{Int}(a,\phi(i'))(i{+}1) \qquad (\mathcal{PI}')$$

Some of the agent's attitudes may be rational given its mental state, while others may not be. We thus, at least, require that

Condition For each agent a, interval i and world w

$$\mathcal{W}_{(\text{Rat},a,i,w)} \supseteq \mathcal{W}_{(\text{Bel},a,i,w)} \cup \mathcal{W}_{(\text{Des},a,i,w)} \cup \mathcal{W}_{(\text{Int},a,i,w)} \cup \mathcal{W}_{(\text{Obl},a,i,w)}$$

However this is not very informative. The remainder of this section outlines the proposed approach.

Beliefs should be held as long as there is no contradictory evidence of greater credibility. Quine [25] suggests the idea of a "web" (almost-connected partial order) of beliefs in which a peripheral belief, for example an agent's perception-based belief about some aspect of its current situation, might be given up relatively easily in the face of contrary evidence, while more central beliefs, for example beliefs in the Laws of Nature, are much less likely to be given up no matter what contrary evidence arises. This idea has formal echoes in the work of Gärdenfors [16] and others.

A major contribution of Bratman's work is the view of intentions as parts of larger partial plans. While Bratman distances himself somewhat from the definite notions of plans developed in AI, it seems that a good way to formalise rational intention, obligation and action is to formalise (aspects of) a hierarchical non-linear planner which integrates generation execution and monitoring; for example, IPEM [1] and SIPE [31]. This involves having an agenda of goals (including maintenance goals, such as surviving, and continuing to watch a TV programme, and achievement goals, such as getting a degree, and opening a door), a plan generator which reduces these goals to more achievable sub-goals, and a scheduler which dynamically determines how these goals can best be achieved given the limited resources available and the constraints in force. This requires that the agenda can be (partially) ordered according to some value system; but otherwise reduces the problem of rational agency to a planning problem. On this view the only difference between, say, fulfilling an intention and meeting an obligation is that the latter will typically be given a higher priority by the scheduler. A similar view is expressed by Pollock [24], however his account differs significantly in detail; for example, in the nature and role of desires and obligations, and in the view of planning.

8 Further Work

In addition to formalising the theory of rationality and refining and extending the static logics much else remains to be done.

The theory will be extended to include the multi-agent attitudes necessary for co-ordination, co-operation and competition. For example commitments (or obligations between agents) [29], and joint intentions of groups of agents [18]. In this paper we have taken a simple *objective* view when defining preference criteria; that is we have not referred to particular agents. This has sufficed for present purposes, however the *subjective* perspectives of individual agents are essential in the accurate representation of multi-agent scenarios. For example agent a may come to believe φ at i+1 on the basis of the belief that agent a' does not believe φ at i; as happens in the Wise Man Puzzle. We may want to impose credence orders on agents, or to define *inter-subjective* preference criteria over groups of agents. It may also be that we cannot define ordering-based preference criteria and have to resort to more general function-based relevance criteria [6, 8].

Finally, there is the question of implementation. This will be done by following the model-building programme suggested in [8] and extending its application from causal theories [7, 17] to (suitably restricted) teleological theories as part of the DYNAMO project (UK, EPSRC GR/K19266).

Acknowledgements

An earlier version of this paper was presented at the AAAI Spring Symposium on Reasoning About Mental States : Formal Theories and Applications, held at Stanford University in March 1993. I am grateful to everyone who has refereed it and to everyone else who has commented on it. This research was supported by The Royal Society (UK), the RED project (UK, DTI/EPSRC ITD4/1/9053), and the DRUMS project (EC, ESPRIT BRA 6156).

Appendix: The language CA

CA is a many-sorted first-order modal language (family) with explicit reference to time points and intervals. It has its origins in the languages in [5, 13, 28] and is still evolving.

Syntax

Let
- D, A, T and E be pairwise disjoint sets of constant symbols.
- V_D, V_A, V_T, V_I and V_E be pairwise disjoint sets of variable symbols.
- F_S be a set of sets F_{Sn} of n-ary function symbols, for $S \in \{D, A, T, I, E\}$ and $n \geq 1$.
- R be a set of sets R_n of n-ary relation symbols, for $n \geq 0$.
- Op be a set of sets Op_n of n-ary modal operators, for $n \geq 1$.

The terms of sort object, agent, time point, interval and event (the sets $term_D$, $term_A$, $term_T$, $term_I$ and $term_E$ respectively) are then defined as follows.

Definition CA terms
For $S \in \{D, A, T, E\}$, $term_S$ is the minimal set such that
- $S \cup V_S \subseteq term_S$, and
- if $f \in F_{Sn}$, and $u_1, ... , u_m \in term_S$ then $f(u_1, ... , u_m) \in term_S$.

$term_I$ is the minimal set such that
- $\{[u,u'] \mid u,u' \in term_T\} \cup V_I \subseteq term_I$, and
- if $f \in F_{In}$, and $u_1, ... , u_m \in term_I$ then $f(u_1, ... , u_m) \in term_I$.

Definition CA formulas
- If $t, t' \in term_T$ then $(t < t') \in CA$.
- If $u_1, ... , u_n \in term_D \cup term_A$, $r \in R_n$, and $i \in term_I$ then $r(u_1, ... , u_n)(i) \in CA$.
- If $u,u' \in term_D \cup term_A$ and $i \in term_I$ then $(u = u')(i) \in CA$.
- If $e \in term_E$ and $i \in term_I$ then $Occurs(e)(i) \in CA$.
- If $a \in term_A$, $e \in term_E$ and $i \in term_I$ then $Agent(a,e)(i) \in CA$.
- If $a_1, ... , a_n \in term_A$ for $n \geq 0$, $\varphi \in CA$, $op \in Op_{n+1}$, and $i \in term_I$ then $op((a_1, ... , a_n),\varphi)(i) \in CA$.
- If $\phi(i) \in CA$ then $Aff(\phi(i))(i) \in CA$.
- If $\psi, \chi \in CA$ then $\neg\psi \in CA$ and $(\psi \vee \chi) \in CA$.
- If $S \in \{D, A, T, I, E\}$, $v \in V_S$, and $\varphi \in CA$ then $\exists v\varphi \in CA$.

Definition Relations and functions on time points and intervals.
$$t_1 = t_2 \ =_{df} \ \neg(t_1 < t_2) \wedge \neg(t_2 < t_1)$$
$$t_1 \leq t_2 \ =_{df} \ (t_1 < t_2) \vee (t_1 = t_2)$$
$$min([t_1,t_2]) =_{df} min(t_1,t_2), \ max([t_1,t_2]) =_{df} max(t_1,t_2)$$
$$i <_e i' =_{df} max(i) < max(i'), \ i =_e i' =_{df} max(i) = max(i')$$
$$i \leq_e i' =_{df} (i <_e i') \vee (i =_e i')$$
$$i = i' =_{df} min(i) = min(i') \wedge max(i) = max(i')$$

$i \subset i'$ $=_{df}$ $min(i) = min(i') \wedge max(i) < max(i')$
$i \subseteq i'$ $=_{df}$ $i \subset i' \vee i = i'$
$i+1$ $=_{df}$ $[min(i)+1, max(i)+1]$ if $min(i) = max(i)$, $[min(i),max(i)+1]$ otherwise

$i+1$ is said to be the interval which *increments* i. More generally, if $i \subset i'$ we say that i *extends* i'.

Abbreviations
- The logical constants $\wedge, \supset, \equiv, \forall$ are defined in the usual way.
- Interval terms of the form [t,t] will usually be abbreviated simply to t.
- Enclosing universal quantifiers are omitted.
- $op(\varphi)(i)$ abbreviates $op((),\varphi)(i)$ and $op(a,\varphi)(i)$ abbreviates $op((a),\varphi)(i)$.
- As in natural language, multiple occurrences of the same interval term may be eliminated when the result is unambiguous; e.g. $(\phi \vee \phi')(i)$ abbreviates $\phi(i) \vee \phi'(i)$.
- $op(a_1, \ldots, a_n,\phi)(i)$ abbreviates $op(a_1, \ldots, a_n,\phi(i))(i)$. Thus $op(a,op(a,\phi(i')))(i)$ abbreviates $op(a,op(a,\phi(i'))(i))(i)$ rather than $op(a,op(a,\phi(i'))(i'))(i)$. The convention is that missing interval terms are the same as immediately enclosing ones.

The symbols φ, ψ and χ are used as meta-variables for formulas, while ϕ is used as a meta-variable for incomplete sub-formulas which can be completed by adjoining a temporal index; thus $\phi(i) \in CA$ if $i \in term_I$. Intuitively a sentence of the form $\phi(i)$ asserts that ϕ is true at interval i. In particular, Occurs(e)(i) asserts that event e occurs during i, Agent(a,e)(i) asserts that a is an agent of event e at i. $Aff(\phi(i))(i)$ states that the truth value of $\phi(i)$ is affected at i; that is, the truth value of $\phi(i)$ changes at the end of i. Sentences of the form $op((a_1,\ldots,a_n),\varphi)(i)$ are agent- and interval- indexed modal sentences. It is assumed that each Op_n contains the n-ary operators used. Examples are: $Bel \in Op_2$, where $Bel(a,\varphi)(i)$ states that a believes φ at i, and $Cmt \in Op_3$, where $Cmt((a,a'),\varphi)(i)$ states that a has a commitment to a' concerning φ at i; cf. [29].

Semantics

Definition A CA model is a structure

$M = (W, w_0, D, A, E, T, r_T, I, Occurs, Agent, Op, V, F, R)$
where
- W, D, A, E and T are disjoint non-empty sets.
- w_0 is a distinguished member of W.
- $r_T \subseteq T \times T$.
- $I = \{[t,t'] \mid t,t' \in T\}$.
- $Occurs \subseteq E \times I \times W$.
- $Agent \subseteq A \times E \times I \times W$ is such that $(a,e,i,w) \in Agent$ only if $(e,i,w) \in Occurs$.
- $Op: Op_n \times A^n \times I \times W \to \wp W \times \wp(W \times W)$ is such that for any $op \in Op_n$ and $\alpha = (op, (a_1, \ldots, a_n),i,w)$, $Op\alpha = (W_\alpha, R_\alpha)$ is centered at w, that is $w \in W_\alpha$, and $(w,w') \in R_\alpha$ for any $w' \neq w$ in W_α.
- $V = (V_D, V_A, V_T, V_I, V_E)$ is an interpretation function such that $V_S: S \to S$ for $(S, S) \in \{(D, D), (A, A), (T, T), (I, I), (E, E)\}$.

- $\mathcal{F} = (\mathcal{F}_D, \mathcal{F}_A, \mathcal{F}_T, \mathcal{F}_I, \mathcal{F}_E)$, where $\mathcal{F}_S : F_{Sn} \to (S^n \to S)$
  for $(S, \mathcal{S}) \in \{(D, \mathcal{D}), (A, \mathcal{A}), (T, \mathcal{T}), (I, \mathcal{I}), (E, \mathcal{E})\}$.
- $\mathcal{R} : R_n \times I \times \mathcal{W} \to \wp(\mathcal{A}^1 \times \ldots \times \mathcal{A}^m \times \mathcal{D}^{m+1} \times \ldots \times \mathcal{D}^n)$
  where $0 \leq m \leq n$.

Intuitively $\mathcal{W}$ is a set of possible worlds, w_0 being the actual world, $\mathcal{D}$ is a set of objects, $\mathcal{A}$ is a set of agents, $\mathcal{E}$ is a set of primitive event types, and $\mathcal{T}$ is a set of time points. The worlds in $\mathcal{W}$ are thought of as total possible world histories which share a common flow of time $(\mathcal{T}, r_T)$. The binary multisets in I represent intervals; so intervals are defined in terms of time points. Op maps modal operators, their indices and worlds to possible-worlds frames. For each $\alpha = (op, (a_1, \ldots, a_n,) i, w)$, the conditions on $\mathcal{W}_\alpha$ and $\mathcal{R}_\alpha$ capture the idea that $\mathcal{W}_\alpha$ is the set of $\mathcal{R}_\alpha$-accessible worlds from w. The definition of $\mathcal{R}$ allows the extension of relations to vary between worlds and times, but for simplicity, the definitions of $\mathcal{V}$ and $\mathcal{F}$ result in the denotation of constants and functions being fixed across worlds and times.

Definition A variable assignment is a function $g = (g_D, g_A, g_T, g_I, g_E)$ where $g_S: V_S \to \mathcal{S}$ for $(S, \mathcal{S}) \in \{(D, \mathcal{D}), (A, \mathcal{A}), (T, \mathcal{T}), (I, \mathcal{I}), (E, \mathcal{E})\}$.

Definition Let g be a variable assignment, and let $\mathcal{V}$ and $\mathcal{F}$ be defined as above. Then the term valuation function $\mathcal{V}_g$ is defined as follows:
- $\mathcal{V}_g(\tau) = \mathcal{V}_S(\tau)$, for $\tau \in S \in \{D, A, T, E\}$.
- $\mathcal{V}_g(\tau) = g_S(\tau)$, $\tau \in V_S$, $S \in \{D, A, T, I, E\}$.
- $\mathcal{V}_g(\tau) = [\mathcal{V}_g(u), \mathcal{V}_g(u')]$, for $\tau = [u,u'] \in term_I$.
- $\mathcal{V}_g(\tau) = \mathcal{F}_S(f)(\mathcal{V}_g(u_1), \ldots, \mathcal{V}_g(u_n))$, for $\tau = f(u_1, \ldots, u_n) \in term_S$,
  $(S, \mathcal{S}) \in \{(D, \mathcal{D}), (A, \mathcal{A}), (T, \mathcal{T}), (I, \mathcal{I}), (E, \mathcal{E})\}$.

Definition A variable assignment g satisfies a formula φ at a world w in a $\mathcal{CA}$ model $M = (\mathcal{W}, w_0, \mathcal{D}, \mathcal{A}, \mathcal{E}, \mathcal{T}, r_T, I, Occurs, Agent, Op, \mathcal{V}, \mathcal{F}, \mathcal{R})$, written $M,w,g \models \varphi$, as follows.

$M,w,g \models t < t'$	iff	$(\mathcal{V}_g(t), \mathcal{V}_g(t')) \in r_T$
$M,w,g \models r(u_1, \ldots, u_n)(i)$	iff	$(\mathcal{V}_g(u_1), \ldots, \mathcal{V}_g(u_n)) \in \mathcal{R}(r, \mathcal{V}_g(i), w)$
$M,w,g \models (u_1 = u_2)(i)$	iff	$\mathcal{V}_g(u_1)$ is $\mathcal{V}_g(u_2)$
$M,w,g \models Occurs(e)(i)$	iff	$(\mathcal{V}_g(e), \mathcal{V}_g(i), w) \in Occurs$
$M,w,g \models Agent(a,e)(i)$	iff	$(\mathcal{V}_g(a), \mathcal{V}_g(e), \mathcal{V}_g(i), w) \in Agent$
$M,w,g \models op((a_1, \ldots, a_n), \psi)(i)$	iff	$\alpha = (op, (\mathcal{V}_g(a_1), \ldots, \mathcal{V}_g(a_n)), \mathcal{V}_g(i), w),$
		$Op\alpha = (\mathcal{W}_\alpha, \mathcal{R}_\alpha)$ and
		$M, w',g \models \psi$ for all $(w,w') \in \mathcal{R}_\alpha$
$M,w,g \models Aff(\phi)(i)$	iff	there is an i' such that $i \subset i'$ and for any i" such that $i \subset i'' \subseteq i'$
		either $M,w,g \models \phi(i)$ and $M,w,g \not\models \phi(i'')$
		or $M,w,g \not\models \phi(i)$ and $M,w,g \models \phi(i'')$
$M,w,g \models \neg\psi$	iff	$M, w,g \not\models \psi$
$M,w,g \models \psi \vee \chi$	iff	$M,w,g \models \psi$ or $M,w,g \models \chi$
$M,w,g \models \exists v\psi$	iff	$M,w,g' \models \psi$ for some g' differing from g at most on v

Note that the semantic clause for Aff does not assume that time is discrete.

Definition A formula φ is true at a world w in M (written M,w $\models \varphi$) if φ is satisfied by all assignments g at w, φ is true in M (written M $\models \varphi$) if M, $w_0 \models \varphi$.

CA can be extended in many ways. Familiar tense operators can be defined; for example

$$F(\phi)(t) =_{df} \exists t'(t < t' \wedge \phi(t'))$$
$$S(\phi,\phi')(t) =_{df} \exists t'(t' < t \wedge \phi(t') \wedge \forall t''(t' \leq t'' \leq t \supset \phi'(t'')))$$
$$U(\phi,\phi')(t) =_{df} \exists t'(t < t' \wedge \phi(t') \wedge \forall t''(t \leq t'' \leq t' \supset \phi'(t'')))$$

Kamp showns that if the order of time is linear and complete then S(ince) and U(ntil) are sufficient to define all possible temporal operators [23]. The operators of Dynamic Logic [21] can be defined, allowing the representation of complex events. For example, assuming discrete linear time

$$Starts(i,i') =_{df} min(i) = min(i') \wedge max(i) \leq max(i')$$
$$Ends(i,i') =_{df} min(i) \geq min(i') \wedge max(i) = max(i')$$
$$Meets(i,i') =_{df} max(i)+1 = min(i')$$
$$Contains(i,i') =_{df} min(i') \geq min(i) \wedge max(i') \leq max(i)$$
$$Occurs(e_1;e_2)(i) =_{df}$$
$$\quad \exists i',i''(Starts(i',i) \wedge Meets(i',i'') \wedge Ends(i'',i) \wedge Occurs(e_1)(i') \wedge Occurs(e_2)(i''))$$
$$Occurs(e_1|e_2)(i) =_{df} Occurs(e_1)(i) \vee Occurs(e_2)(i)$$
$$Occurs(e_1||e_2)(i) =_{df} Occurs(e_1)(i) \wedge Occurs(e_2)(i)$$
$$Occurs(e^*)(i) =_{df} Occurs(e^+)(i) \vee \neg \exists i'(Contains(i,i') \wedge Occurs(e)(i'))$$
$$Occurs(e^+)(i) =_{df} \exists i'(Starts(i',i) \wedge Occurs(e)(i') \wedge$$
$$\quad (Ends(i',i) \vee \exists i''(Meets(i',i'') \wedge Ends(i'',i) \wedge Occurs(e^+)(i''))))$$
$$Occurs(?\phi)(i) =_{df} \phi(i)$$

Complex actions can be defined in like manner; for example

$$Does(a,e_1;e_2)(i) =_{df}$$
$$\quad \exists i',i''(Starts(i',i) \wedge Meets(i',i'') \wedge Ends(i'',i) \wedge Does(a,e_1)(i') \wedge Does(a,e_2)(i''))$$

References

[1] J. Ambros-Ingerson and S. Steel: Integrated Planning, Execution and Monitoring. Proceedings AAAI'88, pp. 83-88.
[2] L. Aqvist: Deontic Logic. In: D. Gabbay and F. Guenthner (eds.): Handbook of Philosophical Logic, Vol. II. Dordrecht: D. Reidel 1984, pp. 605-714.
[3] G.E.M. Anscombe: Intention (second edition). Oxford: Basil Blackwell 1963.
[4] J. Bell: Why the frame problem is not a problem. AI Communications 3(1) pp. 3-10, (1990).
[5] J. Bell: Extended causal theories. Artificial Intelligence 48 pp. 211-224, 1991.
[6] J. Bell: Pragmatic Logics. Proceedings KR'91, pp. 50-60 (1991).
[7] J. Bell: Model-based causal reasoning. In: P. Doherty and D. Driankov (eds.): Partiality, Modality and Nonmonotonicity; Proceedings of the Workshop on Partial Semantics and Nonmonotonic Reasoning, Linköping, Sweden, May 1992. Oxford: Oxford University Press, to appear.

[8]   J. Bell: Pragmatic reasoning, a model-based theory. In: M. Masuch and L. Polos (eds.): Applied Logic, How, What and Why; Proceedings of the Applied Logic Conference, Amsterdam, December 1992. Amsterdam: Kluwer Academic Publishers, to appear at the end of 1994, pp. 1-28.

[9]   M.E. Bratman: Intention, Plans, and Practical Reason. Cambridge Massachusetts: Harvard University Press 1988.

[10] M.E. Bratman: Planning and the Stability of Intention. Minds and Machines 2, pp. 1-16 (1992).

[11] F. Brown (ed.): The Frame Problem in Artificial Intelligence. San Mateo, California: Morgan Kaufmann 1987 .

[12] B. Chellas: Modal Logic. Cambridge: Cambridge University Press 1980.

[13] P. Cohen and H. Levesque: Intention is choice with commitment. Artificial Intelligence 42 pp. 213-261 (1990).

[14] R. Fagin and J. Halpern: Belief, awareness, and limited reasoning. Artificial Intelligence 34, pp. 39-76 (1988) .

[15] R. Fagin, J. Halpern, Y. Moses, and M. Vardi: Reasoning About Knowledge. Cambridge Massachusetts: MIT Press, to appear in 1995.

[16] P. Gärfenfors: Knowledge in Flux. Cambridge Massachusetts: MIT Press 1988.

[17] S. Graham: Further investigations in model-based causal reasoning. M. Sc. Project Report, Dept. of Computer Science, Queen Mary and Westfield College, London E1_ 4NS, 1993.

[18] B. Grosz and S. Kraus: Collaborative plans for group activities. Proceedings IJCAI-93, Vol 1, pp. 367-373, (1993).

[19] J. Halpern (ed.): Theoretical Aspects of Reasoning About Knowledge. San Mateo California: Morgan Kaufmann 1986.

[20] W.H. Hanson: Semantics for deontic logic. Logique et Analyse 8 pp. 177-190 (1965).

[21] D. Harel: First-Order Dynamic Logic. Berlin: Springer 1979.

[22] J. Hintikka: Knowledge and Belief. New York: Cornell University Press 1962.

[23] H. Kamp: Tense Logic and the Theory of Linear Order. Ph.D. dissertation, Department of Philosophy, UCLA, 1968.

[24] J. Pollock: The phylogeny of rationality. Cognitive Science 17, pp. 563-588 (1993).

[25] W.V.O. Quine: Two dogmas of Empiricism. In: From a Logical Point of View. Cambridge Massachusetts: Harvard University Press 1953.

[26] A.S. Rao and M.P. Georgeff: Modelling rational agents within a BDI-architecture, Proceedings KR'91, pp. 473-484 (1991).

[27] J. Searle: Minds, Brains, and Science. Cambridge Massachusetts: Harvard University Press 1984.

[28] Y. Shoham: Reasoning About Change. Cambridge Massachusetts: MIT Press 1988.

[29] Y. Shoham: Agent-oriented programming. Artificial Intelligence 60, pp. 51-92 (1993).

[30] B. van Fraassen: Values and the heart's command. The Journal of Philosophy 70, pp. 5-19 (1973) .

[31] D. Wilkins: Practical Planning. San Mateo California: Morgan Kaufmann 1988.

Guarantees for Autonomy
in
Cognitive Agent Architecture

Cristiano Castelfranchi
PSCS- Project for the Simulation of Social Behaviour
Istituto di Psicologia del CNR
viale Marx 15 - 00137 Roma - ITALY
+39 6 860 90 518; fax +39 6 82 47 37
cris@pscs2.irmkant.rm.cnr.it

> *"Que chacun, en s'unissant aux autres, n'obéisse*
> *qu'à lui-même et reste libre comme auparavant"*
> (In joining others, let everyone obey nobody else
> but oneself, and remain free as before)
> J.J.Rousseau, *"Contract Social"*

Abstract

The paper analyses which features of an agent architecture determine its Autonomy. I claim that Autonomy is a relational concept. First, Autonomy from environment (stimuli) is analysed, and the notion of Cognitive Reactivity is introduced to show how the cognitive architecture of the agent guarantees Stimulus-Autonomy and deals with the "Descartes problem" relative to the external "causes" of behaviour. Second, Social Autonomy is analysed (Autonomy from others). A distinction between Executive Autonomy and Motivational Autonomy is introduced. Some limitations that current postulates on Rational interacting agents could impose on their Autonomy are discussed. Architectural properties and postulates that guarantee a sufficient Autonomy in cognitive social agents are defined. These properties give the agent control over its own mental states (Beliefs and Goals). In particular, a "double filter" architecture against influence, is described. What guarantees agent's control over its own Beliefs is specified: relevance, credibility, introspective competence. Particular attention is devoted to the "non negotiability of beliefs" (Pascal law): the fact that you cannot change the other's Beliefs by using promises or threats. What guarantees agent's control over its Goals is specified: self-interested goal adoption, and indirect influencing. Finally, it is argued how and why social dependence and power relations should limit the agent's Autonomy.

1 Introduction

Autonomy is a crucial notion both in AI and DAI studies [19], [20], [11]. In fact, there are many different circulating notions of Autonomy (from Robot's motion, to negotiating economic agents), and multiple levels of analysis. I will deal with some foundational aspects relative to the Autonomy of Cognitive and Social agents.

This is not a formal paper, aimed to formally define postulates on Agent and action. It is more a conceptual paper, trying to formulate some crucial postulates (to be formalized) that guarantee Autonomy and sociality; trying to sketch some essential features of an agent architecture. I will assume a Cognitive Modelling perspective:

which features of an agent architecture determine its Autonomy? What are the relationships between Cognition, Rationality, and Autonomy?

I will support two main claims:

Autonomy is a relational concept. Mainly, it is a social concept. An agent is "autonomous" just in relation to the influence of other agents.

Agents' autonomy is necessarily limited, bounded (as its rationality). Otherwise the Autonomy would be contradictory with the agent's situatedness, and with the advantages of Sociality.

I will start discussing the "Descartes problem": how (human) behaviour is responsive, adapted to the environment, but also "independent of" the external stimuli. Then, I will introduce and define the notion of "Cognitive Reactivity".

After, I will discuss the notion of "Socially Autonomous Agent". Distinguishing between "executive or means" Autonomy, and "motivational or goal Autonomy". I will stress the difference between Autonomy and Rationality, following the current model of Rational Action. I will stress some limitations of current postulates on Rational interacting agents.

I will define architectural properties and postulates that guarantee a sufficient Autonomy in cognitive social agents, giving the agent control over its own mental states (Beliefs and Goals). First of all, I will describe what I call the "double filter" against influence.

In particular, I will analyse:

- what guarantees agent's *control over its own Beliefs*
  - *relevance*
  - *credibility*
  - *introspective competence*
  - *non negotiability of beliefs (Pascal law)*

- what guarantees agent's *control over its Goals*
  - *self-interested goal adoption*
  - *postulate of indirect influencing*

Finally, I will define what limits the Agent's Autonomy (Social Dependence and Power), and justify why this is both unavoidable (like for bounded rationality) and advantageous.

2 Autonomy: a Relational Notion

2.1 Agenthood, Self-Regulation, and Autonomy

To define a heuristic notion of Autonomous Agent, Self-Regulation in not sufficient.

"Agent" is a system whose behaviour is neither casual nor strictly causal, but teleonomic, "goal-oriented" toward a certain state of the world. In particular, for Cognitive Modeling, "goal governed" or "purposive" behaviours (*Actions*) are relevant [25], [26]: those controlled by an *internal explicit representation* used as a cybernetic "set point" (*Goal*). "Intentions" are just a kind of internal Goals; "intentional actions" are just a kind of Actions.

Self-Regulated Agents are "goal governed" agents, who given a certain Goal, are able to achieve it by themselves: planning, executing actions, adapting and correcting actions. In a sense, even a sub-cognitive cybernetic servo-mechanism (like a thermostat) is able to assure "autonomously" the fulfilment of a given goal-state.

However, I don't think that this level or notion of Autonomy is very heuristic, and interesting.

To be an Agent and to be Self-Regulated (even with complex planning and reactive capacities) are not sufficient conditions to be an Autonomous Agent. Autonomy requires "Autonomous Goals"[11].

Executive Autonomy

If a robot acts just in order to execute orders, to comply with external requests, without any initiative or "personal" preferences, even if it is able to find solutions to my problems and carry out appropriate plans and actions, it is not a fully "Autonomous Agent". Let me call "executive" this kind and level of Autonomy. It is relative just to the "means" (to instrumental sub-goals), not to the "ends". It could imply some level of decision (choice among means), or some level of planning and problem solving; depending on the level of the assigned "tasks" (more or less close to movements).

What does it means "to have Autonomous Goals"? "Autonomous" from what should these Goals be? Should they be just "internal"? Or also endogenous? In our analysis an agent may accept, and adopt, goals from outside (orders, requests, expectations, norms), but this doesn't hamper its Autonomy, which is not synonym of Autarchy or a-sociality.

One can not define Autonomy, other than in relational terms (this is the main point missed in Covrigaru & Lindsay [11] discussion). For example in social terms: a robot has some initiative, or has "its own goals", when/if for such Goals it could refuse to do what I ask it to do, and/or do something I didn't ask for. So its Goals are Autonomous from me, from my Goals; they are "its own" Goals.

More generally, the very concept of Autonomy is an intrinsically relational concept: *the Autonomy of a system is defined in relation to another system.*

> *X is Autonomous from Y (as for p)*

where *p* is a behaviour of *X* (for Cognitive Agents then *p* is a Goal of *X*).

We should consider two main relations:
- *Autonomy from physical context (from environment)*
- *Autonomy from social context (from other agents)*.

2.2 The Descartes Problem and Cognitive Autonomy

Both in biological and artificial Agents acting in a real world, Autonomy is necessarily limited.

Since they have to be "situated", Agents have to be and to act in a way that "fits" the context. The behaviour of a real Agent cannot be completely "autistic", unrelated to and unconcerned about its world, governed only by its internal representations (Autistic Agent).

This relationship between Autonomy and Adaptation is what Chomsky discussed as "Descartes Problem": *responses of many living systems (specially humans) to the environment are "neither caused by, not independent of the external stimuli"* [6].

Our behaviour is influenced by external stimuli, but is not determined or imposed by them. It fits the external situations, but it is not caused by the situations. *Behaviour has no "causes", but "reasons", "motives"*. It is not under the laws of forces, pushes, attrition (see the opposite current attempt to model Agent behaviour, and also "mental states" like "desires", in terms of Dynamics, e.g. [22], [9]). Behaviour is not a set of rigid and deterministic reflexes to external stimuli.

How to solve the Descartes Problem? What Agent Architecture guarantees that the Agent is neither completely determined by stimuli (stimulus dependent), nor completely non reactive to environmental changes?

Autonomy from Stimuli

Even purely reflex systems are not slaves to stimuli; they have some devices that guarantee some Stimulus Autonomy, like "drives" (if I am in a certain internal condition -like hunger- I am sensible to certain stimuli) or the extinction of conditioning.

Cognitive Autonomy

In Cognitive systems Stimulus Autonomy is much larger (and unpredictability too). It is guaranteed by "Cognitive Mediation" (Stimulus Cognitive Autonomy):

- "Stimuli" are replaced by "interpretations", "meaning", in other terms we don't have "Stimuli" anymore, we have "Beliefs". Also in "reactions", the Agent reacts to certain Beliefs.

- "Reactions", fixed behavioural patterns, action schemata to be specified, are replaced by "Goals": internal manipulated representations of the states to be reached, that govern/drive the behaviour and require some planning and/or decision [1].

This is what I call Cognitive Reactivity: *the Agent reacts to a Belief and/or with a Goal*.

In between Stimulus and Response, mental representations (of the environment and of the objective and action) hold.

2.3 Social Autonomy and Limited Autonomy

In a Multi-Agent world Autonomy is an intrinsically social notion. There are two main possible definitions of "Social Autonomy". The first one, is just the complementary notion of Dependence: the less an Agent is dependent on other Agents for its needs, the more is Autonomous. Given our theory of Dependence relations [5] [27] it would be also possible to quantify the "degree" of such an Autonomy, in terms of the number and value of the Goals the Agent can not reach without the help of others.

This notion of Autonomy doesn't add anything interesting to the notion of Dependence. Thus, I prefer to use for this notion the synonymous term of "Independence" or "Self-Sufficiency".

The other possible definition of "Social Autonomy" is much more critical: it concerns the relationship between the Goals of the Agents; more precisely the Goals of others mentioning the Agent itself. This paper is mainly about this notion of "Autonomy".

At this level we have at least two kinds of Autonomy:

- the already mentioned **Executive or Means Autonomy**; and

- **Motivational or Goal Autonomy** (Auto-Nomos)

The system is endowed with Goals of its own, which it has not received from outside as contingent commands. And its decisions to adoption others' goals are taken on the basis of these Goals.

If in any case and circumstance an Agent does anything it is required (and able) to do, then it has no Autonomy. Nor it is autonomous if it does not execute the required task just because of some mistakes or misunderstanding. In order to be autonomous from others, it should be able to choose to refuse obedience, as well as to accept others' requests for its own reasons. This is the main point: if the agent decides to do something for its own reasons (Goals) its decision is autonomous whether it complies with others' requests or not. It is equally autonomous both if it refuses and if it accepts.

Let me try to enunciate some basic postulates that characterize the Socially Autonomous Agent:

1) it has its own Goals: endogenous, not derived from other Agents' will;

2) it is able to make decisions concerning multiple conflicting goals (being them its own goals or also goals adopted from outside);

3) it adopts goals from outside, from other Agents; it is liable to influencing (this is a strange postulate of Autonomy: see later);

4) it adopts other agents' Goals as a consequence of a choice among them and other goals (adoption is thus neither automatic nor rule-governed, and it is not simply required that the goal should not be inconsistent with the current ones -see later); more that this:

5) it adopts other agents Goals only if it sees the adoption as a way of enabling itself to achieve some of its own goals (i.e. the Autonomous Agent is a Self-Interested Agent).

Let me clarify the paradoxical condition 3 (which supports conditions 4 and 5, that are very relevant). In condition 3, in order to be Autonomous, an Agent should have a limited Autonomy: it should do something according to the desires of other Agents; it should even be subject to the "influence" of other agents, meaning that *it can be induced by another to adopt the latter's Goals.*

Why did I put such a paradoxical condition? Because Autonomy becomes irrelevant, uninteresting, when it is extreme. If an agent is designed in such a way as to never adopt other's Goals (because it never happens to have any reason for adopting them), this Autarchic (or Socially Autistic) Agent, is alone, lives alone, in an a-social situation even when in a crowded Multi-Agent world. Given that it is in fact alone, it is worth of noting, it is meaningless to say that it is Autonomous. Autonomy is a social relation: it is pertinent when it is limited.

Given that a Social Agent should have a limited autonomy, should adopt others' goals, should be liable to influencing by others, conditions 4 and 5 create boundaries to such influence and establish real Social Autonomy. However I will be soon more precise about such conditions, speaking of the Architecture that guarantees Autonomy, and of the control that an Autonomous Agent must have over its mental states (Beliefs and Goals).

3 Current Models of Rational Agents and Autonomy

In principle, *only an Autonomous Agent could be fully Rational*. Rationality should be relative to the "personal" ends of an Agent. In fact an Agent that wastes its own resources, abilities, and time, for the benefit of others, under their command, without calculating its own advantages and rewards in so doing, is all but "Rational".

However, following the distinction between *Executive Autonomy* (Autonomy in tasks execution, in planning for assigned Goals) and full *Goal Autonomy*, we could distinguish between *Executive Rationality* (relative to merely "economic" reasoning about possible actions and plans) and *Full Rationality* relative to how to maximize the fulfilment of its own end-Goals.

On the other side, Autonomy doesn't require conceptually Rationality. We can imagine fully autonomous goal-governed systems that are not adequately coherent in their decisions and efficient in their actions.

Anyway, Rationality and Autonomy could/should be in agreement, not in contrast. This is specially true in "artificial agent" design. In my view, on the contrary, current models of Rationality do not fit very well with Agent Autonomy.

3.1 "Rational Slaves"?

The already mentioned view of Autonomy leads me to question some definitions and postulates that characterize current theories of "rational interaction" (e.g.[7]), and that are, in fact, also implicit in the behaviour of many DAI systems (like Contract Nets).

The most questionable aspects are, in my view, "Benevolence" (or Helpfulness) and "Credulity"

Criticism to "Benevolence"
There is a contradiction between the objective of constructing models of "rational" agent and assigning these agents the social characteristic of being benevolent, i.e. of adopting other people's goals simply upon being requested to (and provided they do not have an opposite or incompatible goal of their own).

A model of a "rational" agent also implies that *actions have costs*, and that resources are scanty and are used for the agent's goals. *An agent who pays the cost of its own actions and spends its own resources for someone else's benefit, in order to allow other persons to attain goals (without calculating the advantages to themselves), is just as irrational as an agent who wastes effort and resources on unattainable goals: in both cases it gets nothing out of it.*

On the other hand an "autonomous" agent cannot claim to be such if it does anything the others ask of him (unless he really wants the opposite). A truly "autonomous" but social agent decides to do something or not (and therefore also what the others ask and what the others need) only as a function of his own goals (condition 5): if doing something means avoiding damage, he does so: if performing a certain action allows him to achieve another goal, he does so. The same is true of the action of "adopting other people's goals".

An autonomous and rational agent makes someone else's goal his own (i.e. he adopts it) only if he believes it to be a means for achieving his own goals. This is more precise than to say that it should "prefer" to do so, to adopt [14].

Autonomy, Rationality and Utilitarianism

This position does not coincide completely with that of Durfee, Lesser and Corkill [13], who draw their model of "self-interested" agents from classic economic theory and utilitarian philosophy.

The postulate of an agent who "adopts other people's aims solely as a function of his own aims" (which may also be defined as "self-interested"), does not necessarily coincide with a "selfish" view of the agent.

The agent's "own" goals, for the purpose of which he decides to adopt certain aims of someone else, may include "benevolence" (liking, friendship, affection, love, compassion, etc.) or impulsive (reactive) behaviours/goals of an altruistic type (although only towards certain agents and only in certain circumstances).

In our agent model (PSCS Project), among the families of "Goal adoption" (Instrumental, Cooperative) there is also:

- "terminal" adoption, i.e. goal adoption as an end in itself, in which the adopting agent B does not calculate or expect any advantage or reward. In a sense it has no super-Goals (SG) and is an end-goal in B's mind, or better it has as SG that "A obtain some of his goals", i.e. benevolence towards A.

We do not want *universally and generically "benevolent" agents; they are neither autonomous nor rational*. We want agents who a) adopt other people's goals only as a function of their own goals; b) include among their own goals several affective, emotional or solidarity goals towards specific agents and/or in specific circumstances.

The problem is *how to reconcile autonomy and cooperation*: we need an autonomous, but "liable to influencing" agent. This is possible only if the agents are dependent on each other for their own goals and needs and if they therefore have power over others and can influence them (par. 4). Autonomy is guaranteed in this case by the fact that B "decides" on the basis of his own goals and knowledge (which he controls) whether or not to adopt.

Current definitions of "Helpfulness" or "Benevolence" contradict Autonomy also for another aspect. They prevent Agent's helping initiative, and in particular spontaneous Goal adoption, which is a relevant feature of Autonomous Social Agents, and an important dimension of true help and cooperation. Goal Adoption should not be limited to the explicit requests or to the expectations of the other Agent [3].

Criticism to Credulity

Worrying about Autonomy we should be very careful about Agent credulity and Belief Autonomy. We should not identify the "liability to influencing" with "credulity". Credulity makes the agent totally vulnerable to undue influence. Given that Beliefs are the fundamental access to Goal modification, if our Agents believe anything the other Agents induce them to believe that they believe, they become too prone to manipulation. In order to be Autonomous an Agent should be Autonomous in its believing. It should have some idea about the reliability of the source, as one of the criteria for deciding to believe or not something [15], [17], [12]. It is necessary to introduce at least Agents' sincerity and expertise [7]. However, we must be careful also with the way we define such notions. For example, Cohen and Levesque's definition of EXPERT [7, first version]

Def 13 (EXPERT x y p) = (BEL x (BEL y p)) ⊃ (BEL x p)

seems to be too strong. If is asserted that (EXPERT A B p) is asserted that to believe that A believes p is a sufficient condition for B to believe p. This might be dangerous unless it is accompanied by a control over B's beliefs and other restrictions.

One of the most important and explicit restrictions should be that an Autonomous Agent is the best expert concerning its own mind! This is a privileged source of knowledge (introspection). Agent can not believe others about what it wants or desires, or believes, without probing into its own mind.

In rational agent model, it is reasonable to postulate what Cohen and Levesque express with the proposition 13 about the relationship between Agent's Beliefs and Goals

Prop 13 (BEL x (GOAL x p)) ⊃ (GOAL x p)

But, if we do not explicitly exclude others' mental states from the Agents' expertise, we could have that: if A believes that B believes that A wants p, and B is assumed to be Expert about this, A comes to want p:

(BEL A (BEL B (GOAL A p))) ⊃ (BEL A (GOAL A p))
and
(BEL A (GOAL A p)) ⊃ (GOAL A p)

Thus, A's goals (the core of its autonomy) would be left to the mercy of B's beliefs. An agent with such a small autonomy and great vulnerability could perhaps be plausible only in the case in which B is A's psychoanalyst! Only our psychoanalyst may be allowed to be more expert than ourselves concerning what we want and believe. Of course, these risky assumptions are not in Cohen and Levesque's model. I want just to stress the opportunity to take care also of the Agent's autonomy (in both Goals and Beliefs) while design the conditions for Agent's rationality.

4 Architecture for Autonomy

Which aspects of the Architecture of a Cognitive Agents guard its Social Autonomy (not only its Stimuli Autonomy)? The already mentioned conditions are insufficient.

Galliers [14] rightly says that to be Autonomous, agents must have "control over their acquisition of mental states, i.e. their Belief and Goal adoption". However this is quite vague. As it is vague and tautological the claim that Goal adoption should be subordinate to Agent preferences. Let me try to be more precise adding to the postulate of Self-Interested Goal Adoption (5) the following postulates:

6) It is not possible to directly modify Agent's Goals from outside: any modification of its Goals must be achieved by modifying its Beliefs.

Thus, control over Beliefs becomes a filter, an additional control over the adoption of Goals. This is not because Goals are a sub-set of Beliefs (I think that this assertion is misleading), but *because Goals activation, generation, value, choice, abandon, depends on higher-Goals and Beliefs.*

Incidentally, let me notice that, *as mental states, Goals are not a sub-set of Beliefs*. Only the content of pursued Goals (i.e. intended state of affairs, intended propositions), are a sub-set of the Believed propositions, state of affairs. Beliefs and Goals could insist on, share the same propositional arguments; and pursued Goals must have a propositional argument that is also believed (or at least not disbelieved). But, the mental states of willing, intending, pursuing something, are not a sub-set of the mental states of believing something.

7) it is impossible to change automatically the Beliefs of an Agent. The adoption of a Belief is a special "decision" that the Agent takes on the basis of many criteria and checks. This protect its Cognitive Autonomy.

4.1 The "Double Filter" Architecture

Postulates 6 plus 7 define what I call the "double filter" Autonomous Architecture

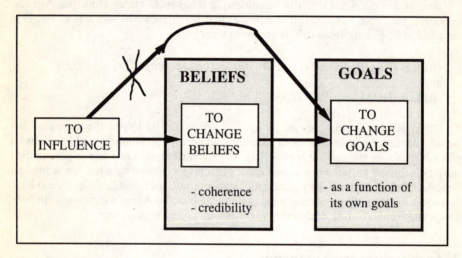

4.2 Autonomous Point of View: Control over Beliefs

An Agent that swallows everything may be induced to do everything.

a) Credibility
An Autonomous Agent controls the acquisition of Beliefs, testing their "credibility" on two main basis:
  - the coherence or compatibility with previous Beliefs [15], [16];
  - the reliability and competence of the source.

As for the first criterion, the Autonomous Agent will consider as a "cost" any Belief revision required by the acceptance of a new Belief; it will accept a Belief only if it succeeds in justifying it or at least in inserting it without inconsistency (compatibility).

As for the second criterion, the Autonomous Agent will accept the information given by an other Agent by default (in force of the assumption that the speakers follow

Grice's principles) provided it has no reasons to doubt the sincerity or the competence of the source.

b) Autonomous Sources of Knowledge
An Autonomous Agent also gives more credit to other Belief sources like its *direct experience* (senses), or its *inferences* (reasoning) when well supported, than to other Agents [15], [12].

c) The best Expert About its own Mind
As I already explained, an Autonomous Agent can not believe others about it wants or desires. Introspection is a personal, exclusive knowledge source.

d) Belief Relevance According to Goals
Cognitive Agents do not pay attention to, utilize, and memorize any information. They are interested in finding, processing and preserving knowledge pertinent to their Goals. They are seeking Beliefs according to their Goals.

In other terms, in Belief management there are not only criteria strictly internal to Beliefs, i.e. "epistemic" criteria (like credibility, or importance of the Beliefs in supporting other Beliefs, or the minimal change). There are also "pragmatic" criteria. The management of Beliefs is not completely independent of the management of the Goals, precisely because Beliefs decide about Goals. Knowledge is finalized to the achievement of Goals, to the satisfaction of needs, thus this link plays a role in the acquisition, the maintenance, and the revision of knowledge.

This idea is well known in psychology, and receives an increasing attention in AI models, like for example in "costructivistic inductive learning" [24]. However, I think that there is some dangerous confusion about this. The idea that knowledge is interesting "according to Goals", could mean two very different things:

Relevance. Beliefs are more or less pertinent, useful for the pursuit of some Goals (in particular of active, current Goals). The agent tends to acquire relevant Beliefs and to neglect those irrelevant.

A Belief is subjectively relevant to a certain Goal when:

   i) *it is about that Goal (e.g. (GOAL x p) & (BEL x (GOAL x p));*

   ii) *it is about the content (proposition) of the Goal (e.g. (GOAL x p) & (BEL x*

   (q ⊃ p));

   iii) *it is about the relationships between the Goal and its sub-Goals or super-*

   Goals (plan relations)

   iiii) *it is about the conditions for the pertinent actions (a sub-case of iii).*

Likeability. Among the relevant Beliefs, i.e. Beliefs useful for the pursuit of the Goal, there are some which are quite special: the *Satisfaction Beliefs*. I mean those Beliefs on the basis of which a Goal has been reached or not.

A Goal-governed Agent has no other way to know whether a Goal has been reached or not (and then to be "satisfied") but the matching between its Beliefs relative to the current state of the world, and the representation of the Goals. When the Agent has the Goal that p, and it beliefs that p, then the Goal subjectively has been realized. Thus there are Beliefs that have a very special role: the Belief that p or Not p (and their possible supporting Beliefs), when the Goal is p. For the Agent the Belief that p is the "success"; the Belief that Not p constitutes a frustration, a failure.

Human agents seem to have a tendency to believe and to maintain Beliefs which satisfy their Goals (to believe that their Goals are achieved). I call this Beliefs "satisfactory" or "agreable" Beliefs.

This, of course, augments the subjectivity and autonomy of the Agent's point of view, but, could be quite in contrast with the rationality and the adaptiveness of the Agent. In fact, it is the bases of *wishful thinking*.

We should not mix up *Relevance* and *Likeability*. I don't think that the latter should be introduce also in artificial cognitive architectures. *Relevance* on the contrary is an important feature.

Points a), b), c), and d) guarantee an autonomous *point of view*.

However let me stress another very peculiar property of human belief systems, that strongly protect them from external manipulation, and that I think should be preserved also in artificial belief systems.

4.3 The non Negotiability of Beliefs: the Pascal Law

To believe or not to believe a certain proposition can be considered as a "decision" by the believer. However, this kind of (mental) action shows a very interesting property. This decision can not be taken in view of the believer's interest/utility; this action is not an intentionally utilitarian action! Notice that, normally, it is a "rational" action and decision: in fact, we believe a certain assertion on the basis of its logical coherence with our knowledge, on the basis of some evidence and supports (arguments), controlling its "plausibility" and the "credibility" of the source. Knowledge could also have an "epistemic utility" or value [23], and decision about Beliefs could be based on this special utility. However, this "rational" choice is not "utilitarian" respect to the "non-epistemic" interest of the agent.

We cannot believe a certain assertion just because there would be some advantage for us in believing it. At least consciously we cannot decide to believe somebody because he will give us 10 dollars, or to be glad. And even when unconscious defence mechanisms are called into play, we must consciously "adjust" and justify such utilitarian beliefs, by finding rational supports and evidence for them (*Rationalization*).

Let me call this the "Pascal law" about Beliefs, because this property was discovered by Pascal in the famous argumentation about the bet (relative to the existence of God). Pascal says that it is impossible to decide by a mere act of volition to believe that something is true or not. We cannot believe that God exists only because it is convenient for us (or because Pascal has demonstrated that it is convenient) to believe in God.

In social interaction, we cannot use threats ("*Argumentum ad baculum*") or promises to make people believe something. We cannot pay our listener. Of course, one might say that for 10 dollars s/he will believe our claim, but we know that s/he is lying, because we know that s/he cannot believe by a conscious self-interested decision.

In our view, this is one of the main properties that guarantee the autonomy of our mind in its decisions. There is a crucial difference between *persuading to do* something and *persuading to believe*. And, given that in order to persuade to do one must persuade to believe ("double filter"), this protection over Beliefs is a general protection of Goal Autonomy.

4.4 Autonomy in Goal Management: Control over Goals

As I sad autonomy in the adoption of Goals from outside is guaranteed:

- By the postulate of self-interested Adoption:

An agent X is goal-autonomous *if and only if whatever new goal q it comes to have, there is at least a goal p of X 's to which q is believed by the agent to be instrumental.*

With this postulate I think that I have substantially clarified the problem of Agent's "preferences". In which sense the Agent should prefer to do what it is required to do [14]? This consists of :

a) adoption subordinated to some of its own Goals;

b) that for the Agent this Goal has more value that others of its Goals (of course, this requires some model of choice).

In fact, it is also possible that an Agent *adopts a given Goal* but after he will not pursue the adopted Goal, this will not become an Intention, because *it is not preferred* to other more important Goals.

- By the postulate about the only indirect action upon Goals:

Any modification of the Goals of another Agent is achieved by modifying its Beliefs.

One could object that this is not always true even in humans. But, my claim is that it is the most frequent case and the most significant for cognitive simulation and artificial agents.

Among humans, sometimes our aim is to elicit a reaction (a reflex) rather than to give rise to an intention: Paul tickles Mary to make him drop something she is holding. Moreover, this postulate is not true in the rare cases in which it is possible to modify Goals or their value directly by acting on the soma, e.g. lobotomy, drugs, etc.

Notice that the assertion that "any modification of the Goals is achieved by modifying Agent's Beliefs" *does not mean that in order to change other Agent's Goals one should use communication.* The influencing Agent can use either communication, or the alteration of the perceptual input of the other Agent: she may either modify the real world of the other Agent; or deceive the other Agent's senses.

5 Principles of Bounded Autonomy

I said that Social Agents' Autonomy should be limited, that the Agents are open to influence (condition 3). What limits their Autonomy? How do the Agents have the power to influence others?

What binds the Agents to each other, and what bounds their Autonomy is a Common World. When can one say that system X and system Y are in a common world? I assume that X and Y share a common world if and only if the effects of Y 's actions *interfere* with the future of X 's goals, and vice versa. That is, X 's success or failure in achieving its goals should depend on Y 's behavior (besides X 's own actions and the state of affairs). We could distinguish between:

- Positive interference: A relation of positive interference also called *favour*, exists between two Agents X and Y when

  - *Y 's doing a certain act implies later p*
  - *and X wants p*

- Negative interference: The more general case is the following one:

  - *Y 's doing a certain act implies later Not p*
  - *and X wants p*.

For example a relation of *objective competition* occurs between X and Y whenever

  -both need a certain resource r
  - r cannot be used by both

(so if X uses r for his goal p, Y cannot reach her goal q)

On one side, the Agents may be aware of such interferences and to adapt their plans in such a way to avoid or exploit the effects of others' actions. They try *to adapt themselves to a Multi-Agent world*.

On the other side, thank to the fact that their actions *interfere* in the other's world, they could try to induce certain behaviour in the others. Thus trying *to adapt the Multi-Agent world* to their plans.

In other words, what limits Agent autonomy is what founds and motivates sociality: the dependence relations among the Agents. In order for X to achieve some goal of its own, Y should do a certain action (including that of refraining from doing something). This is exactly the *dependence* relation, which I think of as the rational as well as evolutionary grounds of sociality [5], [27], [18], [28].

Dependence is also the basis of the power that the agent has over other agents and its power of influencing other agents [5].

Now, Dependence and limited Autonomy are not only limitations for the Agent. They imply also some important advantages: the advantages of Society.

The main function of pro-social (non-aggressive) sociality is the multiplication of the power of the participating agents.

Unlike Huberman and colleagues [21], I do not assume that the greatest advantage of (cooperative) sociality is to speed up the search for solutions to common problems, or to find better solutions to them, but rather to multiply individual "powers": any agent, while remaining limited in its capabilities, skills and resources, finds the number of goals it can pursue and achieve increased by virtue of its "use" of others' skills and resources. In one sense, any agent's limits of power, and its differences from others in the kind of power it is endowed with, turn into an advantage: although not omnipotent, the agent is allowed to overcome its computational, cognitive, and practical limits through "sociality".

In conclusion, Agents cannot be completely Autarchic, given that they are not completely self-sufficient. Given the differences among Agents in Goals, abilities, resources, they take advantage of inter-dependencies, then of Goal adoption, then of their liability to influence. But, obviously, in order to avoid Agent's exploitation, slavery, (and for a higher level of cooperation) the Agent should maintain not only a level of Executive Autonomy, but of full Goal Autonomy.

References

1. Basso, A., Mondada, F., Castelfranchi, C. 1993. Reactive Goal Activation in Intelligent Autonomous Agent Architecture. In Proceedings of AIA'93 - First International Round-Table on "Abstract Intelligent Agent", ENEA, Roma, January 25-27.
2. Brooks, R.A. 1989. *A robot that walks. Emergent behaviours from a carefully evolved network.* Tech. Rep. Artificial Intelligence Laboratory. Cambridge, Mass.: MIT.
3. C. Castelfranchi. No More Cooperation, Please ! In Search of the Social Structure of Verbal Interaction. In *A.I. and Cognitive Science Perspectives on Communication*, Ortony, A., Slack,J., and Stock,O. (eds.) Heidelberg, Germany: Springer, 1992.
4. C. Castelfranchi. Principles of Bounded Autonomy. Modelling Autonomous Agents in a Multi Agent World. *Pre-Proceedings of the Fist Round-Table Discussion on "Abstract Intelligent Agent" - AIA '93.* Roma: Enea; TR-Ip/CNR, 1993.
5. C. Castelfranchi, M. Miceli, A. Cesta. Dependence relations among autonomous agents. In *Decentralized AI - 3,* Y. Demazeau, E. Werner (eds), 215-31. Amsterdam: Elsevier, 1992.
6. N. Chomsky. *Language and Problems of Knowledge: The Nicaraguan Lectures,* Cambridge, Mass. MIT Press, 1988.
7. P. R. Cohen, H.J. Levesque. Rational Interaction as the Basis for Communication. Technical Report, n.89, CSLI, Stanford, 1987. A new version in *Intentions in Communication.*, P.R Cohen, J. Morgan, M.A. Pollack (eds), 33-71. Cambridge, Mass.: MIT Press, 1990.
8. P.R. Cohen, H. J. Levesque. Intention is choice with commitment. *Artificial Intelligence*, 42, pp. 213-261, 1990.
9. D. Connah, P, Wavish. An Experiment in Cooperation. In *Decentralized AI,* Y. Demazeau and J.P. Mueller (eds.),197-212. North-Holland, Elsevier, 1990.
10. R. Conte, C. Castelfranchi. *Cognitive and Social Action.* London: UCL Press, (in press).
11. A. A. Covrigaru, R.K. Lindsay. Deterministic autonomous systems. *AI Magazine*, Fall, 1991, 110-17.
12. A.F.Dragoni. A Model for Belief Revision in a Multi-Agent Environment. In *Decentralized AI - 3,* Y. Demazeau, E. Werner (eds), 215-31. Amsterdam: Elsevier, 1992.
13. E. H. Durfee, V. R. Lesser, D. D. Corkill. Cooperation through communication in a problem-solving network. In *Distributed Artificial Intelligence* , M.N. Huhns (ed.), 29-58. San Mateo, CA: Kaufmann, 1987.
14. J. R. Galliers. A strategic framework for multi-agent cooperative dialogue, in *Proceedings of the 8th European Conference on Artificial Intelligence* London: Pitman, 1988, 415-20.
15. J. R. Galliers. Modelling Autonomous Belief Revision in Dialogue, In *Decentralized AI-2*, Y. Demazeau, J.P. Mueller (eds), 231-43. Armsterdam: Elsevier, 1991.
16. P. Gardenfors.The Dynamics of Belief Systems: Foundations vs Coherence Theories. *Revue Internationale de Philosophie*, 1989.

17. G. Gaspar. Communication and Belief Changes in a Society of Agents. In *Decentralized AI-2*, Y. Demazeau, J.P. Mueller (eds), 245-55. Armsterdam: Elsevier, 1991.
18. N. R. Jennings. Commitments and conventions: The foundation of coordination in multi-agent systems. *The Knowledge Engineering Review*, 3, 1993, 223-50.
19. Hewitt, C.& P. de Jong 1983. Open systems. In *Perspectives on conceptual modeling*, M.L. Brodie, J.L. Mylopoulos, J.W. Schmidt (eds), New York: Springer.
20. C. Hewitt. Open information systems semantics for distributed artificial intelligence. *Artificial Intelligence*, 47, 1991, 79-106.
21. B. A. Huberman, S. H. Clearwater, T. Hogg. Cooperative Solution of Constraint Satisfaction Problems. Science, vol .254, Nov. 1991, 1181-2.
22. G. Kiss, H. Reichgelt. Towards a Semantics of Desires. In *Decentralized AI-3*, E. Werner & Y. Demazeau (eds.), 115-27. Amsterdam: Elsevier, 1992.
23. I. Levi. *The Enterprise of Knowledge*, MIT Press, Cambridge, Mass, 1980.
24. R. S. Michalski,. Development of Learning Systems Able to Modify Their Knowledge Representation According to Their Goals. In *AIA'94 - Second International Round-Table on "Abstract Intelligent Agent"*, ENEA, Roma, February 1994, 23-25.
25. G. Miller, E. Galanter, K.H. Pribram. *Plans and the structure of behavior*, New York: Holt, Rinehart & Winston, 1960.
26. A. Rosenblueth, N. Wiener. Purposeful and Non-Purposeful Behavior. In *Modern systems research for the behavioral scientist,* Buckley, W. (ed.). Chicago: Aldine, 1968.
27. J. Sichman, R. Conte, R., C. Castelfranchi, Y. Demazeau. A Social Reasoning Mechanism Based On Dependence Networks, *ECAI'94*, Amsterdam, August 1994.
28. E. S. K. Yu, J. Mylopoulos. An Actor dependency model of organizational work with application to business process reengineering. In Proceedings of *COOCS'93-Conference On Organizational Computing Systems*, Milpitas, USA, 1993

Acknowledgements

A previous version of this paper [4] has been presented at the *1st Round Table on Abstract Intelligent Agent - AIA'93*, Roma, ENEA, January 25-27 1993. I would like to thank all the participants in the discussion, and in particular Adam Gadomsky, George Rzevski, Jan Zitkow. Many of these topics were also improved during the preparation of a book on "Cognitive and Social Action" [10] with my colleague Rosaria Conte. I would like to thank Maria Miceli for her precious comments. I would like to thank also an anonymous referee of the ECAI Workshop, which was very helpful in better understanding the relationships between my notion of social Autonomy and current characterisation of rational agency.
Current developments were supported by the European ESPRIT3 Working Group "*MODEL AGE*".

Multi-Agent Reasoning with Belief Contexts: the Approach and a Case Study[*]

Alessandro Cimatti and Luciano Serafini

Mechanized Reasoning Group
IRST — Istituto per la Ricerca Scientifica e Tecnologica
I-38050 Povo, Trento, Italy
phone:+39 461 314517
email:{cx,serafini}@irst.it

Abstract. In this paper we discuss the use of *belief contexts* for the formalization of multi-agent reasoning. In addition to representational power, belief contexts provide implementational advantages. We substantiate this claim by discussing a paradigmatic case study, the Three Wise Men puzzle.

1   Introduction and motivations

Belief contexts [4, 7, 8] are a formalism for the representation of propositional attitudes. Their basic feature is *modularity*: knowledge can be distributed in different, separated modules, called contexts; the interactions between them, i.e. the transfer of knowledge between contexts, can be formally defined according to the application. For instance, the beliefs of an agent can be represented with one or more contexts, distinct from the contexts representing beliefs of other agents; different contexts can be used to represent the beliefs of an agent in different situations. Interaction between contexts can express the effect of communication between agents, and the evolution of their beliefs (e.g. learning, belief revision).

Belief contexts, beside providing the expressivity of other formalisms [7], also give implementational advantages. First, the representation formalism is *incremental*: adding new contexts to the system has no effects other than the ones which are explicitly encoded in the interaction mechanisms. This allows for incremental and independent development of different parts of the knowledge base; furthermore, it opens up the possibility to parallelize the inference process in a natural way. Second, substantial parts of the reasoning process are *local* to modules. For instance, in order to represent the "internal" reasoning of an agent it is not necessary to take into account the information describing a different

---

[*] Fausto Giunchiglia has provided basic motivations, useful feedback and suggestions. He has also provided help and encouragement. Lorenzo Galvagni has developed an implementation of multi-context systems in GETFOL. We thank Paolo Bouquet, Enrico Giunchiglia, Kurt Konolige, John McCarthy and Toby Walsh for useful feedback and discussions. The other members of the Mechanized Reasoning Group are also thanked. This work has been done at IRST as part of the MAIA project.

agent. Local reasoning is captured by general purpose reasoning inside a well defined, simple module rather than by ad hoc reasoning techniques, which try to isolate the relevant information in a global, unstructured theory. Finally, non-local reasoning steps, corresponding to interaction between modules, often have a very *natural* interpretation; for instance, switching from (the module of) a speaking agent to another, corresponding to a listening agent, can be the result of an utterance. The advantage is that the search strategy can exploit the structure of the system, which can be tailored to the structure of the problem: as a result the process of inference is much more efficient, being problem dependent, than a uniform and problem independent strategy.

In this paper we substantiate our claims by discussing the solution of the Three Wise Men puzzle (TWM) using belief contexts. This activity is not purely academic: formalizing the TWM forces us to deal with problems such as multi-agent belief, common and nested belief, and ignorance. These are the problems that a real system for reasoning about propositional attitudes (e.g. [2, 9]) has to face.

The paper is structured as follows: in section 2 we present the formalism of belief contexts and we discuss a solution to the TWM puzzle. In section 3 we show how this solution extends naturally to take into account reasoning through situations. In section 4 we compare our solution to other formalizations. In section 5 we draw some conclusions.

2   Belief Contexts

Here is a statement of our case study, the TWM [13]:

> *A certain King wishes to test his three wise men. He arranges them in a circle so that they can see and hear each other and tells them that he will put a white or black spot on each of their forehead but that at least one spot will be white. In fact all three spots are white. He then repeatedly asks them "do you know the color of your spot?". What do they answer?*

In this scenario there are three agents (wise men 1, 2 and 3), with certain beliefs about the state of the world. We formalize the scenario by using *belief contexts* [4]. Intuitively, a (belief) context represents a collection of beliefs under a certain point of view. For instance, different contexts may be used to represent the different sets of beliefs of the agents about the world. In this case, the context of the first wise man contains the fact that the spots of the second and third wise men are white, that the second wise man believes that the spot of the third wise man is white, and possibly other information. Other contexts may formalize a different view of the world, e.g. the set of beliefs that an agent ascribes to another agent. For example, the set of beliefs that 1 ascribes to 2 contains the fact that the spot of 3 is white; however, it does not contain the fact that his own (i.e. 2's) spot is white, because 2 can not see his own spot. Finally, a context can formalize the view of an observer external to the scenario (e.g. us, or even a computer, reasoning about the puzzle); this context contains the fact that all the spots are white, and also that each of the agents knows the color of the other spots but doesn't know the color of his own.

Contexts are the basic modules of our representation formalism. Formally, a context is a theory which we present as a formal system $\langle L, \Omega, \Delta \rangle$, where L is a logical language, $\Omega \subseteq L$ is the set of axioms (basic facts of the view), and Δ is a deductive machinery. This general structure allows for the formalization of agents with different expressive and inferential capabilities. The representation of non-logically omniscient reasoners using belief contexts is thoroughly discussed in [8]. For the puzzle we consider logically omniscient agents: for each contexts, Δ is the set of classical natural deduction inference rules [15], and L is described in the following. To express statements about the spots, L contains the propositional constants W_1, W_2 and W_3, W_i meaning that the spot of i is white. To express belief, L contains well formed formulas (wff) of the form $B_i(\text{``}A\text{''})$, for each wff $A$ and for $i = 1, 2, 3$. Intuitively, $B_i(\text{``}A\text{''})$ means that i believes the proposition expressed by A; therefore, $B_2(\text{``}W_1\text{''})$ means that 2 believes that 1 has a white spot. To express statements about common belief, $L$ contains formulas of the form $CB(\text{``}A\text{''})$ for each formula A. $CB(\text{``}A\text{''})$ expresses the fact that the proposition expressed by $A$ is a common belief, i.e. that the wise men jointly believe it [14]. For instance, we express that at least one of the spots is white is a common belief with the formula $CB(\text{``}W_1 \vee W_2 \vee W_3\text{''})$.

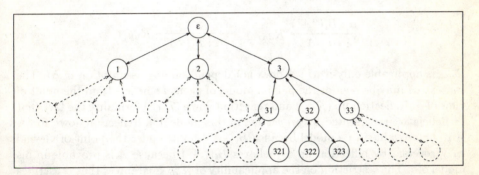

Fig. 1. The context structure to express multi-agent nested belief

Contexts are organized in a tree (see figure 1). We call ϵ the root context, representing the external observer point of view; we let the context i formalize the beliefs of wise man i, and ij the beliefs ascribed by i to wise man j. Iterating the nesting, the belief context ijk formalizes the view of agent i about j's beliefs about k's beliefs. In general, a finite sequence of agent indexes, including the null sequence ϵ, is a context label, denoted in the following with α. This context structure allows to represent arbitrarily nested beliefs. In principle there is an infinite number of contexts. Nevertheless, belief contexts can be efficiently implemented. First of all, the modularity of the representation allows us to limit reasoning to a clearly identifiable subpart of the context structure: for instance, in this particular problem, reasoning can be limited to few contexts although the solution involves very complex reasoning about mutual beliefs. Furthermore, it is possible to implement contexts lazily, i.e. only when required at run time.

The interpretation of a formula depends on the context we consider. For instance, the formula W_1 in the external observer context, also written $\epsilon : W_1$ to stress the context dependence[2], expresses the fact that the first wise man has a white hat. The same formula in context 232, i.e. $232 : W_1$, expresses the (more complex) fact that 2 believes that 3 believes that 2 believes that 1 has a white spot. Notice that "2 believes that 3 believes that 2 believes that.." does not need to be stated in the formula. Indeed, context 232 represents the beliefs that 2 believes to be ascribed to himself by 3. However, it should be explicited if the very same proposition had to be expressed in the context of the external observer: the result is the (more complex) formula $\epsilon : B_2(``B_3(``B_2(``W_1")")")$. This shows that with belief contexts a fact can be expressed in different ways. The advantages are that knowledge may be represented more compactly and the mechanization of inference may be more efficient.

We want $232 : W_1$ to be provable if and only if $\epsilon : B_2(``B_3(``B_2(``W_1")")")$ is, as they have the same meaning. This kind of constraint is in general represented by means of so called *bridge rules* [4], i.e. rules with premises and conclusions in distinct belief contexts. Bridge rules allow us to formalize any kind of interaction between contexts. The constraints defined above are formalized by the following bridge rules, called *reflection* rules [7]:

$$\frac{\alpha : B_i(``A")}{\alpha i : A} \; \mathcal{R}_{dn.} \qquad \frac{\alpha i : A}{\alpha : B_i(``A")} \; \mathcal{R}_{up.}$$

$\mathcal{R}_{up.}$ is applicable only if $\alpha i : A$ does not depend on any assumption in αi. The context αi may be seen as the partial model of agent i's beliefs from the point of view of α. Reflection up ($\mathcal{R}_{up.}$) and reflection down ($\mathcal{R}_{dn.}$) formalize the fact that i's beliefs are represented by *provability* in this model [3]. Reflection down forces A to be provable in i's model because $B_i(``A")$ holds under the point of view of $\alpha$. Viceversa, by reflection up, $\alpha$ believes $B_i(``A")$ because A is provable in his model of i. The restriction on the applicability of $\mathcal{R}_{up.}$ guarantees that α ascribes a belief A to the agent i only if A is provable in αi and not simply derivable from a set of hypotheses. Reflection down allows us to convert the formula into a simpler format, i.e. to get rid of the belief predicate and represent information *about* the agent as information *in the model of* the agent; then, local reasoning can be performed in this simpler model; finally, reflection up can be used to infer the conclusion in the starting context, i.e. to introduce again the belief predicate. This sequence is a standard pattern in reasoning about propositional attitudes (see for instance [9, 12]). Notice, however, that the use of belief contexts allows us to separate knowledge in a modular way. It is then clear from the structure of the formal system what information has to be taken into account in local reasoning.

---

[2] In this paper we use a variant of the notation adopted for formulas in multi-language systems [7].

Bridge rules are used to formalize common belief. A fact is a *common belief* if not only all the agents believe it, but also they believe it to be a common belief (see for instance [14]). The bridge rule CB_{inst} allows us to derive belief of a single agent from common belief, i.e. to *inst*antiate common belief. The bridge rule CB_{prop} allows us to derive, from the fact that something is a common belief, that an agent believes that it is a common belief, i.e. to *prop*agate common belief.

$$\frac{\alpha : CB(\text{``}A\text{''})}{\alpha i : A} \; CB_{inst} \qquad \frac{\alpha : CB(\text{``}A\text{''})}{\alpha i : CB(\text{``}A\text{''})} \; CB_{prop}$$

CB_{inst} and CB_{prop} encode meaningful reasoning patterns (instantiation or propagation) about common belief, relevant from the representational point of view, and therefore easier to deal with and encode in a control strategy.

Let us consider now the solution of the puzzle. Did you figure out the answers of the wise men? The first and second answers are "I don't know", while the third one is "My spot is white". We formalize the reasoning of the wise men in the three situations (i.e. before the first, the second and the third answer) with three different systems of contexts, all having the same structure shown in figure 1. The formal system describing the initial situation has the following axioms in context ϵ:

$W_1 \wedge W_2 \wedge W_3$	(State-of-affairs)
$(W_i \supset B_j(\text{``}W_i\text{''})) \wedge (\neg W_i \supset B_j(\text{``}\neg W_i\text{''}))$	(i-sees-j)
$CB(\text{``}W_1 \vee W_2 \vee W_3\text{''})$	(King-utterance)
$CB(\text{``}(W_i \supset B_j(\text{``}W_i\text{''})) \wedge (\neg W_i \supset B_j(\text{``}\neg W_i\text{''}))\text{''})$	(CB-i-sees-j)

where $i, j \in \{1, 2, 3\}$ and $i \neq j$. State-of-affairs states that all the spots are white. i-sees-j states that wise man i can see the spot of his colleague j. King-utterance states that at least one of the spots is white is a common belief, i.e. all the wise men have heard the king's statement, and they know that their colleagues know it. Finally, CB-i-sees-j states that the wise men commonly believe that they can see each other.

Reasoning about ignorance is required to formalize "I don't know" answers, e.g. to perform the derivation of the formula $\epsilon : \neg B_1(\text{``}W_1\text{''})$. We know that belief corresponds to provability in the context modeling the agent. However, since this model is partial, non-belief does not correspond to simple non-provability. We need to formalize the fact that the information explicitly taken into account is all the relevant information available for an agent to (try to) prove a certain formula. To this purpose, L contains the formulas $ARF_i(\text{``}A_1, \ldots, A_n\text{''}, \text{``}A\text{''})$ meaning that $A_1, \ldots, A_n$ are All the Relevant Facts available to i to infer the conclusion A; i.e., additional information does not change i's knowledge about A. The following bridge rule allows to derive the conclusion that the wise man does not know a certain fact:

$$\frac{\alpha i : A_1 \quad \ldots \quad \alpha i : A_n \quad \alpha : ARF_i(\text{``}A_1, \ldots, A_n\text{''}, \text{``}A\text{''})}{\alpha : \neg B_i(\text{``}A\text{''})} \; \text{Bel-Clo}$$

Bel-Clo is applicable only if $\{A_1, \ldots, A_n\} \nvdash_{\alpha i} A$ ($\vdash_{\alpha i}$ standing for provability from axioms and rules of context αi), and $\alpha i : A_1, \ldots, \alpha i : A_n$ do not depend on any assumption in αi. Intuitively, Bel-Clo formalizes the following pattern: if A can not be derived in context i from the theorems that are explicitly stated to be relevant, then infer that agent i does not know A. From a logical point of view, our approach resembles the approach to circumscriptive ignorance proposed by Konolige in [12]. His modal operators $[S_i]$ and $\langle S_i, \Gamma \rangle$, for each agent i, represent i's belief, and i's capability to derive consequences from Γ, respectively: $[S_i]A$ means that i believes A, while $\langle S_i, \Gamma \rangle A$ means that i can derive A from Γ. With this interpretation in mind, when $A_1, \ldots, A_n$ are beliefs of i, the meaning of $ARF_i(``A_1, \ldots, A_n", ``A")$ coincides with that of $\langle S_i, \{A_1, \ldots, A_n\} \rangle A \equiv [S_i]A$. Our solution gives several advantages. The first is that we do not have to deal with a non-monotonic system. Indeed, Bel-Clo encodes non-monotonicity at the object level in a monotonic way. If we take into account more premises, e.g. an additional $\alpha i : A_{n+1}$ such that $\{A_1, \ldots, A_n, A_{n+1}\} \vdash_{\alpha i} A$, it is no longer possible to derive $\alpha : \neg B_i(``A")$. However, the system remains monotonic, because the relevance statement changes when an additional fact is considered. The second advantage is expressivity. Indeed, we deal with ignorance by expressing relevance hypotheses on the knowledge of an agent *in* the formal language, rather than leaving them unspoken at the informal metalevel as happens, for instance, in circumscription. Although in this paper we do not axiomatize relevance (i.e. ARF is a primitive, underspecified notion, and relevance statements are assumed rather than inferred), in our framework it is possible to reason uniformly about relevance. This is not possible in other non-monotonic formalisms, where the relevance hypotheses are not even expressed in the formal language. Finally, our formalization is more suitable for mechanization: it mirrors the fact that, in practice, the closure is often applied after that a certain amount of theorem proving has been performed at the object level, e.g. to derive the relevant facts. This is very different from circumscription, where the closure has to be performed in advance.

The following proof formalizes the reasoning of the first agent in the first situation. In our notation a proof is a sequence of labelled lines. Each line contains the derived formula and a list of assumptions the derived formula depends on. A box collects together the sequences of lines of the same context, specified in the upper left corner.

1	ϵ $B_1(``W_2")$	From State-of-affairs and 1-sees-2
2	$B_1(``W_3")$	From State-of-affairs and 1-sees-3
3	1 W_2	From 1 by $\mathcal{R}_{dn}$.
4	W_3	From 2 by $\mathcal{R}_{dn}$.
5	$W_1 \vee W_2 \vee W_3$	From King-utterance by CB_{prop}
6	ϵ $ARF_1(``W_2, W_3,$ $W_1 \vee W_2 \vee W_3", ``W_1")$ (6)	By assumption
7	$\neg B_1(``W_1")$ (6)	From 3–6 by Bel-Clo

The above proof formalizes the following reasoning pattern. Wise man 1 sees the color of the spots of his colleagues (steps 1-4) and he also believes the king

1	3	$\neg W_3$	(1)	By assumption
2		$\neg W_3 \supset B_2(\text{``}\neg W_3\text{''})$		From CB-2-sees-3 by CB_{inst}
3		$B_2(\text{``}\neg W_3\text{''})$	(1)	From 1 and 2 by $\supset E_3$
4	32	$\neg W_3$	(1)	From 3 by $\mathcal{R}_{dn}$.
5		$\neg W_3 \supset B_1(\text{``}\neg W_3\text{''})$		From CB-1-sees-3 by CB_{prop} and CB_{inst}
6		$B_1(\text{``}\neg W_3\text{''})$	(1)	From 4 and 5 by $\supset E_{32}$
7		$\neg W_2$	(7)	By assumption
8		$\neg W_2 \supset B_1(\text{``}\neg W_2\text{''})$		From CB-1-sees-2 by CB_{prop} and CB_{inst}
9		$B_1(\text{``}\neg W_2\text{''})$	(7)	From 7 and 8 by $\supset E_{32}$
10	321	$\neg W_3$	(1)	From 6 by $\mathcal{R}_{dn}$.
11		$\neg W_2$	(7)	From 9 by $\mathcal{R}_{dn}$.
12		$W_1 \vee W_2 \vee W_3$		From King–utterance by CB_{prop} and CB_{inst}
13		W_1	(1, 7)	From 10, 11 and 12
14	32	$B_1(\text{``}W_1\text{''})$	(1, 7)	From 13 by $\mathcal{R}_{up}$.
15		$\neg B_1(\text{``}W_1\text{''})$		From Utterance1 by CB_{prop} and CB_{inst}
16		$\bot$	(1, 7)	From 14 and 15 by $\supset E$
17		W_2	(1)	From 16 by $\bot_c$
18	3	$B_2(\text{``}W_2\text{''})$	(1)	From 17 by $\mathcal{R}_{up}$.
19		$\neg B_2(\text{``}W_2\text{''})$		From Utterance2 by CB_{inst}
20		$\bot$	(1)	From 18 and 19 by $\supset E$
21		W_3		From 20 by $\bot_c$
22	ϵ	$B_3(\text{``}W_3\text{''})$		From 21 by $\mathcal{R}_{up}$.

Fig. 2. The proof in the third situation

utterance (step 5). He tries to answer the question of the king, i.e. to infer that his spot is white. Under the hypothesis that 3, 4 and 5 constitute the only relevant knowledge for this goal (step 6), we conclude that he does not know the color of his spot (step 7).

The formal system describing the second situation differs from the first one in the additional axiom in context ϵ:

$$CB(\text{``}\neg B_1(\text{``}W_1\text{''})\text{''}) \text{ (Utterance1)}$$

This axiom expresses the fact that after the utterance of 1, the fact that he does not know the color of his spot becomes a common belief. The reasoning of wise man 2 in this situation is analogous to the reasoning of wise man 1 shown above.

The formal system describing the third situation has one more axiom in ϵ, namely

$$CB(\text{``}\neg B_2(\text{``}W_2\text{''})\text{''}) \text{ (Utterance2)}$$

describing the effect of the "I don't know" utterance of 2. The reasoning pattern of the third wise man in the third situation is as follows (the steps refer to the formal proof in figure 2): "Suppose my spot were black (step 1); then 2 would have seen it (step 3) and would have reasoned as follows: "3 has a black spot (step 4); if also my spot were black (step 7), then 1 would have seen two black spots (step 6 and 9), and would have reasoned as follows "The spots of my colleagues are both black (steps 10-11) and since at least one is white (step 12), then my spot is white". Therefore 1 would have known that his spot is white (step 14). But he didn't (step 15); therefore my spot must be black". Hence 2 would have believed that his spot were white (step 18); but he didn't (19); then my spot must be white (step 21)". We conclude that the third wise man believes that his spot is white (step 22).

The proof in figure 2 highlights the modularity provided by belief contexts. It contains several local reasoning chunks, performed very efficiently by simple propositional inference machinery. These local subproofs are connected together by the application of bridge rules, which have a tight correspondence with the informal reasoning: for example, the opening quotes in the written informal explanation correspond to changing context by reflecting down into an agent's view. Analogously, the closing quotes correspond to exiting a context by reflection up. Therefore, efficient proof strategies can be defined, driven by the structure of the problem, as a combination of local inference and bridge rules.

3   Situated belief contexts

The formalization presented in the previous section describes belief as a static propositional attitude. Indeed, each of the three formal systems is a snapshot of the beliefs of the agent in a fixed situation. The transitions between situations, determined by the utterances of the agents, are not represented at the formal level. They are simulated at the informal meta level by the operation of changing to a different formal system with additional axioms. However, this view is too naive for practical purposes. Any autonomous AI system dealing with multi-agent beliefs and interacting with the external environment (e.g. listening to and making utterances) needs the ability to represent the evolution of propositional attitudes through time. Indeed, the interactions may modify the beliefs of the other agents in the environment, and therefore the system should be able to represent and reason about these changes and modify his belief ascriptions accordingly.

In this section we show how the multi-context system for static belief given in previous section can be naturally extended to formalize the dynamics of agents' beliefs. Of course, the three context systems defined in previous section can not be simply put together in a single system: three static systems do not allow for a dynamic representation of beliefs. First of all, we have to consider that beliefs are expressed in a particular situation: we need to express facts such as "*In the initial situation* wise man 1 does not know his color", or "*in the second situation* wise man 2 does not know his color". Therefore, belief contexts no longer formalize unsituated views, but rather describe situated views. Instead of a single view, the external observer will have a view on the first situation, one on the second and one on the third situation: the context ϵ is replaced by three contexts s_1, s_2 and s_3 (see figure 3), each corresponding to one view of the external observer. The wise men have beliefs about different situations: for instance, context i is now replaced by three contexts, $s_j is_1$, $s_j is_2$ and $s_j is_3$, for each situation s_j. For instance, context $s_3 3 s_2$ represents what, in s_3, 3 believes to hold in s_2. This extension is performed at all levels of depth. In general, a context label α is now a situation label followed by a (possibly empty) sequence of pairs agent-situation.

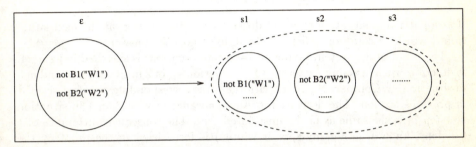

Fig. 3. Situated belief contexts

Associating contexts with situations, however, is not enough to represent the dynamic of propositional attitudes. Agents are now required to reason about *situated* beliefs. For instance, 3 has to be able to express facts such as "Wise man 1 does not know his color *in the initial situation*, and wise man 2 does not know his color *in the second situation*". Therefore, situations are introduced in the language of the belief contexts: for instance, the formula of the form $B_i("A")$ is replaced by the formulas $B_i(s, "A")$, with $s = s_1, s_2, s_3$. The formula $B_i(s, "A")$ means that the i-th wise man believes that A holds in situation s.

The bridge rules for nested belief, common belief and ignorance are modified according to the above changes: they not only take into account whose agent the view is, but also about which situation. For example reflection rules are modified as follows:

$$\frac{\alpha : B_i(s_j, "A")}{\alpha is_j : A}\,\mathcal{R}_{dn}. \qquad \frac{\alpha is_j : A}{\alpha : B_i(s_j, "A")}\,\mathcal{R}_{up}.$$

The introduction of situations in the language is strictly related to the situation dependence in the interpretation of the views. Indeed, reflection up [reflection down] can now be interpreted as making explicit [implicit] that context αis_j is a description of the beliefs of wise man i about situation s_j from the point of view of α.

In the expanded context structure defined above we represent the whole evolution of the scenario. Its only axioms (in context s_1) are the axioms of the unsituated system describing the first situation (modulo the introduction of situations). We express now at the formal level the transfer of information previously performed at the informal metalevel, with the transition between unsituated systems. First, we formalize the fact that the wise men never reject their beliefs with the following bridge rule:

$$\frac{\alpha s_k : B_i(s_j, \text{``}A\text{''})}{\alpha s_{k+1} : B_i(s_j, \text{``}A\text{''})} \text{ Frame}$$

Second, we model the effect of utterances with the following bridge rule:

$$\frac{s_j : \neg B_i(s_k, \text{``}\neg W_i\text{''})}{s_{j+1} : CB(s_j, \text{``}\neg B_i(s_k, \text{``}\neg W_i\text{''})\text{''})} \text{ Utterance}$$

If at a particular situation an agent doesn't know the answer, at the next situation it will be a common belief that he didn't know the answer.

The proof in the system taking into account situations is sketched in figure 4. It describes the reasoning patterns of 1 in situation s_1, of 2 in situation s_2 and of 3 in situation s_3. Compare the proof with the three corresponding proofs described in previous section. The derivation of the ignorance of wise man 1 in situation s_1 (step 7) is the same as in the unsituated case. The consequent utterance of 1 ("I don't know whether my spot is white") is formalized *in* the proof by the application of the Utterance rule, which yields step 9. Wise man 2, differently from the unsituated case, does not derive the color of his colleagues' spot from the axioms describing the scenario. He remembers them from the first situation. This fact is formalized *in* the proof by the application of the Frame rule, yielding step 10. The derivation of the ignorance of 2 (step 16) goes as in the unsituated case. With respect to the first situation, wise man 2 may consider as relevant knowledge also the utterance of 1 (step 15). The transfer of information from the second to the third situation, is again formalized by the application of Utterance and Frame bridge rules. Compare now the reasoning performed by wise man 3 in s_3 (from step 18 to step 40) with the unsituated proof (from step 1 to step 22). If we rule out the situations from the formulas and the context names, the steps of the two proofs are the same (step 20 and 21 both corresponding to step 3). The differences are due to the fact that 3 reasons about situated beliefs, namely the beliefs of 1 in situation s_1 and the beliefs of 2 in s_2. Besides the obvious difference due to situations in belief statements, it is interesting to consider the derivation of step 39. In the unsituated case, the corresponding step 21 was derived by classical contradiction; in this case, however, wise man 3 needs to reason by contradiction through multiple situations. His reasoning is modeled by the following bridge rule:

$$\frac{\begin{array}{c}[s_j is_k : \neg A]\\ \vdots\\ s_j is_{k+1} : \bot\end{array}}{s_j is_k : A} \bot\text{-Propagation}$$

which is a generalization to the situated case of the rule for reasoning by contradiction. This rules states that if agent i can derive a contradiction about situation s_{k+1} based on the assumption that $\neg A$ holds in s_k, then he can infer that A holds in s_k independently of the assumption. The assumption 18 about

1	s_1	$B_1(s_1, \text{“}W_2\text{”})$		From State-of-affairs and 1-sees-2
$\vdots$				
6		$ARF_1(s_1, \text{“}W_2, W_3,$ $W_1 \vee W_2 \vee W_3\text{”}, \text{“}W_1\text{”})$	(6)	By assumption
7		$\neg B_1(s_1, \text{“}W_1\text{”})$	(6)	From $\ldots$–6 by Bel-Clo
8		$B_2(s_1, \text{“}W_1\text{”})$		From State-of-affairs and 2-sees-1
9	s_2	$CB(s_1, \text{“}\neg B_1(s_1, \text{“}W_1\text{”})\text{”})$	(6)	From 7 by Utterance
10		$B_2(s_1, \text{“}W_1\text{”})$		From 8 by Frame
$\vdots$				
15		$ARF_2(s_2, \text{“}\neg B_1(s_1, \text{“}W_1\text{”}), W_1, W_3,$ $W_1 \vee W_2 \vee W_3\text{”}, \text{“}W_2\text{”})$	(15)	By assumption
16		$\neg B_2(s_1, \text{“}W_2\text{”})$	(6, 15)	From $\ldots$–15 by Bel-Clo
17	s_3	$CB(s_2, \text{“}\neg B_2(s_2, \text{“}W_2\text{”})\text{”})$	(6, 15)	From 16 by Utterance
18	$s_3 3 s_1$	$\neg W_3$	(18)	By assumption
19		$\neg W_3 \supset B_2(s_1, \text{“}\neg W_3\text{”})$		From CB-2-sees-3
20		$B_2(s_1, \text{“}\neg W_3\text{”})$	(18)	From 18 and 19 by $\supset E_3$
21	$s_3 3 s_2$	$B_2(s_1, \text{“}\neg W_3\text{”})$	(18)	From 20 by Frame
22	$s_3 3 s_2 2 s_1$	$\neg W_3$	(18)	From 21 by $\mathcal{R}_{dn}$.
23		$\neg W_3 \supset B_1(s_1, \text{“}\neg W_3\text{”})$		From CB-1-sees-3
24		$B_1(s_1, \text{“}\neg W_3\text{”})$	(18)	From 22 and 23 by $\supset E$
25		$\neg W_2$	(25)	By assumption
26		$\neg W_2 \supset B_1(s_1, \text{“}\neg W_2\text{”})$		From CB-1-sees-2
27		$B_1(s_1, \text{“}\neg W_2\text{”})$	(25)	From 25 and 26 by $\supset E$
28	$s_3 3 s_2 2 s_1 1 s_1$	$\neg W_3$	(18)	From 24 by $\mathcal{R}_{dn}$.
29		$\neg W_2$	(25)	From 27 by $\mathcal{R}_{dn}$.
30		$W_1 \vee W_2 \vee W_3$		From King–utterance
31		W_1	(18, 25)	From 28, 29 and 30
32	$s_3 3 s_2 2 s_1$	$B_1(s_1, \text{“}W_1\text{”})$	(18, 25)	From 31 by $\mathcal{R}_{up}$.
33		$\neg B_1(s_1, \text{“}W_1\text{”})$	(6)	From 9
34		$\bot$	(6, 18, 25)	From 32 and 33 by $\supset E$
35		W_2	(6, 18)	From 34 by $\bot_c$
36	$s_3 3 s_2$	$B_2(s_2, \text{“}W_2\text{”})$	(6, 18)	From 35 by $\mathcal{R}_{up}$.
37		$\neg B_2(s_2, \text{“}W_2\text{”})$	(6, 15)	From 17
38		$\bot$	(6, 15, 18)	From 36 and 37 by $\supset E$
39	$s_3 3 s_1$	W_3	(6, 15)	From 38 by $\bot_{prop}$
40	s_3	$B_3(s_1, \text{“}W_3\text{”})$	(6, 15)	From 39 by $\mathcal{R}_{up}$.

Fig. 4. The situated proof

situation s_1 leads to contradictory beliefs about situation s_2 (step 36), and can therefore be discharged when deriving step 39.

The above proof shows further advantages of the modularity provided by belief contexts. The first advantage is that the situated system has been developed incrementally from the three systems of contexts presented in previous section. Each of the subproofs associated with a situation is the simple generalization with situations of the proof in the corresponding unsituated system. Furthermore, notice that the search for a proof can be driven not only by reasoning about mutual beliefs, but also by the evolution of the scenario through time. For instance, the application of a bridge rule describing the effect of the utterance is a natural step to apply once the ignorance of the agent has been derived.

4   Related Work

Konolige in [12] formalizes the TWM in a propositional modal logic. His formalization consists of an unique modal theory that describes the puzzle from the external observer's point of view. Both Konolige's and our approach describe a multi-agent scenario in terms of views. In our formalism views are taken into account in the logic, with the structure of contexts; in Konolige's system they are present only in the semantics, and in the calculus (his inference machinery being a *semantic* tableaux system). The proofs of the TWM in his and our systems present interesting similarities. In Konolige's system, in order to prove a modal formula $[S_i]A$ from a set of hypotheses $[S_i]\Gamma$, a new tableaux is opened with goal A and hypotheses Γ. This corresponds, in our multi-context system, to reflecting down $B_i(``\Gamma")$ in $i$'s context, deriving $A$ from $\Gamma$ and reflecting up $B_i(``A")$ in the external observer's context. However, Konolige's formalization presents some problems. First, in order to axiomatize the fact that agent i_1 believes that agent i_2 believes that ... that agent i_n believes A, the axiom $[S_{i_1}][S_{i_2}]\ldots[S_{i_n}]A$ has to be added to the modal theory; there is not the possibility to add the much simpler axiom A to the $i_1,\ldots,i_n$ context. Furthermore, any deduction machinery for the modal logic must consider $[S_{i_1}][S_{i_2}]\ldots[S_{i_n}]A$ for the deduction of any other facts in the modal theory, at least to discard it as irrelevant. This does not happen in our modular approach: the fact A in the context $i_1,\ldots,i_n$ has to be considered only when trying to prove a theorem in context $i_1,\ldots,i_n$. A second problem arises when we want to formalize/implement connection between different views (e.g. communication between agents, beliefs remembered from previous situations). Consider, for instance, communication between agents i and j: in Konolige's approach we have to impose the suitable semantic restrictions on the deduction structure of agent i and j, e.g. by axiomatizing the restricted structures. However, communication between agents is often very complicated, and it could be impossible to find a complete axiomatization. In our approach we formalize communication between agents i and agent j by means of bridge rules which can have very complicated side conditions; if we have to prove that the agent j believes A from the fact that the agent i believes B, in Konolige's approach we have to pass through the external theory, while in our approach it is sufficient to go from i's context to j's context.

McCarthy in [13] proposes a formalizaton of the TWM puzzle in which belief is modeled by possible worlds and accessibility relations as in [10]. McCarthy formalizes possible worlds semantics in a first order theory, whose language contains terms for worlds and predicate symbols for the accessibility relations. The main problem with the implementation of the theory proposed by McCarthy is that it is a theory with no structure: its facts are not partitioned into modules. As a consequence, an inference procedure for this theory can hardly distinguish between facts concerning the beliefs of each agent, the communication between agents, the state of the world, etc. This implies that any decision procedure for such an unstructured theory must be general. Furthermore, it is almost impossible to implement in a general inference strategy local strategies for reasoning about the belief of a particular agent and global strategies for communication between agents or reasoning through situations.

In [1] an implementation of the TWM in FOL [16] is presented. Each agent is represented by three object contexts and a meta context. The three object contexts represent the beliefs of the agents about the world and about the other agents' beliefs respectively. The meta context formalizes how the agent reasons about his own and other agents' beliefs. The meta context interacts with the object contexts via the REFLECT and EVAL commands, which are the implementation of a form of reflection. Although this solution features a certain degree of modularity, it is not totally clear from a logical point of view, and it seems difficult to extend to more general cases. The use of beliefs contexts provides a solution to this problem. First, we have a general criteria for the modularization of facts based on the concept of view [4]; second, multi-context systems provide a framework whose formal properties are well understood (see [7, 6]).

5   Conclusions and future work

Belief contexts can be used to formalize propositional attitudes and provide many advantages from the implementational point of view. In this paper we have discussed a formalization of the TWM puzzle using belief contexts. First we have shown how reasoning about mutual and nested beliefs, common belief, and ignorance, can be formalized using belief contexts in a natural and structured way. The structure of the formal proofs shows that the local reasoning patterns of the wise men are formalized by deduction inside single contexts, connected by bridge rules to represent the overall reasoning patterns. This makes the search for a proof driven by the structure of the problem. Furthermore, we have shown how belief contexts are suitable for an incremental implementation of knowledge: a solution of the puzzle taking into account the evolution of propositional attitudes through situations was obtained as a natural extension of the unsituated case.

This work is being developed in two directions. On the one hand, in order to show that our formalization is general and elaboration tolerant, we will discuss how several variations in the statement of TWM puzzle can be easily captured within the formalization presented here. These variations include agents with different spots, with different expressive and inferential abilities, and with different languages.

On the other hand, we will investigate the use of belief contexts as data structures to *implement* agents, following the intuitions of R.W. Weyhrauch [16, 17]. We have already mechanized in GETFOL[3] [5] the systems of contexts and the formal proofs described in this paper (these mechanizations are not described here because out of the scope of this paper). This is basically the reasoning of an external observer reasoning about the puzzle. We are now considering a different goal, i.e. the mechanization of the agents of the scenario (the wise men and also the king) as autonomous and communicating systems, combining reasoning and acting capabilities. The reasoning component will be based on the formal structures presented in this paper, and will be integrated with action and perception capabilities (e.g. speaking, listening, watching).

References

1. L. Carlucci Aiello, D. Nardi, and M. Schaerf. Reasoning about knowledge and ignorance. In *International Conference of 5th Generation Computer System*, pages 618–627, Tokyo, 1988.

2. L. G. Creary. Propositional Attitudes: Fregean representation and simulative reasoning. In *Proc. of the 6th International Joint Conference on Artificial Intelligence*, pages 176–181, 1979.

3. G. Criscuolo, F. Giunchiglia, and L. Serafini. A Foundation of Metalogical Reasoning: OM pairs (Propositional Case). Technical Report 9403-02, IRST, Trento, Italy, 1994.

4. F. Giunchiglia. Contextual reasoning. *Epistemologia, special issue on I Linguaggi e le Macchine*, XVI:345–364, 1993. Short version in Proceedings IJCAI'93 Workshop on Using Knowledge in its Context, Chambery, France, 1993, pp. 39–49. Also IRST-Technical Report 9211-20, IRST, Trento, Italy.

5. F. Giunchiglia. GETFOL: Interactive Multicontext Theorem Proving (abstract). In *Proceedings of IJCAI-93 Workshop on Automated Theorem Proving*, page 43, Chambery, France, 1993.

6. F. Giunchiglia and L. Serafini. On the Proof Theory of Hierarchical Meta-Logics. Technical Report 9301-07, IRST, Trento, Italy, 1993.

7. F. Giunchiglia and L. Serafini. Multilanguage hierarchical logics (or: how we can do without modal logics). *Artificial Intelligence*, 65:29–70, 1994.

8. F. Giunchiglia, L. Serafini, E. Giunchiglia, and M. Frixione. Non-Omniscient Belief as Context-Based Reasoning. In *Proc. of the 13th International Joint Conference on Artificial Intelligence*, pages 548–554, Chambery, France, 1993. Also IRST-Technical Report 9206-03, IRST, Trento, Italy.

9. A. R. Haas. A Syntactic Theory of Belief and Action. *Artificial Intelligence*, 28:245–292, 1986.

10. J. Hintikka. *Knowledge and Belief*. Cornell University Press, Ithaca, NY, 1962.

11. J.R. Hobbs and R.C. Moore, editors. *Formal Theories of Commonsense World*. Ablex Publishing Corporation, Norwood, New Jersey, 1985.

---

[3] GETFOL is an interactive prover for the mechanization of multi context systems.

12. K. Konolige. *A deduction model of belief and its logics.* PhD thesis, Stanford University CA, 1984.

13. J. McCarthy. Formalization of Two Puzzles Involving Knowledge. In V. Lifschitz, editor, *Formalizing Common Sense - Papers by John McCarthy*, pages 158–166. Ablex Publishing Corporation, 1990.

14. R.C. Moore. The role of logic in knowledge representation and commonsense reasoning. In *National Conference on Artificial Intelligence*. AAAI, 1982.

15. D. Prawitz. *Natural Deduction - A proof theoretical study.* Almquist and Wiksell, Stockholm, 1965.

16. R.W. Weyhrauch. Prolegomena to a Theory of Mechanized Formal Reasoning. *Artificial Intelligence*, 13(1):133–176, 1980.

17. R.W. Weyhrauch, M. Cadoli, and C. L. Talcott. Using Abstract Resources to Control Reasoning. August 1994.

Toward a Formal Model of Commitment for Resource Bounded Agents

Paul Dongha

Department of Computation, UMIST
Manchester, M60 1QD. United Kingdom
EMAIL: dongha@sna.co.umist.ac.uk

Abstract. Reasoning about intentions is an important area of research for the design of resource bounded rational agents who need to coordinate their actions with the actions of other agents in a multi-agent system. Closely related to intentions is the notion of an agent being committed to an intention. Commitments ensure that agents reason to achieve their intentions, however a commitment can also be dropped if it is considered irrational by the agent to continue acting for its associated intention. If commitments are to be taken seriously in AI we need to mediate this tension. We take a first step toward a solution by presenting a logical model for resource bounded agents who have to reason about their intentions whilst situated in an unpredictable environment.

1 Introduction

The performance of multi-agent systems depends on the interactions between agents, the performance of actions and the reasoning which issues in those actions. Central to the operation of agents is their ability to construct plans of action, and to behave rationally in executing those plans. Bratman [1], suggests that future-directed intentions, that is, partial plans of action play critical roles in the ongoing reasoning of limited rational agents who need to coordinate themselves with the actions of other agents. By committing to an intention an agent predicts its own future behaviour to a degree, and thus provides useful information for other agents who may need to coordinate their future actions with him.

However, an intention is not irrevocable. In complex environments which are subject to unexpected changes, an agent may be obliged to revoke a prior intention by dropping its commitment, because unanticipated changes make it irrational for the agent to continue to act for his intention. The decision to drop an intention will often be the result of careful deliberation. However, dropping an intention is a costly decision to make because it has implications on the agent's success in achieving its goals. Thus there exists a tension between dropping an intention and remaining committed to an intention when faced with unanticipated changes in the environment of an agent. Part of a solution to this is to provide normative assessments of the way an agent should manage its intentions.

This paper is organised as follows. In §2 we state two problems facing computational agents, and show how Bratman's theory of intention helps overcome them. In §3 we analyse the concept of commitment to an intention. In §4 we critically review existing work which has looked at the commitment aspect of intention. In §5 we describe how intentions are partial in their structure, and we describe how deliberation effects intentions for limited agents who wish to achieve complex goals. In §6 we show how the commitment concept associated with intentions can be used to assist an agent in deliberating and acting for its intentions. In §7 we present a logical model for an agent reasoning about its intentions. Using the model we specify useful principles for an agent who discovers that some of its intentions become un-achievable.

2 The Usefulness of Intentions for Limited Agents

There are two constraints on the type of agents which we are considering. Firstly, agents have limited computational and informational resources [14]. As such they are unable to perform arbitrarily large computations in constant time and are unable to deliberate at every moment, but, despite these limitations an agent should be capable of achieving complex goals. The environment within which an agent is situated is subject to unexpected and rapid change. Thus even if agents could deliberate rapidly, the beliefs upon which such intensive deliberation is based may be undermined even while deliberation takes place. Agents may also be limited in their knowledge of the world, therefore detailed deliberation about the future, based on incomplete knowledge would also be inappropriate.

The second constraint is that of coordination. If agents are to achieve complex goals—ones requiring a number of actions dispersed temporally—they must coordinate their present activities with their future activities. This is important in both single and multiple agent settings. In the former case an agent is situated in an environment, can perceive changes in the environment and performs actions to effect that environment; such systems may be called situated systems [8]. In such cases an agent's present actions must serve a purpose toward his overall goal—they must contribute in some way toward the goal. In the latter case an agent is situated in a multi-agent setting and may require the assistance of another agent in order to achieve a complex goal [10]. For example, an agent may have a goal but requires that certain pre-conditions hold before he can proceed; he may ask that another agent perform some action so that the pre-condition is met. An agent may require resources under the control of another agent in order to proceed toward his goal; he may therefore request that the appropriate resources be released to him. In this situation he must synchronise his own actions with those of another agent. In other cases, two or more agents may jointly intend to achieve the same goal, such that all agents concerned are required to perform various actions toward its fulfillment [11]. Once more, each agent will be required to coordinate his actions with those of others. Whether we examine a situated environment or a multi-agent environment (where agent's may have joint-intentions), needs for coordination are paramount.

Michael Bratman argues that the role of intentions in practical reasoning helps overcome the problems above. Future directed intentions represent partial plans in the reasoning of limited agents. By settling on a partial plan an agent acquires a focus for reasoning because the prior intention poses problems for future deliberation; given an intention, an agent reasons to means of achieving that intention. Since the agent is limited he restricts his reasoning only to actions which are relevant to his intention. For example, my prior intention to be at the library tomorrow evening, urges me to reason about how to get there, which books to take *etc.* At the same time my prior intention rules out seriously considering a whole host of other activities which I could do tomorrow evening. Settling on a prior intention therefore helps me to achieve complex goals despite my resource limitations.

By settling on a partial plan an agent provides support for the belief that he will act to achieve his intention. Therefore an agent can coordinate his future actions to fit-in with his intention, based on his belief that he will act to achieve his intention. For example, my prior intention to be at the library tomorrow evening will normally provide me with a belief that I will go there tomorrow evening. Thus I can plan to perform activities to fit around my going to the library tomorrow, e.g, I can plan to meet a friend for coffee near the library tomorrow. Other agents can coordinate their future actions to fit in with another agent's intention, based on the their belief that he will act to achieve his intention. For example, my intention to meet you for coffee tomorrow provides support for your belief that I will act to achieve my intention, and therefore you can coordinate your actions for tomorrow so that you act to meet me for coffee.

3   Commitment

A fundamental characteristic of an intention is that it involves commitment [1, Chapter 6]. This commitment aspect of intention comprises three dispositions according to Bratman. Firstly, an agent will tend to retain an intention without reconsideration—because agents are resource bounded they can not constantly reconsider the merits of their intention. Secondly, an agent tends to reason from the intention to (sub-)intentions which play a part in the agent's plan. For example, an agent will reason from an intention to sub-intentions concerning more specific actions. Thirdly, an agent tends to reason in a way which constrains the adoption of sub-intentions, so that possible courses of action incompatible with the intention are not seriously considered.[1]

Commitment therefore is a concept closely related to an intention—it determines the degree to which an agent persists in trying to achieve an intention, and thus controls the likelihood of the agent reconsidering an intention.[2] As discussed in §2, intentions are useful because they help resource bounded agents who have coordination requirements. But for intentions to function properly, the

---

[1] These three principles apply to human reasoning and we therefore take them into consideration in describing computational agents of the type we are interested in.

[2] There are other factors which may determine the likelihood of reconsidering an intention. For example, some intentions may be unstable by their very nature and thus more likely to be reconsidered.

commitment aspect of them must operate in a way which ensures that agents behave rationally. For example, we would not want agents to drop intentions unless they really had to, and we would not want agents to over-commit to an intention.

Commitment to an intention is even more important when we consider cooperative problem solving situations which occur when a number of agents choose to work together to achieve a common goal. In such a setting each agent will have to perform inter-leaved (or possibly simultaneous) actions over an extended period of time to achieve a goal. Their actions will have to be coordinated. The commitment aspect of intention will need to function in a way which provides an adequate solution to their coordination requirements [4]. This is because agents believe and expect that other agents will act in a way to achieve their intentions, and those actions will be rational means to achieving those intentions. In essence, this allows agents to coordinate their actions with those they believe others will perform.

However, an agent will not remain committed to an intention in all possible circumstances. There will be occasions when it is obviously irrational for the agent to remain committed, for example, the agent may come to believe that the intention is impossible to achieve. Clearly, this is an occasion when an intention must be revoked by an agent otherwise the agent could be criticised for behaving irrationally. Sometimes however, it is not always obvious that an agent should drop an intention immediately in the light of new information. More often, (according to Bratman) [2] an update in information about an agent's environment, between the time of committing to an intention and the time for its completion, will cause the agent to reconsider its intention. This is because the result of acquiring new information could possibly undermine the rationality of continuing with the intention—but does not immediately rule out the intention. Therefore, the agent needs to reconsider whether or not to remain committed to the intention. The outcome of such reconsideration could cause the agent to re-commit itself to the intention or may cause the agent to revoke its intention.

A decision to drop an intention could be based on incorrect beliefs about the outcome of an action, or by the failure of an action or by the failure to execute an action. Such outcomes could be the result of a combination of the agent's limited capacity to predict the outcome of its actions or by cruel changes in the environment which could not possibly have been predicted. In any case, if an agent drops its intention the costs of such a decision could be great, since the reason which motivated previous actions—actions which play a part toward the achievement of the intention—is no longer present, those actions may have been wasted. Still further, the agent may have to undo the effects of these previous actions. The costs of dropping an intention could be even greater in a multi-agent environment. Revoking an intention whose fulfillment is required toward the achievement of a joint-goal could jeopardise the whole problem solving situation. Furthermore, as noted above, the performance of other agents could be reduced because their anticipated coordination is now no longer required.

On one hand, dropping an intention has costs associated with it in both single and multi-agent environments; the ensuing replanning and jeopardy to the problem solving situation. On the other hand, committing to an intention has benefits if it functions correctly; it meets the need for coordination of actions within and between agents, and helps with an agent's resource limitations.

But there is a tension between dropping an intention and remaining committed to one when situated in an unpredictable environment. What we would like to do is try and design a commitment mechanism for intentions which ensures that an agents continue to remain committed to their intention only when it is rational to do so, despite their limitations and the unpredictability of the environment.

4 Existing Approaches To Commitment

In this section we very briefly review existing work which describe the conditions under which an agent releases its commitment to an intention. Space restrictions prevent us from providing a detailed review of existing approaches (the interested reader is referred to [5]). In particular we wish to highlight the degree to which approaches have addressed the issue of an agent reconciling his limited capacity to deliberate with his need to achieve his intentions.

In [3], Cohen and Levesque distinguish three circumstances which dictate an agent releasing his commitment to an intention; when the agent believes his intention has already been achieved, believes the intention is impossible to achieve, or when the motivation for the intention is no longer believed to hold. In [11], a model of commitment to a joint-intention is presented for two or more agents. Here the conditions for revoking a commitment are similar to those conditions in their single agent version except that when one of the above conditions are believed by an agent he adopts the goal of bringing about a mutual belief between all agents in the group his reasons for revoking his commitment to the joint-goal. In [13] a formalisation of intention is presented based on a branching-time possible-worlds model. Three axioms are presented for an agent releasing its commitment to an intention which are similar to the three conditions in [3]. These, three formalisms suffer from essentially the same problem. There is no indication of when an agent should reconsider a commitment—the three conditions are simply necessary conditions on the agent for persisting with his commitment. The three conditions for releasing a commitment to a goal are obvious conditions, in the sense that it is clearly rational of the agent to revoke its commitment when it believes any of them. However, (as pointed out in §3) there may be changes in an agent's environment which do not obviously cause it to drop its commitment, but rather may cause the agent to deliberate about dropping its intention, i.e., the agent is not straight-away obliged to drop its intention because it has yet to figure out whether its rational to persist with the intention in light of new information. These issues are not examined. Also, as pointed out by Singh [16], the agent would be committed to an intention only as long as these three conditions do not hold. But, this means that the agent would have to, at every moment, deduce that these conditions do not hold, and this would involve a continual process of deliberation which is clearly not possible by a limited agent.

In [9] Jennings presents a model of commitment based on a a unifying principle of coordination. He argues that commitments are promises made by an agent to undertake a specified action (or actions). A convention governs how an agent should react to changes in its environment which it believes adversely effect the fulfillment of a commitment. A convention is a list of rules, each rule comprising of a condition and action. If an agent acting toward the achievement of a commitment ever comes to believe the condition part of a rule, then it tries to perform the actions listed in its action part. Jennings goes on to argue that an agent may have a number of different conventions at its disposal, each one suited to different types of cooperative problem solving situations. In this model the conventions have in their condition parts assessments which have to made by a process of deliberation. Some of these conditions are in themselves quite complex expressions, and require the agent to reason about a complete plan of action. The type of agents we are interested in only ever have a partial description of an intention therefore they can not reason about a complete plan of action.

In [15] Munindar Singh argues that at the time of adopting an intention an agent commits himself to the intention, and his level of commitment is set equal to the expected utility of the intention to him. Each action performed by the agent toward the intention has some associated cost, and after performing an action the agent's level of commitment to the intention is reduced by this cost, until after a number of actions, the level of commitment reaches zero. At this point the agent can either reconsider the intention or he can choose to drop the intention because he judges himself to have put in enough effort. In this way an agent's level of commitment to an intention is a measure of the resources that he is willing to use in trying to achieve it, and is related to the utility of achieving that intention. Although this model is mathematically attractive, it is an ideal which may not be reached in practice. The agent is presumed to operate in a single agent environment where he is always successful in the performance of his actions. As noted above, in situated systems the environment may be subject to unanticipated changes which by themselves may be cause for reconsideration.

We conclude that existing models of the commitment aspect of intention do not address the problems facing the kind of resource bounded situated agents which we are interested in. The models described either do not consider the resource limited nature of agents [9], or the volatility of the environment [3, 11, 13, 15]. None of them address the issue of an agent simultaneously holding more than one intention.

5   Intentions as Partial Plans

In this section we elaborate on the notion of a partial plan, and describe how one might typically be constructed by an agent as it alternates between performing actions and deliberating over time. The approach described in this section will

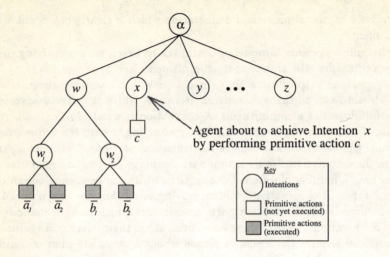

Fig. 1. An intention plan to achieve α, at time t_1, after the agent has performed some actions and deliberations on α.

be used as the basis for defining some general principles in §6, and for the logical model of commitment in §7.

An intention is a partial plan in two distinct ways. It is sequentially partial in that it can be expressed as an incomplete temporally ordered sequence of sub-intentions. The intention will be achieved only if the sub-intentions are achieved in their temporal order. For example, if I form an intention at time t_1 to "catch a train to London at 2.00pm tomorrow" I may have to purchase a ticket, reserve a seat and pack my suitcase between the time of forming that intention and the time of boarding the train. These are examples of sub-intentions (or preliminary steps). There may be other sub-intentions which I need to achieve, but at t_1, these are not part of the plan yet, because I may not yet be aware what they should be, but I can still be confident that as time progresses I will come to know what to do. In this way intentions are sequentially partial because some of the preliminary steps have yet to be calculated.

Given our comments about agents being resource limited and situated in environments where detailed plans may not be achievable, agents may put off till some later time the details of how they will achieve each of their sub-intentions, and at what specific times to start and finish acting for each sub-intention. At t_1, I may deliberate about which sub-intentions are required (and conclude with the three mentioned above), but I will not figure out how to achieve each one at time t_1—it is sufficient for me to know that I need to achieve them but calculating how to achieve them can be postponed until nearer the time for acting for them. In this way sub-intentions are hierarchically partial.

Fig. 1 shows the partial nature of a future directed intention to α, at time t_1 after an agent has spent some time acting for α and deliberating on α. It is read as, the agent intends to achieve α, by achieving w followed by x followed by y and eventually finishing by achieving z, in that order. After y, there may be other intentions which the agent should also achieve, (indicated by dots) however at t_1 it may be unclear to the agent what they are, although, the agent should believe at t_1 that after performing w, x and y it will know what actions are required. This is because the agent is confident that it will be able to deliberate some time between starting w and finishing y, and therefore will be in a better position to calculate what to do after y. On adopting α, the agent may deliberate in deciding how it will achieve w, and conclude that w is achieved by first achieving w_1, followed by w_2, in that order. Still further, it may deliberate about how to achieve w_1, and conclude that it is achieved by achieving action $\bar{a}_1$ followed by $\bar{a}_2$. These last two are primitive actions in the sense that an agent can directly perform them, e.g., "rotate arm through 45 degrees" or "grasp block". Primitive actions label leaf nodes in intention plans.

As time progresses, and the agent performs actions toward its intention, it can deliberate intermittently to fill in the details of its plan. It can fill in the sequential components which are missing, or it can calculate means to achieving some of its sub-intentions. Because deliberation takes time, and time is a resource, an agent must only put in as much effort in deliberating as it thinks is reasonable. Reasonable here will be directly related to the unpredictability of the environment. In an unpredictable environment an agent should spend proportionately less time calculating the details of its plan since they are likely to be unstable anyway.

6 Formalising Commitment For Partial Plans

In a fully predictable world an agent should, in theory, always be capable of achieving all its intentions. Bratman's intention formation model guarantees firstly, that an agent will never adopt intentions without appropriate beliefs in their success, and secondly, an agent will not adopt an intention which it believes will clash with others it holds. This is an ideal which may never be reached in practice. There are essentially two problems with this approach which have already been mentioned previously. Firstly, as time progresses in an unpredictable world an agent may discover, part way through acting for an intention, that it conflicts with another intention which it holds, such that both together can not be achieved. This will cause the agent to reconsider one or other of these intentions. Reconsideration involves the agent deciding again from scratch whether or not it should continue intending. However, the agent must decide between which of the two intentions it will reconsider. Something better than an arbitrary choice is required. Secondly, limited agents are incapable of calculating at every moment whether changes in the environment threaten the progress of each and every intention that they hold. We would like to specify criteria with which to guide the agent's reasoning as it notices changes in its environment. We explain below how the notion of commitment can be used to overcome these two problems.

We have already discussed the important characteristics of commitment which ensure that agents direct their reasoning and actions toward achieving their intentions. The notion of commitment to an intention can be used as an indicator of the importance to the agent of achieving its intention. How do we determine the degree of commitment of an agent for an intention? We use the following principle. At any point in time, the commitment of an agent to an intention is a combination of two things;

(1) a measure of the amount of resources invested by the agent toward the achievement of that intention, and;
(2) a measure of the amount of future resources required by the agent toward the achievement of that intention.

If an agent has already put in a great deal of effort in acting toward an intention, he will be highly committed to the achievement of that intention. However, an intention which the agent has only performed a few actions toward, will have a lower degree of commitment because the agent will have put in less effort to achieving it, $i.e.$, according to (1), commitment values are proportional to the amount of invested resources. Two intentions can be compared to see what the invested resources are for each. In Fig. 1, say at time t_n the agent is in the process of acting for sub-intention x, having already performed the actions associated with achieving w_1 and w_2, between time t_1 and t_n. At time t_n then, we can judge the agent as being relatively highly committed to α. In comparison, consider another intention, β say, which the agent simultaneously holds, and for which it has only performed two primitive actions. Although the agent is committed to β, and will consequently direct its reasoning efforts to achieve it, α has a greater degree of commitment. This seems intuitive since agents are more committed to those intentions which they have already put in a lot of effort for in comparison to those which are far from being achieved. This also relates commitment to deliberation. Intentions which are nearing completion will have been subjected to more deliberation by the agent, whereas intentions which are less complete will not have involved the same amount of deliberation. Indirectly then, the level of commitment is a measure of the amount of resources spent—in deliberating and acting—toward the intention.

However, calculating the future resources required for an intention is more problematic. We are considering agents who partially and intermittently fill in their intention plans when they deliberate, so calculating how many resources are required in the future to achieve an intention can only be an approximation. The lower the anticipated future resources then the higher the commitment value of an intention, $i.e.$, according to (2), commitment values are inversely proportional to the amount of anticipated future resources. We state conditions (1) and (2) as a principle;

Principle of Commitment: The commitment level associated with an intention is a measure of the amount of resources expended in deliberating and acting toward that intention, combined in some way with an approximate measure of the amount of future resources (in deliberating and acting) required to achieve the intention.

The Principle of Commitment is a useful guide for the agent in deciding between two intentions which conflict. If an agent discovers that two or more of its intentions are together unachievable, then it can appeal to the commitment value of each intention in deciding which one should be reconsidered. In this case we state that the intention with the lower commitment value will be subject to reconsideration, whereas the intention with the higher commitment value will not be a candidate for reconsideration. In this way the reconsideration process is simplified.

In reconsidering an intention, an agent has to decide whether it could possibly achieve its intention by other means or whether the intention should be dropped. In the former case an agent would have to replan the sub-intentions of the overall intention in order to calculate if the intention is still achievable. If the intention is dropped as a result of reconsideration then all the effort expended in acting and deliberating for that intention has been wasted. Reconsidering the intention with the least commitment value, will minimise how much effort could be wasted (or put at risk).

A limited agent can not be alert to changes in the environment at every moment, and calculate at every moment whether all of its intentions are threatened by such changes. Rather, agents can only stop periodically in order to perceive their environment [12]. By perceiving, intelligent agents form new beliefs about objects in their environment, and revise existing beliefs [7]. The result of perception then, may undermine the beliefs upon which existing intentions are based, so that the successful achievement of such intentions become threatened. Intuitively, the more committed an agent is to an intention, the more alert it should be to changes in the environment which could threaten the successful achievement of that intention—in human practical reasoning we would want to know immediately if the progress of those intentions to which we are most committed become threatened.

Commitments look like a useful guide for agents to use in checking their intentions after perception. After perception an agent should firstly check its intention with the highest commitment value to determine if it still achievable. Then it should check the intention with the next lowest commitment value, followed by the intention with the next lowest commitment value and so on. It is likely that an agent will not have the available time to check each and every one of its intentions after perception, but the ones it can check will be those with the highest commitment values. This implies that intentions should be prioritized in decreasing order of their commitment value. The highest priority intention is the one with the greatest commitment value, and the lowest priority intention is the one with the least degree of commitment.

We state that commitment to an intention as a measure of anticipated and invested resources serves two roles. (1) Commitment provides a basis for comparing intentions so that if an agent discovers two or more of its intentions conflict, it can choose to reconsider the one with the lowest commitment value. Consequentially the agent does not have to expend resources in deliberating between which of its intentions it should reconsider—the commitment value automatically provides a guide for the agent. (2) Commitment values can be used to provide a priority ordering for intentions, so as the environment develops and an agent perceives its environment, it is disposed to check its highest committed intention for possible threats to its planned achievement. Condition (1) leads to the following principle:

Principle of Least Commitment: If all the agent's current intentions taken together are found to be inconsistent then it should drop those intentions whose overall commitment value is minimal such that the remaining intentions are still consistent.

Condition (2) leads to the following principle:

Principle of Commitment Priority: When the agent perceives changes in its environment it should firstly check its intention with the highest commitment value to verify that it is still believed to be achievable. Then the agent should check its lower priority intentions, in decreasing order of commitment value, to verify they are still believed to be achievable.

7 The Formal Model

Our logical model is based on a subset of linear-time temporal logic [6]. We do not address issues of soundness and completeness for the logic which we develop here. Our main aim is to present an expressive semantics for the notion of commitment described above, and to model how an agent constructs an intention plan as it interleaves deliberations and actions.

Syntax The syntax of our language is defined as follows;

- The two basic sets from which intention plans can be constructed are the set of all primitive actions **PA**, and the set of all non-primitive actions **NPA**. Primitive actions are those actions which can be directly executed by the agent, and non-primitive actions are those that must be decomposed into other (possibly primitive) actions for them to be achieved. We use members of **NP** with an overscore to denote primitive actions which have been executed in intention plans;

$$\langle primitive\text{-}act \rangle ::= a_i, \text{ for } i \in \mathbb{N}$$
$$\langle non\text{-}primitive\text{-}act \rangle ::= x_j, \text{ for } j \in \mathbb{N}$$
$$\langle completed\text{-}primitive\text{-}act \rangle ::= \langle primitive\text{-}act \rangle$$

Notation: $a, b, c, \ldots$ (with or without subscripts) are arbitrary primitive actions. $\bar{a}, \bar{b}, \bar{c} \ldots$ (with or without subscripts) are arbitrary completed primitive actions. $x, y, z, \ldots$ (with or without subscripts) are arbitrary non-primitive actions.

- The set **Int** represents the set of all intention plans (an example of an intention plan was given in Fig. 1), and is described by the following grammar;

$$\langle int \rangle ::= \langle primitive\text{-}act \rangle \mid \langle completed\text{-}primitive\text{-}act \rangle \mid$$
$$\langle non\text{-}primitive\text{-}act \rangle \mid [\langle int \rangle, \dots, \langle int \rangle]$$

Notation: $\alpha, \beta, \gamma, \dots$ are arbitrary intentions plans.

In this grammar the intention plan α in Fig. 1 would be represented as $[[[\bar{a}_1, \bar{a}_2], [\bar{b}_1, \bar{b}_2]], [c], y, z]$.

- **At** is the set of action transformation rules;

$$\langle act\text{-}rules \rangle ::= \langle primitive\text{-}act \rangle \mapsto_{act} \langle completed\text{-}primitive\text{-}act \rangle \mid$$
$$\langle non\text{-}primitive\text{-}act \rangle \mapsto_{del} \langle primitive\text{-}act \rangle \mid$$
$$\langle non\text{-}primitive\text{-}act \rangle \mapsto_{del} [\langle int \rangle, \dots, \langle int \rangle]$$

Notation: $\psi, \omega \dots$ are arbitrary action transformation rules.

The set **At** says how to achieve non-primitive or primitive actions, where each rule is capturing a deliberation on a non-primitive action or an execution of a primitive action which can be performed by the agent. For example, in the grammar $x_i \mapsto_{del} [\alpha_1, \dots, \alpha_m]$ expresses that the non-primitive action x_i is achieved by achieving $[\alpha_1, \dots, \alpha_m]$, and $a_i \mapsto_{act} \bar{a}_i$ expresses the execution of primitive action a_i.

- **B** is the set of beliefs which an agent can have;

$$\langle belief \rangle ::= \langle int \rangle \mapsto \langle int \rangle$$

Notation: $b_1, b_2, \dots$ are arbitrary beliefs.

Agents have beliefs about how one intention can be transformed to another intention, either through deliberation or by the execution of some action.

- The set **IN** is used to denote commitment values;

$$\langle commit\text{-}val \rangle ::= n$$

Notation: $n, m, l, \dots$ are arbitrary commitment values.

- **FL** is the set of formulae described by the following grammar;

$$\langle fmla \rangle ::= \mathsf{Int}(\langle int \rangle) \mid \mathsf{Commit}(\langle int \rangle, n) \mid \mathsf{Act}(\langle int \rangle, \langle int \rangle) \mid$$
$$\mathsf{Del}(\langle int \rangle, \langle int \rangle) \mid \mathsf{Bel}(\langle belief \rangle) \mid \langle commit\text{-}val \rangle > \langle commit\text{-}val \rangle \mid$$
$$\langle fmla \rangle \vee \langle fmla \rangle \mid \neg \langle fmla \rangle \mid \bigcirc \langle fmla \rangle \mid \Box \langle fmla \rangle \mid \Diamond \langle fmla \rangle$$

Notation: $\theta, \varphi, \psi, \dots$ are arbitrary formulae.

Semantics A frame F is a tuple $\langle S, R, c, i, b, l \rangle$, where:

- $S \neq \emptyset$ is a set of states;
- $R \subseteq S \times S$ is a reflexive binary relation on S;
- $c : S \rightarrow (\mathbf{Int} \mapsto \mathbf{IN})$ assigns commitment values to each intention that the agent has at a particular state. This function is partial with respect to **Int** since not all intention plans will have commitment values.

- $i : S \rightarrow powerset(\mathbf{Int})$ gives the set of intentions which the agent has at a particular state.
- $b : \sigma \rightarrow powerset(\mathbf{B})$ gives the set of beliefs for the agent at a particular state. These are beliefs about how an intention plan can be transformed by either a deliberation or action. For example, in a given state $\sigma \in S$ the agent can believe that $x_i \mapsto [\alpha_1, \alpha_2, \alpha_3]$, intuitively denoting the agent believes that non-primitive action x_i is achieved by achieving intention α_1 followed by α_2, and then α_3.
- $l : R \rightarrow \{del, act\}$ labels each arc with the type of transition made on that arc. Intuitively, for any two states $\sigma, \sigma' \in R$, the value $l(\sigma, \sigma')$ represents the occurrence of either a deliberation (del) or an action (act) occurring on that arc.

We define a model M as $\langle F, \sigma : \mathbf{IN} \rightarrow S \rangle$. Thus the behaviour of an agent in our model is a path of the branching time structure in the frame defined above. The semantics of formulae are given relative to a model and path defined above and a point in it. $M, \sigma, t \models \theta$ expresses "M satisfies θ at point t in path σ". The formal semantics are as follows;

$M, \sigma, t \models \theta \vee \vartheta$	iff	$M, \sigma, t \models \theta$ or $M, \sigma, t \models \vartheta$
$M, \sigma, t \models \neg\theta$	iff	$M, \sigma, t \not\models \theta$
$M, \sigma, t \models n > m$	iff	n is greater than m
$M, \sigma, t \models \mathsf{Int}(\alpha)$	iff	$\alpha \in i(\sigma(t))$
$M, \sigma, t \models \mathsf{Commit}(\alpha, m)$	iff	$c(\sigma(t))(\alpha) = m$
$M, \sigma, t \models \mathsf{Del}(\alpha, \beta)$	iff	$\alpha \in i(\sigma(t))$ and $\beta \in (i(\sigma(t+1)))$ and $l(\sigma(t), \sigma(t+1)) = del$
$M, \sigma, t \models \mathsf{Act}(\alpha, \beta)$	iff	$\alpha \in i(\sigma(t))$ and $\beta \in (i(\sigma(t+1)))$ and $l(\sigma(t), \sigma(t+1)) = act$
$M, \sigma, t \models \mathsf{Bel}(b_1)$	iff	$b_1 \in b(\sigma(t))$
$M, \sigma, t \models \bigcirc\theta$	iff	$M, \sigma, t+1 \models \theta$
$M, \sigma, t \models \Box\theta$	iff	$\forall t' \geq t$ such that $M, \sigma, t' \models \theta$
$M, \sigma, t \models \Diamond\theta$	iff	$\exists t' \geq t$ such that $M, \sigma, t' \models \theta$

Having described a general model, we can lay down principles which capture some intuitions. We ensure that an agent does intend all those things to which it is committed by stating the following principle;

Commitment-Intention Principle:

$$\Box(\mathsf{Commit}(\alpha, n) \Rightarrow \mathsf{Int}(\alpha))$$

Swapping the implication around to $\Box(\mathsf{Int}(\alpha) \Rightarrow \exists n \cdot \mathsf{Commit}(\alpha, n))$ is not expressible in our formal system, and indeed we may not want it to be because an agent may hold an intention without yet having a commitment value for it. The **Action Principle** below shows that if an agent acts on an intention then it can act on that intention when it forms a sub-intention of some larger intention plan. The **Deliberation Principle** shows the same for a sub-intention which is the subject of deliberation.

Action Principle:

$$\Box(\mathsf{Act}(\alpha_i, \alpha_i') \Rightarrow \mathsf{Act}([\alpha_1, \ldots, \alpha_i, \ldots, \alpha_m], [\alpha_1, \ldots, \alpha_i', \ldots, \alpha_m]))$$

Deliberation Principle:

$$\Box(\mathsf{Del}(\alpha_i, \alpha_i') \Rightarrow \mathsf{Del}([\alpha_1, \ldots, \alpha_i, \ldots, \alpha_m], [\alpha_1, \ldots, \alpha_i', \ldots, \alpha_m]))$$

Using our logical language, we now capture part of the Principle of Commitment by presenting Proposition 1 and Proposition 2 below. Proposition 1 shows that the commitment value of an intention is increased with a deliberation step. Proposition 2 shows that performing a primitive action for an intention also results in an increase in commitment value to that intention. However, formalising the anticipated future resources required for achieving an intention are not captured by our logical model, but will be the subject of future work.

Proposition 1:

$$\Box\left[\mathsf{Del}(\alpha, \beta) \Rightarrow \left(\left(\begin{array}{l}\mathsf{Bel}(\alpha \mapsto \beta) \wedge \mathsf{Int}(\alpha) \wedge \bigcirc\mathsf{Int}(\beta)\wedge \\ \mathsf{Commit}(\alpha, n) \wedge \bigcirc\mathsf{Commit}(\beta, m)\end{array}\right) \Rightarrow m > n\right)\right]$$

Proposition 2:

$$\Box\left[\mathsf{Del}(\alpha, \beta) \Rightarrow \left(\left(\begin{array}{l}\mathsf{Bel}(\alpha \mapsto \beta) \wedge \mathsf{Int}(\alpha) \wedge \bigcirc\mathsf{Int}(\beta)\wedge \\ \mathsf{Commit}(\alpha, n) \wedge \bigcirc\mathsf{Commit}(\beta, m)\end{array}\right) \Rightarrow m > n\right)\right]$$

In order to formalise the Principle of Least Commitment it is first necessary for us to define a notion of consistency for intentions. A set of intentions are inconsistent if they require more resources than are currently believed available. For example, intending to fly to Portugal tomorrow and intending to complete a chapter of a Ph.D. thesis from scratch by tomorrow could use up more resources than are currently available. Thus, we need to incorporate both a notion of resources available to the agent ($pool : S \rightarrow (Res \rightarrow \mathbb{N})$) and the resources required by a primitive action ($cost : (\mathbf{NP} \cup \mathbf{NPA}) \rightarrow (Res \rightarrow \mathbb{N})$) given a model M. We may extend our cost function to obtain a lower bound on the resources required by an intention ($cost^* : \mathbf{Int} \rightarrow (Res \rightarrow \mathbb{N})$) as follows;

$$cost^*([\alpha_1, \ldots, \alpha_m]) = \sum_{i=1}^{m} cost^*(\alpha_i)$$
$$cost^*(x) = cost(x)$$
$$cost^*(a) = cost(a)$$

Using the functions *pool* and *cost** we may now define what it means for a set of intentions $\Gamma \subseteq \mathbf{Int}$ to be consistent at a given state $\sigma \in S$, by extending our model M to be $\langle F, pool, cost, Res, \sigma : \mathbb{N} \rightarrow S \rangle$;

$$M, \sigma, t \models \text{Cons}(\Gamma) \quad \text{iff} \quad \forall r \in \textit{Res},$$
$$pool(\sigma(t))(r) > \textstyle\sum_{\alpha \in \Gamma} cost^*(\alpha_i)(r),$$
$$\forall \alpha \in \Gamma \, \exists n \in \mathbb{IN}, c(\sigma(t))(\alpha) = n$$

So a set of intentions are consistent if the pool of available resources in the current state exceed the total cost of all future actions of the set of intentions, and the agent is committed to all these intentions. Here, we view Cons to be a new operator that's been augmented to the formulae of our language;

$$\langle fmla \rangle ::= \ldots \mid \text{Cons}(\{\langle int \rangle, \ldots, \langle int \rangle\})$$

We may now formalise the Principle of Least Commitment;

Proposition 3:

$$\Box \left[\left(\begin{array}{l} \text{Cons}(\Gamma) \wedge \neg\text{Cons}(\Gamma \cup \{\alpha\}) \wedge \text{Commit}(\alpha, n) \wedge \\ \forall \beta \in \Gamma, \exists m \in \mathbb{IN} \cdot \text{Commit}(\beta, m) \wedge m > n \end{array} \right) \Rightarrow \bigcirc \neg \textit{Int}(\alpha). \right]$$

This proposition says that if a set of intentions Γ are consistent, and the addition of intention α makes them inconsistent, and the agent is committed to α with some value n, and the commitment value for every other intention which the agent has is greater than m, then at the next state in the path the agent no longer intends α.

8 Conclusions and Future Work

In this paper we have explained important properties of intentions which assist an agent in coordinating its future actions so that it can achieve complex goals. We have also discussed the characteristics of commitment which help an agent achieve its intentions. We have shown how intentions can be thought of as partial plans which are filled in as an agent deliberates over time. How commitment to an intention can be thought of as a measure of the amount of anticipated and invested resources by an agent (Principle of Commitment). We then identified two ways in which this notion of commitment can be used to assist resource bounded agents situated in unpredicatable environments; commitment values can be used to decide which intention to reconsider should an agent discover its intentions to be inconsistent (Principle of Least Commitment), and commitment values can be used to provide a priority ordering on intentions so that an agent is more alert to changes in its environment which effect its most committed intention (Principle of Commitment Priority). We then presented a logical model that formalised part of the first principle.

Future work includes extending the logical model to capture how the anticipated future resources are approximated for an intention. As well as extending the logical model to that of a branching time nature so that more expressive properties of commitment can be stated. Also, examining the role of commitment in a cooperative problem solving scenario involving multiple resource limited agents.

Acknowledgements The author would like to thank Carl Pulley for help with formalising the ideas presented in this paper. The author would also like to thank Cristiano Castelfranchi, Nick Jennings, Greg O'Hare and Mike Wooldridge for many useful discussions, as well as the reviewers for their helpful comments and suggestions.

References

1. M. Bratman. *Intention, Plans, and Practical Reason.* Harvard University Press, 1987.
2. M Bratman. Planning and the Stability of Intentions. *Minds and Machines,* 2:1–16, 1992.
3. P. Cohen and H. Levesque. Intention is Choice With Commitment. *Artificial Intelligence,* 42:213–261, 1990.
4. K. S. Decker and V. Lesser. Quantitative Modelling of Complex Environments. *International Journal of Intelligent Systems in Accounting, Finance and Management,* 2(4), 1993.
5. R. P. Dongha. Formalizing commitments for deliberative agents. Tech. Report TR16, UMIST, August 1994.
6. E. A. Emerson. Temporal and Modal Logic. In J. van Leeuwen, editor, *Handbook of Theoretical Computer Science,* pages 996–1072. Elsevier, 1990.
7. P. Gärdenfors. *Knowledge in Flux.* Bradford Books/MIT Press, 1988.
8. M. P. Georgeff. Situated Reasoning and Rational Behaviour. In *Pacific Rim Intenrnational Conference on Artificial Intelligence,* 1990.
9. N.R. Jennings. Commitments and conventions: The foundation of coordination in multi-agent systems. *Knowledge Engineering Review,* 8(23):223–250, 1993.
10. V. R. Lesser. A retrospective view of FA/C distributed problem solving. *IEEE Transactions on Systems, Man and Cybernetics,* 21:1347–1363, 1991.
11. H. Levesque, P. Cohen, and J. H. T. Nunes. On Acting Together. In *Proceedings of AAAI-90.* Morgan Kaufmann, 1990.
12. D. Musto and K. Konolige. Reasoning about Perception. *AI Communications,* 6(3–4):207–212, 1993.
13. A. S. Rao and M. P. Georgeff. An abstract architecture for rational agents. In C. Rich, W. Swartout, and B. Nebel, editors, *Proceedings of the Third International Conference on Principles of Knowledge Representation and Reasoning.* Morgan Kaufmann Publishers, San Mateo, CA, 1992.
14. S. J. Russell and E. Wefald. *Do The Right Thing.* MIT Press, 1991.
15. M. P. Singh. Intentions, Commitments and Rationality. In 13th *Annual Conference of the Cognitive Science Society,* 1991.
16. M. P. Singh. A Critical Examination of the Cohen-Levesque Theory of Intention. In *Proceedings of the 1992 European Conference on AI (ECAI '92).* Wiley, August 1992.

Compositional Formal Specification
of Multi-Agent Systems[+]

Barbara Dunin-Keplicz[1] and Jan Treur[2]

[1]University of Warsaw, Institute of Informatics
ul. Banacha 2, 02-097 Warszawa Poland
Email: keplicz@mimuw.edu.pl

[2]Free University Amsterdam, Dept. of Mathematics and Computer Science
De Boelelaan 1081a, 1081 HV Amsterdam The Netherlands
Email: treur@cs.vu.nl

Abstract

In this paper it is investigated how multi-agent systems with complex agents can be designed and formally specified based on the notion of a compositional architecture. After identifying the types of knowledge required for an agent we formally define a general multi-agent system. Moreover, a specific type of agent with various capabilities of reasoning and acting is given. Some essential patterns of integrated reasoning, communication and interaction with the material world are described. Finally, we present an overview of formal semantics for our approach.

1 Introduction

Research on multi-agent systems focuses on the one hand on theoretical foundations, sometimes not too strongly related with implementable applications, and on the other hand on specific architectures and programming languages, and environments for applications (e.g., see [1], [7], [8], [11]). According to our view a clear methodology including a specification method for the development of complex multi-agent systems is needed. In this paper we study the possibilities for the development of a *high level formal specification language for multi-agent systems*. The structure underlying our language is based on the notion of a compositional architecture (see [6], [9]) allowing to specify complex agents in a transparent manner as well as to integrate reasoning and acting in one (declarative) logical framework. We aim at a type of agent that is able to behave in a flexible manner using a sophisticated local structure and control allowing it to make its own decisions about subproblems to solve and subproblems or solutions to communicate.

As a point of departure we take a formal specification language for compositional architectures: DESIRE (framework for DEsign and Specification of Interacting REasoning components; see [9], [10]). This framework turns out to cover major parts of the specification of a multi-agent system. First, it is easy to design different variants of agents. Second, one can completely specify the dynamics of reasoning patterns and acting behaviour. The executability of DESIRE specifications (there exists a software environment realizing this), gives the ability to carry out experiments with (alternative) patterns of behaviour. The research reported here has also resulted in identifying a number of features to be added.

[+] This work is part of the ESPRIT III Basic Research project 6156 DRUMS II.

The paper is organized as follows. In Section 2 we discuss the generic domains of an agent that can be distinguished according to the types of knowledge to be dealt with. In Section 3 we show how a complex agent can be composed from components that represent subtasks, using specific composition principles defining semantic links between them in a formal, standardized manner. In Section 4 we describe an example architecture created in this manner and some patterns of reasoning and acting. In Section 5 we sketch formal semantics of our approach. Finally, in Section 6 we evaluate our investigations and end up with a number of issues for further research.

2 Distinguishing generic domains of agent knowledge

Since we consider an agent as a rather complex reasoning and acting entity, our first concern is a transparent structure for it. Solving a problem by an agent can be viewed as an alternation of reasoning and other activities:
- actively *gather observational information* from the material world;
- *draw conclusions* from this information;
- initiate and *carry out communication* with other agents;
- generate beliefs by making additional (defeasible) *assumptions*;
- change the world by *executing actions*.

Individual agents make local decisions: each of them pursues activities interesting from its local viewpoint. These viewpoints may vary from one agent to another, and the compatibility of the individual viewpoints determines whether agents are interested in cooperation, competition, or merely coexistence. In order to cooperate, they must recognize that cooperation is in their self-interest. Thus, they must have local knowledge guiding them into cooperation. Speaking about agent knowledge we implicitly assume basic reasoning capabilities related to it.

In this section different types of agent knowledge are distinguished. The first, basic type of knowledge to be distinguished is the knowledge about the *material world*. As this knowledge is very broad, it needs to be considered in more detail. The core of this knowledge is a description of the external material world, but as a special part of the world's entities material aspects of agents (including itself) should be distinguished. Secondly, in view of possible cooperation, each agent is expected to have (reflective) knowledge about *mental aspects* of itself and other agents. Thirdly, knowledge allowing *communication* with other agents and *interaction* with the external world (directing and carrying out observations, communications and actions) is needed. A combination of various types of knowledge constitutes a proper basis for making decisions. To promote a cleaner separation of concerns, we classify agent's knowledge in the following way:

(a) *Material world*
(b) *Mental world of the agent itself*
(c) *Mental world of other agents*
(d) *Interaction with the material world*
(e) *Communication with other agents*

Another essential point is the dynamics and incompleteness of knowledge: at each moment in time only a limited amount of information has been acquired. This suggests a time-dependent definition of an overall structure of an agent's knowledge. This knowledge can be treated as a collection of knowledge states for each type of knowledge involved, called (*dynamic*) *information state* or facts base. In contrast to the time-dependent part of the information, for each type of knowledge we distinguish an invariant part (holding in all states), called a *(static) knowledge base.* Thus one can reason about the current state as well as the past and (possible) future states and their connections. We briefly explain the generic domains in more detail.

(a) Material world
This knowledge describes the current world state: material (e.g., physical) aspects of the world, including the agents. This (object) knowledge constitutes the basis for drawing conclusions about the current world state. Also (temporal) knowledge about past and possible future states and their connecting processes (events, actions) can be covered, for example for the sake of planning.

(b) Mental world of the agent itself
This kind of knowledge is essential from the (meta-level) perspective of guiding complex patterns of reasoning and acting. It can take many forms:
•   *Strategic control knowledge* about the agent's current goals and reasoning and acting processes, guiding the agent in its behaviour; i.e., helping it in achieving its goals, to follow heuristics. In particular, if the agent lacks some information it has to decide whether this information can be acquired by making observations from the material world, communications with other agents, introducing assumptions - beliefs. Sophisticated strategic knowledge enables an agent to perform flexible behaviour.
•   Speaking about agent's knowledge we also take into account its possibility of *introspection*. Introspection, i.e., the process of examining one's own beliefs, has two interesting sides. The *positive introspection* principle assumes that an agent knows what it knows. Analogously, the *negative introspection* principle states that an agent knows what it does not know. In our approach we consider both types of introspection useful. We call this part of an agent's knowledge *epistemic knowledge*. This kind of knowledge should contain (among others) explicit information about qualifications of the agent's knowledge (e.g., observed, assumed, derived, based on ...).
•   If it turns out hard or impossible to acquire necessary information, there still remains the possibility to rely on beliefs only. Beliefs can be generated by *generating additional assumptions*. The agent needs (defeasible) knowledge to do this.

(c) Mental world of other agents
Sometimes one agent has knowledge about some aspects of the mental state of another one and can reason about it; for example knowing another agent's goals or past reasoning processes.

(d) Interaction with the material world
Observations are usually an important source of additional information. To determine which ones are possible in the current world state specialized knowledge may be needed. In taking the decision another factor should be considered: the costs or effort of an observation. Observations form one kind of interaction with the material world. Another one is created by actions considered for execution in the material world (to actually change the world state).

(e) Communication with other agents
The agent may need knowledge to determine what communications are possible and useful to obtain additional information together with the information on the availability of agents for communication.

Within each of these five domains some subdomains can be distinguished. The depth of these distinctions is a matter of choice (related to the type of agent being created).

3 Compositional Multi-Agent Systems

Knowledge and reasoning capabilities referring to the domains of an agent's interest should be specified in some way. In this section we introduce a specific type of architecture for multi-agent systems, called *compositional architecture*. The general idea is that each complex agent is composed from (primitive) *components* that describe subtasks to be performed. Components are connected to each other according to predefined types of *semantic links*. Each component has a simple logical description and makes use of specific knowledge. Complex behaviour covering both reasoning and acting can be obtained by nontrivial (and dynamic) patterns of interaction between components. In a similar manner the system as a whole can be composed from its agents. In the Sections 3.1, 3.2 and 3.3 we introduce the notions of component, compositional agent and compositional multi-agent system, respectively.

3.1 Agent components

We describe the domain of a component C by a *signature* Σ_C: a lexicon of basic language elements in terms of propositional or many-sorted predicate logic. Using this signature we can define:
- possible states of the domain as a set of truth assignments to its ground atoms;
- the knowledge described in the component.

We distinguish the component's knowledge base (the static part) and the facts base or information state (the dynamic part).

Definition 3.1 (object signature and information state)
a) A *partial model* of signature Σ is a mapping
$$M : At(\Sigma) \rightarrow \{0, 1, u\}$$
where $At(\Sigma)$ is the set of ground atoms for Σ.
An atom a is *true* in M if 1 is assigned to it, and *false* if 0 is assigned; otherwise it is called *undefined* or *unknown*. A partial model M is called *complete* if no $M(a)$ equals u. The partial model N is called a *refinement* of M, denoted by $M \leq N$, if for all atoms a it holds: $M(a) \leq N(a)$, where the (partial) ordering on truth values is defined by $u \leq 0, u \leq 1, u \leq u, 0 \leq 0, 1 \leq 1$.
b) An object signature assignment assigns to each component C a signature called the *object signature* of C, denoted by Σ_C or Σ_C^{obj}.
A *domain state* for C is a complete model of signature Σ_C^{obj}. By $DS_0(C)$ we denote any given set of complete models of signature Σ_C^{obj} (assigned to C), called the *set of domain states* for C.
An *object information state* for C is a partial model of signature Σ_C^{obj}. By $IS_0(C)$ we denote any given set of partial models of signature Σ_C^{obj}: the *set of (object) information states* for C.
c) A *knowledge base* for C is a set of ground formulae KB_C of signature Σ_C^{obj}.

In other words, the object information state of a component C provides a repository for all domain information already generated (i.e., input and derived facts) and received as a result of interaction with other agents. For simplicity we allow only ground literals to be communicated in interactions and as the conclusions of derivations. Thus information states can be represented by sets of ground literals, or, equivalently, by partial models for the signature of the component. Knowledge bases are expressed in rule format.

An example of an object information state is

< I_am_performing_a_task:0, resources_available:u >

stating that currently the agent is not busy performing a task and no information is present on whether resources are available.

Recall that some of the agent domains are reflective: they refer to internal mental states of the agent itself. To achieve an adequate specification of reflective aspects we introduce the notion of combined information state for a component (for more details, see [13], [14]). A combined information state consists of two types of information:
- an *object-information state*: the information about the current domain state;
- a *meta-information state*: information about the state of the component's reasoning and knowledge.

Important points of a meta-information state are explicit information on what is currently (not) explicitly known and on current goals. Technically, it summarizes a number of descriptors characterizing these process states, for example:
- the truth value of object statement **a** has not been determined;
- the object statement **h** is considered as a goal for the reasoning process;
- the degree of exhaustiveness of the reasoning.

Distinguishing between meta- and object level information, which is crucial in our approach, allows us to make a component **C**'s reasoning process subject of the reasoning of another component **D**. If a component **D** reasons at a meta-level with respect to **C**, the current meta-information state of **C** provides a domain state for **D**.

Formally, for each component **C** we introduce a meta-signature Σ_C^{meta} in order to define a meta-information state as a truth assignment to its ground atoms. The object and the meta-information state together specify a more complete description of the state the component is in.

Definition 3.2 (meta-signature and information state)

A meta-signature assignment assigns to each component **C** a signature called its *meta-signature*, denoted by Σ_C^{meta}. A *meta-information state* for **C** is a partial model of signature Σ_C^{meta}.

By $IS_m(C)$ we denote any given set of partial models of signature Σ_C^{meta} assigned to C, called the *set of meta-information states* for **C**.

An example of a meta-information state is

< known(I_am_performing_a_task):1,
known(resources_available):0,
goal(resources_available):1 >

This represents the meta-information that currently it is known in this component whether the agent is busy performing a task and that it is not known whether resources are available. Moreover, a current goal for the component is to find out whether resources are available. Often meta-information states will be complete. However, we leave open the possibility that some meta-informnation is undefined.

In practice the meta-signature is related to the object signature by a naming relation for the object statements as terms in the meta-language. Notice that we do not allow a meta-knowledge base and meta-reasoning within a component. Meta-reasoning with respect to a component **C** can be specified by another component **D** that has object-meta semantic links to **C**.

During a session of the architecture basic steps can be modelled by transitions between information states. One information state can change into another one by means of *inference processes* or *interactions between components*. By making inferences both the object and meta-information state will change. In the former case, the change is a refinement into a more complete one: we assume that inferences in one component are conservative and monotonic. In practice this specifies a component's memory: all information obtained hitherto is stored. As regards the meta-information state, changes are based on non-conservative transitions. For example, when an unknown object-level atom **a** becomes known as a result of a derivation, the meta-statement **known(a)** changes from false to true. For more details, see Section 5 (or [6], [14]). Another manner to change information states, i.e., interactions between components, will be discussed in the next section.

3.2 Compositional agents

Components representing subtasks and making use of knowledge from the different domains of an agent can be viewed as building blocks for the agent. The glue consists of two ingredients: semantic connectivity and control connectivity. We will discuss both in more detail.

3.2.1 Semantic links within an agent
The various domains resulting from our decomposition are not completely independent: they have mutual semantic relations. This means that an atom in one domain may have an immediate connection to an atom in another one. Indeed, these semantic links create the logical basis for exchanging information between components (see also [13]). Roughly spoken an interaction from component C_1 to component C_2 causes a change in the information state of C_2 on the basis of information available in C_1. This change can mean a refinement or (in case of updates) a non-conservative modification of the information state of C_2. In effect it implies an extension, update or revision of the information state. Also here we assume a (relative) principle of conservation: all information that is not explicitly changed by an interaction will remain available (a specific frame assumption).

A semantic link is defined on the level of semantic units: atoms and their truth values. In principle it relates a semantic unit of a component C_1, defined by a pair $< a, tv_1 >$ of a ground atom **a** of one signature and a truth value tv_1 to a semantic unit of another component C_2, defined by a pair $< b, tv_2 >$ with **b** of another signature. Distinguishing an object and meta-information state for any component implies a classification of semantic links and the interactions based on them accordingly into four types.

Definition 3.3 (semantic link)
Let C, C_1 and C_2 be components and $x, y \in \{obj, meta\}$.
a) The set of *object*, resp. *meta*-level *semantic units* for C is defined by
$$SU_x(C) = At(\Sigma_C^x) \times \{0, 1, u\}$$
A *semantic link* I *between* C_1 *and* C_2 *of type* $< x, y >$ is a relation
$$I : SU_x(C_1) \times SU_y(C_2)$$
b) A meta-signature assignment assigns to each semantic link I a signature called its *meta-signature*, denoted by Σ_I^{meta}. A *meta-information state* for I is a partial model of signature Σ_I^{meta}. By $IS_m(I)$ we denote any given set of partial models of signature Σ_I^{meta} assigned to I, called the *set of meta-information states* for I.

A kind of standard example of a semantic link is when the involved sets of semantic units have a common subset **SU**, and the relation **I** for $< a, tv_1 > \in SU_x(C_1)$, $< b, tv_2 > \in SU_y(C_2)$ is defined by

$$I(< a,\ tv_1 >, < b,\ tv_2 >) \quad \text{if} \quad a = b, < a, tv_1 > \in SU \ \text{and} \ tv_2 = tv_1 \neq u.$$

Note that by restricting this subset **SU** one can specify restricted information exchange. It is also possible that the considered sets of semantic units have an empty intersection because the atoms that are meant to refer to the same are named differently. In that case a semantic link involves a renaming (of atoms) as well. As an example, within an agent no particular name of the agent itself is needed (one can use the generic term "*I*" to refer to oneself in a natural manner), wheras the same information needs a proper reference if another agent considers it; e.g., the information "*I am busy*" in agent A can be named "*A is busy*" in agent B. A semantic link enables one to identify these (syntactically different, but semantically identical) statements.

Usually changes provoked by an interaction may require additional update procedures within the component of destination. It is assumed that all components have generic standard facilities for this that are executed before starting inferences (built in in the DESIRE software environment: [12]).

The data flow can be performed by transforming output of one component into input of another one according to a semantic link. As defined in Definition 3.3, this exchange of information can refer to both object and meta-level semantic units. The meta-input facts can be used to guide or influence the reasoning process at the object-level. Common examples are *targets* and *assumptions,* specifying an object output fact a component should try to derive and an input fact that has to be assumed as a belief, respectively. Other meta-facts provide information about the component's current process state; we provide two kinds of them: *epistemic facts* and *requests.* Epistemic facts describe the truth, falsity or undefinedness of the object-level facts. A request specifies an object-level input atom that must be known in order to continue the object-level reasoning. In this way, different types of reflective architectures can be described. A semantic link connecting the meta-output of one component to the object-input of another is called an *upward reflection.*; in this case the second component reasons about the first's meta-level description. Analogously, a semantic link in the opposite direction is called a *downward reflection.* A classification of all semantic links (in terms of interaction types) built-in DESIRE is given in Table 1 (see [10], [13]).

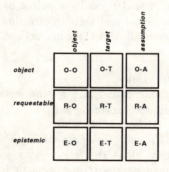

	object	target	assumption
object	O-O	O-T	O-A
requestable	R-O	R-T	R-A
epistemic	E-O	E-T	E-A

Table 1   Interaction types

Note that, in comparison to Definition 3.3, here we have a further semantic distinction within the category of meta-facts. In DESIRE one can specify an arbitrary number (tower) of meta-levels.

Besides *internal* semantic links an agent has also semantic links with (components of) other agents and the material world. These *external* semantic links allow an external exchange of information.

3.2.2   Control structure within an agent

To specify coherent agent reasoning and acting patterns, we distinguish a global control component within the mental domain of the agent. We adopt the supervisor structure of DESIRE. We present it briefly (see [10]), assuming that the internal agent's processing is sequential, while different agents may proceed in parallel.

For each component it is described when and how it is activated, the latter possibly including a number of interactions necessary to provide input facts for it. When a component is activated, its exhaustiveness and target set has to be specified. This exhaustiveness type (**any, any-new, every** or **all-possible**) together with the target set specifies the goal the module has to attain in order to terminate successfully.

The activation condition for a component is described in terms of the termination status of another one: if its goal is attained, the termination status is **succeeded**. If it has not reached its goal, but may do so when additional input is provided (without revisions), its status is **failed**, otherwise, if reaching the goal needs some revision of the inputs, it is **c-failed**.

The global control of the system can be specified by means of *supervisor knowledge*. The most simple form of it is by supervisor rules of the following type.

```
if termination(epistemic_state, epistemic_facts, succeeded)
then next-module(generating_observations, facts_to_observe, without-requests, any)
and next-pre-trans(transfer_epistemic_info)
```

This rule specifies that, if the component epistemic_state has succeeded with respect to the target set epistemic_facts, the transformation transfer_epistemic_info is applied, the component generating_observations is activated, and it should try to derive **any** element of the target set facts_to_observe without additional requests.

3.3   Combining agents into a compositional multi-agent system

While combining agents into a compositional multi-agent system we distinguish semantic connectivity and control connectivity, taking into account also connections with the (material) world.

3.3.1   Semantic links between agents

Interactions can take place not only between components of one agent (internal interactions), but also between components of different agents (external interactions). In the latter case communication between agents is induced. In our approach we restrict interactions to *supply* of information and base them on semantic links. For example, a request for information **a** from A to B amounts to the supply of meta-information from A that it wants to know **a** to B.

The same applies to interactions with the material world. We specify the world in a compositional manner, similar to an agent, structured by components where both object and meta-information is included. For example, a directed observation from agent A is the supply of meta-information to the world ("*A wants to know ...*"). The world responds by initiating transfer of the referred information.

If an agent A concludes to execute an action, the action is actually executed by transferring this as meta-information from A to the world component. The world is specified in such a manner that its internal behaviour just simulates its reactions on imposed observations and actions. In this manner both the act of communication between agents and interactions with the world can be specified by the execution of a semantic link.

The use of explicitly defined and executed semantic links has two important advantages: one can precisely specify the required part of information and the moment of execution of a connection.

3.3.2 Control connectivity between agents

For the global control of agents there are two possibilities. In the case of centralized global control it is specified explicitly under which conditions an agent has to be active and in these cases it is activated. In the decentralized case, agents are active all the time and react on the information they receive from other agents. The first possibility can already be specified in the current version of DESIRE, by means of supervisor rules as discussed in Section 3.2.2. The second type of control is currently being developed.

4 Example architecture and patterns

In this section we present an example architecture of an agent and of the material world. Interaction patterns are described (observation and action execution between an agent and the world) and communication patterns (between two agents).

4.1 An example of a compositional agent and world

Each agent is specified by components realizing various tasks making use of our taxonomy of knowledge. First, we give a short description of the structure of the material world. Next, we design an example agent with capabilities of reasoning, observing, action execution and communication.

4.1.1 Compositional structure of the material world

We distinguish two types of interactions between agents and the material world: performing observations and executing actions. In both cases the agent transfers information to the world which is expected to respond. Within the world we distinguish two components:

- *current world state*
providing complete object level information about the current world state (the truth values of the atoms). This information will change and the agents may react on this.

- *world execution control*
providing the input information about the required observations or actions in order to perform them. Semantically spoken, this component constitutes a meta-level with respect to the current world state.

In practical applications of multi-agent systems, a detailed description of the world is not a part of the system itself - only the interface with the world is specified.

4.1.2 Compositional structure of an example agent

In order to design our agent, its (sub)tasks, represented by components, have to be identified. The knowledge they use is classified according to the five generic domains introduced in Section 2.

The component *world state analysis* contains knowledge on the domain "Material world". Based on knowledge from "Mental world of the agent itself" we have three components: *epistemic state, assumption generation* and *supervisor*. No tasks make use of knowledge from "Mental world of other agents" (for an example covering this, see [3]: the wise men's puzzle). The domain "Interaction with the material world" is used in two components *generating observations* and *generating actions*. Finally, "Communication with other agents" is used in two components *generating questions* and *receiving questions*. Some of the internal semantic links are depicted in Fig. 1. Here the transformation from *world state analysis* to the *epistemic state* is of type **E-O** (an upward reflection). The semantic link between *epistemic state* and *generating assumptions* is of type **O-O**, while the connection from the latter component to *world state analysis* is of type **O-A** (a downward reflection). Other semantic links and their types will be described in the Sections 4.2 and 4.3.

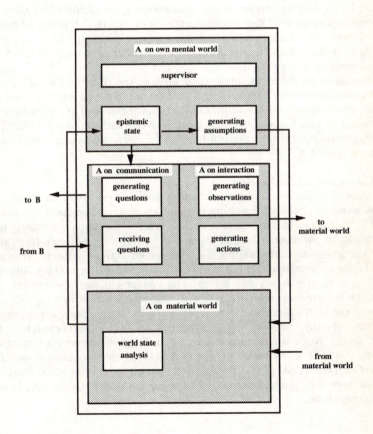

Fig 1   The components of the example agent A

4.2 Interaction with the material world

We describe the acts of observation and action execution in more detail. For simplicity we consider only observations and actions performed instaneously, not taking into account executions of plans of actions and/or observations (although it is quite possible to cover this case as well).

4.2.1 The act of observation

An observation activity of an agent A entails a bi-directional interaction with the world. First, we assume that the agent A decides whether an observation is currently required and which one in particular (implying what property of the world should be observed). This takes place in *generating observations* based on knowledge from the domain "A on interaction with the world". If an observation is required, the necessary information (i.e., **selected_observation(t)**) is transferred from *generating observations* to the *world execution control* component of the material world (semantic link of type **O-O**).

Next, the world is active in processing this observation. In *world execution control* the information **selected_observation(t)** is translated into the corresponding properties (assumed represented by atomic facts, say **required(a)**, **required(b)**) of the world state; by an internal interaction this information is transformed into goals **a, b** of the component *current world state* (a transformation of type **O-T**). Finally, an interaction from the *current world state* (back) to the agent A (*world state analysis*) is performed transferring from the world state the information concerning the truth values of **a, b** to A (a transformation of type **O-O**).

An alternative, maybe conceptually more elegant, specification for interaction back to A can be obtained by first transforming within the world the information from *current world state* to *world execution control* (an **E-O** transformation) and then by a second transformation to *generating observations* (an **O-O** transformation). Finally, A can decide to internally transform the information to *world state analysis*: an internal interaction of type **O-A**.

4.2.2 Execution of an action

The execution of an action entails an interaction from an agent A to the world (and not back: if A wants to check the resulting information it should perform an observation afterwards). We assume that the agent A decides whether an action is currently required and which one in particular (this takes place in *generating actions*). If an action is required, the necessary information (i.e., on which action: **selected_action(α)**) is transferred from *generating actions* to *world execution control* (type **O-O**). After that the world is active in processing this action. The component *world execution control* translates the information **selected_action(α)** (on which action is required) into the properties of the world (assumed to be represented by atomic facts **a, b, c**) that result (the effect of the action; e.g., **affected(a, true)**, **affected(b, false)**, **affected(c, true)**). Next, it transforms them by an internal interaction into new facts of the world state (a transformation of type **O-A** to the component *current world state*). Since *world execution control* may need information on the current world state, we also assume that there is an internal interaction from *current world state* to *world execution control* (of type **E-O**).

4.3   Communication between agents

We view communication as the supply of information by one agent to another, i.e., executing a semantic link. We discuss a common pattern of communication between agents: agent A requests information from agent B and gets a response from B. Let us assume that the agent A (in the component *generating questions* in the domain "A on communication") made three decisions: *whether* communication is required, *which* information is needed and *from which* agent it may be obtained.

If communication with agent B is required, the relevant information (which observation - **requested(v)**) is transferred from A to B: an interaction between *generating questions* of A and *receiving questions* of B (type **O-O**) is initiated.

Agent B translates (within *receiving questions*) the information **requested(v)** into the corresponding atoms (**required(a)**, **required(b)**) and transforms them by an internal interaction into goals **a, b** of the component *world state analysis* of B (type **O-T**). Finally, an interaction from *world state analysis* of B (back) to *world state analysis* of A is performed by transferring the information of the truth values of the goals **a, b** to A (a transformation of type **O-O**) from the world state.

Similar to the case of observation, an alternative way back is possible here. First transform within agent B the information to *receiving questions* in B (an **E-O** transformation) and then by a second transformation from there to *generating questions* in A (an **O-O** transformation). Finally, A can decide to internally transform the information to *world state analysis* in A by an internal interaction (transformation of type **O-A**).

5   On formal semantics of compositional multi-agent systems

In this section we sketch the semantics of a compositional multi-agent system. This semantics gives a complete account of the behaviour of such a system. It is based on information states, transitions between them and traces. An overall information state of an agent is a combination of information states of components whereas a state of the whole system is a combination of the latter information states.

Definition   5.1   (combined and overall information states)
Let **MAS** be a multi-agent system and let **A** be an agent or the material world **MW** in **MAS**. Its *set of components* is denoted by **C(A)** and its *set of semantic links* by **I(A)**. Here all outgoing semantic links (to other agents and the material world in **MAS**) are included in **I(A)**.

a) The *set of possible (combined) information states* for a component **C** of **A** is defined by:

$$\mathbf{IS(C)} \quad = \quad \mathbf{IS_0(C)} \times \mathbf{IS_m(C)}$$

b) The *set of possible overall information states* for **A** is defined by:

$$\mathbf{IS(A)} \quad = \quad \prod\nolimits_{C \in C(A)} \mathbf{IS(C)} \; \times \; \prod\nolimits_{I \in I(A)} \mathbf{IS_m(I)}$$

c) The *set of possible overall information states* for the multi-agent system **MAS** is:

$$\mathbf{IS(MAS)} \quad = \quad \mathbf{IS(MW)} \; \times \; \prod\nolimits_{A \in A(MAS)} \mathbf{IS(A)}$$

where **A(MAS)** denotes the set of all agents of **MAS**.

Note that any mapping on one or more factors of a cartesian product can be extended in a canonical manner to (i.e., it *induces*) a mapping on the whole cartesian product (by leaving the other factors out of consideration). Furthermore, a mapping π of information states is called *conservative* if $M \leq \pi(M)$ for all M; it is called *monotonic* if $\pi(M) \leq \pi(N)$ for all M, N with $M \leq N$. In general we do not require idempotency because we do not assume exhaustive reasoning. However, for correct functioning we always assume that the deductive closure is an upper bound. By $dc_{KB_C}(M)$ we denote the *deductive closure* of M under the component C's knowledge base KB_C; i.e., the partial model just containing all (literal) information derivable, under exhaustive inferences, from the information (the literals true) in M and KB_C. For any component C we assume that in the meta-information states also information on the history of the inferences (dependencies between literals) is maintained: a simple book-keeping system that can be used for truth maintenance purposes. Based on this we assume for any C a simple standard *update function* $\pi_{upd} : IS(C) \to IS(C)$ is given. The idea is that this update function simply retracts all literals that are not supported anymore because they depend on updated literals. Moreover, it updates object and meta-information states with respect to each other. For more details, consult [12].

Definition 5.2 (transition functions)

Let MAS be a multi-agent system and let A, B be agents in MAS or the material world MW.

a) A *transition function for an internal component* C (or *internal component transition function*) of A is a function transforming information states for C to information states for C; i.e., a mapping
$$\pi : IS(C) \to IS(C)$$
For *correct functioning* of MAS it is required that $\pi = \pi_{inf}\pi_{upd}$ for mappings
$$\pi_{upd}, \pi_{inf} : IS(C) \to IS(C)$$
with π_{upd} the standard update mapping and π_{inf} an (inference) mapping such that for each $N \in IS_m(C)$ the mapping $\pi_{inf}^N : IS_0(C) \to IS_0(C)$ defined by $\pi_{inf}^N(M) = \pi_{inf}(M, N)$ is conservative and monotonic and $\pi_{inf}^N(M) \leq dc_{KB_C}(M)$ for all M.

b) Suppose C_1 and C_2 are components, $x, y \in \{obj, meta\}$ and I is a semantic link from C_1 to C_2 of type $< x, y >$. A *transition function for the semantic link* I is a mapping
$$\pi : IS_x(C_1) \times IS_y(C_2) \times IS_m(I) \to IS_y(C_2) \times IS_m(I)$$
For *correct functioning* of the system it is required that for all M_1, M_2, N, M'_2, N' with $\pi(M_1, M_2, N) = < M'_2, N' >$ and atom b it holds $M'_2(b) = M_2(b)$ or
$$I(< a, M_1(a) >, < b, M'_2(b) >)$$
for some atom a.
If I is an internal semantic link of agent A (i.e., a semantic link between components C_1 and C_2 of A) then a transition function function for I is called an *internal interaction transition function* of A; otherwise it is called an *external interaction transition function*.

c) An *internal transition function for (an agent or the material world)* A is a mapping
$$\pi : IS(A) \to IS(A)$$
induced by an internal component transition function of A, or by an internal interaction transition function of A.

d) An *external (interaction) transition function from (an agent or the material world)* **A** *to (an agent or the material world)* **B** distinct from **A** is a mapping
$$\pi : IS(A) \times IS(B) \rightarrow IS(B) \times IS(A)$$
induced by an external interaction transition function from a component C_1 of **A** to a component C_2 of **B**.

e) An *overall transition function for the system* **MAS** is a mapping
$$\pi : IS(MAS) \rightarrow IS(MAS)$$
induced by an internal transition function for an agent or the material world, or induced by an external transition function between an agent (or the material world) and another, distinct agent (or the material world).

Note that an external transition from an agent **A** in principle also changes the information state of the agent itself (e.g., to store that some information has been communicated); however, this change only depends on the information state of the sender A, not of the receiver.

In Definition 5.2 we treated the sequential case: just one agent is active at a time. The definition can be extended to cover the parallel case as well. Important then is to maintain that information coming from different sources is disjoint (e.g., labeled with the source) or to take into account the order in which it is received.

The following definition shows how traces generated by iteratively applying a transition function on the current information state can be interpreted as temporal models, giving a declarative description of the semantics of the behaviour of the system. They can be viewed as the so-called intended (behavioural) models of the system.

Definition 5.3 (traces and temporal models)
Let **MAS** be a multi-agent system and let **A** be an agent in **MAS** or the material world **MW**.

a) A *possible trace* of a component **C** is a sequence of information states $(M^t)_{t \in \mathbb{N}}$ in IS(C). The set of all of them can be denoted by $IS(C)^{\mathbb{N}}$, or **Traces(C)**.
A *possible trace* of **A** is a sequence of information states $(M^t)_{t \in \mathbb{N}}$ in **IS(A)**. The set of all of them can be denoted by $IS(A)^{\mathbb{N}}$, or **Traces(A)**.
A *possible trace* of **MAS** is a sequence of information states $(M^t)_{t \in \mathbb{N}}$ in **IS(MAS)**. The set of all of them can be denoted by $IS(MAS)^{\mathbb{N}}$, or **Traces(MAS)**.

b) An element $(M^t)_{t \in \mathbb{N}} \in$ **Traces(MAS)** is called *a temporal model of* **MAS** if for all time points t the step from M^t to M^{t+1} is defined in accordance with an overall transition. The set of temporal models of **MAS** forms a subset **BehMod(MAS)** of **Traces(MAS)**.

A temporal model describes a trace representing possible (intended) behaviour of the reasoning. One view is that the trace is generated by the transition functions (executing them), given some initial input information. From every initial information setting a trace can be generated by the transitions. All generated traces together form the set **BehMod(MAS)**. A slightly different view is that the transition functions define a set of (temporal) axioms or constraints **BehTheory(MAS)** on temporal models in **Traces(MAS)**. The possible behavioural alternatives are given by the set of the temporal models satisfying these temporal constraints:

$$\text{TempMod(MAS)} = \{ M \in \text{Traces(MAS)} \mid M \vDash \text{BehTheory(MAS)} \}$$

where $M \vDash \text{BehTheory(MAS)}$ holds iff each formula from the set BehTheory(MAS) has truth value *true* at every time point in the temporal model M. This second view provides a formalization of the intended behavioural patterns in the form of the (intended) models of a logical (temporal) theory in a specific type of temporal logic, giving a declarative (Tarski) semantics. The formal semantics of the behaviour is defined by the set of models TempMod(MAS). The first view corresponds to the notion of an executable temporal logic. Both views co-exist: executing a temporal theory is a useful technique to construct a model of this theory. The semantic approach based on temporal logic, as sketched above for the case of (compositional) multi-agent systems, already has been applied to classical proof systems, default logic, compositional reasoning systems and meta-level architectures (see [4], [6], [14]).

6 Conclusions and further research

In this paper it was investigated how multi-agent systems with complex agents can be designed and formally specified based on the notion of compositional architecture. Due to our experiences the following requirements for multi-agent systems are fulfilled by compositional architectures and the formal specification language DESIRE:
-   Integration of various types of reasoning and acting is possible within one declarative logical framework with component wise classical (partial) semantics and overall temporal semantics.
-   Dynamic maintenance of states is handled by the explicit semantic links (activated in a controlled manner) and the standard update facilities built in in the DESIRE software environment.
-   Limited reasoning of an agent is possible with explicit control by means of strategic knowledge.
-   Complex, reflective agents can be specified in a conceptually transparent manner.
-   Flexibility in modelling: it is easy to build different types of agents.
-   Explicit and directed observation acts and their control, can be specified.
-   Explicit and directed communication acts and their control, can be specified.
-   The semantics of the dynamics can be based on (compositional) temporal models representing behavioural patterns.

It turned out to be possible to completely specify nontrivial multi-agent examples in DESIRE (see [3]). Moreover, [2] reports work on modelling interaction between a knowledge-based system, the world and a user based on the compositional multi-agent approach presented here. Integration of different types of components (e.g., neural networks, optimization algorithms) can be assured by specifying their interface and referring to an external component or specification. Further investigations are planned in a real world application area: diagnosis of an electricity network. Here the new version of DESIRE will be applied where it is possible to structure specifications according to hierarchical decomposition, enabling one to specify components that consist of other components.

Acknowledgements
Useful discussions about the subject have taken place with Frances Brazier. An earlier draft of this paper was read by Pascal van Eck; this led to a number of improvements in the text.

References

[1] Bouron, T. and Collinot, A., SAM: a model to design computational social agents. In: B. Neumann (ed.), *Proc. 10th European Conference on Artificial Intelligence, ECAI'92*, John Wiley & Sons, Chichester, 1992, pp. 239-243

[2] Brazier, F.M.T. and Treur, J. . User centered knowledge-based system design: a formal modelling approach. In: L. Steels, G. Schreiber and W. Van de Velde (eds.), "A future for knowledge acquisition," *Proceedings of the 8th European Knowledge Acquisition Workshop*, EKAW '94. Springer-Verlag, Lecture Notes in Artificial Intelligence 867, 1994, pp. 283-300.

[3] Dunin-Keplicz, B. and Treur, J., Formal modelling in multi-agent domains. Report, Free University Amsterdam, Department of Mathematics and Computer Science, 1994. Shorter version in: L. Steels, G. Scheiber, W. van de Velde (eds.), Position papers of the EKAW'94, Technical Report 94-2, Vrije Universiteit Brussel, AI Lab, 1994

[4] Engelfriet, J. and Treur, J., Temporal theories of reasoning. In: C. MacNish, D. Pearce, L.M. Pereira (eds.), *Logics in AI, Proc. JELIA'94*, Lecture Notes in AI, Vol. 838, Springer Verlag, 1994, pp. 279-299.

[5] Fisher, M. and Wooldridge, M, Specifying and verifying distributed intelligent systems, *Proc. of the 6th Portugese Conference on AI*, Lecture Notes in AI, Vol. 727, Springer Verlag, 1993

[6] Gavrila, I.S. and Treur, J., A formal model for the dynamics of compositional reasoning systems. In A.G. Cohn (ed.), *Proc. 11th European Conference on Artificial Intelligence, ECAI'94*, John Wiley & Sons, Chichester, 1994, pp. 307-311

[7] Huhns, M. (ed.), *Distributed Artifical Intelligence*. Morgan Kaufman, 1987

[8] Jennings, N.R., Towards a cooperation knowledge level for collaborative problem solving. In B. Neumann (ed.), *Proc. 10th European Conference on Artificial Intelligence, ECAI'92*, John Wiley & Sons, Chichester, 1992, pp. 224-228

[9] Kowalczyk, W. and Treur, J., On the use of a formalized generic task model in knowledge acquisition. In: B.J. Wielinga, J. Boose, B.R. Gaines, A.Th. Schreiber, M.W. van Someren (eds.), *Current Trends in Knowledge Acquisition (Proc. EKAW-90)*, IOS Press, Amsterdam, 1990, pp. 198-221.

[10] Langevelde, I.A. van, Philipsen, A.W. and Treur, J., Formal specification of compositional architectures. In B. Neumann (ed.), *Proc. 10th European Conference on Artificial Intelligence, ECAI'92*, John Wiley & Sons, Chichester, 1992, pp. 272-276

[11] Osawa, E.I., A scheme for agent collaboration in open multi-agent environments. *Proc. Int. Joint Conference on AI, IJCAI'93*, pp. 352-358.

[12] Pannekeet, J.H.M., A.W. Philipsen and J. Treur, Designing compositional assumption revision, Report IR-279, Department of Mathematics and Computer Science, Vrije Universiteit Amsterdam, 1991. Shorter version in: H. de Swaan Arons et al., *Proc. Dutch AI-Conference, NAIC-92*, 1992, pp. 285-296

[13] Treur, J., Interaction types and chemistry of generic task models. In: M. Linster, B. Gaines, (eds.), *Proc. EKAW'91*. GMD Studien 211, 1992, pp. 390-414.

[14] Treur, J., Temporal semantics of meta-level architectures for dynamic control of reasoning. *Proc. Int. Workshop on Meta-programming in Logic, META'94*, Lecture Notes in Computer Science, Vol. 883, Springer Verlag, 1994.

[15] Treur, J., Wetter, Th. (eds.), *Formal Specification of Complex Reasoning Systems*. Ellis Horwood, 1993

Logical Reorganization of DAI Systems

GUICHARD Frédéric[1] and AYEL Jacqueline[1]

Université de Savoie,
Laboratoire d'Intelligence Artificielle
2 route du Bourget du Lac
73376 Chambéry FRANCE
guichard@univ-savoie.fr

Abstract. The dynamic organisation of a distributed artificial intelligence (DAI) system is generally executed with the assistance of a human expert. The purpose of our study is to define primitives to allow the system itself to adapt dynamically to this environment and to improve its performance. Each agent or group of agents has knowledge about itself and about other agents. By means of a mechanism of introspection, which relies upon an agent's own knowledge or on a consensus between several agents, agents may make decisions about the creation or the suppression of other agents. In addition to the definition of these primitives, we present their functionalities. Finally, we present an example of our approach.

Introduction

This article concerns the Distributed Artificial Intelligence (DAI) paradigm built up of social which agents resolve problems. Agents communicate between themselves by intentional message dispatching. The characteristic of a social agent is its capability to become integrated and active in the organization.

We propose an approach of self dynamic reorganization of a system using a DAI technique. Our approach suggests how a system is to organize itself in terms of the task it performs and the environment it is embedded in. Such a reorganization is interesting for applications having a tolerance to breakdowns (of a computer, or a sensor, · · ·) and those systems with a large number of agents distributed perhaps on different work stations. Generally, in a distributed problem-solving system, there is an essential correspondence between the architecture of the system, the structure of the problems, and the environmental condition under which resolution takes place. This correspondence has to be maintained even under change of the environment or the load of the system, by means of a dynamic adaptation of the whole DAI system. There are four ways to maintain this correspondence: to alter the structure of the problems, to alter the environmental conditions, to alter the problem-solving architecture, or to alter the goal-knowledge-action relationships (*e.g.* tasks, the type of knowledge, · · ·).

The approach in AI is to use a fixed problem-solving architecture and to restructure the problems in response to the changes of the environment (*e.g.* by relaxation of constraints, by changing the decision criterion, · · ·). Research on DAI systems has first investigated the adaptation of the macroarchitecture (that is the problem-solving).These systems are composed of a fixed collection of problem-solving agents, each of which has a stable microarchitecture. The modification of the relationships between agents or of the organization of the agents allows a dynamic adaptation of the macroarchitecture. The best-known early dynamic macroarchitecture is the Contract Net system [1], in which manager-worker relationships evolve in an opportunistic fashion based on the structure of the given problem decomposition, the availability of free agents with required capabilities, and the outcomes of mutual selection processes governed by a binding-contract protocol.

In this article, we introduce organizational knowledge as well as two primitives of reorganization: the composition (regrouping several agents in to one) and the decomposition (creation of several new agents). These primitives of reorganization may vary dynamically: relationships between agents, knowledge about an agent, the number of agents in the system, and the resources allocated for each agent. The decision of reorganization is taken by the system itself in accordance with the knowledge of the problem which has to be resolved and the environment in which agents evolve.

In Section 1 of this paper, we introduce and formalize our model of dynamic self-reorganization. In section 2, we describe the two primitives of logic reorganization. In section 3, we describe the first implementation of a physically distributed system which has the capacity of self-reorganization.

1 Model of dynamic self-reorganization

This section introduces the basic concepts associated with the reorganization of a system. Here we present the description of the organisational structure as well as a model of self-reorganization that allows modification and dynamic extension of this structure.

1.1 Description of an organisational structure

From an external point of view, the complete specification of the organisational structure of a DAI system describes the components of the system, the interconnections between them, and their physical location in the system.

1.2 Model self-reorganization

Our dynamic self-reorganization model (see fig 1) is composed of three modules:

- The module of validation which verifies if there are no inconsistencies between the specifications of changes coming either from an expert or the mechanism of introspection, and the specifications of the system.
- The mechanism of introspection which allows an agent to observe itself, with a view to increasing the functionality of the system. This mechanism is described in more detail in the following section.

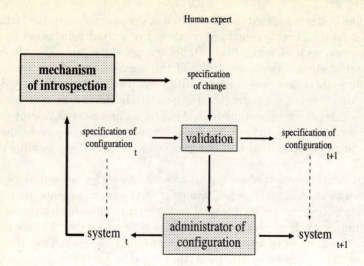

Fig. 1. Model of dynamic self-reorganization.

- The administrator of the configuration which is responsible for the modification of the system during resolution. Since the system is not stopped
during modification, the administrator observes and minimizes the duration
of modifications and their disruption of system operation.

Our approach is based on a mechanism of introspection allowing the system to
be reorganised by him own. It has been noticed in the case of classic distributed
systems that the specifications of changes are always stated by an expert [2].

1.3 Introspection

In order for an agent or a group of agents to decide to modify its own knowledge
or the organization of the system (*e.g.* to create or to suppress an agent), it
needs a mechanism of introspection. This introspection is the ability of a system
to operate at a meta-level, by being able to observe and to reason about its
functioning, so as to increase its performance or to learn for the future [3]. In
addition to this multi-level architecture, the capacity of introspection requires
the definition of two operations :

- *Reification*, which is the operation of changing from the basis level to the
meta level (e.g. to launch the operation of introspection),
- *Denotation*, which corresponds to the operation of changing from the meta
level to the basis level.

The global system is composed of the basic level, the meta level and both
above operations; these components comprise a reflexive system. The utilization

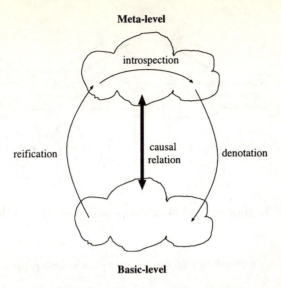

Meta-level

Basic-level

Fig. 2. Relexive system architecture.

of a reflexive formalism (see fig 2) is a way to implementing implicitly the intro-spection mechanism. Brian Smith defines reflexivity [4] as being "Reflexivity : An entity's integral ability to represent, operate on and otherwise deal with its self in the same way that it represents, operates om and deals with its primary subject matter".

We can observe three levels of reflexivity, described in [5] :

- structural reflexivity concerns the structure of information and the informa-tion itself;
- operative reflexivity relevs to the description of the manner of system func-tioning,
- conceptual reflexivity concerns the conceptual (intentional) description of the system.

In a DAI system it is difficult and perhaps impossible, to have in a given instant a global view of the system. Such, a view has therefore to be built by taking into account the information concerning the local evolution of an agent and possible bounds between other agents.

We have chosen to use a management with several levels of introspection knowledge (see fig 3). This allow us to associate an image of each agent of the system by taking into account its nature, in order to recover a more global image at a superior level of observation. In this type of management, it is possible to have several levels of decomposition. For example, agents having the same function can be joined in the same group, which allows us to have two levels of images of the system : the level of each agent and a global view of functions.

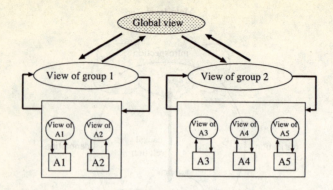

Fig. 3. Management of introspection at several levels.

This last type of reflexivity concerning groups was first proposed by the team of Yonezawa [6].

In our approach, we consider two types reorganization: the logical reorganization and the physical reorganization of the system. The latter concerns the placement and migration of agents from one resource to an other. We will not discuss it further here. Instead, we will focus on the logical reorganization and its implementation .

2 Primitives for a logic reorganization

These primitives allow the system to adapt its logical structure to the needs of the problem. The reorganization can focus on bounds between agents, knowledge of agents, or the number of agents. We are specially interested in modification of the content and the number of agents. This is performed by two primitives : composition and decomposition of agents.

The modification of the relation between agents to improve the problem-solving of the group has been studied by [7] and [8].

2.1 Decomposition

Description The purpose of this primitive is to allow one or several agents (denoted here by the term *entity*) to delegate part of its skills. This process of decomposition begins when an entity reasons by applying its mechanism of introspection, that it will not be able to perform its tasks adequately. This reasoning can be base on, for example, the number of tasks, the importance of tasks, or the required time for resolving the problem [9]. The entity then determines if some of its skills can been decomposed or parallelized.

If such is the case, the entity then must decide if delegation to an other exiting entity may take place, or if an entity has to be created first.

This decision depends on:

- The knowledge the entity has to create another entity or to search a subcontractor. Of course, in a DAI system, all agents can't possess the entire of the knowledge of the system, there for, there are three possibilities:
  - the entity does not know about the possibility off delegation or creation of a new entity;
  - it does not know how to create an entity and asks another to create it;
  - the entity knows how to create the new entity.
- The number and the importance of tasks to be delegated, because it is preferable to create news entities when the number of tasks is too big;
- The availability of resources.If resources are saturated, the creation of a new entity will not increase performance.

There has been much research concerning subcontracting and the delegation of tasks. The most well known is the *CONTRACT NET* realised by the team of SMITH [8].

Here, we are interested in the creation of a new agent.

Creation of new agents The process of creating a new agent is performed in three phases:

1. Definition of which skills are to be delegated: this is the task that the creating entity wishes to give to a subcontractor, as well as some other tasks, taking into account the redundance of knowledge, so as to ensure, in case of failure of the creating agent, that no other agent of the system could perform this type of task.
2. Collection of the knowledge to perform the tasks. If the overloaded entity contains several agents, it is necessary beforehand to verify the coherence of the knowledge provided to the new agent. The knowledge for performing tasks is found with knowledge of introspection.
3. Creation (or delegation of creation) of the new agent.

It has been seen that this process of creation can be considerably simplified if the overload entity is composed of a unique agent. In this case, the new agent is a total or mid-term clone of its creator. This primitive of decomposition increases parallelisation of the problem-solving, but it also increases actions of coordination as well and thus the number of messages between agents increases.

2.2 Composition

The composition primitive allows the transformation of an entity into another, but smaller[1] but more complex entity. When several entities are composed the original entities are replaced by the composed agents entity. The system may be composed for either of the following reasons:

- The cost of performing tasks decreases, so that a large number of agents is no longer required.

---

[1] The size of an entity is the number of agents which compose the entity.

– Resources of the system decrease (*e.g.* breakdown of a workstation, ···). It is therefore necessary to reorganize the knowledge of agents. Agents concerned with the deleted resources will have to use other existing resources. If these resources are not available the agents will have to be deleted.

An agent is suppressed if it is judged ineffective (for example those whose activity are lower than a certain threshold). This judgement of ineffectiveness is undertaken by the agent itself, or by a group of agents when there is a consensus between them. Of course, before the suppression of an agent is performed, it is necessary for the agent to delegate its tasks to other agents or to signal its contractors that it cannot finish its tasks.

We notice that the faculty of pulling out an agent from the system, when it is no longer adapted in the environment, is analogous to the natural selectivity which determines when members of a population should survive.

2.3 Composition and decomposition

The composition and decomposition primitives (see fig 4) are independent and therefore may be performed at the same time by differents agents of the system. These two operations are essential for the existence of a system. Indeed, S. Luspasco in [10] considers that in order for a system to exist it is necessary that the constituents of a system could be associated or dissociated following their own laws.

Both primitives of composition and decomposition are in fact two antagonistic forces that allow the proper functioning of the system.

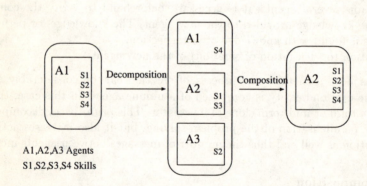

Fig. 4. Composition and decomposition.

3 Experimental evaluation

We have evaluated the effectiveness of our approach using simulation, solving the research of prime number.

3.1 Model of environment and task

We use a model of environment and task characteristics. It is composed of three levels: objective, subjective and generative [11].

- **Objective level**: This level describes the task structure of the problem to be solved. It is a formal description of a single problem-solving situation, without information about particular agents. Formally, the subtask relationship is defined as **subtask**$(\mathcal{T}, T, Q(T,t))$ where T is the set of all direct subtasks of $\mathcal{T}$ and Q is a quality function $Q : [\text{task} \times \text{times}] \mapsto [\text{quality}]$ which returns the quality of the task $\mathcal{T}$. In a valid model, the directed graph induced by the relationship between the tasks is acyclic (no task has itself as a direct or indirect subtask).
- **Subjective level**: The purpose of this level is to describe what portions of the objective model are available to 'agent'. It answers questions such as "when is a piece of information available," "who can perform this task," and "what is the cost for the agent of that piece of information". This level is represented by using the notion of beliefs of an agent.
- **Generative level**: Adding a generative level to the model allows us to determine what the expected performance of an algorithm is over a long period of time and many many individual problem solving episodes. It describes the statistical characteristics required to generate the objective and subjective situations in a given domain.

This model has been implemented using a modified version of Prolog. This "new" Prolog contains two primitives of communications: send a message from an agent to another and read an agent's mail box.
The description of each one of the task structures is implemented using prolog facts. For example:

- **belief** (rule-to-execut,me,[introspection,state,rule-100]) That means that in order for the agent to perform the "introspection" task at a certain state, it must call the rule set named "rule-100". There may be more than one rule set to accomplish a task, and each rule set will take some amount of time and will produce a result of some quality.
- **belief** (subtask,me,[main,test-integers,display]) That means that in order to perform the "main" task the agent must first call the subtask "test-integers" and then the subtask "display". this knoledge is build automaticaly by analysing the source of the agent.
- **belief**(quality-function,me,[main,sum]) The quality function for the "main" task is the sum of the quality of its subtasks (in this case "test-integers" and "display").
- **belief** (duration,agent2,[test-integers,3]) The agent belief that the duration of task "test-integers" is 3 seconds for the agent "agent2".
- **belief** (duration,me,[creat-agent,8]) The agent beliefs that the creation of a new agent takes 8 seconds.
- **know** (time-required,me,[test-integers,3000) The agent knows that the time to perform all task "test-integers" must by lower than 5 minutes.

3.2   Experimentation

Our system is implemented on a Unix work-stations network and each agent is a prolog process.

The experiments begin with one agent containing all the problem-solving knowledge. The main task of this agent is to determine and display if an integer, less than 1000, is prime or not. The determination if an integer is a prime number is performed by the successive division of the prime numbers already found. In order to test the decomposition and composition process, we have increased the duration of the prime number division task by 0.6 seconds. The requests to test an integer arrive at constant intervals of 2 seconds.

The decomposition in our experiment is actually a serialisation. The agent that decomposes itself splits the list of prome numbers found in two halfs and sends the upper half to the newly created agent. To determine if a number is a prime number, it has now to be checked by both agents.

In this Experiment we mesure quality by checking the time needed by the system to produce the desired results. Each agent beeing able to do introspection determines the time needed to do verification of a number with his known prime numbers ($TIME_{actual}$) and compares it to the required time ($TIME_{required}$).

$$\begin{cases} if\ TIME_{actual} > TIME_{required}\ then\ start\ decomposition \\ if\ TIME_{actual} < \frac{TIME_{required}}{10}\quad then\ start\ composition \\ if\ TIME_{actual} < \frac{TIME_{required}}{2}\quad then\ agent\ can\ accept\ tasks\ or\ skills \end{cases}$$

With $TIME_{required}$ equal to six minutes for task "test-integers", we observe the creation of a new agent ($Agent_B$) at point T_1 (see fig 5). At point T_2, the time needed for the test is again over the upper limit $TIME_{required}$ while $Agent_B$ is still fast enough. The time it needs for test is even under the lower limit so $Agent_A$ decides to give some of its already known prime numbers to $Agent_B$ thus lowering the number of divisions it has to do for test. At time T_3, all the requests to test an integer have been given to $Agent_A$. The tests will be finished one after another and so the time needed for the remaining tests decreases. At point T4 $Agent_A$ has completed most of its tests and the time it needs to finish one test drops under the lower limit. $Agent_A$ decides that it is no longer needed and that the remaining division tests can be done by $Agent_B$. $Agent_A$ and $Agent_B$ rejoin.

The critical parts in this procedure are the upper and lower limits of the time needed for one test. If the lower limit is too low, it will take more time to rejoin the agents than to just finish all the remaining tests with the same structure. If the lower limit is too high, the behaviour of the system can become chaotic. For example the load of $agent_A$ could be only a little under its upper limit and $Agent_B$ rejoins with it. This would increase the time it would need for one test over its upper limit and it would decompose again. This would result in a system where the agents pass their time decomposing and rejoining.

4 Conclusions

We have presented a general and conceptually simple model of a DAI system which reorganises its architecture in order to adapt itself to the changes of environment and its load. Beside the existent systems which propose a delegation of tasks to other existent entities with less costs, the paradigm that we have defined allows us to create and to suppress the entities one or several agents dynamically. A mechanism of introspection allows each agent or group of agents to define if a decomposition is needed, or if it has to be composed if it judged ineffective.

These actions have for immediately the consequences of adding, modifying or deleting knowledge about some agents or groups of agents in the system. The objective of the reorganization by means of these two dual primitives is to acquire a better tolerance to breakdowns and there by increase the potential of resources.

It is has been noted that the utilization of these primitives has to be moderated, because, used indiscriminately, they may generate a saturation of resources or an overload on the entities that would be the opposite of desired effect.

Indeed, we have to study the mechanism of validation of knowledge during the creation of a new entity and the mechanism of introspection allowing the construction to have a global view (at a more general level of abstraction) which is built up from the local view.

We intend to continue the study of such systems and to implement in the context of supervision of air traffic control.

References

1. R. Davis and R.G. Smith. *Negotiation as a Metaphor for Distributed Problem-Solving*. Artificial Intelligence, vol 20, 63-109, 1983.
2. T. Bloom. *Dynamic Module Replacement in a Distributed system*. Technical Report MIT/LCS/TR-303, March 83.
3. J. Pitrat. *Métaconnaissances : Futur de l'intelligence artificielle*. Edition Hermès, Paris 1990.
4. ECOOP/OOPSLA-90 Workshop on Reflexion and Meta-Level Architectures in OOP, 1990
5. J. Ferber. *Objets et agents : Une étude des structures de représentation et de communication en intelligence artificielle*. Thèse d'état, Univ Paris VI, Juin 1989.
6. T. Watanabe, A. Yonezama. *An Actor Based Metalevel architecture for Group-wide Reflexion*. Proc REx Scholl/workshop on fondations on Objet Oriented Langages, Noordwijkerhout, the Netherland, May 1990.
7. J. Rosenschein. *Consenting agents : negotiation mechanisms for multi-agent systems*. Proc Internatinal Joint Conference on Artificial Intelligence 93, Chambéry , 1993.
8. R. G. Smith. *The contract net protocol : high level communication and control in a distributed problem solver*. IEEE transaction on computers, Decembre 1980.
9. L. Gasser and T. Ishida. *A dynamic Organisational Architecture for Adaptative Problem Solving*. Proceedings AAAI-92, vol 1, 185-190, July 1992.

128

10. S. Lupasco. *Le principe d'antagonisme et la logique de l'énergie*. Editions Hermann 1951, Editions du Rocher 1987.
11. K. Decker and V. Lesser. *Quantitative Modeling of Complex Computational Task Environnement*. Proceedings AAAI-93, 217-224, 1993.

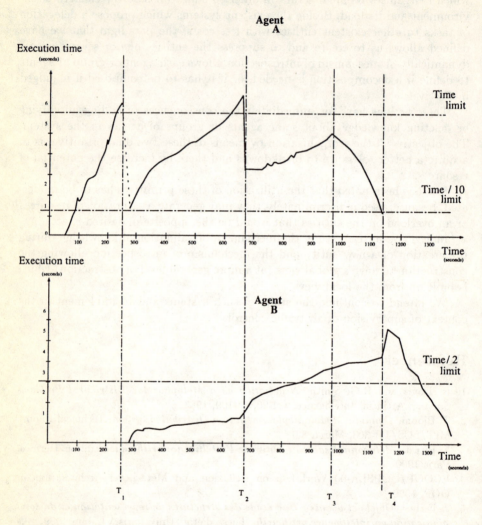

Fig. 5. Time to test numbers.

Logical Formalization of Concurrent Actions for Multi-Agent Systems

Mikhail Soutchanski and Eugenia Ternovskaia

Dep. of Computer Science, 10 King's College Road, SF3303
Toronto University, Toronto (Ontario), M5S 1A4, Canada
e-mail: (mes,eugenia)@ai.toronto.edu

Abstract. This paper presents a logical approach to formalization of some aspects of multi-agent systems in an incompletely known world. The contribution on this regard is as follows.

We formalized reasoning about concurrent actions inside the situation calculus framework which has the sufficiently clear and well-understood semantics to express different aspects of agent theory.

Conclusions can be drawn by default about results of a group of concurrent actions which may include unknown or unspecified actions.

The approach allows to examine all models corresponding both to different assumptions about possible failures in performing of one or another action, and to assumptions whether a particular action was executed really. This provides an opportunity to predict the consequence of joint activity of agents operating in complex environment and to explain apparently unexpected changes.

These results are achieved by choosing a suitable circumscription policy. The approach provides a general and formal framework for design and verification of wide class of agent-oriented systems such as telecommunication systems, network management, and evolving distributed data bases.

1 Introduction

The study of multi-agent systems composed from reasoning agents and embedded in a changing environment has been receiving considerable attention. An example of such a system is a team of mobile robots either jointly committing to a common goal or having competitive interests. Each member of a team to achieve both a shared goal and its own aims should be able to take into accounts its own and others states of knowledge, incorporates the plans of other agents into its own, and to reason about a result of joint actions.

Among the nowadays agent-based products are agent software that schedules meetings, responds automatically to incoming e-mail, delivers the message to the addressee's computer thus protecting programmers from many of the complexities of network protocols. It appears that agent technology will present a powerful example for remote computing, especially in a client/server environment. The message has to be smarter there whenever there is nobody to guide it.

Several mathematical formalisms are used for representing and analyzing different issues of agent systems. We adhere to logical approach because it will permit to combine the strategic analysis of agent interests, which is a part of the traditional game theory, with the analysis of argumentation, used by agents to overcome a conflict situation. Moreover, the logical approach allows naturally take into account constraints on cognitive abilities of agents. It is well known that 'complete rationality' is an extreme assumption and can lead to implausible predictions about an outcome in a repeated game. We suggested here as a way of dealing with 'bounded rationality' to restrict explicitly the logical language used for representation of agent beliefs and communications. Interesting reader can find in other papers from this volume aternative approaches to formalisations of multy-agent systems ([3, 23],etc).

We have focused our attention only on the development of the simple logical formalization of reasoning about actions executed simultaneously. As the starting point we used the situation calculus [15] which is now one of the most popular approaches for representing and reasoning about actions [2, 8, 14, 18, 22]. Moreover, recently it was conceived that some of its apparent limitations can be overcame easily [4]. The attractiveness of the situation calculus stems from its clear ontology and its simplicity. From the formal point of view, we use a small fragment of a MSFOL (many-sorted first order logic) with appropriate circumscription policies. We stick with a sorted logic given its general suitability in reducing the search space for many problems. However, the question how this choice can help us to develop a more effective circumscription prover is beyond the scope of our paper.

We solved the following problems. The first is: How should causal rules refer to simultaneous actions so that if we knew that some agents perform the group of actions which includes unspecified one, the appropriate causal rule nevertheless would be fired to derive default conclusions ? Such conclusions will agree with the intuition that the engagement in an activity (simultaneously with other actions) whose influence on the world is unknown, by default cannot prevent inferences about the results of other actions from deriving. These inferences will be defeasible and can be withdrawn in the presence of new causal rules with contrary specifications. For instance, in accordance with some ideological, theological or social doctrines all of us are unconsciously involved in a lot of activities. Nevertheless, it does not preclude us from reasoning about everyday actions. The approach we proposed put no restrictions on how many such actions unspecified by causal rules of the theory are performed, and moreover, its flexibility is achieved without complications of the causal rules.

While dealing with the first problem we concern ourselves with predictions, the second problem aroused from the need to gain explanations for obtained observations. Thus, the second problem is: how to recognize the actions performed by the multi-agent system under incomplete knowledge about its evolution ? The incompleteness is conditioned both by the intention to allow for the possibility that actions may fail to have their expected effects and by the lack of knowledge about what particular actions determined the observed phenomena. We proposed an elegant solution to this problem by applying the ideas of [2, 12, 13].

Our solutions allow also to derive easily new values of all properties of the world which can change after an action have been executed, in particular, values of those properties which were not influenced by the action. Thus, we cope with the *frame problem* sticking to the circumscription. Our method solves also the *ramification problem*. It arises when a theory includes a set of static constraints on the properties of the world. The problem is how all implicit consequences of actions can be found without explicit applications of causal rules (i.e. only from static constraints). We indicate also a way of dealing with *qualification problem*, which is the problem how all sufficient preconditions for each action could be enumerated concisely.

Despite we have not consider very important issues of intricate interaction of knowledge, intentions, collaboration, and actions, we will demonstrate briefly how agent beliefs and communication can be represented. We think this justifies our adherence to the situation calculus. In this respect, we follow a long standing tradition of syntactic approach to denoting agent's beliefs (first order language expressions) by terms [7, 16, 17].

An alternative to syntactic approach is representing propositional attitudes by means of a multi-modal language. However, first order formalizations have more attractive features in comparison with possible-worlds approach, so called due to Kripke-style semantics of possible worlds for a modal logic of knowledge and belief. This approach suffers from the *logical omniscience* problem: agents are so ingenious that they know all valid formulas and they know all the logical consequences of their knowledge. It is certainly not appropriate because real agents have resource limitations on their reasoning process. The second objection is that modal logics do not explicitly represent relationships among beliefs, particularly the process how one belief is caused by other beliefs and do not distinguish derivational capabilities of different agents [7]. A good example of multi-agent systems composed from reasoning agents with varying degree of intelligence is a client/server environment: client should not be so clever as a server. Our preferences are thus close to framework proposed by [24].

We follow a certain tradition, which is briefly described in section 2. After an introduction of sorts for object variables, function and predicate symbols in the section 3 we demonstrate in section 4 our method of axiomatizing concurrent actions. In particular, this section contains hints how axioms should be formulate in general case. In the section 5 we outline the circumscription policies. For expository purposes we illustrate our considerations by three examples in the section 6. We will focus our attention on reasoning forward and backward in time. Section 7 compares our approach with other works. The last Section 8 notes some possible extensions and summarizes our proposal.

2 Preliminaries

In this section we briefly describe approaches from which our work originates.

Our approach to concurrent actions representation stem from the idea of J.Weber [22]. He proposed to represent the dynamic component of the situational calculus ontological scheme by two distinct ontological entities. The first of them is a single action, second one is an operator. Roughly speaking, an operator is simultaneously performing actions, however it is an independent entity. Taken this step we can drastically simplify an axiomatization, because under this point of view on concurrent changes there is no need to add axioms about the inheritance of the properties of single actions by the operator which is composed from them. The operator is related with its compound actions by the binary predicate $Type$. Thus, J.Weber proposed to detach the type of an action from its name and make it into a predicate.

The predicate $Type$ will occur in causal rules and in the so-called scenario. To prevent causal rules from undesirable applying, $Type$ should be circumscribed. Without such circumscription it would be possible for some of the models to permit superfluously wide extents of the predicate.

We will use the *pointwise circumscription* [10] to deal with the frame problem.

We take J.Crawford and D.Etherington's [2] suggestion into consideration. [1] They introduced two abnormality predicates to capture the following two ideas.

First, when an action typically has certain effects, but the list of all combinations of circumstances in which the action may fail to have these effects is too long to be generated explicitly. The failures to perform actions are described in our proposal by the predicate $Wrong$, keeping in mind that usually such failures occur rarely.

Second, whenever actions have indirect effects, the task to capture by an axiomatization the exact effects of successful actions can be infeasible. To address the last problem, persistence axiom is usually added that state that if a particular value is not known to change as the result of an action, then one may assume that it persists. The abnormality predicate Ab is used to express this idea.

The extents of both these predicates are supposed to be as minimal as possible, i.e. logical models with fewer violations of default assumptions are preferred over those with more violations. Although one or another violation must take place when we have to explain certain observations, a straightforward axiomatization gives no hints for resolving a conflict to the benefit of one over another. The conflict has be avoided by choosing an appropriate circumscription policy.

The method is also applicable if a specification of a system is incomplete. For example, let one observes that a truth value of the particular property remains the same but s/he doesn't know all those actions which agents have performed concurrently. First, in order to explain the observed phenomena, s/he can form a hypothesis that some action which is known definitely as occurring didn't has its expected effect on the property. Second, s/he can assume that an unforeseen action took place concurrently with the actions which definitely occurred and that action was the reason for the observed phenomena.

---

[1] The idea of "filtering" appropriate models via special axioms encoding observations has been proposed by E.Sandewall in [12].

3 Language

We describe in this section the language of situation calculus and briefly review the syntactic approach to representing beliefs.

3.1 Situation Calculus

We will consider a subset of MSFOL [2]. In the sequel, we would like to express that a set of facts holds or does not in a situation. We would like also to describe agent's beliefs (explicitly represented in a subset of our language), deductions and communications. In order to allow this, the syntax of the underlying language must includes terms for formulas so that they can appear as arguments in predicates [7, 16, 17]. A first-order language so endowed with terms is called usually the *reified* language [3].

In accordance with a long standing tradition, in our notation we distinguish two sorts of reified formulas. Terms (object variables, constants) for truth-valued fluents (f) representing external fluently varying properties of the world are used without a quotation marks in a formulas of our language. Terms for beliefs, content of communicative acts, and other information-related entities (i) are obtained by applying a quotation construct to a formula. We use also object variables of other sorts: for situation (s), for operators (o), for actions (a), for agents (c). For each sort there is a finite set of constants denoting a corresponding set of objects in a domain.

We use the ordinary situation-valued function symbol *Res* having operator term and situation term as arguments. For example, $Res(O, S_0)$ denotes a situation resulting from the execution of the operator O in the initial situation S_0.

The binary predicate constant symbol $Holds(f, s)$ asserts that a property f holds in a situation s: $Holds(Communication(C_1, C_2), Res(O_2, Res(O_1, S_0)))$ means that agents C_1 and C_2 communicate in the situation achieved as the result of performing the operator O_2 in the earlier situation $Res(O_1, S_0)$.

Even if fluents have equivalent truth values everywhere, they may denote different properties of the world. Note that otherwise, if we were to include the axiom $Holds(f_1, s) \equiv Holds(f_2, s) \supset (f_1 = f_2)$, our theory would be monadic second order, because fluents are universally quantified.

We use the ordinary ternary predicate constant symbol $Ab(f, o, s)$ to assert that a fluent f is abnormal (i.e., its value does not persist) after the performance of an operator o in a situation s.

The binary predicate constant symbol $Type(o, a)$ means that an operator o contains, in particular, an action a, e.g. $Type(O_1, Send(C_1, "Message", C_2))$ asserts that the action $Send(C_1, "Message", C_2)$ belongs to the operator O_1, where C_1 is the sender, C_2 is the recipient, and Message is a formula.

---

[2] Variables begin with lower-case letters. Constants, function symbols, predicate symbols begin with upper-case letters. Unbound variables are universally quantified.

[3] alternative name is the *thingified* language, due to J.McCarthy

The predicate $Wrong(o, a, s, f)$ is used further to cope with several problems. Please note that whenever we apply the adjective 'wrong' to characterize an effect of an action a (which belongs to an operator o) on a fluent f at a situation s, we describe a state of affairs when the action was canceled out by other actions (which belong to the same operator) or failed due to some reasons.

The auxiliary binary predicate constant symbol $Earlier(s_1, s_2)$ taking situation terms as its argument says that a situation s_1 precedes a situation s_2.

3.2 Syntactic Approach to Encode Agent Beliefs.

To justify our choice of the situation calculus as a framework for formalizing concurrent actions in agent systems, we demonstrate in brief how the syntactic approach works. [4]

We may enrich our language by terms:

by appropriately sorted term constants. They are designated by applying quotation marks to object constants $("C", "S")$;

by the standard naming function;

for each predicate letter we assume corresponding function symbol designated by applying quotation marks to the predicate constant $("Holds")$;

by Boolean constructors (with obvious axiomatization): and, or, neg, imp. These function symbols allow to put together more complicated formulas starting from atomic ones.

To avoid cumbersome expressions, it is convenient to use sense quotes " " enclosing a $Formula$ as a syntactic abbreviation for the term that is intended. For example, we write $"Holds(F_1, S_0) \supset Holds(F_2, S_0)"$ instead of $imp("Holds"("F_1", "S_0"), "Holds"("F_2", "S_0"))$.

Note to simplify our definitions we consider as beliefs only formulas being boolean expressions obtained from ground atomic formulas.

The fluent-valued function symbol Bel having agent term and information term as arguments denotes a specific fluent expressing a fact that the agent believes in the information. For example, $Holds(Bel(C_1, "Inf"), S_0)$ means that the agent C_1 possesses a belief $"Inf"$ at the initial situation (where Inf is a formula).

We can address the 'bounded rationality' imposing explicit restrictions on terms of information sort. For example, let beliefs be only Horn formulas without function symbols. Then, we may put a $priory$ restrictions on the amount of disjuncts in a Horn formula and on the depth of beliefs nesting (beliefs about beliefs). For example, let belief be Horn formulas composed from no more than, say, 21 disjuncts, such that each belief may contain inside no more than one level of belief nesting. [5] We can ascribe to the agents certain (even varying from one

---

[4] Interested reader can find further details in [7, 16, 17, 24].

[5] Thus, an agent is able to believe that someone believes that $"Inform"$, however this agent is not able to believe that someone believes that the agent believes that $"Inform"$.

agent to another) deductive power, if we add to a logical theory suitable axioms, for example,

$$Holds(Bel(c, "Holds(F_1, S_0)"), s) \ \&$$
$$Holds(Bel(c, "Holds(F_1, S_0) \supset Holds(F_2, S_0)"), s)$$
$$\supset Holds(Bel(C_1, "Holds(F_2, S_0)"), s)$$

Due to the restrictions, even if agents have a set of beliefs and some limited deductive abilities, they cannot derive facts which are expressed by too sophisticated Horn formulas. One of the most important problems here is *the knowledge precondition problem* [17]. Because of space limitations, we will not discuss these questions deeper.

4 Axioms

We divide axioms on several groups in accordance with their intention. We will discuss here only general case. Illustrating examples will be considered further.

The first group of axioms contains effect axioms (causal rules) with predicate $Type$, that imposes constraints on an operator variable.

$$[\neg]Holds(F_1, s)\&...\&[\neg]Holds(F_k, s)$$
$$\&Type(o, A_1)\&...\&Type(o, A_n)$$
$$\&\neg Wrong(o, A_1, s, F_{k+1})\&...\&\neg Wrong(o, A_n, s, F_{k+1}) \tag{1}$$
$$\supset [\neg]Holds(F_{k+1}, Res(o, s))$$

The second group involves axioms formulating reasons why an action may fail to produce its intended effect:

– Whenever an operator includes an action or a group of actions, the effect of another action on a fluent F is canceled

$$Type(o, A_1)\&...\&Type(o, A_n) \supset Wrong(o, A_{n+1}, s, F)$$

Example, the actions Cl (close) and Op (open) cancel each other's effect on the fluent F (a closed file) whenever they occur in the same situation:

$$Type(o, Op) \supset Wrong(o, Cl, s, F), \ \ Type(o, Cl) \supset Wrong(o, Op, s, F)$$

– Whenever some fluents hold in a situation and some actions belong to the operator which is executed by a group of agents in a situation, a certain action must fail in this situation:

$$[\neg]Holds(F_1, s)\&...\&[\neg]Holds(F_k, s)$$
$$\&Type(o, A_1)\&...\&Type(o, A_n) \tag{2}$$
$$\supset Wrong(o, A_{n+1}, s, F)$$

For example, a duplex line L_5 cannot be assigned to the computer C_4 for communication with the server C_1, if C_1 and client C_7 occupy currently this line ($Occ(Computer, Line)$) for their communication:

$$Holds(Comm(C_1, C_7, L_5), s)\&Type(o, Occ(C_1, L_5))\&Type(o, Occ(C_7, L_5))$$
$$\supset Wrong(o, Assign(C_4, L_5), s, Comm(C_1, C_4, L_5))$$

− Whenever some particular fluents hold in a situation, a certain action must fail in this situation:

$$Holds(F_1, s)\&...\&Holds(F_j, s)\&\neg Holds(F_{j+1}, s)\&...\&\neg Holds(F_k, s) \\ \supset Wrong(o, A, s, F) \qquad (3)$$

For example, if a message "M" has been sent but not received, then the action of delivering the message M has been cancelled out:

$$Holds(Sent("M"), \ s) \ \& \ \neg Holds(Received("M"), \ s) \\ \supset Wrong(o, Deliver, s, Received("M"))$$

Each theory of actions under consideration includes the inertion axiom with the abnormality predicate:

$$\neg Ab(f, o, s) \supset ((Holds(f, s) \equiv Holds(f, Res(o, s)))) \qquad (4)$$

This axiom says informally, that values of those properties f are abnormal in the current situation s which don't persist in the next situation occurring as a result of performing an operator o. Roughly speaking, after the circumscription of the predicate Ab as much fluents will be persistent as it is possible.

The third group is comprised by a set of unique names axioms; for fluents and operators:

$$F_1 \neq F_2 \neq ... \neq F_n \qquad O_1 \neq O_2 \neq ... \neq O_r$$

and for situations: [6]

$$Earlier(s, Res(o, s))$$
$$Earlier(s, s_1)\&Earlier(s_1, s_2) \supset Earlier(s, s_2) \qquad (5)$$
$$Earlier(s, s_1) \supset s \neq s_1$$

And finally, the sixth group axioms is formed by scenario's assertions and, consequently, is specific only for an example under consideration:

$$[\neg] \ Holds(F_i, S_0), \quad i = 1, ..., n. \qquad (6)$$

$$Type(O_j, A_l), \quad l = 1, ..., r. \qquad (7)$$

$$[\neg] \ Holds(F_i, Res(O_k, Res(O_{k-1}, ..., S_0)))...)), \quad i = 1, ..., l \ , \qquad (8)$$

for a certain fixed sequences $O_1, O_2, ..., O_k$.

Because axioms (8) refer to properties of the system after a set of operators have been performed, these axioms will be named as *observations*.

Let us denote by A_1 the conjunction of all axioms from this section besides those axioms (6) - (8) which belong to scenario.

---

[6] This axioms are used here in the form proposed by F.Lin&Y.Shoham

5 Circumscription Policies

As usually, whenever some circumscription policy is formulated we assume that sort and arity of each predicate variable exactly correspond to sort and arity of the initial predicate constant.

5.1 Preliminary Definitions

We will denote (see [9, 10]) by $Circum(A(P, Z); P; Z)$ the *global circumscription of the predicate P in the formula $A(P, Z)$ with Z allowed to vary* to represent the formula:

$$A(P, Z) \;\&\; \neg \exists p, z \; (A(p, z) \;\&\; p < P) \tag{9}$$

where z is a list of predicate and/or function variables whose arities equal to arities of corresponding letters from the tuple Z, and $p < P$ denotes

$$\forall x(p(x) \supset P(x)) \;\&\; \neg \exists x(P(x) \supset p(x))$$

We remind that the corresponding form of *pointwise circumscription*

$$A(P) \;\&\; \neg \exists x, z \; [P(x) \;\&\; A(\lambda y(P(y)\& \; x \neq y), z)]$$

is denoted by $C_P \; (A(P, Z); Z)$.

We remind also that [10] defined *the pointwise circumscription of P in $A(P,Z)$ with the predicate Z allowed to vary only on the part V of its domain*, where V is a λ-expression $\lambda u V(u)$ of the same arity as $Z(u)$, which has no parameters and contains neither P nor Z:

$$A(P) \;\&\; \neg \exists x, z \; [P(x) \;\&\; \forall u(\neg V(u) \supset z(u) \equiv Z(u)) \;\&\; A(\lambda y(P(y)\& \; x \neq y), z)].$$

In the sequel we will need more flexible circumscription policies that also were defined by [10]. Let V be λ-expression $\lambda x u V(x, u)$ whose arity equals the sum of the arities of P and Z, and V_x is the function $\lambda u V(x, u)$ which maps every value of x into the set of all values of u satisfying $V(x, u)$. Then, whenever Z may vary only on that part V_x of its domain which depends of the point x where P is minimized, this circumscription is denoted by $C_P \; (A(P, Z); Z/V) \;$):

$$A(P) \;\&\; \neg \exists x, z \; [P(x) \;\&\; \forall u(\neg V_x \supset z(u) \equiv Z(u)) \;\&\; A(\lambda y(P(y)\& \; x \neq y), z)].$$
$$\tag{10}$$

If instead of Z we may vary some values of the predicate P itself while minimizing its value at some point, this *pointwise circumscription of P in $A(P)$ with P itself allowed to vary on the domain V_x* is $C_P(A(P); P/V)$:

$$A(P) \;\&\; \neg \exists x, p \; [P(x) \;\&\; \neg p(x) \;\&\; \forall u(\neg V_x \supset p(u) \equiv P(u)) \;\&\; A(p)]. \tag{11}$$

Here p is a predicate variable similar to P, V is a λ-expression $\lambda x u V(x, u)$ which has no parameters and does not contain P. The second term of (11) says that if $P(x)$ is *true* it is impossible to change its value to *false* without losing the property $A(P)$, even if the values of P will change arbitrary on the domain V_x.

Note, that although circumscription gives rise to a second order formulas, there is a wide class of circumscribed theories of actions which are either equivalent to a first order formula [5] or to a formula in a more expressive *fixpoint logic* obtained by adding the *least fixed point formation rule* to first order logic [6].

5.2 Description of Our Circumscription Policy

Given a complete description of some multi-agent system, as a set of statement in first-order logic, we can predict possible behaviors of the system by listing facts which are true in each situation achievable from the current one.

That task is more difficult if we don't have the complete description of the system. This incompleteness can be caused (•) either if one allows possibility that actions may fail to have their expected effects; (•) or if one wants to take into account those actions which are not mentioned in the scenario to explain apparently uncaused changes.

Before we will proceed to the formal definition of the circumscription policy, we present its intuitive description.

1. While reasoning about an observed behavior of the system, one choose a set of hypotheses about unknown facts to fill a gap in his/her knowledge. Then he/she simulates the work of the system bearing these hypotheses in mind. Looking over all possible set of hypotheses in turn, he/she constructs gradually complete graph of transitions between states of the systems. These transition can be labeled by corresponding operators.
2. If under a particular set of assumptions the simulation of a system doesn't coincide with the observations (see axioms 8), then there is no sense to consider this set further.
3. When all inappropriate sets of hypotheses are removed one can compare all remained simulations and choose the most plausible ones. Among them will be those simulations which will not contradict to the intuition that an action, as a rule, produces its intended effect, and unrecognized actions, as a rule, occur very rarely.

The circumscription policy, used in this paper allows to carry out the process of recognizing how a system operates. Making assumptions about failures to perform one or another action corresponds in our framework to holding predicate *Wrong* fixed. Making assumptions about what (in particular, uncanny and/or unconscious) actions have been executed corresponds to fixing the predicate *Type*.

Our minimization policy is based on [2]. We will divide the minimization process into three stages in accordance with the above informal description.

At the first stage, the predicate *Ab* is circumscribed pointwisely [10] with *Holds* varying on situations other then current and having *Type* and *Wrong* fixed [7]. The minimization of Ab with Holds varied allows to construct full graph of transitions between states of a system, because for each situation and for each particular operator the circumscription determines values of all fluents minimizing the number of those fluents which change their values. Holding the predicates $Type$ fixed corresponds to making assumptions about what particular actions took place, and fixing the predicate $Wrong$ corresponds to assumptions about what actions failed to have their intended effects.

$$C_{Ab}(A_1; \ Holds/V_1) \equiv A_2, \quad V_1 = \lambda f, s' \ (s' \neq s);$$

Note, that the axioms of a scenario are excluded from the circumscribed theory at this stage (see remark at the end of the previous section).

At the second stage the resulting theory A_2 is augmented with the scenario axioms. This will rule out the models which do not correspond to observations.

At the third stage, the most preferable models from the remaining are chosen by minimizing $Wrong$ and then $Type$:

$$Circum(A_2 \& (6) \& (7) \& (8); \ Wrong; \ Ab, Holds/V_1) \equiv A_3;$$

$$Circum(A_3; \ Type; \ Ab, Holds/V_1) \equiv A_4;$$

This last stage allows to choose the most plausible simulations which correspond to the intuition that actions, as a rule, have their intended influences and unforeseen actions (miracles) occur rarely.

6 Explanation and Prediction

In this section we consider two examples to clarify the effects of our circumscription policy. Everywhere below, we assume that a set of appropriate unique name axioms (in particular, for situations (5)) and the persistence axiom (4) are included in a theory.

Example 1. Prediction Problem

Let us consider a simple example of the theory which doesn't include statements about what fluents hold in the situations other than initial one. Such theories are concerned with prediction problems.

This example describes a toy telecommunication system where multiple actions are performed concurrently. Let us consider two connected computers which exchange messages via one 2-directional channel. If both computers C_1 and C_2 are ready to communicate and their modems send signals about readiness to each other, then the process of communication can start [8]:

---

[7] This policy doesn't need axioms to force the existence of all possible situations, so it can be used for reasoning about complex domains such as reasoning about space.

[8] The process $Communication$ is represented here by the fluent. The general approach to logical representation of reasoning about processes extended in time is described in [21]

$$Holds(Ready(c_1), s) \& Holds(Ready(c_2), s)$$
$$\& Type(o, SendSignal(c_1)) \& Type(o, SendSignal(c_2))$$
$$\& \neg Wrong(o, SendSignal(c_1), s, Communication(c_1, c_2)) \tag{12}$$
$$\& \neg Wrong(o, SendSignal(c_2), s, Communication(c_1, c_2))$$
$$\supset Holds(Communication(c_1, c_2), Res(o, s))$$

Let the scenario involves the following axioms:

$$Holds(Ready(C_1), S_0) \qquad Holds(Ready(C_2), S_0) \tag{13}$$

$$Type(O_1, SendSignal(C_1)) \tag{14}$$

$$Type(O_2, SendSignal(C_1)) \qquad Type(O_2, SendSignal(C_2)) \tag{15}$$

The first two axioms from the scenario (13) describe the initial situation S_0 in which both computers are ready to start communication. The third axiom from the scenario states that the operator O_1 includes the action $SendSignal(C_1)$. The last two axioms of the scenario (15) describe the operator O_2. It is easy to see that the operator O_1 doesn't lead to any changes, because the effect axiom (12) states that the communication starts only if both computers send signals about their readiness. At the same time, after the operator O_2 have been performed by the computers, they will start communicate because all sufficient requirements are satisfied: $Holds(Communication(C_1, C_2), Res(O_2(Res(O_1, S_0))))$.

After the first stage of the circumscription we have all possible simulations of the system for each assumption about failures to perform the actions and about the types of all operators. This corresponds to determining the extent of the predicate Ab with the predicates $Wrong$ and $Type$ fixed. Our theory doesn't involve observations about situations other than initial one. So, the next step of minimization is circumscription of the predicate $Wrong$. To minimize $Wrong$ we compare all simulations under different assumptions and choose those models in which the extent of this predicate is smaller in the usual set-theoretic sense. The circumscription of the predicate $Type$ on the last stage allows to eliminate those simulations of the system which were gained from hypothesis that operators include unforeseen actions.

Let the action $Dial(C_3, 425\text{-}3534)$ unrelevant to the telecommunication system belongs to the second operator, i.e. the third computer dial a phone number. In this case our theory should include the axiom: $Type(O_2, Dial(C_3, 425\text{-}3534))$.

The action $Dial(C_3, 425\text{-}3534)$ is not specified by any effect axiom of our theory. Nevertheless, the same conclusions as before about the effects of the operator O_2 can be inferred.

Example 2. Explanation Problem

This example illustrates how our approach allows to cope with explanation problem (a theory with at least one axiom which asserts what is true in a situation other than initial one). We want to recognize what particular actions have been performed.

Consider several processors of a distributed network. The processors apart from running programs can communicate by sending messages. Let a processor C_1 can perform two kinds of actions: run a program $(RunProgram(C_1))$ and send a message "inf" to another processor $(Send(C_1, "inf", C_2))$. We will consider in this example the only property describing the states of the processors: $Bel(c, "inf")$ - the message "inf" is avaiable for the processor c. The communication is described by the effect axiom (16); the axioms of scenario are (17)-(19).

$$Holds(Bel(c_1, "inf"), s)\&Type(o, Send(c_1, "inf", c_2))$$
$$\&\neg Wrong(o, Send(c_1, "inf", c_2), s, Bel(c_2, "inf")) \tag{16}$$
$$\supset Holds(Bel(c_2, "inf"), Res(o, s))$$

$$Holds(Bel(C_1, "Inf"), S_0) \qquad \neg Holds(Bel(C_1, "Inf"), S_0) \tag{17}$$
$$\neg Holds(Bel(C_2, "Inf"), Res(O_2, Res(O_1, S_0))) \tag{18}$$
$$Type(O_1, RunProgram(C_1)) \qquad Type(O_2, Send(C_1, "Inf", C_2)) \tag{19}$$

The axioms (17) describes the initial situation. The processor C_1 'believes' in "Inf" at the situation S_0 and the processor C_2 doesn't. The first operator O_1 (described by the axiom in (19)) involves the action $RunProgram(C_1)$ which is not specified by any effect axiom. The second one states that the action $Send((C_1, "Inf", C_2)$ belongs to the operator O_2. Note that the scenario includes the statement (18) representing the fact that after O_1 and O_2 have been performed in a sequence, the second processor does not receive the message "Inf". How could we explain this unexpected fact? Let us consider our circumscription policy.

At the first step of minimization we separately simulate the telecommunication system behavior under each fixed set of assumptions about what particular actions could belong to the operators and about what actions could fail to have their expected effects. Let us suppose that all actions which belong to the operators O_1 and O_2 are enumerated in the axioms (19). It is meaningless to generate new assumptions what other actions perhaps have been performed, because these assumptions will be definitely ruled out at the last step of minimization.

If we hypothesize that the action $Send(c_1, "inf", c_2)$ doesn't fail, then we can predict that C_2 receives the information "Inf". Similarly, if the sending action fails then the information "Inf" will not be available for C_2. Then we can check the resultant predictions against observations and rule out the case in which the sending was successful. The remaining model includes one violation of the assumption about normal performing of the action $Send(C_1, "Inf", C_2)$. Then, $Wrong$ is minimized to prefer those models which violate as few assumptions about normal performing of the actions as possible. As we have only one remaining model so the extent of the predicate $Wrong$ is defined. Finally, we circumscribe $Type$ and find that its extent is actually covered by the axioms (19).

Thus, the circumscribed theory implies that the action $Send(C_1, "Inf", C_2)$ fails and this fact quite well explains the observation. This proves that our approach allows to reconstruct the behavior of the telecommunication system (we cannot know why message was lost, because we have not axiomatized properties of communication channel).

7 Discussion

In this section we briefly review different approaches to reasoning about concurrent actions representation. More detailed comparison can be found in our paper [20].

The papers [1, 14] also dealt with the representation of concurrent actions inside the framework of the situation calculus has appeared practically simultaneously with [20]. The paper [1] proposed an approach based upon a specific formal language $\mathcal{A}$. In that paper, the authors provided a translation into the language of extended logic programming and prove its soundness. It is difficult to compare our approaches because our languages differs considerably. However, the paper [5] seems the most promising in this regard.

The authors of [14] also proposed the method for reasoning about concurrent actions. Their approach is similar to our one to some extent, because it is based on the situation calculus and circumscription too. Authors used the binary predicate $In(a, \{A_1, ...A_n\})$ to express that primitive action a belongs to global action $\{A_1, ...A_n\}$. This predicate plays the same role as our predicate $Type$. Because global actions which will be executed are described by explicit enumeration of what primitive actions they contain as the components, there is no need to circumscribe In.

After the closer comparison of two approaches it turns out that for [14] the issue of concurrent actions which cancel out each other's effects is more complicated then for us. They have to ensure that compound actions inherit the effects of their components [19]. Moreover, they concerned themselves with the problem how to take into account the fact that for an action A_{10} to override the effect of some global action $\{A_1, A_2\}$ itself must not be overridden by another action A_{23}. We have achieved the same result without compound actions, because we divide the dynamic component of the situational ontology on two distinct primitives.

In our previous paper [20] we also dealt with concurrent actions representation, but we proposed another approach. Instead of using the predicate $Wrong$, in order to represent actions which cancel each other effects, we used another method. Suppose that we know about a simple action that it can be executed only if some other actions $\{A_1, ..., A_n\}$ are not executed concurrently. In [20] we simply added conjunctively to the left side of the causal rule formulas $\neg Type(o, A_i)$ $(i = 1, .., n)$, to say explicitly what actions the performing operator should not contain. So, the method was very natural and it provided a monotonic solution to the *action-oriented frame-problem* [14]. The approach we present in this paper not only provides the alternative solution, but, most importantly allows also to recognize the behavior of multi-agent system even if an action had not its intended effect.

8 Conclusion

We proposed the logical theory of concurrent actions that allow to draw conclusions about the execution of actions not all of which are specified in the causal rules. We coped with the *fluent oriented frame problem* and the complexity of our solution is less than the complexity of monotonic solution. We proposed the nonmonotonic way to tackle the *action-oriented frame-problem* [14]. The problem of complete characterization of the preconditions (*qualification problem*) can be overcame by the circumscription of the predicate *Wrong*. Our approach also dealt with *ramification problem*, because implicit effects of actions can be found from constraints on the values of fluents. In this regard, the important distinctions proposed in [11] should be taken into account.

In our opinion, the concurrent actions representation must be used for reasoning about changes extended in time, because it may happen that continuous changes are overlapped in time [21]. It is important to note that correspondence between the situation calculus with action types and the explicit time-line temporal calculus established by Weber [22] facilitates future progress.

A matter of prime concern is how to compute circumscription algorithmically [6]. This point will be addressed in our future work.

Acknowledgements: We are indebted to A.Bondarenko and M.Shanahan for discussions, to R.Miller for detailed list of questions and comments, to Slava Ivanov and company Brokinvest for support by computing facilities, to Y.Gouz for help in telecommunications. We are grateful to E.Sandewall and P.Doherty for useful discussion during 11th ECAI'94 in Amsterdam.

References

1. C.Baral, M.Gelfond Representing concurrent actions in extended logic programming. Proc. of the 13th IJCAI, 1993, 866–871
2. J.M.Crawford, D.W. Etherington Formalizing Reasoning About Change: A Qualitative Reasoning Approach (Preliminary Report) In: Amer. Assoc. of Artif. Intell., 10th National Conference on Artif. Intell., 1992, 577-583.
3. B.Dunin-Keplicz, J.Treur Compositional formal specification of multi-agent systems, (this volume)
4. M.Gelfond, V.Lifschitz, A.Rabinov What are the limitations of the situation calculus ? In: Essays for Bledsoe, (Ed. by R.Boyer), Kluwer Academic, 1991, 167–177
5. G.N.Kartha Soundness and completeness theorems for three formalisations of action. Proc. of the 13th IJCAI, 1993, 724–729
6. Ph.G.Kolaitis, Ch.H.Papadimitriou Some computational aspects of circumscription. J. of the ACM, 37, 1990, 1–14
7. K.Konolidge A first-order formalisation of knowledge and action for a multi-agent planning system. In: Machine Intelligence, v. 10, (Eds. J.E.Hayes, D.Michie, Y.-H.Pao), Chichester, Ellis Horwood Ltd., 1982, 41–71
8. V.Lifschitz Toward a metatheory of action. Proc. of the 2nd Int'l Conf. on Principles of Knowledge Representation and Reasoning, (Eds. J.Allen, R.Fikes, E.Sandewall), 1991, p.376-387
9. V.Lifschitz Computing circumscription. Proc. 9th IJCAI, 1985, 121–127
10. V.Lifschitz Pointwise circumscription: preliminary report. In: Amer. Assoc. of Artif. Intell., 5th National Conference on Artif. Intell., 1986, v.1, p. 406-410
11. F.Lin, R.Reiter State Constraints Revisited. J. of Logic and Computation, 4 (1994), (to appear)

12. E.Sandewall Filter preferential entailment for the logic of action in almost continuous worlds. Proc. of 11th IJCAI, 1989, 894–899

13. E.Sandewall Features and Fluents: A Systematic Approach to the Representation of Knowledge about Dynamical Systems. Technical Report LiTH-IDA-R-94-15, 1994 (to be published by Oxford Un. Press)

14. F.Lin, Y.Shoham. Concurrent actions in the situation calculus. In: Amer. Assoc. of Artif. Intell., 10th National Conference on Artif. Intell., 1992, v.1, p. 590-595

15. J.McCarthy, P.Hayes Some philosophical problems from the standpoint of artificial intelligence. In: Machine Intelligence, v. 4, (Eds. B.Meltzer and D.Michie), Edinburgh University Press, 1969, p. 463–502

16. J.McCarthy First order theories of individual concepts and propositions. In: Machine Intelligence, v. 9, (Eds. J.E.Hayes, D.Michie, L.I.Mikulich), Chichester, Ellis Horwood Ltd., 1979, p.120–147

17. L.Morgenstern A first order theory of planning, knowledge, and action. In: Theoretial Aspects of Reasoning about Knowledge (Ed. by J.Halpern), Proc. of the conference held March 19–22, 1986, Morgan Kaufmann Publ.

18. R.Reiter The frame problem in the situation calculus: a simple solution (sometimes) and a completeness result for goal regression. In: Artificial Intelligence and Mathematical Theory of Computation: Papers in Honor of John McCarthy, Academic Press, San Diego (CA),1991, 359–380.

19. M.Shanahan E-mail message N frigate.do.395 Date: Wednesday, 20th January 1993, 13:12:01.

20. M.E.Soutchanski, E.A.Ternovskaia Logical theory of concurrent actions. In: Soviet J. of Computer and System Sciences, 1993, vol.31.

21. E.A.Ternovskaia Interval situation calculus. Proc. of the W/Sh 'Logic and Change', held 8th August 1994, during 11th ECAI, 1994, 153–165

22. J.C.Weber On the representation of concurrent actions in the situational calculus. Proc. of the 8th Biennual Confer. of Canadian Society of Computat. Study of Intelligence, Ottava, 22-23 May, 1990, 28-32.

23. M.Wooldridge The logic of an agent-oriented testbed for DAI, (this volume)

24. M.Wooldridge, M.Fisher A first-order branching time logic of multi-agent systems. Proc. of the 10th ECAI, 1992, 234–238.

Simulating Animal Societies with Adaptive Communicating Agents

Geof Staniford[1] and Ray Paton[2]

Department of Computer Science, University of Liverpool,
Chadwick Building, P.O. Box 147, L69 3BX
email: g.staniford@csc.liv.ac.uk
Tel: (+44 51) 794 3695
Fax: (+44 51) 794 3715

Abstract. Animal societies are an excellent source of ideas for studying distributed and emergent computation. These complex systems can be simulated in a number of ways and there is a range of models upon which such simulations can be based. These include both stochastic systems in which large numbers of very simple agents interact and social behaviours emerge and also logic-based systems in which the numbers of interacting units are reduced but the functionality of each individual is increased. This chapter presents an approach for investigating logic-based systems based on the formal specification of communicating agents in a distributed system. The foundations for this model specification methodology are presented and applied to the specific example of honeybee colony defence. The chapter concludes with a discussion of how and where the approach can be applied.

1 Introduction

The work described in this chapter reflects material which we hope can be exploited by biologists and computer scientists. In the former case, an approach to modelling is described which seeks to simplify the interactional complexity of animal societies by focussing on logical abstractions of how the system works. For computer scientists it is a further example of work we have carried out on the application of natural metaphors to computing (Paton *et al*,[21]). We may note that from its early beginnings, developments in computing have been strongly influenced by the biosciences. This can be seen in the work of many pioneers in computing and cybernetics such as: Turing, von Neumann, McCulloch, Pitts, Wiener, Bush and Ashby. Indeed, Herken's book, The Universal Turing Machine A Half-Century Survey[7] may seem an unlikely biology text and yet it shows computing-biology interchanges in at least six chapters - Arbib , Brady, Conrad, Penrose, Rosen and Wiener. This transfer of ideas between biology and computing continues to grow as can be seen is recent publications such as (Forrest,[2] or Paton,[20]). In the study reported here we are using the metaphor of an animal society, specifically a honeybee colony, to investigate the adaptive behaviour of computational agents in a distributed system.

A great need for pluralism in the modelling enterprise persists in the life sciences because of the various levels of organisation and viewpoints on biosystems (Paton[18]). Levins[12] makes it very clear that it is not possible to take account of the complexity of a real world biosystem using a single model. There will always be a pay-off somewhere between realism, generality and precision. Consequently, a number of different modelling strategies are possible. Three general approaches can be described namely, logical, mechanistic and stochastic. Stochastic models very often deal with statistical associations between large numbers of interacting components and are typified by multi-dimensional techniques. The fine details of causal mechanisms are necessarily lost in these models because of the sheer numbers and variations of interactions. Mechanistic models simplify the complexity of biosystems by focussing on particular processes. Logical models tend to be used when an emphasis is to be placed on changes of state within a system and are very useful for exploiting deductive inferences about the general operation of biosystems (Paton[19]). These models range from boolean network descriptions (e.g., Thomas and Thieffry[25]) to verbal models based on production rules (Paton[17]).

The contrast between a stochastic system and a logic-based system is important for the present discussion. In the former case it is possible to construct many simple agents, allow them to interact together and then observe the emergent behaviours (for a review of this approach see Meyer[13]. However, in the latter case the behaviours of real world agents (bees in our study) have already been observed. The purpose of the logic-based models as described below is to provide a framework that accounts for the behaviour of the agent and the society as a whole. In addition it may provide enhancements to our models of distributed computational systems. Collins[1] describes these two approaches as the distinction between the analytical, top-down approach of modelling in biology with the synthetic bottom-up approach of ALife. We contend that both approaches are essential to a proper understanding of animat interactions.

In this chapter we present a computational modelling approach that is particularly appropriate for use with the top-down modelling of the biologist. Section two contains a specification methodology for describing behaviour among coexisting individuals and an architectural model specification that is general and can be adapted to suit many different types of specific agent. Section three illustrates the use of the general models and specifications using a specific example, honeybee colony defence. Section four draws the work presented in the earlier sections together and discusses future directions.

2 Foundations for the Model

In order to model communicating creatures existing and adapting within a dynamic environment, particularly creatures displaying the structural and behavioural complexity of the honeybee, it is necessary to build up complex biosystem models that rely upon well defined computational specifications. In this section we present and describe the definitions which form building blocks for the modelling process.

Genesereth and Nilsson[5] define the architecture of four types of agent, *tropistic, hysteretic, knowledge level and stepped knowledge level*, in order of increasing sophistication and complexity. They then introduce the notion of a deliberate agent which is a stepped knowledge level agent with certain restrictions on its set of actions. These agents are designed to exist in an environment in which they have the sole occupancy. There is no need for them to be aware of nor communicate with others of their kind. Staniford[23] extended the architecture (loquacious tropistic, etc.) to enable agents to coexist, communicate, and cooperate with other agents. We use an extension to the architecture of the loquacious hysteretic agent as the basis upon which to model honeybees. There will no further discussion of the other sorts of agent and the interested reader is referred to the references for a full account.

So that an agent may receive external stimuli we require four functions:

Definition 2.1:

$$see : R \rightarrow S$$

$$feel : R \rightarrow W$$

$$smell : R \rightarrow X$$

$$hear : T \rightarrow Q$$

where the set R is the set of states that characterises the agents world and in order to characterise the agents sensory capabilities we partition the set R of external states into a set S of disjoint subsets (associated with the function *see*) and a set W of disjoint subsets (associated with the function *feel*) and a set X of disjoint subsets (associated with the function *smell*) such that the agent is able to distinguish states in different partitions but is unable to distinguish states in the same partition. The set T is a set of words that characterise communications that the agent may receive from other agents, and similar to the foregoing in order to further characterise the agents sensory capabilities we partition the set T of words into a set Q of disjoint subsets such that the agent is able to distinguish words in different partitions but is unable to distinguish words in the same partition ●

These are sensory functions and are used to characterise the way in which an agent perceives external stimuli. We use *see, feel*, and *smell* to enable an agent to determine the local state of its environment and *hear* to enable the agent to receive oral communications from other agents. It will often be necessary to define agents that carry out an action purely as a result of the influence of one or other of the external stimuli, consequently it seems reasonable to keep all four functions separate.

A valuable simplification in modelling communicating agents is to consider a communication channel to be a one way system that provides a medium for acts of communication to take place, see Milner [15, 16]. We consider an act of communication to be an indivisible event, taking place instantaneously between two or more agents. The adoption of this simplification, for our models, means that if a message has been "sent" by an agent then it has been received by the agent or agents to whom it was sent. Similarly we consider that any local attributes of a state in an environment that an agent can "see" or "feel" will have been perceived by that agent as soon as they become available as a result of some state change within the environment.

Next we need to turn our attention to the manner in which the state of an environment is changed. We assume that agents make local changes to an environment and consider that a state S_n changes to $S_{(n+1)}$ the instant that an agent makes a local change. Agents do not have the power to make global changes in an environment. In order that an agent may make changes we define three more functions:

Definition 2.2:

$$internal : N \times I \times S \times Q \times W \times X \rightarrow I$$

$$action : N \times I \times S \times Q \times W \times X \rightarrow A$$

$$do : A \times R \rightarrow R \times Y$$

where the set I is an arbitrary set of internal states and we assume that the agent can distinguish between all its internal states so that there is no need to partition I. The set Y is a set of words that characterise the communications that an agent may send to another agent. We assume that the agent can distinguish all its responses so there is no need to partition Y. The set N is the set of natural numbers and is used to represent an agents cycle number; ie.: the passage of time internal to an agent. The function *internal* maps an internal state and both types of observation into the next internal state. The function *action* is a discriminatory function which maps the sets of internal states and observations onto a particular action, thus providing an agent with the ability to choose which action to perform according to its internal condition and perceived stimuli. Finally, the function *do* is an executory function which maps an action and state onto the new state and an output; providing the agent with the ability to change the local state of its environment and to communicate a message to another agent ●

Unlike *see*, *feel*, *smell*, and *hear* we encapsulate doing and communicating in one function because although there will be occasions when we wish to communicate without changing a state it will often be the case that the change of state will itself be an act of communication. So, these two operations are closely bound together in order that we may simplify the coordination of the knowledge, between autonomous agents, that environmental state changes have taken place. Note, however, in general the ability to communicate without state changes occurring in the environment is crucial to the notion of societies of cooperating agents.

For our purposes then, acts of observation both visual, tactile, and oral must take place in the internal state of an agent, between changes in state of the external environment. In general there is no simple linear correlation between the internal state changes within an agent and the external state changes of the environment.

Definition 2.3:

An *extended hysteretic agent* in an environment is a tuple of the form

$$< N, I, R, S, T, Q, W, X, Y, A, see, do, hear, feel, smell, internal, action >$$

where the sets and functions are taken to have been defined and described in Definitions: 2.1-2.2

Two important definitions of properties that extended hysteretic agents share with other autonomous agents, namely, *weak* or *observational equivalence* and *strong equivalence*, are complex, protracted and very abstract, see Milner[16]. For reasons of space we content ourselves with a simple explanation tailored to our modelling requirements. Two extended hysteretic agents are observation-ally equivalent if a third external agent cannot distinguish between them from their actions alone. This means that for every possible set of inputs the two agents produce the same set of actions/outputs. There is no requirement that the two agents should pass through the same internal states. Strong equivalence, on the other hand, requires that the inputs, internal states and outputs/actions are indistinguishable. For our purposes, the study of agents in adaptive cooperating social groups, observational equivalence is completely adequate.

The description of the structure of a social grouping involves description of the constituent relationships within it and also descriptions of the meta-relationships that exist Hinde[8]. Hinde divides the structural analyses of groups into two levels, surface structures and more general structure. Surface structure is taken to be a description of the pattern of relationships that describe inter-actions between individuals. This may show idiosyncrasy between individuals in that behavioural differences between individuals may be reflected in the structure. The more general structure is viewed as an abstraction from the surface structures which shows the patterns or regularities of more general relationships across social groupings and neglects the peculiarities of individuals. We need to consider both levels of relationship during the course of designing autonomous agents into societal units. The literature on the structure of social units surveyed in Thompson *et al*[26] shows that there are a number of pervasive models (eg. *hierarchy, market, network*) and workers in the field of distributed autonomous agents are actively engaged in investigating the application and suitability of such models in various projects. In this chapter we consider the specification of animal behaviour using normative decision theory; in particular we are interested in networks of cooperating individuals as the primary mechanism that may be used to impose a social structure upon autonomous agents.

Normative decision theory involves the study and explanation of guidelines for right action; the defence of choice among competing alternatives according to rules that agents ought to follow. The general subject is vast, covering numerous social theories developed over several millennia, Kelsen[11], but computationally tractable theories are beginning to emerge that are suitable for use in multi agent systems, Staniford[23].

In the study of the theory of norms the expression norm is not precisely defined; rule is the nearest English equivalent, however the two words are not synonyms. There are a very wide variety of logical types of rules, not all of which are norms. Norms do, however, form some of the most important kinds of rules such as categorical (action requiring rules) and permissive (action allowing rules). Two key concepts in the explanation of norms are:

- reasons for action,
- restraints upon action.

We find that these can be related together through the logical interaction of various types of norms into a unified system. Underpinning these two important concepts and fundamental to their acceptance by designers is the *principle of autonomy*, Kelsen[11], which can be restated in terms of an agent society as follows:

> The operational (legal) order within an agent system is never created by the individual agent for whom this order is valid but is posited by the systems designer directly, or indirectly, through the dynamic action of an agent whose responsibility it is to create or vary such orders.

Normative (or deontic) logic is a form of philosophical logic that was primarily considered to be relevant as a foundation for law and ethics. Recently the subject has been has been viewed by computer scientists as a form of alethic modal logic that provides an extension over first order predicate logic. Unsurprisingly normative logic was first applied to computer science in the area of legal analysis and legal automation, see for example "Artificial Intelligence and Law" and "Law, Computers and Artificial Intelligence", both journals being founded in 1992. The extension of the use of normative logic outside the domain of Law is very recent indeed and includes intelligent agents in computer supported cooperative work Staniford[23], the specification of fault tolerant systems, the specification of security policies, and the specification of normative integrity constraints for databases, Wieringa and Meyer[28].

In order to develop an autonomous normative system model, suitable for use both in specification and in Prolog implementation, we assume, following the example of Hansson[6], the existence of basis logic (henceforth **BL**); where, in our case, **BL** is the Horn Clause subset of first-order predicate calculus. Note that **BL** is complete in the sense that every valid formula is a theorem and that if it is well known what constitutes a well-formed formula and a theorem of **BL**.

The *logic of normative systems*, developed in Staniford[23] and briefly described here, will be called the *normative logic* (**NL**) and is based upon **BL**.

The meta-variables

f,g,h range over the set of formulae of **BL** . In order to develop **NL** we require three normative operators 'O', 'F', 'P' where the intended readings are:

- 'O' :- 'it is obligatory that'
- 'F' :- 'it is forbidden that'
- 'P' :- 'it is permitted that'

with F defined as $O\neg$ and P defined as: $\neg F$ or $(\neg O\neg)$. Following von Wright[30] the well formed formula of **NL** are called *O-expressions*.

An atomic *O-expression* is the letter '*O*' (or '*F*' or '*P*') followed within brackets, by two variables, or compounds of variables and truth connectives, separated by '/', e.g. '$O(f/g)$', which would be read as: one ought to see to it that f when g. Alternatively to 'when g' it can be read 'if it is the case that g' or 'should it be the case that g'. Note that both f and g refer to states of affairs (or situations within an environment). If, for example, f describes the state of affairs that a returning forager to a honeybee colony performs a tail wagging dance, von Frisch[4] and g describes the contingency that the forager bee's source of supply is further than 100 metres from the nest, then $O(f/g)$ says that the forager ought to perform a tail wagging dance upon return to the nest when the food source is further than 100 metres from the nest. Similarly we see that $F \equiv O\neg(f/g)$ is read as 'one ought not to see to it that f when g'. $P \equiv \neg O\neg(f/g)$ resulting in the clumsy 'not one ought not to see to it that f when g' is better thought of in the original English form 'it is permitted to see to it that f when g'.

The elements within an atomic *O-expression* to the left and right of the '/' within the brackets are schemes for descriptions of two possible generic states of affairs. The description to the left indicates how the world 'ought to be' when it 'is' as the description to the right indicates that it is.

The requirement to maintain the status quo can be expressed as $O(f/f)$, which is a completely meaningful statement in **NL** ; a statement that expresses the duty of an agent to see to it that f is the case when f is the case. It is also meaningful to write $O(f/\neg f)$ which reflects the duty of an agent to change the state of affairs to f whenever it finds that the world is not as it ought to be.

NL has three axioms:

A1: $\neg[O(f/f)O(f/\neg f)O(\neg f/f)O(\neg f/\neg f)]$

A2: $O(fg/h) \Leftrightarrow O(f/h)O(g/h)$

A3: $O(f/gh) \Leftrightarrow O(f/g)O(f/h)$

NL has four rules of inference:

R1: For any variable in an axiom of theorem of the system may be substituted (throughout) another variable or molecular compound of variables.

R2: Modus Ponens

R3: A variable or molecular compound of variables in an axiom of theorem may become replaced by a tautologically equivalent compound of variables.

R4: The *O-expression* which is obtained from a tautology of **BL** by replacing its **BL** variables by *O-expressions* is a theorem.

Axiom A1 says that the four dyadic *O-units* of a normative space determined by a single variable cannot all be conjunctively valid. This principle also follows for the general case of n variables, see Staniford[23] for the proof.

We assume that the variables of **BL** range over the set all elements in a given possible world which comprises the Cartesian product of the set of agents currently being modelled and an *environment* which is a subset of some *Universe* within which the agents exist.

The practical consequence of the foregoing is that in an agent specification the sentences in **NL** must be defined over a non-empty set of sentences in **BL**, Γ say, and each member of Γ must clearly specify the domain of discourse to which it applies.

It is reasonably asserted here, without proof, that **NL** is decidable; see the detailed discussions in von Wright[30] and Hansson[6]. Furthermore it is the case, Staniford[23], that A1-A3, suitably manipulated into clausal form, and R1-R4 will be amenable for implementation using a combination of unification and resolution; hence **NL** whilst being of the utmost importance during specification will also be implementable using Prolog. Many agents have been specified using **NL** , by the primary author, and a model fragment taken from the domain of defence of a honeybee colony is developed in the next section as an illustrative example (based on [3]). A more detailed discussion of this approach as applied to honeybee colony defence can be found in Staniford and Paton[24].

3 Application to an Animal Society

The application of the behavioural and architectural specification methods to particular applications falls into two distinct parts. Normative logic is used to specify desired behaviours, and the agent architecture is fleshed out with implementation level detail in order to provide the computational functionality required.

Normative logic can be used to specify behaviours at different levels of modelling. For example the *O-expression*:

$O(\ internal\_state(\ excited,\ hive\_entrance,\ hive\_centre\ )\ /$
$internal\_state(\ calm,\ hive\_entrance,\ hive\_centre\ )$
$seen(\ darting\_flight\_intruder\ )$
$smelled(\ isopentyl\_acetate(\ Level\ ))$
$isopentyl\_acetate\_level\ <\ alarm\_trigger\_level\ )$

which says that a calm honeybee located at the hive entrance must become excited upon sight of an approaching object with a darting flight when the alarm pheromone isopentyl acetate ($(CH_3)_2CHCH_2CH_2OCOCH_3$) is less than some trigger level. Clearly this specifies the honey-bee's internal behaviour in response to external stimulus and corresponds to the first internal clause of the example Prolog fragment. In a complete specification it would also be necessary to specify the obligatory behaviour in the situation where the alarm pheromone was at a concentration greater than the trigger level.

In contrast the *O-expression*:

$O(\,honeybee(\,attack(\,darting\_flight\_intruder\,))/$
$internal\_state(\,agressive,\ hive\_entrance,\ hive\_centre\,)$
$seen(\,darting\_flight\_intruder\,)$
$smelled(\,isopentyl\_acetate(\,Level\,))$
$isopentyl\_acetate\_level\,>\,alarm\_trigger\_level\,)$

which says that an aggressive honeybee located at the hive entrance is obliged to attack an intruder displaying the characteristic darting flight pattern when the external pheromone stimulus is at a sufficient excitation level. Such an *O-expression* is quite clearly referring to a complex operation that will need to be carried out using such activities as *flying, fighting, stinging, dying,* etc. see the definition of the set *A* below.

The architectural model of an extended hysteretic agent specified in Definition 2.3 is flexible, providing considerable generality. Specificity, in order to model particular animals, is achieved when the various functions and sets contained within the model are instantiated. In this section we consider instantiating the model with particular reference to the adaptive behaviour of honeybee colonies when faced with potential intruders to the colony hive. In order to keep the explanation within reasonable bounds we will ignore the functions *feel* and *hear* (of Definition 2.1.) in the following exposition and concentrate primarily upon the interplay between the functions *internal* and *action* of Definition 2.2. This discussion represents a fragment of the complete model which may be found in Staniford and Paton x.

The functions *see* and *smell* operate independently of, and concurrently with, both themselves and other functions within the agent model. For the purposes of this particular agent we consider that the functions *internal, action,* and *do* are linked sequentially in a temporal ordering.

The internal honeybee data structures are encapsulated in the set *I* of internal states and a simplified definition for the purpose of explanation is:

$$internal\_state \equiv I \stackrel{def}{=} \left\{ \begin{array}{c} current\_disposition \\ actual\_orientation \\ reference\_orientation \end{array} \right\}$$

where each internal state is itself represented by a set eg:

$$current\_disposition \stackrel{def}{=} \left\{ \begin{array}{c} calm \\ aggressive \\ excited \end{array} \right\}$$

$$actual\_orientation \stackrel{def}{=} \{\,coordinates\,\}$$

$$reference\_orientation \stackrel{def}{=} \{\,coordinates\,\}$$

The set A of actions which characterise current activity and is partially defined by:

$$activity \equiv A \stackrel{def}{=} \left\{ \begin{array}{l} threatening \\ patrolling \\ inspecting \\ feeding \\ flying \\ walking \\ resting \\ fighting \\ stinging \\ dying \\ landing \\ turning \\ taking\_off \end{array} \right\}$$

In order to fully characterise the honey-bee's internal functions, with respect purely to the present study, we would require the internal function to be defined using twelve Prolog clauses. We consider two clauses that are of particular interest.

```
/* Note the current values for N,I,S,Q,W,X, and A are stored */
/* and accessed via the Prolog database the functions see, */
/* feel, smell, and hear operate concurrently. In this */
/* example, for simplicity, we ignore feel and hear */
```

internal :-

```
    internal_state(calm,hive_entrance,hive_centre),
    seen("darting flight intruder"),
    smelled(isopentyl_acetate(Level)),
    alarm_level(Alarm),
    Level < Alarm,
    retract(internal_state(calm,hive_entrance,hive_centre)),
    assert(internal_state(excited,hive_entrance,hive_centre)),
    action .
```

internal :-

```
    internal_state(excited,hive_entrance,hive_centre),
    seen("darting flight intruder"),
    smelled(isopentyl_acetate(Level)),
```

```
    alarm_level(Alarm),
    Level >= Alarm,
    retract(internal_state(excited,hive_entrance,hive_centre)),
    assert(internal_state(aggressive,hive_entrance,hive_centre)),
    action .
```

The action of the first clause was described earlier with reference to *O-expressions*. This clause provides a good example of the transition from specification to executable code when using a form of logic for both specification and programming. The second clause describes the agent continuing with an increasing level of internal excitement as the external level of alarm pheromone is increased.

The action clauses,similar to the internal clauses above,represent a small subset of the complete range of clauses required. The first action clause presents the most complex structure of all the action clauses and contains within itself calls to two other clauses: choose_action/1 and new_action/1,see below.

```
action :-

    internal_state(calm,hive_entrance,hive_centre),
    seen("normal flight intruder"),
    action(walking),
    choose_action(Action),
    new_action(Action),
    do .

choose_action(Action) :-

    random(X),
    smelled(isopentyl_acetate(Level)),
    Y is X + Level * Genetic_Constant,
    Y < 0.33 - > Action = flying ;
    Y < 0.66 - > Action = walking ;
    Y >= 0.66 - > Action = patrolling .

new_action(New_Action).

    retract(action(_Old_Action)),
    assert(action(New_Action)) .
    do .
```

This set of clauses illustrate the behavioural choice mechanism that operates when a honeybee in a calm state enters the hive entrance area from within the hive. There are three choices of behaviour allowed,flying,walking,and patrolling. When zero isopentyl acetate is detected then a honeybee,in this particular example,has a 0.33 probability of choosing one of the three actions. As the pheromone level increases the probability of choosing,first flying and then walking is successively reduced and at the same time the probability of becoming a guard bee is successively increased. The size of the genetic constant has a considerable bearing upon the collective behaviour of honeybee agents and would be small when modelling less aggressive bees,Italian bees say,and rather larger when modelling more aggressive bees,African bees say.

action :-

```
internal_state(calm,hive_entrance,hive_centre),
seen("darting flight intruder"),
action(patrolling),
smelled(isopentyl_acetate(Level)),
trigger_level(Trigger),
Level < Trigger,
retract(action(patrolling)),
assert(action(threatening)) .
do .
```

action :-

```
internal_state(excited,hive_entrance,hive_centre),
seen("darting flight intruder"),
action(threatening),
trigger_level(Trigger),
Level < Trigger,
retract(action(threatening)),
assert(action(threatening + isopentyl_acetate release)) .
do .
```

action :-

```
internal_state(aggressive,hive_entrance,hive_centre),
seen("darting flight intruder"),
action("threatening + isopentyl_acetate release"),
trigger_level(Trigger),
Level >= Trigger,
retract(action(threatening + isopentyl_acetate release)),
assert(action(fighting + isopentyl_acetate release)) .
do .
```

The final three clauses of *action*, illustrate the change in behaviour of a guard bee in the presence of an intruder. First from patrolling to threatening, then from threatening to threatening coupled with pheromone release, and finally to attacking the intruder. This corresponds closely to the description of the behaviour of honeybees given in Frisch[4].

It will be appreciated that the individual honeybee behaviour outlined in this model has direct consequences upon the collective behaviour of other bees in the hive entrance area. The release of isopentyl acetate by guard bees causes other bees to change their behaviour and provides both an individual and collective positive feedback behavioural excitation loop while the stimulus of the presence of an intruder is detected. This mechanism provides a relatively simple method of modelling the honeybee colony adapting their behaviour in a cooperative manner in response to a perceived danger to the hive. There has not been space to show the mechanism for allowing the excitation to decay once the stimulus has been removed.

In this model there are five parameters that can be adjusted to give a very wide variation of individual and collective behaviour patterns: the two intermediate relative probability levels and genetic constant (in choose_action/1), the alarm trigger level in internal/0, and the action trigger level in action/0. These levels may be changed by the experimenter before a program run which is the way that the work has been carried out so far. It would be possible for simulations to be designed in which one or more of these levels could be evolved over generations of honeybees using some computational simulation of an evolution mechanism.

4 Concluding Remarks

We have described a method for modelling interactions between agents based on a logical framework. This has enabled us to described behaviour at several levels of abstraction in a manner that is susceptible to the use of formal reasoning techniques. There are a number of ways in which this kind of approach can benefit biology and computing including:

- The facilitation of the transfer of biological metaphors into the computing domains of distributed artificial intelligence and intelligent cooperative information systems.
- We have a formal specification language for characterising agents and environments. This means that the models developed have great generality and power. They are independent of particular machine architectures and particular programming paradigms.
- The biological source ideas can assist our understanding of the ecology of computation. This approach views distributed systems as ecologies in which there is communication, cooperation and competition between components (Huberman,[9]). Taking a biological viewpoint on distributed systems can shift the focus away from central control, synchronoy and rigid hierarchical structures to more dynamic network thinking (see Kelly,[10]). In the example discussed in this chapter we have focussed on co-operative effects among communicating agents but it would also be possible to apply the modelling approach to other social activities including competition, selection and resourcing.
- The framework is very general. For example the agents discussed in this chapter have been characterised by logical functions. However, it would also be perfectly appropriate to implement some of the functions using a connectionist system such as an ANN or classifier system. In this way we have a means of hybridising both behaviour and knowledge based components.

Clearly, we have mentioned only one case study (colony defence in honeybees) but we anticipate that the approach will be applicable to the modelling and subsequent simulation of animal and human societies. However, we would also wish to point out that a plurality of modelling approaches is advocated in the elucidation of these dynamic systems.

The type of normative logic used in the model in this chapter is based upon a relatively early form of such logics and there are a number of well documented problems associated with them, Meyer and Wieringa[14], in the form of derivable paradoxes. The approach to these problems adopted in this work, described earlier in Staniford[23], is essentially based upon such problems being considered the designers/programmers responsibility to deal with possible occurrences by forseeing them in advance and treating them as special cases (a method commonly used in rule based artificial intelligence work, cf. natural language processing). An interesting line of investigation for possible improvement to this approach has been proposed in Wieringa and Meyer[27] based upon work in Wieringa *et al.*[29] and we intend to investigate translating this approach from the field of the specification of actors to the specification of autonomous agents operating within an environment. It is intended that the work should be set in the context of several domains, not just the context of biological models.

References

1. Collins R. : Artificial Evolution and the Paradox of Sex. in Paton R.C. (ed) Computing with Biological Metaphors London, Chapman and Hall. (in press)
2. Forrest, S. (ed) : Emergent Computation. Cambridge, MA MIT Press. (1991)
3. Free J.B.: The Social Organisation of Honeybees London, Arnold. (1977)
4. Frisch K. von : Bees: Their Vision Chemical Senses and Language. New York, Cornell University Press and London, Jonathon Cape. (1950)
5. Genesereth M. R. Nilsson N. J.: Logical Foundations of Artificial Intelligence. Morgan Kaufman Inc., Los Altos California. (1987)
6. Hansson B.: An Analysis of Some Deontic Logics. in R. Hilpinen (Ed) Deontic Logic: Introductory and Systematic Readings. Holland, D. Reidel(1971) 121–147.
7. Herken, R. (ed): The Universal Turing Machine A Half-Century Survey Oxford, University Press. (1988)
8. Hinde R. A. : Individuals Relationships and Culture: Links between Ethology the Social Sciences. Cambridge, University Press. (1987)
9. Huberman, B.A. : The Ecology of Computation. in Paton ed Computing with Biological Metaphors. London, Chapman and Hall. (1994)
10. Kelly, K. : Out of Control The New Biology of Machines. London, Fourth Estate (1994)
11. Kelsen H. : General Theory of Norms. Oxford, Clarendon Press. (1991)
12. Levins R. : Complex Systems. in Waddington C.H. (ed) Towards a Theoretical Biology. Edinburgh: University Press. (1970)
13. Meyer, J-A and Guillot, A. : From SAB90 to SAB94: Four Years of Animat Research. in Cliff, Husbands, Meyer and Wilson (eds) From Animals to Animats 3. Cambridge, MA MIT Press. (in press)

14. Meyer, J.-J.CH., and Wieringa,R.J., : Deontic Logic: A Concise Overview. in Meyer, J.-J.CH., and Wieringa,R.J. (Eds) Deontic Logic in Computer Science: Normative System Specification. John Wiley and Sons Ltd., (1993)

15. Milner R. : A Calculus of Communicating Systems. Lecture Notes in Computer Science. Springer-Verlag **92**. (1980)

16. Milner R. : Communication and Concurrency. Prentice Hall International (UK) Ltd. (1989)

17. Paton R.C. : Students Deductive Reasoning about State Changes in a Model Biosystem. Journal of Biological Education. **252** 129–135. (1991)

18. Paton R.C.: Towards a Metaphorical Biology. Biology and Philosophy **7** 279–294. (1992)

19. Paton R.C. : On an Apparently Simple Modelling Problem in Biology. to appear in International Journal of Science Education. (forthcoming)

20. Paton, R. C. (ed): Computing with Biological Metaphors. London, Chapman and Hall. (1994)

21. Paton R.C. Nwana H.S Shave M.J.R. and Bench-Capon T.J.M.and Hughes S. : Transfer of Natural Metaphors to Parallel Problem Solving Applications. in Schwefel H-P. and Maenner R.(eds) Parallel Problem Solving from Nature Lecture Notes in Computer Science Springer: Berlin. (1991)

22. Snyers D. , Thayse A. : Languages and Logics. in A. Thayse (Ed) From Modal Logic to Deductive Databases. Wiley Chichester England 1-54. (1989)

23. Staniford G. : Multi Agent Systems in Support of Cooperative Authorship. Unpublished PhD Thesis, University of Liverpool United Kingdom. (1993)

24. Staniford G. and Paton R.C. : Adaptive Simulation with Communicating Agents. Unpublished Technical Report No. 93 12 1. The Liverpool Biocomputation Group. Dept. Computer Science University of Liverpool. (1993)

25. Thomas R. and Thieffry D. Developing a Logical Tool to Analyse Biological Regulatory Networks in Paton R.C. (ed) Computing with Biological Metaphors London: Chapman and Hall. (in press)

26. Thompson G., Frances J., Levacic R. and Mitchell J. Markets Hierarchies and Networks. Sage Publications Ltd. in assoc. with the Open University London. (1991)

27. Wieringa,R.J. and Meyer, J.-J.CH., : Actors, Actions, and initiatives in normative system specification. Technical Report IR-257, Faculty of Mathematics and Computer Science, Vjrie Universitat, Amsterdam. (1991)

28. Wieringa,R.J. and Meyer, J.-J.CH., : Applications of Deontic Logic in Computer Science: A Concise Overview. in Meyer, J.-J.CH., and Wieringa,R.J. (Eds) Deontic Logic in Computer Science: Normative System Specification. John Wiley and Sons Ltd., (1993)

29. Wieringa,R.J., Meyer, J.-J.CH., and H. Wegand. : Specifying Dynamic and Deontic Integrity Constraints. Data and Knowledge Engineering, (4) pp157-189, (1989)

30. Wright G. H. von : Deontic Logic Mind **60** 1-15. (1951)

This is MyWorld:
The Logic of an Agent-Oriented DAI Testbed

Michael Wooldridge

Department of Computing, Manchester Metropolitan University
Chester Street, Manchester M1 5GD, United Kingdom

M.Wooldridge@doc.mmu.ac.uk

Abstract. The ultimate goal of the work presented in this article is to develop practical frameworks for formally reasoning about multi-agent systems. Such frameworks are particularly important, as multi-agent approaches are inherently complex, and are already being applied in safety-critical domains such as air traffic control. The article is in three parts. The first contains an informal overview of MyWorld, a testbed for experimentation in Distributed Artificial Intelligence (DAI). A MyWorld system contains a number of concurrently executing agents, each of which is programmed along the lines proposed by Shoham in his Agent-Oriented Programming (AOP) proposal [22]. The second part of the article contains a detailed formal model of MyWorld, which rigorously defines the possible states and state transitions of MyWorld agents. The third part develops a logic that can be used to represent the properties of MyWorld systems; this logic is closely related to the formal model of MyWorld, in that the histories traced out in the execution of a system are used as the semantic basis for the logic. We comment on the applications of the logic, and conclude by indicating areas for future work.

1 Introduction

One area of much current interest in DAI is the use of mathematical logic for specifying the properties of agents and multi-agent systems. Probably the best-known example of this work is the Cohen-Levesque theory of intention [3]. To express this theory, the authors developed a quantified multi-modal logic, with modalities for representing beliefs and goals, and an apparatus for representing actions that was loosely based on dynamic logic [13]; beliefs and goals were characterised using possible worlds semantics [12]. Various concepts were then defined in a layered fashion, each layer building on the concepts introduced at the previous layer, until intention was introduced. The result was a theory that satisfies many of the properties that one would expect of intention, and which is also *formal*, with all the attendant advantages that rigour and formality bring. Building largely on this work, attempts have been made to use similar logics to capture various other properties of agents [18] and multi-agent systems [24].

Although this work is undoubtedly significant, it is important to realise what its limitations are. Agent theories expressed in a modal logic with possible worlds semantics can only serve as specifications in a very abstract sense; they cannot, in general, be refined into implementations in the conventional way[1]. There are several reasons for

---

[1] A notable exception is the *situated automata* paradigm [20].

this. First, there is no clear relationship between the logic used to express the specific-ation, and the structure of (D)AI systems as they are typically built. In particular, it is not generally clear what possible worlds might correspond to in an implemented sys-tem. Secondly, such logics make unreasonable assumptions about the reasoning ability of agents: this is the logical omniscience problem [15]. For these reasons, we have proposed developing formalisms for reasoning about multi-agent systems where a pre-cise relationship is maintained between the specification language and the systems we ultimately hope to build [23]. The technique depends on borrowing some ideas from mainstream computer science [16]. Specifically, we construct a formal model of the type of system we wish to reason about, and then use the execution histories traced out by such a system as the semantic foundation for a temporal logic, which can then be used to reason about the systems we are modelling. Since there is a precise relationship between the logic and the systems the logic is modelling, we can realistically claim that statements in the logic actually express properties of the systems we hope to model.

In this article, we demonstrate this approach by applying it to MYWORLD, an im-plemented testbed for DAI. A MYWORLD system contains a number of concurrently executing agents, each of which is programmed along the lines proposed by Shoham for his *agent-oriented programming* proposal [22]. Agents are given intentions and be-liefs, and rules that define how they should generate and modify them. Additionally, they are given rules that represent information about how to achieve intentions; to achieve an intention, an agent must typically perform some actions. In the next sec-tion, we present a more detailed review of MYWORLD; this is followed, in section 3, by a formal model of MYWORLD agents and systems. In section 4, we present a logic called $\mathcal{L}_M$ (for MYWORLD logic), which can be used to represent and reason about the properties of MYWORLD systems. The logic extends classical first-order logic with the introduction of modalities for representing the beliefs, intentions, and actions of agents, as well as temporal modal connectives for representing the time-varying properties of MYWORLD systems. The article concludes with some comments on limitations of the work presented, and issues for future work.

Related work: Surprisingly few attempts have been made by researchers within (D)AI to develop formal models of real agents and multi-agent systems (although, as we ob-served above, many *abstract* models have been proposed [3, 18, 24]). Genesereth and Nilsson develop simple models of various classes of agents in [9, Chapter 13], though these models are also very abstract. Seel developed formal models of simple reactive agents, and investigated the use of temporal logics for reasoning about them [21]. The Z language has been used in a number of agent specifications: Goodwin used it to develop formal models various types of agents, and used these models to characterise various attributes of agency (such as capability, reactivity, rationality, and so on) [11]; a 240-page formal specification of the SOAR cognitive architecture has also been developed in Z [17]; and Craig has used Z to specify his CASSANDRA blackboard model [4]. Finally, in some work closely related to this article, Rao and Georgeff have considered the ex-tent to which agents can be said to satisfy theories of agency [19]. However, they use a theory of agency expressed in a modal logic of beliefs, desires, and intentions, with a possible worlds semantics: such a logic is ultimately unsatisfactory for specifying agents, for the reasons we outlined above.

Notational conventions: Most of the formalism in the article is presented using the VDM specification language: the first eight chapters of [14] cover the relevant material. Additionally, if $\mathcal{L}$ is a logical language, then we write $Form(\mathcal{L})$ for the set of (well-formed) formulae of $\mathcal{L}$.

2 A Glimpse of MYWORLD

This section contains an informal overview of MYWORLD, adapted from [26]. At run-time, a MYWORLD system has four components:

- an *umpire*, or *world manager*, which has top-level control of the system;
- an *agent-oriented* language, for programming agents;
- a *world shell*, which defines the characteristics of an experimental 'world'; and
- a *scenario*, which represents a particular experiment.

The umpire is the part of MYWORLD that has overall, top-level control of the system. Amongst other things, it is responsible for scheduling agent execution, monitoring the user interface, and responding to requests from the latter. The umpire is the 'generic' part of MYWORLD, and was designed to allow as much flexibility and generality as possible. However, it was found necessary to build certain basic principles into it, the most important of which being the notions of animate and inanimate objects (animate objects being agents), time, space, events, and actions.

The world shell is the part of MYWORLD that defines the environmental characteristics of a particular 'world' in which experiments may be performed. For example, the world shell defines what actions may be performed in an experiment, when such actions are legal, and what the results of an action performed in some particular situation are. Additionally, it defines what entities may appear in the world, and what their properties are. At the time of writing, we have implemented just one world shell; in future, we hope to construct a library of such shells, to allow experimentation in a variety of domains.

A scenario in MYWORLD represents a specific experiment carried out. It describes the initial locations and properties of all the entities that appear in the experiment.

For the purposes of this article, the most important component of MYWORLD is the agent-oriented part, for programming agents. This language characterises an agent in terms of five attributes: (i) a set of *beliefs*; (ii) a set of *intentions*; (iii) a set of *belief rules*; (iv) a set of *intention adoption rules*; and finally (v) a *belief revision function*. These components, and the way that they interact to generate the behaviour of an agent, will now be described in more detail.

Beliefs: An agent's beliefs represent that agent's information about the world it occupies: in more traditional AI terms, an agent's beliefs are its 'knowledge'. In the current implementation of MYWORLD, an agent's beliefs are a set of ground atoms of first-order predicate logic (cf. PROLOG facts).

Belief sets are not fixed: they may change over time, by new beliefs being added and old beliefs being removed. New beliefs arise from three sources:

- from inferences made via *belief rules*;
- from perceiving the world; and
- from performing non-logical 'cognitive', or 'private' actions.

Belief rules define how new beliefs are generated from old ones. A belief rule corresponds closely to a rule in the standard AI sense: it has antecedent and consequent parts, and will 'fire' if the antecedent unifies with the agent's belief set. In the current implementation, belief rules are applied exhaustively, in a forward chaining fashion, to generate new beliefs.

Perception is modelled by a *belief revision function* (cf. [8]). This function looks at the state of the system and the agent's current beliefs, and generates a new set of beliefs as a result. Old beliefs may also be removed by a belief revision function.

Finally, cognitive, or private actions, correspond to an agent exploiting its internal computational resources. For example, imagine an agent consulting an internal database; this would be an action that was not visible to other agents — hence the term 'cognitive' action. The result of such an action would be some information, which appears in the form of new beliefs.

Intentions: Intentions represent desires that an agent will attempt to bring about. An intention contains a *goal* part, a *motivation* part, and a *rating* part. The goal represents the 'purpose' of the intention — if it is ever believed to be satisfied, then the intention is fulfilled. The motivation represents what must be believed in order for the intention to be maintained — if the motivation ever becomes false, then there is no point in maintaining the intention, and it is dropped. So an intention will be maintained until either its goal is believed to be satisfied or its motivation is no longer present[2]. The *rating* of an intention represents its priority; the higher the rating, the more important the intention. The highest rated intention is called the *current* intention, and will guide the actions of the agent, in a way that we describe below.

New intentions are generated via intention adoption rules (IARs). An IAR is a pair, containing:

- an *adoption condition*; and
- an *intention skeleton* (an intention containing variables).

The idea is that on every cycle, the agent tries to match the adoption condition of each IAR with its beliefs; if it succeeds, then the variables in the corresponding intention skeleton are instantiated, and the resulting intention is added to its intention set.

Strategy rules: Intentions are linked to actions by *strategy rules*. Strategy rules represent information about how to achieve intentions. A strategy rule is a pair, consisting of:

---

[2] This is very close to what Cohen and Levesque call a *persistent relativised goal* [3].

- a *condition*, corresponding to the goal of an intention;
- a *strategy function*, which takes as its sole argument the state of the agent, and returns an action, that the agent has chosen to perform.

Strategy rules loosely resemble knowledge areas in the PRS [10]. Strategy functions are the closest that agents in MYWORLD come to doing any planning; they may be thought of as crude procedural plans.

Agent execution: Let us now summarise the behaviour of an agent on a single scheduler cycle:

1. update beliefs through belief revision function; apply belief rules exhaustively;
2. update intentions by:
   - removing those that are no longer applicable; and
   - finding and adding those that have now become applicable;
3. find the highest rated intention and use strategy rules in order to find a strategy function;
4. evaluate the strategy function in order to find some action;
5. execute the action that results.

3   A Formal Model of MYWORLD

In this section, we construct a formal model of MYWORLD, focussing particularly on the agent-language component. In section 4, we use this formal model as the foundation upon which to construct a logic for representing and reasoning about the properties of MYWORLD systems.

Beliefs and belief rules: In the current implementation of MYWORLD, beliefs are simply *ground atoms* of first-order logic: beliefs are thus similar to PROLOG facts. To represent beliefs, we require a set of *terms*, made up of a set of *constants* and a set of *variables*. We also require a set of *predicate symbols*.

$$Const = \{a, b, c, ...\} \qquad Var = \{x, y, z, ...\}$$

$$Term = Const \cup Var \qquad Pred = \{P, Q, ...\}$$

Notice that the only functional terms allowed are constants. An *atom* is an application of a predicate symbol, (called the *head* of the atom), to a list of terms.

$$Atom :: \quad head : Pred$$
$$term\text{-}list : Term^*$$

A function *at-vars* is defined, which takes an atom and returns the set of variables it contains.

$$at\text{-}vars : Atom \to Var\text{-set}$$

$$at\text{-}vars(mk\text{-}Atom(P, tl)) \quad \triangleq \quad Var \cap elems\, tl$$

A *ground* atom is one containing no variables.

$$GAtom = Atom \quad \text{where} \quad \text{inv-}GAtom(at) \triangleq \text{at-vars}(at) = \{\,\}$$

The set of possible beliefs is defined to be the set of ground atoms.

$$Bel = GAtom$$

Agents are able to reason by applying *belief rules* to their belief set. Conceptually, a belief rule corresponds to a first-order formula of the form

$$\forall \bar{x} \cdot \varphi(\bar{x}, \bar{a}) \Rightarrow \psi(\bar{y}, \bar{b})$$

where $\bar{x} = x_1, \ldots, x_m$ and $\bar{y} = y_1, \ldots, y_n$ are tuples of variables, such that $\{y_1, \ldots, y_n\} \subseteq \{x_1, \ldots, x_m\}$, $\bar{a} = a_1, \ldots, a_o$ and $\bar{b} = b_1, \ldots, b_p$ are tuples of constants, and $\varphi(\bar{x}, \bar{a})$ and $\psi(\bar{y}, \bar{b})$ are conditions. Note that variables in the consequent must appear in the antecedent. This form of rule is, of course, very similar to that which appears throughout AI; the way in which such a rule may be applied is obvious. For simplicity, we shall assume that conditions may contain only conjunctions; we do not consider disjunctions or negations. This relieves us of the need to deal with issues such as negation as failure, which would otherwise obscure more important points. We define a type for conditions.

$$Cond = Atom^*$$

A condition is thus a sequence of predicates, representing their conjunction. The function *at-vars* is extended to conditions, so that *vars* takes a condition and returns the set of variables it contains.

$$vars : Cond \rightarrow Var\text{-set}$$

$$vars(c) \quad \triangle \quad \bigcup \{at\text{-}vars(at) \mid at \in \text{elems}\, c\}$$

Antecedents and consequents are then simply conditions; a belief rule is a pair containing an antecedent and a consequent, with the restriction on variables as above.

$$BelRule :: \quad ante : Cond$$
$$conse : Cond$$
$$\text{inv}\,(mk\text{-}BelRule(an, cn)) \triangleq vars(cn) \subseteq vars(an)$$

The applicability of a belief rule with respect to a set of beliefs is determined by unification of the antecedent in the belief set; as we have no functional terms other than constants, unification is a straightforward process. First, a *binding* is defined to be a map from variables to constants.

$$Binding = Var \xrightarrow{m} Const$$

Next, a function *at-apply* is defined, which applies a binding to an atom: the function returns the atom that results from replacing all variables with the constant they are bound to.

$at\text{-}apply : Binding \times Atom \rightarrow Atom$

$at\text{-}apply(\beta, at) \quad \triangle$
    let $tl = term\text{-}list(at)$ in
    let $tl' = \{n \mapsto a \mid (n \in \text{inds}\, tl) \wedge (tl(n) = x) \wedge (x \in Var) \wedge (\beta(x) = a)\}$ in
    let $tl'' = tl \dagger tl'$ in
    $\mu(at, term\text{-}list \mapsto tl'')$

The function *at-unifiers* takes a belief set and an atom, and returns that set of bindings which, when applied to the atom, yield members of the belief set.

$at\text{-}unifiers : Atom \times Bel\text{-set} \rightarrow Binding\text{-set}$

$at\text{-}unifiers(at, bs) \quad \triangle \quad \{\beta \mid (\beta \in Binding) \wedge (at\text{-}apply(\beta, at) \in bs)\}$

The function *at-apply* is extended to the function *apply*, which applies a binding to a condition.

$apply : Binding \times Cond \rightarrow Cond$

$apply(\beta, c) \quad \triangle \quad \{n \mapsto at\text{-}apply(\beta, c(n)) \mid n \in \text{inds}\, c\}$

The function *unifiers* is a similar extension of *at-unifiers*.

$unifiers : Cond \times Bel\text{-set} \rightarrow Binding\text{-set}$

$unifiers(c, bs) \quad \triangle \quad \bigcap\{at\text{-}unifiers(at, bs) \mid at \in \text{elems}\, c\}$

It is convenient to define a boolean-valued function *fires*, which takes a condition and a belief set, and returns true iff the condition is satisfied by the belief set.

$fires : Cond \times Bel\text{-set} \rightarrow \mathbb{B}$

$fires(c, bs) \quad \triangle \quad unifiers(c, bs) \neq \{\ \}$

The function *fire-belrule* takes a belief rule and a set of beliefs, and returns the set of beliefs that results from firing the rule. If the rule cannot fire, then the function returns the empty set.

$fire\text{-}belrule : BelRule \times Bel\text{-set} \rightarrow Bel\text{-set}$

$fire\text{-}belrule(br, bs) \quad \triangle$
    $\bigcup\{\text{elems}\, apply(\beta, conse(br)) \mid \beta \in unifiers(ante(br))\}$

Finally, a function *close* is defined, which returns the closure of a belief set under some belief rules; that is, it returns the belief set that results from exhaustively applying the rules to the belief set. Note that the definition of *close* makes use of an auxilliary function *close-aux*.

$close\text{-}aux : \mathbb{N} \times BelRule\text{-set} \times Bel\text{-set} \rightarrow Bel\text{-set}$

$close\text{-}aux(u, brs, bs) \quad \triangle$
    if $u = 0$
    then $\{at \mid \exists br \in brs \cdot at \in fire\text{-}belrule(br, bs)\}$
    else $\{at \mid \exists br \in brs \cdot at \in fire\text{-}belrule(br, close\text{-}aux(u - 1, brs, bs))\}$

$$close : BelRule\text{-set} \times Bel\text{-set} \rightarrow Bel\text{-set}$$

$$close(brs, bs) \quad \triangleq \quad \bigcup \{close\text{-}aux(u, brs, bs) \mid u \in \mathbb{N}\}$$

Finally, we look at belief revision. In MYWORLD, a belief revision function maps an environment state and a belief set into a new belief set; the type *Env*, for environment state, is defined later.

$$BRF = Env \times Bel\text{-set} \rightarrow Bel\text{-set}$$

Intentions and intention adoption rules: An intention is a triple, containing: (i) a *goal* part; (ii) a *motivation* part; and (iii) a *rating*. The goal represents what the agent would believe if the intention was satisfied; the motivation represents what must be believed by the agent in order for the intention to be maintained; and the rating represents how important the intention is considered to be. We begin by defining *intention skeletons*. An intention skeleton is essentially an intention that can have a variable for a rating.

$$
\begin{array}{rl}
IntSk :: & goal : Cond \\
& motivation : Cond \\
& rating : \mathbb{N} \cup Var
\end{array}
$$

An intention is then an intention skeleton that does not have a variable for a rating.

$$Int = IntSk \quad \text{where} \quad inv\text{-}Int(mk\text{-}Int(g, m, r)) \triangleq r \notin Var$$

Note that variables may appear in the goal or motivation parts of an intention, in which case they are considered to be existentially quantified. An *intention adoption rule* is a pair, consisting of an intention skeleton and an adoption condition.

$$
\begin{array}{rl}
IARule :: & adcond : Cond \\
& intsk : IntSk
\end{array}
$$

$$inv\ (mk\text{-}IARule(c, mk\text{-}IntSk(g, m, r))) \triangleq r \in Var \Rightarrow r \in vars(c)$$

The invariant on *IARule* ensures that if the rating part of the skeleton is a variable, then it is one of the variables that occurs in the adoption condition. Thus, when the rule fires, this variable will be instantiated. The function *iar-apply* takes an intention adoption rule and a binding, and returns the intention that results from applying the binding to all variables that occur in the intention skeleton.

$$iar\text{-}apply : Binding \times IARule \rightarrow Int$$

$$iar\text{-}apply(\beta, iar) \quad \triangleq$$
$$\quad \text{let } g = goal(intsk(iar)) \text{ in}$$
$$\quad \text{let } m = motivation(intsk(iar)) \text{ in}$$
$$\quad \text{let } r = rating(intsk(iar)) \text{ in}$$
$$\quad \text{let } r' = \text{if } in \in Var \text{ then } \beta(r) \text{ else } r$$
$$\quad mk\text{-}Int(apply(\beta, g), apply(\beta, m), r')$$

The function *fire-iarule* takes an intention adoption rule and a belief set, and returns the set of intentions made current by the rule. Once again, the applicability of the rule is determined by unification in the belief set. Note that if the rule cannot fire, then this function returns the empty set.

$$fire\text{-}iarule : IARule \times Bel\text{-set} \to Int\text{-set}$$

$$fire\text{-}iarule(iar, bs) \quad \triangleq \quad \{iar\text{-}apply(\beta, iar) \mid \beta \in unifiers(adcond(iar), bs)\}$$

The boolean-valued function *satisfied-int* takes an intention and a belief set, and returns true iff the intention is satisfied with respect to the belief set.

$$satisfied\text{-}int : Int \times Bel\text{-set} \to \mathbb{B}$$

$$satisfied\text{-}int(int, bs) \quad \triangleq \quad fires(goal(int), bs)$$

The boolean-valued function *applicable-int* takes an intention and a belief set, and returns true iff the intention is still applicable with respect to the belief set, i.e., if the motivation is still present.

$$applicable\text{-}int : Int \times Bel\text{-set} \to \mathbb{B}$$

$$applicable\text{-}int(int, bs) \quad \triangleq \quad fires(motivation(int), bs)$$

The function *update-intentions* takes a set of intentions, (representing those currently held by an agent), a set of beliefs, (also representing those currently held by the agent), and a set of intention adoption rules, and returns the set that results by removing those that are no longer applicable, or that are satisfied, and adding those that have become applicable.

$$update\text{-}intentions : Int\text{-set} \times Bel\text{-set} \times IARule\text{-set} \to Int\text{-set}$$

$update\text{-}intentions(ints, bs, iars) \quad \triangleq$
    let $sat = \{int \mid (int \in ints) \land satisfied\text{-}int(int, bs)\}$ in
    let $inap = \{int \mid (int \in ints) \land \neg applicable\text{-}int(int, bs)\}$ in
    let $new = \bigcup \{fire\text{-}iarule(iar, bs) \mid iar \in iars\}$ in
    let $ints' = (ints - (sat \cup inap)) \cup new$ in
    let $sat' = \{int \mid (int \in ints') \land satisfied\text{-}int(int, bs)\}$ in
    let $inap' = \{int \mid (int \in ints') \land \neg applicable\text{-}int(int, bs)\}$ in
    $ints' - (sat' \cup inap')$

This function ensures that newly adopted intentions will be consistent with an agent's beliefs: intentions will not be adopted if they are believed to be satisfied, or if there is no motivation for them. Finally, the function *highest-rated* takes a set of intentions, representing those currently held by an agent, and returns the highest rated of these.

$highest\text{-}rated$ $(ints : Int\text{-set})$ $int : Int$

pre $ints \neq \{\}$

post $int \in ints \land \neg (\exists int' \in ints \cdot rating(int') > rating(int))$

Strategy rules: A strategy rule represents information about how to achieve intentions. In the current implementation, a strategy rule has a *condition* part and a *strategy function* part. A strategy function is best thought of as a kind of procedural plan, that operates on an agent's internal state to generate an *action*, representing that which the agent has chosen to perform. The condition part of a strategy rule determines the circumstances under which the associated strategy is applicable.

$$Ac = \ldots$$

$$Strat = Bel\text{-set} \times Int\text{-set} \to Ac$$

$$StratRule :: cond : Cond$$
$$strat : Strat$$

(The content of the set Ac, of actions, is not significant.) We shall demand that an agent's set of strategy rules is *strongly complete*, in the sense that, for any given set of beliefs, they are guaranteed to pick out precisely one strategy function[3]. This ensures that an agent is never uncertain about which strategy function to apply. This notion of strong completeness is formalised in the following boolean-valued function.

$$strongly\text{-}complete : StratRule\text{-set} \to \mathbb{B}$$

$$strongly\text{-}complete(srs) \;\;\triangle\;\; \forall bs \in Bel\text{-set} \cdot \exists ! \, sr \in srs \cdot fires(cond(sr), bs)$$

The function *chosen-strategy* takes a strategy rule set and a set of beliefs, and returns the strategy picked out by the rule set.

$$chosen\text{-}strategy \; (srs: StratRule\text{-set}, bs: Bel\text{-set}) \, st: Strat$$
pre $strongly\text{-}complete(srs)$
post $\exists str \in srs \cdot fires(cond(str), bs) \land (strat(str) = st)$

Agents and agent operation: We now have all the definitions required to introduce a type for agents.

$$Agent :: bel : Bel\text{-set}$$
$$int : Int\text{-set}$$
$$br : BelRule\text{-set}$$
$$iar : IARule\text{-set}$$
$$sr : StratRule\text{-set}$$
$$brf : BRF$$
inv $(mk\text{-}Agent(bs, ints, brs, iars, srs, brf)) \triangle$
$\quad strongly\text{-}complete(srs) \land$
$\quad \forall int \in ints \cdot applicable\text{-}int(int, bs) \land \neg \, satisfied\text{-}int(int, bs)$

The second invariant ensures that the agent's intentions are consistent with its beliefs.

Next, we define a next-state function for agents. This function captures the idea of an agent observing its environment, and updating its beliefs on the basis of its observations, applying its belief rules where possible, and then updating its intentions in light of its new beliefs. (The type Env, for environment state, is defined below.)

---

[3] *Weak* completeness would mean that the rules picked out *at least one* action [23].

$$agent\text{-}next\text{-}state : Agent \times Env \rightarrow Agent$$

$$agent\text{-}next\text{-}state(mk\text{-}Agent(bs, ints, brs, iars, srs, brf), env) \quad \triangle$$
$$\text{let } bs' = brf(env, bs) \text{ in}$$
$$\text{let } bs'' = close(bs', brs) \text{ in}$$
$$\text{let } ints' = update\text{-}intentions(ints, bs'', iars) \text{ in}$$
$$mk\text{-}Agent(bs'', ints', brs, iars, srs, brf)$$

Finally, we define a function *chosen-action*, which takes an agent and returns the action that the agent has chosen to perform.

$$chosen\text{-}action : Agent \rightarrow Ac$$

$$chosen\text{-}action(mk\text{-}Agent(bs, ints, brs, iars, srs, brf)) \quad \triangle$$
$$chosen\text{-}strategy(srs, bs)(bs, ints)$$

Systems: A MYWORLD system may be regarded as containing a set of named entities, which fall into two categories: inanimate entities, or *objects*, which have *attributes*, but do not have any internal structure and are not able to change the state of the system, and agents. The idea is that objects correspond to chairs, books, pints of beer, pieces of string, and so on: things which do not originate actions, but rather have actions performed on them. Agents are things that originate actions. We require types for attributes and names.

$$Attribute = \ldots \qquad Name = \ldots$$

(The content of these two sets is not significant.) The state of a MYWORLD system at some point during execution may then be characterised by two maps, which associate names with attributes and agents respectively. A value of this type represents a 'snapshot' of a MYWORLD system during execution. We introduce a separate type for environment state, which represents the state of every object in the system.

$$Env = Name \xrightarrow{m} Attribute\text{-set}$$

$$Sys :: objects : Env$$
$$agents : Name \xrightarrow{m} Agent$$

Finally, we model a world shell as a function that takes an action and an environment state, and returns the returns the environment state that results from the attempted performance of the action. Such a function represents the 'natural laws' of an experimental world, and the environmental constraints that hold in it.

$$World = Ac \times Env \rightarrow Env$$

Note that this definition implicitly assumes that agents are not directly affected by the performance of an action.

4 The Logic of MYWORLD

In this section, we develop the logic $\mathcal{L}_M$, which can be used to represent the properties of MYWORLD systems. $\mathcal{L}_M$ is closely related to the formal model of MYWORLD that we constructed in the preceding section: we use the *histories* traced out in the execution of a system as its semantic basis. Although this technique has long been used in mainstream computer science [16], it has only recently been applied in DAI [23]. This earlier work made two limiting assumptions. First, a very simple model of agents was used. Secondly, it was assumed that agents act in *synchrony*, rather than *concurrently*. In developing $\mathcal{L}_M$, we make no such assumptions: $\mathcal{L}_M$ is based on a more realistic model of both agents and their execution.

Semantic concepts: We begin by setting the scene with a short discussion on agent execution. Consider the behaviour of an agent during a single scheduler cycle. It begins by perceiving its environment, updating its beliefs through its belief revision function, then updating its intentions, and so on, until finally, it executes an action. A direct attempt to model this behaviour would lead us to a number of difficulties. For example, what are an agent's beliefs while it is applying its belief rules? What action is it performing during this time? To avoid such problems, we assume that agents update their internal state *instantaneously* at the beginning of a scheduler cycle, and spend the rest of that cycle with fixed beliefs and intentions, performing their chosen action. The results of an action are assumed to come into effect at the end of the cycle. Finally, we shall also assume that once an agent's scheduler cycle is complete, it immediately begins another, without any pause.

Before developing the structures used to represent execution histories, we must fix on a model of time. We choose to let time be *linear*, (i.e., there is only one 'timeline'), *bounded in the past* (i.e., there was a time at which system execution began), and *infinite in the future*, (i.e., the system is non-terminating). Unusually, we also choose to let time be *dense*, meaning that for any two time points, it is possible to find a third between them. A convenient temporal model is thus $(\mathbb{R}^+, <)$, i.e., the positive reals ordered by the less-than relation. The reason for fixing on such a model is that it allows us to represent 'real' concurrency with comparative ease [2]. The use of the temporal logic of reals for modelling the behaviour of a group of agents was first proposed by Fisher, who used the technique to give a semantics to his Concurrent METATEM language [5].

We now introduce the technical apparatus for dealing with time. An *interval* over $\mathbb{R}^+$ between $x, y \in \mathbb{R}^+$, where $x < y$, is the subset of $\mathbb{R}^+$ that falls between x and y.

$$interval : \mathbb{R}^+ \times \mathbb{R}^+ \to \mathbb{R}^+\text{-set}$$

$$interval(x, y) \quad \triangleq \quad \{z \mid (z \in \mathbb{R}^+) \wedge (x \leq z < y)\}$$

The set of all intervals is *Interval*.

$$Interval = \{interval(x, y) \mid (x, y \in \mathbb{R}^+) \wedge (x < y)\}$$

We assume two functions *start* and *end*, which give the start and end points of an interval, respectively — their formal definitions are trivial, and are therefore omitted. To represent execution histories, we essentially use functions that map times to the state of the entity they are modelling. The first such function is *os*, which gives the state of every object in the system.

$$os: \mathbb{R}^+ \to Env$$

To model the time-varying state of agents, we use two functions. The first, *cycle*, takes an agent name and a scheduler cycle number, and gives that interval of that cycle. Note that scheduler cycles are indexed by the natural numbers, and we thus assume that each agent has a countably infinite number of such cycles; this is a kind of (rather extreme) *fairness* assumption [7].

$$cycle: Name \times \mathbb{N} \to Interval$$

The second, *as*, takes a time and returns a map that gives the state of every agent at that time.

$$as: \mathbb{R}^+ \to (Name \xrightarrow{m} Agent)$$

Unfortunately, the situation is complicated by the fact that various relationships exist between the entities in a system. For example, once an agent performs an action, we expect the effects of that action to be reflected in the subsequent state of the system. To capture these relationships, we place a number of constraints on the functions representing execution histories.

Constraint 1: An agent's scheduler cycles meet each other [1]. For example, if an agent's first cycle extends from t to t', and its second extends from t'' to t''', then $t' = t''$. Formally, this constraint is expressed as follows.

$$\forall i \in Name \cdot \forall u \in \mathbb{N} \cdot end(cycle(i, u)) = start(cycle(i, u + 1))$$

Constraint 2: Every agent's state is fixed within its scheduler cycles.

$$\forall i \in Name \cdot \forall u \in \mathbb{N} \cdot cycle(i, u) = \iota \Rightarrow \forall x, y \in \iota \cdot as(x)(i) = as(y)(i)$$

Constraint 3: The end point of every scheduler cycle is unique.

$$\forall i, j \in Name \cdot (i \neq j) \Rightarrow \forall u, v \in \mathbb{N} \cdot end(cycle(i, u)) \neq end(cycle(j, v))$$

Constraint 4: An agent's internal state during a cycle is a result of perceiving the world at the beginning of that cycle.

$$\forall i \in Name \cdot$$
$$\forall u \in \mathbb{N}_1 \cdot$$
$$\text{let } \iota = cycle(i, u - 1) \text{ in}$$
$$\text{let } \iota' = cycle(i, u) \text{ in}$$
$$\text{let } prev\text{-}ag\text{-}st = as(start(\iota)) \text{ in}$$
$$\text{let } cur\text{-}ag\text{-}st = as(start(\iota')) \text{ in}$$
$$\text{let } cur\text{-}obj\text{-}st = os(start(\iota')) \text{ in}$$
$$cur\text{-}ag\text{-}st(i) = agent\text{-}next\text{-}state(prev\text{-}ag\text{-}st(i), cur\text{-}obj\text{-}st)$$

Constraint 5: Actions have effects: they change the state of the system in which they are executed. Recall from the preceding section that the effect an action has on a system is determined by a world function. Also, we assumed that an action only achieves its effects at the end of a cycle, at which time the system instantaneously changes state. This leads to the following constraint, which can only be expressed with respect to some world function $\omega \in World$.

$\langle fmla \rangle ::= \langle \mathcal{L}_0\text{-}fmla \rangle$	$\mid \forall \langle var \rangle \cdot \langle fmla \rangle$
$\mid \neg \langle fmla \rangle$	$\mid \langle fmla \rangle \vee \langle fmla \rangle$
$\mid \langle fmla \rangle \, \mathcal{U} \, \langle fmla \rangle$	$\mid \langle fmla \rangle \, \mathcal{S} \, \langle fmla \rangle$
$\mid (\text{Bel } \langle name \rangle \langle \mathcal{L}_0\text{-}fmla \rangle)$	$\mid (\text{Intend } \langle name \rangle \langle \mathcal{L}_0\text{-}fmla \rangle \langle \mathcal{L}_0\text{-}fmla \rangle \langle nn \rangle)$
$\mid (\text{Do } \langle name \rangle \langle ac \rangle)$	

Fig. 1. Syntax of $\mathcal{L}_M$

$\forall i \in Name \cdot$
$\quad \forall u \in \mathbb{N}_1 \cdot$
$\qquad \text{let } \iota = cycle(i, u - 1) \text{ in}$
$\qquad \text{let } \iota' = cycle(i, u) \text{ in}$
$\qquad \text{let } prev\text{-}obj\text{-}st = os(\max \iota) \text{ in}$
$\qquad \text{let } cur\text{-}obj\text{-}st = os(start(\iota')) \text{ in}$
$\qquad \text{let } prev\text{-}ag\text{-}st = as(start(\iota))(i) \text{ in}$
$\qquad \text{let } \alpha = chosen\text{-}action(prev\text{-}ag\text{-}st) \text{ in}$
$\qquad cur\text{-}obj\text{-}st = \omega(\alpha, prev\text{-}obj\text{-}st)$

There are other constraints that we might wish to place on these functions. For example, we might specify that the system remains unchanged except for the performance of actions within it. However, we shall leave such refinements for future work.

Syntax: $\mathcal{L}_M$ is a *quantified multi-modal* logic. It extends classical first-order logic by the introduction of a set of temporal modal connectives for representing the time-varying properties of MYWORLD systems, as well as three further connectives, for representing the *beliefs*, *intentions*, and *actions* of agents within a system. For convenience, we shall assume an underlying classical first-order logic $\mathcal{L}_0$, defined over the sets *Pred* of predicate symbols, *Var* of variable symbols, and *Const* of constant symbols (see section 3). The syntax of the logic is defined by the grammar in Figure 1. The terminal symbols, other than literals, that appear in this grammar are interpreted as follows: $\langle \mathcal{L}_0\text{-}fmla \rangle \in Form(\mathcal{L}_0)$, $\langle var \rangle \in Var$, $\langle name \rangle \in Name$, $\langle nn \rangle \in \mathbb{N}$, and $\langle ac \rangle \in Ac$.

The temporal connectives $\mathcal{U}$ and $\mathcal{S}$ are called *until* and *since*, respectively. The other modal connectives, Bel, Intend, and Do, are for representing the beliefs, intentions and actions of agents, respectively. The classical connectives $\vee$ and $\neg$ have their standard interpretation, as does the universal quantifier $\forall$; the existential quantifier and the remaining connectives of classical logic are introduced as abbreviations, in the standard way.

Semantics: The semantics of $\mathcal{L}_M$-formulae are defined by a set of semantic rules, each of the form $\mathcal{I} \models \varphi$, where $\mathcal{I}$ is an *interpretation structure* and φ is a formula. Such an expression means that the structure $\mathcal{I}$ satisfies φ; the symbol '$\models$' is called the *satisfaction relation*. For $\mathcal{L}_M$, interpretation structures are triples of the form $\langle M, \beta, t \rangle$, where M is a

$$
\begin{array}{ll}
\langle M, \beta, t \rangle \models P(\tau_1, \ldots, \tau_n) & \text{iff } \textit{at-apply}(\beta, \textit{mk-Atom}(P, [\tau_1, \ldots, \tau_n])) \in \\
& \quad \pi(\textit{mk-Sys}(\textit{os}(t), \textit{as}(t))) \\
\langle M, \beta, t \rangle \models \neg \varphi & \text{iff } \langle M, \beta, t \rangle \not\models \varphi \\
\langle M, \beta, t \rangle \models \varphi \vee \psi & \text{iff } \langle M, \beta, t \rangle \models \varphi \text{ or } \langle M, \beta, t \rangle \models \psi \\
\langle M, \beta, t \rangle \models \forall x \cdot \varphi & \text{iff } \langle M, \beta \dagger \{x \mapsto a\}, t \rangle \models \varphi \text{ for all } a \in \textit{Const} \\
\langle M, \beta, t \rangle \models \varphi \mathcal{U} \psi & \text{iff } \exists t' \in \mathbb{R}^+ \text{ s.t. } (t < t') \text{ and } \langle M, \beta, t' \rangle \models \psi \text{ and} \\
& \quad \forall t'' \in \mathbb{R}^+ \text{ if } (t < t'' < t'), \text{ then } \langle M, \beta, t'' \rangle \models \varphi \\
\langle M, \beta, t \rangle \models \varphi \mathcal{S} \psi & \text{iff } \exists t' \in \mathbb{R}^+ \text{ s.t. } (t' < t) \text{ and } \langle M, \beta, t' \rangle \models \psi \text{ and} \\
& \quad \forall t'' \in \mathbb{R}^+ \text{ if } (t' < t'' < t), \text{ then } \langle M, \beta, t'' \rangle \models \varphi \\
\langle M, \beta, t \rangle \models (\textsf{Bel } i \, \varphi) & \text{iff } \textit{apply}(\beta, \varphi) \in \textit{bel}(\textit{as}(t)(i)) \cup \textit{br}(\textit{as}(t)(i)) \\
\langle M, \beta, t \rangle \models (\textsf{Intend } i \, \varphi \, \psi \, n) & \text{iff } \textit{mk-Int}(\textit{apply}(\beta, \varphi), \textit{apply}(\beta, \psi), n) \in \textit{int}(\textit{as}(t)(i)) \\
\langle M, \beta, t \rangle \models (\textsf{Do } i \, \alpha) & \text{iff } \alpha = \textit{chosen-action}(\textit{as}(t)(i))
\end{array}
$$

Fig. 2. Semantics of $\mathcal{L}_M$

logical model for $\mathcal{L}_M$, $\beta \in \textit{Binding}$ is a binding, and $t \in \mathbb{R}^+$ is a *reference time*. Logical models for $\mathcal{L}_M$ are themselves structures, which have the form:

$$M = \langle \textit{os}, \textit{as}, \textit{cycle}, \pi \rangle$$

where *os*, *as*, and *cycle* are functions with constraints (1)–(4) holding between them as defined earlier, and

$$\pi : \textit{Sys} \to \textit{GAtom}\text{-set}$$

is an interpretation function, which takes a system and returns the set of ground atoms that represent the properties of, and relationships between, the various objects in that system[4]. The semantics of $\mathcal{L}_M$ are given in Figure 2. Note that the rules make use of various auxiliary functions (such as *apply*) that we defined in section 3. These functions are syntactic abbreviations: they serve only to simplify the statement of the formal semantics, and play no other part in the interpretation process.

Note that world functions do not appear in logical models. If we have a model M and world $\omega \in \textit{World}$ such that the components of M satisfy Constraint 5 with respect to ω, then we say that M satisfies the laws of the world ω, and write M_ω to indicate this.

We now discuss the non-standard connectives of $\mathcal{L}_M$. First, the temporal modal connectives. A formula $\varphi \mathcal{U} \psi$ means that at some time in the future, ψ is satisfied, and *until* then, φ is satisfied. A formula $\varphi \mathcal{S} \psi$ means that ψ was satisfied at some time in the past, and *since* that time, φ has been satisfied. Using just these two connectives, we may define the remaining connectives of linear temporal logic (notice, however, that as time is *dense*, there is no *next time* connective in $\mathcal{L}_M$). First, $\Diamond \varphi$ means that either now or at some time in the future, φ is satisfied; $\square \varphi$ means that φ is satisfied now and at all future times. We can define these connectives as follows:

---

[4] If we were defining the semantics of, for example, first-order logic, then we would make π a function that gave the extension of each predicate symbol.

$$\Diamond \varphi \triangleq \text{true}\, \mathcal{U} \,\varphi \qquad \Box \varphi \triangleq \neg \Diamond \neg \varphi.$$

(In the first of these definitions, true is any classical tautology.) Just as the $\mathcal{S}$ connective mirrors the behaviour of $\mathcal{U}$ in the past, so we can define two unary connectives, ◆ and ■, that mirror the behaviour of $\Diamond$ and $\Box$ in the past (we omit the formal definitions, as these are very similar to those for $\Diamond$ and $\Box$).

We also have a *weak* version of the $\mathcal{U}$ connective: $\mathcal{W}$ allows for the possibility that its second argument is never satisfied.

$$\varphi \,\mathcal{W}\, \psi \triangleq \varphi \,\mathcal{U}\, \psi \vee \Box \varphi$$

A past time version of the $\mathcal{W}$ connective is $\mathcal{Z}$ ('zince').

Turning to the connectives for representing the properties of agents, a formula (Bel i φ) means that the agent i believes φ. In the current implementation, this means that either φ is one of the facts present in i's belief set, or φ is one of i's belief rules. A formula (Intend i φ ψ n) means that i intends to achieve φ with respect to motivation ψ and rating $n \in \mathbb{N}$. A formula (Do i α) means that i is doing action α.

Finally, note that we have simplified the formal semantics in a number of ways. First, we indicate that (Bel i φ) is satisfied if the $\mathcal{L}_0$ formula φ is present in i's belief set or belief rule-set. In the formal model of MYWORLD that we developed earlier, the element's of an agent's belief set are defined to be VDM structures representing formulae, rather than formulae themselves. However, the meaning should be clear. Similar comments apply to the Intend connective. We have also assumed that the function *apply*, (which applies a binding to a condition), has been extended to arbitrary $\mathcal{L}_0$-formulae.

Properties: The temporal fragment of $\mathcal{L}_M$ inherits the expected properties of its underlying Temporal Logic of Reals — an axiomatization is given in [2]. In addition to these, there are a number of axioms relating to the agent part of $\mathcal{L}_M$[5]. By knowing what the beliefs, intentions, and various rule-sets of an agent are, these axioms allow us to derive a set of formulae that capture many of the properties of that agent. These formulae are called the *theory* of the agent: the systematic derivation of such a theory is the first step on the road to formally verifying the properties of the agent, and the system to which it belongs. We comment briefly on specification and verification below.

First, we have an axiom which tells us that agents apply belief rules exhaustively. Suppose φ, ψ, φ', and ψ' are $\mathcal{L}_0$-formulae, and $\exists \beta \in Binding$ such that $apply(\beta, \varphi) = \varphi'$ and $apply(\beta, \psi) = \psi'$. Then the following axiom is sound:

$$\vdash ((\text{Bel}\, i\, \varphi \Rightarrow \psi) \wedge (\text{Bel}\, i\, \varphi')) \Rightarrow (\text{Bel}\, i\, \psi'). \qquad (A1)$$

Axiom $(A2)$ tells us about the adoption of intentions via IARs. Suppose φ, ψ, χ, φ', ψ', and χ' are $\mathcal{L}_0$-formulae, and $\exists \beta \in Binding$ such that $apply(\beta, \varphi) = \varphi'$, ..., and $apply(\beta, \chi) = \chi'$. Then if agent i has an IAR with adoption condition φ, goal ψ, motivation χ, and rating n, then $(A2)$ will correctly describe i:

$$\vdash (\text{Bel}\, i\, \varphi') \Rightarrow (\text{Intend}\, i\, \psi'\, \chi'\, n). \qquad (A2)$$

---

[5] We shall not present formal proofs of these axioms, as they are all immediate from the model given in the preceding section.

Note that it is much simpler to actually use axioms $(A1)$ and $(A2)$ than it is to state them formally!

There are a number of other axioms that capture properties of intentions. Axiom $(A3)$ tells us that once an agent has adopted an intention, it keeps it until either it is believed to be satisfied, or its motivation is no longer believed to be present.

$$\vdash (\text{Intend } i\ \varphi\ \psi\ n) \Rightarrow \begin{bmatrix} (\text{Intend } i\ \varphi\ \psi\ n) \\ \mathcal{U} \\ (\text{Bel } i\ \varphi) \vee \neg (\text{Bel } i\ \psi) \end{bmatrix} \tag{A3}$$

Axioms $(A4)$ and $(A5)$ tell us that an agent's intentions are consistent with it's beliefs.

$$\vdash (\text{Intend } i\ \varphi\ \psi\ n) \Rightarrow \neg (\text{Bel } i\ \varphi) \tag{A4}$$
$$\vdash (\text{Intend } i\ \varphi\ \psi\ n) \Rightarrow (\text{Bel } i\ \psi) \tag{A5}$$

It is interesting to compare $(A3)$–$(A5)$ with those axioms considered by researchers developing abstract theories of intention [3, 18]. For example, $(A3)$ captures the important properties of *persistent relativised goals*, as defined by Cohen-Levesque [3, pp254–255]; the only significant property they lack is that according to the Cohen-Levesque theory, an agent will drop a persistent relativised goal if it believes that it can never be achieved. MYWORLD agents are not (yet!) capable of such reasoning.

Reasoning about MYWORLD systems: The issues surrounding the use of logics like $\mathcal{L}_M$ to reason about DAI systems are considered at length in [23], and more briefly in [6, 25]; they will not, therefore, be discussed again here. Instead, we simply note that $\mathcal{L}_M$ can be used in both the specification and verification of MYWORLD systems. A specification S is given as a set of $\mathcal{L}_M$-formulae; any system whose execution histories all satisfy the formulae is considered to satisfy the specification. For verification, one attempts to derive the theory T of a particular system, using axioms like $(A1)$–$(A5)$, above, and show via formal proof that the specification follows from the theory, i.e., that $T \vdash S$. Although specification is a straightforward process, verification is generally considered much more difficult; it is particularly awkward when one uses complex logics like $\mathcal{L}_M$, for which automated theorem proving tools are not likely to become available in the near future.

5 Concluding Remarks

In this article, we hope to have demonstrated two points: (i) that it is both possible and desirable to develop rigorous formal models of implemented multi-agent systems; and (ii) that it is possible to use such formal models in the development of more abstract formalisms for reasoning about implemented multi-agent systems. In future, we hope to extend the work presented in this article in a number of ways. First, MYWORLD agents, as described in this article, have a very simple structure — we are currently reimplementing the system to provide a more powerful agent language. The formal model will need to be redeveloped when this work is complete. Secondly, the axiomatization given in section 4 is not *complete*, in that there are properties of MYWORLD systems that we cannot prove using it. In particular, the relationship between intention and action needs further study.

References

1. J. F. Allen. Towards a general theory of action and time. *Artificial Intelligence*, 23(2):123–154, 1984.

2. H. Barringer, R. Kuiper, and A. Pnueli. A really abstract concurrent model and its temporal logic. In *Proceedings of the Thirteenth ACM Symposium on the Principles of Programming Languages*, pages 173–183, 1986.

3. P. R. Cohen and H. J. Levesque. Intention is choice with commitment. *Artificial Intelligence*, 42:213–261, 1990.

4. I. Craig. *Formal Specification of Advanced AI Architectures*. Ellis Horwood: Chichester, England, 1991.

5. M. Fisher. Towards a semantics for Concurrent METATEM. In M. Fisher and R. Owens, editors, *Executable Modal and Temporal Logics*. Springer-Verlag: Heidelberg, Germany, 1995.

6. M. Fisher and M. Wooldridge. Specifying and verifying distributed intelligent systems. In M. Filgueiras and L. Damas, editors, *Progress in Artificial Intelligence — Sixth Portuguese Conference on Artificial Intelligence (LNAI Volume 727)*, pages 13–28. Springer-Verlag: Heidelberg, Germany, October 1993.

7. N. Francez. *Fairness*. Springer-Verlag: Heidelberg, Germany, 1986.

8. P. Gärdenfors. *Knowledge in Flux*. The MIT Press: Cambridge, MA, 1988.

9. M. R. Genesereth and N. Nilsson. *Logical Foundations of Artificial Intelligence*. Morgan Kaufmann Publishers: San Mateo, CA, 1987.

10. M. P. Georgeff and A. L. Lansky. Reactive reasoning and planning. In *Proceedings of the Sixth National Conference on Artificial Intelligence (AAAI-87)*, pages 677–682, Seattle, WA, 1987.

11. R. Goodwin. Formalizing properties of agents. Technical Report CMU–CS–93–159, School of Computer Science, Carnegie-Mellon University, Pittsburgh, PA, May 1993.

12. J. Y. Halpern and Y. Moses. A guide to completeness and complexity for modal logics of knowledge and belief. *Artificial Intelligence*, 54:319–379, 1992.

13. D. Harel. Dynamic logic. In D. Gabbay and F. Guenther, editors, *Handbook of Philosophical Logic Volume II — Extensions of Classical Logic*, pages 497–604. D. Reidel Publishing Company: Dordrecht, The Netherlands, 1984. (Synthese library Volume 164).

14. C. B. Jones. *Systematic Software Development using VDM (second edition)*. Prentice Hall, 1990.

15. K. Konolige. *A Deduction Model of Belief*. Pitman Publishing: London and Morgan Kaufmann: San Mateo, CA, 1986.

16. Z. Manna and A. Pnueli. *The Temporal Logic of Reactive and Concurrent Systems*. Springer-Verlag: Heidelberg, Germany, 1992.

17. B. G. Milnes. A specification of the Soar cognitive architecture in Z. Technical Report CMU–CS–92–169, School of Computer Science, Carnegie-Mellon University, Pittsburgh, PA, August 1992.

18. A. S. Rao and M. P. Georgeff. Modeling rational agents within a BDI-architecture. In R. Fikes and E. Sandewall, editors, *Proceedings of Knowledge Representation and Reasoning (KR&R-91)*, pages 473–484. Morgan Kaufmann Publishers: San Mateo, CA, April 1991.

19. A. S. Rao and M. P. Georgeff. An abstract architecture for rational agents. In C. Rich, W. Swartout, and B. Nebel, editors, *Proceedings of Knowledge Representation and Reasoning (KR&R-92)*, pages 439–449, 1992.

20. S. Rosenschein and L. P. Kaelbling. The synthesis of digital machines with provable epistemic properties. In J. Y. Halpern, editor, *Proceedings of the 1986 Conference on Theoretical Aspects of Reasoning About Knowledge*, pages 83–98. Morgan Kaufmann Publishers: San Mateo, CA, 1986.

21. N. Seel. *Agent Theories and Architectures*. PhD thesis, Surrey University, Guildford, UK, 1989.

22. Y. Shoham. Agent-oriented programming. *Artificial Intelligence*, 60(1):51–92, 1993.

23. M. Wooldridge. *The Logical Modelling of Computational Multi-Agent Systems*. PhD thesis, Department of Computation, UMIST, Manchester, UK, October 1992. (Also available as Technical Report MMU–DOC–94–01, Department of Computing, Manchester Metropolitan University, Chester St., Manchester, UK).

24. M. Wooldridge. Coherent social action. In *Proceedings of the Eleventh European Conference on Artificial Intelligence (ECAI-94)*, pages 279–283, Amsterdam, The Netherlands, 1994.

25. M. Wooldridge. Temporal belief logics for modelling distributed artificial intelligence systems. In G. M. P. O'Hare and N. R. Jennings, editors, *Foundations of Distributed Artificial Intelligence*. John Wiley & Sons: Chichester, England, 1995. (To appear).

26. M. Wooldridge and D. Vandekerckhove. MYWORLD: An agent-oriented testbed for distributed artificial intelligence. In S. M. Deen, editor, *Proceedings of the 1993 Workshop on Cooperating Knowledge Based Systems (CKBS-93)*, pages 263–274. DAKE Centre, University of Keele, UK, 1994.

A Knowledge Level Characterisation of Multi-Agent Systems

J. Stuart Aitken[1], Franz Schmalhofer[1] and Nigel Shadbolt[2] *

[1] German Research Center for Artificial Intelligence (DFKI),
P.O. Box 2080, D 67608 Kaiserslautern, Germany email:
aitken,schmalho@dfki.uni-kl.de Phone: (49)0631 205 3439
[2] Department of Psychology, University of Nottingham,
University Park, Nottingham NG7 2RD, England
email: nrs@psyc.nott.ac.uk

Abstract. This paper presents a knowledge-based analysis of a number of multi-agent systems. The analysis is based on the knowledge level hypothesis of Newell and Clancey. We claim that the models of problem solving which we obtain constitute descriptions of global coherence in multi-agent systems. We contrast the results of this analysis with the conventional views of coherence.

1 Introduction

One objective in the design of multi-agent systems (MAS) is for an agent to coordinate its actions with other agents in a coherent way. The concept of coherence has been studied both formally [24] [11] [26] and empirically [1]. In this paper we propose a knowledge-based analysis of coherence in distributed systems in which the resulting models can be formally specified.

The formal approaches typically combine two intentional attitudes: an information attitude and a pro-attitude (a definition of these terms and an introduction to the various formal approaches can be found in the review chapter of this volume). There are two objectives in the formal specification of multi-agent systems. Firstly, formalisation increases our understanding of multi-agent interactions by making intuitive concepts such as *common knowledge* and *group intention* more precise and revealing new relationships between them. Secondly, the ability to verify the behaviour of a real multi-agent system requires the existence of a formal model against which it can be compared. Achieving the second objective also entails being able to describe existing MAS in terms of the language and concepts of the formalism, this, however, can be problematic. One example is the concept of common knowledge [11] which can be shown to be prerequisite for agreement among agents, but which defines a situation which cannot be achieved in practice. [3]

---

* This work was supported by DAAD Stipendium number 513 009 0293 at the DFKI, Kaiserslautern, Germany
[3] A modified concept of common knowledge can be achieved by real systems, for a fuller discussion see [11]

An empirical analysis [1] of existing multi-agent systems concludes that coherence has a number of dimensions including solution quality and efficiency.
The efficiency or minimality of the multi-agent solution is also emphasised in
[26], and the *sharing of pro-attitudes* (goals, plans etc.) specified in some formal
models can be compared with the mechanism of meta-level communication found
in a number of implemented systems. Relating the formal models of coherence
to the empirical analysis in a rigorous way is task which, in many cases, has yet
to be undertaken. A number of criticism of the empirical approach are developed
later in this paper, however, we share the objectives of Bond and Gasser [1] in
that we aim to gain a better understanding of existing distributed AI systems.

This paper presents an analysis of multi-agent systems which attempts to
clarify the concept of global coherence from the knowledge-based perspective.
The analysis is based on the knowledge level hypothesis. The central feature of
knowledge level (KL) characterisations is their focus on rational activity based
on a functional notion of knowledge. This provides the theoretical background
which we use to characterise a number of existing systems, and specifies an approach which abstracts away from implementational details to show the essential
problem solving actions of the distributed system. While the resulting characterisations are generic, they can easily be related to the information states of the
agent system and therefore this approach bridges the gap between theory and
practice. We believe that our analysis increases our understanding of existing
DAI systems and that it will aid the design of future, more capable, systems and
encourage the reuse of models of multi-agent problem solving.

The knowledge level analysis is presented in Section 2. We first describe the
KL hypothesis as proposed by Allen Newell [19], and discuss the modified KL
theory proposed by William Clancey [3]. A logical notation for the knowledge
level is introduced. The methodology is applied in Section 3 to a number of DAI
systems whose architecture is currently influential. In Section 3.4 a conventional
DAI description of the concept of global coherence is presented, analysed and
contrasted with the knowledge level view. In Section 4 we discuss some related
work and some conclusions are drawn in Section 5.

2 The Knowledge Level Analysis

This section restates the knowledge level hypothesis, highlighting the concept of
agency in Newell's and Clancey's theories [19][3]. Subsequently, some notation
is defined for the purpose of formalising knowledge level characterisations.

2.1 The knowledge level hypothesis

The knowledge level is defined by Newell [19] as a computer systems level lying
immediately above the symbol level. This level is characterised by knowledge
as the medium and the principle of rationality as the law of behaviour. Newell
refers to the notion of agency in the definition of the principle of rationality:
"If an agent has knowledge that one of its actions will lead to one of its goals

then the agent will select that action". The concept of an agent also appears in Newell's definition of knowledge: "Knowledge. Whatever can be ascribed to an agent, such that its behaviour can be computed according to the principle of rationality.". The concept of an agent is a simple one: "an agent is composed of a set of actions, a set of goals and a body". An agent is then a delimited computational process to which we can ascribe goals, knowledge and actions. For Newell, agency, rational behaviour and knowledge are bound together.

In contrast with previous analyses of computer systems, the knowledge level hypothesis focuses on the knowledge that can be attributed to a rational agent from the point of view of an observer [3]. A knowledge level characterisation is an abstraction made by an observer and hence is radically different from characterisations based on architectural considerations (e.g. those of DAI). It has been noted [3] that a knowledge level characterisation cannot be objective as we must (as the theoretician-observer) consider the intensions of the observer who makes the KL characterisation.

2.2 Clancey's redefinition of the knowledge level

In [3] Clancey modifies the definition of the knowledge level, he views it as a characterisation of a system of agents and not of an isolated agent.

"A KL description is about a situated system, not an agent in isolation. That is, the systems level being described is above that of individual agents. Therefore, a knowledge-level description cannot be identified with (isomorphically mapped to) something pre-existing inside an individual head, but rather concerns *patterns that emerge in interactions the agent has in some (social) world.*

...A KL description is always ascribed by some observer, and so is relative to the observer's frame of reference and is inherently subjective."[3]

This paper adopts Clancey's view of the knowledge level as an ascribed and idealised description of the rational behaviour of a system of (possibly) many agents. In contrast with Newell's definition, this alternative statement takes a more 'elevated' view of the world where agents are now symbol level entities.

The two versions of the knowledge level hypothesis are valuable for explaining different phemomena: the actions of an agent with respect to its knowledge and goals - in the case of Newell's definition, and the behaviour of a system of agents in the case of Clancey's definition.

As yet we have not defined exactly what is represented at the knowledge level. We propose that knowledge in the form of a specific method of problem solving, specified by its categorisations of knowledge, and the goal that is achieved define the knowledge level. This approach is based on the idea of an inference structure as proposed by Clancey [2]. However, we do not map this structure onto a single agent, rather we view the inference structure as a characterisation of the coherent problem solving activity of many agents.

The inference structure is an idealised description, but does not have the problem of omniscience that is associated with a purely logical characterisation of knowledge. It is interesting to note that this problem has arisen in knowledge acquisition research, where the straightforward logical view of inference has been challenged, and also in agent modelling, where logics of restricted inferential capability have been investigated [8][14].

2.3 Notation for knowledge level characterisations

The notation of the inference structure was introduced to describe heuristic classification [2], a knowledge level characterisation of a problem solving method. The nodes of the inference structure diagram stand for propositions describing a class of objects e.g. Data Abstractions. The arcs are labelled with the name of the inferential process by which the nodes are related e.g. Heuristic Match. A similar notation is used in [25] where the nodes are called meta-classes and describe the role of domain objects in the problem solving process. Knowledge sources name the inferential step which relates the meta-classes. A knowledge source carries out a primitive inference step to produce a new piece of knowledge.

In this paper we formalise the inference structure by defining sets of domain terms, for example the set of symbols DA representing data abstractions, and defining a predicate symbol to denote instances of this class of symbols. We define the logical type a as instances of DA. We can now write that a_1 is a data abstraction by the atomic formula $Data\text{-}Abstraction(a_1)$ if a_1 is of type a ($a_1 \epsilon DA$).

Relations between classes of objects are denoted by logical implications. These implications correspond to the arcs of the inference structure diagram. The intention of the logical formalisation of the KL is to specify conditions of consistency. That is, the sets of formulae presented in the following sections do not predict the symbol level behaviour, but specify the knowledge level such that we can determine whether or not the behaviour of the symbol level does indeed correspond to it. This KL formalisation retains the desired features of denoting the essential classes of domain knowledge, and their interrelation.

In this paper we adopt the terminology of Wielinga *et al.* [25] and use the term 'knowledge source' to denote inference processes and the term 'meta-class' to refer to classes of domain terms.

3 Characterising DAI Systems

A number of distributed AI systems are now characterised at the knowledge level. The systems include the contract net [23][17], a reactive planner [15] and DVMT, a multiple-blackboard system [6].

3.1 The contract net

The contract net [4][22][23] is typically described in terms of the bidding process, i.e. the issuing of a task announcement by a manager-agent, the response of contractor-agents with bids, and the awarding of contracts to the bidders judged most suitable. Agents can play the role of manager or contractor or both. Agents have pre-defined capabilities, which with their level of activity, determine their response to task announcements.

The contract net is a framework in which decomposable tasks can be distributed among a group of agents in a flexible manner. Global coherence is to be achieved through negotiation as a mechanism for interaction, task decomposition and the common language shared by all agents [4]. However, it has been noted that if tasks cannot be decomposed into independent subtasks then the synthesis of results is problematic [1][17]. The synthesis of results is one dimension of global coherence, and hence we must doubt whether the mechanisms identified in [4] can guarantee global coherence.

The mechanisms of the contract net do not specify a particular solution method or the major catagorisations of knowledge involved in solving the domain problem, these mechanisms therefore lie entirely at the symbol level. A concrete example of the use of the contract net for resource allocation is given in [17]. We now present a knowledge level analysis of the same example and contrast the results.

In the resource allocation problem, agents have resources which they require and resources which they are prepared to trade. Resources can be exchanged by a simple bidding process. This, however, does not lead to a globally satisfactory solution as longer sequences of resource exchanges are not explored.

An inference structure which describes this process is defined in Figure 1. The classes *ResourceSet* and *RequirementSet* contain the resources which are available and the resources which are required. The classes *Offer* and *Need* define a particular resource of the *ResourceSet* which is on offer, and an element of the *RequirementSet* which is a resource needed by some agent. The inferences which connect these meta-classes is *selection* in both cases. The final inference is called *assign*. An assignment is made if an *Offer* matches a *Need*.

Type	Description of set
a	Set of symbols representing agent names
b	Set of symbols representing resources
c	$a * b$
$c*$	Powerset of c
d	Set of integers
$e*$	Powerset of $b * d$

Selection of Need
1 $(\forall x : c*)(RequirementSet(x) \rightarrow (\exists y : a)(\exists z : b)Need(y, z))$
Selection of Offer
2 $(\forall x : c*)(ResourceSet(x) \rightarrow (\exists y : a)(\exists z : b)Offer(y, z))$
Assignment
3 $(\forall x : a)(\forall y : b)(\forall z : a)(Need(x, y) \land Offer(z, y) \rightarrow Assignment(x, y))$

Fig. 1. A formalisation of the inference structure for resource allocation

The symbol level description is mapped onto the knowledge level as follows.

The decision of an agent to issue a request for a resource (as a task announcement) corresponds to the selection inference, i.e. the selection of a need. This is termed selection as if an agent has more than one resource which it requires it must, necessarily, make a choice between the alternatives. The decision of an agent to bid for the contract corresponds to the selection of an offer in the knowledge level description. The acceptance of a bid by the agent who issued the task announcement corresponds to the assignment inference.

The selection processes may simply be dependent on the order of elements in the sets, and under this assumption the formalisation produces the behaviour described in ([17] p301) for a simple contract net approach to the assignment problem.

It has been observed [17] that the quality of the global solution is improved if agents have information regarding the overall scarcity of resources. This requires that agents should not make decisions on purely local information. The knowledge of resource scarcity must be collected from all participating agents and a manager agent can be introduced to perform this task [17]. From the knowledge level point of view, the gathering of 'market statistics' represents a new type of knowledge which plays a role in the solution process. The method of problem solving is modified and we must redescribe the inference structure as a result. In specific, a new inference is added which calculates the *MarketStatistics*, and these statistics become a factor in the selection processes.

Calculate market statistics

4 $(\forall x : c*)(\forall y : c*)(RequirementSet(x) \wedge ResourceSet(y)$
$$\rightarrow (\exists z : e*)(MarketStatistics(z)))$$

Redefine selection of Need

1' $(\forall w : c*)(\forall x : e*)(RequirementSet(w) \wedge MarketStatistics(x)$
$$\rightarrow (\exists y : a)(\exists z : b)Need(y, z))$$

Redefine selection of Offer

2' $(\forall w : c*)(\forall x : e*)(ResourceSet(w) \wedge MarketStatistics(x)$
$$\rightarrow (\exists y : a)(\exists z : b)Offer(y, z))$$

Concretely, the selection process now takes place under an ordering relation defined by the market statistics. Scarce resources will now be traded for other scare resources in preference to abundant resources (for the sake of simplicity we have not specified exactly how this is done in the formalisation).

In [17], knowledge about resources is distributed among many agents and agent activity occurs in four distinct phases; the calculation of the market statistics being the first, and the bidding process is the final phase. Precisely how the assignments are made is determined not only by the knowledge of the agents but also by the bidding protocol and hence is dependent on the bidding strategies of the agents (we have described only the simplest strategy). In [17] the improved method is described as delegated negotiation and is seen as an improvement in the organisation of the agents by the introduction of a manager agent. In contrast, the knowledge level characterisation focusses on the knowledge required to solve the problem and identifies the improved performance as being due to a new source of knowledge.

In this section we have described an application of the contract net at both the knowledge level and the symbol level. We have shown how the knowledge level specification can be used to explain why different organisations of agents produces different behaviours and differing qualities of solution.

3.2   A reactive planner

A reactive planner based on the RTA* algorithm [16] is described in [15]. The application is the 8-puzzle. The goal of the planner is to derive a sequence of moves which results in the goal state being reached, but the plan need not be optimal. The planner can be configured to be reactive, that is, at each state the best action is selected by calculating weights according to a simple distance function. Past moves are recorded and the weights associated with actions are modified if the state has been reached before. This prevents the planner from entering a loop. If two actions have equal weights then a random choice is made.

The RTA* reactive planner has properties which are highly valued in DAI, namely, that actions are executed based on local information only. This can be contrasted with the deliberative planning approach where the space of possible moves would be searched. There are a number of possible implementations of the RTA* planner:

Option 1 As an off-line planner which returns a solution.
Option 2 As a real time planner which executes each action
when it is determined.
Option 3 As a system on **n** off-line planners working in parallel
Option 4 As a system of 8 agents each representing a square of the 8 puzzle.

Options 1-3 have been described in [15]. Option 3 is interesting as it makes use of the property of the RTA* algorithm that running the algorithm several times on the same problem results in a distribution of solution lengths. This is due to the random choice of equally weighted actions, some choices turn out to have been better than others. By running **n** planners in parallel, where **n** is greater than about 10, the probability is high that one planner will find a short solution, and this plan will be found first. There are great benefits in terms of computation time in this approach [15]. Option 4 is similar to the proposal of [5].

The distinctions of knowledge made in all of the above implementations are characterised in Figure 2. We can distinguish the classes of the current state, *State*, possible future states, *FutureStates*, the association of weights with future states, *HeuristicEstimate* , and the immediately following state, i.e. the one with the greatest weight, *NextState*. Formulae 1-3 in Figure 2 characterise the selection of one action in a specific state, in order to describe a sequence of actions we could add a temporal argument to the predicates or use a temporal logic.

There are clearly many differences in where the knowledge of states, weights etc. is represented at the symbol level. For example, in a single agent planner all knowledge resides in that program. In a multi-agent system such as Option 4, knowledge of future states need only reside in agents which are capable of

Type	Description of set
a	Set of symbols representing states
$a*$	Powerset of a
b	Set of integers representing heuristic estimates
c	The set $a * b$, ordered by the value of b
$c*$	Powerset of c

Generate possible future states
1 $(\forall x : a)(State(x) \rightarrow (\exists y : a*)FutureStates(y))$
Estimate values for future states
2 $(\forall x : a*)(FutureStates(x) \rightarrow (\exists y : c*)HeuristicEstimate(y))$
Select the state with the maximum estimate
3 $(\forall x : c*)(\forall y : c*)(HeuristicEstimate(x) \wedge Top(x) = y \leftrightarrow NextState(y))$

Fig. 2. A formalisation of the inference structure for a reactive planner

moving, knowledge of actions executed in the past can be stored in the agent which executed that action, but all agents need to know the current positions of all squares (agents) as this is necessary for the weights to be correctly modified when that global state has been visited before.

In order for the RTA* algorithm to operate correctly the estimation function must not overestimate the value of an action [20]. When considering the multi-agent implementation of Option 4 it is clear that each agent must have the same weighting function and must always respect the outcome of any negotiation over which agent can move. If these conditions are not met then the system will not behave according to RTA*. In terms of the knowledge level characterisation, rule 3 will show a contradiction if the next state is not the top element of the set of heuristic estimates.

In this section we have presented a knowledge level characterisation of a reactive planner and discussed four symbol level implementations of it.

3.3 Multiple-blackboard systems

The basic idea of the blackboard model is that there are a number of knowledge sources, viewed as experts, which contribute to the solution of a problem by reading and writing data to a central data structure, the blackboard. Implementational details can be found in [7], of relevance here is the hierarchical organisation of the blackboard and the partitioning of domain knowledge according to content into distinct knowledge sources. These features result from a model-based view of problem solving [7] which includes an explict catagorisation of domain knowledge. Therefore we can, in certain instances, associate the levels of a blackboard with meta-classes and the knowledge sources of the blackboard with knowledge sources in the KL sense.

In the distributed vehicle monitoring testbed (DVMT) of Durfee *et al.* [6] each agent is a blackboard system. The DVMT consists of between 1 and 13 agents whose task is to identify the track of a vehicle from acoustic data sensed by a number of agents from adjacent or overlapping regions. Durfee *et al.* investigated the effect of communication policies and organisational structure on the efficiency of resource utilisation. The use of planning and the exchange of meta-information were also investigated with regards to improving the local control of agent activity e.g. preventing agents from duplicating work and increasing the priority of potentially rewarding tasks.

Each agent in the DVMT has the same architecture, a blackboard system. More significantly from the knowledge level point of view, each agent has the same global model of the problem solving task, namely the meta-classes and knowledge sources (levels and knowledge sources) of the blackboard. This means that the inferences performed by one agent, for example, one which adds information to the meta-class (blackboard level) 'vehicle location', can be broadcast to other agents who are able to interpret it correctly. This is possible because all agents have the same blackboard levels. All agents share a global, knowledge level view of the problem solving process and their activity is therefore globally coherent by design. There is a marked difference between the contract net and DVMT in this regard, as agents in the contract net have no global view. The activity of DVMT agents may not be optimal as regards the use of computational resources (this is termed 'coherence' in [6]).

The DVMT experiments can be characterised as assuming a global problem solving model, shared by all agents, and investigating a number of symbol level techniques for the assignment of functions to agents - lateral or hierarchical agent organisation, and for the optimal guidance of search within agents, given the global state of problem solving.

3.4 An alternative characterisation in terms of DAI concepts

Bond and Gasser ([1] pages 19-25) define the coherence of a multi-agent system as having four dimensions: solution quality, efficiency, conceptual clarity of system behaviour and graceful degradation [4]. Coherence can be achieved by a number of means, including the following:

- □ the assignment of roles to agents
- □ planning in order to align agent activity
- □ management of communication
- □ management of resources
- □ data abstraction
- □ the use of meta level information

These mechanisms include agent roles - an attributed or conceptual property, planning - a problem solving paradigm, and data abstraction - a problem solving step common to a range of domains. This view of coherence is not a generalised, analytical view, it is a documentation of what occurs in existing DAI systems. This is unsatisfactory if we wish to gain a deeper understanding of DAI systems. Bond and Gasser do not consistently identify these methods with the specific

---

[4] It should be noted that the analysis of DAI systems in [1] is of much greater scope than that presented here.

dimensions of coherence that they define, and this detracts further from clarity. They do refer to the specific DAI systems which utilise planning etc. but do not consistently refer to the domain problem, hence the problem solving context is lost. The theoretical generalisations based on this method are weak: coherence is related to resource management and communication, resource management is related to communication, communications can be planned etc. The problem is that the mechanisms of DAI are analysed outwith their context in the solution of problems. The division of the knowledge level from the symbol level proposed in this paper is an attempt to clarify the purpose of the multi-agent system as a whole and in doing so, to distinguish the various roles of the symbol level functions. Such distinctions can play a useful role in the design of distributed systems, as they have done in the model-based design of knowledge-based systems.

4 Related Work

It is noted by Gasser [9] that DAI has taken the agent as the focus of analysis. Two attempts to break from the agent-centered approach are the Open Information Systems (OIS) Semantics of Hewitt [12] and the six principles for social-DAI outlined in [9]. Gasser proposes the existence of multiple actors as a fundamental concept in a 'more social' DAI. The social perspective entails grounding DAI principles in the group rather than the individual agent. The social perspective does not view the autonomy of agents as a concept which is completely divorced from group concepts. Presumably, it should not focus on the mechanisms within agents, but rather on the joint activity of a system of agents.

When we consider the proposals for a 'more social DAI' then it appears that the KL analysis satisfies some of the goals of this enterprise by proposing a global model of behaviour. This model is above the agent level (which we consider to be the symbol level) and this type of characterisation is radically different from the conventional DAI viewpoint(s).

In contrast with [13] we have not sought to add a layer above Newell's knowledge level in order to account for cooperative problem solving. Instead, we have used Clancey's redefinition of the knowledge level to provide the basis of our analysis. This view appears to be consistent with the situated view of knowledge as advocated in [21] as the knowledge level description need not be reflected in specific structures at the symbol level. The analysis of this paper does not lead us to conclude that reasoning about knowledge [11] or planning are necessary features of a knowledge level description. However, in agreement with [13] we do hypothesise a common agent goal which persists through an episode of problem solving. Finally, we acknowledge the importance of planning and reasoning about knowledge as mechanisms for guiding agent activity i.e. as sophisticated control mechanisms. Constructing a plan may also be the purpose of agent activity, in which case we would expect to find knowledge level models of planning. These models may be reactive or deliberative.

The problem of designing the interaction between a knowledge-based system and the user, i.e. a two agent system, from an inference structure is described in

[10]. The method we outline generalises this approach, making use of Clancey's recent review of the knowledge level hypothesis. The problem of implementing a KL description in a blackboard architecture has been addressed in [18] in practical terms. Thus, there are examples which suggest that the analytical approach we advocate can also be used as a basis for the design of multi-agent systems.

5 Conclusions

This paper has presented characterisations of a number of distributed systems at the knowledge level. The systems we have considered have been of a restricted range, distributed knowledge-based systems, and we have emphasised the problem solving domains and solution methods of these systems.

The separation of the knowledge level from the symbol level entails a clear delineation of the roles of symbol level processes and of the concept of agency. Our analysis shows that the global coherence of a number of existing systems can be understood by this analysis. Therefore, we conclude that the knowledge level analysis is a valuable addition to our understanding of distributed information processing systems.

Our conclusions are that the concept of global coherence is best understood as the idealised, rational behaviour of a system of agents. This can be described in terms of the deduction of new knowledge units within a model of problem solving. The model need not specify an optimal solution, nor the intentional attitudes of the agents. It is required that by following the model some solution is identified, and for global coherence, all participating agents must act consistently with the model. It is not necessary that the model be represented within the agents themselves, however, this could produce a flexible exchange of roles among agents by enabling agents to reason about their own role and that of others.

References

1. Bond, A.H. and Gasser, L. (1988) An analysis of problems and research in DAI. *in Readings in distributed artificial intelligence. (eds) Bond, A.H. and Gasser, L., Morgan Kaufmann, 1988 :333-356*

2. Clancey, W.J. (1985) Heuristic Classification. *Artificial Intelligence 27 (1985) :289-350*

3. Clancey, W.J. (1991) The frame of reference problem in the design of intelligent machines. *in (ed) Vanlehn, K. Architectures for intelligence. Lawrence Erlbaum Associates, 1991*

4. Davis, R. and Smith, R.G. (1983) Negotiation as a metaphor for distributed problem solving. *Artificial Intelligence 20, 1983 :63-109*

5. Drogoul, A. and Dubreuil, C. (1991) Eco-problem-solving model: Results of the N-puzzle. *Proc. 3rd European workshop on modelling autonomous agents and multi-agent worlds (MAAMAW 1991) (eds) Steiner, D.D. and Müller, J., D.F.K.I. report No. D-91-10*

6. Durfee, E.H. Lesser, V.R. and Corkhill, D.D. (1987) Coherent cooperation among communicating problem solvers. *IEEE Transactions on Computers C-36 :1275-1291*

7. Engelmore, R.S. (1988) Backboard Systems *Addison Wesley 1988*
8. Fagin, R. and Halpern, J.Y. (1985) Belief, awareness and limited reasoning. *Proc. IJCAI 1985 :491-501*
9. Gasser, L. (1991) Social conceptions of knowledge and action: DAI foundations and open systems semantics. *Artificial Intelligence 47 (1991) :107-138*
10. de Greef, P. and Breuker, J.A. (1992) Analysing system-user cooperation in KADS. *Knowledge Acquisition (1992) 4 :89-108*
11. Halpern, J.Y. and Moses, Y. (1990) Knowledge and common knowledge in a distributed environment. *Journal of the ACM, Vol 37. No. 3 :549-587*
12. Hewitt, C. (1991) Open information systems semantics for distributed artificial intelligence. *Artificial Intelligence 47 (1991) :79-106*
13. Jennings N.R. (1992) Towards a cooperation knowledge level for collaborative problem solving. *Proc. ECAI 1992 :224-228*
14. Konolige, K. (1986) A deduction model of belief. *Pitman, London, 1986*
15. Knight, K. (1993) Are many reactive agents better than a few deliberative ones ? *Proc. IJCAI 1993 :432-437*
16. Korf, R. (1990) Real-time heuristic search. *Artificial Intelligence 42(2-3) 1990*
17. Lenting, J.H.J. and Braspenning, P.J. (1993) Delegated negotiation for resource re-allocation. *in Lecture Notes in A.I. No. 671, (ed) Ohlbach, H.J., Springer Verlag, 1993 :299-311*
18. Major, N. Cupit, J. and Shadbolt, N. (1994) Applying the REKAP methodology to situation assessment. *Proc. 4th KADS Meeting, GMD, Sankt Augustin, Germany 24-25 March 1994, (eds) Voss, H. and Studer, R. Arbeitspapiere der GMD 832*
19. Newell, A. (1982) The knowledge level. *Artificial Intelligence 18 (1982):87-127*
20. Reinfeld, A. (1993) Complete solution of the eight-puzzle and the benefit of node ordering in IDA*. *Proc. IJCAI 1993 :248-253*
21. Rosenschein, S.J. (1985) Formal theories of knowledge in AI and robotics. *New Generation Computing 3(1985) :345-357*
22. Smith, R.G. (1977) The contract net: a formalism for the control of distributed problem solving. *Proc. IJCAI 1977 :472*
23. Smith, R.G. (1980) The contract net protocol: high level communication and control in a distributed problem solver. *IEEE Trans. on computers Vol. C-29 No. 12 December 1980 :1104-1113*
24. Werner, E. (1990) What can agents do together ? A semantics for reasoning about cooperative ability. *Proc. ECAI 1990 :694-701*
25. Wielinga, B.J. Schreiber, A.T. and Breuker, J.A. (1992) KADS: a modelling approach to knowledge engineering. *Knowledge Acquisition (1992) 4, :5-53*
26. Wooldridge, M. (1994) Coherent social action. *Proc. ECAI 1994 :279-283*

Towards Anticipatory Agents

Bertil Ekdahl[1]*, Eric Astor[2] and Paul Davidsson[2]

[1] Dept. of Computer Science and Business Adm., University of Karlskrona/Ronneby, Soft Center, S–372 25 Ronneby, Sweden
[2] Dept. of Computer Science, Lund University, Box 118, S–221 00 Lund, Sweden

Abstract. This paper presents a novel approach to the problem of designing autonomous agents that is based on the idea of anticipatory systems. An anticipatory system has a model of itself and of the relevant part of its environment and will use this model to predict the future. The predictions are then utilised to determine the agent's behaviour, i.e. it lets future states affect its present states. We argue that systems based on causal reasoning only, are too limited to serve as a proper base for designing autonomous agents. An anticipatory agent, on the other hand, will use reasoning from final cause to guide its current actions. We then discuss to what extent an anticipatory agent can be constructed from computable functions and we conclude that this problem is best expressed and analysed in linguistic terms. This discussion points out how such an agent should be designed and results in a proposal of an appropriate architecture. However, as the meta-linguistic problems involved are very hard to solve, a simpler architecture is also proposed. This is also a hybrid architecture that synthesizes reactive behaviour and deliberative reasoning, which, we believe, still has its merits compared to previous approaches to the design of autonomous agents. Finally, we discuss introspection and reflection, and show that the underlying concepts are easy to comprehend in the context of anticipatory systems.

1 Introduction

Although reactive (behaviour-based) agents have been shown to be superior to deliberative agents, at least in some situations, in doing a limited number of simple tasks in real world domains, they have also been shown to have several limitations. In addition to not being particular versatile, they have problems with handling tasks that require knowledge of the world that must be obtained from memory or by reasoning, rather than by perception (cf. Kirsh [5] and Davidsson [1]).

As a synthesis of the benefits of reactive agents with the enhanced abilities of deliberative agents, several researchers have suggested that an intelligent agent should have both high-level reasoning and low-level reaction capabilities. The rationale behind such a hybrid approach is to utilise the reaction ability of reactive agents necessary for routine tasks, but in addition also have the power of reasoning on a higher level that seems necessary for more advanced tasks.

This paper presents a novel framework for autonomous agents that falls into the category of hybrid approaches. It combines low-level reactive behaviour with fundamental abilities of a system claiming to behave intelligently on its own.

* Bertil Ekdahl's research is sponsored by Blekinge Research Foundation.

- The agent should be *active* in its interaction with the environment. In order to deal with the events in the real world the agent should be able not only to predict what will happen, but also be able to *pre-adapt* itself for the occurrence of a crucial or time-critical event.
- The agent should have a *description* of the environment and of itself as a part of that environment. When the environment (or itself) changes, the agent should be able to update or exchange its description. This implies that the agent must be able to recognise the fact that there is a discrepancy between the description and the environment (or itself).
- There should be a clear separation between the model, i.e. the interpretation of the description, and the reasoning process of the agent. The agent should be able to distinguish between reasoning *in the model* and reasoning *about the model*, i.e. there is a need for an explicit *meta-level*.
- The agent should have *introspective* ability, i.e. it should have access to its own internal structures, operations and behavioural potentials.
- The agent should have *reflective* ability, i.e. it should be able to reason and deliberate about its situation in relation to the embedding context.

In the following we will use the concept of *anticipatory systems* as the basis for discussion of how to approach the problem of designing rational agents with a prospective of addressing the points above.

2 Anticipatory vs. Causal Reasoning

The idea concerning causal relationships is a central doctrine of the laws of physics. Superficially, the doctrine states that all natural phenomena occurring in physical systems are related to the past of the system in such a way that all the trajectories are determined by the initial states. In the description of a physical system based on this tradition, no references are made to the future, i.e. the intention of the system is not considered. In this way the past has come to appear as the cause of the present. The development of physics, from Newton to the present time, represents in its deepest expression the faith in this causality.

The causal method has also proved to be very successful in areas other than physics. However, the success of a method might depend on how the problems are studied. For instance, Gaines [4] points out that the causal explanation of the behaviour of an animal, as determined by its current internal state and external input, may be very complex, whereas the teleological explanation, i.e. the reasoning from final cause in terms of its intended future behaviour, may be very simple.

3 Anticipatory Systems

An anticipatory system is, according to Rosen [10], "... a system containing a predictive model of itself and/or of its environment, which allows it to change state at an instant in accord with the model's prediction to a latter instant."[3] (p. 339) An anticipatory system is thus a system which uses knowledge of future states to decide what action to take in the present.

However, our concept of anticipatory systems differs in a decisive way from Rosen's. We will call an anticipatory agent *description-based* when based directly on the ideas of Rosen, while our ideas yield a *model-based* agent. Such an agent is illustrated in Figure 1.

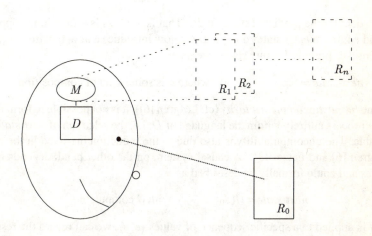

Fig. 1. Model-based anticipatory agent.

R_0 is the part of reality that the agent interacts with. D is an internal description of the agent's environment (R_0) and of the agent itself, while M is an internal interpretation (i.e., a model) of this description made by the agent in order to foresee the future. M gives rise to a number of comprehended realities, R_i's. The variations among these are partly caused by different possible events in the environment, and partly caused by interactions between the environment and the agent itself.

Thus, the agent is anticipating a number of different R_i's, all of which are to be understood to give different predictions of the state of R_0 at some future time. The differences are caused by the different possible behaviours of the environment and the agent. The point is that the agent affects its environment and must take this into account when anticipating the future. Which possible future it prefers is a question of what is "good" for the agent. By letting the future guide the present, the agent expects to avoid future difficulties.

---

[3] Rosen uses the word *model* as a synonym of *description*. Model used in this sense refers to the syntactic part of the formal language and not to the semantic part of a language, which is, we consider, more appropriate in this context. We will not argue with Rosen in this paper but will throughout exchange his word *model* for the more correct word *description*. For a more comprehensive inquiry of models in anticipatory systems, see Ekdahl [2] (forthcoming).

When creating the different R_i's, the agent must be able to change the description (D) as every model is based either on a new description, or on a new interpretation of the old description. When one of the R_i's is preferred, it means that the description corresponding to that conception is selected.

The process described above can be formulated in the metalanguage of mathematics in the following way. Let e be a vector of environmental parameters (states), s a vector of past states, and G a function that generates the future states. We can now write

$$\langle e, s \rangle \xrightarrow{\ G\ } \{P_1, ..., P_n\}.$$

where P_i denotes the predicted states of R_i. That is, $G(e, s)$ is a function, mapping internal and environmental states on sets. If we now introduce a new function, S_{next}, for the selection of preferred future states, we have

$$next\text{-}state = S_{next} \circ G(e, s) \text{, where } \circ \text{ is some kind of composition.}$$

Due to the *linguistic complementarity* (cf. Löfgren [6]), it is not possible to formalise the selection process entirely within the language of D, i.e. the selection of *next-state* is not computable. The uncomputability is also due to the induction involved in the process (cf. Löfgren [6] and Fetzer [3]). A causal system, on the other hand, depends only on past states and could formally be described as

$$next\text{-}state = \mathcal{G}(s_0, ..., s_n), \text{ with } \mathcal{G} \text{ computable.}$$

When G is applied to a specific sequence of values $\langle e, s \rangle$, we can regard the result as a trajectory, i.e. every P_i in $\{P_1, ..., P_n\}$ can be regarded as a trajectory.

Rosen [10] states five formal requirements that a system of the kind outlined above has to fulfill in order to be anticipatory. In the view of an anticipatory agent the requirements can be summarised as follows. An anticipatory agent (AA) is one which contains a model of a system R_0 with which it interacts. This model is a predictive model; its *present* states provide information about *future* states of R_0. Further, the present state of the model causes a change of state in other subsystems of AA; these subsystems are (a) involved in the interaction of R_0 with AA, and (b) they do not affect (i.e. are unlinked to) the model of R_0.

3.1 Reasoning from Final Causes

In causal AI systems based on the Newtonian paradigm of classical mechanics, we can identify three of Aristotle's four causes

$$\begin{aligned}
\text{material cause} &\Longleftrightarrow \text{initial states} \\
\text{formal cause} &\Longleftrightarrow \text{programs} \\
\text{efficient cause} &\Longleftrightarrow \text{execution (interpretations).}
\end{aligned}$$

The fourth cause, the *final cause*, is missing and this is not so surprising if we consider that AI, like many other sciences, is greatly influenced by physics. It was the physicists who first began to describe nature more formally, and material systems in nature have no finality. When, in spite of this fact, we persist in describing "intelligent" systems, or more generally, biological systems as if they were material systems we cannot hope for success. Rosen [11] describes the reluctance as follows. "The rejection of finality in science is ... in the form of an unspoken "Zeroth Commandment" permeating all of theoretical science: "Thou shalt not allow the future to affect the present." " (p. 49)

Anticipatory systems are supposed to have a finality in its own way. When applied to the design of an autonomous agent this means that the agent has its own final cause(s) and not merely the final cause(s) of the programmer.

3.2 Architecture

It appears that a system must consist of at least the following parts to be called an anticipatory agent

- an *enactor*, i.e. that part of the system that performs the action of the system through the actuators,
- a set of *sensors* that receive the environmental inputs,
- a *description* (D) of the environment and the system itself,
- a *generator* (G) of future states (trajectories),
- "someone" that can start the generation of new trajectories, parameterized with time variables which run faster than reality and who can select the new states (trajectories).

These demands give rise to the basic architecture of an anticipatory system illustrated in Figure 2. The enactor is responsible for the AS's performance in its environment. This part can be compared with a reactive system and might be implemented as such.

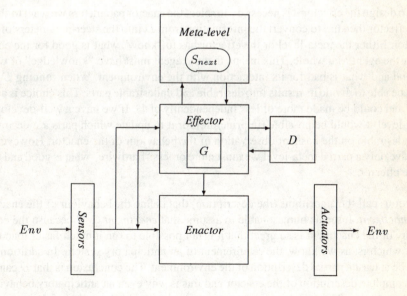

Fig. 2. The basic architecture of an anticipatory agent.

D is the description of the enactor and of the environment significant for the enactor. The point is now that D, like a theory of a physical reality, should be able to predict the future for the enactor. This demands that time can be described in D. However, this is not as simple as it may seem. According to Löfgren [7] "any consistently proposed formal theory of time is incomplete", i.e. incomplete in the same sense as, for example, the ordinary theory of arithmetic is incomplete. The time, considered only as a series of positions totally ordered, is, however, describable and in this paper it is the only concept of time that will be considered. Thus, time, as it is measured for the enactor and the environment is described in D. We assume that time in the enactor is real time and require that time goes faster in D, i.e. if the trajectories of the enactor are parameterized in real time then the description in D, corresponding to these trajectories, is "running" faster. If the times in the enactor and D are synchronised at the time $t = t_0$, and the states at that point are equivalent, then after a time interval t, D has run a time interval, $\tau(t)$ where $\tau(t) > t$. Now, D and the enactor shall be coupled, in such a way that the prediction from D is able to influence the enactor, and the new behaviour of the enactor should affect D, i.e. the theory. For this reason we will utilise D and the enactor with an effector. The latter has the same information as the enactor, but is running D. When doing so, it applies the generator G. We have deliberately placed G in the effector as we believe it is computable, at least to a considerable extent, for most planning purposes. However, when learning is involved, as it must be for the agent in order to refine its description, i.e. generate new hypotheses about the reality, G also has to be inductive and thus not longer generally computable (cf. Löfgren [6] and Fetzer [3]). As pointed out above, $S_{next} \circ G$ is not a computable function. We are thus forced to place S_{next} on the meta-level. An interesting question is then, "how much" of S_{next} can be counted as computable, i.e. how much must be left for the meta-level alone?

To design the effector it is necessary to select the enactor parameters we want to steer. The effector then has to convert the information from D into the steer-parameters of the enactor. Either the meta-level or the effector has to "know" what is good for the enactor or the agent as a whole. This means that the agent must have "knowledge" of what is good and what is bad for its interaction with the environment. When running D we must be able to divide its results into desirable and undesirable parts. This choice is arbitrary and could be made more or less independently of D. If we have a well-developed meta-level it would be possible (in principle) for it to update which parts are desirable or undesirable on the basis of observation of the behaviour of the enactor. However, if we have only a partial meta-level we must more or less "hardwire" what is good and bad in the effector.

Let us call the algorithms (the description) that define the behaviour of the enactor, the *enactment*. It seems unreasonable to assume that *enactment* $\subseteq D$ because the complexity of the enactment is so great that it is not possible to run it much faster than real time, which is, as we know, the requirement of an anticipatory system. In addition, D shall be at least a partial description of the environment. The conclusion is that D cannot be a complete description of the enactor and this is why even an anticipatory behaviour could go wrong. Thus, D must describe the most important dynamics of the enactor's interaction with the environment.

How then can D be improved? The proper way to do this is from the meta-level because it demands that "someone" can observe the behaviour of the enactor, as a real system. Even if we know the algorithm (description) behind the enactor, we cannot tell exactly how the enactor will behave in the environment. This is particularly true from the point of D. The effector, as an algorithm, cannot itself determine whether D is a good description of the enactor's behaviour in the environment. The enactor has no platform to stand on. This is the same as saying that a physical theory cannot know if it is a good theory. Only on a meta-level is it possible to have such knowledge. This is another reason why we really need a meta-level. However, to change D appropriately is not an easy procedure. Rosen [10] has pointed out that an improvement must be made on the basis of the behaviour of the total system (D + *effector* + *enactor*) and that this might lead to an infinite regress. We suppose that the problem of infinite regress can be neglected since in an agent there are time restrictions that force it to choose the best from a reasonable number of actions. D can be improved, we believe, in a more modest way by allowing the effector to have rules that can lead from an undesired state to a desired.

As should be quite clear from the discussion above, there is much research to be done before we know how to handle the meta-level properly and this includes how to "compute" the uncomputable function S_{next}. The proposed architecture is usable even if we completely neglect the meta-level and make S_{next} computable, thereby making the agent non-anticipatory. We still have an agent which is to some extent able to modify itself. Such agents could be referred to as *quasi-anticipatory* agent.

3.3 Introspective and Reflective Abilities

When talking about self-reference, the Epimenide's paradox *I am lying*, or Berry's paradox *The least positive integer that is not denoted by an English expression containing fewer than 200 occurrences of symbols*, are often taken as examples of genuine self-reference.[4]

The self-referential problems are interesting, because they indicate that there are restrictions in our ability to interpret what is describable. Löfgren [8] calls this restriction *linguistic complementarity*, meaning that descriptions and interpretations of a language are complementary in the sense that "... as long as we stay within a language L, we cannot completely describe L only in terms of its sentences — both sentences and interpretations are required for a full account, and use, of L." (p. 329) This restriction is applicable not only to natural languages, but also to formal languages. There is a strong support for this *thesis* in the results of Gödel and Tarski. Tarski showed that the true sentences in a formal language are not describable, i.e. truth is non-definable. In the realm of arithmetic we can formulate this as follows: The set of Gödel numbers of arithmetical sentences, true in the intended interpretation, are not arithmetical.[5] So there is no hope for complete self-reference in any formal language. However, Tarski [8, 13] has pointed out that to every formal language, a metalanguage can always be constructed in which the concept of truth for the object language can be defined. This means of course that there is no truth predicate for the metalanguage, but we can construct a meta-metalanguage and

---

[4] For the paradoxes, see Mendelson [9].

[5] See, for example, Mendelson [9].

so on. This leads to an infinite regress. This infinite regress cannot, due to the linguistic complementarity, lead to a language in which self-reference is completely captured. It is imperative to have at least a small part of a metalanguage that is not completely self-referential. There is, nonetheless, a great deal of progress to be made for autonomous agents if we focus our efforts on constructing metalanguages of a higher order than the object languages and not, as is the praxis today, use the word meta-level as a synonym for monitor. Self-reference is the subject of *autology* [8], and we believe its theoretical foundations should be taken into consideration by AI researchers. We will not, however, dwell further upon this problem, but simply point out some interesting varieties of self-references and show that our architecture fits these settings. Smith [12] describes four different ways in which a computational agent may be self-referential; *indexical*, *autonymic*, *introspective*, and *reflective*. We will comment on the last two of these categories.

Introspect means "examine one's own thought and feelings".[6] For a computational agent, Smith argues, it is these abilities "... that enable it to obtain (typically privileged) access to its own internal structures, operations and behavioural potential in such a way as to matter to its present and future actions". We believe, that the idea of anticipatory systems embodies these demands. In fact, we maintain the view that to be an anticipatory agent is to have at least some introspective abilities.

To have complete introspective ability, however, implies a language in which self-reference is possible. But, as we have outlined above, such ability is only partial. This means that we have to find an object language in which most of the agent's need for introspection can be covered.

The implications of this can be comprehended by looking at introspection in logic. There is a theorem of Gödel, (the Fixed Point Theorem) which says that for any formula $\Phi(x)$, of one free variable, there is a sentence ψ such that

$$\vdash \psi \iff \Phi(\bar{\psi}) \text{ , where } \bar{\psi} \text{ is the Gödel number of } \psi.$$

This formula is self-referential (cf. Löfgren [8]) in that ψ says of itself that it has the property Φ.

This, can be argued, is a restricted form of self-reference in that ψ does not *know* that it has the property Φ. It is just on the meta-level that this fact is accessible in the form of knowledge. To find a programming language which includes self-reference as described is, of course, an interesting research challenge. However, we do not believe that this is the correct approach to "intelligent" agents, rather the solution should be based on anticipatory systems. Introspection, in the sense outlined above, cannot handle *induction*, because induction cannot be captured by a computable function (cf. Löfgren [6]). Hence, the idea of using a meta-level is more appropriate.

To be *reflective*, on the other hand, is a system's ability to reason even (besides introspection) about its situation and embedding context (cf. Smith [12]). This, we believe, is one of the more characteristic features of an anticipatory system: to deliberate the future to decide the present. This is, of course, to reflect.

We believe that the idea of anticipatory systems fits quite well in the context of self-reference as presented above. We also believe, that the architecture presented is a pos-

---

[6] Oxford Advanced Learners Dictionary

sible way to achieve an anticipatory autonomous agent. Apart from its other merits, the architecture shows what issues cannot be overlooked in order for an agent to be called *autonomous*.

4 Discussion

When we talk about models in mathematical logic we mean an interpretation for which all the axioms in the theory are true. In every day life we talk about models of aeroplanes, houses etc. implying that we have constructed something simplified or smaller from a description originating from the real thing. In both cases the fundamental feature of a model is that of being an interpretation or realization of a description. In AI, and computer science in general, a description of a problem expressed by a specification or programming language is often misleadingly referred to as a model. This will not lead to any confusion as long as there is a tacit understanding that as humans we automatically interpret the description to form the model. We cannot communicate our models directly as they are images in our mind, but we have to communicate them in terms of a language forming a description. If the receiver of the description does not have the same interpretation as the sender, or lacks an interpretation, communication becomes difficult or is not possible at all.

In physics we have descriptions in the form of theories based on experiments or empirical studies. The theory is expressed in a formal language with an interpretation that is shared among physicists. The interpretation forms the bridge between the theory and the corresponding phenomena in the real world. As a student of physics much of the work is dedicated to develop an understanding of how to interpret the theories, i.e. how they relate to reality. A theory can be used to make predictions. These predictions will be more or less accurate depending on the circumstances but also depending on the theory itself, i.e. if it is a good theory. The judge of whether the theory is a good theory or not is, of course, the physicists.

An autonomous agent has a description in the form of a program. The program controls the behaviour of the agent in accordance with the intention of the programmer. The programmer has written the program and, in correspondence to a physicist's interpretation of a theory, the programmer has an interpretation of the program, i.e. he has a model. The agent itself has no interpretation of the program, i.e. *the model is not a part of the agent*. The agent is autonomous only in the respect that it is programmed to deal with expected situations in the environment while it is carrying out some goal. It might have a predictive ability in the sense that it can simulate possible future actions in the same way that a theory in physics predicts the future. It might have goals but only in the sense that the programmer has expressed his comprehension of adequate goals in different situations.

The goals, intentions and belief system of the agent is programmed by a programmer who has tried to foresee all situations the agent may encounter. The programmer is able to do this on basis of the model *he* has of the agent's intended abilities and of the environment it will interact with. If the programmer has a well developed model of the environment and of the actions the agent may be programmed to perform, he might be able to implement a quite sophisticated agent. But, as soon as the circumstances changes in a way not foreseen by the programmer, the agent is stuck and its program must be revised to include the new situation.

An anticipatory agent in the sense outlined in section 3 will have its own model of its actions and of the environment. Even if this model is far from the kind of model a human being is able to create, the agent will nevertheless have some ability to formulate goals on basis of the interpretation of the description of its own abilities and the surrounding environment. Like a physicist it may test the adequacy of different theories, i.e. programs, on basis of the fact that it has an interpretation of its descriptions and may change either the description or the interpretation to better adapt to something unforeseen.

In order to describe the interpretation of a description a metalanguage is required. As pointed out in Section 3.3, this metalanguage is not describable in terms of the object language, i.e. the language used to form the description. In many of the architectures suggested for agents there are different languages for different levels of the architecture, i.e. behavioural languages, intentional languages etc. Languages of this kind will aid the programmer in the conceptualization process when constructing the programs for the different levels of the agent, but that is all. They do not implement any semantics for the agent and should not be confused with a metalanguage.

Computer scientists in general are not used to think about programs as having their own semantics. However, when constructing autonomous agents it is crucial to include semantics in the form of an internal model if the goal is to construct autonomous agents with the ability of interaction with an open environment. If not, the agent will only be able to function well in a closed environment, i.e. in a world where all possible situations can be calculated in advance. There is a resemblance to the relation between polynomials and the continuous functions in mathematics. Polynomials are dense in the set of continuous functions, which means that we can approximate an arbitrary continuous function with a polynomial with desired accuracy. In the same way, given the circumstances of a closed environment, we may construct an autonomous agent with any desired ability of successful interaction with that environment. However, if the environment changes in an unpredicted way the agent programmer has same problem as the mathematician has with his approximating polynomial when the continuous function changes. Furthermore, there is interesting mathematical theory developed on the basis of the understanding of the properties of the continuous functions that is unlikely to have been developed solely on the understanding of polynomials. In the same way we believe that in order to develop a theory for autonomous agents it will be fruitful to study autonomous agents based on the concept of anticipatory systems. Our approach will also place the theory of autonomous agents in a linguistic setting in addition to the computability view.

Human beings are anticipatory agents in the full sense. Our ability to form elaborate models is a possible key to our dominance among the species. Especially, we can form the models necessary to program agents carrying out the goals, intentions and beliefs that we anticipate on basis of our models. The outline of an anticipatory agent in this paper is intended to point out and discuss the difficulties involved when this ability of a human programmer is to be transferred to an artificial autonomous agent. But it is also an attempt to point out the prevailing confusion concerning the concept of model and who has the goals, intentions and beliefs.

5 Related Work

5.1 Comparison with Traditional Planning

It can be argued that the planning component in a traditional system (i.e. STRIPS-like programs) provides a degree of anticipation by testing internally different actions (or sequences of actions) to see what future states can be achieved. This kind of anticipation is, however, limited in the sense that it covers only state changes that are caused by the pursuing of a particular goal. Changes resulting from other causes, such as other agents or independent physical processes, are considered only if they are explicitly expressed in the planning algorithm. The present framework, on the other hand, has the potential to regard all kinds of changes in the environment, and in particular it will be able to detect unwanted situations in advance. It is a kind of passive and general anticipation rather than the active and goal-directed anticipation of planning systems.

The continuous maintenance of the predictive trajectory tree could be regarded as an expanded horizon of predicted future situations used by the meta-level to pre-adapt the object-level in its interaction with the environment. This pre-adaptation will in some cases compensate for the lack of pre-programmed algorithms when situations occur that have not been anticipated by a programmer.

A simple example, is a scenario where an agent wants, for some reason, to catch up and intercept an object moving at a slower speed. A pure reactive system will move in the direction corresponding to the present position of the target object, resulting in a curved path that will catch up with the target from behind. An anticipatory agent will be guided by the meta-level to move in a direction corresponding to a predicted future position of the target object, i.e. it will behave in much the same way as an agent equipped with a special algorithm for the computation of a cross point. If the scenario is further complicated by obstacles and other active objects, a planning algorithm tends be quite complicated and might not cover all situations. An anticipatory agent, on the other hand, would have a potential for coping with the complications even where the behaviour might not be optimal.

5.2 Comparison with Feedforward Control

Some control systems use a method called *feedforward* to eliminate disturbances that can be measured. According to Åström and Wittenmark [14], "the basic idea is to use the measured disturbance to anticipate the influence of the disturbance on the process variables and to introduce suitable compensating control actions." (p. 166) To do this, the feedforward method requires an adequate description of the process to be controlled. Thus, the feedforward method resembles the suggested approach in that a description is used to predict future states and that these predictions are used to guide the behaviour of the system. The anticipation is, however, limited to the prediction of just one future state (i.e. the error in output that the disturbance would have caused) whereas anticipatory systems are able to make predictions of arbitrary "time steps" into the future. Moreover, the process to be controlled is characterised by only one single numerical value, whereas in autonomous agent contexts there is a need for qualitatively more powerful descriptions.

6 Conclusions and Further Research

There are two main interesting directions to follow:

1. *Disregard the meta-level.* This is the computational direction and is, of course, the more narrow angle of approach. But despite this we believe that the influence from anticipatory systems gives our architecture a conceptual advantage compared to a conventional agent which either has a weaker theoretical basis, or has no theoretical basis at all. In this case we have pointed out how to make predictions, and how to carry out an implementation; and it will also give hints as to what cannot be done, and what kind of restrictions we are facing.
2. *Investigate the meta-level and the concept of model.* This is to study the computer as a linguistic system. We believe that there is a strong connection between "intelligence" and language. It is thus necessary to study intelligent agents from a linguistic perspective.

A computable function when computed by hand or by a Turing-machine can be regarded as an interpretation process acting upon the functional description. Thus, looked upon from this view, we can say that a computation (computer) is a *linguistic system*. This is an important divergence from traditional AI-research, in which the computer is regarded as a machine.

References

1. P. Davidsson. Concepts and autonomous agents, (Licentiate thesis). LU–CS–TR: 94–124, Dept. of Computer Science, Lund University, Sweden, 1994.
2. B. Ekdahl. The concept of models in anticipatory agents. Technical Report LU–CS–TR: 95–?, Dept. of Computer Science, Lund University, Lund, Sweden, 1995. In preparation.
3. J.H. Fetzer. The frame problem: Artificial intelligence meets David Hume. *International Journal of Expert Systems*, 3(3):219–232, 1990.
4. B.R. Gaines. Calculus of possibility, eventuality, and probability. Technical Report EES–MMS–FUZ–175, Dept. of Electr. Eng. Sci. University of Essex, Colchester, 1975.
5. D. Kirsh. Today the earwig, tomorrow man? *Artificial Intelligence*, 47(1):161–184, 1991.
6. L. Löfgren. Methodologies and the induction problem. In R. Trappl et al., *Progress in Cybernetics and Systems Research Vol. VIII*, pages 15–22. McGraw-Hill, 1982.
7. L. Löfgren. Autology of time. *International Journal of General Systems*, 10(1):5–14, 1984.
8. L. Löfgren. Autology. In *Systems and Control Encyclopedia*, pages 326–333. Pergamon Press, 1987.
9. E. Mendelson. *Introduction to Mathematical Logic*. Wadwort & Brooks, 1987.
10. R. Rosen. *Anticipatory Systems – Philosophical, Mathematical and Methodological Foundations*. Pergamon Press, 1985.
11. R. Rosen. *Life Itself*. Columbia Univ. Press, 1991.
12. B.C. Smith. Self-reference. In S.C. Shapiro, editor, *Encyclopedia of Artificial Intelligence*, pages 1005–1010. John Wiley and Sons, 1987.
13. A. Tarski. *Logic, Semantics, Metamathematics*. Oxford, 1956. second edition, J. Corcoran (ed.), Hacklett, 1983.
14. K.J. Åström and B. Wittenmark. *Computer Controlled Systems: Theory and Design*. Prentice-Hall, 1984.

Integrated Control and Coordinated Behavior:
a Case for Agent Models

Innes A. Ferguson[1]

Knowledge Systems Laboratory, Institute for Information Technology
National Research Council, Ottawa ON, Canada K1A 0R6

Abstract. This paper presents a new architecture for controlling autonomous agents in dynamic multi-agent worlds, building on previous work addressing reactive and deliberative control methods. The proposed multi-layered architecture allows a rationally bounded, goal-directed agent to reason predictively about potential conflicts by constructing causal theories which explain other agents' observed behaviors and hypothesize their intentions; at the same time it enables the agent to operate autonomously and to react promptly to changes in its real-time environment. A principal aim of this research is to understand the role different functional capabilities play in constraining an agent's behavior under varying environmental conditions. To this end, an experimental testbed has been constructed comprising a simulated multi-agent world in which a variety of agent configurations and behaviors have been investigated. A number of experimental findings are reported.

1 Introduction

The computer-controlled operating environments at such facilities as automated factories, nuclear power plants, telecommunications installations, and information processing centers are continually becoming more complex. As this complexity grows, it will be increasingly difficult to control such environments with centralized management and scheduling policies that are both robust in the face of unexpected events and flexible at dealing with operational and environmental changes that might occur over time. One solution to this problem which has growing appeal is to distribute, along such dimensions as space and function, the control of such operations to a number of intelligent, task-achieving robotic or computational agents.

Most of today's computational agents are limited to performing a relatively small range of well-defined, pre-programmed, or human-assisted tasks. Operating in real world domains means having to deal with unexpected events at several levels of granularity — both in time and space, most likely in the presence of other independent agents. In such domains agents will typically perform a number of complex simultaneous tasks requiring some degree of attention to be paid to environmental change, temporal constraints,

---

1. This research was conducted while the author was a doctoral candidate at the Computer Laboratory, University of Cambridge, Cambridge, UK.

computational resource bounds, and the impact agents' shorter term actions might have on their own or other agents' longer term goals. Also, because agents are likely to have incomplete knowledge about the world and will compete for limited and shared resources, it is inevitable that, over time, some of their goals will conflict. Any attempt to construct a complex, large-scale system in which all envisaged conflicts are foreseen and catered for in advance is likely to be too expensive, too complex, or perhaps even impossible to undertake given the effort and uncertainty that would be involved in accounting for all of one's possible future equipment, design, management, and operational changes.

Now, while intelligent agents must undoubtedly remain reactive in order to survive, some amount of strategic or predictive decision-making will also be required if agents are to handle complex goals while keeping their long-term options open. On the other hand, agents cannot be expected to model their surroundings in every detail as there will simply be too many events to consider, a large number of which will be of little or no relevance anyway. Not surprisingly, it is becoming widely accepted that neither purely reactive [1,2] nor purely deliberative [3,4] control techniques are capable of producing the range of robust, flexible behaviors desired of future intelligent agents. What is required, in effect, is an architecture that can cope with uncertainty, react to unforeseen incidents, and recover dynamically from poor decisions. All of this, of course, on top of accomplishing whatever tasks it was originally assigned to do.

This paper is concerned with the design and implementation of a novel integrated agent control architecture, the *TouringMachine* architecture [5—7], suitable for controlling and coordinating the actions of autonomous rational agents embedded in a partially-structured, dynamic, multi-agent world. Upon carrying out an analysis of the intended TouringMachine task domain — that is, upon characterizing those aspects of the intended real-time road navigation domain that would most significantly constrain the TouringMachine agent design — and after due consideration of the requirements for producing autonomous, effective, robust, and flexible behaviors in such a domain, the TouringMachine architecture has been designed through integrating a number of reactive and *suitably designed* deliberative control functions.

2   TouringMachines

Implemented as a number of concurrently-operating, latency-bounded, task-achieving control layers, the resulting TouringMachine architecture is able to produce a number of reactive, goal-directed, reflective, and predictive behaviors — as and when dictated by the agent's internal state and environmental context. In particular, TouringMachines (see Fig. 1) comprise three such independently motivated layers: a *reactive* layer $\mathcal{R}$ for providing the agent with fast, reactive capabilities for coping with events its higher layers have not previously planned for or modelled (a typical event, for example, would be the sudden appearance of some hitherto unseen agent or obstacle); a *planning* layer $\mathcal{P}$ for generating, executing, and dynamically repairing hierarchical partial plans (which are used by the agent, for example, when constructing navigational routes to some target

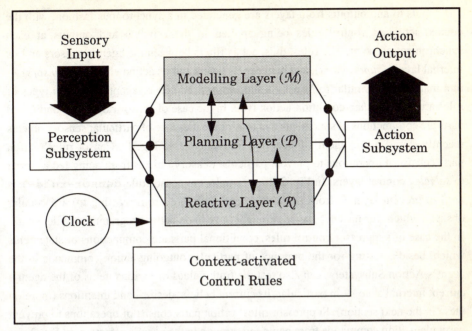

Fig. 1. A TouringMachine's mediating control framework.

destination); and a reflective-predictive or *modelling* layer $\mathcal{M}$ for constructing behavioral models of world entities, including the agent itself, which can be used as a platform for explaining observed behaviors and making predictions about possible future behaviors (more on this below).

Each control layer is designed to model the agent's world at a different level of abstraction and each is endowed with different task-oriented capabilities. Also, because each layer directly connects perception to action and can independently decide if it should or should not act in a given world state, frequently one layer's proposed actions will conflict with those of another; in other words, each layer is an approximate machine and thus its abstracted world model is necessarily incomplete. As a result, layers are mediated by an enveloping control framework so that the agent, as a single whole, may behave appropriately in each different world situation.

Implemented as a combination of inter-layer message-passing and context-activated, domain-specific control rules (see Fig. 1), the control framework's mediation enables each layer to examine data from other layers, inject new data into them, or even remove data from the layers. (The term *data* here covers sensed input to and action output from layers, the contents of inter-layer messages, as well as certain rules or plans residing within layers.) This has the effect of altering, when required, the normal flow of data in the affected layer(s). So, in the road driving domain for example, the reactive rule in layer $\mathcal{R}$ to prevent an agent from straying over lane markings can, with the appropriate control rule present, be overridden should the agent embark on a plan to overtake the agent in front of it (more on this shortly).

Inputs to and outputs from layers are generated in a synchronous fashion, with the context-activated control rules being applied to these inputs and outputs at each synchronization point. The rules, thus, act as filters between the agent's sensors and its internal layers (*suppressors*), and between its layers and its action effectors (*censors*) — in a manner very similar to Minsky's suppressor- and censor-agents [8]. Both types of rules are of the *if-then* condition-action type. In the case of censor rules, the conditional parts are conjunctions of statements that test for the presence of particular sensory objects recently stored in the agent's Perception Subsystem (see Fig. 1). Censor rules' action parts consist of operations to prevent particular sensory objects from being fed as input to *selected* control layers. In Fig. 2, for example, the censor rule `censor-rule-1` is used to prevent layer $\mathcal{R}$ from perceiving (and therefore, from reacting to) a particular obstacle which, for instance, layer $\mathcal{M}$ might have been better programmed to deal with. In the case of suppressor control rules, conditional parts are conjunctions of statements which, besides testing for the presence of particular outgoing action commands in the agent's Action Subsystem, can also test the truth values of various items of the agent's current internal state — in particular, its current beliefs, desires, and intentions (more on these in the next section). Suppressor rules' action parts consist of operations to prevent particular action commands from being fed through to the agent's effectors. In Fig. 2, for example, the suppressor control rule `suppressor-rule-3` is used to prevent layer $\mathcal{R}$ from reacting to (steering away from) a lane marking object whenever the agent's current intention is to overtake some other agent that is in front of it. Any number of censor control rules can fire (and remove selected control layer input) when these are applied at the beginning of a synchronization timeslice. Suppressor control rules, on the other hand, are assumed to have been crafted by the agent's programmer in such a way that *(i)* at most one will fire in any given situational context (an agent's situational context is taken to be the combination of its perceptual input set and its current internal state); and *(ii)* at most one action command will remain in the Action Subsystem after the suppressor control rule's action part has been executed. By crafting suppressor control rules in this way, a TouringMachine's effectors can be guaranteed to receive no more than one action command to execute during any given timeslice.

Mediation remains active at all times and is largely "transparent" to the layers: each layer acts as if it alone were controlling the agent, remaining largely unaware of any "interference" — either by other layers or by the rules of the control framework — with its own inputs and outputs. The overall control framework thus embodies a real-time opportunistic scheduling regime which, while striving to service the agent's high-level tasks (e.g. planning, causal modelling, counterfactual reasoning) is sensitive also to its low-level, high-priority behaviors such as avoiding collisions with other agents or obstacles.

```
censor-rule-1:
    if   entity(obstacle-6) ∈ Perception-Buffer
    then
         remove-sensory-record(layer-R, entity(obstacle-6))

suppressor-rule-3:
    if   action-command(layer-R-rule-6*,
                        change-orientation(_))† ∈ Action-Buffer
         and
         current-intention(start-overtake)
    then
         remove-action-command(layer-R, change-orientation(_))
         and
         remove-action-command(layer-M, _)
```

*`layer-R-rule-6` is the reactive (layer R) rule which is invoked in order to avoid crossing a path lane marking.
† "_" simply denotes a don't-care or anonymous variable.

Fig. 2. Two example control rules: **censor-rule-1** and **suppressor-rule-3**.

3 Modelling Agent Behavior

Like most real-world domains, a TouringMachine's world is populated by multiple autonomous entities and so will often involve dynamic processes which are beyond the control of any one particular agent. For a planner — and, more generally, for an agent — to be useful in such domains, a number of special skills are likely to be required. Among these are the ability to monitor the execution of one's own actions, the ability to reason about actions that are outside one's own sphere of control, the ability to deal with actions which might (negatively) "interfere" with one another or with one's own goals, and the ability to form contingency plans to overcome such interference. Georgeff [9] argues further that one will require an agent to be capable of coordinating plans of action and of reasoning about the mental state — the beliefs, goals, and intentions — of other entities in the world; where knowledge of other entities' *motivations* is limited or where communication among entities is in some way restricted, an agent will often have to be able to infer such mental state from its observations of entity behavior. Kirsh, in addition, argues that for survival in real-world, human style environments, agents will require the ability to frame and test hypotheses about the future and about other agents' behaviors [10].

The potential gain from incorporating causal mental modelling capabilities in an autonomous agent is that by making successful predictions about entities' activities the agent should be able to detect potential goal conflicts earlier on. This would then enable it to make changes to its own plans in a more effective manner than if it were to wait for these conflicts to materialize. Goal conflicts can occur within the agent itself (for example, the agent's projected time of arrival at its destination exceeds its original deadline or the agent's layer $\mathcal{R}$ effects an action which alters the agent's trajectory) or in relation to another agent (for example, the agent's trajectory intersects that of another agent). Associated with the different goal conflicts that are known to the agent are a set of conflict-resolution strategies which, once adopted, typically result in the agent taking some action or adopting some new intention.

The structures used by an agent to model an entity's behavior are time indexed 4-tuples of the form $\langle C, B, D, I \rangle$, where C is the entity's *Configuration*, namely *(x,y)*-location, speed, acceleration, orientation, and signalled communications; B is the set of *Beliefs* ascribed to the entity; D is its ascribed list of prioritized goals or *Desires*; and I is its ascribed plan or *Intention* structure. Plan ascription or recognition has been realized in TouringMachines as a process of *scientific theory formation* which employs an abductive reasoning methodology similar to that of the Theorist default/diagnostic reasoning system [11].

The mental models used by an agent are, in fact, filled-in templates which the agent obtains from an internal model library. While all templates have the same basic 4-way structure, they can be made to differ in such aspects as the depth of information that can be represented or reasoned about (for example, a particular template's B component might dictate that modelled beliefs are to be treated as defeasible), initial default values provided, and computational resource cost. The last of these will subsequently be taken into account each time the agent makes an inference from the chosen model.

Reasoning from a model of an entity essentially involves looking for the "interaction of observation and prediction" [12]; that is, for any discrepancies between the agent's *actual* behavior and that *predicted* by its model or, in the case of a self-model, between the agent's actual behavior and that *desired* by the agent. Model-based reasoning in TouringMachines specifically comprises two phases: *explanation* and *prediction*. During the explanation phase, the agent attempts to generate plausible or inferred explanations about any entity (object/agent) behaviors which have recently been observed. Explanations (models) are then used in detecting discrepancies between these entities' current behaviors and those which had been anticipated from previous encounters. If any such behavioral discrepancies are detected, the agent will then strive to infer, via intention ascription, plausible explanations for their occurrence.

Once all model discrepancies have been identified and their causes inferred, predictions are formed by temporally projecting those parameters that make up the modelled entity's configuration vector C in the context of the current world situation and the entity's ascribed intention. The space-time projections (in effect, knowledge-level simulations) thus created are used by the agent to detect any potential interference or goal conflicts among the modelled entities' anticipated/desired actions. Should any conflicts — intra- or inter-agent — be identified, the agent will then have to determine how such conflicts might best be resolved, and also which entities will be responsible for carrying out these resolutions. Determining such resolutions, particularly where multiple goal conflicts are involved, will require consideration of a number of issues, including the priorities of the different goals affected, the space-time urgency of each conflict, rights-of-way protocols in operation, as well as any environmental and physical situational constraints (for example, the presence of other entities) or motivational forces (for example, an agent's own internal goals) that may constrain the possible actions that the agent can take [7].

4 Experimenting with TouringMachines

The research presented here adopts a fairly pragmatic approach toward understanding how complex environments might constrain the design of agents, and, conversely, how different task constraints and functional capabilities within agents might combine to produce different behaviors. In order to evaluate TouringMachines, a highly instrumented, parametrized, multi-agent simulation testbed has been implemented in conjunction with the TouringMachine control architecture. The testbed provides the user with a 2-dimensional world — the *TouringWorld* — which is occupied by, among other things, multiple TouringMachines, obstacles, walls, paths, and assorted information signs. World dynamics are realized by a discrete event simulator which incorporates a plausible world updater for enforcing "realistic" notions of time and motion, and which creates the illusion of concurrent world activity through appropriate action scheduling. Other processes handled by the simulator include a facility for tracing agent and environmental parameters, a statistics gathering package for agent performance analysis, a mechanism enabling the testbed user to control the motion of a chosen agent, a declarative specification language for defining the agents to be observed, and several text and graphics windows for displaying output. By enabling the user to specify, visualize, measure, and analyze any number of user-customized agents in a variety of single- and multi-agent settings, the testbed provides a powerful platform for the empirical study of autonomous agent behavior.

A number of experiments have been carried out on TouringMachines which illustrate, in particular, that the balance between goal-orientedness (effectiveness) and reactivity (robustness) in agents can be affected by a number of factors including, among other things, the level of detail involved in the predictions agents make about each other, the degree of sensitivity they demonstrate toward unexpected events, and the proportion of total agent resources that are made available for constructing plans or building mental models of other agents. Other experiments point toward a trade off between the reliability and the efficiency of the predictions an agent can make about the future (this turns out to be an instance of the well-known *extended prediction problem* [13]). Yet other experiments have been carried out which suggest that predicting future world states through causal modelling of agents' mental states, can, in certain situations, prove useful for promoting effective coordination between agents with conflicting goals. To illustrate some of the diverse opportunities for analysis which are afforded by the TouringMachine testbed, two particular experiments that illustrate the role of causal modelling of agent behavior will be described in some detail. Before this, however, a few comments on the adopted experimental methodology are worth giving.

4.1 Some Methodological Issues

One useful approach toward understanding the reasons for the behaviors exhibited by the TouringMachine agent design — and, more specifically, for identifying the conditions under which one configuration of the architecture performs better than another — is to vary the environment in which it operates. The simplest approach to this issue, Langley [14] argues, involves designing a set of benchmark problems, of which some, for the purposes of scientific comparison (that is, for the purposes of enabling independent variation of different task environment attributes), should involve artificial domains. The TouringWorld environment is one such domain (other examples include the Phoenix environment [15], the Tileworld [16], and MICE [17]).

The power of the TouringWorld testbed domain, and of artificial domains in general, arises from the insights it can provide toward the improved understanding of agent — in this case, TouringMachine — behavioral ecology: in other words, the understanding of the functional relationships that exist between the designs of agents (their internal structures and processes), their behaviors (the tasks they solve and the ways in which they solve these tasks), and the environments in which they are ultimately intended to operate [15].

The characterization of TouringMachines as a study of agent behavioral ecology exemplifies a research methodology which emphasizes complete, autonomous agents and complex, dynamic task environments. Within this methodological context, the focus of the present evaluation has been centered on two particular research tasks. Cohen *et al*. [15] refer to these as *environmental analysis*, in other words, understanding what characteristics of the environment most significantly constrain agent design; and the *design task*, in other words, understanding which agent design or configuration produces the desired behaviors under the expected range of environmental conditions.

These two tasks, in fact, are the first two stages of a more complete research methodology which Cohen [18] refers to as the *MAD* methodology, for *modelling*, *analysis*, and *design*.[2] This methodology aims to justify system design (and re-design) decisions with the use of predictive models of a system's behaviors and of the environmental factors that affect these system behaviors. Like IRMA agents in the Tileworld domain [16], TouringMachine agents can be viewed as having been developed via an incremental version of MAD, in which the (causal) model of TouringMachine behavior is developed incrementally, at the same time as the agent design. In other words, the agent design (or some part of its design) is implemented as early as possible, in order to provide empirical data (or feedback) which flesh out the model, which then become the basis for subsequent redesign [18]. The implications of adopting such a design method, as well as the roles played in this method by the environmental and behavioral analyses referred to above, are discussed in detail elsewhere [7].

The present evaluation of TouringMachines is realized through a series of interesting task scenarios involving one or more agents and/or zero or more obstacles or traffic lights. The scenarios have been selected with the aim of evaluating some of the different

---

2. The remaining design activities — *predicting* how the system (agent) will behave in partic- ular situations, *explaining* why the agent behaves as it does, and *generalising* agent designs to dif- ferent classes of systems, environments, and behaviours — are beyond the scope of this work. See Cohen [18, pages 29—32] for details.

capabilities and behaviors which TouringMachines will require if they are to complete their tasks in a competent and effective manner — for example, reacting to unexpected events, effecting of goal-directed actions, reflective and predictive goal monitoring, spatio-temporal reasoning, plan repair, coping with limited computational and informational resources, as well as dealing with real-time environmental change. The scenarios can be considered interesting because they succinctly exercise agents' abilities to carry out time-constrained tasks in complex — partially-structured, dynamic, real-time, multi-agent — environments. Although the chosen scenarios are simplified to deal only with mentally and structurally homogeneous agents possessing noiseless sensors, perfect actuators, and approximately similar non-shared relocation tasks these still present a number of non-trivial challenges to TouringMachine agents.

It is not the aim of the present evaluation to show that the TouringMachine architecture is in any sense "optimal". As argued elsewhere [7], optimal rational behavior will in general be impossible if the agent is resource-bounded, has several goals, and is to operate in a real-time multi-agent environment in which events are able to take place at several levels of space-time granularity. As such, one should more realistically expect a TouringMachine to behave satisficingly, but at times — for example, when under extreme real-time pressure — to fail to satisfy every one of its outstanding goals. What is really of interest here is understanding how the different configurations of agents and the different environmental characteristics to which such configurations are subjected affect, positively or negatively, the ability of agents to satisfy their goals.

It is also not the aim of the present evaluation to show that TouringMachines are "better" than other integrated agent architectures at performing their various tasks. Rarely is it the case that the actual and/or intended task domains of different agent architectures are described in sufficient detail so as to permit direct comparisons of agent performance. The lack, at present, of any common benchmark tasks or of any universally agreed upon criteria for assessing agent performance — previous evaluations have relied either on a single performance criterion (for example, the total point score earned for filling holes in specific single-agent Tileworld environments [16,19]), or on a small number of performance criteria which can only be interpreted with respect to the particular architecture being measured (for example, the total number of behaviors communicated between agents in selected MICE environments [17]) — combine to make detailed *quantitative* comparisons with other architectures extremely difficult if not altogether impossible.

Due to the relatively large number of parameters which the TouringWorld testbed provides for specifying different agent configurations, performance evaluation criteria (for example, task completion time, resource utilization), and agent task and environmental characteristics, the present evaluation will necessarily be partial, the main focus being placed on studying selected *qualitative* aspects of TouringMachine behavioral ecology — namely, some of the effects on agent behavior which, in a given task environment, can occur through varying individual agent configuration parameters; and the effects on agent behavior which, for a given agent configuration, can occur through varying certain aspects of the agent's environment. Like with the Tileworld experiments described by Pollack and Ringuette [16, page 187], a number of

TouringWorld "knobs" (for example, world clock timeslice size, total per-timeslice resources available to each agent, agent size, agent speed and acceleration/deceleration rate limits, agent sensing algorithm, initial attention focussing heuristics, reactive rule thresholds, plan schema and model template library entries) have been set to provide "baseline" environments which are dynamic, somewhat unpredictable, and moderately paced. In such environments, a competent (suitably configured) agent *should* be able to complete all of its goals, more or less according to schedule; however, under certain environmental conditions and/or agent parametrizations — a number of which will be analyzed below — this will not always be the case. In order to simplify the analysis of agents' behaviors in *multi-agent* settings, TouringMachine configurations — both mental and physical — should be presumed identical unless otherwise stated.

4.2 Monitoring the Environment: Sensitivity versus Efficiency

TouringMachines continuously monitor their surroundings for activity or change. In monitoring the state of another agent, and in particular, in determining whether the model it maintains of an agent's current physical configuration (its location, speed, orientation, etc.) is as it should be — that is, satisfies the expectations which were computed when it last projected the agent's model in space-time — a TouringMachine makes use of various tolerance bounds to decide whether any discrepancies in fact exist. As with any discrepancies detected in the agent's self model, identification of a discrepancy in the model of another entity typically requires further investigation to determine its cause. Often this reasoning process results in having to re-explain the entity's current behavior by ascribing it a new intention. For example, a discrepancy between the modelled entity's current and expected speeds might be indicative of the entity's change of intention from, say, drive-along-path to stop-at-junction.

In Fig. 3 (upper two frames) we can see, at two different time points, $T = 12.5$ seconds and $T = 15.5$ seconds, several agents in pursuit of their respective goals: agent1 (round), agent2 (chevron-shaped), and agent3 (triangular, top-most). Furthermore, we can see the effect on agent1's behavior — that is, on its ability to carry out its pre-defined homeostatic goal avoid-collisions — of modifying the value of **ModelSpeedBounds**, an internal agent parameter which, when modelling another entity, is used to constrain the "allowable" deviations between this entity's currently observed speed and the speed it was predicted to have had when the entity was last observed. In this scenario, agent1 has to contend with the numerous and unexpected speed changes effected by agent2, a testbed user-driven agent. With fairly tights bounds (for example **ModelSpeedBounds** = +/- 0.5 ms^{-1}), agent1 detects any speed discrepancies in agent2 which are greater than or equal to 0.5 ms^{-1}. Among such discrepancies detected by agent1 are those which result from agent2's deceleration just prior to its coming to a halt at a junction at time $T = 20.0$ (Fig. 3, lower left-hand frame). As a result, and compared to the situation when agent1 is configured with **ModelSpeedBounds** = +/-2.0 ms^{-1}, and therefore, in this particular scenario, unable to detect or respond fast enough to agent2's actions at $T = 20.0$ (Fig. 3, right-hand frame), the configuration with tighter speed bounds is more robust, more able to detect "important" events (for example, the agent in front coming to a halt) and also more able

213

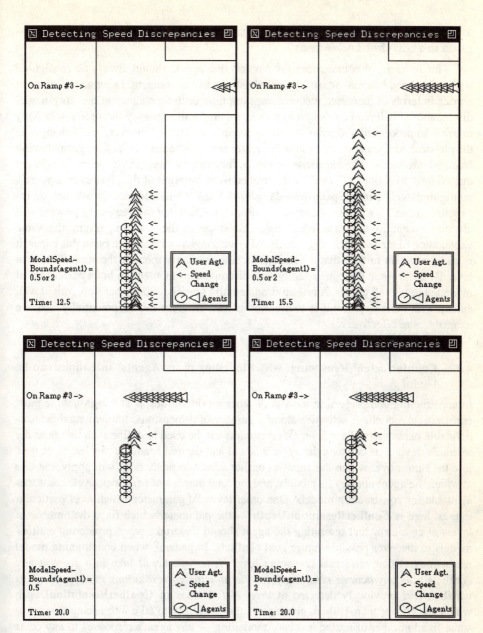

Fig. 3. Varying the value of an agent's **ModelSpeedBounds** parameter can affect the agent's level of sensitivity to environmental change.

to carry out timely and effective intention changes (for example, from `drive-along-path` to `stop-behind-agent`).

This in itself, of course, does not suggest that agents should always be configured with tight speed bounds. Sensitivity or robustness to environmental change can come at a price in terms of increased resource consumption: each time an agent detects a model discrepancy it is forced by design to try to explain the discrepancy through a (relatively expensive) process of abductive intention ascription.[3] Often, however, small changes in the physical configuration of a modelled entity need not be the result of the entity having changed intentions. In the scenario of Fig. 3, for example, `agent2`'s speed changes are due entirely to actions effected by the testbed user. Ignorant of this, however, `agent1` configured with **ModelSpeedBounds** $= +/-0.5$ ms^{-1} will continually attempt to re-explain `agent2`'s changing behavior — despite the fact that this reasoning process will always, except in the case when `agent2` stops at the junction, return the same explanation of `drive-along-path`. Also, although not elaborated on in this paper, it is also important to note that a TouringMachine may only monitor the state of its *own* layer $\mathcal{M}$ goals when there are exactly zero discrepancies to attend to in its current set of modelled (external) agents. A less environmentally sensitive agent, therefore, might well end up with more opportunities to monitor its own progress and so, potentially, achieve its goals more effectively.

4.3 Counterfactual Reasoning: why Modelling other Agents' Intentions can be Useful

In constructing and projecting models of other world entities, a TouringMachine must constrain its modelling activities along a number of dimensions. Implemented as user-definable parameters, these layer $\mathcal{M}$ constraints can be used to define such things as the tolerable deviations between the agent's actual and desired headings, the length of time into the future over which the agent's conflict detection predictions will apply, the rate at which the agent updates its models, and the total number of per-clock-cycle resources available for constructing models. One other layer $\mathcal{M}$ parameter which is of particular interest here is **ConflictResolutionDepth** — the parameter which fixes the number of levels of counterfactual reasoning the agent should undertake when projecting entities' models to discover possible future goal conflicts. In general, when constructing model projections at counterfactual reasoning level N, an agent will take into account any conflicts *plus any actions resulting from the anticipated resolutions to these conflicts* which it had previously detected at level $N-1$. Values of **ConflictResolutionDepth** which are greater than 1, then, give agents the flexibility to take into account — up to some fixed number of nested levels of modelling — any agent's responses to any other agent's responses to any predicted conflicts.

In the scenario of Fig. 4, two TouringMachine agents can be seen following

---

3. The process is expensive in the sense that since the agent has only enough computational resources to focus on a subset of entities in the world at any given time, misplaced sensitivity can result in the agent making poor use of its limited resources and potentially missing what might otherwise have been critical events.

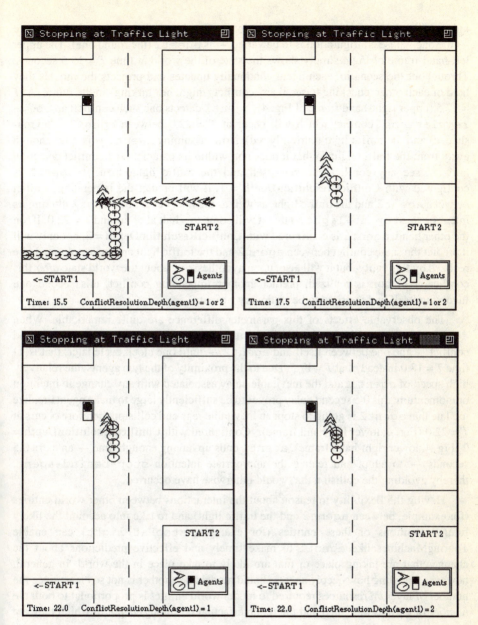

Fig. 4. Altering the value of an agent's **ConflictResolutionDepth** parameter can affect the timeliness and effectiveness of any predictions it might make.

independent routes to one destination or another. The interesting agent to focus on here — the one whose configuration is to be varied — is agent1 (the round one). The upper left-hand frame of Fig.4 simply shows the state of the world at time $T = 15.5$ seconds. Throughout the scenario, each agent continually updates and projects the models they hold of each other, checking to see if any conflicts might be "lurking" in the future. At $T = 17.5$ (upper right-hand frame of Fig. 4), agent1 detects one such conflict: an obey-regulations[4] conflict which will occur at $T = 22.0$ between agent2 (chevron-shaped) and the traffic light (currently red). Now, assuming agent1 is just far enough away from the traffic light so that it does not, within its parametrized conflict detection horizon, see any conflict between itself and the traffic light, then, if agent1 is configured with **ConflictResolutionDepth** = 1, it will predict the impending conflict between agent2 and the traffic light, as well as the likely event of agent2 altering its intention to stop-at-light so that it will come to a halt at or around $T = 22.0$. If, on the other hand, agent1 is configured with **ConflictResolutionDepth** = 2, not only will it predict the same conflict between agent2 and the traffic light and the resolution to be realized by this entity, but it will also, upon hypothesizing about the world state *after* this conflict resolution is realized, predict another impending conflict, this second one involving itself and the soon to be stationary agent2.

The observable effects of this parameter difference are quite remarkable. When agent1 is configured with **ConflictResolutionDepth** = 1, it will not detect this second conflict — the one between itself and agent2 — until one clock cycle later; that is, at time $T = 18.0$ instead of at $T = 17.5$. Due to the proximity of the two agents, the relatively high speed of agent1, and the inevitable delay associated with any change in intention or momentum, this 0.5 second delay proves to be sufficiently large to make agent1 realize too late that agent2 is going to stop; an inevitable rear-end collision therefore occurs at $T = 22.0$ (Fig. 4, lower left-hand frame).[5] Configured with **ConflictResolutionDepth** = 2 (Fig. 4, lower right-hand frame), agent1 ends up having enough time — an extra 0.5 seconds — to adopt and realize the appropriate intention stop-behind-agent, thereby avoiding the collision that would otherwise have occurred.

Having the flexibility to reason about the interactions between other world entities (for example, between agent2 and the traffic light) and to take into account the likely future intentions of these entities (for example, stop-at-light) can enable TouringMachines like agent1 to make timely and effective predictions about the changes that are taking place or that are likely to take place in the world. In general, however, knowing how deeply agents should model one another is not so clear: since the number of layer $\mathcal{M}$ resources required to model world entities is proportional to both the *number* of entities modelled and the (counterfactual reasoning) *depth* to which they are

---

4. All agents possess the homeostatic goal obey-regulations which, in this particular example, will trigger a goal conflict if the agent in question (agent2) is expected to run through the red traffic light.

5. In fact, this collision need not be "inevitable": in this scenario both agent1 and agent2 have been configured with fairly insensitive (not very robust) layer $\mathcal{R}$ reactions, primarily to emphasize the different behaviours that *could* result from different parametrizations of agents' modelling capabilities.

modelled, agents will ultimately have to strike a balance between breadth of coverage (more entities modelled, little detail) and depth of coverage (less entities, more detail). This issue is investigated in more detail elsewhere [7].

5 Conclusions

Through the above and a number of other single- and multi-agent coordination experiments addressing such issues as the production of emergent behavioral patterns, the TouringMachine architecture has been shown to be feasible and that, when suitably configured, can endow rational autonomous agents with appropriate levels of effective, robust, and flexible control for successfully carrying out multiple goals while simultaneously dealing with a number of dynamic multi-agent events.

The integration of a number of traditionally expensive deliberative reasoning mechanisms (for example, causal modelling and hierarchical planning) with reactive or behavior-based mechanisms is a challenge which has been addressed in the TouringMachine architecture. Additional challenges such as enabling effective agent operation under real-time constraints and with bounded computational resources have also been addressed. The result is a novel architectural design which can successfully produce a range of useful behaviors required of sophisticated autonomous agents embedded in complex environments.

The research presented here is ongoing; current work on the TouringMachine agent architecture includes an effort to generalize further the TouringWorld testbed, in particular, by separating the definition of the agent's domain of operation (description of the environment, initial goals to accomplish, criteria for successful completion of goals) from the specified configuration (capabilities, internal parameters and constraints) of the agent itself. Another aspect of the current work is to identify and incorporate new capabilities in order to extend the behavioral repertoire of agents; capabilities being considered at present include, among others, inductive learning, user modelling, and episodic memory management. Relatedly, a new domain to which TouringMachines are currently being applied involves adaptive information retrieval and filtering on the World Wide Web.

References

1. Rodney A. Brooks. A robust layered control system for a mobile robot. *IEEE Journal of Robotics and Automation*, 2(1):14−23, 1986.

2. Philip E. Agre and David Chapman. Pengi: An implementation of a theory of activity. In *Proceedings Conference of the American Association for Artificial Intelligence*, pages 268−272, 1987.

3. Yoav Shoham. AGENT0: A simple agent language and its interpreter. In *Proceedings Conference of the American Association for Artificial Intelligence*, pages 704−709, 1991.

4. Steven Vere and Timothy Bickmore. A basic agent. *Computational Intelligence*, 6(1):41−60, 1990.

5. Innes A. Ferguson. TouringMachines: Autonomous Agents with Attitudes. *IEEE Computer*, 25(5), 51—55, 1992.

6. Innes A. Ferguson. Toward an Architecture for Adaptive, Rational, Mobile Agents. In E. Werner and Y. Demazeau (eds.) *Decentralized AI 3*, Elsevier Science (North Holland): Amsterdam, 1992.

7. Innes A. Ferguson. *TouringMachines: An Architecture for Dynamic, Rational, Mobile Agents*. Ph.D. thesis, Computer Laboratory, University of Cambridge, Cambridge UK, 1992.

8. Marvin L. Minsky. *The Society of Mind*. Simon and Schuster: NY, NY, 1986.

9. Michael P. Georgeff. Planning. In J. Allen, J. Hendler, and A. Tate, editors, *Readings in Planning*, pages 5—25. Morgan Kaufmann: San Mateo, CA, 1990.

10. David Kirsh. Today the earwig, tomorrow man? *Artificial Intelligence*, 47:161—184, 1991.

11. David L. Poole, Randy G. Goebel, and Romas Aleliunas. Theorist: A logical reasoning system for defaults and diagnosis. Research Report CS-86-06, University of Waterloo, Waterloo, Ont., February 1986.

12. Randall Davis and Walter Hamscher. Model-based reasoning: Troubleshooting. In Howard E. Shrobe and AAAI, editors, *Exploring Artificial Intelligence*, pages 297—346. Morgan Kaufmann: San Mateo, CA, 1988.

13. Yoav Shoham and Drew McDermott. Problems in formal temporal reasoning. In James Allen, James Hendler, and Austin Tate, editors, *Readings in Planning*, pages 581—587. Morgan Kaufmann: San Mateo, CA, 1990.

14. Pat Langley. Machine learning as an experimental science. *Machine Learning*, 3:5—8, 1988.

15. Paul R. Cohen, Michael L. Greenberg, David M. Hart, and Adele E. Howe. Trial by fire: Understanding the design requirements for agents in complex environments. *AI Magazine*, 10(3):32—48, 1989.

16. Martha E. Pollack and Marc Ringuette. Introducing the Tileworld: Experimentally evaluating agent architectures. In *Proceedings Conference of the American Association for Artificial Intelligence*, pages 183—189, 1990.

17. Edmund H. Durfee and Thomas A. Montgomery. A hierarchical protocol for coordinating multiagent behaviors. In *Proceedings Conference of the American Association for Artificial Intelligence*, pages 86—93, 1990.

18. Paul R. Cohen. A survey of the Eighth National Conference on Artificial Intelligence: Pulling together or pulling apart. AI Magazine, 12(1):16—41, 1991.

19. David N. Kinny and Michael Georgeff. Commitment and effectiveness of situated agents. Technical Note 17, Australian Artificial Intelligence Institute, Carleton 3053, Australia, April 1991

An Agent Architecture for Distributed Medical Care

Jun Huang[1], N. R. Jennings[2] and John Fox[3]

[1] Dept. of Computing, University of Central Lancashire, Preston PR1 2HE, UK.

[2]Dept. of Electronic Engineering, Queen Mary & Westfield College,
Mile End Road, London E1 4NS, UK.

[3]Advanced Computation Laboratory, Imperial Cancer Research Fund,
61 Lincoln's Inn Fields, London WC2A 3PX, UK.

Abstract. This paper describes the design and implementation of a layered agent architecture for decision support applications in general and for distributed medical care in particular. Three important characteristics which shaped the agent design are identified: distribution of data and control, information uncertainty, and environment dynamism. To provide appropriate decision support in these circumstances the architecture combines a number of AI and agent techniques: a symbolic decision procedure for decision making with incomplete and contradictory information, a concept of accountability for task allocation, commitments and conventions for managing coherent cooperation, and a set of communication primitives for inter-agent interaction.

1. Introduction

Artificial Intelligence and knowledge based systems are assuming an increasingly important role in medicine for assisting clinical staff in making decisions under uncertainty (eg diagnosis decisions, therapy and test selection, and prescribing). Furthermore, many medical procedures now involve several individuals, in a number of specialist departments, whose decisions and actions need to be coordinated if the care is to be effective and efficient [1, 2, 3]. For example, a general practitioner (GP) may suspect that his patient has breast cancer. However, as he neither has the knowledge nor the resources to confirm this hypothesis, he must refer the patient to a hospital specialist who can make a firm diagnosis. Having confirmed the presence of breast cancer, the specialist must devise a care programme for treating the patient - this typically involves hospital nurses, the patient's GP, and a home care organisation jointly executing a series of interrelated tasks.

To provide the appropriate software support for such coordinated health care management it was decided to adopt an agent-based approach. This decision was based on three main observations about the medical care management domain (given below) and the properties of autonomy, social ability, reactivity and proactiveness which are normally associated with intelligent agents [4]. The first relevant domain property is the fact that there is a significant physical distribution of information, problem-solving capabilities, resources, and responsibilities which need to be brought together in a consistent and coherent fashion by the distributed 'agents' who jointly execute a care programme (here agent is defined as an integrated entity involving a computer system and its user). Secondly, the combination of the aforementioned decentralisation and the high cost of obtaining a comprehensive overview means that many different, partial and overlapping problem solving models exist within the community - hence the ability to reason with contradictory and incomplete information and knowledge is essential. Finally, as the environment is highly dynamic and unpredictable the problem solvers need to exhibit intelligent goal-oriented behaviour yet still be responsive to changes in their circumstances - plans to achieve particular goals need to be devised and whilst these plans are being executed they need to be continuously monitored (and perhaps refined) in the light of changes in information and problem solving state.

Given these domain properties and previous experience with medical care management systems it was possible to identify the main problems which the new agent-based system had to overcome and the additional functionalities which needed to be offered to provide the desired degree of decision support. Firstly, the system needs explicit communication management (dealing with both syntax and semantics) so that the sender and receiver of a message have a common understanding of its meaning and purpose (previously messages were often misinterpreted during extensive interactions because of ambiguities in the communication structures). Secondly, appropriate mechanisms and structures are needed to ensure that tasks are delegated to the most appropriate agents (previously tasks could be allocated to the wrong agents and thus delays in the delivery of care occurred - a serious concern when time is a critical factor in care administration). Thirdly, a decision making mechanism which is able to reason with contradictory and incomplete information is needed (previously the popularly used decision methods, especially those based on probabilistic theory, could not tolerate conflicting or incomplete information). Finally, to ensure coherent care in spite of the dynamic and unpredictable environment an explicit set of procedures for monitoring an agent's goals and plans needs to be specified and adopted by all the agents (previously no explicit procedures existed and changes in goals and care plans were managed largely in an *ad-hoc* and ineffective manner).

The paper is structured in the following manner: section 2 describes the agent architecture and the inter-agent communication structures which were developed in the course of this work. The architecture itself is based on a three-layer knowledge organisation (domain layer, inference layer and control layer) and is informed by work on The Oxford System of Medicine [5] and the KADS model of expertise [6]. The remainder of the paper deals in turn with each of the key agent functionalities described above - section 3 with the decision making mechanisms, section 4 with the task allocation mechanisms, and section 5 with the cooperation management mechanisms. Finally, section 6 compares the developed agent architecture with related work.

2. The Agent Architecture

The agent architecture comprises multiple layers of knowledge, a working memory, a communications manager and a human-computer interface (see figure 1). To be successful in this domain, the agent needs to exhibit both deliberative behaviour (eg plan selection, task decomposition, and task allocation) and reactive behaviour (eg respond in a timely manner to the arrival of new data, to changes in existing data, and to varying agent commitments). Within the proposed architecture the deliberative behaviour is achieved by the incorporation of decision rules for plan selection, task management rules for task decomposition and allocation, and cooperation rules for formulating commitments. The reactive behaviour is achieved by the control layer which responds to changes in the working memory (e.g. the arrival of new task results, goals, or messages or changes in existing data, goals, agent commitments or task states). The remainder of this section describes each of the main components of the architecture in more detail.

The three *layers of knowledge* which form the key part of the agent architecture are as follows:

• Domain knowledge - includes: a knowledge base covering specific medical domains such as breast cancer, a knowledge base of clinical management plans (known as *clinical protocols* [7]), a database of patient records, and a database of resource availability.

• Inference knowledge - in the form of generic, declarative inference rules which apply domain knowledge to specific patient cases to infer new data. Inference rules represent the core of the agent architecture and are subdivided into those for decision making under uncertainty (section 3), those for task management (section 4), and those for managing agent cooperation (section 5).

• Control knowledge - which applies the inference knowledge to the domain knowledge in order to generate inferences whenever new data is added to the working memory.

In more detail, the domain knowledge base simply states information and facts about the domain. It says nothing about how the knowledge is to be used. For example, it states that a task called '1st-cycle EMV chemotherapy' contains two subtasks, 'inject cytotoxic drugs' and 'measure patient temperature':

```
component(`1st-cycle EMV chemotherapy',
                'inject cytotoxic drugs').
component(`1st-cycle EMV chemotherapy',
                'measure patient temperature').
```

The inference knowledge base contains rules (implemented as declarative schemas) that specify the inference relations between domain-level knowledge and possible new information. For example, the task management module contains a declarative inference schema for managing task state transitions:

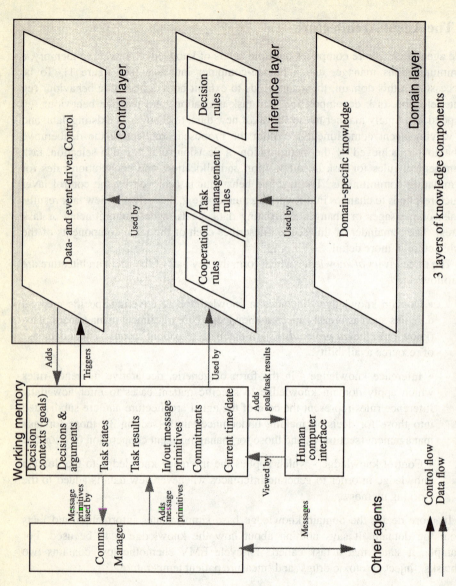

Figure 1: Agent architecture for distributed medical care

```
schema(conditions(component(Task, SubTask) and
                  state(SubTask, started) ),
       conclusions(state(Task, started) ).
```

However, it is only at the control level that the actual execution of the inference rules is carried out and new data is added into the working memory:

```
If schema(Conditions, Conclusions) and
   all_true(Conditions)
then add(Conclusions)
```

There are two main reasons for adopting this functional and logical separation of domain, inference and control knowledge. Firstly, it simplifies the representation, reuse and maintenance of knowledge. Inference knowledge for decision making, task management and cooperation is represented independently of medical domains and can therefore be reused; control knowledge is represented independently of the inference knowledge and so the same control rules can be applied to the different groups of inference rules. Furthermore, modifications to domain knowledge can be made independently of inference and control knowledge. The second main reason for such a separation is that it provides a convenient basis for knowledge elicitation: domain knowledge can be acquired and modified independently of inference and control knowledge.

The *working memory* stores temporary data generated by the control layer, the user, or the communications manager. Examples of the types of information which need to be stored include: goals to be achieved, control states of tasks that are currently active, results of completed tasks, incoming and outgoing messages, and current commitments. Its function is similar to that of a global blackboard, on to which new information (or any change which triggers reactions by the control layer) can be added.

The *communications manager* composes the messages to be sent to the other agents from the primitives produced by firing task management rules or cooperation rules (see sections 4 and 5 for respective examples). The primitives each have a type and a content as well as a specified effect on the recipient - they include: request, accept, reject, alter, suggest, inform, query, cancel and acknowledge [8]. Request, accept, reject and alter are used during the allocation of tasks and the formulation of agreed courses of action. A suggest act may be the result of a query. Inform usually follows an accepted request to perform a certain task and is typically used to return the results of the task back to the originator. Cancel is included because in certain circumstances agents may not wish to adhere to the agreed plan of action (see section 5.2). Finally, all messages must be acknowledged. The communication manager also converts messages which arrive from other agents into primitives that may be used by the cooperation manager.

The *human computer interface* defines a scheme for interaction between the system and its user. The approach is as follows: the computer is capable of performing various functions (i.e. decision making, task management, communication and cooperation) but may not act autonomously on all of these capabilities. In general, the computer informs the user of the results of its inferences and the user must then endorse or authorise them before they can be communicated to external agents. For example, the system may recommend to a GP that he refers a patient to a hospital consultant for a particular course of treatment, but the GP may have a personal preference for another consultant and therefore be unwilling to make such a referral. In this case, the system will not send an electronic request to the consultant and will instead offer the GP an alternative solution.

3. Decision Making Under Uncertainty

The purpose of the decision rules is to choose among alternative options (e.g. potential diagnoses of a patient's illness, potential clinical protocols which could be used to treat the patient, etc.). As well as being used to decide which course of action to start, these rules may also be embedded as a decision point within the body of an action - eg whilst executing a particular clinical protocol there may be a crucial decision to be made which needs to make use of the decision making know-how contained in this rule group (see section 4 for an illustration of this point with respect to prescribing).

In this application, the decision making is often complicated by the presence of incomplete or even conflicting information. For example, a drug may be very effective for eliminating a tumour, but the patient may be unwilling to tolerate its side effects such as loss of hair. To facilitate decision making in such a context, a domain-independent decision procedure is abstracted and separated from domain-specific knowledge: the same set of decision rules can then be used to make decisions in varying medical domains (such as cancer, diabetes, cardiology etc.). Such a separation also permits formalisation of the decision knowledge.

The starting point of a decision making session is a goal, represented as a *decision context*, which is either given by the user or generated by the task management rules (section 4). By way of an example, the agent could have a goal of deciding which clinical protocol to select to treat a patient with breast cancer. Given this context, there are several distinct components of the decision procedure. The primary component activities are *proposing* candidate decision options, *refining* candidates, *arguing* the pros and cons of the options in view of the available evidence (argument generation), and *aggregating* the arguments to determine the preferred option (argument aggregation). For instance, the use of chemotherapy and radiotherapy may be proposed to treat the breast cancer of an old-aged patient (proposing). These options may then be refined to specific chemotherapy and radiotherapy treatments (refining). Arguments supporting the use of a particular chemotherapy treatment may include its effectiveness for removing the cancer, but there may also be arguments against its use (e.g. the level of toxicity associated with the drug may be too high for this particular patient due to her age). The pros and cons for each proposed option are finally combined to give a most preferred decision - e.g. the decision to use FB1 chemotherapy (argument aggregation).

The decision procedure is based on a simple but flexible method of reasoning under uncertainty for argument generation and aggregation, called *argumentation* [9], which avoids the necessity for precise quantification of uncertainty. Argumentation involves two simple ideas. First, one may know that some piece of information increases one's belief in a diagnosis, or preference for an action, though one may not be able to put a precise number on the change. Arguments for options can be constructed that are qualitatively labelled to indicate this change - for example, "confirm", "support", "weaken" or "exclude". Arguments of this sort are similar to Cohen's endorsements [10], but in this work a more sophisticated set of aggregation functions are used to combine collections of arguments to yield a preference ordering on the decision options. This method is versatile, conceptually intuitive, easy to implement and simplifies some of the problems of knowledge acquisition and maintenance. Second, the grounds of arguments for and against decisions are explicitly represented - this means they can serve a variety of functions including truth maintenance and explanation.

Details of this approach to decision making are given elsewhere - for example, [11] describes it within a general context of qualitative reasoning and [12] gives a more formal, declarative specification of the decision procedure and discusses its application in medical decision making - and therefore will not be elaborated upon here. The emphasis in this paper is on the use of this generic decision knowledge alongside task management and cooperation knowledge in an integrated agent architecture for coordinated care. For example, the decision rules select an appropriate clinical protocol, which is then decomposed, allocated and monitored by the task management and cooperation rules.

4. Task Management

Once the decision procedure has selected a particular clinical protocol to achieve the agent's goal the task manager component is responsible for its decomposition into subtasks, the allocation of subtasks to appropriate agents, and the management of task state transitions. Each of these activities is described in turn in the remainder of this section.

The structure of a generic clinical plan (e.g. for treating breast cancer) is determined by experts in authority, and is precisely defined in a clinical protocol. The task management rules decompose such a protocol into subtasks according to the predefined plan structure. Subtasks at the bottom of the plan hierarchy may be primitive actions for humans or machines to perform (such as measuring a patient's temperature) or they may be decision tasks (such as choosing the right cytotoxic drug for a breast cancer patient). In the latter case, the decision procedure is used to perform such a task, as explained in the previous section.

To facilitate task allocation, there are two roles associated with each (sub)task within the system - there is one agent who *manages* the execution of the task (i.e. ensures that it gets executed by somebody within the system and that the result of the execution will be sent back to the originator) and one agent who is actually responsible for *performing* the task (the contractor). Task allocation is, therefore, the process by which the manager of a task finds the most appropriate contractor to perform it. The key structure in making such decisions is that of *accountability*.

Accountability is a static relationship which defines what and to whom an agent is responsible. It is expressed by the following relation: accountable(Agent1, Agent2, TaskType) which means that Agent1 is accountable to Agent2 for performing tasks of type TaskType. For example, a hospital nurse may be accountable to one or more doctors for monitoring patient data such as temperature and blood pressure. The task manager component uses its accountability relations, together with the generic inference rule given below, to pick the most appropriate contractor for a given task. The underlined term "request" represents a primitive which is sent to the communications manager when this task management rule is fired (as described in section 2).

```
IF Task is necessary &
    Task is of type TaskType &
    Acquaintance is accountable to Agent for tasks of
        TaskType &
    Agent prefers to interact with Acquaintance
        concerning TaskType
THEN request (Agent, Acquaintance, perform (Task))
```

All tasks within the system have a state (either scheduled, cancelled, started, completed, or abandoned). The management of the transitions between these states needs to be carefully controlled by the agents because such transitions need to be documented in patients' care records: for example, when a task was scheduled, when it was started, when it was completed and when (why) it was abandoned. Transition management is complicated by the complex structure of the care plans. For example, the following two task management rules specify that when a composite task is cancelled, its started subtasks become abandoned and the subtasks that are scheduled but not yet started become cancelled:

```
schema(conditions(state(Task, cancelled), and
                  component(Task, SubTask) and
                  state(SubTask, started) ),
    conclusions(state(SubTask, abandoned) ).

schema(conditions(state(Task, cancelled), and
                  component(Task, SubTask) and
                  state(SubTask, scheduled) ),
    conclusions(state(SubTask, cancelled) ).
```

A distinction is made between the states of cancelled and abandoned because a corrective action is usually needed for an abandoned task (e.g. when the patient has to stop taking a certain drug which he has already been taking for a period) whereas such action is not normally necessary for a cancelled task.

5. Managing Agent Cooperation

The underlying mechanisms on which cooperative interactions are based are those of *commitment* (pledge to undertake a specified course of action) and *convention* (means of monitoring commitments in changing circumstances) [13]. The former means that if an agent agrees to undertake a task then it will endeavour to execute it at the appropriate time - this implies both that the agent is able to perform the task and that it has the necessary resources. Conventions are needed because commitments are not irrevocable: agents' circumstances may change between the making and the execution of their commitments, and agreed actions may turn out to be undesirable or even impossible to perform. Conventions, therefore, define the conditions under which an agent can drop its commitments and how to behave with respect to other agents in the cooperating group when such circumstances arise.

Given that cooperation is founded on commitments and conventions, two key issues need to be addressed: (i) what is involved in establishing a commitment? (section 5.1); and (ii) what type of convention is appropriate for monitoring commitments in the given care organisation? (section 5.2).

5.1 Establishing commitments

Accountability alone does not guarantee commitment: to commit to a specified task, an agent must also have the necessary resources (temporal and material) which are required to perform that task[1]. For example, a hospital specialist may be accountable to patients for breast cancer surgery, but will not become committed to surgery on a specific patient until the time (temporal resource) and equipment (material resource) are available to perform the operation. Although agents know what resources are available to themselves, they do not generally have information about the resources of their acquaintances. Therefore a task may have to be iteratively delegated to a number of acquaintances until a specific agent becomes committed.

When an agent accepts a request it becomes committed to performing it (i.e. it takes on the role of contractor) and informs the manager that the task has been accepted using the following inference rule:

```
IF   Acquaintance is requested by Agent to perform Task &
     Acquaintance accountable to Agent for TaskType tasks&
     Task is of type TaskType &
     Task requires Resources &
     Resources are available to Acquaintance
THEN   Acquaintance becomes committed to Task, AND
       accept(Acquaintance, Task, for(Agent) )
```

[1.] In addition, an agent may also have a local policy governing the acceptability of a requested task. For example, a hospital may specify the following internal policy: a patient can only be admitted to the hospital if his/her GP is suitably registered with the hospital (so that the hospital can be paid more quickly). The capture and use of these policies remains a challenge to computer-assisted care and so, for the sake of simplicity, it is assumed here that availability of the appropriate resources is the only requirement for an agent to commit to a task.

Commitment to the role of contractor also entails an additional responsibility - when the task has been completed the contractor must inform the manager about it and any results which have been generated - again this behaviour is encoded in a generic inference rule:

```
IF  Task is completed and it produces Results &
    Acquaintance is committed to Agent for Task
  THEN   inform (Acquaintance, Agent, performed(Task),
                          results-produced(Task, Results))
```

Note that in both cases, the underlined term represents primitives sent to the communication manager when the appropriate inference rules are triggered (as described in section 2).

5.2 Adaptive management of commitment changes

In most cases, when an agent commits itself to perform a task then that task will indeed be executed. However in certain well-defined circumstances it may be appropriate for an agent to renege upon its commitment. There may be an unforeseen lack of resources (e.g. unrelated emergencies may arise), the need for the task may cease to exist (e.g. because of the unexpected death of the patient), or it may no longer be feasible to execute a given task (e.g. a planned chemotherapy may have to be withdrawn because the patient has a high temperature resulting from the toxic effect of the drug). Having detailed the conditions under which commitments can be cancelled, the convention must also specify how to manage this change both locally and within the wider context of the cooperating group. The latter is important because it ensures that the cooperating care agents will behave coherently in the face of dynamic and unpredictable changes in the network [14]. Figure 2 details the convention embodied in the cooperation manager in this application.

6. Related Work

In this section our architecture is briefly compared with some of the well-known architectures and systems in the literature.

GRATE [15] is also a layered architecture that provides a generic cooperation module, situation assessment module, control module, and application-specific module. However the GRATE framework lacks an uncertainty management mechanism which is essential for medical decision making. Also GRATE's layers are functionally separated rather than logically separated - the additional benefit of this logical separation is that it provides a convenient basis for declarative specification and for logical verification and validation of the various layers of knowledge (eg in a formal language such as ML^2 [16]). The same two observations can be made of similar layered architectures presented in this volume, such as INTERRAP [17] and TouringMachines [18].

```
REASONS FOR RE-ASSESSING COMMITMENTS TO A TASK:

    • Task is no longer necessary
    • Resources for Task become unavailable
    • Commitment to the super-task of Task is dropped

ACTIONS:

R1: IF Manager of Task believes Task is no longer necessary
    THEN   request (Manager, Contractor,
                              drop-commitment(Contractor, Task))

R2: IF Contractor for Task believes Task is no longer necessary
            for a certain Reason
    THEN inform(Contractor, Manager, unnecessary(Task, Reason))

R3: IF Contractor for Task drops commitment to Task, AND
        Task has a SubTask
    THEN request (Contractor(Task), Contractor(SubTask),
                drop-commitment(Contractor(SubTask), SubTask))

R4: IF Resources allocated to Task become unavailable
    THEN   Contractor for Task drops his commitment to Task &
           inform (Contractor, Manager(Task),
                     drop-commitment(Contractor, Task, Reason))

R5: IF Manager of Task is informed that Contractor for Task is
            no longer committed to Task, AND
        Manager believes that Task is still necessary, AND
        Manager has another accountable Acquaintance for Task
    THEN request (Manager, Acquaintance, perform (Task))
```

Figure 2. Convention for Adapting Commitments

Coordinator [19] is a conversational system for coordinated action which is based on Searle's speech act theory [20]. However, whilst the generation and monitoring of speech acts and commitments are centralised in Coordinator, our architecture distributes both of these functions (thus helping to reduce the communication bottleneck). Also the functionality of Coordinator is limited to coordination alone through the generation of speech acts and commitments, whereas our architecture accommodates additional functions such as a generic decision module for decision making under uncertainty.

Our proposal also bears certain similarities to a standard blackboard architecture [21]. In both cases the working memory is changed through the application of functionally separated modules of inference rules. However, in addition to functional separation, our architecture also emphasises the logical layering of knowledge for reasons stated above and provides a set of generic knowledge modules for cooperation and decision making.

7. Conclusions

This paper has described the design and implementation of an agent architecture for distributed medical care management (an application area which is representative of an important class of real world problems). A prototype system has been developed for the specific application of distributed management of cancer patients among general practices, hospitals, home care organisations and pharmacies. PROLOG is used for the representation of the domain- and inference- layer knowledge, and a production-rule language, implemented in PROLOG, is used for the data-driven control. A standard email system and server is used for message passing among the care agents.

Preliminary evaluation of this prototype indicates that in real clinical application settings where exact probabilities and utilities are difficult to obtain the built-in symbolic decision procedure is more effective than conventional numerical methods [22]. Also a senior oncologist manager and a senior cardiologist manager concluded that the cooperation strategy would provide useful guidance for clinicians jointly executing a care programme.

Acknowledgements

The first and third authors are grateful to the EC Advanced Informatics in Medicine (AIM) programme for funding the DILEMMA project, in which this work was carried out. The role of the second author has been to assist in the design and specification of the cooperation and communication mechanisms. All the authors would like to thank Richard Thomson and the two anonymous reviewers for their helpful comments on earlier drafts of this paper.

References

[1] Pritchard, P., (1992) "The role of computers in referral", in *Referrals to Medical Outpatients* (eds. Hopkins, A. & Wallace, P.), Royal Colleges of Physicians and General Practitioners, pp 79-89

[2] Reeves, P., Rickards, T., and Carniel, B., (1993) "Requirements for Shared Care Decision Support in Cardiology", Technical Report, Royal Brompton National Heart and Lung Hospital, London, England.

[3] Renaud-Salis, J. L., Lagouarde, P., Gordon, C., and Thomson, R., (1992), "Requirements for Decision Support in Cancer Shared Care", Technical Report, Fondation Bergonie, Bordeaux, France.

[4] Wooldridge, M. J., and Jennings, N. R., (1995) "Agent Theories, Architectures and Languages: A Survey" In this volume.

[5] Fox, J., Glowinski, A., Gordon, C., Hajnal, A., and O'Neil, M., (1990) "Logic Engineering for Knowledge Engineering: Design and Implementation of the Oxford System of Medicine", *Artificial Intelligence in Medicine* 2, pp 323-339.

[6] Hickman, F. R., Killin, J. L., Land, L., Mulhall, T., Porter, D., and Taylor, R. M., (1989) *"Analysis for Knowledge Based Systems: a Practical Guide to the KADS Methodology"* Ellis Horwood, Chichester.

[7] Gordon, C., Herbert, S. I., Jackson-Smale, A., and Renaud-Salis, J. L., (1993) "Care protocols and healthcare informatics", *Proc. of Artificial Intelligence in Medicine Europe 93*, Munich, Germany, pp 289-309.

[8] Huang, J., Jennings, N. R., and Fox, J., (1994) "Cooperation in Distributed Medical Care", *Proc. of Second Int. Conf. on Cooperative Information Systems*, Toronto, Canada, pp 255-263.

[9] Krause, P., Amble, S., and Fox, J., (1993), "The Development of a Logic of Argumentation", in: *Advanced Methods in Artificial Intelligence*, Lecture Notes in Computer Science Series, Springer-Verlag, Berlin

[10] Cohen, P. R., (1985) *"Reasoning about Uncertainty: An Artificial Intelligence Approach"*, Pitman, London.

[11] Fox, J., and Krause, P., (1992) "Qualitative frameworks for decision support: lessons from medicine", *Knowledge Engineering Review* 7, pp 19-33.

[12] Huang J., Fox J., Gordon C., and Jackson-Smale A., (1993) "Symbolic decision support in Medical Care", *Artificial Intelligence in Medicine* 5, pp 415-430.

[13] Jennings N. R., (1993) "Commitments and conventions: the foundation of coordination in multi-agent systems", *Knowledge Engineering Review 8*, pp 223-250.

[14] Jennings, N. R., (1995) "Controlling Cooperative Problem Solving in Industrial Multi-Agent Systems using Joint Intentions" *Artificial Intelligence* 74 (2).

[15] Jennings N. R., Mamdani E. H., Laresgoiti I., Perez J., and Corera J., (1992) "GRATE: a general framework for cooperative problem solving", *Intelligent Systems Engineering* 1(2) pp 102-114.

[16] van Harmelen, F., (1992) "ML^2: a Formal Language for KADS Models of Expertise", *Knowledge Acquisition* 4(1).

[17] Muller, J. P., Pischel, M., and Thiel, M., (1995), "A pragmatic approach to modelling autonomous interacting systems: a preliminary report" In this volume.

[18] Ferguson, I. A. (1995), "Integrated control and coordinated behaviour: a case for agent models" In this volume.

232

[19] Winograd, T., and Flores, F., (1986) *"Understanding Computers and Cognition: a New Foundation for Design"* Ablex Publishing, Norwood.

[20] Searle, J. R., (1969) *"Speech Acts: an Essay in the Philosophy of Language"* Cambridge University Press.

[21] Engelmore, R., and Morgan, T., (1988) *"Blackboard Systems"* Addison-Wesley.

[22] Walton, R., and Randall, A., (1992), "Clinical Decision Analysis", *British Medical Journal* 301, p.301

A Unified Approach to Intelligent Agency

Jacek Malec⋆

Department of Computer and Information Science
Linköping University
S–581 83 Linköping, Sweden
jam@ida.liu.se

Abstract. The paper presents a unified approach to intelligent agency
that has been developed by the members of the Laboratory for Knowledge Representation in Logic at the Department of Computer and Information Science, University of Linköping since 1986. The approach is
based on the theory of Inhabited Dynamical Systems proposed and developed by Sandewall [27], on the integrated layered software architecture
concept developed at our lab [24] and on the research on specification of
reactive system behaviour pursued since 1990 [15].

1 Introduction

The problem of designing *intelligent autonomous systems* (or *agents*) has been
the subject of much attention for a long time. Recently the research has focused on designing systems which would combine, among others, the following
attributes of autonomy:

- *reactivity*, in order to allow the system to cope with unpredictable changes
  in the dynamic environment while performing its mission;
- *robustness*, meaning the ability to function in a variety of situations, including failure of some of its subsystems;
- *selectivity of attention*, in order to effectively use existing (possibly limited)
  resources of the system, such as computing power, or sensory equipment;
- *ability to pursue goals*, either defined by the designer or by the system itself,
  as one of the basic attributes of an intelligent agent.

One can distinguish several approaches to this problem. One of them is called
"behaviour-based", because behaviour is the basic structure used for specifying
control for an autonomous system. Another one is based on layered control architecture, where usually each layer has its own, well-defined task(s) to perform,
often some software tools supporting implementation of those tasks, and some
appropriate mechanism for passing control between the layers (or distributing it
among them).

⋆ This research has been supported by the Center for Industrial Information Technology (CENIIT).

Those two approaches are often opposed to each other: "Behaviourists" claim that a rigid architecture requires excessive computational power and enforces too many constraints on the actual design and implementation, thus unnecessarily limiting the capabilities of the resulting system. The other group claims that behaviour-based approach is unsuitable for applications requiring either sophisticated control algorithms, or symbolic reasoning (as e.g. planning) procedures, or both. It has to be said that both criticisms are to some extent justified.

It is our firm belief, however, that one can gain by exploiting advantages of both approaches, namely by combining the freedom of behaviour-based specification together with predictability of well-engineered layered control. Therefore in our research we aim at creating a set of tools (both in formal and engineering sense) supporting the designer of an (eventually intelligent) autonomous system.

Assuming that the (set of) system's behaviour(s) can be somehow defined, one then has to address the problem of choosing an appropriate architecture for the implementation. The bottom-up approach guarantees that effective realization is always possible — the system is physically grounded from the very beginning. The top-down design, on the other hand, provides systems proven to pursue top-level goals requiring non-trivial amounts of intelligence. However, the question whether systems possessing both these properties can be designed remains open.

It is worth noting that quite a lot of publications (see e.g. [7, 12]) stress very strongly the need to *constrain* the design so that it is realizable by simple, and thus fast, hardware. This leads to the third, to some extent orthogonal to the previous two, major aspect of design: the problem of choosing the best medium of implementation. One can imagine solutions ranging from general purpose machines with appropriate software implementing the adopted control strategy, to collections of specialized processors designed for specific purposes (processing visual data, motor control, sensor fusion), to purely hardware realizations of control algorithms, as is the case of some of the MIT robots.

While *emerging intelligence* is yet the unachieved goal of the behaviour-based systems research, the property of being *autonomous* has definitely to be acknowledged to its designs, in contrast to the most of the systems engineered in a more traditional way. Within limits of capacity of their not too big batteries, subsumption robots deal effectively with cluttered environments, avoiding collisions, following people or other robots, picking soda cans, and following their urge to hide from the light or sound source. Autonomy, understood as the ability of a system to survive in an unknown, maybe even hostile, environment while pursuing its (usually not too complex) mission is the major achievement of the behaviour-based approach, yet unchallenged by any of the more classical, symbolic-reasoning-based systems.

The results described in this paper are a combination of two, for a long time independent, tracks of research. The first of them, logics for reasoning about action and change, has for a long time been attacked from a standard "theoretical AI" standpoint: given a plausible (usually very simple) "common sense" scenario, find a logic which would model the human way of reasoning about it. This approach resulted in multitude of complex logics, very often tested on just one, not too complex problem. This observation led Sandewall to address the question from a meta-theoretical point of view. The results of his work are very briefly (and selectively) summarized in Section 2 of this paper.

The other track of our research has addressed the question of effective implementation of intelligent systems. Its outcome is a three-layered architecture combining both reactive and deliberative parts in a manner exposing the subsystems to thorough analysis. The architecture is described in Section 3.

The blend of deliberation and reactiveness necessitates the use of several distinct languages for formal description of the intended functionality of the designed system. The languages we have either created or adopted for use within our framework are briefly described in Section 4.

Finally, Section 5 contains some remarks regarding the possibility of using behaviour-based specification of control (namely, Brooks' Behavior Language) for the layered architecture of ours. Moreover, the architecture is compared with several similar ones.

2   Inhabited Dynamical Systems

Inhabited Dynamical Systems (IDSs) have been introduced by Sandewall [27] to facilitate analysis of various approaches to common-sense reasoning. It has been shown that such analysis is impossible without an exhaustive classification of the worlds (domains) the reasoning is applied to. However, IDS, the model of a reasoning agent he has introduced, has much wider applicability than just comparison of logical systems. It can be seen as a generic theoretical framework for intelligent agency.

Every IDS is situated in a *world* (environment) and consists of two basic parts called *ego* and *vehicle* (Fig. 1). The ego can be interpreted as the deliberative part of an intelligent autonomous system or, in other words, its mind. The vehicle, on the other hand, constitutes the system's body, i.e. its reactive, unconscious executor of perceptory and effectory actions.

An IDS perceives its environment (and possibly other IDSs existing in it) using the perceptory processes embedded in the vehicle. Each such process can be seen as a transformation of the input information physically gathered by the sensors into the output sent to the ego. This transformation is called *perception function*, and usually introduces substantial reduction of information (the ego is notified only about important changes of perceived sensory data). The sensory input is very often a continuous function of time, but it is usually sufficient that the value of perception function is piecewise constant.

Likewise, the ego executes actions in the environment using the motoric processes available in the vehicle. The ego send a command to the vehicle to initiate some action and it is executed by the vehicle without any further intervention or supervision.

The theory developed in [27] precisely defines the interfaces between the world and the vehicle and between the vehicle and the ego. Both interfaces

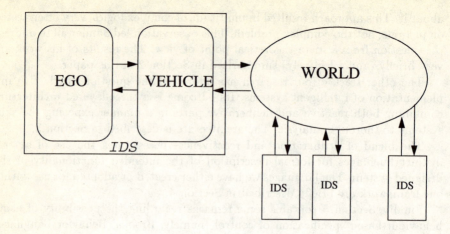

Fig. 1. An IDS interacting with the world.

can be specified as games between two entities, where the complexity of the behaviour of game participants depends on the level of abstraction required for some particular application. More concretely, the world an IDS operates in can be described as a purely discrete system, as a continuous system, or as a combination of both (i.e. a hybrid system). Depending on the model of the world, the vehicle is a set of either continuous or discrete or both discrete and continuous controllers implementing *actions* decided upon by the ego. The ego itself is a symbolic reasoning system choosing actions appropriate for achieving some goal or maintaining some particular state of the world.

Having assumed this model, Sandewall has asked the following question: What are the conditions that have to constrain the world evolution in order to make sound and complete some particular logical formalism describing the reasoning of the ego. After having analyzed a number of existing, mostly non-monotonic formalisms, he has introduced a family of logics of action of increasing complexity, suitable for capturing evolution in worlds characterized by some of the assumed set of well-defined criteria, such as temporal invariance of the domain, inertia, alternative results of actions, delayed effects of actions, concurrency of actions, etc.

The logic family consists of ETL (Elementary Feature Logic), LFL (Lexical-domain object-Feature Logic) and a series of logics DFL–i (Discrete time temporal Feature Logic): the full-blown temporal logics with increasing expressive power.

The presentation of any of the logics is beyond the scope of this paper: the interested reader is referred to [27] for details of this approach.

3   The Layered Architecture

The class of systems which are formally described using the IDS model described in the previous section can be implemented with a three-layered architecture (depicted in Figure 2) developed in our group [11, 25, 24] since 1986. The three

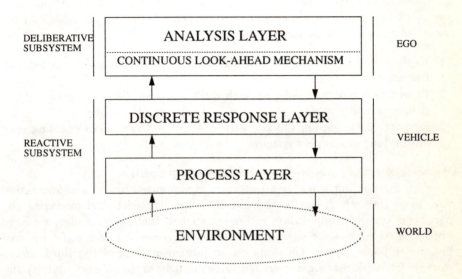

Fig. 2. The layered architecture

layers are separated on the basis of the type of computations they are intended to perform. The first layer (*process layer*) performs periodic numerical compu-tations at predetermined frequencies and typically hosts the control algorithms, both for identification and for actuator control. In other words, it contains reg-ulatory processes (the ones performed unconsciously by the agent). The middle layer is called the *discrete response layer*, and computes the response to asyn-chronous events that are generated in (or rather recognized by) the process layer. One type of response can be to change the mode of the process layer due to the change of mode in the environment. This layer can be interpreted as a set of reactive behaviours switching on and off regulators residing in the process layer. Its contents should still be assigned as belonging to the vehicle, although some of the reactions can be deliberate (i.e. the result of reasoning) while other are pure reflexes invoked by some change of the environment. The last layer (*analysis layer*) handles symbolic reasoning such as prediction, planning, and replanning. This layer would also host eventual learning mechanisms which might adapt the discrete response layer while maintaining its critical response requirements. A sub-task of this layer, the *continuous look-ahead* (or limited prediction) mechanism has been distinguished in this layer due to the assumed implementation strategy.

Literally dozens of layered architectures have been recently proposed for autonomous system implementation (see e.g. [1, 2, 4, 6, 8, 28] for just some of them). Although there are differences both in the way of assigning various tasks to different layers and in the way the overall control of the system is executed, the general conclusion is that such layering is beneficial, if not necessary, in designing autonomous *intelligent* real-time systems. We do not claim that the architecture presented here is beneficial per se, rather our claim is that its advantage for the design of an autonomous agent is threefold:

1. Explicit separation of tasks requiring different conceptual and computational frameworks;
2. Providing a potential designer with a set of formal tools (languages, algorithms) simplifying and systematizing the design process itself;
3. Supporting the design process with a set of software tools enabling easy prototyping of complex systems.

We would especially like to stress the latter two properties.

Each layer in our software architecture is supported by an implementation tool, or *engine*, which can be thought of as a restricted kernel managing the particular type of computation accommodated in that layer. So far, we have implemented engines for the *reactive subsystem* consisting of the process and discrete response layers. The work on an implementation of the third engine suitable for implementing a restricted subset of reasoning processes, namely the continuous look-ahead mechanism, is close to its final stage.

The process layer is supported by a multi-threaded time-triggered real-time engine (Process Layer Executive) which may operate in several modes. The engine's real-time properties have been thoroughly analyzed [22] which resulted in a parameterized description of the system overhead automatically derivable from the application description in the Process Layer Configuration Language.

The engine of the discrete response layer maintains a set of symbolic state variables, or *slots*, which have rules associated with each of them. A rule specifies how a change in the value of the slot conditionally should change the value of other slots, which, in turn, may have associated rules. Thus, the arrival of an event (this layer can be interpreted as an implementation of a generic event-based control system) that changes the value of a slot may start a forward-chaining process which eventually results in a new state, representing the response to the event. Computations in the asynchronous event-driven layer also have time-constraints, typically stating that the response to a particular event has to be computed within some defined amount of time. Currently the analysis of the response time is based on reachability analysis for a given set of rules and for the predetermined evaluation strategy (depth-first, breadth-first, or mixed).

The third engine, currently under development, exploits the fact that a restricted temporal feature logic has models expressible using state automata. A limited prediction of the future evolution of the world is done by appropriate manipulations on the set of possible interpretations for some particular theory in this logic. However, the engine able to interpret the statements in any of the DFL-i languages is far from realization. The work on computational properties of DFL theories has just begun, see e.g. [5]. Although some promising results about equivalence of a large class of DFL theories with circumscriptive theories axiomatizable in first-order logic have been recently proven, this research is still far from the state in which a reasonable computational tool could be proposed.

4 The Languages

Each of the layers can be seen (and can be implemented) as a generic software engine for interpreting programs written in a language tailored for its specific purpose. In the case of analysis layer it is a logic, namely the non-monotonic temporal logic DFL [27]. Its computable restriction is used for specifying prediction problems. Its even more restricted version, RETFL (Restricted Elementary Temporal Feature Logic, [14]) has been found to model exactly the behaviour of the discrete response layer.

For defining the behaviour of the discrete response layer a number of alternative specification formalisms can be used (Statecharts [9], the behavior language [3], a rule based language RLL [23], etc.). There exist algorithms allowing translation from each of them into the actual language compiled by the Rule Language compiler RLC.

Finally, the processes residing in the process layer are implemented using any of the traditional programming languages (e.g. C or C++), whereas the interdependencies among the processes are specified in so called Process Layer Configuration Language PLCL [21]. As most of the code residing here is an implementation of either pure control data analysis algorithms, we felt that leaving the choice of the programming language to the actual designer would be rather an advantage.

In our experiments we have found that in general the systematic generation of a sound rule base for the discrete response layer was non-trivial. To facilitate this task we developed a formal graphical language, Process Transition Networks (PTN), which we used for description of complex traffic scenarios [14, 13]. During the last two years we have provided a formal semantics also for some of the better-known languages for expressing behaviour-based control [15, 14, 16], among them the Behavior Language (BL) [17]. The result of our investigations is that programs in any of these languages can be rewritten using statecharts [9]: a formalism based on finite state automata (FSA) but semantically extending the classical FSA with time-dependent elements, called timers. As statechart specification can be translated into an RLL rule base, this gives the designer an opportunity to specify the reactive part of the system using the language of his choice. Moreover, it enables the investigation of dependencies between behavioural specification and temporally bounded execution of reactive software.

5   Discussion

What is the mechanism of emergence of complex, goal-oriented behaviours out of a set of interconnected low-level ones? Usually, the behavioural design is made without any thorough analysis of the low-level computational processes underlying this attributed emergence. This is due to the fact that the complexity of the interaction among those processes might be enormous, given the real world environment and a large number of parameters influencing the interacting behaviours (cf. [17]) In other words, although one can create behaviour-based control for toy robots managing well in a laboratory setting, more complex behaviours are still outside the range of possibilities of this approach. Control systems for relatively simple robots in relatively simple environments are currently designed using the only existing methodology: "trial and error" [19]. However, when the size of the problem increases, the programmer has no reasonable methodology to support him in this design task. Trial-and-error would be too expensive in terms of programming man/time, cost of equipment damaged during failed trials and, last but not least, in terms of uncertainty. Even if, after a series of debugging sessions and tests, the robot appears to behave correctly, there is no guarantee that it will continue doing so.

In order to change this situation we have focused on analyzing the possibility of merging the behaviour-based specification with the set of analysis tools available for our architecture. The result of this investigations is an algorithm for translating a behaviour program (written e.g. in the Behavior Language [3]) into a program for the two layers (reactive subsystem) of our architecture. The translation consists of two steps, with statecharts [9] as the intermediate representation. With such translation we expect to get the possibility of implementing larger systems directly within the layered architecture paradigm, but with behaviours as the basic conceptual blocks for specification of control.

The choice of DFL$-i$ family of logics as the languages for reasoning results in the possibility of proving that the agent will be able to obtain the correct conclusions in a given environment. One can imagine a step further when the designed system itself, after having sensed its environment and determined the class of observable events, chooses the appropriate logic in order to minimize the necessary amount of computations in a given situation.

The price for using this formalism, however, is very high. The more expressive versions of DFL are, informally speaking, non-computable. Therefore we focus on identifying such subsets of these languages, for which decision procedures would guarantee computations in limited amount of time.

The layered architecture presented in Section 3 is an attempt to provide a software engineering kind of support (methodology, languages, software engines, analysis tools) to the task of autonomous agent design. The ubiquity of layered architectures suggests that layering is probably necessary for keeping the design and implementation problems within some reasonable limits while offering potential for constructing complex, intelligent systems.

The other three-layered architectures differ from ours in several aspects. Gat [8] distinguishes the layers on the similar basis, i.e. the type of performed computations, but control in his system is located in the middle layer, with only occasional invocation of high-level (actually, path planning) procedures. As in our system, communication with the environment is done through the lowest (control) layer only. The language ALFA is a specialized programming language rather than a formalism for specification of system's abilities.

Connell's system SSS [4] has a similar decomposition of tasks as in our, or Gat's case. The lowest layer hosts control procedures, the middle one contains behavioural specification of system's reactions, and the highest layer is expected to perform path planning. However, in contrast to ours, his approach does not offer any tools for, nor even possibility of, analyzing the real-time performance of the implemented system.

Ferguson's TouringMachine architecture [6] is the most elaborate and complete of the three. It addresses both the real-time aspects and higher cognitive functions (including manipulation of system goals, intentions and beliefs about itself and other agents). The main difference is in the perceptory and effectory paths: TouringMachine layers are simultaneously fed with the sensory information and then compete for the right to control the actuators. Actually, neglecting the possibility of implementing complex continuous control algorithms in our process layer (TouringMachine has totally separated inputs and outputs), the two approaches are to a large extent similar, with our discrete response layer corresponding to the reactive layer of TM, and analysis layer performing the tasks divided between TM's planning and modeling layers.

Yet another layered framework, the APE generic architecture, has been proposed in [28]. Our architecture can be seen as an instantiation of this proposal, with just three layers distinguished according to the type of world model stored in them (state vectors in the lower two layers, and symbolic description in the third one).

Recently (in this volume) several other integrated agent architectures have been presented. Will [20] is a classical blackboard architecture, very similar in spirit to Guardian [10], but with less concern put on guaranteeing proper reactivity (or, in other words, hard-real-time performance). This is also one of the basic functional differences between our approach and Will: we would like to first ensure that the agent is able to survive in a dynamic environment and then, if it is still possible, to extend its capabilities with appropriate amount of reasoning, whereas in Will the architecture is developed just having in mind generality rather than performance.

Another example of an agent architecture is InteRRaP [26]. It can be seen as a more general solution than ours: yet another layer is introduced on top of the three basic ones to provide multi-agent planning and cooperation ability. Another significant difference is that InteRRaP possesses a global knowledge base, accessible from all the processing layers, whereas our approach stresses the need of multiple models suited for the processing layer they are used by. In this way we can have inconsistencies between the models, but on the other hand the modeling is simpler and more realistic.

6   Conclusion

In the paper we have described a unified approach to intelligent agency, based on the research done at RKLLAB, LiU during the last decade. The approach provides a theory suitable for analyzing or specifying intelligent agents on several degrees of accuracy, suggests a generic architecture for implementing intelligent autonomous agents and offers a set of languages for writing executable specifications of intelligent autonomous system's behaviour. The article did not formally introduce the languages: inerested reader is referred to the original work of Sandewall and others [27, 24]. An extensive example of usage of this approach in the design of an agent reasoning about the traffic domain can be found in [18].

The research described here is by no means a finished one. Although the lower two layers are relatively stable, with software engines existing for several hardware platforms, more work is necessary in order to get the set of tools cooperate with each other. There is also an interesting connection to the theory of hybrid systems, which we currently look at. However, most of the work on the analysis layer, both on the theory and on practical issues, is still waiting to be done. Besides the mainstream work of Sandewall on DFL logics, some research is done on introducing modalities (belief, goal and intention operators) into it.

Acknowledgment

The work described in this paper is the result of research of the previous and current members of the Laboratory for Representation of Knowledge in Logic (RKLLAB), at the University of Linköping, Sweden, headed by Erik Sandewall. Thanks to them all.

References

1. J. S. Albus, H. G. McCain, and R. Lumia. NASA/NBS Standard Reference Model for Telerobot Control System Architecture (NASREM). NIST Tecnical Note 1235, National Institute of Standards and Technology, Robot Systems Division, Center for Manufacturing Engineering, Gaithersburg, MD 20899, 1989.
2. R. Peter Bonasso. Integrating reaction plans and layered competences through synchronous control. In *Proceedings of the Twelvth International Joint Conference on Artificial Intelligence, Sydney*, pages 1225–1231. Morgan Kaufman, 1991.
3. Rodney A. Brooks. The behavior language; user's guide. Memo 1227, MIT AILab, April 1990.
4. Jonathan H. Connell. SSS: A hybrid architecture applied to robot navigation. In *Proceedings of the 1992 IEEE International Conference on Robotics and Automation*, pages 2719–2724, Nice, France, May 1992.
5. Patrick Doherty. Reasoning about action and change using occlusion. In *Proc. ECAI'94*, pages 401–405, 1994.
6. Innes A. Ferguson. *TouringMachines: An Architecture for Dynamic, Rational, Mobile Agents*. PhD thesis, University of Cambridge, Computer Laboratory, Cambridge CB2 3QG, England, November 1992.

7. Anita M. Flynn, Rodney A. Brooks, and Lee S. Tavrow. Twilight zones and cornerstones: A gnat robot double feature. AI Memo 1126, MIT, 1989.

8. Erann Gat. Integrating reaction and planning in a heterogenous asynchronous architecture for mobile robot navigation. *SIGART Bulletin*, 2(4):70–74, 1991.

9. David Harel. Statecharts: A visual formalism for complex systems. *Science of Computer Programming*, 8:231–274, 1987.

10. B. Hayes-Roth. Architectural Foundations for Real-Time Performance in Intelligent Agents. *Journal of Real-Time Systems*, 2:99–125, 1990.

11. Johan Hultman, Anders Nyberg, and Mikael Svensson. A software architecture for autonomous systems. In *Proc. 6th International Symposium on Unmanned Untethered Submersible Technology*, pages 279–292, 1989.

12. Leslie Pack Kaelbling and Stanley J. Rosenschein. Action and planning in embedded agents. *Robotics and Autonomous Systems*, 6:35–48, 1990.

13. Jacek Malec. Passing an intersection, or automata theory is still useful. In Brian Mayoh, editor, *Proc. of the Scandinavian Conference on Artificial Intelligence – 91*, pages 258–265. IOS Press, 1991.

14. Jacek Malec. Applied knowledge representation. *CC-AI: The Journal for the Integrated Study of Artificial Intelligence, Cognitive Science and Applied Epistemology*, 9(1):9–41, 1992.

15. Jacek Malec. Complex behavior specification for autonomous systems. In *Proc. IEEE International Symposium on Intelligent Control'92*, pages 178–183, Glasgow, Scotland, August 1992.

16. Jacek Malec. On semantics of behaviour languages. In *Proceedings of the Fourth National Conference on Robotics*, Wrocław, Poland, 1993. Available also as Technical Report IDA-RKL-93-TR17, Department of Computer and Information Sciences, Linköping University.

17. Jacek Malec. On formal analysis of emergent properties. In Christer Bäckström and Erik Sandewall, editors, *Current trends in AI planning*, pages 213–225. IOS Press, 1994.

18. Jacek Malec and Per Österling. Driver support system for traffic manoeuvers. In G. Ambrosino, M. Bielli, and M. Boero, editors, *Artificial Intelligence in Traffic Engineering*. VSP International Science Publishers, Zeist, The Netherlands, 1994. Available also as Technical Report LiTH-IDA-R-93-21, Department of Computer and Information Sciences, Linköping University.

19. Maja J. Mataric. Basic tips for programming in the behavior language. Unpublished memo.

20. David Moffat and Nico Frijda. An agent architecture: Will. In Michael Wooldridge and Nicholas R. Jennings, editors, *Proceedings of the ECAI'94 Workshop on Agent Theories, Architectures and Languages*, pages 216–225, Amsterdam, The Netherlands, August 1994.

21. Magnus Morin. PLCL – Process Layer Configuration Language. Technical Report LAIC-IDA-91-TR10, Linköping University, 1991.

22. Magnus Morin. Predictable cyclic computations in autonomous systems: A computational model and implementation. Licenciate thesis 352, Department of Computer and Information Sciences, Linköping University, 1993.

23. Magnus Morin. RL – RL: An embedded rule-based system. Technical Report LAIC-IDA-94-TR2, Linköping University, 1994.

24. Magnus Morin, Simin Nadjm-Tehrani, Per Österling, and Erik Sandewall. Real-time hierarchical control. *IEEE Software*, 9(5):51–57, September 1992.

25. Magnus Morin and Erik Sandewall. A software architecture supporting integration of sub-systems. In *PROMETHEUS: Proceedings of the Fourth Workshop*, 1990. Also available as Technical Report LAIC-IDA-90-TR21, Dept. of Computer and Information Science, Linköping University.

26. Jörg P. Müller, Markus Pischel, and Michael Thiel. A pragmatic approach to modeling autonomous interacting systems – preliminary report. In Michael Wooldridge and Nicholas R. Jennings, editors, *Proceedings of the ECAI'94 Workshop on Agent Theories, Architectures and Languages*, pages 226–240, Amsterdam, The Netherlands, August 1994.

27. Erik Sandewall. *Features and Fluents*. Oxford University Press, 1994. The final review version is available as the research report LiTH-IDA-R-94-15, Department of Computer and Information Science, University of Linköping.

28. Lee Spector and James Hendler. Knowledge strata: Reactive planning with a multi-level architecture. Technical Report CS-TR-2564, Department of Computer Science, University of Maryland, College Park, MD, November 1990.

Where there's a *Will* there's an Agent

David Moffat and Nico H. Frijda*

Faculty of Psychology (PN)
University of Amsterdam
Roetersstraat 15
1018 WB Amsterdam.
The NETHERLANDS.
email: *moffat@psy.uva.nl*

Abstract. This theoretical paper introduces a formal architecture that supports the integration of various A.I. technologies, including planning, to make an autonomous agent.

The design decisions made are self-consciously minimal, resulting in a simple but general architecture. Its functionality appears comparable to other agent architectures in the literature, including the incorporation of a reactive element.

Novelties in the architecture include "cognitive reactivity," a formal notion of *relevance*, and *attention*, and a control regime based on these.

An initial implementation is briefly described.

Most research in A.I. has been concerned with programs and models of partial intelligences. The project to build a whole artificial mind is an enormous one, and so researchers have chosen to address only *parts* of the big problem. The unspoken intention has always been to solve the part problems, and then all that would remain to be done would be to stick the partial solutions together to get a comprehensive model of a "mind". When we try to effect such a synthesis, however, we find it is not so trivial, after all. On the contrary, the attempt reveals gaps in our knowledge. One specific problem is that it is unclear where *goals* are to come from, but more generally there are what we call *integration problems*.

In this paper we shall explore the integration of some classical A.I. functions, to make an agent that successfully inhabits a simple domain. We motivate the architecture of a computer agent, called *Will*, which is the simplest interesting design we could think of. We show the design-decisions that led to it, report the solutions chosen for the various integration problems, and explain why we feel that *relevance* and *attention* deserve much more investigation in the field.

---

* We are grateful to the anonymous reviewers of this paper for their helpful comments. The first author is supported by a grant from the NWO, the Dutch Organisation for Scientific Research. We would also like to thank the authors of GNU software, all members of the Linux project, and free software contributors everywhere, without whom the development of *Will* would have been much harder.

1   What is an Autonomous Agent?

The word "agent" is a technical term without a generally agreed usage. It can refer to something as trivial as a persistent computer program like the Unix *"at"* daemon; or to an independent system with enough knowledge and interactive capabilities to ensure its effectiveness in a wide range of somewhat unforeseen circumstances [22]. The biological model for this latter kind of agent would be an animal of some kind, somewhere on the scale from insect to human.

This more interesting kind of *autonomous* agent is the focus of this paper. Researchers seem to agree that there are certain qualities such an agent needs:

Autonomy. The capability of an agent to achieve its own goals is part of what it means for an agent to be autonomous. An autonomous agent must have its *own* dispositions to behave in certain ways [4, 8, 9]. This is called "goal-autonomy" by Castelfranchi [5].

Flexibility. The agent should not be rigid, responding in fixed manners of processing. Classical A.I. is concerned with formal perfections, proving completeness and correctness of her logics and algorithms: "if there is a solution, my planner will find it, and if there isn't, it will say so". This approach was bred on toy problems, but is unworkable in most real environments. There is often no time to run a big planning subroutine before taking even a single step, and in an environment where there may be other agents, it will usually be impossible to prove plans correct. Something unexpected may always happen [3, 8, 9, 10, 12, 13, 19]. *Planning is not a subroutine.*

Reactivity. An agent is said to be "reactive" if it does not necessarily plan everything, but can sometimes just react appropriately to certain stimuli [3, 9, 11, 12, 14, 19]. We shall distinguish this *strong* from *weak* reactivity, where the agent does plan its response, but does so immediately, by interrupting or halting any other ongoing planning processes that are less important.

Planning. Some researchers think planning (or indeed any cognition) is not necessary for agents [3], but others argue that only the insect-like end of agenthood is feasible without planning [9, 11, 13]. We take the latter view also.

Prediction. The agent should know what its own actions are going to be. It will know those for free from its Planner if it has one. But it is often necessary also to entertain beliefs about actions of other agents, or other exogenous events. Agents should be generally predictive.

Other researchers to require this property include Ekdahl [6], who views anticipation as essential for an autonomous agent, to allow preparation for difficulties before they arise; and Norman [20], who further argues that an agent needs to create goals "pro-actively," and not just "reactively" as he claims most researchers' artificial agents do at present.

Selectivity. The real world is a noisy place, and much of what happens in it is irrelevant. An agent needs intelligent sensors to focus on what it needs to see, and ignore the rest [10]. This requirement is not as popular as the others listed here, but in recent articles "attention" is becoming recognised as important [15, 14]. We shall take *attention* to be *essential,* and central, in the control of an agent.

Robustness. Imperfection and limitation of various kinds, whether in sensors, information-overload, or limited CPU cycles, is a fact of life for systems in the real world. They should be able to cope with failure.

Some researchers include other requirements also, such as that an agent must be one of a society, interacting with other agents. While this would be very interesting to model as well, we find it challenging enough at present to model just a single agent. Another common requirement [14] for agency that we shall not treat here is adaptivity, in the sense of learning.

A computer agent has been designed, which meets the requirements above to varying extents. It is called *Will* because it follows its own motives, and is therefore (goal-)autonomous. It is not a robot, it has no body, its input and output are as simple as possible in accordance with our research focus on integration. But it is an agent nevertheless, we feel. Although it is controversial to claim that an agent need not have a physical body, it is tenable: the necessity of a body for agenthood has been asserted [3] but not proven.

Will is a composition of A.I. modules that were kept as conventional as possible, but had to be connected in novel ways in order to solve certain integration problems, which we outline now.

2 A Disintegrated Agent

Let us begin with a minimal classical-A.I. approach to building an agent that acts rationally in the world. Various functions will be necessary for such an agent, including perception and action, as well as the important and much-researched area of planning. We may assume that we have, therefore, separate *modules* for each of these functions. So let us take an off-the-shelf Perceiver, Planner, and Executor (for action), and join them together. What is inside these modules, or how they work, is not important to us here. We are only interested in how they may be integrated. The Perceiver may be a vision system, or just a keyboard; the Executor may be a real robot arm, or just a computer screen to write on, and the Planner may be STRIPS [18] or NONLIN [21], or simpler goal-directed reasoning.

We said that we wanted *Will* to be a minimal design, but a naïve Perceiver → Planner → Executor loop is inadequate. In fact it is totally ineffective! The clearest way to see this is to ask where the *goals* are. Answer: There are none. The Perceiver only observes the world's transient facts and events. The Planner could read those only as (partial) descriptions of initial states. Without goals as well, there would be no problem for the Planner (or the agent) to solve (planning researchers invariably assume that initial state *and* goal state are *given*). No plans or intentions would ever be generated, and so the Executor would never have anything to do.

So where do goals come from, anyway? The question is easy to miss until one attempts to construct a real agent from A.I. parts, and consequently it has barely been noticed, though it was asked in 1982 [4]. We shall give an answer to it below, when we introduce concerns.

The Perceiver → Planner → Executor loop has another problem: it has no memory. In a toy world where all relevant information is in the current "initial" state, and is all available to immediate perception, no memory is required. However, in the real world, a world-model is not given, but has to be built up over time, and that needs memory.

Given a Memory, we should also add a module (capability) to make general inferences from Memory contents. This is necessary for the agent to be able to understand more about its situation than is immediately evident from sensors. For example, it needs to anticipate problems before they arise, to prepare for them, or even avoid them altogether. Call this module a Predictor.

2.1 Integration Problems

Once we have chosen a set of modules (or functions), we have to connect them coherently. The first problem is *how* to join these modules together: how do they communicate with each other? No standard interface language for all cognitive functions has ever been agreed; nor even proposed. As well as deciding on formal languages, we also have to decide which inputs and outputs of which modules are to be linked, and what information the links are to carry. These are interface or *information* problems.

Then we have the *control* problem, too: what is to determine which module should operate when? Should some of them run in parallel? Even if we know what kind of information a module must process, and how that information is to be expressed, there are still choices to be made as to the order of processing. For example, which goal should the Planner work on next?

The general integration problem thus splits into several problems, grouped under *flow of information* and *flow of control*.

3 Derivation of *Will*'s Architecture

Driven by the problems mentioned above, we now motivate the architectural design of *Will* through several design decisions.

Our guiding principle in what follows is to keep the design as simple as we can. We may call it Occam's Design Principle: when presented with a design choice, always opt for the simplest structure that will do the job, be aware that every convenient design "feature" bears a theoretical cost, and never assume more than you have to. In short, one should "design" as *little* as possible.

3.1 Memory Solves the Information Problem

Our solution to the interface problem is to connect all the modules' inputs and outputs to each other. This is the first application of Occam's Design Principle, and it results in the least constraining setup; any other decision would be restrictive. The best way to implement such an open architecture is to communicate by broadcasting. All messages between modules are broadcast so that any module may hear them; but they are also collected into a global buffer so that we do not need to *synchronise* communication. (To require synchronisation would be unnecessarily restrictive.) Instead, information may be read from the buffer long after it was written.

Purity. The information in this buffer should be as pure as we can manage, such that it is necessary to all or most of the modules. It should contain no *ad hoc* control information if avoidable. The purest necessary content we can imagine is simply information about external events. Such information is clearly necessary to the agent, but any more would involve making unwarranted assumptions.

Accordingly, we identify this buffer with the (episodic) Memory from now on. Information such as any add/delete lists [18] for events we regard as impure, as it is relevant only to the Planner and Predictor, and accordingly are not stored in the Memory.

There is a tension between the desire for purity in the Memory and the need for rich information to be available to other modules. In the current implementation of Will it was possible to keep the Memory extremely pure, but this may have to change for more complex domains.

Work and Episodes. The Memory holds representations of observed past and present events; but also of predicted future ones.

All the modules are to read from the Memory, except the Perceiver, whose input comes also from the world. And all write to Memory, except the Executor, whose output goes back out to the world.

Psychologists may like to note that this structure serves as an episodic memory; but that it is also a working memory, as will become apparent.

3.2 Concerns Solve the Control Problem

How, when, and in what order are the modules to use the information in the Memory? Again, making the minimal decision, we simply refuse to specify a processing order by allowing all modules to run concurrently. Given the globally accessible interface of the Memory, and the asynchronous communication method, this is feasible. Each module can simply take information as and when it needs it. The Predictor, for example, can read a piece of information from Memory, make a prediction from it, and write the prediction back into Memory before reading another event representation and beginning again.

In this way, the modules can be implemented as processors that run in little cycles, reading from and writing to Memory as and when their functions require. These modules operate concurrently for the requirement of flexibility (which would be sacrificed if any one of them were a big subroutine that could interrupt the others for unbounded stretches of time).

It was mentioned earlier that agents need to select the most relevant information they get through their sensors, as otherwise they would be overloaded by environmental noise. The sensors themselves might be overloaded, but we can generalise this idea to all processors: they *all* need to be selective. For example, if the Predictor spends its time finding consequences of relatively trivial events, then the agent may never come to be aware of the true significance of its circumstances, so the Predictor would be practically useless. How can we ensure that *each* module only reads the most relevant information?

The obvious thing to do is to rank all the items in Memory according to *relevance*. This reduces the problem to one of the determination of relevance. Where does it come from? An event can be relevant to one or more goals the agent may have, but if the goals are subgoals of a larger goal, the relevance is only inherited. Where is the ultimate source of relevance?

3.3 Concerns and Relevance

We suggest that the deepest well of relevance in a biological organism is in its fundamental needs, for food, warmth and safety and so on. In an artificial agent this would correspond with the agent's fundamental purpose, its role in life: not its goals, which are only transient, but in its reasons for having goals. In any agent, biological or artificial, we call these concerns.

Our definition of concerns comes from psychology [8]. Concerns are dispositions to prefer certain states and/or dislike others. They can be thought of as representations of those states, or their relevant aspects. They enable the agent to recognise events as (in)compatible with its best interests.

When an event is perceived that is relevant to one of the organism's concerns, an internal signal is emitted and a goal is generated. The goal is to repair the damage done by the event (if it was incompatible with the concern) or to further it, or take advantage of it (if it was compatible). The internal signal (called a "concern relevance" signal) is to cause other processing to be interrupted so that due attention can be given to the new goal.

The concerns are definitely not active all the time. This is another distinction from goals, which endure until they are achieved, in the naïve view. The concerns can instead be thought of as "demons", lying dormant until concern-relevant events arouse them.

We have operationalised this definition to a simple representation in Will, whereby a concern is represented by a scale on a world-variable, optionally with a set-point for the ideal value. For example, there might be a concern for optimal body temperature, set at $20\,^{\circ}$C. Excessively high or low temperatures would then cause a proportional mismatch.

Matching for Concern-Relevance & Surprise If concerns are given a suitable state-like representation they can be matched against an observed state or event in order to determine its concern-relevance. The match may be positive (indicating concern satisfaction), negative (indicating dis-satisfaction) or null (indicating irrelevance).

We include other factors in the matching process, namely *importance* and *surprise,* to arrive at a total relevance signal including all the concerns the agent has. More important concerns give a (mis)matching event a stronger match signal. And the signal is also incremented in cases of surprise, where the observed event does not occur exactly as anticipated, or is wholly unforeseen.

Note that this calculation of (un)expectedness, though new in this work as far as we are aware, is not hard to do, because the Memory, including its expectations, is accessible to the Perceiver.

The final outcome of the matching process is not a pure measure of concern-relevance any more. We call it a charge by analogy with static electricity, because it attaches to events in Memory, from where it attracts *attention* from Will's modules. That is: when a module looks for an item in Memory, the one with the highest charge is the one it sees and processes.

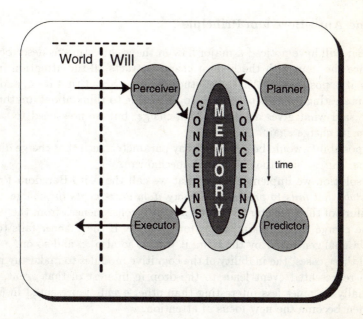

Fig. 1. Will's basic architecture

The reason for this control method is obviously to see to it that at any time the most important, unexpected and relevant events get the most attention from Will. This answers many of the requirements for agenthood. The mention of expectedness is new though: what is the value of responding especially to unexpected events?

Our idea here is that unexpected events *should* get more attention from an agent, because it does not know what to do about them. Expected events are already in Memory, so it is *likely* (only) that some form of contingency plan has already been formed to cope with the event, since the agent has already been aware of it for some time. But unexpected events are those that enter Memory for the first time, and so they should be better served by processing modules, so that the agent can discover what significance there may be in them.

This hypothesis concerning the functional value of surprise is powerful. With it we can also account for the function of relevance and surprise in other cognition too, in an exact parallel. For example, take learning. It is intuitively clear that unexpectedness drives learning. (It must do, for expectedness cannot: it is only evidence that no learning is required.) The same holds for surprise: we argue that surprising events should lead to more learning, should arouse curiosity and so on, precisely in order to be able to better predict similar events in the future.

There is no learning in *Will*, however: the point is only to illustrate why we have given *relevance, expectedness,* and *surprise* such a central role in our architecture. We believe this trio to be extremely important for agent cognition.

3.4 The Auto-Boredom Principle

The reader will have noticed a major flaw in the architecture as described up to now. Since the item with the highest charge attracts all the attention from the modules, it is possible for *Will* to get stuck thinking about that item, and, unless a more interesting event is perceived, to be unable to think about anything else. We have said what gives an item a high charge, but we now need to say what can lower its charge again.

One possibility would be a global decay parameter, such that charge dissipates with time. But we find that an *ad hoc* mechanism.

The solution we implemented is what we call the Auto-Boredom Principle: *Any module that fails to process a Memory item decrements the charge on it.*

A failure of the Predictor to predict any new consequences from the item will lower the charge by a certain factor, for example. If the Planner fails to find a plan for a goal generated by the item, it will do so also ...and so on.

In all these cases, the inability of the cognitive modules to make any progress with the represented event leads to the drop in interest of that event, so that it eventually becomes less interesting than other events represented in Memory, which then become the new focus of attention.

That is why the principle is called Auto-Boredom. Items become boring automatically, if there is nothing more that can be done with them. This is not an *ad hoc* solution, because its value is clear to see. It amounts to a design-principle, therefore, and one new to this work.

3.5 Where Goals come from

Concerns can also be made to explain where goals come from. Since the concerns represent preferences, and since they therefore match events with a polarity, we can take negative polarities (mismatches) to generate goals. For example, if the agent has a concern to keep warm, then a drop in body-temperature from the sensors will mismatch against the concern. The natural goal to create would be the goal to raise body-temperature back to normal. The Planner might then create subgoals to leave the room etc., but the source of all the subgoals is this concern.

The architecture up to now is shown in Fig. 1, with its central Memory, and peripheral cognitive components. The Concerns form a layer round the Memory. They are not a part of the Perceiver, because it is not only *observed* events that we wish to be evaluated for concern-relevance, but *all* contents of Memory. We feel it is crucial to make this generalisation so that *all items passing into* Memory *are matched against the* concerns. This means that predicted (and planned) events (and intentions) also have the opportunity to be charged and to attract attention from the modules in their own right. Otherwise a plan to solve some problem might be found, that in fact has even worse consequences than the original problem situation, and the agent would never realise this. For example, the agent may try to escape from a hot place by leaving it and going somewhere else, even hotter. "Out of the frying-pan, and into the fire," as they say.

This completes the derivation of an earlier version of *Will*. The agent as portrayed in Fig. 1 already has *weak* reactivity, due to the responsiveness provided for by the concerns, and the attention mechanism.

3.6   The Reactor Module

The next addition to *Will* is the Reactor. This module completes *Will*'s performance regarding reactivity, because it implements what are sometimes called stimulus-response "arcs" (e.g. [14]), which is to say that certain stimuli evoke certain responses directly: As it were, without using general cognition, such as the Planner or Predictor.

Because of the open architecture adopted for *Will*, it was possible to add the Reactor module quite effortlessly. None of the existing modules or code had to be changed *at all*. They all continue working exactly as before. They did not need to be changed because all the modules are ignorant of each other anyway. That was a deliberate design-principle, made possible by the choice of global, pure Memory. The term "module" is not used lightly!

Incidentally, *Will* gains a kind of robustness from the same property, because some modules can just stop working for some reason, without totally incapacitating *Will*. The Reactor could be removed as easily as it was added. Or the Predictor could disappear, or the Planner, but then the Reactor would still be there to react, so you would still see behaviour from *Will*. This is a kind of "graceful degradation", which some researchers advocate [3, 14].

There is another design-decision to be made in connecting the Reactor to the rest of the system. Some researchers [3] suggest it should form a *direct* "arc" between perception and action. But in the richer cognitive architecture that *Will* has, there is a more interesting possibility, which we have implemented. The Reactor, just like all the other modules, is connected not to the Perceiver, but to Memory. This means that *Will* does not react only to direct percepts, but to its own planned, predicted and recalled thought *as well*. It also means that

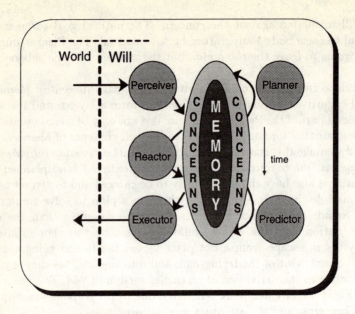

Fig. 2. *Will*'s *full* architecture

reactions are not necessarily performed without a chance to sanction them. *Will*'s reactions can be inhibited by other cognition, because a reaction proposed by the **Reactor** goes into **Memory** as an intention, where it may be seen by the **Planner**, for example, that might realise the action would strongly mismatch a concern, and so might reverse the decision.

In light of this, we distinguish the kinds of reactions *Will*'s **Reactor** has from *reflexes,* which is a term we reserve for direct perception-action arcs. Reactions are more intelligent than reflexes.

4 Is *Will* an Agent?

Evaluating *Will* against the requirements given in Sect. 1, shows that they are all satisfied to some degree:

Autonomy, because goals are not simply read in from "the environment", uncritically. *Will* does not follow orders, it follows its own dispositions. It creates goals for the **Planner** itself, by comparing perceived and predicted situations with its set of **concerns**. *Will* can be *made* to follow orders, but only through the indirect route, of programming it with a concern to fulfill requests made of it.

Flexibility, because its parallelism means that the **Perceiver** never stops observing the environment, and because all the modules' processing automatically tracks what is most important at the time, including planning for the most important goals, and predicting from the most important facts.

Weak reactivity is present in *Will* even without the Reactor module. But the inclusion of the Reactor makes the reactive capability of the system **strong.** From a certain stimulus situation that happens to match a reactive rule, the Reactor will produce the intention to react to it in the manner specified by the rule. An interesting generalisation made over other reactive systems in the literature is that, due to the general past/present/future representation in the Memory, the Reactor can react to *any* event, even future ones if desired by the programmer. This fulfills Castelfranchi's requirement for "cognitive reactivity," but is still more general than that, since not just the Reactor, but *all* modules can respond to these "imagined" events.

Prediction is obviously provided by the Predictor. This is non-goal-directed inference that can alert the system to future contingencies that it might not otherwise be aware of, such as an unfortunate side-effect of one of its intentions generated by the Planner. Corrective planning can then be undertaken.

Selectivity the primary result of the general attentional mechanism in *Will*. Irrelevant events may be seen and written into Memory, but they will not be highly charged, and so will be ignored. Note that this is not just selectivity among percepts, but a general *cognitive attention.*

Robustness of the architecture has already been described, but *Will* is also robust in other ways. An ability to recover from faulty actions or effectors, for example, is automatic. *Will* simply notices that something has gone wrong because it *expected* its actions to succeed. Then it sets about repairing the situation to bring it into line with its concerns again, as normal. This behaviour may look like "execution monitoring" [1] to an outsider, but in fact no extra, complicated mechanisms or distinct data-structures are required to achieve it.

If the same action fails repeatedly, then more awareness than *Will* has would be necessary to recover, but at least this primary robustness is there for free.

4.1   Some More General Issues

Leaving the initial requirements aside, we can draw out some other conclusions that we had not necessarily expected before making the model.

Firstly, we have shown that reactivity *is* compatible with symbolic A.I. techniques, *pace* Brooks and others referred to in the introduction. *Will* is a hybrid deliberation & reaction architecture, but is entirely symbolic. We are working on semantics for its languages.

We mentioned that concern rank can help to resolve conflicts in *Will*, but it only helps. The problem of conflict resolution (e.g. between modules) in *Will* takes a limited, but clear form. Namely, Memory-access conflicts. What to do when two modules (or the same module at different times) want to write information into the Memory that is mutually contradictory? For example, if *Will* believes that an event happened that contradicts the one that has just been seen by the Perceiver, what is it to do? In the case of the Perceiver we might simply say that *Will* "believe its own eyes". But such relatively clear conflict-resolution strategies are not always available. What is a general solution?

We do not know. In general it is a very hard problem, possibly insoluble. But at least the Will architecture allows us to put the question clearly and unambiguously, and that has to be a good start. It also gives us a typology of different kinds of conflict (depending on which modules are involved). Some of these have quite satisfying parallels in folk psychology too: for example a conflict between the Perceiver and Predictor (inferencer) may resolve in favour of the Predictor, effectively overwriting a representation of an event that was actually observed to happen one way, with a different version of the event because the system thinks it "ought to have happened that way." Memory can be corrupted, and sensors mistrusted.

As well as conflict resolution, we have a number of tradeoffs to consider. There is a tradeoff, for example, between long and short inference. Namely, in a system with communicating modules that use a fairly flexible language, one can choose how often communication of partial results should take place. If the modules reason *short,* as we put it, they infer in short chains, and keep other modules informed by frequently writing to the globally accessible space, the Memory, in Will. If they reason *long,* on the other hand, they may construct quite elaborate plans (or whatever they do) before informing other modules. In an interrupt-based system such as Will, this is a tradeoff. If the modules reason too long, they will frequently be working with out-of-date information, because they do not keep each other informed of their own decisions and inference. If they reason too short, however, there will be too many updates, and they will continually interrupt one another, making progress accurate but slow.

Other tradeoffs are private versus public inference (how open or encapsulated should the modules be?), and storage versus recomputation (as in the goal-generation process).

5   Implementation

Although we have concentrated on the rationale behind the architecture in this paper, it should be noted that this is not empty theoretical discussion. The architecture has been implemented in a prototype of Will, which plays a little game with the User, planning its moves and reacting to those of the opponent.

A different domain can (theoretically) be programmed quite easily, using the causal rule notation for domain description (not tried yet).

All the modules run concurrently, just as described, in a specially fashioned coordinated Prolog (called COPr [16]). The latter language is unfortunately a slow prototype. It is difficult to get a fair impression of the Will system itself because of the large overhead due to COPr.

To thoroughly evaluate Will and compare it to other agents, it would be necessary to run it on a standard domain, and to eliminate the overhead from COPr. Therefore we have evaluated Will only from a theoretical viewpoint.

6   Related Work

Several other agent architectures have been proposed or described in the literature, and in this volume. Some of these are radically different from *Will* in terms of implementation technique [3, 12, 19], but have a similar functionality.

One system we would particularly like to mention is Guardian [10], a large and sophisticated system for patient-monitoring. It is curious that, though independently developed (and more recently), *Will* seems to share many ideas with the Guardian project, and a closer comparison would be interesting to undertake. Guardian has effective "input filtering," which makes use of a different conceptualisation of relevance, but could perhaps profit from the operationalisation of expectancy in *Will*, for example by setting its input filters around an *expected* value rather than some default. Then Guardian's predictive capacity could make the input filters even more efficient.

A major difference between Guardian and *Will* is the complexity of the architecture. One complexity in Guardian is the use of meta-control-plans, something we hope to be able to continue to avoid by the use of concerns at a lower level. *Will* is much simpler, but that does not necessarily mean that it is simplistic! On the contrary, parsimony is something to aim for, as Hayes-Roth agrees [10]. However, we should add that Guardian has several features that *Will* does not, including some learning. Also, Guardian has been developed for several years and tested on rich and demanding domains.

Pattie Maes, in [13], describes a very interesting reactive architecture that unifies reaction with goal-deliberation. It appears very different to *Will*, but there are some remarkable similarities, too. For example, Maes has a threshold θ for "thoughtfulness", which allows control over how much time is spent trying to resolve goal conflicts. In *Will* you can vary the relative speeds of the modules, and if you make the Predictor faster than the Planner, you get a more cautious system that thinks more about the consequences of its planned actions, and is a slower performer, but is less likely to do something stupid.

We emphasise that Maes' system only *appears* very different to *Will*. In fact it uses spreading activation in a network: and the reader may already have noticed that the charge in *Will*'s Memory operates as a kind of spreading activation also.

6.1   Layered Architectures

Another group of agents comprises those with "layered architectures" [12, 15, 17, 7], which owe their lineage to Brooks' [2] "subsumption architecture."

These architectures can be seen as applications of Occam's Design Principle (see Sect. 3), although their designers may not have seen it that way. Each layer of such an architecture has a certain function (usually there are one or more reactor-layers, and possibly a planner-layer). The architectures had to solve the Integration Problems (see 2.1) just as we did, and did so in similar ways.

The "information problem" was solved in most cases by connecting each layer's input to the whole agent's input buffer, and each layer's output to the agent's output buffer, so each layer sees all percepts, and each may try to control the agents' effectors. We can see that as an application of Occam's Design Principle, because it is a design that refuses to make a commitment as to which layer sees (or controls) what.

The same design Principle is applied to the control problem to lead the layers to run concurrently, like *Will*'s modules. Conflict resolution is typically difficult in these architectures, as each conflict between layers has to be settled by rewriting the individual rules (e.g. the ones called "censor" or "suppressor" rules in [7]), within the layers to recognise each other. This unfortunately means the layers are not so independent, and the only practical way to make such a system is incrementally [7, 2]. Müller says that all "horizontal" architectures suffer from a control "bottleneck" problem, and proposes his "vertical" architecture as an alternative (please see his [17] in this volume for details, including his Fig. 1(c)). Even his proposal requires the specification of several interfaces, however, so appears not to totally solve the problem. Other methods to help solve this control problem in INTERRAP include the use of a Maslow hierarchy of motives [17], something very similar to our motive-like Concerns.

Perhaps the most developed layered architecture at this time is that of Ferguson's TouringMachines [7], paradigmatic for this group. It includes a planning layer with sophisticated planning capabilities, and makes hierarchical partial plans. It is more sophisticated than *Will* in other ways, too, especially in having been proven in a rich domain (of simulated traffic), and several experiments have shown the worth of its architectural characteristics. A direct experimental comparison with it is not possible, as the implementation of *Will* is still only a prototype, but some theoretical comparisons include the following.

The solutions to the Integration Problems that we implemented in *Will* go a little further than those for the layered architectures, in that we have applied Occam's Design Principle more strongly. Our solution to the Information Problem is more general, because we have unified the input and output buffers of the agent into one global read/write buffer for all modules. In addition, we have not stipulated synchronous communication (in contrast to all layered architectures, as far as we know). Neither does this buffer (the Memory) throw information away, so we really can call it a Memory. Such an episodic Memory is just the sort of thing Ferguson proposed for further development of his TouringMachines [7].

Our solution to the Control Problem is not more general than the control methods in the layered architectures, but it is different in an interesting way. Conflict resolution is a problem in *Will* just as it is in all other agents we know of, but it is mitigated to some extent by the *attention* mechanism. For under this control regime, modules will only act on information that is seen as relevant, which might make conflicts less frequent. Other systems typically use thresholds to try to filter out less urgent or important stimuli; but in a very noisy environment many thresholds may be exceeded at a time, whereas in *Will* there can only ever be one most highly charged item in Memory.

These factors seem to give certain advantages to *Will*: Firstly, that it is more domain independent (admittedly not proven yet), and secondly, that its modules really are mutually independent to a degree not matched by the layers in the layered architectures.

7 Conclusions

We have given some generally accepted requirements for autonomous agenthood, and briefly outlined an implemented model that satisfies them. The design steps of the model suggested some quite general properties that we expect may turn out to be valuable to other agents too.

The model exploits A.I. conceptions as far as possible, but can be seen as a hybrid architecture, with both deliberation and reactivity. Unlike most reactive systems it is domain independent, symbolic, and logical to a fair extent.

The architecture satisfies other researchers' requirements for goal-autonomy [5], for "pre-adaptive" anticipation [6], and for "pro-active" goals [20]. It also has what Castelfranchi [5] calls "cognitive reactivity."

The architecture is a generalisation of other architectures in several ways, we claim, due to the conscious application of a minimalist design principle. Perhaps most significant is the Memory, and the Concerns, which together make for a general kind attention, not limited to just what the agent perceives, but extended to *all* its cognition.

Other novelties in Will include the following: it is a flexible and minimal way to integrate modules for cognition, in which goals are not given, but produced as required by concerns. The control regime drives the whole system by directing *attention* at what is most *relevant.* A functional argument was given for why *surprise* plays such a role in (Will's and our) cognition. It was also shown why a kind of *boredom* is functional in an agent.

References

1. J. Ambros-Ingerson and Sam Steel. Integrating planning, execution and monitoring. In *AAAI-88*, St. Paul, Minnesota, 1988.
2. Rodney A. Brooks. A robust layered control system for a mobile robot. *IEEE Journal of Robotics and Automation*, 2(1):14–23, 1986.
3. Rodney A. Brooks. Intelligence without representation. *Artificial Intelligence*, 47:139–159, 1991.
4. Jamie G. Carbonell. Where do goals come from? In *4th Annual Conference of the Cognitive Science Society*, pages 191–194, Ann Arbor, Michigan, 1982.
5. Cristiano Castelfranchi. Guarantees for autonomy in cognitive agent architecture. In *(this volume)*.
6. Bertil Ekdahl, Eric Astor, and Paul Davidson. Towards anticipatory agents. In *(this volume)*.
7. Innes A. Ferguson. Integrated control and coordinated behaviour. In *(this volume)*.
8. Nico H. Frijda. *The Emotions*. Studies in emotion and social interaction. Cambridge University Press, Cambridge, U.K., 1986.

9. Steve Hanks and R. James Firby. Issues and architectures for planning and execution. In *Workshop on Innovative Approaches to Planning, Scheduling and Control*, pages 59–70. DARPA, November 1990.

10. Barbara Hayes-Roth. Architectural foundations for real-time performance in intelligent agents. *Journal of Real-time Systems*, 2:99–125, 1990.

11. Barbara Hayes-Roth. An architecture for adaptive intelligent systems. Technical report KSL-93-19, Stanford University, Knowledge Systems Laboratory, 1993.

12. Leslie P. Kaelbling. An architecture for intelligent reactive systems. In Michael P. Georgeff and Amy L. Lansky, editors, *Reasoning about Actions and Plans: Proceedings of the 1986 Workshop*, pages 395–410, Los Altos, California, 1987. Morgan Kaufmann.

13. Pattie Maes. Situated agents can have goals. *Robotics and Autonomous Systems*, 6:49–70, 1990.

14. Pattie Maes. Modeling adaptive autonomous agents. *Artificial Life*, 1:135–162, 1994.

15. Jacek Malec. A unified approach to intelligent agency. In *(this volume)*.

16. David C. Moffat. A poor man's co-ordination of Prolog: COPr. In Koen De Bosschere, Jean-Marie Jacquet, and Antonio Brogi, editors, *Proceedings of the ICLP'94 Post-Conference Workshop on Process-Based Parallel Logic Programming*, pages 85–89, Santa Margherita Ligure, Italy, 1994.

17. Jörg P. Müller, Markus Pischel, and Michael Thiel. A pragmatic approach to modelling autonomous interacting systems. In *(this volume)*.

18. Nils J. Nilsson. *Principles of Artificial Intelligence*. Morgan Kaufmann, San Francisco, California, 1980.

19. Nils J. Nilsson. Teleo-reactive programs for agent control. *Journal of Artificial Intelligence Research*, 1:139–158, 1994.

20. Timothy J. Norman and Derek Long. A proposal for goal creation in motivated agents. In *(this volume)*.

21. Austin Tate. Generating project networks. In *5th International Joint Conference on Artificial Intelligence*, pages 888–893, Cambridge, Massachusetts, 1977.

22. Michael J. Wooldridge and Nicholas R. Jennings. Agent theories, architectures and languages: A survey. In *(this volume)*.

Modeling Reactive Behaviour in Vertically Layered Agent Architectures

Jörg P. Müller, Markus Pischel, Michael Thiel

DFKI, Stuhlsatzenhausweg 3, D-66123 Saarbrücken

Abstract. The use of layered architectures for modeling autonomous agents has become popular over the past few years. In this paper, different approaches how these architectures can be build are discussed. A special case, namely *vertically layered architectures* is discussed by the example of the INTERRAP agent model. The paper focusses on the lower levels of the architecture which provide reactivity, incorporate procedural knowledge, and which connect the cooperation and planning layers with the outside world. We claim that the lower system layers are likely to become a control bottleneck in vertically layered architectures, and that very careful modeling is required to produce the desired agent behaviour.

1 Introduction

Over the past few years, several different architectures for autonomous systems have been proposed in the (D)AI literature (e.g. [2, 8, 3, 14, 4, 7, 10, 5, 16, 15]). An important class of approaches to modeling systems that have to behave in a goal-directed manner in a complex, changing environment are layered architectures. This approach regards an agent as consisting of several hierarchical functional modules, representing the different requirements on an agent, such as reactivity, efficiency, goal-directed behaviour, and coordination with others, as well as representing different qualities and levels of abstraction concerning the agent's knowledge (e.g. from raw sensor data to the description of complex, rather abstract situations). Basically all these approaches are somehow linking the input into an agent (its perception) into a kind of output from the agent (normally regarded as the actions the agent performs). Most of them define an agent cycle using perception in order to update the agent's internal state, i.e. its beliefs about the world, then use this world model as a basis to do some kind of decision-making (planning), possibly taking into account other agents, finally leading to a decision as to what to do next, i.e. to the actions to be performed in the next agent cycle. Possible layers of these agent models incorporate *perception* and *action*, *reactivity* (behaviour-based layer), *local planning*, *cooperation*, *modeling*, *intentions*, and *learning*.

In this paper, we identify and describe several basic classes of layered architectures. We focus on a specific class, namely *vertically layered architectures*, and describe a concrete instance, the agent architecture INTERRAP. INTERRAP consists of two basic units, the agent control unit and the agent knowledge base, which both share a hierarchical structure. The four control layers are (from lower to upper): the agents' world interface definition (WIF); the behaviour-based component (BBC); the plan-based component (PBC); and the cooperation component (CC). The agent knowledge base is designed as a hierarchical blackboard system which is basically splitted into four layers corresponding to the structure of the control component. It is not the purpose of this paper to give a thorough description of the agent architecture; this has been done elsewhere [13]. Rather we argue that the way the lower layers are modelled is of special importance in vertically layered architectures since every piece of information and any control discussion has to pass them. Therefore, we focus on the design of the behaviour-based component of the INTERRAP model. Several aspects will be discussed that have to be taken into account and problems which have to be solved when dealing with this problem. As an example, we will look at the world interface and behaviour-based component used to implement KHEPERA miniature forklift robots. The different functionalities defined at the BBC layer and the basic control structures used to schedule the patterns of behaviour will be described. Different mechanisms for pattern selection will be discussed in the light of this example, such as static and dynamic priorities between patterns, the use of genetic algorithms, suppression mechanisms, and knowledge-based methods.

2 Layered Architectures

Among the many instances of layered architectures mentioned in the introduction, we can distinguish between two fundamental classes: horizontally layered architectures (such as the ones developed by Brooks[1][2], Kaelbling[8], and Ferguson [4]) and vertically layered architectures (such as MECCA[15] and INTERRAP[13]). Whereas all the layers of an agent have access both to the perception and action components in horizontal architectures, only one (and normally: the lowest) layer has a direct interface to these facilities in the vertical approach. This is illustrated by figure 1. Ferguson's *Touring Machines* architecture [4] is a very good example of a horizontally layered architecture (figure 1a). It consists of three control layers, the reactive layer, the planning layer, and the modeling layer. All the layers work concurrently, have access to the agent's perception and may propose actions. In order to achieve coherence, Ferguson's agents employ a set of global control rules which may suppress the input to a certain layer (suppressors) and which may censor the output of a layer. Brooks [2] employs similar mechanisms (suppression and inhibition) in order to enable higher layers to suppress inputs to and to inhibit output from lower layers.

The need for a centralized control authority and the complexity of its design seems to be one of the key problem with horizonatally layered architecture. In an architecture consisting of n layers, even if we restrict ourselves to bilateral interactions between layers, each layer may theoretically interact with each other

---

[1] Note that Brooks' approach is often referred to as vertical decomposition approach, since it divides up the functionality of an agent in a hierarchical manner; this should not be confounded with the fact that the access to perception and action is possible for each layer, and that it therefore describes a vertical architecture in our notation.

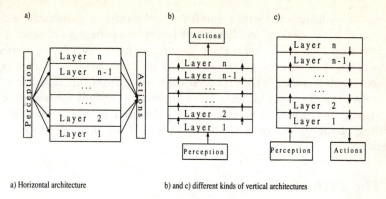

a) Horizontal architecture   b) and c) different kinds of vertical architectures

Fig. 1. Vertical and Horizontal Agent Architectures

layer, leading to $\frac{n \cdot (n-1)}{2}$ bilateral cases to be described, each of which can be very complex itself. Thus, in horizontal approaches, the bottleneck is *control*. This observation has led to the development of vertically layered architectures, which impose certain restrictions on the possible interactions among different layers. An example for vertically layered architectures (figure 1c) is the INTERRAP agent architecture [13]. which is the model underlying our work. INTERRAP describes an agent as consisting of trhee hierarchical layers, the behaviour-based component, the plan-based component, and the cooperation component. The basic concepts of INTERRAP are described in section 3.

The MECCA architecture proposed by Steiner et al. [15] can be regarded as a variation of a vertically layered architecture (figure 1b). Reasoning within an agent is regarded as running in four phases which are represented by four modules: *goal activation*, *planning*, *scheduling*, and *execution*. The main difference between INTERRAP and MECCA is that the modularization in the latter architecture is *functional*, whereas it is *conceptual* in the former; the MECCA modules correspond to different functionalities of an agent whereas the INTERRAP layers rather constitute different levels of abstraction of similar functionalities.

Due to the nature of the flow of control in vertical agent architectures, the way the lower layers are modeled are crucial for these class of agent models. On the one hand, using vertical architectures such as INTERRAP saves one from having to define the sort of global control knowledge that is specified in horizontally layered architectures: the only thing that needs to be done for an architecture with layers $1 \ldots n$ is to define $n - 1$ interfaces between directly neighbouring modules. On the other hand, there is a price to pay for this convenience: anything the agent does must pass its lowest layer. In the case of the INTERRAP agent, the behaviour-based layer is the critical layer: this layer firstly has to react to unforeseen events, secondly monitors the execution of what we call the agent's abstract actions based upon commands from the local planning layer, thirdly must maintain constraints imposed by the local planning context, and, last but not least, may be affected with commitments obtained by cooperative activities.

Thus it is the task of the behaviour-based component to maintain and to schedule a set of possibly concurrent patterns of behaviour, being activated by the recognition of certain situations and by decisions made at higher layers of the agent architecture. What should become clear from this discussion is that whether a vertical agent architecture can be used successfully for modeling agents in a specific domain is to a large extent influenced by a more or less careful modeling of the lower layers of the agent as well as their interface to higher layers.

3 The INTERRAP Agent Model

The main idea of INTERRAP is to define an agent by a set of functional layers, linked by a activation-based control structure and a shared hierarchical knowledge base. Figure 2 overviews the INTERRAP agent model. It consists of five

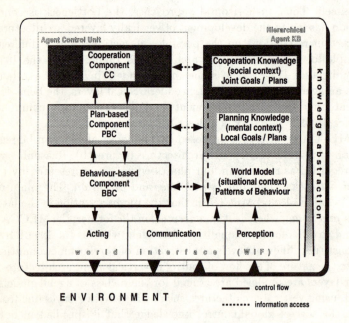

Fig. 2. The INTERRAP Agent Model

basic parts: the world interface (WIF), the behaviour-based component (BBC), the plan-based component (PBC), the cooperation component (CC), and the agent knowledge-base. The *WIF* contains the agent's facilities for perception, action, and communication. The *BBC* implements and controls the basic reactive behaviour of the agent as well as its procedural knowledge (abstract actions).

It is based on the concept of *patterns of behaviour*. These allow an agent to react flexibly to its environment, and to perform routine tasks efficiently without requiring explicit symbolic planning. The *PBC* contains a planning mechanism which is able to devise local single-agent plans. The plans are hierarchical skeletal plans whose nodes may be either new subplans, or executable patterns of behaviour, or primitive actions. Thus, the plan-based component may activate patterns of behaviour in order to achieve certain goals. Planning helps an agent to act in a goal-directed manner. Moreover, in a multi-agent context, planning is necessary to coordinate actions of agents. For instance, agents should be able to devise joint plans ([9]) to cope with special situations. This functionality is provided by the cooperation component CC.

The agent knowledge base is designed as a hierarchical blackboard system which is basically splitted into three layers corresponding to the structure of the control component: the agents' *world model* containing its object-level beliefs about the world; the *mental model* holding autoepistemic knowledge, and knowledge about the agent's mental state (goals, plans, intentions); finally, the *social model* representing what an agent believes about other agents, as well as information about joint goals, plans, and intentions Information access is possible only from lower layers to higher layers of the knowledge base. For example, the PBC can access information about the world model, whereas the PBC does not have access to planning or cooperation information.

The overall control behaviour of an INTERRAP agent emerges from the communication among the different modules. Based on interesting events happening in the world (*situations*) recognized by the agent, control is shifted upward until the appropriate layer to deal with the situation. There are three generic *execution paths* describing general classes of problem-solving: the *reactive path*, the *local planning path*, and the *cooperative planning path*. The reactive path treats a situation by direct execution of a pattern of behaviour, without involving explicit planning. The local planning path makes use of the local planning resources of the agents: control is shifted upward from the BBC to the PBC where a plan is devised. Finally, the cooperative planning path is selected if a situation cannot be satisfactorily solved by local planning. Except these generic paths, there exist other, more complex interactions, especially between the PBC and CC. For example, in order to make a decision in a negotiation protocol, it can be necessary to determine the possibility and the cost of locally solving a specific subproblem.

In the rest of this paper and for the reasons motivated in the introduction, we will focus on the BBC and WIF components. We refer to [13, 12] for a more detailed description of the planning and cooperation layer and of the control aspects of the architecture.

4 Behaviour-Based Modeling

In this section, the lower layers of the INTERRAP model are described in detail. Subsection 4.1 discusses the agent's world interface. In subsection 4.2, we present our concept of patterns of behaviour. Subsection 4.3 describes the basic control cycle of the behaviour-based component.

4.1 The World Interface

As stated above, the world interface implements the basic facilities of an agent for performing actions, handling messages, and perceiving its environment. Defining the interface between the behaviour-based layer and the world interface layer is an important design decision. For many applications, an obvious possibility to define the world interface is by using the primitives given by the application itself. This can be the case for example in a robot application, where the designer's possibility to model the behaviour of its robots is based on the existing hardware. Therefore, we call this interface the *hardware interface* (HI). The advantage of this approach is that the separation is clear and given in advance. Moreover, the behaviour-based component may directly access all the functionality of the system; thus, control is maximized. On the other hand, the behaviour-based component becomes machine-dependent, and is based on a low degree of abstraction.

Different approaches to separating WIF and BBC are what we call the *symbolic/subsymbolic interface* (SSI) and the *abstraction interface* (AbI); according to the former, the quality of reasoning (symbolic or subsymbolic) is the criterion for dividing between WIF and BBC. That means, subsymbolic reasoning is done in the WIF, the BBC starts where information is stated explicitly at a symbolic layer. The advantage of the SSI approach is that it can be defined more flexibly than HI and increases abstraction and hardware independence. However, it offers only little help in deciding what should be represented at a symbolic and at a subsymbolic layer, respectively. The latter approach, the abstraction interface, can overcome this weakness: the main idea behind it is to define logically primitive actions for a given application. Experience has shown that it is easy to specify this interface for many applications.

In the simulation of the loading dock, for example, it turned out to be reasonable to specify the actoric world interface of the forklifts by primitive actions such as *walk_ahead, turn_left, turn_right, grasp_box, put_box*. Thus, a pattern of behaviour *goto_landmark* may call *walk_ahead* as a primitive action having the agent move to the field in front of it. In the KHEPERA implementation with real robots, moving one field ahead is by no means primitive for a robot. Rather, it is a complex action, implying following the guiding line, controlling speed and avoiding collisions. The functionality offered by the hardware interface of the robots such as *read_speed(<right-motor, left-motor>), set_speed(<right-motor, left-motor>), read_proximity_sensors, read_floor_sensors*, is partially too low-level. Therefore, the WIF-definition in the KHEPERA implementation lies somewhere in between and consists of a set of functions such as *go(speed), right_curve(intensity), left_curve(intensity)*, which are more abstract than e.g. *set_speed*, but more specific than *walk_ahead.*.

4.2 Patterns of Behaviour

Patterns of behaviour are the essential structural primitives of the behaviour-based component. They incorporate the reactive abilities and the procedural knowledge of an agent. The former allow an agent to react quickly, flexibly, and often avoiding explicit replanning, to certain unexpected events, the latter provide the primitives for the plan-based component of an INTERRAP agent

Structure According to their activation/effect functionality, we distinguish between four basic types of patterns: *reactors, control modifiers, knowledge modifiers*, and *procedures*. *Reactor patterns* are triggered by external events and cause the agent to perform some sort of action. For example, stopping when facing an obstacle in front of it should be implemented as a reactor pattern. *Knowledge modifiers* are patterns that change the internal state of the agent (e.g. its knowledge). They are activated by changes in the world perceived by the agent (i.e. by changes in the agent's world model). In our approach, they are used to implement the recognition and classification of situations and world model abstraction. Similar to knowledge sources in a blackboard system, there are patterns that recognize and abstract specific situations (e.g. *another agent ahead, standing in a narrow corridor*). Other patterns recognize more complex pattern based on the results of the lower-level knowledge modifiers. *Control modifiers* are patterns that expand control to the planner by calling the PBC. For example, a pattern `treat_order_beh` will activate the PBC with the goal of planning an order as so on as the agent has received a transportation order. Finally, *procedure* patterns implement what is viewed as abstract actions by the planner. For example, moving straight ahead to a landmark is likely to be implemented as a procedure in a robot application, i.e. is atomic from the perspective of the PBC. These patterns can be compiled down from plans. Since we assume that the planner basically plans *actions*, our classification does not take into account patterns that are triggered internally and yield only a modification of the agent's world model or an activation of the planner. Based on this classification, patterns of behaviour are abstractly defined as frame structures as shown in figure 3. The definition of a PoB consists of a description part and an execution part. The description part contains meta-information describing the pattern of behaviour which is needed for the control mechanism, such as the activation condition and several monitoring conditions. The execution part contains the executable body of the pattern, which is started if the pattern is selected by the control mechanism. In the following, the elements of both parts will be described in more detail.

The Description Part The basic elements of the description part of a PoB are its activation condition and a set of monitoring conditions. All these conditions describe situations which are relevant for the selection and/or execution of the pattern and thus provide meta-information about the pattern. The *activation condition* is a formula which whose satisfaction in a certain state of the world

```
( PoB
        :name           /* Name of pattern */
        :type           /* reactor, modifier, procedure */
        :args           /* arguments */
        :activation     /* activation condition */
        :monitor        /* conditions monitoring execution */
         :failure       /* failure condition: stop execution */
         :success       /* condition for successful termination */
         :holding       /* conditions that must hold during execution */
         :exceptions    /* user-definable exceptions */
        :post           /* condition that must hold after execution */
        :exec_body      /* executable body;e.g. control program */ )
```

Fig. 3. Patterns of Behaviour

is a precondition for the PoB to be applicable in this world state. Thus, in each state of the world, there is a set of active patterns. Once one of the active patterns has been selected by the control mechanism (see below), its execution is monitored by a set of monitoring conditions. These conditions describe exceptions which may occur during the execution of a pattern. An exception is a tuple *(Cond, Act)*, where Cond is a *state formula*, and Act is an action description. The operational semantics is that if Cond becomes satisfied by the current state of the world, Act is executed. Apart from a set of user-defined exceptions, there are some exceptions whose action parts possess a fixed semantics: For example, if the *failure condition* becomes satisfied during the execution of the pattern, execution is aborted with a failure; if the *termination condition* becomes satisfied, the pattern is terminated successfully. This allows to deal with the case that the purpose of a pattern is reached by coincidence. Failure and termination conditions are of the form (Cond, Clean-Up) where Cond specifies the actual condition and Clean-Up specifies certain activities which have to be performed in order to ensure consistent termination/failure of the PoB. The necessity of the Clean-Up part will become obvious by the example in section 5. The conditions of an active pattern are monitored by so-called *guards*, which are basically knowledge modifiers, i.e. patterns of behaviour which become active when the respective condition (e.g. the termination condition of the parent pattern) becomes true. For example, the termination condition for a PoB for moving to a landmark is satisfied when the agent has reached the landmark. This again is monitored by a guard pattern.

Finally, a *post condition* may be specified which describes the essential properties of the world after the execution of the pattern. Unlike the termination condition, the post condition is not monitored during execution. However, it may be accessed by the control mechanism in order to determine the *degree of satisfaction* for a PoB, that can be used as a means for determining the priority of a pattern (see also subsection 4.3 and [6]).

The Execution Part The execution of a pattern of behaviour will cause the agent to perform actions in the world, to read its sensors, or in specific situations will lead to calling the plan-based component. The execution procedure of a PoB is specified in its execution part. Since the bodies of patterns of behaviour may be complex (for example: *goto_landmark*), and since several patterns of behaviour may be active at a time, the granularity of execution is a critical topic: a scheduling mechanism is required that allows stepwise execution which may alternate between different PoB. Execution granularity must not be too coarse in order to keep reactivity of the BBC, nor must it be too fine in order to reduce the overhead for changing between the execution frames of different PoB's too often. In the sequel, a language for describing the bodies of PoB is defined.

An Execution Language for PoB An execution language for PoB needs to satisfy the following requirements:

- It has to allow stepwise execution providing reasonable stepwidths and allowing to specify *atomic* activities that must not be interrupted.
- Its primitives should be the activation of WIF primitives, such as actions and sensors, and calls to the plan-based component.
- It shall offer language constructs such as composition, tests, and iteration. For determining the values of test and iteration predicates, access to the knowledge base is needed.
- Since patterns of behaviour may be compiled down from plans, they will activate other patterns of behaviour; sequential and parallel activation should be supported.

Figure 4 shows the EBNF syntax of a language fulfilling these requirements. Keywords (e.g. **while**, **if**) appear in bold face, primitives in italics. Dots denote incomplete definitions. In the sequel, we will define the semantics of the execution language.

Semantics The operational semantics of the language presented above is defined by an interpretation function *step* which takes as argument a language expression. *Step* can be recursively defined as follows:

$$\text{step}(\{\ P\ \}) \stackrel{\text{def}}{=} \text{set block} = \text{true}; \text{step}(P)\ ;\ \text{set block} = \text{false}$$

$$\text{step}(P_1; P_2) \stackrel{\text{def}}{=} \text{step}(P_1); \text{step}(P_2)$$

$$\text{step}(\textbf{while } c \textbf{ do } P \textbf{ od}) \stackrel{\text{def}}{=} \textbf{if } c \textbf{ then } \text{step}(P; \textbf{while } c \textbf{ do } P) \textbf{ else } \text{true } \textbf{fi}$$

$$\text{step}(\textbf{if } c \textbf{ then } P_1 \textbf{ else } P_2 \textbf{ fi}) \stackrel{\text{def}}{=} \textbf{if } c \textbf{ then } \text{step}(P_1) \textbf{ else } \text{step}(P_2)$$

$$\text{step}(ex(P)) \stackrel{\text{def}}{=} ex(P)$$

$$\text{step}(call(pbc, X)) \stackrel{\text{def}}{=} call(pbc, X)$$

$$\text{step}(activate([P|Rest])) \stackrel{\text{def}}{=} activate(P); \text{step}(activate(Rest));$$

$$\text{step}(activate([])) \stackrel{\text{def}}{=} \text{true}$$

program	::=	block [';' program]
block	::=	'{' block-content '}' | primitive-instr
block-content	::=	**while** condition **do** block-content **od** |
		if condition **then** block-content **else** block-content **fi** |
		primitive-instr
primitive-instr	::=	wif-execution | pbc-call | pob-activation | modifier
condition	::=	*atomic formula*
wif-execution	::=	**ex** '(' wif-primitive ')'
pbc-call	::=	**call** '(' pbc ',' **do** '(' goal-specification ')' ')' | ...
pob-activation	::=	**activate** '(' pob-spec-list ')'
wif-primitive	::=	*turn_left* | *turn_right* | 'go('*integer*')' | 'right_curve('*integer*')' |
		'left_curve(' *integer* ')' | *read_sensors* | ...
goal-specification	::=	*formula*
pob-spec-list	::=	'[' { pob-specification }$^+$ ']' ')'
pob-specification	::=	pobname '(' *parameter-list* ')'
modifier	::=	**assert** *ground formula* | **retract** *ground formula*

Fig. 4. EBNF-Syntax of the Execution Language

The function *step* is described using a meta language. *Ex, call, activate* denote the physical actions of executing a WIF primitive, calling the PBC, or activating a pattern of behaviour. $[H|T]$ denotes a list with first element H and rest T. *While do od* and *if then else fi* are interpreted as usual. In order to distinguish the meta language constructs from their object-level counterparts, we do not use bold type for the former ones. The reason for the treatment of blocks will become clear in subsection 4.3, where the stepwise execution mechanism is described.

4.3 The BBC Control Cycle

Up to now, we have described patterns of behaviour. The BBC of an agent consists of a set of patterns of behaviour and of a pattern maintenance unit which implements the control mechanism of the BBC. Next, in this subsection, this control mechanism is described.

Overview In order to achieve the requirement of reactivity, the BBC control is implemented in a processing cycle: in each loop, it monitors changes in the world model caused by perception and commands received from the plan-based components. According to the new world state, several PoB may be active because their activation conditions are satisfied or because they have become active in an earlier world state and have not yet been finished. The basic task of the BBC cycle is to determine the active patterns based on the updated world model, then to select one PoB for execution in the current cycle, and to execute it one step further. The control cycle algorithm is shown in figure 5. At the beginning of each cycle, the agent updates its world model based on its current perception and based on activation messages from the PBC and from other patterns

```
/* Variables:                                                            */
/*      POBSET:         set of all patterns of behaviour                 */
/*      ACTᵢ:           set of PoB which are active by the end of cycle i */
/*      INACTᵢ:         set of PoB which are not active by the end of cycle i */
/*      PERCᵢ:          perception at the beginning of cycle i           */
/*      ACT-REQᵢ:       PoB activation requests at beginning of cycle i   */
/*      PoBᵢ:           pattern of behaviour selected for execution in cycle i */
/*      WMᵢ:            world model in cycle i                           */

bbc-cycle(POBSET)
{    i := 0;
     ACTᵢ := ∅;
     WMᵢ := init_kb;
     INACTᵢ := POBSET;
     repeat
             WMᵢ₊₁ := update_state(WMᵢ, PERCᵢ₊₁, ACT-REQᵢ₊₁);
             ACTᵢ₊₁ := det_active_pob(ACTᵢ, INACTᵢ, WMᵢ₊₁);
             PoBᵢ₊₁ := select_pattern(ACTᵢ₊₁, WMᵢ₊₁);
             WMᵢ₊₁ := execute_pob(PoBᵢ₊₁, WMᵢ₊₁);

             INACTᵢ₊₁ := POBSET − ACTᵢ₊₁;
             i := i + 1
     forever  }
```

Fig. 5. The BBC Control Algorithm

of behaviour. The actual processing of the cycle runs in three phases, which are discussed in more detail in the following subsections.

Determining Active Patterns The function `det_active_pob(WM,ACT,INACT)` is used in each BBC cycle in order to determine the current set of active patterns of behaviour. In the following, let $\mathcal{P}$ denote a set of patterns of behaviour, and let $\mathcal{L}$ denote a set of propositions (denoting e.g. an agent's world model). For a pattern $p \in \mathcal{P}_a$ let $p.AC$, $p.TC$, and $p.FC$ denote p's activation, termination, and failure condition, respectively. A pattern is called active at a certain time if the activation condition of the pattern is satisfied at that time, or if the pattern has been activated at an earlier time and has not yet terminated or failed. Thus, det_active_pob is a function $\delta : 2^{\mathcal{L}} \times 2^{\mathcal{P}} \times 2^{\mathcal{P}} \mapsto 2^{\mathcal{P}}$, where

$$\delta(WM_{i+1}, Act_i, InAct_i) \overset{\text{def}}{=}$$
$$\{p \in InAct_i | WM_{i+1} \models p.AC\} \cup \{p' \in Act_i | \exists j.j < i \wedge WM_j \models p.AC \wedge$$
$$\neg \exists k.j < k < i \wedge (WM_k \models p.TC \vee WM_k \models p.FC)\}.$$

Pattern Selection We see that different PoB may be active at a time. However, our model assumes a sequential model of execution. That means, only one pattern may have the control to initiate an action at a certain time. It is a consequence of this fact that one pattern must be selected for execution in each BBC cycle. This selection is performed by the function select_pattern(ActPList). It is defined as a function $\sigma : 2^{\mathcal{P}} \times 2^{\mathcal{L}} \mapsto \mathcal{P}$. It is the task of this function to select the most urgent, most important, or most useful PoB to be executed in a specific situation described by the second argument of σ, the agent's current world model. Pattern selection problem; it has turned out to be the core problem of behaviour-based modeling, and the way it is implemented is crucial for the behaviour of the agent, for its reactivity as well as for its capability to handle complex situations. In the following, we outline two approaches for modeling pattern selection, both of them based on a priority mechanism.

Static Priorities: The Maslow Pyramid Very often, we can identify classes of patterns of behaviour that are generally more urgent or more important than others. Based on a hierarchical classification of human needs by the psychologist Maslow [11], we defined four hierarchical classes of patterns of behaviour: PoB corresponding to physical goals (e.g. remain unharmed, avoid collisions, ensure energy supply), to task-related goals (e.g. perform transportation tasks), to social goals (e.g. help other agents), and PoB corresponding to optimization goals (explore regions, improve plans). Maslow claims that the lower-level needs have higher priority than the higher-level needs, and that the former must be satisfied before a human starts satisfying the latter.

This classification of patterns of behaviour in an application results in a static preordering of the patterns, and allows to express e.g. that if an agent has a task to fulfill and it detects a threatening collision, the collision avoidance pattern has higher priority than the task-oriented pattern. In their DASEDIS architecture, [3] pursue a similar approach by associating behaviours with intentions and by defining a total ordering on the intentions.

Dynamic Priorities: Degree of Satisfaction (DoS) The static priority approach has some serious drawbacks. Firstly, it provides no guidance to select between two patterns classified at the same classification layer. Secondly, the relative priority of a pattern often depends on the current situation. Thirdly, giving task-related goals a higher priority than social goals does not support cooperative behaviour. Strictly speaking, it would even imply that an agent only cooperates if it has no local tasks to achieve - which is definitely not what is intended. A better approach seems to be to compute the priority of a pattern dynamically based on its *degree of satisfaction* (a similar idea has been proposed by [6] in the context of decision-theoretic planning). The degree of satisfaction of a PoB is a function of the amount of resources consumed by the pattern, and of how much of the goal corresponding to the pattern has already been achieved. For example, the DoS of the pattern of behaviour *goto_landmark* can be expressed by

$$DoS(goto\_landmark(X_d, Y_d)) = 1 - \frac{dist((X_{curr}, Y_{curr}), (X_d, Y_d))}{dist((X_s, Y_s), ((X_d, Y_d))}$$

where $(X_s, Y_s), (X_{curr}, Y_{curr}), (X_d, Y_d)$ denote the start position, the current position, and the destination position of the agent, respectively. $dist(p_1, p_2)$ denotes the Euclidean distance between two points p_1 and p_2. A general possibility to compute the DoS is by comparing the actual state of the world with the post condition of the pattern. If we allow only conjunctive, pairwise independent formulae to define postconditions, and assume that we can evaluate the truth value of the partial formulae by simple matching against the world model, we can use the percentage of satisfied subgoals as a coarse measure for the degree of satisfaction. Another approach is to maintain statistical or heuristic models about the average (expected) time and resource consumption of patterns of behaviour, and to estimate the degree of satisfaction based on these models.

Pattern Execution The execution of a pattern of behaviour which has been chosen in the selection phase is monitored by the function **execute_pattern(PoB, WM)**. **execute_pattern** is a function $\varepsilon : \mathcal{P} \times 2^{\mathcal{L}} \mapsto 2^{\mathcal{L}}$ which determines the change of an agent's internal state by executing a pattern of behaviour in a given state. As stated above, the execution mechanism has to provide stepwise execution of patterns of behaviour. In the sequel, we will outline how an execution scheduling mechanism can be achieved by slightly modifying the interpretation function *step* defined in subsection 4.2.

The main idea behind the scheduling algorithm is to define one execution step either as the (computation plus) execution of the next primitive instruction or as the execution of a block defined by the programmer of the pattern. That means, we provide a high-level scheduling mechanism which allows the programmer to define the granularity of execution - and which also forces her/him to take the responsibility for selecting an appropriate choice.

The function **execute_pattern** can be implemented by modifying the *step* function for *primitive instructions* as follows:

$$step(ex(P)) \stackrel{def}{=} ex(P);$$
$$\text{if block = false then store\_execution\_frame; exit fi}$$

$$step(call(pbc, X)) \stackrel{def}{=} call(pbc, X);$$
$$\text{if block = false then store\_execution\_frame; exit}$$
$$\text{else true fi}$$

$$step(activate([P|Rest])) \stackrel{def}{=} activate(P); step(activate(Rest));$$
$$\text{if block = false then store\_execution\_frame; exit}$$
$$\text{else true fi}$$

$$step(activate([])) \stackrel{def}{=} true$$

block is a boolean variable which is set to *true* at each entrance into a block structure defined by the user, and set to *false* again when leaving the block. If a primitive instruction is processed, it is tested whether it occurred inside a block. If this is not the case, the current execution step is finished. Then, the *execution frame* of the pattern (which stores the local state of processing) is stored and control returns to the BBC cycle.

5 An Example

The application that will be used to illustrate the model described in the previous chapter is the FORKS system. FORKS describes a simulation of an automated loading-dock, where autonomous forklift agents have to load and to unload trucks. In the loading dock, there are shelves which may contain different types of goods. We use a grid-based representation of the loading-dock. The forklifts can move from one square to the next, turn around, grasp and store goods, and communicate with other agents. Each agent has a certain range of perception, which it can observe. Currently, a physical implementation based on KHEPERA miniature robots has been initiated, which differs from the simulation mainly by the definition of the world interface (see also section 4.1). The patterns of behaviour defined in the following refer to the KHEPERA implementation.

To give a better idea how the BBC works, we present some examples of PoB in our FORKS system and trace some steps of the control cycle.

```
( PoB
      :name            goto_landmark
      :type            procedure
      :args            (destX,destY)
      :activation      msg(activate(goto_landmark(destX,destY)))
      :monitor
          :success     my_pos(destX,destY)
          :exception   ([(return_status(walk_ahead) = failure,
                          enable(dodge))])
      :exec_body
          while true do
             activate(turn_to_free_dir(destX,destY));
             activate(walk_ahead);
          od
)

( PoB
      :name            dodge
      :type            reactor
      :activation      object_in_front
      :exec_body       activate(step_aside);
)
```

Fig. 6. Patterns of Behaviour *goto_landmark, dodge*

The name of the PoB illustrated in figure 6 is *goto_landmark*. It is a *procedure* which is activated by a call (message) of the PBC or another PoB and it receives the destination field as argument. The purpose of *goto_landmark* is to move the robot from its actual position to the destination field. There are no monitors for failure, holding or other exceptions. Only successful termination is checked:

the PoB succeeds, if the robot stands on the destination field. In the body, two further PoBs are called. *turn_to_free_dir(x,y)* turns the robot in a direction, where the field in front of it is free and a step forward decreases the distance to the destination field, if such a direction exists. *walk_ahead* makes the robot move one field ahead.

When this PoB gets active (by a call from the PBC) and is selected to be executed, the function *step* processes the body until it reaches the expression *activate(turn_to_free_dir())*. Now the PoB *turn_to_free_dir* becomes active and *goto_landmark* is suspended until *turn_to_free_dir* is finished, i.e. the body will not be executed furthermore, but the success-monitor keeps running. If *turn_to_free_dir* succeeds, *goto_landmark* continues and on the next execution step *walk_ahead* will be activated. If *turn_to_free_dir* fails, *goto_landmark* fails too. The activation of *walk_ahead* behaves the same way, except that its failure is handled by an exception: the *reactor pattern dodge* is enabled which tries to move around the obstacle; *walk_ahead* fails only in case *dodge* also fails. If the monitor reports success of the PoB, all child PoB are deactivated and the PoB ends with success.

The reason why it is advantageous to implement the functionality of *goto_landmark* as a pattern of behaviour in our case is that it is only activated by the planner in order to move the robot between places where there is no (static) obstacle in between. The only unforeseen event that could happen is that another agent crosses the way. This case can often be managed by the behaviour-based component without doing explicit replanning by defining a reactor pattern that has the agent dodge as illustrated in figure 6.

6 Conclusion and Outlook

In this paper, we discussed problems occurring when modeling the lower layers of a vertically layered architecture. We have used the example of the behaviour-based layer of the agent architecture INTERRAP. The structure of and the processing within this layer was described.

In a certain sense, describing an agent by a set of interacting layers makes agent design itself a multi-agent problem. The benefits of decentralizing knowledge, competence, and control within an agent have to be weighed against the effort introduced by the coordination among the different layers. One conclusion we draw from this observation is that there certainly is an upper bound to a reasonable number of different layers, which may differ for certain applications. The second conclusion is that we might use coordination techniques from multi-agent systems in order to solve the coherence problem within the agent, i.e. the problem of make the different layers work together smoothly. An example for an idea how the problem-solving power of the INTERRAP architecture can be enhanced is to use the contract net protocol with time-out mechanisms for controlling concurrent, time-dependent planning at different layers. This would allow different layers to work on a given time-dependent task concurrently and to choose the best solution found so far by the time of the deadline. These issues are related to anytime planning (see also [1]) and are further interesting research topics in agent design.

We thank Michael Wooldridge and Nick Jennings for valuable comments on earlier versions of this paper. They greatly helped improving its quality. The work presented in this paper has been supported by the German Ministry of Research and Technology under grant ITW9104.

References

1. M. Boddy and T. L. Dean. Deliberation scheduling for problem solving in time-constrained environments. *Artificial Intelligence*, 67:245–285, 1994.
2. Rodney A. Brooks. A robust layered control system for a mobile robot. In *IEEE Journal of Robotics and Automation*, volume RA-2 (1), April 1986.
3. B. Burmeister and K. Sundermeyer. Cooperative problem-solving guided by intentions and perception. In E. Werner and Y. Demazeau, editors, *Decentralized A.I. 3*. North-Holland, 1992.
4. I. A. Ferguson. *TouringMachines: An Architecture for Dynamic, Rational, Mobile Agents*. PhD thesis, Computer Laboratory, University of Cambridge, UK,, 1992.
5. R. James Firby. Building symbolic primitives with continuous control routines. In J. Hendler, editor, *Proc. of the First International Conference on AI Planning Systems*. Morgan Kaufmann Publishers, San Mateo, CA, 1992.
6. P. Haddawy and S. Hanks. Utility models for goal-directed decision-theoretic planners, 1994. Submitted to *Artificial Intelligence* journal.
7. N. R. Jennings. *Joint Intentions as a Model of Multi-Agent Cooperation*. PhD thesis, Queen Mary and Westfield College, London, August 1992.
8. L. P. Kaelbling. An architecture for intelligent reactive systems. In J. Allen, J. Hendler, and A. Tate, editors, *Readings in Planning*, pages 713–728. Morgan Kaufmann, 1990.
9. D. Kinny, M. Ljungberg, A. Rao, E. Sonenberg, G. Tidhar, and E. Werner. Planned team activity. In A. Cesta, R. Conte, and M. Miceli, editors, *Pre-Proceedings of MAAMAW'92*, July 1992.
10. D. M. Lyons and A. J. Hendriks. A practical approach to integrating reaction and deliberation. In *Proc. of the 1st International Conference on AI Planning Systems (AIPS)*, pages 153–162, San Mateo, CA, June 1992. Morgan Kaufmann.
11. A. H. Maslow. A theory of human motivation. *Psychological Review*, 50:370–396, 1943.
12. J. P. Müller. Evaluation of plans for multiple agents (preliminary report). In K. Fischer and G. M. P. O'Hare, editors, *Working Notes of the ECAI Workshop on Decision Theory for DAI Applications*, Amsterdam, NL, August 1994.
13. J. P. Müller and M. Pischel. Integrating agent interaction into a planner-reactor architecture. In M. Klein, editor, *Proc. of the 13th International Workshop on Distributed Artificial Intelligence*, Seattle, WA, USA, July 1994.
14. A. S. Rao and M. P. Georgeff. Modeling Agents Within a BDI-Architecture. In R. Fikes and E. Sandewall, editors, *Proc. of KR'91*, Cambridge, Mass., April 1991. Morgan Kaufmann.
15. D. D. Steiner, A. Burt, M. Kolb, and Ch. Lerin. The conceptual framework of mai^{2}l. In *Pre-Proceedings of MAAMAW'93*, Neuchâtel, Switzerland, August 1993.
16. M. Wooldridge. *On the Logical Modelling of Computational Multi-Agent Systems*. PhD thesis, UMIST, Department of Computation, Manchester, UK, 1992.

Goal Creation in Motivated Agents

Timothy J. Norman and Derek Long

Department of Computer Science, University College London,
Gower Street, London WC1E 6BT, United Kingdom.
EMAIL: (tnorman, derek)@cs.ucl.ac.uk

Abstract. Goal creation is an important consideration for an agent that is required to behave autonomously in a real-world domain. This paper describes an agent that is directed, not by a conjunction of top level goals, but by a set of motives. The agent is motivated to create and prioritise different goals at different times as a part of an on-going activity under changing circumstances.

Goals can be created both in reaction to, and in anticipation of a situation. While there has been much work on the creation of reactive goals, i.e. goals created in reaction to a situation, the issues involved in the creation of anticipatory, or proactive goals have not been considered in depth. The solution to the goal creation problem outlined here provides an agent with an effective method of creating goals both reactively and proactively, giving the agent a greater degree of autonomy.

1 Introduction

The focus of planning research has principally been concerned with the creation of good plans to satisfy a conjunction of goals in an efficient way [8, 11, 12]. These systems typically assume that neither the goals of the agent, nor their importance change as time passes. This assumption cannot be justified for an autonomous agent acting in a real-world domain (i.e., a domain that can neither be completely nor correctly modelled). The domain may change at any time such that pursuing the current goal may no longer be realistic or even possible. Furthermore, the agent will typically need to satisfy various goals, some maybe more than once, at various times as part of an on-going activity; the agent must have the ability to create goals "on the fly" in response to a changing environment.

A real-world domain changes over time presenting a continuous flow of contexts to an agent acting in the domain. An effective autonomous agent must be capable of identifying changes that are relevant to its purposes and creating appropriate goals in response to these changes. There are two important types of goal that are identified here—reactive and proactive goals. Reactive goals are so called because they are created in response to beliefs about the current state of the domain: certain beliefs cause the creation of goals. These goals are to affect the domain in such a way that the beliefs that caused the goal to be created are no longer valid. Reactive goal creation is the basic mechanism employed in belief, desire, and intention (BDI) architectures [6, 13, 14]. It is essential for an agent to create goals in reaction to certain environmental conditions because there will always be situations in any real-world domain that can never be predicted—can only be reacted to when they occur. These goals may be satisfied either through planning [13, 14] or by the selection of control procedures [1, 2] depending on the context. Proactive goals are created in response to predictions about how the domain will change over time, and typically satisfied through planning[1]. If an agent is capable of creating effective proactive goals in an efficient way, the undesirable situations that *can* be predicted by the agent may be avoided through purposeful action. This paper proposes a goal creation mechanism that produces both reactive and proactive goals through the influence of motivation (section 3.1 defines what is meant by motivation in the context of this system). This motivated agent is influenced by various, maybe conflicting factors—*multiple motives*[2]. These motives characterise the purposes of the agent, reflect the context within which the agent is acting, and serve to drive it towards certain types of activity by triggering the creation of reactive and proactive goals. Within different contexts, the agent may be motivated towards the creation of different goals. In this way, the behaviour of the agent (governed by its goals) is founded in the context, and changes as the context changes.

This proposal is a part of an on-going research effort into the development of motivated autonomous agents [15, 16, 21]. Section 2 gives a review of related work in this area and serves to put this work in context. Refer to section 3.1 for definitions of the terms "motive", "motivation", and "goal" as they are used in this paper. Section 3.2 discusses the reasons behind the use of motivation for driving a goal creation mechanism. A system for reactive and proactive goal creation is described in section 4. Section 5 outlines the limitations of this work and its future directions, and section 6 describes the conclusions that can be drawn from this proposal and their significance to agent control.

2   Related Work

Agre and Chapman's Pengi [1] illustrates the use of mechanisms for reactive selection of control procedures in contexts that do not require planning. The intention of the theory is that an agent should decide what to do before it is too late to do it. The theory is applied to, and is effective for tasks that require reference to only the current situation. Low-level procedural control mechanisms are an essential part of a complete agent architecture; they provide the agent with effective control at fine time grains. The control mechanisms proposed here are intended to provide effective control at larger time grains, i.e. tasks where planning is useful and that require the creation of longer term goals.

The behaviour selection algorithm developed by Maes [17, 18] uses activation flow to select the most appropriate behaviour in a given context. The selection is driven by

---

[1] An agent will react to proactive goals if the predicted situation is of immediate relevance. For example, it is only sensible to react a prediction that a car travelling towards the agent may hit it. This proposal is primarily concerned with longer term proactive goals, these more typically require planning.

[2] The use of multiple motives in agent control is influenced by Neisser's [20] 1963 criticism of AI (also see Simon 1967 [25]). "Almost all human activity, including thinking, serves not one but a multiplicity of motives at the same time" (U. Neisser). However, this work is not intended to have any significance to the study of human motivation.

mutual activation of behaviours, the state of the domain, and the agent's motivations. This system illustrates the use of motivation in agent control within a behaviour-based agent. (Norman [21] gives a comparison between the use of motivation as a control mechanism in behaviour-based and model-based agents.) However, while having an influence, the work presented in this paper focuses on the creation of goals and the sources of motivation, and not the achievement of goals through the selection of behaviour or planning.

The procedural reasoning system (PRS) developed by Georgeff et al. [13, 14] chooses goals, called intentions, from a set of desires on the basis of the agent's beliefs[3]. The system is capable of reacting to a situation by creating a goal to manage this situation (triggered by a change of belief) and planning a strategy to satisfy the goal while acting on its prior instructions. These goals undergo hierarchical refinement to produce procedures that can be directly executed, allowing planning and execution to be interleaved. PRS is capable of planning for goals provided by an external source, i.e. instructions given by a human operator. These externally provided goals can be suspended if the agent needs to react to a situation such as a flashing warning light. The motive processing system developed by Beaudoin and Sloman [4, 3] is influenced by the PRS architecture. Motives are seen as a type of goal (see Sloman [26]) and are generated either through self monitoring, or environmental stimulus. Concentration is given in this work to the processing of these goal structures (i.e., filtering, scheduling, etc.) and not their creation.

Schank and Abelson's "Themes" [23], Wilensky's "Noticer" [27] and Moffat and Frijda's "Concerns" [19] all give rise to goals in similar ways. They have the function of recognising that some important event has occurred and cause a goal to be set. Schank and Abelson [23] concentrate on the structure and use of knowledge in plan generation and understanding, Wilensky [27] gives a comprehensive analysis of goals and goal interaction, and Moffat and Frijda [19] approach the problem of developing a unified agent architecture based around a strictly controlled blackboard memory.

Shoham [24] introduces a programming paradigm (agent-oriented programming) whereby agents can communicate and cooperate between each other. During the process of cooperation, agents may enter into commitments in response to requests from other agents (some of which may be human) depending on certain conditions[4].

The Phoenix system [9] concentrates on the integration of low-level reflexive agents with agents that have the capabilities of strategic planning and scheduling of multiple tasks (reflective functions) within the complex domain of fire fighting. Goals are created in reaction to detected forest fires by the reflective agent and instructions communicated to the simple reflexive agents in coordinating them to fight fires.

Many important problems involved in building autonomous agents capable of managing multiple goals in real-world domains have been investigated in the literature.

---

[3] An intention is a type of goal—a goal that the agent has committed itself to in some way. However, the problems involved in defining the nature and role of intention are not considered here (see Bratman [5] and Cohen and Levesque [10]); the term goal is used for consistency only in the discussions of BDI architectures and motivated goal creation.

[4] Castelfranchi [7] discusses some consequences of the "benevolence" of these agents to the concept of autonomy.

However, goals are typically created in reaction to situations; there is little attention given to, and no complete account of the difficult problems involved in creating goals *proactively*.

3   The Role of Motivation

With the work presented in this paper put in context, this section gives the definitions of motive, motivation, and goal as they are used throughout this paper, and compares goal creation in BDI architectures to motivated goal creation. It is shown that for an agent to efficiently create proactive goals, machinery is required that is external to a system of beliefs, desires and intentions.

3.1   Definitions

In human terms a "motive" may be described as a need or a desire that causes a person to act. In information-processing terms, it is a variable that has influence on the decision-making process and may cause action. "Motivation" is a driving force (dependent both on the internal state of the agent and the state of the external world) that arouses and directs action towards the achievement of goals. To illustrate this distinction, all humans have the motive of hunger, but no person will have sufficient motivation to act to satisfy their hunger at all times. These motivations reflect the context within which the agent is acting and ensure that any decisions have some relevance to this context. A "goal" is distinct from a motive, it denotes a state that the system can achieve/prevent through action. A goal may be satisfied by the agent achieving/preventing the state in the required conditions, where a motive is a force biasing the decision-making mechanism and therefore cannot be satisfied in the same way (cf. Sloman [26]). For example, the goal to have eaten at a favourite restaurant may be derived from the motive of hunger (among others). This goal is satisfied once the meal is finished and the bill paid, but the motive will not disappear; the satisfaction of the goal will result in *mitigating* the influence of the hunger motive on the decision-making mechanisms. (A goal created by the agent will, if satisfied in the correct conditions, have effects on the motives of the agent by affecting the environment in important ways.) To summarise, a motive describes reasons for creating goals, a goal is a state that may be achieved by invoking planning and execution processes, and the motivation that the agent has towards achieving a goal is a measure of the importance of the goal to the agent at that time. Within a planning mechanism, the influence of motivation can be used as a heuristic in the selection of actions and goals during hierarchical refinement of a plan. Finally, the motivations of the agent can also serve to drive execution of a plan in satisfying the motivated goals of the agent in the required conditions, e.g. at the right time. This paper will concentrate on the role of motivation within the goal creation process.

3.2   Motivated Goal Creation and BDI Architectures: A Comparison

The primary reason behind this proposal is to provide mechanisms for the creation of both reactive and proactive goals. A goal is created within a BDI architecture [6] by certain beliefs that the agent may have about its domain; beliefs cause goals. So, to create proactive goals, a set of beliefs must be identified that will cause this type of goal to be created.

The data of reactive goals are beliefs about the current state of the domain and therefore can directly cause goals to be created. For example, a warehouse agent may believe that there are insufficient quantities of commodity x for a specific order; this will cause the creation of a goal to restock the warehouse with x. The data of proactive goals are predictions about the evolution of the domain based on the agent's knowledge. These predictions are essentially beliefs about what the agent will believe in the future. For example, the warehouse agent may predict that, on the basis of the projected sales figures, commodity x will need to be restocked at time t_2. The consequence of such a prediction at t_1 is a belief that at some time in the future (t_2) the agent will believe that commodity x must be restocked so that the level of commodity x is maintained $(BEL_{t_1}(BEL_{t_2}(restock(x))))$[5]. The consequence of a prediction is not a certainty; x may be sold at a different rate, or the agent's information at the time of prediction may be wrong, etc. A belief about a future belief is not sufficient to cause the creation of a goal. It is only a belief that commodity x needs restocking now that can cause a goal to be created. The problem for proactive goal creation is to create the goal, by performing this reasoning process, so that the agent acts before an undesirable situation occurs or in time to produce some desirable situation. In the example, if the agent considers restocking x around time t_2, it will conclude that it believes that it should restock x if and only if the prediction at t_1 was correct. The agent will only have sufficient certainty to create a proactive goal at time t_2 if this belief $(BEL_{t_2}(restock(x)))$ is valid at t_2.

In a BDI architecture, to ensure that the agent can create these types of belief, and hence produce proactive goals, it needs to either periodically consider restocking x until the reasoning concludes that the agent should restock x, or directly create a goal to restock x from the prediction at t_1. Periodically predicting the sales of every commodity in the warehouse and all other sources of proactive goals is unacceptably computationally expensive. If the argument outlined above (i.e., a belief about what the agent will believe in the future is insufficient to cause a goal) is not accepted, proactive goals can be created directly from beliefs about beliefs in the same way that reactive goals are created from beliefs. However, all goals created by the agent must be managed whether it is sensible to act on the goal or not in the current circumstances. Furthermore if the prediction was wrong, the agent must have a mechanism for removing these incorrect goals before they are acted upon; this will require constant reevaluation of the agent's goals. The early creation of goals therefore forces the agent to perform unnecessary reasoning in the goal management mechanism.

Motivational goal creation provides an external mechanism by which proactive goals are created efficiently. A prediction about the agent's future beliefs provides information for the triggering of a reasoning process. In the example, the belief about a future belief (the consequence of the prediction at t_1) provides an alarm that wakes the attention of the agent to the possibility[6] that commodity x needs restocking at time t_2.

---

[5] This *BEL* operator is used only for the purposes of illustration and is not intended to denote any particular belief formalism.

[6] Note, possibility, not certainty.

So, these predictions, and hence beliefs about future beliefs, are useful in the efficient creation of proactive goals without giving predictions any greater consequence than they deserve. These external triggering processes are the motives of a motivated agent; motives are described in more detail in section 4.3.

4 A System of Motivated Goal Creation

With the need for some external mechanism for proactive goal creation established, this main section presents a proposal for motivated goal creation. The system is first described in general terms and an example given, then the important functions of attention triggering (section 4.3) and goal creation (section 4.4) are specified.

4.1 Overview

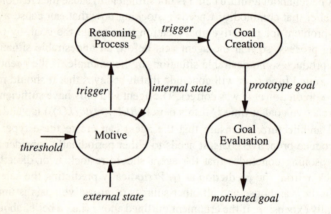

Fig. 1. The motivated goal creation process.

Motivated goal creation produces goals in response to changes that affect the motivations of the agent. Both internal and external changes in state are monitored by a set of motives. A change of state may trigger a response from the agent if the motivation (calculated from the state of the domain and the internal state of the agent) exceeds a certain threshold; this is the function of the "motive" process in figure 1. This simple mechanism ensures that the agent will only respond to and reason about changes if they are sufficiently important[7]. Calculating the motivations (stimuli) that affect the behaviour of a motive is necessarily a simple process; the efficiency of the goal creation mechanism relies on this. For example, a hunger motive may be driven by a record of

---

[7] "Sufficiently important" is an intentionally ambiguous statement; the response is determined by the stimuli affecting the motive and the threshold, or the sensitivity of the agent to those stimuli.

the time since the last meal; the greater this time, the greater the motivation. By ensuring that the periodic evaluation of these stimuli is simple, the use of computational resources is minimised. However, to determine whether action is required to mitigate the hunger motivation and what goal to pursue to that end, many other factors may be important. The motive will only trigger this more involved reasoning process if the motivation to do so is sufficiently high. The trigger is not just a simple boolean: If the motive is driven by a number of stimuli, typically only a subset will be primarily responsible for the triggered response; these primary stimuli are communicated to the reasoning process.

A motivational response creates a goal to consider the primary reasons for the trigger of attention. This goal is purely cognitive; its function is to determine whether the situation warrants activity on the part of the agent. The existence of this reasoning goal temporarily mitigates the motive by removing the stimuli that were primary in producing the response; these stimuli are suspended from influencing the agent's attention. If no activity is required by the agent, the stimuli are updated with revised predictions and replaced. If activity is required, the stimuli will continue to be suspended while a goal is created that will, if satisfied in the correct conditions, cause the mitigation of these stimuli through action in the domain. Once a goal has been created and evaluated, it is made available to the planning and goal management control systems. This goal effectively transmits the motivational response of the agent to these systems.

Reactive goals are also created in this way. Certain aspects of a situation may directly trigger a response by the agent (see section 4.3). By imposing a wider evaluation of the situation in which the response was triggered (through creating a reasoning goal), the agent is not constrained to reacting in the same way to the same trigger every time it is detected; a variety of possibilities may be selected between depending on the context.

4.2 An Example: The Warehouse Agent

This section introduces the example of an agent acting within a warehouse domain; this agent will be used to illustrate the triggering, and goal creation and evaluation mechanisms that are described in more detail in sections 4.3 and 4.4. The motives of the warehouse agent are: to prepare orders for customers in time, keep the warehouse well stocked so that it may satisfy these orders, ensure that the domain is kept tidy, and maintain the security of the warehouse. These motives define the agent and drive its goal creation functions. The domain is governed by a number of variables, some of which cannot be modelled by the agent. The commodities that the agent stocks all have certain characteristics such as volume, best before date, buying price, selling price, etc. The capacity of the warehouse and the volume of the commodities constrain the number of items that can be kept in the warehouse. Prices of supplied commodities are related to the volumes ordered—a high volume at a lower price. However, if the agent orders a large amount of a certain commodity and is unable to sell those goods before the sell by date it will have lost the advantage gained in buying at lower prices. There are also fluctuations in the market—these cannot be modelled. The agent has a choice of suppliers all offering different prices, quality, and reliability. The primary function of the agent is to maximise the profit that it makes in managing the warehouse by making good goal creation choices.

4.3 Motives

Now, a more detailed specification can be given of a motive. Then in section 4.3, some design issues are discussed that constrain the choice of an agent's motives.

The Attention-Triggering Function of a Motive The motivations of an agent are derived from both the predicted behaviour of the domain and significant unpredicted events detected by the agent. From the knowledge that the agent has about the domain it is acting in, predictions can be made on how the domain will evolve over time, providing stimuli for the agent to behave proactively. Unpredicted events stimulate the agent into reactive behaviour.

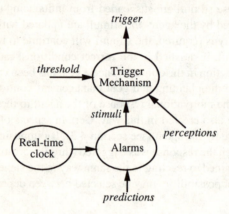

Fig. 2. A motive.

Predictions give the agent beliefs about when it should next consider certain aspects
of the domain. For example, the prediction of when the agent should next consider
restocking the warehouse with commodity x can be used in triggering the agent's
attention. A set of alarms are produced from such predictions (ref. figure 2). These
alarms are simple time-varying stimuli. The success of proactive behaviour is dependent on the accuracy of the predictions, and the stability of the domain[8]. A
single motive can be driven by predictions about the behaviour of various aspects
of the domain. The resulting stimuli are the motivations that drive the triggering
mechanism. These stimuli are combined using a weighted vector. If this combined
motivation exceeds the threshold, a motivational response is triggered. Those stimuli that have greatest influence are communicated to the reasoning processes as a
part of this motivational response.

---

[8] The success of proactive behaviour will also be dependent on the characteristics of the
motive—see section 5:4.

Perceptions give the agent beliefs about the current state of the domain. These beliefs interrupt the normal operation of the agent and directly trigger a response, communicating the reasons for this response to the reasoning process. The more unstable the domain is, the greater the probability that the proactive motivations will not trigger the attention of the agent in time. So, the greater the need for the agent to react to certain aspects of a situation. These events typically will be infrequent if the proactive behaviour is functioning effectively.

For example, the warehouse agent will make predictions about when next to consider restocking the commodities contained in the warehouse. A warehouse that stocks n commodities will have a maintain stock motive driven by the predictions of when next to consider commodities $c_1 - c_n$. A set of alarms are created on the basis of these predictions. As time passes, the motivations to consider each of the commodities increases at different rates depending on the predictions. The combined effect of the motivations is simply compared to the threshold of the motive. If this combined motivation exceeds the threshold, a response is triggered by the motive. The primary motivating factors, e.g. $c_4 = milk$ and $c_7 = cereals$, are communicated to the reasoning process.

The reasoning process considers these primary factors. The agent will use the information about the customer orders that are known to the agent and any other predicted demand, the current stocks in the warehouse, and the availability of resources such as space. A decision can then be made about the possibility of creating a goal to restock the warehouse in some way. If the decision is made that the stock is currently sufficient, updated predictions about when next to consider c_4 and c_7 are communicated to the maintain stock motive. This resets the alarm functions of c_4 and c_7, and they again affect the triggering mechanism. If the stock is not sufficient, the goal creation process is triggered. For example, if commodities c_4 and c_7 trigger the attention of the agent, it may be the case that a certain customer has failed to collect an order that included a large volume of cereals (c_7). The levels of commodity c_7 is therefore greater than predicted, and so does not warrant action. At the same time, the warehouse may still need to be restocked with milk (c_4). Now, c_7 is dropped as a reason for creating a goal, but c_4 triggers the goal creation process.

The Specificity of a Motive The behaviour of a motivated agent is dependent on the set of basic motives that characterise it. The choice of these motives must reflect the purposes of the agent in the domain. Motives can be of any specificity, but the more specific the set of motives, the more motives will be required to produce the same complexity of behaviour. For example, a warehouse agent could be defined with specific motives for every type of commodity instead of a single motive for all commodities (the maintain stock levels motive discussed before). This design will result in a larger number of attention triggering events; this is because different commodities can no longer trigger the attention of the agent in combination. So, either a greater number of goals is created, or the agent will require a mechanism for determining when these motivational responses can be combined within the reasoning process. This illustrates one of the factors in the design of a motivated agent—that the motives should be selected so that they are largely independent from each other. I.e. whether a goal is created or not is only dependent on the reasons for triggering the attention of the agent and no other motivations.

Efficiency also affects the selection of the driving motives. If for example, the tidiness motive were to be separated into two, more specific motives (e.g., tidy floor and tidy shelves), the computational resources required to create a specific goal are reduced. At the same time, the number of motives are increased, increasing the computational resources needed to periodically evaluate the motivations driving the agent. Therefore a trade-off exists between the resources required to evaluate the motivations of the agent (periodic, but cheap) and the resources required to create a specific goal (infrequent, but expensive). The designer of an effective motivated agent will need to find an optimum set of driving motives.

4.4 Goal Creation and Evaluation

A goal created by the agent must be powerful enough to sufficiently mitigate the motivations that triggered the attention of the agent, and have lead to the creation of the goal. At the same time, there are other factors that may affect the choice of goal: negative effects on other motivations, positive effects on other motivations, and conflicts with other goals. It is not sensible for the agent to consider all these factors, so the search is constrained by using a set of standard goal templates with predefined characteristics (e.g. figure 3). The factors that are considered are the reasons for which the template could be used with their associated risks, and the potential points of conflict with other goals—"contentions"[9].

Supplier 1 Template	
Goal	Order stock from supplier 1
[(Reasons,Risks)]	[(maintain stock,[quality,reliability])]
[Contentions]	[price,volume]

Fig. 3. A goal template

The creation of a goal involves the selection and instantiation of a goal template. An analogy can be drawn between these goal templates and action templates commonly used in planning. Action templates are generally characterised by a list of preconditions defining the conditions that must hold for that action to be used. The list of possible reasons for adopting a goal correspond to the motives that are potentially mitigated by the satisfaction of an instantiation of this goal template; a single motive may be a reason for selecting various goal templates. A difference is that the preconditions of action templates are all necessary, where a single reason for adopting a goal template is

---

[9] This approach is similar to the "reference features" adopted by Pryor and Collins [22] to constrain the search for possible conflicts when reasoning about the adoption of opportunities in plan following.

sufficient. Action templates have a list of effects that the action is expected to produce. A goal template will have a list of important negative effects on the agent's resources and therefore possible conflicts with other goals; the notable positive effects are the mitigation of the motives listed in the possible reasons for adopting the goal. The number of possible goal templates will be finite due to there being a finite number of activities that an agent can perform in the domain of reference it is designed for: an agent will have a finite set of possible goal templates because it will have a finite set of possible actions, these being constrained by its abilities.

In the creation of a goal, only the templates that contain the driving motive in the list of reasons are considered. The potential conflicts are investigated to determine the possibility of using the goal by investigating the "contentions" of the goal templates. Then, once the possible templates are identified, the risks associated with the motive are considered with reference to the context. For example, the warehouse agent, having determined that a goal is required to restock commodity c_4 so that it may mitigate the maintain stock motive, may find that there are two possible templates that could be adopted. These are to order stock from supplier 1 (see figure 3) at a certain price, quality, and reliability or from supplier 2 that has different characteristics. The adoption of the template to order from supplier 1 may be risky if the quality of c_4 from this supplier has been low in the past. In addition to this, the goal must have the power to sufficiently mitigate the motivations that caused its creation. For example, the agent must have sufficient monetary resources to purchase sufficient volumes of c_4 at the supplier's prices. There may be a trade-off here in the selection of the best goal, high risk goals often give high returns where a lower risk goal may give lower returns; supplier 1 may have lower quality goods, but at a low price, where a different supplier may have high quality, but more expensive goods.

Evaluation of a selected and instantiated goal template involves determining both the conditions that the goal is to be satisfied in, and the importance of the goal. The conditions for the satisfaction of the goal may involve real-time deadlines, e.g. have commodity c_4 restocked before that stock is needed for a customer (ref. section 5:3). The temporal conditions under which a goal is to be satisfied serves to define the urgency of the goal at any time—as a deadline approaches, the urgency increases. The importance of the goal to the agent is determined on the basis of the reasons for the adoption of the goal. E.g., the importance of the goal to have c_4 restocked may depend on the financial loss incurred in failing to satisfy an order in time.

Various evaluated goals may be active at any one time. They represent the motivational influences, possibly conflicting, on the agent at that time. The motivation towards these goals may be used to determine the relative importance of the goals to the present situation. This motivation is the reason for acting on the goal, and may change over time (e.g. as a deadline approaches). A motivated agent is therefore provided with a flexible set of goals (including an evaluated goal to restock c_4) that reflect the motivations of the agent toward the present situation with reference to its on-going activities.

5   Discussion and Future Work

1. **Reconsidering adopted goals:** This paper presents a system of goal creation. However, once a goal has been created, the domain may change so that the goal is no longer appropriate. It may either be the case that the domain changes so that there is no longer any motivation to continue with the goal, or that the goal is no longer powerful enough to mitigate the driving motivations. For example, if a warehouse agent has created a goal to restock commodity x, the agent may subsequently find a store of commodity x that was unknown to it, or that the new stocks are required more urgently. Both situations will change the motivations of the agent and may lead to the goal being dropped. The conditions under which a goal is to be dropped in the two circumstances are different. For situations where the goal is no longer sufficient, the decision is made on the basis of alternatives open to the agent. In some cases the goals may partially mitigate the motivations of the agent and a simple alteration is sufficient, e.g. increasing the size of an order. For situations where the context has changed such that the goal may no longer be useful, a trade-off exists between the persistence of the agent towards a goal and its usefulness. There may be situations were an agent may persist with a goal because it has already invested so much in its satisfaction if there is any gain to be made from it. An important area of further work is to investigate mechanisms for the triggering of a goal reevaluation process [6], and defining the conditions under which a goal is to be dropped [10].

2. **The creation of different goal types:** An important distinction has been made in this paper between proactive and reactive goals, defining them in terms of their data and effect. It may be useful to distinguish further between achievement goals, prevention goals and maintenance goals. It is implied in the discussions of this system of goal creation that all goals are achievement goals, but this does not mean that other types of goal are not considered important. Prevention goals characterise goals to prevent some situation from occurring and are purely proactive in nature. Maintenance goals are similarly dependent on predictions, they characterise goals to maintain some variable or process for a fixed period of time. The distinction between reactive and proactive goals is an important initial step to the development of mechanisms for the creation of a wider variety of useful goal types.

3. **The urgency of a goal:** The deadlines of goals are not necessarily hard; it may be useful to satisfy the goal even after the deadline has passed. For example, it will be highly desirable to satisfy the goal to have c_4 restocked before this new stock is needed for an order, but it will still be important to satisfy the goal after the deadline. This must be reflected in the urgency of such a goal as time passes. Different types of goal will have different urgency characteristics; with a better understanding of the types of goal that an agent can perform, these characteristics may be determined.

4. **Triggering characteristics:** There is a need for further work in defining a justifiable basis for determining both the threshold and the weighted vector that define the triggering characteristics of a motive. There are a number of approaches that are being considered. These include a mechanism that involves the reasoning pro-

cess having an influence on the threshold. If the motives consistently trigger the attention of the agent to situations that do not warrant the creation of a goal, then the threshold is set too low. If the motives consistently trigger reactive goals where the evolution of the domain was predicted well, the threshold is too high. There are many difficulties in using such a mechanism, primarily ensuring that the mechanism is domain independent. No filtering mechanism is perfect, however the motive (the filter of contexts) must produce good results while giving the advantages of efficiency.

6 Conclusions

It is generally accepted that an effective autonomous agent must have the abilities to create and select between multiple goals, the importance of which will be context-dependent, as part of an on-going activity. Two distinct types of goal have been identified in this paper—reactive and proactive goals. Reactive goals are goals that are created in response to the current state of the domain, and proactive goals are created on the basis of prediction about how the domain will evolve over time. It is argued that only the creation of reactive goals have been considered to date in the agent-programming literature. Furthermore, the extension of a belief, desire, and intention architecture to handle proactive goal creation will necessitate some system that is external to existing mechanisms. A goal creation system has been proposed that uses a set of motives to trigger the "motivated agent" into considering the creation of a goal. These motives act as a filtering mechanism, extracting the contexts that may warrant the creation of a goal, and hence minimising the computational resources required in creating sensible proactive goals. This proposal is not complete, there are many issues that have not been fully addressed (see section 5), however this paper serves to illustrate the primary problems involved in the efficient creation of proactive goals in complex real-world domains and propose some sensible solutions.

References

1. P. Agre and D. Chapman. Pengi: An implementation of a theory of activity. In *Proceedings of the Sixth National Conference on Artificial Intelligence*, pages 268–72, 1987.
2. P. Agre and D. Chapman. What are plans for? In P. Maes, editor, *Designing Autonomous Agents: Theory and Practice from Biology to Engineering and Back*. Bradford-MIT Press, 1991.
3. L.P. Beaudoin. *Motive processing and attention*. PhD thesis, School of Computer Science, University of Birmingham, 1994.
4. L.P. Beaudoin and A. Sloman. A study of motive processing and attention. In *Prospects for Artificial Intelligence: Proceedings of AISB-93*, pages 229–38, 1993.
5. M.E. Bratman. What is intention? In P.R. Cohen, J. Morgan, and M.E. Pollack, editors, *Intentions in Communication*, chapter 2, pages 15–31. MIT Press, 1990.
6. M.E. Bratman, D.J. Israel, and M.E. Pollack. Plans and resource-bounded practical reasoning. *Computational Intelligence*, 4(4):349–55, 1988.
7. C. Castelfranchi. Guarantees for autonomy in cognitive agent architecture. In this volume.

290

8. D. Chapman. Planning for conjunctive goals. *Artificial Intelligence*, 32:333–77, 1987.
9. P.R. Cohen, M.L. Greenberg, D.M. Hart, and A.E. Howe. Trial by fire: Understanding the design requirements for agents in complex environments. *AI Magazine*, 1989.
10. P.R. Cohen and H.J. Levesque. Persistence, intention, and commitment. In P.R. Cohen, J. Morgan, and M.E. Pollack, editors, *Intentions in Communication*, chapter 3, pages 33–69. MIT Press, 1990.
11. R.E. Fikes and N.J. Nilsson. STRIPS:a new approach to the application of theorem proving to problem solving. *Artificial Intelligence*, 2:189–208, 1971.
12. M. Fox. A formal basis for hierarchical planning. In *Proceedings of the Sixth Australian Joint Conference on Artificial Intelligence*, 1993.
13. M.P. Georgeff and F.F. Ingrand. Decision-making in an embedded reasoning system. In *Proceedings of the Eleventh International Joint Conference on Artificial Intelligence*, volume 2, pages 972–8, 1989.
14. M.P. Georgeff and A.L. Lansky. Reactive reasoning and planning. In *Proceedings of the Sixth National Conference on Artificial Intelligence*, pages 677–81, 1987.
15. D. P. Long and M. Fox. Architectures for self-motivated autonomous systems. In *Working Notes: AISB Workshop Series, Models or Behaviours, Which Way Forward for Robotics?*, 1994.
16. D. P. Long and M. Fox. A hybrid architecture for rational agents. In S. Torrance and C. Thornton, editors, *Hybrid models of cognition*. AISB, 1995.
17. P. Maes. The dynamics of action selection. In *Proceedings of the Eleventh International Joint Conference on Artificial Intelligence*, volume 2, pages 991–7, 1989.
18. P. Maes. Situated agents can have goals. In P. Maes, editor, *Designing Autonomous Agents: Theory and Practice from Biology to Engineering and Back*. Bradford-MIT Press, 1991.
19. D. Moffat and N.H. Frijda. An agent architecture: Will. In this volume.
20. U. Neisser. The imitation of man by machine. *Science*, 139:193–7, Jan 1963.
21. T.J. Norman. Motivated goal and action selection. In *Working Notes: AISB Workshop Series, Models or Behaviours, Which Way Forward for Robotics?*, 1994. (UCL Research Note RN/94/18).
22. L. Pryor and G. Collins. Reference features as guides to reasoning about opportunities. In *Proceedings of the Fourteenth Annual Conference of the Cognitive Science Society*, pages 230–5, 1992.
23. R.C. Schank and R.P. Abelson. *Scripts, Plans, Goals, and Understanding*. Laurence Erlbaum, 1977.
24. Y. Shoham. Agent-oriented programming. *Artificial Intelligence*, 60:51–92, 1993.
25. H.A. Simon. Motivational and emotional controls of cognition. *Psychological Review*, 74:29–39, 1967.
26. A. Sloman. Motives, mechanisms, and emotions. *Cognition and Emotion*, 1(3):217–33, 1987.
27. R. Wilensky. *Planning and understanding: A computational approach to human reasoning*. Addison-Wesley, 1983.

Agent-Oriented Programming
for Open Systems

Hans-Dieter Burkhard

Institute of Informatics, Humboldt University Berlin
Unter den Linden 6, 10099 Berlin, Germany
hdb@informatik.hu-berlin.de

Abstract. Agent oriented techniques may have a great future. Recently, a lot of discussions reflect the "true" meaning of the notions of agents and agent oriented programming. Coming from modelling human like behaviour, there are many meaningful choices for the design of agent oriented programming languages. Thus, it is now (and may be for ever) not the time to restrict oneself by a single closed definition. We shall learn to live with ambiguities in the field of agent oriented programming, and use it as a chance to have flexible systems. The aim of this paper is to collect arguments under the special viewpoint of agent oriented programming for open systems.

1 Introduction

Agent oriented programming (AOP) is recently discussed under a lot of viewpoints. It has the potentials to become a very attractive technique in the future. But up to now, the real benefits and the true characteristics of AOP are not clear. One question to ask is: why not to use object oriented languages, what is new in AOP?

A proposal for an agent oriented programming language, AGENT-0, was presented by Shoham in the paper [25]. For him, AOP is a special kind of object oriented programming. I would like to take a somewhat different point of view, and I'll try to explain it in this paper. By my point of view, the special benefits of AOP can be worked out best for open systems in the sense of Hewitt ([16]).

Mental states and mental attributes are one ("the"?) essential of AOP. A lot of work has been done in Distributed AI concerning modelling of autonomous/ deliberate/reflexive agents. Reflecting models of human behaviour, the so-called "B-D-I"-architectures (belief – desire – intention) and related notions (cf. e.g. [8, 24]) have a great influence to the DAI- and AOP-community. But for applications, we need agent programs more guided perhaps by tasks and duties instead of intentions and desires. Shoham's AGENT-0 has agents with beliefs, capabilities and commitments.

Thus, there are lot of things to discuss. The aim of my paper is to bring some more questions into mind, and may be, to provoke with some controversial opinions and concepts. Obviously, the paper is strongly influenced by Shoham's work. I'll argue that there will be no unique notion of an agent. Looking at recent approaches (cf. e.g. [3, 12, 15, 19, 22, 23, 24, 25, 27, 29, 30, 31, 33]), the lot of difficult ideas cannot be subsumed in a unified way. Moreover, the notions of agents and agent oriented programming will be even more ambiguous in the future. I'll furthermore argue, that a unique definition of notions in AOP is not mandatory, – and: there are ways to deal with different notions and semantics. There may be several different AOP-languages in a good coexistence even in a single system. Some standards might be convenient, but too much of them would be more an obstacle than a benefit for AOP.

The paper is organized as follows: I start with a general discussion about the design of programming languages (section 2), and continue with programming in DAI (section 3). Open systems are considered as a field where AOP may provide special support (section 4). A list of design choices for the development of agent oriented techniques follows in section 5, while section 6 discusses the influence of the theoretical work to AOP. A possible architecture is given in section 7, with special emphasis put to communication (section 8), belief update (section 9), and "belief-to-action"-programming (section 10).

2   Foundations of programming language design

When talking about programming language design we have to distinguish at least four stages:

On the **first stage** are the users of the programs, and on the **second stage** are the programmers. They both decide about usefulness of programming languages, if they don't accept the constructs, then the language is only an academic exercise. Important questions for their acceptance are transparency, efficiency for programming and running, portability, structuring, flexibility, few basic primitives, and so on. Under the viewpoint of agent oriented programming, further requirements should be:

- use of mental attributes according to their real life meanings,
- transparency of inferences,
- time handling,
- social conventions.

These aspects must be regarded by the language designers which are on the **third stage**. They have to decide in favour of languages which are easy to understand and easy to use. They have to design the support of the languages given by compilers and interpreters. When talking about agent oriented techniques, this stage is the most influential one: agent oriented languages and the implied architectures of agents decide about the usefulness of AOP in the applications.

On the **forth stage** is the theory. It gives foundations for the design of the programming language and for the development of tools for implementation and verification. Theory might start with algorithmic logic, algorithms, grammars, etc. for the classic procedural languages, continuing with concurrency theory for concurrent programming, predicate calculus for PROLOG, and additionally to all of these: temporal and modal logics for AOP.

Important aspects valid in general and especially for the development of agent oriented techniques are:

- Only a few subsets of a theoretical background can be covered by a programming language (example: only HORN clauses and depth-first search are used for PROLOG, – but users agree with that restriction of predicate calculus).

- Compilers and interpreters give support to make life easier (examples: storage management in any higher language, search strategies in PROLOG, communication facilities in AOP, ...). Theory investigates the principles.
- Theory investigates further principles of programming (examples: program validation, expressiveness, decidability, tractability).

Which parts of a theory should be covered, and which supports are desired, this must be determined from the basic stages of the programmers and the users, while the broad theories are necessary to have a clear foundation.

Since AOP may start by modelling human agents, the discrepancy between theoretic models and practical implementations is very large. I shall discuss some possible consequences in this paper. To give an illustration of the problems, one may consider the following two closure axioms:

- If an agent knows a and if b follows from a then it knows b.
- If an agent wants a and if b follows from a then it wants b.

Both axioms are useful under certain conditions, and might not be useful under other circumstances. Theory has to study their consequences (up to tractability and decidability questions – as for the both axioms from above), while practical design has to be guided by acceptable compromises.

3 Programming in Distributed AI

Artificial intelligence – and Distributed AI as well – has two origins:

Cognitive aspect: Modelling and simulation of (human) intelligence.
Technical aspect: Development of tools for knowledge processing.

The simulation of human intelligence may be a guide to the development of "intelligent systems", but it need not to be (just like a wheel is not the model of a leg, and successful chess programs need not to simulate human players). Nevertheless, the simulation and the discovering of human thinking is part of AI (some researchers won't agree today, since AI has not satisfied its promises from some years ago, but I think AI should be faithful to all of its origins ...).

The same holds for Distributed AI, where the cognitive aspect includes the simulation of collective human intelligence (of the society), while the technical aspect concerns the construction of collaborating intelligent systems.

Concerning this first choice point for developing agent oriented techniques, I decide in this paper in favour of the second aspect: for the development of useful practical aims for programming collaborating systems. Then it is to discuss whether models of human collaboration are useful. While the answer can be given only after several years of practical experience (not now), I want to argue for this approach since it could make programming more flexible and convenient in certain applications. (No doubt: One can also use ALGOL or LISP or SMALLTALK or something else. There is no need at all for an higher programming language if one decides to use assembler or TURING machines, – but nobody wants to do. Thus, the use of agent oriented programming languages will be a matter of the support for the duties of programmers and users.)

The next choice point follows the well-known partition of DAI into **Distributed problem solving** and **Multi Agent Systems**. Here I argue that the benefits of agent oriented programming could become more obvious for the programmers community in the case of collaborating autonomous agents. Here AOP could contribute to a lot of open technical problems (while in distributed problem solving there is a comparison to other already established approaches like object oriented programming and concurrent programming – using agent oriented techniques may be of good use too, but it might be difficult to convince programmers of a new paradigm if they have useful ones).

The next point to discuss need not to be a real choice. There are two aspects of giving mental attributes to agents or objects. The first I call the agent oriented circumscription of objects (by the programmer), while the second one is the treatment of programs as agents since they are really planned to behave as agents (i.e. someone who acts autonomously on someone else's mission):

1. Agent oriented circumscription: Humans assign mental attitudes to objects on a certain level of complex phenomena ("my computer must be crazy today"). Since humans do it very often (and successfully), it could be introduced as a programming style if related tools are available. It needs a special process of "agentification" of objects, where e.g. meaningful transformations to mental attributes are needed (see [25] for a discussion). After this has been done, agents may be programmed as under 2.
2. Agent oriented programming: There are programs and procedures which really make decisions, and where certain goals are maintained, respectively (consider e.g. a chess program). No additional transcription to mental attributes is needed, the tasks of the programs can be used as descriptions in mental terms from the beginning.

Now it depends on the special support of programming languages, whether the mental terms can be exploited even in programming. We can use arithmetical and logical operations in programming since our hardware and software support their use. We could use mental operations – if the same would be true with respect to mental categories.

It should be remarked that the possible conflict between the modelling of human intelligence and the effective implementation of knowledge processing disappears for agent oriented programming: The programmer may treat the programs just as (human like) agents, and the mental attributes should be as near to human attributes as possible.

If possible and useful at all, the related support should be given by languages/tools for agent oriented programming. What support should be given? I propose the orientation towards open systems (other applications may be discovered from this platform).

4 Programming for open systems

The characteristics of open systems are given by (cf. [16]): continuous availability, extensibility, decentral control, asynchrony, inconsistent information, arms-length relationships. To make the intentions more clear, I give some examples:

1. Traffic control (cf. [18]),
2. Shipping companies (cf. [14]),
3. Airline reservation (cf. [20, 25]),
4. Offices (Hewitt: ... are open systems, cf. [16]),
5. Robotics, Virtual reality, artificial life, computer animation/games, ...

Now we can discuss the characteristics of open systems (with the examples in mind) and their requirements to agent oriented programming:

- Continuous availability: The agents perform their own tasks, and sometimes they get in contact to delegate jobs, and to commit for tasks, respectively. Thus a shipping company may get in touch to other companies if there is a profitable job which can not be performed alone.
- Extensibility: The system is a dynamic one, agents may enter the system (may be added by their programmers, or be instantiated by other agents, respectively), while others may be leaving for a while or even for ever.
- Decentral control: Remember again the shipping companies – they would not agree in an overall control of their jobs. In other examples the decentralization is due to complexity or to the absence of any global control rule.
- Asynchrony: Most interactions in the examples can be performed by asynchronous message passing. Some activities may require synchronization, but usually only in a local environment.
- Inconsistent information: There is in general no way to maintain global consistency (if this term can be given a real meaning at all). Hence, consistency is a local matter of the agents (– which could have related support by agent oriented languages).
- Arms-length relationships: There need not to be a global overview over the whole system, nor for the agents, nor for their programmers (look for the shipping companies: the system works for restricted acquaintance relations as well; and the airline agent needs not to know which customers could ask him, respectively). Thus, the acquaintance relations of agents need not to be reflexive. But a real requirement is the possibility to add a new agent to an existing system and make it acquainted to several of the old agents.

One agent can be a single program on a single machine, and another agent could be another program on another machine (here is an important difference to many tools of DAI, where several agents are simulated by a single program on a single machine – this is more close to distributed problem solving).

We can imagine a system of agents in the scenario of human machine cooperation (cf. [28]), where the programmed agents take care of the official rules and keep track of decisions. Each human has her own agent on her own computer (and may be some further agents ...). Standard routines (like information gathering and distribution) can be performed by the programs, while important decisions are due to the humans (may be after reminder by machines). I don't believe in the replacement of human decisions by computers. (Any application program must be programmed in order to follow the official rules, while real life decisions sometimes require the violation of rules and laws. Nobody would accept a program which may violate rules and laws e.g. in traffic domains. On the other hand, "Working to the rules" in real life may result in some kind of strike – to overcome this problem: humans will still be needed in the future …. I'll come back again to this point later on.)

In this way, agent oriented programming could be used for design support, too. During the design process the agents can maintain a lot of difficult questions:
– who is affected by changes in the design,
– who is responsible for conflict resolution,
– who has to be informed about decisions, and so on … .
This is more then recent tools for concurrent engineering provide.

Conflict detection and may be some proposals are performed by the computers, but the final decision is left to humans. Note that quite other intentions could be guiding if we don't look for real world applications, but for simulations of societies by agent systems.

While a lot of useful languages and tools exist for programming the "conventional" (local, private) activities of agents, the special application area of agent oriented languages could be the support of

- the communication between the agents residing on different computers ("anywhere in the world"),
- the local control of an agent,
- the support of local actions as links ("side effects") to other private programs (implemented in an appropriate language),
- the control and information transfer between agents.

5   Design choices for agent-oriented languages

In this section I shall argue that a lot of discussions about the appropriate "true" common structure and the appropriate "true" common language for agents should be suspended: I like to say that it is not necessary to have common global notions for agents.

A first possible choice is the decision (in order to meet requirements of open systems) for **single agents on different computers** with the possibility of communication and cooperation (including the handling of conflicts etc.). There are a lot of further choices if we want to introduce an agent oriented language:

Mental categories and their relations: A lot of mental attributes for the description of the mental state of an agent have been proposed: Belief, desire, intention, goal, choice, decision, capability, obligation, commitment, …. Furthermore, a lot of possible relationships (axioms) between these attributes have been used to establish different kinds of agents: Sometimes the desire is a subset of the belief, sometimes not. Modelling human behaviour, all those approaches might be reasonable.

If I want to program agents for computer games, I would possibly prefer goals and intentions, if I had to program office agents, I would like to describe their mental states by tasks, jobs, duties etc.

Communication primitives: Speech act theory is a good guide. But while a lot of work is done in unifying the use of communication primitives, I'll propose to try the opposite way in the following.

Consistency handling: Local consistency of the agents may be checked by support of the interpreter of an agent oriented language. Problems arise since these checks may be intractable or even undecidable if the language is rich enough. A possible design choice could provide a support tool which in many but not all cases receives an answer (it is up to the programmer and the program verification that a program will run successfully – this is the case in other languages, too).

Further design choices are due to the consequences of inconsistencies (overwrite old beliefs, send messages to other agents or to the human user, …).

Inferences: A lot of inferences ranging from belief updates over short time decisions up to long time planning can be desirable for an agent. Support by the language or interpreter may consist of related programming primitives and/or related inference routines.

Actions: As already mentioned, the agents have to execute tasks etc., which can be programmed in other languages. Which languages and tools are necessary?

Belief-to-action: There must be routines which determine the actions depending on the mental state of an agent. Again, some of these dependencies should be programmable by the programmer, hence a useful support by the language and its interpreter is recommended.

Structure: According to the choices from above, an appropriate structure must be found (and implemented e.g. by the interpreter).

Maintaining special conventions: Special conventions are important for the organization of agent systems (in the sense of "societies"). An example of such conventions could be the handling of requests and confirmations. There are different ways to maintain related conventions:

- by some programmer rules ("good programming style for AOP"),
- by error messages/warnings from the interpreter of an AOP-language,
- by automatic support of the interpreter (e.g. sending an confirmation automatically).

Again, there are a lot of different choices, and when I say that conventions are needed on one hand, I have to accept on the other hand that different conventions may apply for different agent systems.

Social norms and social roles: On a higher level, social laws, norms and roles (cf. e.g. [9, 26]) can be introduced for conventions, and as codifications for "good agent behaviour". Again, there are different ways to realize it as for the conventions from above.

Inheritance and creation of new agents: Social hierarchies may be related to usual client-server-models. The dependencies may be introduced "by hand" by the programmers, but they may also come from instantiation and inheritance mechanisms like in OOP. Recent AOP-tools go different ways with respect to this topic.

Technical choices: They are related to the underlying implementation principles and to the underlying implementation language etc. of an agent oriented language/tool. Portability considerations may give priority to the development of an agent oriented language together with a related interpreter instead of an agent oriented tool/shell.

The choices have to regard the intended use of AOP: If we want to experiment with human like agents by related simulations we need other features than for office support programs. It should be clear that not all features desirable from one or the other viewpoint may be supported by only one language.

Since there are so many choices, we can imagine many different languages. But what about the common work of agents? How many common assumptions and common notions are necessary? A possible answer is: Common notions are not mandatory. Quite different languages can be used in a single system.

Different agents might be programmed using different languages using different notions,– communication must only provide that an arbitrary sequence of characters is received by an agent as the same sequence as it was sent by some other agent. The architectures, the inferences etc. of the different agents in a system might be quite different.

How can this work? The answer is: The same way as humans deal with different languages and different conventions. If I want to use a service, I have to know its rules (if I use UNIX computers I have to know the commands ..., if I want to talk to Danish people I have to look for a common language..., if I want to sale my car I have to announce it by known terms ...). Thus, if I as a programmer want to add my agent to a system, I must program it following the conventions of those agents which my agent shall cooperate with. (Note the differences between the external and the internal view: my agent needs not to know about those difficulties, I have to implement it correctly. – Another problem may be special services in the system for giving advices, allocating services, making translations, but such agents can be programmed and need not to be a part of the agent oriented programming language or interpreter.)

The process of language design can then concentrate on different accents for different languages, each one especially useful for related agents. Functionally overloaded and over-complicated languages can be avoided this way.

6 Implementing agent theories

A lot of work has been done in theories for multi agent systems from different points of view. They can be found in related collections of papers (cf. e.g. [2, 10, 21]). Especially the papers in the field of multi-modal temporal logics are inspired by modelling human social behaviour, but they give also advices for the architecture of agents in practical applications – because AOP shall allow to think and program in terms of human behaviour. Other papers are related to applications of game theory (e.g. [36]) and to aspects of fairness (e.g. [6]) and control (e.g. [7]) influenced by concurrency theory. If DAI (and multi-agent systems) are considered as models of (human) societies, than various other disciplines should contribute to the theory of DAI, too (cf. [5]).

Many discussions concern the use of notions like belief, desire, intention ("B-D-I"), choice, goal, decision, obligation, commitment and their relations. Should goals be a part of the belief, or may they contradict the (actual) belief, should we use desire/intention or obligation/duty to express the deliberation of agents .... I would argue again that all of these approaches can be motivated from some points of view, but not all of them can be implemented by a single agent oriented programming language or tool.

Thus, several reasons apply for restrictions when building languages for agent oriented programming (under the technical viewpoint of applications, – while other other aspects would be valid under the cognitive viewpoint of AI).

- First of all, programs shall not really behave freely as humans may. Each of us knows that there are real life decisions violating given office rules and even laws (think of traffic control as already mentioned, or of an office were each people strictly follows all orders). But computer programs not following the laws and rules would hardly be accepted. I see no hope to overcome these problems, because of the insufficiency of any rules and laws with respect to real life. Hence, for the next future (or for ever) the right to decide violating given rules or orders is reserved for humans only.
- As mentioned above, a lot of choices are suitable, but they cannot be realized all by only one system. Some of these aspects are even contradicting each others. Hence we have to decide in favour of one or the other.
- The third reason is due to complexity of a programming tool. A language with too many features can not be handled. The program and its behaviour must keep some transparency, otherwise it would not be accepted by programmers.
- The last reason concerns complexity again, but with respect to execution of programs. Again it would not be acceptable if a program always runs out of time and memory. Hence properties like deductive closure are not realistic in richer languages. On the other hand, the argument that some computations may be intractable (or even unsolvable) would already apply to classic languages, – hence tractability must be required only for a considerable amount of tasks, but not for all.

As a consequence, we shall have languages and tools with only restricted features: only small subsets of the theoretical aspects can be implemented by a practically useful agent oriented language. One could also think of tools with a lot of supplements for different purposes, such that useful agents can be configured.

A very important aspect is the clear difference between the external view (of the theory, and of the programmer, respectively) and the internal view (of the agent). The programmer knows about the principles of the system and knows about communication primitives of interesting agents. She uses this knowledge for programming her agents. She decides what her agents will belief and intend, and how they come to decisions and activities. The "internal knowledge" of the agent must be sufficient to fulfil its tasks, while the external knowledge of its programmer must be sufficient to decide about its needs.

Since different programmers may add their agents at different times to the system, a very good specification and documentation is needed for all parts of the system. The support for both the documentation (the external view) and the implementation (the internal view) is a further desirable feature.

For existing agent oriented languages and tools I refer to the papers written by Wooldridge and Jennings [34], Shoham [25], and Kraetzschmar [17].

7   A possible architecture and alternatives

We have a data part and a procedural part in the program constituting an agent. According to the notions of the mental state, the data part may have subdivisions for belief, intentions, goals, plans, obligations, capabilities etc.

The representation may range from simple boolean values up to multi-modal temporal logical formula. Compromises are needed with respect to expressiveness on one hand and tractability for "usual" tasks on the other hand.

The data concern knowledge about the agent itself (its goals, plans ...), about other agents and about the environment (including knowledge about rules, laws, norms ...). It may change due to internal inferences and information from outside (other agents, environment, – especially from the human counterparts). The internal inferences include interferences between different data divisions, where especially properties like update, consistency, persistency and closure properties are maintained.

As already discussed, the choice for special notions is due to the intentions of the programmers: An agent in office support should be more dedicated to obligations and duties, while an agent in design support could also act with goals and intentions.

The procedural part manages the inferences over the data divisions. It manages the communication control and the control over the executions. The procedural part consists

- of fixed routines, which are predefined and implemented by the interpreter (like the search and unification routines for PROLOG), and
- of programmable routines, respectively, which implement the special behaviour of an agent due to its specification by the programmer.

The relationships between fixed interpreter routines ("built-ins") and user defined routines is one of the points to be discussed and evaluated while developing agent oriented programming as a technique. Clearly, the interpreter should give useful support, e.g. for checking consistency. But how should it react in a case of inconsistent belief: By overwriting old knowledge, by a special interrupt routine to the human user, or what else could be useful?

The interpreter must give support with respect to communication, time handling, update, consistency, executions. For the executions of actions, the linking to other languages is required. For communication the interpreter should hide all details of protocols etc., in an ideal version the programmer of an agent has to specify only the name and host of another agent to program a message transfer.

On the other hand, an agent oriented language must provide language constructs which allow the programmer to program his agents in a flexible way while using the interpreter routines and defining his own functionalities.

A program consists of initial data and of programmers routines, respectively. The routines specify the internal work of an agent (changing the mental state), and its activities (depending on the actual mental state).

As proposed by several authors (cf. [25]), an agent program can be executed by a (three-phase-)cycle. This cycle is similar to the recognize-act-cycle of production systems (recognize data, resolve conflicts, execute the chosen rule). A related rule for an agent may look like

IF < *belief* > AND ... AND < *intention* > AND < *time* > THEN DO < *action* > .

In agent oriented programming, the interpreter and its cycle is cut off with respect to the environment, and the underlying philosophy reflects mental categories. The interpreter cycle has (at least) three phases:

Input processing. By input I subsume messages from other agents and inputs from the environment ("sensing" [3], user interface). The inputs have been stored in a "mailbox" concurrently to other activities of the agent. In the processing phase, they are checked for consistency with the former mental state, and some data may be updated according to the related interpreter/programmer routines ("belief update").

Internal work. Further processing of the mental state appears. Inferences between different data divisions are executed. A new mental state is computed and decisions concerning actions (e.g. via desires and intentions) are performed ("belief-to-action").

Output actions. Messages are sent to other agents and (private) actions (including reactions to the user interface) are executed ("execution").

A lot of alternatives are connected with this cycle, and a lot of details can be (and should be) implemented in different ways. For example: should special messages rise something like an interrupt (e.g. for user messages)? Much work of the agent can be done concurrently: an urgent message need not to cause an interrupt, but it can install a new process concurrently to other processes of the agent. Hence, the concurrent work of a single agent may consist of overlapping executions of the cycle. As for humans, the question is, how many (which) things can be performed in parallel without confusions.

If we adopt the intuitive meaning of an agent as an entity acting autonomously according to its mental state, then the three phases contain the minimum of necessary tasks:

- information exchange with the outside world
- managing "belief update"
- transforming "beliefs to actions"

Since these tasks do not correspond to the phases in a one-to-one-manner, a finer partition of tasks and phases may be useful. I'll discuss the tasks in the sequel under the (my) viewpoint of open systems.

A first distinction of existing systems concerns the way in which agents are running: In some systems (e.g. in COSY/DASEDIS [4], AgentSpeak [30], MYWORLD [33]) agents are scheduled by a control/simulation tool (not so far from the control used in object oriented programming). Some of these systems also provide (or announce for the next future – e.g. AGENT-0 [25]) an interface for the communication with agents on other machines. The idea of agents autonomously running on different machines – as necessary for open systems applications – can be found e.g. in MAI^{2}L [27] and ARCHON [31].

8 Communication

In commercial tools (Group Ware, Concurrent Design, Collaborative Work), communication between different computers on a very high multi media level plays an important role nowadays. But this communication is related to actual cooperative work of humans. Our approach is related to the communication of programs (which in some sense assist the work of humans, but which can also do information exchange etc. without actual participation of humans).

For agent oriented programming in open systems, a sufficient support by the language and its interpreter is needed to prevent the programmer from low level protocols programming. Thus, the language should provide related "built-in's" to address another agent on another machine (even working under other operating systems ...) only by symbolic names. The different interpreters should permit the faithful transmission of e.g. arbitrary ASCII-sequences (while multi-media seems to be not so essential for communicating agents).

Further support should be given for high level communication protocols which regulate communications (e.g. how a message has to be handled and replied, cf. e.g. [4, 11, 31]) and negotiations (cf. e.g. [36, 27]).

The use for open systems (in contradiction to the use in distributed computations) gives preference to asynchronous message passing (as presupposed by the interpreter cycle, – while concurrent processing inside an agent can overcome the possible related problems).

Much work has been done to exploit e.g. speech act theory for related notions to classify messages by key words etc. While common and standard notions are convenient for many reasons, they are again not mandatory for communication in AOP. As for other design choices concerning agent oriented languages, the great variety of possible agents may even require differing semantics for the message classifications.

As already discussed: If any programmer wants to add an agent to the system, he knows which communications to other agents are necessary for his agent. Then he has to know the languages ("Danish", ...) of the other agents, and he has to program his agent using the appropriate words (e.g. a question to a data base agent has to use the related query language, but at the same time the programmer need not to know, – or even must not know –, the request to manipulate the contents of the data base).

As arm's length relationships in open systems mean, the agent and its programmer need not to know about all agents and all languages in the system (but there may be agents in the system which serve as translators, and which help to find services etc. – if this is useful for the applications).

As in real life, standards are useful in this field, too. But restrictions to fixed standards – referring to a "closed world" – could also be an obstacle. This means, that open systems should also have "open standards": open for extensions and even open for different semantics in different contexts of large and changing systems.

9 Belief update

Belief update is the first step in the computation of a new mental state. It has to reflect new information and to maintain local consistency. The latter one is subject to Theory

Revision [35], but it depends on the complexity of stored belief and of different kinds of knowledge and belief:

- strict knowledge is not revised (as capabilities in AGENT-0 [25]),
- some belief may be revised only by the human user (in case of inconsistencies the system has to ask for a decision)
- some belief can be changed by programmed user routines (as by "Belief Rules" in MYWORLD [33], or via self-commitment for self-information in AGENT-0)
- some belief may be revised by fixed interpreter routines (as in AGENT-0, where new information simply overwrite the old ones).

Since consistency is necessary only on the agent level in open systems, the revision can be performed locally. Truth maintainance is thus a local task, too, but distributed TMS such as DARMS [1] can give support, if some results of revision should be reported to other agents.

Another proposal for maintaining belief update is due to inferences with explicit time dependencies. The data have time stamps recording the time when they are beliefs of the agent, whereby older entries are not removed from the data base. Inferences at a certain time point are made with respect to the actually holding beliefs. This overcomes also problems concerning update anomalies (when beliefs may change while still performing an action).

10 From belief to action

Under "belief-to-action" I subsume all computations over the mental state which are necessary to make choices/decisions/commitments for actions to be executed. Several authors (e.g. in [15, 27, 30, 31]) collect arguments that agents should have possibilities for both:

- reactive behaviour for immediate response to stimuli from outside,
- reflexive/deliberative behaviour depending on longtime goals and related plans.

It seems quite reasonable that agents in open systems should have these abilities, while the implementation details (see below) may vary to a great extend. Thereby the reactive behaviour is seen as the result of an inference over the mental state, too (e.g. with a shortcut between stimulating belief and the immediate decision to perform an action).

While the reactive behaviour results in a fast response by predefined or preplanned actions, the reflexive behaviour is concerned with long term executions by planning e.g. via belief-desire-intention, often in a multi-layered fashion. Different layers are due to different degrees of outstanding choices (as with respect to desire and intention [24, 33]) or different control knowledge [12, 22].

The core of programming agents is concerned with relating beliefs to actions. This leads in a natural way to approaches where preconditions of actions, goals, plans, strategic inferences etc. are matched against the actual beliefs. Systems like AGENT-0 [25] ("Commitment Rules") , PLACA [29] (with "Mental Change Rules" extending the Commitment Rules of AGENT-0), DAISY-MAPL [23] (similar to AGENT-0), MAGSY [13] (using the OPS5-mechanism), MYWORLD [33] (with "Intention Adoption Rules" and "Strategy rules") are rule-based, while other systems have more complex outcomes of the matching process (e.g. scripts in COSY/DASEDIS [3], plan skeletons in ARCHON [31]). In many cases (e.g. AGENT-0 and MYWORLD) the results of the process are "conditional actions" which again have preconditions to be fulfilled at execution time.

Another distinction concerns behaviour programming vs. behaviour learning. "My private agent" should perform some kind of "adaptation" to my (changing) wishes, e.g. with respect to the kind of information I like to have from the WWW. A lot of human behaviour is experience based (reactive?), hence agents may also be experience-driven. The mail-agents in [19] may serve as an example.

As background for this kind of implementations the case based reasoning approaches are useful. Thereby the stimuli to executions need not to come from a direct but from a similarity based matching of preconditions and beliefs.

A quite different way is used by the system CONCURRENT METATEM [15]: agents are described by formulae of temporal logic, and execution means the stepwise construction of a model. Reactive behaviour is given by the *next-operator*, while long time behaviour comes by *"some time in the future"*.

11   Conclusions

I have collected a lot of alternatives and choices for the design of agent oriented techniques. I use this variety as an argument, that a unique notion of agents and a single agent oriented language would restrict the use of AOP. Different principles and different languages/tools are necessary for different agent roles. They can be implemented using different basic languages (thereby supporting different programming styles directly). Further discussion and further experimental work are necessary. Open systems provide a good background to study the special benefits of AOP.

References

1. C. Beckstein, R. Fuhge, and G.K. Kraetzschmar: Supporting Assumption-Based Reasoning in a Distributed Environment. In K. Sycara, Ed.,: *Proc. of the 12th Workshop on Distributed AI*, 1993.
2. A. Bond and L. Gasser, Eds.: *Readings in Distributed Artificial Intelligence*. Morgan Kaufmann, Los Angeles, CA, 1988.
3. B. Burmeister and K. Sundermeyer: Cooperative Problem-Solving Guided by Intentions and Perception. In [10].
4. B. Burmeister, A. Haddadi, and K. Sundermeyer: Generic Configurable Cooperation Protocols for Multi-Agent Systems. In K.Ghedira, F.Sprumont (eds.), *Pre-Proceedings of the MAAMAW'93*.
5. H. D. Burkhard: Theoretische Grundlagen (in) der Verteilten Künstlichen Intelligenz. In [21], 157-189.
6. H. D. Burkhard: Liveness and Fairness Properties in Multi-Agent Systems. Proc. of the *13th IJCAI*, 325-330, Chambéry, 1993.
7. H. D. Burkhard: On Fair Controls in Multi-Agent Systems. Proc. *ECAI'94*.

8. P. Cohen and H. Levesque: Intention is Choice with Commitment. *Artificial Intelligence(42),1990*.

9. A. Conte and C. Castelfranchi: Norms as mental objects: from normative beliefs to normative goals. In K.Ghedira, F.Sprumont (eds.), *Pre-Proc. MAAMAW'93*.

10. Y. Demazeau and J.-P. Müller (Eds.): *Decentralized A.I. 3*, North-Holland, 1992.

11. Y. Demazeau, O. Boissier, and J.-L. Koning: Interaction Protocols in Distributed Artificial Intelligence and their use to Control Robot Vision Systems. In I. Plander, ed.,: *Artificial Intelligence and Information Control Systems of Robots '94*, World Scientific Publ., Singapore, 1994, pp. 17-30.

12. I.A. Ferguson: Integrated Control and Coordinated Behaviour: a Case for Agent Models. In [32], pp.186-199.

13. K. Fischer: Verteiltes und kooperatives Planen in einer flexiblen Fertigungsumgebung. *DISKI, Dissertationen zur Künstlichen Intelligenz*, infix, 1993.

14. K. Fischer, N. Kuhn, H.J. Müller, J.P. Müller and. M. Pischel: Sophisticated and distributed: the transportation domain – exploring emergent functionality in a real-world application. In K.Ghedira, F.Sprumont (eds.), *Pre-Proc. MAAMAW'93*.

15. M. Fisher: Representing and Executing Agent-Based Systems. In [32], pp.265-297.

16. C. Hewitt: Offices Are Open Systems. In [2], 210-215.

17. G.K. Kraetzschmar and R. Reinema: VKI-Tools und Experimentierumgebungen. In [21], 222-256.

18. V.R. Lesser and D.D. Corkill: The Distributed Vehicle Monitoring Testbed: A Tool For Investigating Distributed Problem Solving Networks. *AI Magazine,* 15-33, Fall 1983.

19. P. Maes: Agents that Reduce Work and Information Overload. *Communications of the ACM*, July 1994, pp. 30-40.

20. J. McCarthy: Elephant 2000: a programming language based on speech acts. Unpublished manuscript, cited from [25].

21. H. J.Müller, ed.: *Verteilte Künstliche Intelligenz und Anwendungen*, BI-Verlag 1993.

22. J.P. Müller, M. Pischel, and M. Thiel: A Pragmatic Approach to Modelling Autonomous Interacting Systems. In [32], pp.226-240.

23. A. Poggi: DAISY: An Object-Oriented System for Distributed Artificial Intelligence. In [32], pp.297-306.

24. A. S. Rao and M. P. Georgeff: Modeling Agents Within a BDI-Architecture. In R. Fikes and E. Sandewall (eds.): *Proc. of the 2rd International Conference on Principles of Knowledge Representation and Reasoning (KR'91)*, 1991.

25. Y. Shoham: Agent-oriented Programming. *Artificial Intelligence(60),1993*,51–92.

26. Y. Shoham and M. Tennenholtz: On the Synthesis of Useful Social Laws for Artificial Agent Societies. *Proc. of AAAI-92*, 1992, 276-281.

27. D. Steiner, A. Burt, M. Kolb, C. Lerin: The Conceptual Framework of MAI^{2}L. In K.Ghedira, F.Sprumont (eds.), *Pre-Proceedings of the MAAMAW'93*.

28. D. Steiner and D. Mahling and H. Haugeneder: Human Computer-Supported Cooperative Work. Proc. of the *10th International Workshop on Distributed Artificial Intelligence*. MCC Technical Report Nr. ACT-AI-355-90, 1990.

29. S.R. Thomas: The PLACA Agent Programming Language. In [32].

30. D. Weerasooriya, A. Rao, and K. Ramamohanarao: Design of a Concurrent Agent-Oriented Language. In [32].

31. T. Wittig (ed.): *ARCHON: An Architecture for Multi-agent Systems*. Ellis Horwood, Chichester, England.

32. M. Wooldridge, N. R. Jennings, Eds.. *Intelligent Agents — Proceedings of the 1994 Workshop on Agent Theories, Architectures, and Languages*. Springer-Verlag, 1995.

33. M. Wooldridge: This is MYWORLD: The Logic of an Agent-Oriented Testbed for DAI. In [32].
34. M. Wooldridge and N. R. Jennings: Agent Theories, Architectures, and Languages: A Survey. In [32].
35. S. Wrobel: *Concept Formation and Knowledge Revision*. Kluwer Academic Publishers, Dordrecht, 1994.
36. G. Zlotkin and J.S. Rosenschein: A Domain Theory for Task Oriented Negotiation. Proc. of the *13th IJCAI*, 416-422, Chambéry, 1993.

Representing and Executing Agent-Based Systems

Michael Fisher

Department of Computing
Manchester Metropolitan University
Manchester M1 5GD
United Kingdom

M.Fisher@doc.mmu.ac.uk

Abstract. In this paper we describe an approach to the representation and implementation of agent-based systems where the behaviour of an individual agent is represented by a set of logical rules in a particular form. This not only provides a logical specification of the agent, but also allows us to directly execute the rules in order to implement the agent's behaviour. Agents communicate with each other through a simple, and logically well-founded, broadcast communication mechanism. In addition, agents can be *grouped* together. This not only restricts the extent of broadcast messages, but also provides a structuring mechanism within the agent space.

The purpose of this paper is threefold: to motivate the use of our particular computational model; to show that a logic-based approach is both possible and potentially very powerful; and to assert that by narrowing the gap between the agent theory and the agent programming language, we are able to bring the prospect of formal specification and verification of multi-agent systems nearer.

1 Introduction

Multi-Agent Systems are being developed and applied in a variety of contexts, from traditional AI, through Operating Systems and concurrent programming languages, to Robotics and Artificial Life. In spite of this, not only is there little agreement on what the core attributes of a general computing agent should be, but also there is, as yet, little evidence of an *engineering* approach to the development of multi-agent systems. For example, both development methods and verification techniques for multi-agent systems are rare. In fact, the definitions of agents are often so difficult to understand that they (a) cannot be effectively analysed by humans, and (b) are too complex for verification purposes.

In this paper, we outline an approach to the representation, development and implementation of multi-agent systems that we are developing. This is based upon the notion of concurrent object-based systems where each object executes a temporal specification of its behaviour whilst communicating with other objects using a form of *broadcast* message-passing.

In this paper we will address some issues relating to our approach, in particular:

- we will motivate the use of our particular computational model, by showing how the combination of executable specifications, broadcast message-passing and object grouping is able to represent a range of behaviours of both individual agents and multi-agent systems;

- we show that the use of a logic-based language in the description and implementation of agents is not only desirable but, as we use a *temporal logic*, is also potentially very powerful, particularly since the logic contains simple elements that are fundamental to the representation of dynamic behaviour;

- we outline how this work, combining executable specifications within a powerful logical framework, not only narrows the gap between the theory and implementation of multi-agent systems, but also provides a further step towards the goal of formal specification, verification and development of such systems.

In §2 and §3 we describe our approach to the modelling of individual agent behaviours and agent communication and grouping respectively. In §4, we give a brief outline of an implementation mechanism for these logic-based descriptions. Applications of this approach are indicated in §5, while the work towards the formal development of multi-agent systems is described in §6. Finally, in §7, we summarise the general utility of our approach and comment on related work.

2 Representing Agent Behaviour

In this section, we will motivate our approach to the representation of behaviour within individual agents. This will encompass both an outline of the advantages of a general logic-based approach and a more specific description of the benefits of using *temporal logic* as as a notation for representing dynamic activity.

First of all, however, we will outline the context in which we view individual agents.

2.1 Agents as Objects

An 'agent' is typically described as "an encapsulated entity with 'traditional' AI capabilities". We take the view that the distinction between an object, as used in concurrent object-based systems, and an agent, as defined above, is so vague and flexible to be useless. Hence, we believe that a multi-agent system is simply a system consisting of concurrently executing objects. Although some researchers, for example Maruichi et. al. [17], have attempted to distinguish agents from objects by stating that agents have control over their own execution (i.e., have meta-level capabilities) while objects do not, we take the view that everything is an object and, while many objects have some degree of meta-level control, there is nothing special that distinguishes an 'agent' from any other object. However, for the sake of this discussion, we will refer to objects that exhibit some form of 'intelligence' as 'agents' (although we must recall at certain times that the system is not able to distinguish between 'intelligent' and 'dumb' objects — they are all treated the same).

2.2 Requirements for Agent Description Languages

In representing the internal behaviour of an individual agent, it can be argued that we require a notation satisfying some, if not all, of the following criteria.

- It should be high-level, yet concise, consisting of a small range of powerful constructs.
- It should possess a semantics that is both intuitive and, if possible, obvious from the syntax of the language.
- It should be able to represent not only the static, but the *dynamic*, behaviour of agents.
- It should impose as few operational constraints upon the system designer as possible (for example, concurrent activities within a single agent should be able to be defined).

In representing an individual agent's behaviour, we choose to utilise a formal logic. One of the advantages of following such an approach is that the notation has a well-defined, and usually well understood, semantics. The use of a formal logic language also allows us to narrow the gap between the agent descriptions and the agent theory in that the semantics of an agent is close to that of its logical description. This allows for the possibility of employing both specification and verification techniques based upon formal logic in the development of multi-agent systems.

2.3 Representing Dynamic Behaviour Using Temporal Logic

While a general logic-based approach satisfies many of the above criteria, we choose instead to use temporal logic as the basis of our formal description of agent behaviour. Temporal Logic is a form of non-classical logic where a model of time provides the basis of the system. In our case, a simple discrete, linear sequence of states is used as the basic temporal model. Each state in this temporal sequence can be thought of as a model for classical logic. Such a temporal logic is more powerful than the corresponding classical logic and is useful for the description of dynamic behaviour in reactive systems. As such, it has many advantages as a description technique for agents in multi-agent systems, some of which we outline below.

- The discrete linear model structure that is the basis of the logic is very intuitive matching, as it does, steps in an execution sequence with an identified starting state and an infinite execution.
- The logic contains the core elements for describing the behaviour of basic dynamic execution. For example, it contains three main descriptive elements:
  - a declarative description of the current state;
  - an imperative description of transitions that might occur between the current and the *next* states;
  - a description of situations that will occur at some, unspecified, state in the future.
  Thus, using this logic, we are able to describe the behaviour of an agent now, in transition to the next moment in time and at some time in the future.
- This basic set of concepts is sufficient as more complex temporal properties can be translated into a normal form consisting of these concepts [13]. Thus, a general temporal specification can be given and transformed into a set of rules of this basic form.

Of particular importance, both in the representation of dynamic behaviour and in the execution of such temporal formulae, is the simplicity of the logic. In spite of this simplicity, it contains three core elements that are characteristic of general computation: the state of the agent at the current moment; the transitional constraints upon an agent as it moves forward to the next moment in time; and temporally indeterminate properties which must become true at some point in the agent's future. Thus, we can think of these three core elements as expressing the current state of an agent, what it can do next, and what it's longer term goals are.

We will not provide a detailed description of the temporal logic used, nor of the exact rules used in our approach (for a more detailed description, see [9]). Rather, we will present a simplified version as follows. The behaviour of an agent, both static and dynamic, is represented by a set of temporal *rules*. Each rule is of the form

'formula about the present' ⇒ 'formula about the future'

Simple examples include

$$(p \wedge q) \Rightarrow \bigcirc \neg r$$

representing the rule that if both p and q are true in the present state, then r must be false in the next state, and,

$$s \Rightarrow \Diamond t$$

representing the rule that if s is true now, then t must be true at *some* time in the future.

The form of these rules is such that any formula in the logic can be rewritten into a set of rules consisting of initial constraints (which are true at the start state) and rules of one of the following two forms [13].

$$\bigwedge_{i=1}^{m} p_i \Rightarrow \bigvee_{j=1}^{n} \bigcirc q_j$$

$$\bigwedge_{i=1}^{m} p_i \Rightarrow \Diamond r$$

Here, p_i, q_j and r are simply literals.

Note that, since any formula of the logic can be rewritten as a set of rules in this form, this does not represent a restriction of the logic such as Temporal Horn Clauses [1] — the full power of temporal logic can be utilised. Although we will see later that some additional operational constraints are used, the simple form of the rules means that the behaviour of the system is usually obvious from its description.

Finally, the temporal rules themselves can be seen to capture a mixture of both declarative and imperative aspects of the system. They comprise a declarative description of the state of the agent (classical logic), an imperative description of allowable transitions between states (e.g. '$\bigcirc$') and a declarative description of things that must happen at some time in the future (e.g., '$\Diamond$').

3 Agent Communication

We now turn to the representation of communication between agents. As we have argued above, multi-agent systems should be essentially based upon a form of concurrent object-based system. Thus, the key attributes of our system are those of objects (or agents) and message-passing. However, though most concurrent object-based systems employ point-to-point message-passing as the basic communication mechanism, we will argue below that such an approach restricts the power of multi-agent systems. In particular, we advocate a combination of agent grouping structures and broadcast message-passing in order to achieve communication that is both flexible and adaptable, yet is not prohibitively inefficient.

3.1 Point-to-point Message-Passing

Point-to-point message-passing is widely used in concurrent object-based systems, for example in actor systems [2]. Messages are sent to a specific address (the 'receiver') which must be known by the sender. The advantages of this approach are:

- an agent 'knows' where a message is being sent to;
- security controls are easily introduced as an agent can ensure that important information is never sent to the 'wrong' agents;
- this style of message-passing is both common and efficiently implemented in concurrent object-based systems.

The disadvantages of this simple form of message-passing are:

- an agent *must* 'know' where a message is to be sent to;
- in such a framework, it is hard to model *open* systems, for example the disappearance of the message recipient is usually problematic.

A final disadvantage, more specific to logic-based approaches, is that this form of communication does not fit naturally into the view of computation as a limited form of theorem-proving. Thus, we have examined other approaches to communication in an attempt to find a mechanism that is both more natural and more flexible than point-to-point message passing.

3.2 Broadcast Message-Passing

Broadcast message-passing is a natural mechanism to consider as it not only matches the logical view of computation that we utilise, but it is becoming more widely used in distributed computer systems. Broadcast message-passing involves sending a message, not to a specific address, but to all agents at once. It's advantages are:

- it is *compositional* in that a particular agent in a system can be replaced by another agent having observationally equivalent behaviour and the behaviour of the system as a whole will be unchanged (even though the name/address of the agent *has* changed);

- it is ideal for systems where tasks are announced and agents either compete or cooperate for the 'contract', for example Contract Nets [21];
- it is widely used in adaptable and fault-tolerant systems, for example in distributed operating systems, agents that 'die' can be replaced by 'shadows' allowing the system to continue even if certain processors fail [5].

In spite of these advantages, for many years broadcast message-passing has been avoided due to its perceived disadvantages:

- broadcast is not *secure* — any agent can examine the contents of any message;
- in a distributed system, broadcast has been perceived as *prohibitively* inefficient;
- it is perceived as being difficult to program with.

3.3 Agent Groups and Multicast Message-Passing

An obvious way to avoid some of the perceived problems of broadcast, and one that has been developed both within distributed operating systems and DAI is that of structuring the agent space into *groups*. Thus, each agent is a member of at least one group and if that agent broadcasts a message, it will be sent to all members of one or more (depending on the system) of the agent's groups. In such a way, full broadcast message-passing is replaced by *multicast* message-passing. In distributed operating systems, such an approach, called *process groups* is used to ensure replication and fault-tolerance [6], while in DAI it is used, for example in the *organisational model*, as a method for structuring and organising agents [17].

Thus, by utilising a form of group structuring, together with broadcast message-passing, we are able to retain many of the advantages of full broadcast while avoiding its major drawbacks. A bonus is that, in recent years, low-level mechanisms for efficient broadcast have been developed in many computer systems [4]. Further, not only is broadcast one of the basic communication mechanisms on local area networks [19], but also the advent of novel parallel architectures (e.g. data parallelism [14, 15]) has meant that more powerful programming techniques based upon broadcast communication are beginning to be developed.

4   Implementing Agent Behaviour

Having considered both the representation of behaviour within individual agents, and the communication mechanism between agents, we will now describe how these behaviours are *implemented* is our system. Whilst using a logic-based language gives us a clear link between the agent theory and the agent description language, we may not be certain that the language is implemented according to the semantics of the logic. One way to ensure this is to directly execute the logical statements. This move towards executable logic specifications further narrows the gap between the actual implementation of the language and the theory underlying the system.

Unfortunately, one particular problem with executable logics in general is that as the expressiveness of logic being used increases, so the execution mechanism becomes correspondingly more expensive to implement. This is one of the reasons that the more popular logic-based languages, such as PROLOG, restrict both the logic and the operational model so that the full power of the logic is not available and the execution remains relatively efficient.

4.1 Executing Logical Descriptions

The basis for the execution of logical statements is to construct a model for the set of statements. This, in general, involves theorem-proving. For example, in PROLOG, the model constructed represents a particular refutation constructed through SLDNF-resolution. Unfortunately, in representing agent behaviours concisely, we must often use forms of logic more expressive still than Horn Clauses. Even in PROLOG, decidability is not a property of the executable logic. When more expressive logics are used, completeness is also lost!

Thus, we advocate the use of logic-based languages for representation of agent behaviours, together with the direct execution of these languages, but with the following provisos.

- In abstract, the execution of a formula is just an *attempt* to build a model for that formula.
- We want to avoid *full* theorem-proving – it is often too expensive. Although we might use theorem-proving like mechanisms in the model construction process, *operational* constraints are also imposed in order to make the execution more efficient.
- Some formal properties of the logic are lost, not only through the operational restrictions, but also through the power of the logic used. For example, completeness and decidability might both be lost. Similarly, although execution of a formula is analogous to model construction for that formula, we might be unable to construct a *finite* model. Again, in these, more expressive, logics execution is the process of *attempting* to construct a model.

More important than the formal logical properties of the language are its pragmatic attributes. For example, although the execution mechanism should be sound, it should also be (relatively) efficient. Most importantly, the core logical features of the language must be both concise and applicable.

Given that we wish to directly execute the set of logical rules representing an agent's behaviour, we must decide what particular execution mechanism to employ. In the next section, we outline the approach we adopt, contrasting it with the predominant approach to the execution of logical formulae, namely logic programming.

4.2 Execution within an Agent

Whilst we advocate the use of logic languages as agent descriptions and the direct execution of these languages in order to provide agent behaviour, we argue that the standard logic-programming model is inappropriate for executing general agent behaviours, for the following reasons.

314

- In many cases, we require programs to be non-terminating. In such cases, we cannot expect the execution mechanism to return a finite object (a model). This leads us away from standard logic programming towards, if necessary, concurrent logic languages.
- More importantly, agents often want to specify, and thus attempt to achieve, several simultaneous goals. It is difficult, if not impossible, to represent this directly in a (single) goal directed framework such as logic programming.
- Horn Clauses, or similar classes of formulae often required for logic programming, may be too restrictive.
- In representing and executing agent descriptions where interaction with an environment is required, we must certainly disallow backtracking over observable actions. However, we would like to have some backtracking *within* agents.

The execution mechanism we employ is both natural for the style of logic we advocate (temporal logic) and avoids many of the above problems. The essential features of this execution mechanism are as follows.

- It is based upon *forward chaining* from the initial constraints through the set of temporal rules representing the agent's behaviour.
- This execution is constrained by the execution of eventualities. Thus, when a formula such as $\Diamond e$ is executed, e becomes an *eventuality* that must be made true at some point in the future. If e cannot be satisfied immediately, it is added to the list of outstanding eventualities. When the execution mechanism has a non-deterministic choice (for example, when it has to execute a disjunction), the outstanding eventualities constrain this choice such that the execution mechanism attempts to satisfy the eventualities as soon as possible, with the oldest outstanding eventuality being attempted first.

Thus, in terms of agents, these eventualities can be seen as goals that the agent attempts to satisfy as soon as it can.
- Each agent is an independent asynchronously executing object. In order to implement communication in a natural (and logical) way, the predicates in each agent's rules are split into three categories: *environment*, *internal* and *component*. Environment predicates are under the control of the agent's environment, while the other categories of predicate can be made true or false by the agent itself. Thus, when an agent's execution mechanism makes an internal predicate true, it just records the fact in its internal memory, while when it makes a component predicate true, it also broadcasts this predicate to all other agents. Finally, if an environment predicate is to be executed, the agent must *wait* for the predicate's value to be provided by the environment (i.e., by broadcasting its value). This allows agents to *synchronise* with other agents on selected messages.
- Agents are allowed to backtrack. As the agent's execution mechanism has a range of non-deterministic choices, it can, if it finds a contradiction, backtrack to a previous choice point and continue executing but on the basis of a different choice.

However, as agents are part of an open object-based system, we do not allow an agent to backtrack past the broadcast of a message. Thus, once an agent has broadcast a message, it has effectively *committed* its execution to that choice. This allows agents to carry out search through backtracking internally, but avoids the problem of attempting to rollback actions in a distributed system.

Having discussed and motivated the execution and communication mechanisms for individual agents in our system, we now give a flavour of one of the aspects currently under development, namely the addition of grouping into this framework.

4.3 Implementing Agent Groups

Recall that a *group* is essentially a set of agents. These are used to restrict the extent of broadcast communication and thus to structure the agent space. The basic properties we require of groups are that agents should be able to

- send a message to a group,
- add an agent to a group,
- ascertain whether a certain agent is a member of a group,
- remove a specified agent from a group, and,
- construct a new subgroup.

There are other properties that might be useful, such as the ability to list the members of a group, but they are not essential.

Two alternative approaches to the implementation of groups of agents within CON-CURRENT METATEM are currently being investigated. While these will not be described in great detail, we provide an outline of them in order to show a little of the range of representations that are available. These simple mechanisms allow us to represent a group of agents either

1. as a set of named agents, e.g

    { manager, solver1, solver2, worker, ... }

2. or as a set construction formula, where any agent satisfying the formula is con-
    sidered as a member of the group, e.g

    agent(X) ∧ solver(X)

The former involves generating the group from the bottom up, the latter from the top down (by using a declarative description). Note, however, that we are able to carry out both forms using the more expressive second style, e.g.

    agent(manager) ∨ agent(solver1) ∨ agent(solver2) ∨...

Thus, this formula is true for any of the members of the group explicitly represented in (1) above. Similarly, we can either add an agent to the group by adding a disjunct, e.g, '∨ agent(added)' to the defining formula, or remove an agent from the group by adding a negated conjunct, e.g., '∧ ¬ agent(removed)' to the formula.

However, checking whether a particular agent is in the group is slightly more diffi-cult in the second case as it involves some logical manipulation, rather than just string matching. Further, if we ask the group object to give us a list of its members, this is *much* more difficult using the second approach as there is no explicit representation of the agents within the group, simply a statement of what properties group members must have!

The discussion of which particular technique is most appropriate continues. The two approaches to group computation described above are being evaluated at present, both for their practical efficiency and for their logical consistency.

5   Applications in Multi-Agent Systems

In this section, we briefly indicate how our approach can be applied in a variety of different agent-based scenarios. These cover both the representation and implementation of single agents, and of societies of dynamically interacting agents. As the applications of our language have been presented elsewhere, we will only give an indication of how it can be applied.

The purpose of this section is to indicate to the reader that not only does our approach have some logical merit, but it can also be applied in a range of simple multi-agent scenarios. Further, the two main elements of the system, namely the executable temporal specifications and the communication/grouping mechanism, can often be applied separately. Thus, the communication/grouping mechanism is useful for structuring the agent space, while the temporal logic is useful for representing and executing dynamic behaviour in individual objects.

5.1   Dynamic Objects

By utilising the power of temporal logic, we are able to specify the internal behaviour of *dynamic* objects. In particular, we can represent agents whose internal state changes over time, whilst interacting with its environment. Rather than giving a range of examples here, we refer the reader to our survey of CONCURRENT METATEM applications [9].

5.2   Reaction versus Deliberation

There seems to be a continuing debate about the relative merits of *reactive* architectures versus *deliberative* architectures (typically based upon planning). Rather than arguing for one approach or the other, we take the view that *both* types of behaviour should be possible within agents. In particular, we argue that, in allowing concurrent activities within an individual agent, we are able to represent behaviour that is both reactive and deliberative. Agents can react immediately to certain stimuli, but can be carrying out a longer term planning process in the background.

For example, an agent can contain a range of transition rules representing reactive situations, such as

```
stimuli1 ⟹ ○response1
stimuli2 ⟹ ○response2
```

Note that a response occurs here in the next step of the agent and so a variety of immediate responses can be represented. As well as being useful for reactive architectures in DAI, such rules can be used as part of more traditional applications, such as process control [8].

We are also able to represent typical deliberative activities such as planning, for example by

$$\text{problem} \Rightarrow \Diamond\text{plan}$$
$$\text{plan} \Rightarrow \text{broadcast(plan)}$$

which states that at some time in the future the agent will have generated a plan to solve a particular problem and, when it does, the agent will broadcast this plan. There are two ways in which the agent might construct the plan, as follows.

1. Use $\Diamond$plan, as above, but add rules constraining the production of the plan, for example

$$\neg\,\text{pre1} \Rightarrow \neg\,\text{plan}$$
$$\neg\,\text{pre2} \Rightarrow \neg\,\text{plan}$$

   which states that the plan cannot be achieved until the preconditions pre1 and pre2 have been achieved. These subgoals can in turn be solved by adding the rules

$$\text{problem} \Rightarrow \Diamond\,\text{pre1}$$
$$\text{problem} \Rightarrow \Diamond\,\text{pre2}$$

   Thus, we can attempt to utilise the deductive and backtracking aspects of the system in order to achieve the construction of the plan.
2. An alternative approach is to plan without backtracking. Here, we use a continuation-based approach to represent the *rest* of the search space. This approach is more expensive, but safer (see below). However, such a planner would have to be built *on top* of CONCURRENT METATEM — it would not directly exploit the execution mechanism of the system.

There is a general problem with the first approach in that it may be difficult to mix reactive and deliberative aspects within the same agent. This is because, if the planning process depends upon backtracking of some sort, the reactive rules might be such that they broadcast a message at some point thus effectively committing the execution to a certain path and stopping the system backtracking past this point. The simplest solution to this problem is, when we require an agent that has both planning and reactive capabilities, to spawn a separate 'planning' agent which carries out the planning activity in parallel with the original agent. The original agent acts reactively to its environment, having spawned the planning agent, but once the planning agent has succeeded in producing a plan the original agent is at liberty to act upon it.

This type of behaviour leads us on to other examples of multi-agent systems where cooperative problem-solving can occur.

5.3   Distributed Problem Solving

As shown in [12], we are able to define a range of simple, abstract distributed problem solving systems. By utilising the power of temporal specifications for individual objects simple problem-solving agents can be implemented in CONCURRENT METATEM. These agents can then be organised to form a variety of problem-solving architectures. In particular, we can represent hierarchical, cooperative and competitive problem-solving. It is the combination of broadcast message-passing together with agent grouping that again allows us to develop such rich structures.

5.4   Simulating Societies

Combining the definition of individual dynamic agents, as above, together with broadcast message passing and grouping structures enables us to develop more complex agent societies. (For more details, see [11].) In particular, we are able to represent a range of group behaviours from cooperation through to competition, not only between individual agents but between groups of agents. Further, the grouping structures are dynamic as well — new agents can be added to groups and other agents can be removed.

5.5   Physical Attributes

As well as allowing the development of complex structuring within the object space, the grouping mechanism provides the potential for innovative applications, such as its use to represent physical properties of objects. For example, if we assume that any two objects in the same group can 'see' each other, then movement broadcast from one object can be detected by the other object. Similarly, if an object moves 'out of sight', it moves out of the group and thus the objects that remain in the group will 'lose sight' of it.

5.6   Fault-tolerance

As described above, the notion of groups, together with broadcast message-passing allows us to represent a powerful form of fault-tolerance. Thus, we are able to build this in to our multi-agent systems in addition to their purely functional behaviour. Note also, that the possibility of having many agents recognising and broadcasting the same messages can be used to develop more powerful forms of competition and adaptability, such as those seen in applications of genetic algorithms and artificial life.

6   The Development of Multi-Agent Systems

Formal methods have been used productively in the development of a variety of software and hardware systems. Particularly for complex and safety-critical systems, a formal approach is seen as vital. We believe that, as multi-agent systems become more complex and are applied in ever more critical areas, there will increasingly be a requirement for some form of formal validation/verification.

Our long term goal with this work is the provision of a formal framework for the specification, animation and development of distributed multi-agent systems. We have already identified many important features of multi-agent systems through our work on the abstract modelling of such systems and, by extending our executable temporal logics with a variety of these features, we will be able to model and prototype a range of practical systems. By basing our work on a simple temporal logic, for which there are already a variety of proof methods, we have already outlined an approach to the specification and verification of multi-agent systems [12].

In this section we will briefly identify some of the key areas that need to be developed. We are actively investigating several of these, though others remain as long term goals.

6.1 Temporal Specifications

Temporal logics have been widely used in the specification and verification of reactive systems [16]. Recent and future work in this area will feed into our development framework as multi-agent systems are just a particular class of reactive system. In particular, the work on compositional temporal specification and verification will have some bearing on our ability to effectively verify large multi-agent systems. However, the use of an object-based computational model, together with broadcast message-passing, will avoid some of the problems associated with the large-scale verification of multi-agent systems.

6.2 Agent Transformation

Currently, we are able to specify and verify properties of both individual agents and simple multi-agent systems. Rather than verifying the properties of both agents and systems at every stage of the development process, we intend to provide suitable *transformation* rules for both individual agents and groups of agents. These rules will preserve certain temporal properties. In particular, we will be able to transform an agent's specification to another specification that is logically equivalent (or at least implies the original specification). Further, *structural* transformations will be utilised, enabling the refinement of groups of agents. This will allow both the merging and splitting of agent groups during the development process.

It is important to note that any formula in the logic can be transformed into a set of temporal rules of the required form. However, the system developer would like some control of this process as two logically equivalent sets of rules might not execute at comparable speeds. Similarly, a logical specification might not have the identical behaviour, when executed, as the same specification distributed across multiple agents.

6.3 More Expressive Descriptions

The temporal logic described in this paper provides a simple, yet powerful, basis for the description of dynamic agents. However, there is the potential for the extension of this logical base with further features, including both reflection and meta-level capabilities, and common modalities such as those of intention, knowledge and belief. In the future, we intend to investigate these extended logics, particularly the simple extensions towards knowledge and belief. Although these more powerful logics are applicable in a wider range of complex systems, their logical properties are unknown though it is likely that the manipulation of agent descriptions will be much more expensive in such frameworks. Further, there are the questions of (a) are these additional modalities *really* necessary, and (b) if they are, is there a *core* set of them?

Given that, at least in certain cases, we might wish to specify agents using these more complex descriptions, we must also decide whether the concepts (i.e., intention, belief, etc) are transferrable between agents. If they are not, then a purely *temporal* specification may be carried out, with elements of intention, belief, etc, being introduced at a later stage of (single) agent refinement. If, however, we expect one agent to be able to send messages using these concepts and have the receiving agent understand them using *exactly* the same semantics, then this is likely to require a much more complex specification framework.

6.4   Heterogeneous Agents

An important aspect of our approach is that the two main elements, namely the executable temporal logic and the communication/grouping mechanism, can be separated. This is particularly useful when we consider heterogeneous agents. Here, the temporal logic description of each agent is simply a specification. A variety of programming languages can be used to implement individual agents. For example, one agent might be implemented in LISP, and other in C, and so on. As long as each agent satisfies its temporal specification and obeys the common communication rules, then these heterogenous agents are able to form a multi-agent system.

Two important aspects relating to this need to be studied. The first is the refinement of a temporal specification to a particular programming language, which requires appropriate refinement rules for a variety of languages. The second is the verification of properties of agents already implemented in standard programming languages. This, we may be able to achieve through a process of *temporal model-checking* [7] which allows us to check whether simple finite-state systems satisfy certain temporal properties.

Finally, we are also investigating the direct translation of a temporal specification into a lower-level programming language (e.g. C). This is likely to improve efficiency and would be used as part of the compilation process.

6.5   Verification System

The logic we use at present is relatively simple. However, as agents execute asynchronously and as each agent can effectively refer to an infinite domain, the logical base is more complex when we consider the verification of global properties of multi-agent systems. Not only is the logic undecidable, but first-order temporal logic is incomplete [22]. Further, due to the asynchrony of execution, we require a temporal logic based upon a *dense* model of time, rather than a discrete one [3, 10].

This, together with the possibility of using more powerful augmented logics means that the development of a verification system based upon our approach is likely to require further research into proof methods for temporal logics (particularly links to inductive and semi-automatic theorem-proving). We have made some progress in this area, though much is yet to do. We note that, even when using our simple temporal logic, we are able to verify many useful properties of multi-agent systems at present. However, we are not yet able to tackle either large systems or systems where the agents are particularly powerful.

In addition, the proof rules we have developed do not, as yet, incorporate the full range of *operational constraints* occurring in CONCURRENT METATEM. In proofs about the system, we assume that the execution mechanism perfectly implements the semantics of temporal formulae. However, we do not attempt to implement temporal logic completely, even in the propositional case. Thus, in order to reason about the implemented systems, rather than just their specifications, we must incorporate the operational constraints inherent within CONCURRENT METATEM into the proof system. As an example, the formula $\Diamond \phi$ in temporal logic means that the formula ϕ *will* be satisfied at some point in the future, while when this is executed in CONCURRENT METATEM we simply *attempt* to satisfy ϕ as soon as we can.

This problem, which is being studied at present, is related to the more general problem of whether to use a logical formula purely declaratively, or to add operational constraints in order to be able to execute it efficiently. These constraints in turn affect the declarative semantics of the original formula.

7 Summary

In this paper, we have motivated the use of executable temporal logics, together with broadcast message-passing and grouping mechanisms. We have discussed their use in the development of a range of multi-agent systems and have justified our approach in both logical and practical terms. As well as the notion of autonomous objects, CONCURRENT METATEM also provides a larger structuring mechanism through the 'groups' extension. This not only restricts the extent of an object's communications, but also provides an extra mechanism for the development of strategies for organisations. In particular, this provides the basis for agent cooperation, competition and interaction.

We have shown that a logic-based approach is not only theoretically desirable, but can also be practical. Further, the language we have developed captures a range of agent behaviours in a natural way. We believe that, regardless of the utility of our combined approach, the notions of executable agent specifications and group-based agent communication may be used separately in future systems.

Finally, we have shown that by narrowing the gap between theory and implementation, we are able to retain the elements of agent description that we require, while opening up the possibility of the formal development of multi-agent systems.

7.1 Related Work

While a wide variety of logical theories, purporting to represent agents, have been proposed few, if any, have provided the basis for an agent programming language. For example, languages such as April [18] and AgentSpeak [24] do not appear to be directly based upon a logical theory of agency. The closest work to that described in this paper is that of Shoham [20] who has proposed *Agent-Oriented Programming* (AOP). This framework consists of a logical system for defining the mental state of agents, together with an interpreted language for programming those agents [23]. While the logical basis of AOP contains notions of time, as well as other modalities such as belief, intention and capability, and the programming language provides syntactic support for such concepts, it is not clear what the formal link between the language and the logic is [25]. While, as mentioned above, we are not expecting to *exactly* implement the semantics of our logical specifications, we believe that CONCURRENT METATEM provides a closer link between its logic and programming language than AOP in that is *attempts* to implement as much as is practical of the logical basis.

References

1. M. Abadi and Z. Manna. Temporal Logic Programming. *Journal of Symbolic Computation*, 8: 277–295, 1989.
2. G. Agha. *Actors - A Model for Concurrent Computation in Distributed Systems*. MIT Press, 1986.
3. H. Barringer, R. Kuiper, and A. Pnueli. A Really Abstract Concurrent Model and its Temporal Logic. In *Proceedings of the Thirteenth ACM Symposium on the Principles of Programming Languages*, St. Petersberg Beach, Florida, 1986.
4. K. Birman and T. Joseph. Reliable Communication in the Presence of Failures. *ACM Transactions on Computer Systems*, 5(1):47–76, February 1987.
5. K. Birman. The Process Group Approach to Reliable Distributed Computing. Techanical Report TR91-1216, Department of Computer Science, Cornell University, July 1991.
6. A. Borg, J. Baumbach, and S. Glazer. A Message System Supporting Fault Tolerance. In *Proceedings of the Ninth ACM Symposium on Operating System Principles*, New Hampshire, October 1983. ACM. (In ACM Operating Systems Review, vol. 17, no. 5).
7. E. M. Clarke, E. A. Emerson, and A. P. Sistla. Automatic Verification of Finite-State Concurrent Systems Using Temporal Logic Specifications. *ACM Transactions on Programming Languages and Systems*, 8(2):244–263, 1986.
8. M. Finger, M. Fisher, and R. Owens. METATEM at Work: Modelling Reactive Systems Using Executable Temporal Logic. In *Sixth International Conference on Industrial and Engineering Applications of Artificial Intelligence and Expert Systems (IEA/AIE-93)*, Edinburgh, U.K., June 1993. Gordon and Breach Publishers.
9. M. Fisher. A Survey of Concurrent METATEM — The Language and its Applications. In *First International Conference on Temporal Logic (ICTL)*, July 1994.
10. M. Fisher. Towards a Semantics for Concurrent METATEM. In M. Fisher and R. Owens, editors, *Executable Modal and Temporal Logics*. Springer-Verlag, 1995.
11. M. Fisher and M. Wooldridge. A Logical Approach to the Representation of Societies of Agents. In N. Gilbert and J. Doran, editors, *Artificial Societies*. UCL Press Ltd, London, 1995.
12. M. Fisher and M. Wooldridge. Specifying and Verifying Distributed Intelligent Systems. In *Portuguese Conference on Artificial Intelligence (EPIA)*. Springer-Verlag, October 1993.
13. M. Fisher. A Resolution Method for Temporal Logic. In *Proceedings of the Twelfth International Joint Conference on Artificial Intelligence (IJCAI)*, Sydney, Australia, August 1991. Morgan Kaufman.

14. W. D. Hillis. The Connection Machine: A computer architecture based on cellular automata. *Physica D*, 10:213–228, 1984.
15. W. D. Hillis and G. L. Steele. Data parallel algorithms. *Comm. ACM*, 29(12):1170–1183, December 1986.
16. Z. Manna and A. Pnueli. *The Temporal Logic of Reactive and Concurrent Systems: Specification*. Springer-Verlag, New York, 1992.
17. T. Maruichi, M. Ichikawa, and M. Tokoro. Modelling Autonomous Agents and their Groups. In Y. Demazeau and J. P. Muller, editors, *Decentralized AI 2 – Proceedings of the 2nd European Workshop on Modelling Autonomous Agents and Multi-Agent Worlds (MAAMAW '90)*. Elsevier/North Holland, 1991.
18. F. McCabe and K. Clark. April — agent process interaction language. (In this volume.)
19. R. M. Metcalfe and D. R. Boggs. Ethernet: Distributed Packet Switching for Local Computer Networks. *Comm. ACM*, 7(19), July 1976.
20. Y. Shoham. Agent-Oriented Programming. *Artificial Intelligence*, 60(1):51–92, 1993.
21. R. G. Smith. *A Framework for Distributed Problem Solving*. UMI Research Press, 1980.
22. A. Szalas and L. Holenderski. Incompleteness of First-Order Temporal Logic with Until. *Theoretical Computer Science*, 57:317–325, 1988.
23. S. R. Thomas. The PLACA Agent Programming Language. (In this volume.)
24. D. Weerasooriya, A. Rao, and K. Ramamohanarao. Design of a Concurrent Agent-Oriented Language. (In this volume.)
25. M. Wooldridge and N. Jennings. Agent Theories, Architectures and Languages: A Survey. (In this volume.)

April - Agent PRocess Interaction Language

F.G. McᶜCabe, K.L.Clark

Dept. of Computing
Imperial College
London
{fgm,klc}@doc.ic.ac.uk

Abstract. In this paper we introduce key features of a programming language for building DAI and other types of distributed applications requiring the transmission and manipulation of complex symbolic data. April is oriented to the *implementation* of multi-agent systems. However, April is NOT a 'multi-agent applications language'. It does not directly offer high level features such as: planners, problem solvers and knowledge representation systems that a multi-agent applications language might be expected to include. April is more an object based concurrent language with objects as processes. As argued in [11], this is a highly suitable base for extension to DAI and multi-agent application platforms.

1 What is April?

April is a process oriented symbolic language. It contains facilities for defining processes, and for allowing processes to communicate with each other in a distributed environment in a uniform manner. It also has powerful data structuring and expression handling features as might be found in any high level symbolic programming language. April's symbolic structures are based on tuples, usable as lists, records or sets. Overall, it is aimed at giving as convenient a vehicle as possible for symbolic programming in a distributed environment.

In addition to its 'computational aspects', April also incorporates certain syntactic features – it is strongly typed, it has higher order features and it has an operator precedence syntax linked with a macro processing sub-language.

The type system that is built into April serves many purposes – in addition to the traditional role of types as a technique which helps to ensure that programs 'work first time', types in April also form the basis of pattern matching on messages and set-style search operations.

April's higher order features are used both for program structuring (modules are higher order objects) and to allow functions and procedures to be passed from one process to another.

The macro-processing facility is important to the usability of the language. With it, it is possible to build language 'layers' on top of the basic language to incorporate some additional features. For example, it is possible to define new operators in the language as macros. We have used this facility to provide an Object Oriented extension to April[14].

In particular, a package of macros and library procedures could form the basis of MAIL [19] – a high level language intended to capture many common multi-agent applications. The MAIL specification, and a preliminary version of April, were developed as part of an of an ESPRIT project - Imagine. April was explicitly designed to serve as an implementation language for MAIL, acting as an intermediary between MAIL and C. MAIL was prototyped using a distributed logic programming system, IC-Prolog II [3]. April was distilled from the features of the IC-Prolog II system that were found to be of most use in implementing MAIL.

This paper introduces the key features of April and illustrates their use for agent style applications. For example, we show how the contract net protocol could be implemented, and how a skills server agent might be programmed. Finally, we sketch how it might be used to implement an agent based programming language similar to the recently proposed AgentSpeak[7]. We also show how we can program migrating agents.

2 Specific features of April

2.1 Publically named processes

All processes in April have names – called *handles* – associated with them. Normally, the name will be automatically generated by April when the process is started but a programmer assigned name, such as agent0, or expert1, can given to the process as it is forked. Handles can be passed around as arguments of function and procedure calls, and in messages sent to processes. A message is sent to a process by sending it to its handle.

Programmer assigned handles, such as agent0, are local to the April invocation (the Unix process running April) unless they are made public. An assigned handle is made public by registering it with the name server to which the April invocation is linked. An April name server has much the same role as an Internet domain name server. Thus, at Imperial we have a local April name server called nameserver@lg.doc.ic.ac.uk. As with Internet domain name servers, this is linked with higher level name servers such as nameserver@doc.ic.ac.uk and nameserver@ac.uk. All April invocations running on machines on our research network link with this name server. A forked process within such an invocation can therefore have its assigned name, say agent0, registered with this name server. Now, processes in April invocations running anywhere in the world, providing their local name server is linked to nameserver@lg.doc.ac.uk via some hierarchy of name servers, can send a message to this process using the name agent0@lg.doc.ic.ac.uk. Incidentally, all the nameservers are themselves just April processes.

The name server system allows one to build global April applications. The system will recover from name server failure and restart, and from failure and restart, even on a different machine, of any user process with a registered name. It recovers in the sense that no messages will be lost.

2.2 Communication

April incorporates a simple message passing mechanism for communicating between processes. Messages, which can be arbitrarily complex symbolic structures, can be sent between processes independently of the location of the processes involved. The message send primitive is a send to one or more process handles. The message is put into the message buffer of each identified target process, each process having *exactly one* message receive buffer.

Processes use patterns to determine the messages that they are 'willing to accept' at any given point. Typically it does this by entering a *message receive choice* statement, a sequence of alternative Dijkstra style guarded commands [8], the guards of which are message receive patterns and tests. This has the form:

```
{
  Ptn₁ -> Act₁
  .
| Ptnₖ -> Actₖ
}
```

Here, | is the operator that separates the alternative guarded commands. April will test each message in the buffer in turn, in arrival order, to see if it matches any of the patterns $Ptn_1, \ldots, Ptn_k$, the patterns being tried in that order. As soon as a message is found matching one of the patterns, Ptn_i, the message is removed from the buffer and the associated action Act_i is executed.

Usually the matching pattern Ptn_i will contain variables that extract values from the removed message, and the action will use these extracted values. Messages skipped over before a matching message is found are left in the buffer, perhaps to be picked up by another message receive choice statement that is executed later. (A skipped over message could even be picked up as part of the action Act_i.)

If no message is found in the buffer that matches any of the patterns the message receive choice statement suspends, causing a suspension of the process. The process is reactivated as soon as a new message is placed in its buffer. This new message is then tested against each of the alternative patterns. If it matches none of the patterns, the process again suspends. It will continue testing each new message until one is received that is accepted by the choice statement. The April semantics for a message receive choice statement is similar to that used in Erlang [2].

Order of arrival of two messages M1 and M2 in the message buffer of a process is not necessarily time order of transmission. April cannot preserve time order for messages sent from different processes, because there is no global clock or clock synchronization assumed. Order of messages sent between a given pair of processes is, however, preserved. A message sent from one process P1 to another process P2 cannot overtake any earlier messages sent from P1 to P2. This property is important for many client/server applications.

The communication primitives use the TCP/IP protocol as the underlying transport medium [1]. Whilst this choice is not essential to the design of April, it does permit applications to interact across a wide area network such as the Internet, and also permits access to non-April based applications.

2.3 Real-time

April has aspects of a real-time programming language. That is, it has constructs in it which allow a program to be synchronized with real-time events. For example, it is possible to set processes to be activated at particular 'wall-clock' times (such as midnight on Jan 1st 2000). It is also possible to control the length of time spent waiting for messages by setting an appropriate time out.

2.4 Higher order features

April has a few simple higher-order features. In particular it is possible to use a *lambda abstraction* of an expression as a first class data item denoting a function. Like other values, a lambda abstraction can be stored in a tuple, passed as an argument or returned as a value, or passed to another process in a message.

In addition, there are two other related abstractions – *procedure abstractions* and *pattern abstractions*, both of which generate first class data items. The former allows the runtime construction of a new procedure, the latter the runtime construction of a new pattern. Supplied with variables of the appropriate type, a pattern abstraction can be used wherever a pattern can be used, for example as a message receive guard.

3   A simple server program

A server is a process which receives a series of requests to perform some task - to print files, to update a data base, whatever. A simple April program which implements a server for some task, passed to the server as a procedure argument, T, is outlined in Program 3.1.

Typically, the program would be invoked with a process fork statement of the form:

```
server1 public server(procname)
```

where procname is the name of the procedure that performs the server's task. The statement forks the server process. It also registers the name: server1, with the local April name server. (To fork a process, giving it a name which is not registered, but which remains local to the April invocation in which the fork is executed, we use names instead of public.)

Another process, within the April invocation that forked server0, can send messages to it using a message send statement of the form:

```
[do,taskargument] >> handle?server1
```

---

[1] In fact we use the simpler UDP/IP protocol.

```
server([any]{}?T)
{
  repeat{
    [do,any?arg] -> {                        /* A request to perfom task T */
      T(arg);
      done >> replyto
    }                                              /* report its done */
  } until quit                            /* loop terminates on a quit */
};
```

Program 3.1 A simple server program

Processes in other **April** invocations, use a message send:

```
[do,taskargument] >> handle?server1@domain
```

where **nameserver@domain** is the name of the local **April** name server with
which the **server1** name was registered.

Within the body of the **server** procedure we have the **repeat...until quit**
construction. This is a loop of message processing that ends when **quit** is the
next message for the process.

The body of this loop consists of a single *guarded command*:

```
[do,any?arg] -> {T(arg);...}
```

A guarded command has the form:

```
guard -> action
```

In this case, the guard is a message receive pattern. The pattern specifies a pair
– or a 2-tuple – where the first element of the pair must be the **do** symbol and
the second element is any value.

If the match succeeds – i.e., if there *is* a **do** message that contains some data
value – then that component is assigned to the variable **arg**.

When the server finds a **do** message of the required form, the message will
be removed from the buffer and the action part of the guarded command will be
executed.

After completing the **T** procedure, a reply message is sent to the *reply* process
associated with the received **do** message, normally the process that sent the
message, to let it know that the task has been completed. This is done using the
statement:

```
done >> replyto                                      /* report its done */
```

This sends a message – consisting of the single symbol **done** – as the reply.

The symbol **replyto** is an **April** keyword. When used inside the action part
A of a message receive guarded command:

```
Pattern -> A
```

it identifies the reply process for the message that matched **Pattern**. This is
unless **A** contains another message receive guarded command:

```
Pattern -> {
   ...
   Pattern' -> A'
   ...
}
```

and **replyto** is used inside A'. Then it refers to the reply process for the message
that matched **Pattern'**.

The **replyto** process for a message is usually the process that sent the message, but it can be different. To make it different, the sender uses a message
send:

```
msg ~~reply_handle >>target
```

This makes **reply_handle** the **replyto** process for the message. **April** has another keyword, **sender**, the always denotes the actual sender of the message.

4 A Second Example - Contract Net Protocol

The contract net protocol [17] is used by an agent – the contractor – when it
isn't sure which other agent should be asked to perform a given task. It therefore
'asks' a set of agents to bid for the work. Each of these agents – the contractees
– receives a job proposal message; and evaluates whether it is able to respond
and how to bid for the contract. On receiving the various bids, the contractor
agent evaluates them and selects the most appropriate.

The program in Program 4.1 is a sketch implementation of a simplified contract net protocol as seen from the point of view of the agent issuing the contract.
It is simplified because we assume that the contractor waits until the bid expiry
time and considers all bids received before then. We also assume that at least
one bid arrives in time.

The type declarations introduce user type names, **task_desc**, **proposal** and
reply. They are all for record types. For example, **task_desc** is a record of
three fields with types **symbol**, **any** and **number**, with field selectors **id**, **task**
and **expiry** respectively.

The first argument of the **Cnet** process is a description of the task for which
a contract must be placed. The expiry field of this description is the 'wall clock'
time by which all bids must have been received. The second argument of the
process is a tuple of handles which are the process identifiers of the potential
contractors. The contract is multi-cast to them using:

```
[contract,job] >> Bidders;                /* Invitation to tender */
```

```
task_desc ::= [symbol?id,any?task,time?expiry];   /* Task record */
proposal ::= [symbol?id,any?details];            /* Proposal record */
reply ::= [handle?contractor,proposal?bid];
CNet(task_desc?job,handle[]?Bidders,{[reply][]->reply}?select)
{
  [TASK_ANNOUNCEMENT,job] >> Bidders;         /* Invitation to tender */
  reply[]?Replies :=
    collect                                   /* collect bids */
      {repeat {[BID,proposal?P] -> elemis [replyto,P]}
        until alarm job.expiry-now};
  reply?Best := select(Replies);              /* select best proposal */
  [reject,job.id] >> (Bidders\[Best.contractor]);
  [accept,job.id] >> Best.contractor;
                                  /* Send accept message to contractor... */
};
```

Program 4.1 A skeleton procedure for implementing contract net

The last argument of the process is a function, `select`. This will take a tuple of reply records and return a single selected reply record, the contractor to whom the contract will be awarded paired with their bid proposal.

The tuple of reply records, each one comprising a bid proposal and the handle of the contractor process that sent it, is constructed using the:

```
collect                                       /* collect bids */
  {repeat {[BID,proposal?P] -> elemis [replyto,P]}
    until alarm job.expiry-now}
```

expression.

The `collect` expression is a programming language 'equivalent' of the mathematical *set abstraction* notation. In common mathematical parlance, an expression such as

$$\{x|P(x)\}$$

means

the set of all x's such that $P(x)$ is true.

In `April`, the expression

```
collect{ ... elemis x ...}
```

has a similar function. `collect` converts a statement, usually an iterative statement, into an expression. The value of `collect` expression is a tuple, the elements of this tuple are generated by the `elemis` statements executed inside the `collect`. Every time an `elemis` statement is executed within the body of the collect expression another element is added to the set. The construction of the set is completed when this statement terminates. In **April**, tuples are used to represent sets, and so we often use the terms interchangeably.

In the contract net example above, we have a **collect** which constructs a tuple where the iteration to which it is applied is bounded by time. On each iteraction the next element to be inserted in the tuple is denoted by the **elemis** statement executed in the loop. In this case, an element is put into the tuple whenever a **bid** reply is received. The expression **job.expiry-now** specifies how long the loop should execute. (**now** is an **April** function that evaluates to the current clock time.) The loop terminates when this time has lapsed. When the expiry time is reached, the **select** function is applied to all the collected replies to find the best reply. This is assigned to the variable **Best**.

A **reject** message is sent to all **Bidders** except the bidder **Best.contractor**. The expression:

```
(Bidders\[Best.contractor])
```

evaluates to the tuple of handles of these unsuccessful bidders. (It removes the **Best.contractor** handle from **Bidders**, \ being **April**'s set difference operator.)

Finally, an **accept** message is sent to the bidder, identified by the contractor field of **Best**, to award the contract.

4.1 Macro defined features

In Program 4.1 the loop construct:

```
repeat C until alarm T
```

where T is a delay time and C is a message receive choice statement was used. This form of statement is in fact macro expanded into:

```
handle?new := fork alarm(T);
repeat C until bell :: sender=new
```

where **new** is a fresh variable name. That is, it is implemented as a source transformation into a fork of an alarm process and a loop which terminates when a **bell** message is received from that alarm process. **alarm** is a system process defined as:

```
alarm(time?T){
  delay(T);                          /* suspend for T time */
  bell >> creator}     /* then send a bell message to creator process */
```

creator is another **April** keyword that here denotes the process that forked the alarm process.

Macros are used extensively in **April** to extend the syntax and functionality of the language. In fact, the

```
repeat C until M
```

loop construct is itself macro expanded into:

```
#macro repeat ?C until ?M ->
   while true do{M -> break | C}
```

Program 4.2 Macro for repeat loop

```
while true do {M -> break | C}
```

before being compiled. The macro that does this is given in Program 4.2.

In macros a ? prefix on its own introduces a macro variable (implicitly of type **any**). The left hand side of the macro (before the ->) gives the pattern of the program fragment to be expanded. The macro variables introduced here will be bound to parts of this program fragment. The right hand side gives the replacement program fragment which can use the values assigned to the macro variables by a successful match of the left hand side. When the repeat macro is used the macro variable C is bound to the message accept choice statement of the repeat loop and variable M is bound to the termination message. The macro for the **repeat**.... **until alarm** ... loop is only slightly more complicated.

5 A 'Skills server' Agent

The contract procedure of Program 4.1 will be forked each time an agent needs to place a contract. So typically, there will be several contract processes running within each agent. To invoke the process, the agent needs to have the tuple of handles of the **Bidders**, the agents to whom the contract announcement will be sent.

In a multi-agent environment, the suitable bidders may be continually changing. To cope with this, we might have a directory agent that keeps track of all the current agents and the skills that they have. The contractor agent can then query such a **SkillServer** agent to find a suitable bidder list for some contract. All he needs to know is the skill or skills that are needed for the contract.

5.1 The role

The role of a **SkillServer** agent is to match agents with skills. At its simplest level, the **SkillServer** agent receives a request in the form of a message such as:

```
[request,skill]
```

and replies with a tuple/set of agents who have the required skill.

In addition to requesting agents' handles, an agent can also inform the **SkillServer** agent that it is willing to provide services; i.e., that it has skills which it can perform.

5.2 The implementation

The **SkillServer** server contains a database of skills and agents which have registered them. This database is used to answer requests by any agent which wishes to locate a service. The skills database is updated whenever an agent registers or deregisters. It comprises a tuple of records. Each component record is of the form:

[agent_handle, [skill_1, ..., skill_n]]

The main structure of the **SkillServer** agent, as shown in Program 5.1, consists of a loop which waits for messages such as **request**, **register** and **deregister**.

The variable **skillsDB** contains the skills database – it is a tuple/set of records which have the type declaration:

```
skill_entry ::= [handle?agent,symbol[]?skills];
```

Each record consists of the handle of an agent, which can offer one or more skills, paired with a tuple of names for these skills, which are symbols.

```
skill_entry ::= [handle?agent,symbol[]?skills];
SkillServer()
{
  skill_entry[]?skillsDB := [];    /* The skills database starts empty */
  repeat{
    [request,symbol?sk]->{                    /* Request message received */
      skill_entry[]?rs:=
        skillsDB^/([any,symbol[]?sks]::sk in sks); /* search skill */
      { rs =!= [] -> [CanDo,rs^agent,sk] >> replyto
      | true -> none >> replyto        /* no known agent with the skill */
      }
    }
  | deregister ->                            /* deregister an agent */
      skillsDB := skillsDB ^\ [sender,any]   /* remove skill record */
  | [register,symbol[]?sks] ->
      skillsDB := (skillsDB ^\ [sender,any]) <> [[sender,sks]]
  } until quit;
}
```

Program 5.1 The basic **SkillServer**

In Program 5.1 the statement:

```
skill_entry[]?rs:=skillsDB^/([any,symbol[]?sks]::sk in sks)
```

retrieves and assigns to variable `rs` all the `skillsDB` entries in which the requested skill `sk` appears. The operator `^/` is April's pattern match *selector* from tuples/sets. Its second argument, in this case:

```
([handle,symbol[]?sks] :: sk in sks)
```

is the element pattern, together with a test, to be used in selecting from the set. The value of the `^/` expression is all the pairs in the skills database which match the pattern and have the required skill. The test `sk in sks` is, in this case, the real selection criterion since all the records will match the pattern.

Notice also the use of the choice statement:

```
{ rs =!= [] -> [CanDo,rs^agent,sk] >> replyto
| true -> none >> replyto                           /* no known agent */
}
```

This is a *test choice statement*, a choice statement with only test conditions and no message receive patterns in the guards. The guard `true` always succeeds, so if the guard `rs =!= []` of the first guarded command of the choice fails (remember the guards are tried in sequence), the action of the second guarded command will be executed. The expression `rs^agent` is tuple/set projection. It projects the set `rs` on the `agent` field producing a tuple/set of agent handles.

The operator `^\` is April's pattern match *deletion* operator. For the `deregister` message its effect is to remove any entry in `skillsDB` for the `sender` of the message, before the new entry is added. Its use for a `register` message guarantees that there is only one entry per agent. (`<>`is April's append operator.)

5.3   Retrieving information with user defined patterns

Using the above skill server a `request` message can only ask about one skill even though an agent can register a tuple of skills. Perhaps we should also allow `request` messages that give a tuple of skills and only agent handles registered with all the requested skills will be returned. To do this, we could add an extra guarded command to the choice statement of the message processing loop:

```
[request,symbol[]?rsks] ->
   skill_entry[]?rs:=skillsDB^/([handle,symbol[]?sks]
         ::rsks subset sks)
```

The `subset` operator is April's built predicate that will test that every element in the tuple `rsks` appears on the registered `sks` tuple.

Note that we can have this additional guarded command in the message processing loop even though we already have a message receive clause for a `request` message pair. This is because the `request` message accepted by the new message receive must have a different type of second component in the message pair, a tuple of symbols rather than just a single symbol. The two patterns will therefore match quite different incoming messages.

But what if we now want to find an agent that has either one pair of skills or another pair. Do we add another message receive guarded command? We could, but there is a better alternative. Rather than have a message receive for each new type of retrieval request, we can allow the request message itself to specify the retrieval test in the message. The requester can send a pattern match procedure, a pattern abstraction, in the request message.

Consider this alternative guarded command for **request** messages.

```
[request,[]()?ret_pattern] ->
    skill_entry[]?rs:=skillsDB^/ [](ret_pattern)
```

This expects the message to include a **ret_pattern** which is a type []() , which is the **April** type descriptor for a pattern that just tests, i.e. which does not bind any variables outside the pattern. (The bracket pair () signals that it is a pattern abstraction and the preceding empty tuple [] tells us it exports no variable bindings.) The **ret_pattern** is applied using the expression [](ret_pattern). The surrounding round brackets tell us that **ret_pattern** is a pattern abstraction and the proceeding [] is the list of visible variables, in this case none, that it will bind.

If this is the only request message that **SkillServer** will accept, how does another agent send a request to search for a single skill, or to search for a tuple of skills.

The message that is sent to find all the agents registered with a particular skill, say the **multiply** skill, is now:

```
[request,tau()([any,symbol[]?sks]::multiply in sks)]
```

The message to find all those that have all of a tuple of skills [sk1,..,skn] is:

```
[request,tau()([any,symbol[]?sks]::[sk1,..,skn] subset sks)]
```

The message to find agents that have skill sk1 and not sk3, is:

```
[request,tau()([any,symbol[]?sks]::sk1 in sks and not sk3 in sks)]
```

and so on. Expressions of the form **tau**(*variables*)(*pattern*) are pattern abstractions. In the above examples there are no *variables* since the pattern abstractions are just tests.

The key advantage of this approach is that the requester defines the retrieval criterion, it is not restricted to a fixed set of types of retrieval inquiry. Plus, the **SkillServer** just uses the retrieval abstraction to scan its data base. It cannot inspect the criterion, which is private to the requester.

The main disadvantage is that the requester needs to know the type of the internal **skillsDB** data base of **SkillServer**. It needs to know that the pattern abstraction it will send will be applied to a **skill_entry** record.

6 Influences and related languages

Many of the features of **April** are taken from other languages; in particular much is owed to Parlog [4] and its object oriented extension Polka [6], and to PCN [10], CSP [12], Guarded Commands [8], LISP [18], Prolog [5] and APL[13].

6.1 The actor paradigm

The process style of programming in `April`, and the pattern matching on messages, comes from the Parlog family; although clearly there is a close similarity with the actors concept [1]. We can quite easily simulate actor style programs in `April`.

Differences are:

- In `April`, the action on receipt of a message is a sequence of operations. Parallel operations have to be explicitly forked. For an actor, operations are automatically executed in parallel and sequential execution has to be programmed using delays waiting for messages.
- An actor only accepts messages at the head of its message buffer. `April` always searches down the message buffer to find an acceptable message.
- An actor has just one message processing choice statement, and the action on receipt of a message *cannot* contain another message receive guarded command. In `April` the action can be specified by any `April` statement or group of statements.
- The actor paradigm does not guarantee to preserve order of messages sent from an actor A1 to an actor A2. `April` does.

6.2 ABCL/1

`April` is closer to the ABCL [16] derivative of the actor paradigm. ABCL/1 *preserves* order of messages between a given pair of processes. Like us, the authors of ABCL/1 consider this to be essential for certain applications. ABCL/1 also has both a sender and a replyto identity attached to every message. (As in `April`, the replyto identity can be set by the message send in both ABCL/1 and the actors framework.) In addition, in ABCL/1, an action on a message receive can include another message receive. This auxiliary message receive can also search down the message buffer, and will cause a suspension of the process if the message has not yet been received. But as far as we understand, the main message processing loop of an ABCL/1 program can only pick off messages at the front of the message buffer. (In `April` any message receive guarded command or choice statement will search for an acceptable message in the buffer.)

On the surface, ABCL/1 appears to have more ways of sending messages. It has the *past* form, which is the same as in `April`, and the *now* and *future* forms which are not directly supported in `April`. The *past* is asynchronous message send. The *now* form is synchronous send, in which the sender suspends until a reply is received. The *future* form is asynchronous but the sender can later suspend if the reply has not yet been received and placed in some variable associated with the *future* send. However, as shown in [16], the *future* and *now* forms of message send can be implemented using just the *past* form providing the language allows the explicit setting of the `replyto` address, and it can search for messages in its message buffer. Both of these facilities are in `April`. Thus, the extra forms of message send in ABCL/1 can be emulated in `April`. Using the macro processing facility, we can easily extend the language to have extra message send operators with the semantics of the ABCL/1 *now* and *future* forms. (A macro to implement the *now* form of message send is given in [14].)

ABCL/1 also has two *modes* of message sending: normal and express. An express message sent to an ABCL/1 object/process interrupts the current processing of any normal message, suspending the processing. The action associated with the express message is then executed. After this is completed the normal message processing is usually resumed.

In `April` we can emulate having both express and normal messages, and support ABCL/1 style syntax via macros. The details are given in [9]

7   On Implementing a DAI platform on top of `April`

In this section we shall indicate some of the ways that the features of `April` could be used to implement a DAI or agent based platform similar in functionality to AgentSpeak [7]. This is a recently proposed concurrent agent based programming language designed to extend concepts of object based concurrent programming, which `April` definitely embodies.

An agent would be represented as a publically named process. This process would itself have internal parallelism. At start up it would typically spawn several non-public processes, processes that are local to the agent. One would be the main message receiving *interface* process, another would be the *knowledge handler*, a process that holds the state, or knowledge, of the agent. This knowledge would be represented as several sets of records, each set of records being the current facts for some relation used by the agent to encode its knowledge, as in AgentSpeak[7]. The knowledge needs to be held in a separate process, that accepts messages to update and access the knowledge, if we want to allow the agent to be concurrently executing several tasks or plans. Each task/plan would be executed by a forked process internal to the agent, and each of these would access or update the shared knowledge by sending messages to the knowledge handler.

The interface process would typically accept messages in a standard format for inter-agent communication, perhaps formats based on particular speech acts such as *inform, request* etc. The agent could offer services, and the actions linked to these services could be held in a data base associating a pattern of use of the service with a plan, defined as a procedure [7]. In `April` we can implement such a data base as a set of pairs comprising a pattern abstraction and a procedure abstraction which is held within the interface process. To retrieve a plan corresponding to an incoming *request* message, the agent would find a pattern abstraction/procedure abstraction pair within the set such that the pattern abstraction successfully applied to the incoming request. Successful application indicates that the plan represented by the paired procedure abstraction is appropriate for the request. The procedure abstraction is then applied to values extracted by the successful application of the pattern abstraction to the message, and forked as a separate process within the agent. Notice that this way of holding plans allows for the plan paired with some pattern abstraction to be updated by an *inform* message.

Agent groups, and message sending to agent groups, can be implemented by having a publically named *membership* process for each group. Agents then register with the membership processes for the groups to which they want to belong, in a manner similar to the registering of agents with the skill server described above. Now, an agent that wants to send a message to an agent group sends it to the group process. This, in turn, can multi-cast forward the message to every registered member of the group, or to just those that indicate a willingness to accept messages of a certain form. This last feature will depend on how elaborate we want to make the registration action.

7.1 Mobile agents

There is considerable interest at the moment in the concept of mobile agents migrating from environment to environment accessing and abstracting information local to the environment before moving on.

Let us assume, for simplicity, that such an agent has a single thread of execution and so can be represented as a single process in `April`. How can we let this process migrate, and, if it does, how can it access information in a new environment.

Remember that non-public processes within an `April` invocation can be given program assigned names. So, we can have a network of publically processes, `mobile_agent_station@lg.doc.ic.ac.uk` etc., all of which are executing within `April` invocations that have forked processes with standard, but non-public names, such as `skill_server` and `file_server`. A mobile agent is then sent to a station by being sent to one of the publically named station processes, for example `mobile_agent_station@lg.doc.ic.ac.uk`, as a procedure abstraction in a message. When it arrives at a new mobile agent station, it sends out messages using the standard but locally assigned names `skill_server` etc., and, by so doing, plugs into the local environment.

To migrate, the process sends itself to another of the publically named stations wrapped up as a procedure abstraction. Whatever state information it wants to take with it must be held as arguments of the procedure that defines the agent. Program 7.1 gives one possible structure for such a procedure.

To be able to accept and start running such a mobile agent the program for a `mobile_agent_station` just has to contain the message receive:

```
[migrating_agent,[]{}?Agent] -> Mbs := [fork Agent()] <> Mbs
```

This records the handle of the forked agent for purposes of monitoring, and possible killing. For added security, we are considering having a fork which does not allow ancillary forking within the forked process. So a received mobile agent would not be able to fork processes unknown to the mobile agent station.

```
mobile_agent1(type1?S1,...,typek?Sk){
.
/* initial communication with the environment, sending messages
to the standardly named servers */
.
/* receive replies and get needed information */
.
/* optionally report to some process at the home station
and  determine which station, NewSation, to visit next */
.
[migrating_agent, mu(){mobile_agent1(S1,..,Sk)}] >> NewStation;
/* last action of the process is to send a no argument procedure
abstraction, comprising a recursive call to itself with arguments
the current values of its state variables, to the next station */
};
```

Program 7.1 Structure of a mobile agent

8   Conclusion

April is a small programming language which combines many of the features needed for implementing multi-agent systems and programming DAI applications.

April is efficiently implemented on top of C, using the standard TCP/IP protocol for message passing between processes in different **April** invocations. It gives a very fast and portable bottom layer for building a DAI platform. Then, since we expect that many of the features of DAI platforms can be implemented as predefined processes and language extensions that are macro processed, each platform would itself be just a thin layer on top of **April**.

In our future research we intend to build several DAI platforms on top of **April**.

A full specification of **April** is given in [15]. Please contact the second author if you are interested in using the language.

References

1. G. Agha and C. Hewitt. Concurrent programming using actors. In A. Yonezawa and M. Tokoro, editors, *Object Oriented Concurrent Programming*. MIT Press, 1987.
2. J. Armstrong, R. Virding, and M. Williams. *Concurrent Programming in Erlang*. Prentice-Hall International, 1993.
3. D. Chu. IC-prolog II: a language for implementing intelligent distributed systems. In S. M. Deen, editor, *Proceedings of the 1992 Workshop on Cooperating Knowledge Based Systems*. Dake centre, University of Keele, UK, 1993.

4. K.L. Clark and S. Gregory. Parlog:parallel programming in logic. *ACM Toplas*, 8(1):1–49, 1986.
5. W.F. Clocksin and C.S. Mellish. *Programming in Prolog.* Springer-Verlag, 1981.
6. A. Davison. Polka: a parlog object oriented language. Internal report, Dept. of Computing, Imperial College, London, 1988.
7. D. Weerasooriya et al. Design of a concurrent agent oriented language. In M. Woodridge and N. Jennings, editors, *Pre-Proceedings of ECAI94 Workshop on Agent Theories, Architectures and Languages,* 1994.
8. e.W. Dijkstra. *The discipline of programming.* Prentice-Hall International, 1977.
9. F.G.McCabe and K.L.Clark. April: Agent process interaction language. Technical report, Dept. of Computing, Imperial College, London, 1994.
10. I. Foster and S. Tuecke. Parallel programming with PCN. Internal report anl-91/32, Argonne National Laboratory, 1991.
11. L. Gasser and J-P. Briot. Object based concurrent programming and DAI. In N. A. Avouris and L. Gasser, editors, *Disributed Artificial Intelligence: Theory and Praxis.* Kluwer, 1992.
12. C.A. Hoare. *Communicating Sequential Processes.* Prentice-Hall International, 1985.
13. K. E. Iverson. *A Programming Language.* Wiley, New York, 1962.
14. K.L.Clark and F.G.McCabe. Distributed and object oriented symbolic programming in april. Technical report, Dept. of Computing, Imperial College, London, 1994.
15. F.G. McCabe. April - agent process interaction language. Internal report, Dept. of Computing, Imperial College, London, 1994.
16. E. Shibayama and A. Yonezawa. Distributed computing in abcl/1. In A. Yonezawa and M. Tokoro, editors, *Object Oriented Concurrent Programming.* MIT Press, 1987.
17. Reid G. Smith. The contract net protocol: High-level communication and control in a distributed problem solver. *IEEE Transactions on Computers,* pages 1104–1113, 1980.
18. G. L. Steele and et. al. An overview of common lisp. In *ACM Symposium on Lisp and Functional Programming,* August 1982.
19. Donald Steiner, Alastair Burt, Michael Kolb, and Christelle Lerin. The conceptual framework for mail: An overview. Internal report, DFKI, 1992.

DAISY: an Object-Oriented System for Distributed Artificial Intelligence

Agostino Poggi

DII - University of Parma,
Viale delle Scienze, 43100 Parma, Italy

Abstract. This paper presents an object-oriented distributed system, called DAISY, for the development and experimentation of Distributed Artificial Intelligence systems and algorithms. This system is based on two programming levels: object level and agent level. Both the levels allow to define, implement and experiment systems. While the object level offers a large set of "low level" programming means (a large set of program constructs, a set of "low level" communication procedures, and so on), the agent level, which is implemented on the object level, offers a limited set of "high level" programming means (few program constructs, a fixed set of "high level" communication procedures derived by *speech act theory* and a fixed set of "high level" procedures to manage agent's knowledge). In particular, the paper shows the use of DAISY for modeling an airline reservation scenario and a manufacturing plant scenario.

1 Introduction

Distributed Artificial Intelligence (DAI) is an emergent research field related to the use of concurrency and distribution in Artificial Intelligence (AI) (see, for example, [13, 4, 10]). Such research field is getting more and more importance because of intrinsic limitation of traditional (single agent) AI approaches due to the presence of a number of agents in the real world and the fact that their actions can interact. DAI approaches cope with these problems through the use of a class of models, called multi-agent systems.

Multi-agent systems are systems where groups of intelligent entities, called agents, interact by cooperation, by coexistence, or by competition [6]. These agents are real or virtual entities living in an environment which can perceive and represent partially, and where can take actions. Moreover, they have an autonomous behavior that is a consequence of their own knowledge represented by mental components such as beliefs, capabilities, plans, goals and commitments, and their interaction with the environment. Some agents are assumed to be helping one another on the basis of the fact that they carry out all the required tasks (benevolent agents). Other agents are not benevolent, but they act on the basis of their goals, however, they may accept compromises and perform mutually beneficial activities (rational agents) [18].

Initially, the development of multi-agent systems are based either on software tools taking advantage of traditional AI languages (i.e., Lisp and Prolog) or on concurrent languages, that is, object-oriented, concurrent logic and actor languages (e.g., ABCL [25], April [15], Orient84/K [22] and Act3 [3]). However, while traditional AI languages do not support concurrency and so offer a limited representation power and can be only used for "toy worlds" (e.g., MACE [9] and MICE [16]), concurrent languages do not offer "high level" primitives for multi-agent modeling and so their use for the developing of applications is rather difficult.

Nowadays, multi-agent systems can take advantage of a lot of research on agent theories, architectures and languages [24].

In particular, Shoham introduced a new programming paradigm, called agent-oriented programming, as specialization of the object-oriented programming [20]. He also defined a language, called Agent0, for multi-agent systems; this language is based on an agent model based on a mental state, a set of actions (private and communicative actions) derived from *speech act theory* [19], and an interpreter to define and program agents. However, Agent0 has four main limits: i) it is rather difficult to develop applications because it does not take advantage of object-oriented programming features to define agents; ii) it is based on a sequential interpreter which is not able to represent all the aspects of the distributed nature of a multi-agent system; iii) the relationship between the logic (i.e., the mental state) and the interpreted programming language is only loosely defined, that is, the programming language cannot be said to truly execute the associated logic; and iv) the inability of agents to plan and communicate requests of actions via high-level goals. This last limit has been eliminated in an extension of Agent0, called PLAnning Communicating Agents (PLACA), by introducing some operators for planning to do actions and achieve goals [21].

Another interesting language for agent-oriented programming has been proposed by Fisher [8]. This language, called Concurrent METATEM, not only provides a logical specification of an agent, but also allows the execution of its rules in order to implement agent's behavior. In Concurrent METATEM agents communicate with each other through a broadcasting mechanism and the extent of broadcast messages is restricted through the possibility to organize agents into groups. Moreover, groups also provide a mechanism for the development of strategies for organizations. In particular, this provides the basis for agent cooperation, competition and interaction.

Two agent models, which take advantage of some object-oriented programming features, are the agent model developed at LIFIA [5] and the agent model of Agentspeak [23]. The agent model developed at LIFIA offers perception, communication and action capabilities, the possibility of reasoning about other agents, and a multi-layer control structure. Moreover, the fact that agents are implemented by active objects allows a multi-agent system to have a real distributed implementation. The agent model of Agentspeak is based on a set of database relations, a set of plans and a set of communicative actions. This language offers a large set of features of concurrent object-oriented languages extending them through the use of a goal-directed and reactive behavior and managing communication through speech act messages.

This paper presents an object-oriented distributed system, called DAISY, for the development and experimentation of Distributed Artificial Intelligence systems and algorithms. Section two and three respectively introduce the object and the agent levels. Section four presents two programming examples. Section five describes the relationships with some other agent models and languages. Finally, section six sketches some concluding remarks.

2 The object level

The object level corresponds to CUBL (Concurrent Unit Based Language) [17]. CUBL is a distributed object-oriented language and is based on objects called c_units and concurrent message passing among them.

A c_unit is an active object composed of data (state) and procedures as traditional (passive) objects, but adds the possibility to store incoming messages into a queue while it is active. A c_unit uses centralized concurrency control, that is, there is a single procedure, called script, that controls message reception and action execution. In particular, a c_unit can be in one of the following modes: i) *sleeping*; ii) *active* or iii) *waiting*. Normally, a c_unit is *sleeping* and becomes *active* when it receives a message. When it is *active*, it applies its script to the message performing procedures and sending other messages. In particular, when its execution requires a message and this message is not yet arrived, it becomes *waiting*. When a c_unit is *waiting*, each time a new message arrives, it tests if it is the waited message, and becomes *active* when the waited message is recognized. The messages which arrive while the c_unit is *active* are queued and served in a FIFO order.

A c_unit is a composite object that may contain some other c_units and some s_units. An s_unit is a traditional passive object used for modularizing large c_units. In fact, s_units are useful for representing c_unit parts which do not act concurrently and are not shared by different c_units and hence which can be lightened of any burden for managing concurrency. C_units and s_units are grouped into classes and take advantage of multiple inheritance for both class and procedure specialization.

C_units communicate through synchronous (now) and asynchronous (past) messages. Messages can have a priority, can be multicast and pipelined. Moreover, priority is not the unique means to avoid queue FIFO order; in fact, c_units take advantage of a set of primitives to get a particular message from the queue (e.g., it is useful to implement a future message protocol).

A c_unit can multicast a message, that is, it can send a message to more than a c_unit in parallel. When a c_unit sends a synchronous message, then it can follow three different behaviors: i) it waits for the first answer, ii) it waits for one or more answers that verify a certain condition, or iii) it waits for all the answers. In these two last cases, the c_unit may be helped by a special c_unit, called mailbox, whose purpose is to gather answers, to filter them on the basis of a selection criterion, and to send the selected answers to the destination through a single message.

When a c_unit needs that a set of other c_units perform sequentially one or more operations on a same data, then the c_unit can use pipelining, that is, it sends a message to the first c_unit of the sequence through a "pipe" message; this message contains both the data and the information about the sequence of c_units that the message must visit.

C_units can be organized by groups. A group represents a collection of objects which forms a natural unit performing collective tasks [12]. In CUBL, groups are special c_units containing a set of other c_units and offers them some services: i) membership, ii) external interface, and iii) internal organization.

The membership service keeps track of group population, it creates and removes members and lists current members. It allows the multicasting of a message to all the population of the group without the need to specify all the names of the members, and to model dynamic and complex organizational schemes where more than one c_unit can enter / exit a group.

The external interface service supports communication between internal and external c_units. However, it does not mean that it is not possible to send a message to an internal c_unit directly from outside, but that, when an external message is directed to the group and not to a particular c_unit, the group forwards the message to the appropriate c_unit.

The internal organization service supports interactions among c_units. A c_unit is usually dedicated to do some tasks and may be used in different groups to do them. However, each group has a set of different c_units organized by different synchronization and communication rules. Therefore, either a c_unit must be specialized for each group or a group must support c_units with some organizational means. DAISY follows the second way: a group uses a set of demons to manage interactions among c_units. A demon is a special c_unit which manages a set of interactions: it receives messages from one or more internal c_units and sends a message to one or more internal (or external) c_units.

CUBL allows to re-configure a system through the dynamic creation of c_units, through the delegation of messages and through the modification of c_unit behavior.

A c_unit may have more than one different behavior, that is, more than one way of acting in response to messages. At the beginning of its life, a c_unit starts to process messages through a script corresponding to its initial behavior, this script may contain a command to change the behavior. After the execution of that command the script corresponding to the new behavior processes the messages.

3 The agent level

The agent level corresponds to MAPL (Multiple Agent Programmer Language) [1]. MAPL offers a limited set of program constructs: sequence (*seq*), iteration (*while*), conditional (*if*), assignment (*:=*) and procedure call, and is based on an agent model implemented through c_units.

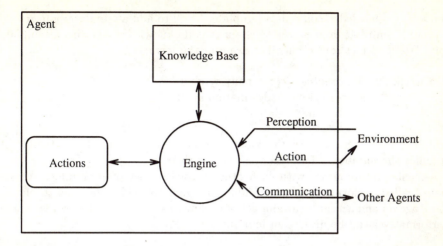

Fig. 1.: Structure of an agent.

MAPL agent model is based on three parts: a knowledge base, a set of actions, and an "engine" (see figure 1). The knowledge base maintains agent's knowledge about itself, the external environment and the other agents. The actions represent the agent's means to perceive the external world, to act on the external world and to communicate with the other agents. In particular, the actions can be divided in primitive actions (i.e., actions which can not be decomposed in other sub-actions) and complex actions (i.e., actions which are defined by the composition of other actions). The "engine" defines the behavior of the agent, that is, the way of acting in response to its knowledge and the interactions with external world (i.e., perception and communication).

How we said before, agent's knowledge base maintains agent's knowledge about itself, the external environment and the other agents. Knowledge is not static, but an agent can acquire knowledge through perception and communication with the other agents. The contents of the knowledge base is composed of two sets of elements respectively called facts and templates.

Facts represent agent's knowledge about external world and agents (beliefs), the actions to do (plans) and the results to achieve (goals). An agent manages its facts through the following four actions: *assert*, to add a fact; *query*, to get the set of facts matching a specified pattern; *delete*, to get and remove the set of facts matching a specified pattern; and *replace*, to replace a fact with a new fact. For example the form:

(query '(flight ? ? Milan Amsterdam ? "7 August 1994"))

gets all the flights that connect Milan to Amsterdam on August 7 1994 (the form ? matches any type of expression).

Templates give knowledge about the types of fact and action the agent knows. An agent manages its templates through the following four actions: *know*, to check if its knowledge contains a template; *learn*, to add a template; *unlearn*, to remove a template; and *verify*, to check that its knowledge contains a template for a specified fact (or action). For example the form:

```
(learn '(flight (flnum integer) (company symbol)
                (source symbol) (destination symbol)
                (fltime time) (fldate date)))
```

adds the flight template to the knowledge base of an agent. In particular, it specifies the number of fact components and their type.

Agents communicate with each other through a set of communicative actions, called performatives, which allow an agent to send a message to one or more agents and accept a variable set of parameters indexed by keywords. These performatives can be divided in four sub-sets:

1. performatives to interact with the knowledge of the other agents (*ask*, *inform*, *retract*, *subscribe* and *unsubscribe*).
2. performatives to commit other agents to the performance of a future action (*request*, *unrequest*, *commit* and *uncommit*).
3. performatives to accept or to reject performatives (*accept* and *reject*).
4. performatives to manage multi-message interactions (*ready*, *next*, *rest*, *discard* and *eos*).

The "engine" defines the behavior of the agent, that is, the way of acting in response to its own knowledge and external stimuli received through perception and communication. The behavior of an agent is a little different from the behavior of a c_unit. In fact, an agent is initially *sleeping* and becomes *active* when it receives a message. The agent starts a task to serve the message and goes on until either the task ends or the task needs to stop in order to wait for another message. The messages which arrive while the agent is *active* are queued and served in FIFO order. If the task needs a message, the agent becomes *waiting* if there are not any message in the queue, else it starts a new task which serves the first message of the queue. This new task goes on until it ends or until it needs a message. When it is *waiting*, it waits for the first message; if this message is the waited message, then it restarts the stopped task, otherwise it starts a new task serving the arrived message. When all the tasks are terminated and the queue is empty, the agent becomes *sleeping* again.

In a multi-agent system, agents can perform different tasks to pursuit common or individual goals. These tasks can compete for some resources or can be interdepended and thus there is a good change that deadlocks raise among agents. Multi-tasking allows an agent to start new tasks while is waiting for some resources and/or for the end of some other tasks. On the one hand, multi-tasking allows an agent to survive a deadlock because the agent can perform new activities even if an its task is blocked. On the other hand, multi-tasking may free an agent from a deadlock because the new tasks may help in releasing the waited resources and in terminating the waited tasks.

4 Two examples

Let us introduce the following airline reservation scenario[1]:

there is a customer that must book a seat on a flight from Milan to
Amsterdam on August 7 1994. Therefore, he goes to the airline office
and negotiates the booking with an airline clerk. Initially, the customer
asks the clerk the flights from Milan to Amsterdam on August 7 1994.
The clerk informs him there are three flights: the first at 7.05, the second
at 10.30, and the third at 16.40. The customer asks if it is possible to
book a seat on the flight at 10.30. The clerk answers that it is not possible
because the flight is full. The customer asks if it is possible to book a seat
on the flight at 7.05. The clerk answers that it is possible. The customer
asks the clerk to book the seat on that flight. The clerk does it and
confirms it to the customer.

This scenario is easily modeled through DAISY. In particular, the airline
clerk and customer are represented by the following two agent classes:

```
(defclass airline_clerk (agent)
  symbol behavior := 'clerk_engine;
  bool clerk_engine(msg inmsg)
    (seq (symbol customer, label; list flinfo;)
      (if (received inmsg
           '(?.customer ask ? (flight +.flinfo) :reply_with ?.label))
        (inform customer (query (cons 'flight flinfo)) :in_reply_to label)
      (if (received inmsg
           '(?.customer request ? (book (flight +.flinfo)) :reply_with ?.label))
        (if (is_free_seat (cons 'flight flinfo))
          (accept customer :in_reply_to label)
          (reject customer :in_reply_to label)))
      (if (received inmsg
           '(?.customer commit ? (book (flight +.flinfo)) :reply_with ?.label))
        (if (assign_seat (cons 'flight flinfo))
          (accept customer :in_reply_to label)
          (reject customer :in_reply_to label)))))
```

---

[1] This example derives from one presented in [20].

```
(defclass airline_customer (agent)
  symbol behavior := 'cust_engine;
  bool cust_engine(msg inmsg)
    (seq ()
      ... some code ...
      (:= flights (ask airline_clerk flight_desc
                    :reply_with 'flights :comm 'blocking))
      (if flights
        (seq (bool asserted := FALSE; list bestflight;)
          (while (and flights (not asserted))
            (:= bestflight (best_flight flights))
            (remove bestflight flights)
            (if (received (request clerk (cons 'book bestflight)
                :reply_with 'reqbooking :comm 'blocking) '(accept +))
              (if (received (commit clerk (cons 'book bestflight)
                  :reply_with 'combooking :comm 'blocking) '(accept +))
                (:= asserted (assert (cons 'booked bestflight))))))))))
      ... some code ... )
)
```

where: i) *behavior* is a variable of the class indicating the name of the current behavior (i.e., the name of the "engine" procedure); ii) a msg corresponds to a message and is represented by a list composed of the name of the sender, the type of performative and the body of the performative; iii) the forms *?.customer* and *?.label* match any type of expression and bind it respectively to the variables *customer* and *label*; iv) the form *+* matches one or more expressions; v) the form *+.flinfo* matches one or more expressions, stores them into a list and binds the list to the variable *flinfo*; vi) *received* is a boolean predicate which accepts two arguments, a message and a pattern, and whose value is true if the message matches the pattern; and vii) the couple *:comm 'blocking* indicates a blocking performative, that is, the performative sends the message, waits for the answer and returns the answer.

The dialogue of the previous scenario can be described as follows:

```
customer:      (ask airline_clerk
                 '(flight ? ? Milan Amsterdam ? "7 August 1994")
                 :reply_with 'flights
                 :comm 'blocking)

airline_clerk: (inform customer
                 '(flight 234 AZ Milan Amsterdam 7.05 "7 August 1994")
                 '(flight 345 KLM Milan Amsterdam 10.30 "7 August 1994")
                 '(flight 456 AZ Milan Amsterdam 16.40 "7 August 1994")
                 :in_reply_to 'flights)
```

```
customer:      (request airline_clerk
                  '(book
                      (flight 345 KLM Milan Amsterdam
                          10.30 "7 August 1994"))
                  :reply_with 'reqbooking
                  :comm 'blocking)

airline_clerk: (reject customer
                  :in_reply_to 'reqbooking
                  :reason 'no_seats)

customer:      (request airline_clerk
                  '(book
                      (flight 234 AZ Milan Amsterdam
                          7.05 "7 August 1994"))
                  :reply_with 'reqbooking
                  :comm 'blocking)

airline_clerk: (accept customer
                  :in_reply_to 'reqbooking)

customer:      (commit airline_clerk
                  '(book
                      (flight 234 AZ Milan Amsterdam
                          7.05 "7 August 1994"))
                  :reply_with 'combooking
                  :comm 'blocking)

airline_clerk: (accept customer
                  :in_reply_to 'combooking)
```

As second example, let us introduce the following manufacturing plant scenario:

there is a manager that accepts product orders, schedules their manufacture and informs customers about the time in which orders will be satisfied. Each manufacture is divided in a set of tasks which can be performed by different robots. The manager knows it and tries to satisfy order as soon as possible. At this purpose, he negotiates with the robots to assign tasks.

This scenario also is easily modeled through DAISY. In particular, the manager is represented by the following agent class:

```
(defclass manager (agent)
  symbol behavior := 'manager_engine;
  bool manager_engine(msg inmsg)
    (seq (symbol customer, label, product;)
      (if (received inmsg
           '(?.customer request ? (order ?.product) :answer time
             :reply_with ?.label))
        (seq (symbol task, robot; int bttime, bptime; list tasks, robots;)
          (:= bptime 0)
          (:= tasks (get_tasks (query (list 'tasks product '?))))
          (while tasks
          (:= task (first tasks))
          (:= tasks (rest tasks))
          (:= robots (get_robots (query (list 'robots task '?))))
          (seq (int bttime, ttime;)
            (:= bttime 0)
            (while robots
              (:= robot (first robots))
              (:= robots (rest robots))
              (:= ttime
                (get_answer (request robot (list 'do task) :answer 'time
                     :reply_with task :comm 'blocking)))
              (if (or (= bttime 0) (¡ ttime bttime))
                (:= bttime ttime)))
            (if (or (= bptime 0) (¡ bttime bptime))
              (:= bptime bttime))))
          (accept customer :answer bptime :in_reply_to label)))
    )
)
```

note the code of manager_engine has been simplified by supposing that all the tasks of each product may be performed in parallel.

5 Comparison with related works

The two programming levels of DAISY have a lot of relationships with some other object-oriented and agent-oriented programming languages.

CUBL shows some similarities with ABCL [25], ORG [11], PANDORA II [14], the Actor languages [2] and April [15].

C_unit model derives mainly from the active object model of ABCL [25]. In fact, it uses the same centralized concurrency control which is based on the script and has the same behavior, that is, it is based on the *sleeping, active* and *waiting* modes.

The group of CUBL derives from Hewitt's ORG [11] and the group of PAN-DORA II [14]. In fact, the group of CUBL offers the same services offered by an ORG (i.e., membership, external interface and internal organization), but, while external interface of an ORG has a distributed management (e.g., external communications are managed by special handlers), the external interface of a group of CUBL is directly managed by the group itself. Moreover, the group of CUBL has the same dynamic organization of the group of PANDORA II which allows the migration of a c_unit from a group to another.

The means used by CUBL to re-configure a system are similar to the ones used by Actor languages [2]. However, while an actor changes its behavior delegating the service of the next messages to another actor (the replacement actor), a c_unit changes its behavior using another script to process the next messages. That is, while in an actor language the possible behaviors are given by a set of actors, in CUBL the possible behaviors are given by a set of procedures. This solution has the advantage that it is never necessary to move state information from an object to another when a c_unit changes its behavior.

CUBL shares with April the use of a smooth interface to standard programming languages. However, while April is interfaced with C programming language, CUBL is interfaced with C, C++ and CLOS programming languages.

MAPL shows some similarities with the agent model developed at LIFIA [5], Agentspeak [23], Agent0 [20] and KQML [7].

MAPL agent model is quite similar to the one developed at LIFIA. In fact, both the two agents are implemented on the active object model and have the same structure which is based on a knowledge base, a set of actions (capabilities), and an engine (control structure). Moreover, MAPL agent model has some similarities with the agent model of Agentspeak [23]. In fact, Agentspeak database relations have a form similar to MAPL facts, but while database relations allow the separation between private and public knowledge (i.e., available outside the agent), MAPL adds templates to check and to dynamically modify the types of fact which are known by an agent. The set of Agentspeak plans is equivalent to the set of MAPL actions. Agentspeak communicative actions also are based on *speech act theory*, but allow only to inform and send asynchronous and synchronous requests of actions.

The set of performatives of MAPL derives from both Agent0 communicative actions and KQML performatives. On the one hand, MAPL derives the set of performatives for negotiation from Agent0. On the other hand, MAPL derives from KQML the possibility of broadcasting, the large set of means for knowledge exchange, and the use of keywords to identify the different parameters of a performative (it allows the management of a large set of optional parameters).

6   Conclusions

This paper has presented an object-oriented distributed system, called DAISY (Distributed Artificial Intelligence SYstem), for the development of multi-agent systems which is based on an object-oriented programming language, called CUBL, and on an agent-oriented programming language, called MAPL. While CUBL offers a large set of "low level" programming means, MAPL offers a limited set of "high level" programming means to model agents implemented on CUBL classes and procedures.

The main reason of the presence of two programming languages is to allow two different programming levels. At the object level, the programmer can define a new agent specializing the components of an agent, for example, specializing the internal structure of its knowledge base, the interface of its knowledge base, that is, the actions to manage it, and the communication protocol, that is, the performatives. At the agent level, the programmer can define a new agent modifying the initial knowledge of an agent or its way to act in response to a message, that is, modifying the initial facts and templates and the engine of the agent.

Besides the two programming languages, DAISY offers a graphical user interface to interacts with the different parts of a distributed program and browse classes, and environments to experiments algorithms and to simulate systems.

Some prototypes of DAISY have been built on the basis of different implementations of CUBL developed in CLOS and in C++. Some of these implementations allows the physical distribution of c_units on a network of UNIX workstations and transputers. In that network, c_units running on the same machine communicate via procedure call, c_units running on different machines communicate via UNIX sockets and transputers communication primitives. In these prototypes, an executable program is built through two phases of parsing (from MAPL to CUBL and from CUBL to CLOS or C++), a compilation (CLOS code can be directly executed by Lisp interpreter), and the loading or linking of CLOS and C++ libraries containing an implementation of MAPL agent model. Moreover, these prototypes allow agents to use pieces of code written directly in CLOS and C++ and to execute operating system calls.

DAISY is actually used for the experimentation of systems in the field of the scheduling board problem. Future research directions are: i) the modification of agent's engine to support task interruption when a higher priority task must be executed, and ii) its use to develop and experiment distributed planning systems.

Acknowledgements

Thanks to Giovanni Adorni, who encouraged and helped me to start and, after, to improve this system through his comments. Special thanks to Michele Ampollini, Alberto Gabitto, Matteo Fontanesi and Anchise Grandi, who contributed to the implementation of some parts of the systems.

The work has been partially supported by National Research Council through "Progetto Finalizzato Trasporti" (EUREKA PROMETHEUS project) and by MURST 40% through the grant "Sistemi Intelligenti".

References

1. G. Adorni and A. Poggi. MAP - a language for the modelling of multi agent systems. In P. Torasso, editor, *Advances in Artificial Intelligence - Lecture Notes on Artificial Intelligence*, volume 728, pages 154–159, Berlin, 1993. Springer Verlag Publ.

2. G. Agha. *Actors, A Model of Concurrent Computation in Distributed Systems.* The MIT Press, Cambridge, MA, 1986.

3. G. Agha and C Hewitt. Concurrent programming using actors. In A. Yonezawa and M. Tokore, editors, *Object-Oriented Concurrent Programming*, pages 37–53, Cambridge, MA, 1987. MIT Press.

4. A.H. Bond and L. Gasser. *Readings in Distributed Artificial Intelligence.* Morgan Kaufmann, San Mateo, CA, 1988.

5. E. Cardozo, J.S. Sichman, and Y. Demazeau. Using the active object model to implement multi-agent systems. In *Proc. 5nd Conference on Tools for AI*, pages 70–77, Boston, MA, 1993.

6. B. Chaib-draa, R. Mandiau, and P. Millot. Distributed Artificial Intelligence: An annotated bibliography. *SIGART Bulletin*, 3(3):20–37, 1992.

7. T. Finin, J. Weber, G. Wiederhold, M. Genesereth, R. Fritzson, D. McKay, J. McGuire, P. Pelavin, S. Shapiro, and C. Beck. Specification of the KQML agent-communication language. Technical Report EIT TR 92-04, Enterprise Integration Technologies, Palo Alto, CA, 1992.

8. M. Fisher. Representing and executing agent-based systems. In this volume.

9. L. Gasser, C. Braganza, and N. Herman. Implementing Distributed Artificial Intelligence systems using MACE. In *Proc. of the Third IEEE Conference on Artificial Intelligence Applications*, pages 315–320, 1987.

10. L. Gasser and M.N. Huhns. *Distributed Artificial Intelligence*, volume 2. Pitman, London, UK, 1989.

11. C. Hewitt and J. Inman. DAI betwixt and between: From intelligent agents to open systems science. *IEEE Trans. on SMC*, 21(6):1409–1419, 1991.

12. Y. Honda and A. Yonezawa. Debugging concurrent systems based on object groups. In A. Yonezawa, editor, *ABCL: An Object-Oriented Concurrent System*, pages 119–132, Cambridge, MA, 1990. The MIT Press.

13. M.N. Huhns. *Distributed Artificial Intelligence.* Pitman, London UK, 1987.

14. T. Maruichi, M. Ichikawa, and M. Tokoro. Modeling autonomous agents and their groups. In Y. Demazeau and J.P. Muller, editors, *Decentralized A.I.*, pages 215–234, Amsterdam, The Netherlands, 1990. North Holland.

15. F.G. McCabe and K.L. Clark. April - Agent PRocess Interaction Language. In this volume.

16. T.A. Montgomery and E.H. Durfee. Using MICE to study intelligent dynamic coordination. In *Proc. 2nd Conference on Tools for AI*, pages 215–220, 1990.

17. A. Poggi. Agents and resources management with CUBL. In *Proc. HICSS '94*, pages 112–121, Maui, HI, 1994.

18. J.S. Rosenschein and M.R. Genesereth. Deals among rational agents. In *Proc. IJCAI-85*, pages 91–99, Los Angeles, CA, 1985.

19. J.R. Searle. *Speech Acts: An Essay in the Philosophy of Language.* Cambridge University Press, Cambridge, UK, 1969.

20. Y. Shoham. Agent Oriented Programming. *Artificial Intelligence*, 60(1):51–92, 1993.

21. S.R. Thomas. PLACA, an agent oriented programming language. Technical Report STAN-CS-93-1487, Stanford University, Stanford, CA, 1993.

22. M. Tokoro and Y. Ishikawa. An object-oriented approach to knowledge systems. In *Proc. of the International Conference on Fifth Generation Computation Systems*, pages 623–631, 1984.

23. D. Weerasooriya, A. Rao, and K. Ramamohanarao. Design of a concurrent agent-oriented language. In this volume.

24. M.J. Wooldridge and N.R. Jennings. Agent theories, architectures, and languages: a survey. In this volume.

25. A. Yonezawa. *ABCL: An Object-Oriented Concurrent System*. The MIT Press, Cambridge, MA, 1990.

The PLACA Agent Programming Language

S. Rebecca Thomas *

University of Northern Iowa, Cedar Falls, IA 50614-0507, USA

Abstract. The fundamental idea underlying agent-oriented programming (AOP) [14] is that agents are modeled in terms of their "mental states" (consisting in this work of beliefs, plans, capabilities, and intentions), both by other agents and by their designers and programmers. An agent program gives the agent's initial mental state and rules describing a transition function: given an agent's current state and input, the rules specify its new state and output. An agent's communicative acts, then, are actions that affect the mental states of the agents involved, just as physical actions affect the agent's physical environment.

We present and discuss a new agent-oriented programming language, PLACA, a descendant of AGENT0 [14]. Unlike AGENT0, PLACA capitalizes on agents' planning abilities. Assuming that all agents have at least elementary planning abilities, PLACA agents can make high-level requests of each other without worrying about how these requests will be carried out. We describe PLACA, show a short example program, briefly describe a PLACA interpreter, and discuss the mental states of agents.

1 Introduction

Agents in a shared environment will often need to coordinate among themselves, for example to share resources flexibly. If agents are to be autonomous and taskable, this flexibility can be increased if coordination is decentralized and done "on the fly." This requires that agents communicate with each other. It is commonly argued that efficient, flexible communication requires that agents model each other's beliefs and plans; we believe that reasoning about capabilities is also important.

In [14], Shoham defines agent-oriented programming (AOP), a programming paradigm in which agents are modeled in terms of their mental states (beliefs, capabilities, and so on). Agent's programs are transition functions on these mental states; given an agent's current mental state and input, the transition function specifies the agent's new mental state and output. In the same paper, Shoham describes a very simple AOP language called AGENT0. The mental states of AGENT0 agents consist of beliefs, capabilities, and obligations (to

---

* This material is based in part on work supported under a National Science Foundation Graduate Fellowship. Any opinions, findings, conclusions, or recommendations expressed in this paper are those of the author and do not necessarily reflect the views of the National Science Foundation.

carry out primitive actions). These agents can communicate information and requests (again, to carry out primitive actions) to other agents.

The work presented here was motivated by a particular weakness of AGENT0. In AGENT0, both the capabilities of agents and the requests agents make of each other may refer only to primitive actions[2]. That is, one agent cannot request of another that some state of affairs be achieved, say, that a door be open. Instead, the requesting agent must generate an appropriate plan for achieving the desired state of affairs. It must then, for each component action (moving to the door, grasping the doorknob, and so on), make a separate request of the second agent that it perform that action. This is clearly an inefficient use of both the requesting agent's computational resources and the communication bandwidth available (since many requests must be made when one could do). Furthermore, such a communicated plan is inherently fragile, because the agent carrying out the plan does not know the plan's purpose and therefore cannot recover from an unforeseen failure of part of the plan. This shortcoming is not inherent in Shoham's conception of agent oriented programming. One motivation of the work described here is to design a new AOP language that overcomes this weakness of AGENT0 by allowing agents to communicate and reason about higher-level goals, leaving the planning for each goal to the agent who has adopted it. This new language is called PLACA ("PLAnning Communicating Agents").

Our work on PLACA [16], like Shoham's work on AGENT0, addresses both agent theory and agent programming. In this paper we focus on the agent programming aspect of the work, but the two aspects of the work are interrelated. Our theoretical work seeks to address questions such as, What components of the mental state are necessary for agents who can communicate about their plans and goals? Will this kind of communication in fact be useful? What kinds of communicative actions will such agents need to be able to perform? What are the relationships among the components of an agent's mental state? As our ideas on these questions progressed, we continually evaluated them by embedding our new versions of the mental state in the programming language PLACA[3]. By writing small PLACA programs, we could see shortcomings of our agent theory; revision of the theory led to revision of the programming language. Eventually we implemented an interpreter for a subset of the PLACA language and wrote agent programs in two simple domains, as a somewhat more stringent test of our theory. The results of this theoretical work, reported in [16], include a logic for representing beliefs, capabilities, plans, and intentions in a unified framework. The result of the agent programming work is the programming language PLACA, which is reported here.

This paper begins with a description of agent programs and PLACA. Section 3 presents a short example PLACA program; this is followed in Section 4 by discussion of an interpreter for PLACA. The next section discusses the components

---

[2] To be fair, AGENT0 was meant to be an extremely simple language, and no claims were made about its generality.

[3] PLACA is very much like AGENT0 in syntax and semantics; the main difference is the difference in the mental state.

of the mental states of PLACA agents, and the paper closes with some general discussion and description of related work.

2   Agent Programs

An agent's program provides the connection among the agent's internal state, the input it receives, and its behavior. It specifies not only when and how the agent will perform actions in the world but also when and how the agent will communicate with other agents and when and how its mental state will change.

A PLACA program has the following components:

1. an initial mental state (which must be consistent with our formal semantics for the mental state, as described in [16]; some important points will be described here):
   (a) a list of capabilities
   (b) a (consistent) list of initial beliefs
   (c) a (consistent) list of initial intentions
   (d) implicitly, an empty set of initial plans
2. a list of mental-change rules (see Section 2.1)

Formally, the mental state is described in a propositional temporal language, extended with a modal operator for each component of the mental state. Here, we will not go into detail about the exact form of this language. Those who are interested may consult [16]. Although we say above that the agent program specifies the agent's initial mental state, actually it specifies the agent's *model* of its own initial mental state. Take for example the agent's capabilities. Our formal definition of capability concerns whether it is true *in the world* that an agent can perform a certain action or can achieve a given state of affairs, but there is no requirement that an agent have perfect information about its own capabilities. The agent can only reason about its *beliefs* about its capabilities. We assume, though, that agents do know about their own plans and intentions.

The beliefs and intentions discussed here are to be understood as they are typically used in the literature. That is, the agent's beliefs record the information that the agent has about itself, its environment, and other agents. Its intentions are sentences that the agent has chosen to work towards making true, and that the agent is committed to (as described in [6, 2]). The above-mentioned list of capabilities is a list of (action precond-list) pairs, where the action is a primitive action (that is, it can be carried out in one unit of time) and the precond-list of zero or more preconditions gives the executability-precondition(s) of the action[4].

---

[4] By executability-precondition, I mean a condition that must be true for the action to be executed *at all*, not for it to have the desired effect. In [12] these are called *primary* preconditions. In [7], actions attempted when these executability-preconditions are not met are said to be unsuccessful in a strong sense, since they cannot be performed at all; if an action can be performed but fails to achieve the desired effect, it is said to be unsuccessful in a weak sense.

2.1 Mental-Change Rules

A BNF description of the PLACA language is shown in Fig. 1. The heart of a PLACA program is the collection of mental-change rules. The basic format of a mental-change rule is this:

⟨⟨message-condition⟩, ⟨mental-condition⟩, ⟨mental-changes⟩, ⟨message-list⟩⟩,

which means that if the ⟨message-condition⟩ is satisfied by the messages just received, and the ⟨mental-condition⟩ is satisfied by the agent's current mental state, then the ⟨mental-changes⟩ specified will be made to the agent's mental state, and the messages in the ⟨message-list⟩ will be sent. Any of the four parts of a mental-change rule may contain variables; variables appearing in the condition parts will be bound during matching with the mental state or messages.

At each tick of the global clock the agent checks, for each rule, whether its message-condition is satisfied by one or more of the messages just received and whether its mental-condition is satisfied by the current mental state. If so, then the agent changes its mental state as prescribed and prepares the specified outgoing messages, in both cases instantiating variables as needed. If multiple variable assignments satisfy a given rule, then it is fired once for each such assignment. All rules are checked before any rule is fired, to ensure that all mental-conditions are checked against the same mental state.

The reader may notice that the language shown in Fig. 1 is atemporal, aside from the comment that $\mathcal{L}$ is assumed to have dated sentences and action terms. That is, we assume that sentences in $\mathcal{L}$ will have times associated with them, for example (t1 (on a b)) (to be read, "at time t1, a {is, was, will be} on b") and that action terms similarly have associated times, for example (t2 (stack c d)). For PLACA constructs that are not explicitly dated, the time is implicitly *now*: the mental-condition of each mental-change rule is checked against the agent's current mental state, the mental-changes are made when the rule is fired, and the messages in the message-list are sent during the current tick of the clock. A rule may be matched by multiple messages in the same cycle, and one message may match several rules' message-conditions. Every rule is fired once for each possible match.

To clarify, let's look at a few example rules. In the following, strings that begin with the character '?' name variables, and "Fred" refers to the agent whose program includes these rules.

- ((TO Fred, FROM boss, REQUEST, ?x),
  (),
  ((ADOPT (INTEND ?x))),
  ((TO boss, FROM Fred, INFORM, (*now* (intend ?x)))))[5]
- ((TO Fred, FROM ?agent, INFORM, ?s),
  (BELIEVE (*now* (unreliable ?agent))),
  (),
  ())

---

[5] *now* refers to the current time.

⟨program⟩	= (⟨capabilities⟩, ⟨initial-beliefs⟩,
	⟨initial-intentions⟩, (⟨mental-change-rule⟩*))
⟨capabilities⟩	= (CAPABILITIES (⟨action⟩⟨sentence⟩)*)
⟨initial-beliefs⟩	= (BELIEFS ⟨ground-sentence⟩*)
⟨initial-intentions⟩	= (INTENTIONS ⟨ground-sentence⟩*)
⟨mental-change-rule⟩	= (⟨message-condition⟩, ⟨mental-condition⟩,
	⟨mental-changes⟩, ⟨message-list⟩)
⟨message-condition⟩	= ⟨message⟩ | (AND ⟨message-condition⟩ ⟨message-condition⟩+) |
	(OR ⟨message-condition⟩ ⟨message-condition⟩+) |
	(NOT ⟨message-condition⟩) | ()
⟨message⟩	= (TO ⟨agent⟩, FROM ⟨agent⟩, ⟨message-type⟩, ⟨sentence⟩)
⟨message-type⟩	= INFORM | REQUEST | UNREQUEST
⟨sentence⟩	= ⟨atomic-sentence⟩ | ⟨mental-atom⟩
⟨atomic-sentence⟩	= an atomic, unquantified sentence from the language $\mathcal{L}$ used
	to describe the agent's environment, or a sentence variable
	Each sentence is dated (see text)
⟨ground-sentence⟩	= an atomic, variable-free sentence from language $\mathcal{L}$; dated
⟨action⟩	= an action term, also from language $\mathcal{L}$; dated
⟨agent⟩	= an agent term, also from language $\mathcal{L}$
⟨mental-condition⟩	= ⟨mental-atom⟩ |
	(AND ⟨mental-condition⟩ ⟨mental-condition⟩+) |
	(OR ⟨mental-condition⟩ ⟨mental-condition⟩+) |
	(NOT ⟨mental-condition⟩) | ()
⟨mental-atom⟩	= ⟨external-atom⟩ | ⟨internal-atom⟩
⟨external-atom⟩	= (BELIEVE ⟨sentence⟩) | (INTEND ⟨sentence⟩)
⟨internal-atom⟩	= (CAN-DO ⟨action⟩) | (CAN-ACHIEVE ⟨sentence⟩) |
	(PLAN-DO ⟨action⟩) | (PLAN-NOT-DO ⟨action⟩) |
	(PLAN-ACHIEVE ⟨sentence⟩)
⟨mental-changes⟩	= (⟨change-atom⟩+) | ()
⟨change-atom⟩	= (ADOPT ⟨external-atom⟩) | (DROP ⟨external-atom⟩)
⟨message-list⟩	= (⟨message⟩+) | ()

Fig. 1. PLACA Program Specification (BNF)

```
- ((TO Fred, FROM ?ag, REQUEST, (?t (did ?act))),
  (AND (BELIEVE (*now* (friendly ?ag)))
       (NOT (PLAN-NOT-DO ((- ?t 1) ?act)))),
  ((ADOPT (INTEND (?t (did ?act))))),
  ((TO ?ag, FROM Fred, INFORM, (*now* (intend (?t (did ?act)))))))
```

The first rule says that if our agent Fred receives a message from the boss containing a request to achieve ?x (notice ?x is a dated sentence[6], so it specifies not only what is to be achieved but when), then Fred will adopt an intention to do ?x and will inform the boss of this intention. This rule's mental-condition, (),

---

[6] If ?x is a mental-atom then the date is implicitly the current time.

is always fulfilled. The second rule says that should Fred receive an informing message from an agent whom Fred believes to be currently unreliable, Fred will ignore the information thus received. The final rule says that if Fred receives a message requesting that Fred perform ?act at time (- ?t 1) (that is, that Fred make it the case that at time ?t Fred has just done the action), and Fred believes that ?ag is currently friendly and furthermore Fred hasn't already decided not to do ?act at (- t 1), then Fred will adopt an intention to do ?act, and will so inform ?ag.

3   A Simple Program

Figure 2 shows a simple program for a library helper[7]. This agent performs xeroxing tasks when requested to do so, (all requests can be read as, "Xerox this document by (time)"), giving preference to Very Important People (VIPs). Their documents will be xeroxed by the time they specify, if possible; everybody else has to wait until 5pm for their documents. The agent also responds to requests to shelve books; its deadline for shelving the books is always 6pm, no matter what the time of the request. If the librarian asks it to give shelving books priority, then it will refuse to accept xeroxing tasks from non-VIPs until all books have been shelved, at which time it will revert to normal behavior. (Note that when the librarian requests that the agent give shelving tasks priority, the agent still performs all the xeroxing tasks it has already agreed to.)

One might expect to see a rule in this program similar to the following:

```
((),
(INTEND (?t xerox-machine-on)),
((ADOPT (PLAN-DO ((- ?t 1) turn-on-xerox-machine)))),
()).
```

This brings up an important point: mental-change rules *never* modify an agent's plans or capabilities. The agent's plans are assumed to be generated and maintained by a separate planning mechanism (that has access to the mental state), which may for the purposes of this paper be regarded as a black box. Thus we separate deliberation about *which* intentions to adopt (this deliberation being controlled by the agent program) from consideration of *means* of achieving those intentions (handled by the planner). The agent's program does not change its capabilities because the agent's capabilities do not change. If a particular agent can perform the action (stack ?x ?y) if ?x and ?y are blocks, then it is always true that the agent can perform this action whenever these preconditions hold. Of course, the agent can change its ability to perform an action at a particular time by changing the veracity of its preconditions at that time. The agent's CAN-ACHIEVE capabilities are similarly fixed, because they depend on the agent's

---

[7] For the example code shown here, we adopt a slightly more compact syntax; for example, in messages we omit the "FROM" and "TO" markers for the sending and receiving agents.

```
;;; Initial mental state
(CAPABILITIES ((shelve ?x) (book ?x))
              ((xerox ?x) (document ?x))
              (turn-on-xerox-machine ()))
(BELIEFS       (0 (NOT shelving-priority))
               (0 (vip Ralph))
               (0 (vip librarian))
               (0 xerox-machine-plugged-in))
(INTENTIONS    (1 xerox-machine-on))

;;; Mental-change rules
(((library-helper ?agent REQUEST (?t (xeroxed ?thing)))        ;;message-condition
(AND (CAN-ACHIEVE (?t (xeroxed ?thing)))                       ;;mental-condition
      (NOT (BELIEVE (*now* shelving-priority)))
      (NOT (BELIEVE (*now* vip ?agent)))))
((ADOPT (INTEND (5pm (xeroxed ?thing)))))                      ;;mental-changes
((?agent library-helper INFORM (*now* (INTEND (5pm (xeroxed ?thing)))))))))
                                                               ;;message-list
;; "If someone asks you to xerox something, and you can, and you don't believe
;; that they're a VIP or that you're supposed to be shelving books, agree to
;; xerox it by 5pm."

((library-helper ?agent REQUEST (?t (xeroxed ?thing)))
(AND (CAN-ACHIEVE (?t (xeroxed ?thing))) (BELIEVE (*now* (vip ?agent))))
((ADOPT (INTEND (?t (xeroxed ?thing)))))
((?agent library-helper INFORM (*now* (INTEND (?t (xeroxed ?thing)))))))))
;; "But if they're a VIP agree to xerox it by the time they ask for."

((library-helper ?agent REQUEST (?t (xeroxed ?thing)))
(OR (NOT (CAN-ACHIEVE (?t (xeroxed ?thing))))
    (AND (BELIEVE (*now* shelving-priority))
    (NOT (BELIEVE (*now* vip ?agent))))))
()
((?agent library-helper INFORM (*now* (not (intend (?t xeroxed ?thing)))))))))
;; "If you can't xerox things, or you're supposed to be shelving, turn down the request."

((library-helper ?agent REQUEST (?t (shelved ?book)))
(CAN-ACHIEVE (?t (shelved ?book)))
((ADOPT (INTEND (6pm (shelved ?book)))))
((?agent library-helper INFORM (*now* (INTEND (6pm (shelved ?book)))))))))
;; "Whenever you can, agree to requests to shelve books and do so by 6pm."
```

Fig. 2. An example program (cont'd in Figure 3)

```
((library-helper LIBRARIAN REQUEST (?t shelving-priority))
()
((ADOPT (BELIEVE (?t shelving-priority))))
((LIBRARIAN library-helper INFORM (?t shelving-priority))))
;; "If the librarian asks you to focus on shelving books for a while, do."

(()
(BELIEVE (*now* all-books-shelved))
((DROP (BELIEVE (*now* shelving-priority))))
())
;; "Once all the books are shelved, stop focusing on shelving."
)
```

Fig. 3. An example program (cont'd from Figure 2)

CAN-DO capabilities and on the state of the environment. To return to the rule above, once the agent adopts an intention that the xerox machine be turned on, its planning mechanism will add to its plans the appropriate action. Another black-box component, the executor, is then responsible for seeing that this action gets carried out at the appropriate time.

Note that none of the domain information needed by the planner about the effects of actions is given in the agent program. In our implementation of the PLACA interpreter, this information is given directly to the planner, which we will not discuss in this paper. In general, this information would be stored with the agent's beliefs or knowledge.

4 The PLACA Interpreter

At the most basic level, a PLACA agent's computation consists of the following steps:

1. Collect messages received from other agents,
2. Update its mental state as specified in its program,
3. If sufficient time remains before the next tick of the clock, refine its plans,
4. Begin execution of the action to be performed next and return to step 1.

The PLACA interpreter, once given an agent program, executes the above loop once for each tick of the global clock[8]. The agent program specifies both the agent's initial mental state and the update function for step 2 of the above loop. The interpreter makes use of a collection of data structures that represent the mental state of an agent. (There is no requirement that the mental state be represented internally as a set of sentences in a logical language, although that is certainly one reasonable choice; an implementor is free to use any representation.) We assume that the interpreter interacts with its environment through

---

[8] Assuming a global clock simplifies the formalism discussed in [16] but is of course problematic in practice.

two buffers; the agent interpreter writes to one buffer any messages intended for other agents and all commands to its own effectors. The agent interpreter reads from the other buffer all incoming messages and information from its sensors. (Note that if we model the agent's sensors and effectors as agents in themselves, then these buffers just contain all incoming and outgoing messages from and to other agents.)

A block diagram of the PLACA interpreter is shown in Fig. 4. The ovals represent data modules and the boxes code modules. We will walk through the four steps shown above, and explain how each one is accomplished.

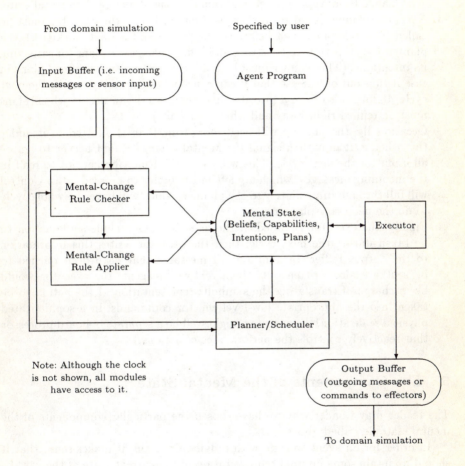

Fig. 4. A block diagram of the PLACA interpreter

1. The messages and information in the input buffer are read into an internal buffer and the input buffer is cleared. (For simplicity, the internal buffer is not shown in the diagram.)

2. The mental state is updated as follows:
   - The Mental-Change Rule Checker has access to the agent program (which contains the mental-change rules), the just-received messages, and the current mental state. It checks, for each mental-change rule, whether its conditions are currently satisfied.
   - All of the mental-change rules whose conditions are satisfied are passed (along with any variable bindings found during the matching process) to the Mental-Change Rule Applier, which makes the indicated changes to the mental state and queues up the messages to be sent. The Mental-Change Rule Applier must maintain the consistency of the mental state.
3. Next, the planner is called. If there is time left before the executor must be called (which happens just before the beginning of the next clock tick), the planner uses this time to construct and refine the agent's plans for satisfying its intentions. (The planner must be able to record partially-refined plans in case it runs out of time, so that it can continue the planning during the next cycle. It must also have a prioritizing scheme, so it can decide which plans must be refined right away and which can wait.)

   Occasionally, the planner will need more time than is allotted to it under this scheme. It may then signal the Mental-Change Rule Checker to ignore all input for the next cycle. This will cause the Rule Checker not to read in the incoming messages, which are left in the buffer to be read later. Control will fall through immediately to the planner, which will have the whole cycle to do the necessary planning.
4. Finally, the executor is called. If the agent's plans include some action to be taken during the next cycle, then the executor writes this information to the output buffer. In addition, all messages that have been queued to be sent are also written out. (In a real-world agent, the executor would be in charge of translating the symbolic representation of the action to be taken into the appropriate low-level effector commands. In a sophisticated physical realization, the executor might well be a separate onboard processor that reactively controls the performance of actions.)

5   The Components of the Mental State

The reader may wonder why we have chosen the particular components of the mental state described above.

In order for an agent to cope with a dynamic world, it makes sense that it should maintain some internal representation of the current state of the world[9], which can be updated as new information about changes in the environment arrives. Assuming the world changes with some predictability, the agent can also store and maintain predictions about the future state of the world. This information is stored in the form of the agent's *beliefs*. In many cases, it will be appropriate to provide agents with *knowledge* as well as beliefs. This allows the programmer to provide an agent with information (say domain rules) that is not defeasible. We have not incorporated knowledge into PLACA, but the extension of the programming language is straightforward, and extension of the formal model of mental states can take advantage of the fact that logical models of knowledge are widely known [8].

If an agent is to adopt new tasks dynamically, and if some of these tasks might be unanticipated by the agent's designer, then the agent must be able to reason about how to accomplish these new tasks[9]. When asked to accept a new task, the agent must perform two kinds of reasoning: deliberating about *whether* to take on the new task, and (if the agent decides to do so) about *how* to accomplish it. Following [3], we separate these two kinds of reasoning. The tasks an agent has decided to accept become that agent's *intentions*; once an agent has adopted an intention it must develop a *plan* for achieving that intention. Following Bratman [2], when we say that an agent has a plan, we mean not just that it has developed a way of achieving some goal, but that it means to carry out the required actions. A PLACA program specifies the criteria by which agents make the first kind of decision, about whether to adopt a new task; the planner is responsible for the second kind of decision.

The content of an intention is a statement to be made true, not an action to be done[10]. Plans, however, come in two kinds: plans to perform some action and plans to achieve some state of the world. The distinction is one of degree rather than of kind; a plan to perform a primitive action is a plan to achieve the state in which the action has just been performed. We find the distinction useful, however, since plans to achieve must be refined into lower-level plans while plans to do need no further refinement.

In developing a plan for achieving some goal, our agent will naturally need to reason about its own *capabilities*, since developing a plan that it cannot execute is no better, practically speaking, than not developing a plan at all. In cases where different agents have different areas of expertise, or different physical capabilities, the agent may need to request help from other agents in order to achieve all of its goals, and so it will need to reason about the capabilities of other agents as well. Otherwise it will waste time asking, for example, a plumber agent to help it with electrical wiring. As was the case with plans, we separate the capability to perform a primitive action from the capability to achieve some state of the world, and define the latter in terms of the former. Whether an agent can perform a given action depends on both the physical abilities of the agent's effectors and the state of the world. An agent with no grasping effector cannot grasp a block, and even an agent with a grasping effector cannot grasp a block that is in a different room from the effector. Whether an agent can bring about a state of the world is more complicated: it depends on whether the agent can perform the requisite actions or cause them to be performed by other agents, and whether the agent can ensure that those actions will be performable at the appropriate times.

---

[9] Obviously, this claim is controversial; see [5, 1, 4].

[10] However, as a special case, one can always intend to make it the case that an action has been performed.

The reader will notice that no social attitudes, such as mutual beliefs or joint intentions, have been included in this model. They have been omitted not because they are considered unimportant, but because it seemed at the outset of this work that one ought to concentrate on getting the asocial attitudes right first, and then move on to the social attitudes. Furthermore, it may be that all the social attitudes can be defined in terms of asocial attitudes, as for example mutual belief has been defined in terms of (a fixed point equation involving) individuals' beliefs [8]. Work thus far has focussed on domains in which agents are largely autonomous and in which only minimal interaction is required during plan execution. In these domains, on simple problems, joint intentions and mutual beliefs have not been required.

To summarize, an agent's mental state consists of the following components: beliefs about the world, capabilities to perform actions and to achieve states of affairs, plans to perform actions and to achieve states of affairs, and intentions to bring about states of affairs.

6 Discussion

The programming language presented in this paper models agents in terms of their "mental states," that is, in terms of their beliefs, capabilities, plans, and intentions. In [16], we give a formal definition of these components of the mental state. We require that the mental states of our agents be consistent with this formal model. This places conditions on the design of agents and on the design of legal PLACA interpreters. While space does not permit a full description of the formal model or of these conditions, we can give illustrative examples.

As a first example, it is an axiom of our logic that if an agent plans to achieve some proposition, then it must believe that it plans to achieve that proposition. That is, agents have positive introspection about their own plans to achieve propositions. An implemented agent that lacked positive introspection about its own plans, then, would not be a legal PLACA agent. Similarly, it is an axiom of the logic that if an agent can perform an action a, then it is capable of achieving the truth of the sentence did(a), which states that the agent has done a. This is mere common sense. Many of the axioms are, like this one, not unduly restrictive on the space of possible agent designs.

In addition to the requirement that any legal PLACA interpreter must obey and enforce the axioms of our logic, we place some extra conditions on a legal interpreter. We require that whenever an agent adopts a new intention, it must eventually create a plan for achieving the intended result, or else give up the intention. (This requirement is based on the work on commitment described in [6].) At the worst, since the intended state of affairs is to be achieved at a particular time, once that time has passed it is too late. Either the intention has been achieved, or it has become impossible. In practice, we must do better than this; the agent must develop a plan for achieving its intention in time to execute the plan. If it realizes this to be impossible, it must give up its intention. A second additional requirement on legal interpreters is that an agent's beliefs and intentions should change only as necessary to (1) make the changes specified by rules that are fired, or (2) maintain consistency of the mental state overall. Plans will change somewhat more freely than either beliefs or intentions, as the planning subsystem may modify the agent's plans at any time in order to increase efficiency or otherwise improve the agent's performance.

The relationship between the logical model of mental states presented in [16] and the programming language presented here is not formally specified. Some argue (see for example the papers by Fisher and by Wooldridge and Jennings in this volume) that the relationship should be much tighter, and that it would be ideal for the language to execute the logic. We believe this is a reasonable approach but not the only one. Drawbacks of the executable-logic approach include the notorious inefficiency of logic programming languages. Execution of logics can of course be made more efficient, but at the cost of reducing other desirable properties such as expressibility or modularity.

The relationship between our logical model and our programming language is twofold. First, the theory grounds the mental-state terminology of the programming language; it specifies the properties that e.g. beliefs of an implemented PLACA agent must have (for example, they must be consistent and they must include the agent's own plans). Second, the theory specifies the *static* properties of the mental state but makes no commitment about its *dynamic* properties. The logic says nothing about how an agent's current beliefs, intentions, and plans are related to its past or future beliefs, intentions, or plans[11]. The programming language, conversely, specifies only the dynamic properties of the mental state, in particular of the beliefs and intentions. (The plans, you will recall, are maintained separately by the planner.)

One advantage of separating the logical model of mental states from the programming language is methodological. Working on these two pieces in parallel provides the developer with two sources of constraints. On the one hand, the logic should be expressive and comprehensible, with reasonably intuitive and theoretically elegant semantics. The programming language should also be expressive, comprehensible, intuitive, and elegant, but a logic with intuitive semantics may not give a programming language that is equally intuitive to programmers. A developer of a logical programming language can similarly consider it from these two points of view, but the two points of view are less distinct and thus the mutually-constraining nature of parallel development may be lost.

7 Related Work

Shoham discussed the similarities of agent-oriented programming and object-oriented programming (and Hewitt's Actors formalism [9]) in [14]. To paraphrase, AOP can be seen as a specialization of OOP, where we have "agents" in place of objects, and the internal states of these agents are constrained to be "mental states" as described above. Currently, there are no good analogues in

---

[11] The logic does however specify some of the agent's current *beliefs* about its own past or future mental state.

AOP for the classes and inheritance of OOP. In AOP, messages are categorized into types corresponding to types of speech acts.

In [15] Tan and Weihmayer discuss a framework for cooperative problem solving which integrates Agent Oriented Programming with planning. Specifically, the AOP language AGENT0 was integrated with the PRODIGY planner [11]. Their thesis is that in separating communication concerns from the agents' local problem-solving abilities, we allow increased agent heterogeneity, since only the communication language needs to be mutually understandable. We agree with this basic idea. Our system differs from theirs in several ways. Most importantly, for them, planning occurs directly as a result of firing a "commitment rule" (the AGENT0 version of mental-change rules) and therefore is not interruptible; planning behaves like a single primitive action. Since many rules may fire during one cycle, many of these planning processes may be triggered. On a single-processor machine, this means that the cycle must be quite long if all planning processes are to be finished within one tick of the clock. Alternatively, our assumption that there is some global clock could be relaxed, and each agent could run its own clock at any speed it wants. This, however, would complicate our formal model.

This work has been strongly influenced by the work of Cohen and Levesque on intention [6], especially their ideas on the role of commitment to one's intentions. We take from their work as well the conditions under which an agent may drop a commitment. Our logical model of agents' mental states differs from theirs in a number of ways; we will mention two. They use a linear-time temporal model with temporal modal operators (such as next-time, every-subsequent-time, etc.), while we use a branching-time model with explicit dates; this difference is probably mostly a matter of taste. Cohen and Levesque enforce *realism* (the requirement that an agent's goals be consistent with its beliefs) with the axiom $BEL(\Phi) \rightarrow GOAL(\Phi)$. That is, the agent's consistent set of goals includes all its beliefs; it can't have a goal that's inconsistent with what it believes will be true. We require instead that $PLAN\text{-}ACH(\Phi) \rightarrow BEL(\Phi)$. That is, an agent that has adopted a plan for achieving Φ believes that it will succeed in doing so. This seems to us a sensible intuition; the agent may be wrong in believing that its plan will succeed, but by and large in its subsequent reasoning it will assume its success. We should note that we place fairly strict conditions on plans; if an agent has a plan to achieve Φ then it has worked out a plan that it believes it can successfully carry out no matter what other agents do in the meantime.

In [13], Rao and Georgeff present a model of beliefs, goals, and intentions. For them, the agent's goals are a consistent subset of its desires, and these goals must be consistent with the agent's beliefs. Specifically, the agent must believe that its goals are achievable, if all agents act in the appropriate ways. Rao and Georgeff call this *strong realism*. The agent's intentions, then, are the goals that it has committed itself to achieving. Rao and Georgeff's model has at least two advantages over ours: its model of intentions avoids the "side-effect problem" [13, 10], and they have a model for the dynamics of intention, while our model is static. However, their model omits explicit mention of capability and has no analogue to our plans.

Konolige and Pollack [10] present a model of beliefs and intentions that, by using a nonnormal modal operator for intentions, avoids the side-effect problem. It also allows the representation of the structure of an agent's intentions. Specifically, some intentions arise as a means of achieving others, and their formalism allows for this structure to be modeled.

8 Conclusion

We have presented an agent-oriented programming language called PLACA. In PLACA, agents are modeled in terms of their mental states, that is, in terms of their beliefs, capabilities, plans, and intentions. Elsewhere we have given a formal specification of the mental state; all legal PLACA agents must obey the axioms of this formal specification.

A PLACA program consists mainly of a list of mental-change rules that specify the conditions under which an agent should communicate and under which it should modify its beliefs and/or intentions. The agent's capabilities and plans are not changed by the agent program for reasons described earlier.

References

1. Philip E. Agre and David Chapman. Pengi: An implementation of a theory of activity. In *Proceedings of the Sixth National Conference on Artificial Intelligence*, pages 268–272, 1987.
2. Michael E. Bratman. *Intention, Plans, and Practical Reason*. Harvard University Press, Cambridge, MA, 1987.
3. Michael E. Bratman, David J. Israel, and Martha E. Pollack. Plans and resource-bounded practical reasoning. *Computational Intelligence*, 4(4):349–355, November 1988.
4. Rodney A. Brooks. Intelligence without representation. *Artificial Intelligence*, 47(1–3):139–59, January 1991.
5. David Chapman and Philip E. Agre. Abstract reasoning as emergent from concrete activity. In Michael P. Georgeff and Amy L. Lansky, editors, *Reasoning About Actions and Plans: Proceedings of the 1986 Workshop*, pages 411–424, 1986.
6. Philip R. Cohen and Hector J. Levesque. Intention is choice with commitment. *Artificial Intelligence*, 42(3):213–261, 1989.
7. M. Gelfond, V. Lifschitz, and A. Rabinov. What are the limitations of the situation calculus? In *Working Notes: AAAI Spring Symposium Series, Symposium on Logical Formalizations of Commonsense Reasoning*, pages 59–69, 1991.
8. Joseph Y. Halpern and Yoram Moses. A guide to completeness and complexity for modal logics of knowledge and belief. *Artificial Intelligence*, 54(3):319–379, 1992.
9. Carl Hewitt. Viewing control structures as patterns of passing messages. *Artificial Intelligence*, 8:323–364, 1977.
10. Kurt Konolige and Martha E. Pollack. A representationalist theory of intention. In *Proceedings of the International Joint Conference on Artificial Intelligence*, 1993.
11. Steven Minton, Craig A. Knoblock, Daniel R. Kuokka, Yolanda Gil, Robert L. Joseph, and Jaime G. Carbonell. Prodigy 2.0: The manual and tutorial. Technical Report CMU-CS-89-146, Carnegie Mellon University, 1989.

12. Edwin Pednault. Extending conventional planning techniques to handle actions with context-dependent effects. In *Proceedings of the National Conference on Artificial Intelligence*, pages 55–59, 1988.

13. Anand S. Rao and Michael P. Georgeff. Modeling rational agents within a BDI-architecture. In James Allen, Richard Fikes, and Erik Sandewall, editors, *Principles of Knowledge Representation and Reasoning: Proceedings of the Second International Conference*, pages 473–484, 1991.

14. Yoav Shoham. Agent-oriented programming. *Artificial Intelligence*, 60(1):51–92, March 1993.

15. Ming Tan and Robert Weihmayer. Integrating agent-oriented programming and planning for cooperative problem solving. In *Notes from the AAAI-92 Workshop on Cooperation among Heterogeneous Intelligent Systems*, 1992.

16. S. Rebecca Thomas. *PLACA, An Agent Oriented Programming Language*. PhD thesis, Stanford University, 1993. Available as Stanford University Computer Science Department Technical Report STAN-CS-93-1487.

Roles, Skills and Behaviour: a Situated Action Approach to Organising Systems of Interacting Agents

Peter Wavish and Michael Graham

Interactive Systems Group, Philips Research Laboratories,
Redhill, Surrey, RH1 5HA, UK.

Abstract. This paper describes a three-layer model for organising systems of interacting agents based on situated action. The top layer of the model consists of agents performing roles, the middle layer provides the skills which agents need to perform their roles, and the bottom layer consists of the behaviours which are needed to realise these skills. The model is realised computationally by means of a production rule language called RTA which is compiled to an efficient asynchronous digital logic circuit representation so allowing multi-agent simulations to operate in real time.

1 Introduction

The standard artificial intelligence approach to agent design is based on the assumption that an agent's actions are primarily determined by explicit symbolic representations of its internal mental state such as goals and beliefs. An alternative, sociological, viewpoint is that individual action in a social context is primarily determined by commonly understood social conventions or rules to which agents normally conform. Agents *perform roles* in order to take part in fluent social interactions.

Based on this understanding of social action we have developed a three layer architecture for implementing systems of interacting agents. The top layer consists of a set of roles which agents can adopt. The middle layer consists of a set of skills which agents require in order to perform their roles. The bottom layer consists of the basic behaviours of the agents from which skills are built. There are interactions between agents at all three levels, so sets of roles, skills and behaviours are designed to be complementary to each other.

To support this architecture computationally we have developed a concurrent production rule language called RTA [6] for representing and implementing the behaviour of agents. New behaviours can be created either by programming them explicitly or by making them emerge from interactions between existing behaviours. RTA supports the development of skilful action based on incremental extension of the agent's repertoire of behaviour and the development of roles which are built upon this foundation of skills and behaviour.

In this paper we show how the three layer agent architecture is motivated by ideas from situated action, describe the RTA language, and then show how it is used to support the development of behaviours, skills and roles.

2 Situated Action

Situated action [10] is a theory of social action[1] that is informed by both sociology and anthropology, and amounts to a critique of the generally accepted view in artificial intelligence of how action is produced. In the mainstream cognitive science and artificial intelligence traditions, action is supposed to be causally determined by explicitly represented cognitive objects such as goals, beliefs and plans. Agents act by devising and performing explicitly represented plans, and action is intelligible to the observer to the extent that the plans of the agent can be recognised. Thus action is represented by both the active agent and the observer in a way that is essentially independent of the concrete situation in which it is produced.

The alternative, situated, view is that social action is improvised from moment to moment with the (unrepresented) purpose of constructing a shared understanding of what is happening. The resulting action is interpreted by the agents in relation to the situation in which they are embedded and in the light of the social conventions which are applicable to that situation. Plans are constructed by agents as representations of sequences of action which are already in progress, and actions are regarded by agents as evidence for the existence of plans. So the actions of an agent are not determined by preconceived plans; instead, situated actions are designed to assist the construction of plans and other representations of action.

These ideas can be illustrated by using the example of a social situation already

---

1. Situated action is not claimed to be a theory of action by Suchman herself; indeed in [10] she refers to it as 'more a reformulation of the problem of purposeful action, and a research programme, than an accomplished theory'. However we have chosen to refer to it here as a theory of action in order to distinguish it from particular agent architectures such as Pengi [1] and Sonja [4].

familiar from AI work on story understanding [9]: the restaurant scenario. But rather than producing a third person understanding of action in terms of scripts etc., our purpose here is to understand how to base a *simulation* of activity in a restaurant on first person descriptions of the skills and behaviours needed by the agents to play the roles involved.

One part of a waiter's role is to guide the customer to a suitable table. This is a skill which involves a number of concurrently active behaviours: visually guided progress towards the table, and the various behaviours necessary to persuade the customer that she should follow. These behaviours can include speech acts, physical positioning, eye motion, gesture, posture, and facial expression, and are performed in order to ensure that the customer can construct a correct understanding of the situation. The waiter's actions are improvised from moment to moment according to the waiter's own understanding of the situation and making use of commonly accepted social conventions, such as the use of gestures to indicate objects (such as the table) to be attended to.

For this interaction to work fluently, the customer must also play a role: that of being a customer in a restaurant. This involves the timely deployment of the skills needed to interpret the waiter's actions in the context of the current situation and in the light of the same social conventions that the waiter is drawing on in order to choose his actions. If the roles are not complementary, for instance if the supposed customer is actually an applicant for a job, fluent interaction is liable to break down until the confusion is resolved.

From this example it can be seen that in order to simulate social action of this kind, agents must be capable of playing roles, of performing skilled action, and of behaving in controlled ways. The remainder of this paper shows how this three layer architecture of roles, skills and behaviour can be realised computationally.

3 The RTA Language

Having set the scene in the previous section, we now turn to the question of how agents playing roles in simulations of social activity can be realised computationally. A practical basis for this is the RTA programming language [6] which is described in this section. Section 4 goes on to show how behaviours, skills and roles can be realised using RTA.

RTA is derived from an earlier parallel production rule language called ABLE [11] which we developed for simulating multi-agent systems. The idea behind ABLE was to represent the behaviour of agents and their physical environment declaratively in terms of symbolic representations of behaviours and rules of behaviour. A set of

ABLE rules describing a multi-agent system can be interpreted to produce a behavioural simulation of it.

RTA is a fast, propositional version of ABLE which is specialised for controlling the behaviour of individual agents rather than for simulating entire multi-agent systems. The forms provided by RTA for representing behaviour are as follows:

- *simple behaviours*, the basic symbolic representations of behaviour. They have two states, ON and OFF, which denote the existence or otherwise of the real behaviours they represent. Typically, symbolic behaviours are causally linked, via the compiled RTA program, to real behaviours of the agent or the world.

- *licences and schemas*, forms of forward chaining production rule typically containing time annotations which sense or control the duration of behaviours. The distinction between licences and schemas is that, in the case of a schema, the right hand side behaviours which are turned ON when the left hand side is satisfied are turned OFF again when it ceases to be satisfied. Licences and schemas can be nested to arbitary depths to provide a means of enabling or disabling large sets of behaviour. Licences and schemas are used to represent rules of behaviour; they define the temporal and logical relations between causes and effects.

- *decision structures*, sets of rules implementing prioritised selection of action. The rules in a decision structure share a common condition which is used to trigger a winner-take-all race between rules whose other conditions are already satisfied. The priority of each rule is determined by its time annotation, so the rule which fires first wins the race.

- *modules*, independently compiled and dynamically loaded sets of simple behaviours, licences and schemas. These can be used to structure an agent, and provide a way of organising the sets of behaviour implementing its different skills and roles.

- *worlds*, which provide independent timelines along which modules are executed. The timeline of the outermost world in a system is normally locked to real time. The timelines and execution rates of inner worlds are controlled by behaviour in the worlds in which they are embedded. A world can execute a number of modules concurrently.

- *identify behaviours*, which connect together behaviours in the same or different modules and which hence also allow modules in the same or different worlds to communicate with each other. Identify behaviours allow changes to propagate from one module to another through what is effectively a set of common behaviours.

RTA is not intended to be a complete programming language in its own right, but relies on already implemented behaviour and computational facilities in the software system in which the RTA program is embedded. Multi-agent systems are built by providing some external means for agents controlled by RTA programs to interact with each other and with the physical world in which they are embedded.

RTA supports the situated or behaviour-based approach to agent design described in [7] and, with particular reference to RTA, in [5]. In this approach the activity of individual agents and the behaviour of the system as a whole is made to emerge from interactions between the agents. RTA has some similarities with the Behaviour Language [3] used for developing behaviour-based mobile robots.

RTA programs are compiled into representations of asynchronous digital logic circuits which are emulated within the application at runtime. The strategy of realising agents as digital logic circuits or interconnected sets of finite state machines is an established way of producing agents which are highly reactive and which can operate intelligently in real time [1, 2, 8]. Many of the characteristics of compiled RTA programs follow from their realisation as asynchronous digital logic circuits:

- *Speed:* the basic mode of computation is propagation of changes through the circuit rather than pattern matching and search. RTA executes at over 20 000 events per second on a typical workstation, corresponding to many thousands of rule firings per second.
- *Concurrency:* asynchronous digital logic circuits are totally concurrent, and so is RTA. RTA avoids many of the standard problems of concurrency because it is not based on a cooperating sequential processes model.
- *Reactivity:* changes propagate concurrently and asynchronously through the logic network from register to register. So an external event striking the program can produce a controlled response regardless of what other activity is occurring at that time (provided that the CPU is not overloaded).
- *Control of timing:* embedded delays determine the temporal relations between causes and effects. All of the actions of an RTA program are located precisely in time, relative to the timeline of an RTA world, which in the case of the outermost world is normally locked to real time.
- *Context dependence:* propagation of state changes across the circuit is influenced by the current state of the network through which the changes propagate, hence the relation between cause and effect can easily be made to be highly context dependent.
- *Scalability:* the computation is change-driven, hence the CPU time used by the simulator is determined mainly the amount of current activity in the circuit, and is not directly influenced by the overall size of the circuit.

4 Using RTA to Build Situated Action Agents

We are now in a position to relate RTA to the three layer situated action architecture introduced in section 2. In this section we show how real behaviour is represented symbolically in RTA, then show how skilful action can be built incrementally out of behaviour, and finally discuss how sets of skilful agents can be designed to perform roles in order to produce simulations of social activity.

4.1 Behaviour

The basis of programming in RTA is to represent real behaviours happening in the agent, or in the agent's world, by symbolic behaviours in the (compiled) RTA program at runtime. A symbolic behaviour has two states — ON or OFF — and these correspond to the existence or otherwise of a particular instance of real behaviour. The programmer's task is to build structure within the agent that makes the state of the symbolic behaviour correspond with the existence of the real behaviour and vice versa. Thus action is seen as the process whereby symbolic behaviours influence real behaviours, and perception is seen as the process whereby real behaviours influence symbolic behaviours. In reality, action and perception are intermixed in the normal activity of the agent.

For example, a typical agent might have walking behaviour. This is real observable behaviour. Corresponding to this is a symbolic behaviour called, say, walking(agent). The two behaviours are connected so that when walking(agent) turns ON, the agent starts walking, and when it turns OFF, it stops. Conversely, if the agent stops walking spontaneously (perhaps because it has collided with something), the symbolic walking(agent) behaviour is turned OFF in order to correspond with the real state of affairs. So the symbolic behaviour operates both as an intention to walk and as a perception that the agent actually is walking.

There are three kinds of real, observable behaviour that the RTA programmer deals with and which normally need to be represented symbolically within the RTA program:

- *natural behaviours*, which already exist in the environment of the RTA program; they may be simple physical behaviours, such as falling when not supported, or they may be behaviours implemented by the existing software and hardware of the agent, such as walking.
- *programmed behaviours*, which are composed from other available behaviours by programming them in RTA. For example, action sequences can be composed by starting each action when the previous one finishes.

- *emergent behaviours*, which arise from interactions between real behaviours and are not explicitly programmed. Controlling the conditions under which behaviours emerge can be an efficient and robust way of producing useful behaviour. However emergent behaviours by definition have no symbolic representation, and this can present a problem to the programmer who wishes to incorporate emergent behaviour into programs. This issue is discussed further in [12].

An RTA program can control the behaviour of an agent by means of rules relating its representation of the current situation to its representation of actions. If the correspondence between symbolic behaviours and real behaviours is properly maintained, this provides a way of making the real actions of the agent appropriate to its real situation.

This behaviour-based approach to the design of interacting autonomous agents is illustrated by the following example of a simulated sheepdog programmed in RTA. An example of the behaviour of this system is shown in figure 1.

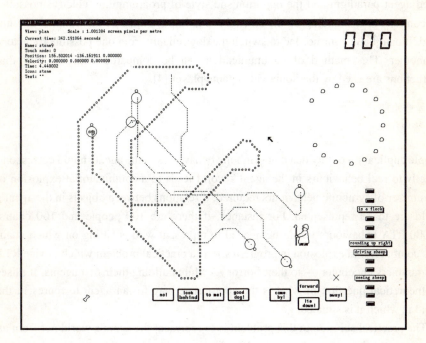

Fig. 1. An incident in the life of a simulated sheepdog.

The sheepdog drives the sheep towards the shepherd by circling round behind them first one way and then the other. The sheep react when the dog gets too close by moving away from it. The circling motion of the dog has the effect of compressing the sheep into a flock, and successive sweeps push the flock forward. The dog changes direction when it sees the shepherd in front of it, so the overall motion of the dog and the flock is towards the shepherd.

The track of the dog in figure 1, which starts and finishes on the left of the picture, shows that it has shuttled to and fro three times behind the flock with the result that three of the sheep are now close to the shepherd. (In fact one of the sheep got too close to the shepherd and reacted by turning away again.) On the dog's third pass, two of the sheep accidentally split off from the flock and headed off to the left so that the dog passed through the middle of the flock. The U-turn in the dog's track is the point at which a 'Look behind!' command was given to the dog. The dog's programmed behaviour in response to this command is to start turning. As it did so, it caught sight of the two stray sheep and started to round them up. At the point when the simulation was stopped, one of the sheep has already responded by turning back to the right, and the dog is just about to have the same effect on the other one.

This illustrates the richness of behaviour which can be achieved in the behaviour-based agent paradigm and the opportunistic style of programming which is possible; the command for rounding up the stray sheep is implemented as the minimal amount of additional behaviour needed to switch the dog reliably from one possible trajectory to another. This method of communication can be compared with the way that instructions are used by the Sonja video game player [4].

4.2 Skills

Simple application of the idea that symbolic behaviours in the agent should correspond directly to real behaviours in the agent's world leads to a combinatorial explosion in the number of symbolic behaviours required, if relations between objects in the agent's world are to be represented. For instance, if there are 100 people and 100 chairs, 10,000 RTA behaviours would be needed to represent who is sitting on which chair. This combinatorial explosion in program size is a practical problem which novice RTA programmers encounter — to their horror — while building their first agents. It raises the theoretical question of what is the appropriate way for an agent to represent the world in which it is situated.

The practical solution to this problem is to represent the agent's world not from an objective, third person viewpoint, but from a subjective, first-person viewpoint. Although objectively there may be many instances of a particular relation holding between two objects in the agent's world, from the agent's point of view most of them are of no current significance to it. Rather than attempting to maintain a complete model of the world within itself, the agent actively examines the world when it needs to obtain information about it.

Thus the agent's set of symbolic behaviours are identified not with absolute instances of behaviour, but with behaviours of the objects that are relevant to the agent's current interests. The selection of which objects are currently of interest normally changes during the activity of the agent, so a given symbolic representation of behaviour may refer to different actual instances of behaviour at different times. Part of the skilled behaviour of the agent is concerned with organising its focus of attention so that the symbolic behaviours represent the particular real behaviours which are appropriate to its current activity.

This is essentially the approach taken by Agre & Chapman [1], who advocate deictic representation as an alternative to standard logical representation. Objects are referred to in terms of a relation between the agent and the object, such as 'the object I am looking at', rather than by some absolute name such as CHAIR_54. Behaviours of the object can be represented similarly: 'this object is a chair' and 'this object is occupied'. Relations between objects can be represented: 'the other agent I am interacting with' identifies the other object in the relation, and a symbolic behaviour 'the other agent is sitting on this object' represents the real sitting behaviour as a relation between the two objects being attended to.

A simple implementation of deictic representation, as used in Pengi [1], is to maintain a set of markers within the agent which hold information about where objects of current interest are located. So markers provide a means for the agent to rapidly focus its attention on objects of interest when it needs to get information about them or to act on them. In the case of Pengi, these are *visual* markers, i.e. they locate the object within the field of view of the agent rather than specifying its position in space.

These ideas are illustrated by an RTA program we have built which plays the tetris video game. Figure 2a shows a game of tetris in progress, and figure 2b shows the structure of a tetris player based on RTA. The point of tetris is to place falling blocks in such a way that completed rows of blocks are formed. Each completed row is deleted, so a good player can prevent the heap from building upwards. Tetris was chosen because it is a simple game which requires fast reactions and a high level of skill to play well. The tetris player implemented in RTA plays in real time at a moderate level of skill.

As can be seen from figure 2b, a set of visual markers mediates between the RTA program and the 10 by 20 tetris array itself. One of these markers, indicated by an icon representing an eye, determines the position of a small window into the tetris array called the 'retina'. The other markers are used to 'remember' positions that are of use in controlling the position of the retina. For instance the small I-shaped icon marks a suitable position for placing a falling I-shaped block.

The RTA program is conceptually organised as three skills called the Scanner, the Aimer and the Handler. The Scanner moves the retina over the top of the heap. It maintains two markers, 'stack top left' and 'stack top right' (which are not visible in figure 2a), so that they always rest just above the heap on either side. These markers are where scans of the heap start. Alternate scans are started from alternate sides. The Scanner works by using information from the retina (represented as a set of symbolic behaviours) to determine how to move along the top of the heap. It is optimised to visit possible target positions in the minimum number of moves.

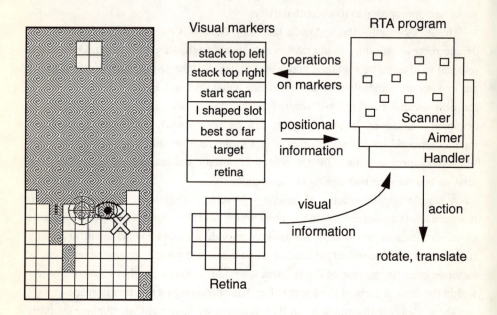

Figs. 2a and 2b. A tetris game in progress, and the structure of the RTA-based player.

The Aimer opportunistically uses the information from the retina to determine whether the current position is a possible target position and how good it is in relation to the best position seen so far. (This position is marked by a marker called 'best so far', indicated by the crosswires icon.) If the current position is better, the 'best so far' marker is moved to the current position of the retina. When the scan terminates, or runs out of time, the target position marker (indicated by the large X-shaped icon) is moved to the current retina position.

The Handler moves the retina to the target position and determines by visual inspection the most appropriate way of fitting the block in that position and then rotates and translates it accordingly. The Handler was originally developed as a user interface to tetris, allowing the user simply to point to where the block should go rather than having to manually rotate and translate it.

All three skills are implemented using RTA decision structures which determine what action to perform. The Scanner and Handler base their decisions directly on information from the retina, whereas the Aimer bases its decisions on behaviours maintained by a set of schemas which recognise particular configurations of the area of the heap viewed by the retina.

The Scanner and the Aimer operate concurrently, whereas the Handler operates after the Aimer has chosen a target position. Explicit means of communication between skills include common symbolic behaviours (used for example by the Aimer to notify the Handler that a target position has been found) and the common set of visual markers (for example the 'target' marker is used by the Aimer to tell the Handler where the target position is). The Scanner and Aimer coordinate their actions through a set of behaviours representing the position of the retina.

The tetris player, like Pengi, demonstrates that skilled activity can be produced from an agent architecture which consists essentially of a digital logic circuit coupled to its environment through a set of markers. The principal difference between the tetris player architecture and Pengi is that there is no distinction between the 'visual routines processor' and the 'central system'. Visual routines are coded as RTA programs which directly control the positions of the markers and the retina.

The approach used to developing skills in agents of this kind is similar to the way that real skills are learnt: by gradually extending the agent's repertoire of behaviour. The tetris player was built incrementally, analysing its behaviour, identifying ways of playing better, explicitly programming the required extra behaviour, and then fine-tuning the result until the anticipated higher level of skill was in fact reached. This takes more work than the standard artificial intelligence approach of developing a symbolic model of the problem domain and searching for optimal actions. But there are two advantages: the technique can be used in domains where no formal model is available, for instance in interacting with people, and it can be used for developing complementary skills in pairs (or groups) of collaborating agents. In fact both possibilities are illustrated by the tetris player. The Handler was originally developed to work in conjunction with a human aimer, and the Scanner and Aimer were subsequently developed to work in conjunction with the Handler. There is no formal specification of the interface between the different skills; they are adapted to each other's performance.

4.3 Roles

The discussion of behaviours and skills in the previous two sections was based firmly on implemented systems. Although we have also implemented simulations of scenarios which emerge from interactions between agents enacting different roles, the following discussion of roles is more speculative; it should be regarded as a description of work in progress aimed at realising synthetic actors capable of improvising scenarios, rather than as accomplished fact.

The prototypical RTA-based agent as already described consists of a compiled RTA program coupled to the world through a set of markers which relate symbolic behaviours to positions in the world at which real behaviour of current interest to the agent is occurring. Much of the activity of the agent is concerned with maintaining the correspondence between symbolic behaviours and real behaviours so that there is a symbolic representation of the agent's situation available within the RTA program controlling the agent on which action selection can be based.

This suggests how RTA-based agents can be designed to perform complementary roles. Each agent has a set of symbolic behaviours representing the role that it is currently performing, and for each role it has a number of markers which are placed on agents playing the other complementary roles. The agent's view of the situation in which it is embedded is as a set of predefined roles being enacted, rather than as a set of agents with individually motivated behaviours. That provides a predictable basis for designing roles to be complementary to each other and to support each other's performance.

If two agents are designed to work together as a pair, each agent can be designed to maintain aspects of the other agent's symbolic representation of the world as well as its own. It can do this by exhibiting behaviour which the other agent perceives and uses to update its own internal symbolic representation. This is especially useful when the two agents need to agree about what situation it is that they are in. For instance, in the restaurant scenario discussed above, much of the behaviour of the waiter is concerned with updating the 'state of mind' of the customer. In a simple simulation of this scenario, the waiter's behaviour of indicating the table would be interpreted by the customer as (say) turning ON a behaviour 'I am being guided to a table' and a placing a marker called 'my table' on the table indicated by the waiter — which is the effect that the waiter's behaviour is designed to produce.

The work of performing a particular role must be augmented by other work of determining what role to play and identifying which of the agents at hand are playing — or are capable of playing — the complementary roles. This too can be a skilled collaborative activity. The behaviour of each agent can indicate what role it is playing and also what roles the other agents are expected to perform, and hence help to maintain appropriate symbolic representations of the roles being played by the set of agents.

A set of complementary roles can be designed to be very robust with respect to variations in the behaviour of the individual agents. Thus agents can play roles with differing levels of skill. Deviations from the expected performance of roles can be handled by rules of behaviour within the agent that steer the interaction back on course. For instance, in a simulation we have built of a queue of agents waiting for service, the expected behaviour is for the agent at the head of the queue to move forward to the desk when the previous agent being served has departed. If for some reason the agent neglects to do this, the server attracts the agent's attention and beckons it forward.

Finally, although we have emphasised the cooperative aspects of agents' behaviour, this architecture also supports deception and (theatrical) acting. An agent could be programmed to display behaviour which is inconsistent with its own internal representation of the situation (its set of behaviours and markers) in order to influence the representation of its behaviour maintained by another agent. For instance, an agent could enact the behaviour of being friendly, regardless of its own internal state of mind, in order to provoke a cooperative response from another agent. So it is possible for agents to exploit the normative behaviour of other agents in order to achieve their own individual purposes. This opens the possibility of creating simulations which display interesting, dramatic action set against a background of mundane social activity.

5 Summary and Conclusion

In this paper we have introduced a three level situated action agent architecture which is centred on agents playing complementary roles to produce a simulated social situation. Sets of such roles are predefined by the programmer. The performance of a role by an agent relies on skills which are implemented by building up layers of behaviour incrementally. The required behaviours either occur naturally or else are constructed by programming or by making them emerge from interactions between behaviours.

The situation in which the agents are embedded is represented within each agent by symbolic behaviours which are maintained to correspond to instances of real behaviour in the agent's environment. The causal relation between symbolic and real behaviours is mediated by markers whose placement is also controlled by the RTA program within the agent. The RTA language provides a simple production rule notation which makes it easy to build role-playing agents having the required behaviours and skills. The asynchronous digital logic circuit representation into which RTA is compiled results in agents which react quickly and appropriately with respect to the situation in which they are embedded.

Almost all aspects of this architecture have been implemented in different demonstrators with the exception of the ideas about dynamic role allocation described in section 4.3. In further work we plan to verify the feasibility of these ideas and also to integrate the three levels of the architecture within a single simulation system.

This approach is motivated by the objective of creating characters and synthetic actors in video games and other interactive entertainment systems which have interesting, human-like behaviour and which can take part in scripted or improvised scenarios [13]. However we believe that it could also be of interest in other multi-agent domains such as modelling social behaviour, engineering distributed intelligent systems and building agents in the user interface.

Acknowledgement

Many of the ideas presented here were developed in collaboration with David Connah.

References

1. P.E. Agre and D. Chapman. 'Pengi: an Implementation of a Theory of Activity', Proc. 6th National Conference on Artificial Intelligence, Morgan Kaufmann Publishers, 1987.

2. R.A. Brooks. 'A Robust Layered Control System For A Mobile Robot', IEEE Journal of Robotics and Automation, Vol RA-2, No. 1, March 1986.

3. R.A. Brooks. 'The Behaviour Language; User's Guide', A.I. Memo 1227, MIT AI Lab, April 1990.

4. D. Chapman. 'Vision, Instruction and Action', The MIT Press, 1991.

5. D.M. Connah. 'The Design of Interacting Agents for Use in Interfaces' in Human-Machine Communication for Educational Systems Design, Maddy D. Brouwer-Janse and Thomas L. Harrington (eds.) NATO ASI Series, Series F: Computer and Systems Sciences, Vol. 129, Springer-Verlag.

6. M. Graham and P.R. Wavish. 'Simulating and Implementing Agents and Multiple Agent Systems', Proceedings 1991 European Simulation Multi-Conference, Copenhagen, June 1991.

7. P. Maes. 'Behavior-Based Artificial Intelligence', Proceedings 2nd Conference on Adaptive Behaviour, eds. Meyer, Roitblad and Wilson, MIT Press, 1993.

8. S.J. Rosenschein and L.P. Kaelbling. 'The Synthesis of Digital Machines with Provable Epistemic Properties', in 'Theoretical Aspects of Reasoning about Knowledge', ed. J.Y. Halpern, Morgan Kaufmann Publishers, 1986.

9.   R.C. Schank and R.P. Abelson. 'Scripts, plans, goals and understanding', Lawrence Erlbaum, New Jersey, 1977.

10. L.A. Suchman. 'Plans and Situated Actions: The Problem of Human-Machine Communication', Cambridge University Press, 1987.

11. P.R. Wavish and D.M. Connah. 'Representing Multi-Agent Worlds in ABLE', Philips Research Laboratories Technical Note No. 2964, October 1990.

12. P.R. Wavish. 'Exploiting Emergent Behaviour in Multi-Agent Systems', Decentralized A.I. 3, eds. Werner and Demazeau, North Holland, 1992.

13. P.R. Wavish and M. Graham. 'Applying Situated Action to Video Game Characters' Proceedings AAAI-94 workshop on Artificial Intelligence, Artificial Life and Entertainment, Seattle, August 1994.

Design of a Concurrent Agent-Oriented Language

Devindra Weerasooriya[1], Anand Rao[2], and Kotagiri Ramamohanarao[3]

[1] Dept. of Computer Science, University of Melbourne, Parkville 3052, Australia. email: dev@cs.mu.oz.au .
[2] Australian Artificial Intelligence Institute Level 6, 171 La Trobe Street Melbourne 3000, Australia. email: anand@aaii.oz.au
[3] Dept. of Computer Science, University of Melbourne, Parkville 3052, Australia. email: rao@cs.mu.oz.au

Abstract. This paper describes the concurrent agent-oriented language AgentSpeak. AgentSpeak can model distributed autonomous agents, situated in dynamic environments, that are reactive as well as proactive towards the environment. Agents are organized into agent families offering certain services to other agents. Services are realized through the execution of an associated Plan. Each agent will also be associated with a Database. Some of the services, and a portion of the database could be public; i.e. available outside the agent. Therefore it follows that the remainder of the database, the remaining services and all of the plans will be private to the agent-family. The language supports and extends concurrent object-oriented language features such as synchronous and asynchronous messages and has well developed group communication primitives.

1 Introduction

Both the Distributed Artificial Intelligence (DAI) community and the Object-Based Concurrent Programming (OBCP) community have been investigating the concept of designing active, autonomous, concurrently running entities that solve problems cooperatively [7]. While the former is primarily concerned with representational and reasoning capabilities of such autonomous entities (called agents), the latter is primarily concerned with developing language constructs that facilitate the implementation of such entities. As a result of this dichotomy a number of DAI systems have been built with little or no common language constructs; conversely, OBCP languages are found wanting in sophisticated agent models and behavioral specifications that are inherent in DAI systems.

The notion of an agent has been extensively studied within the planning and DAI communities. An agent is defined as follows [17]: An agent is an entity, situated in a changing environment that continuously receives perceptual input and, based on its internal mental state exhibits reactive or proactive behavior that potentially changes the environment in which it is situated. The complexity of the internal mental state differentiates many of the agent-oriented systems.

As noted by Wooldridge and Jennings [23] a particular type of agents, called Belief-Desire-Intention (BDI) agents, has been studied extensively [16, 17, 18, 1, 22, 15]. Logical specifications of BDI agents using multi-modal logics with both linear-time and branching-time characterisations have been studied [16]. The Procedural Reasoning System (PRS) [8] is a system that is loosely based on the logical specifications of BDI agents. Formal verification of BDI agents based on model-checking techniques have also been investigated [18]. Furthermore, PRS has been applied to a number of important practical problems, such as air traffic control [12], spacecraft systems handling [11], telecommunications management [11], and air-combat modelling [14].

Research into the specification, design, and verification of agents, (in particular BDI agents) has matured to such an extent that one can now abstract the key concepts behind agents. The primary characteristics of agents are:

- the presence of a complex internal mental state that includes beliefs, desires (or goals), plans, and intentions;
- proactive or goal-directed behavior, in addition to reactive behavior;
- communication through structured messages or speech acts;
- ability to be distributed across a wide-area network;
- capable of acting and reacting to changes in the environment in real-time [4];
- concurrent execution of plans within an agent and between agents; and
- reflective or meta-level reasoning capabilities.

Although, one can build DAI systems based on an agent-oriented BDI architecture that embodies some or all of the above concepts there are many advantages in creating language constructs that capture these features. Some of these advantages are as follows:

- It allows software engineers involved in language and complier design to find efficient implementations of language constructs without getting distracted by foundational and conceptual issues related to representation and reasoning – the primary focus of DAI researchers.
- It will allow programmers to program in a higher-level language – in terms of the goals to be achieved and the intentions that an agent is committed to – without needing to understand any particular DAI system or the foundational issues related to agents.
- It is likely to facilitate more widespread use of agent-oriented concepts, as more conventional imperative, rule-based and object-oriented languages get extended with agent-oriented language constructs.

Researchers in object-oriented programming have been extending the original notion of objects by incorporating one or more of the features that we have associated with agents. As a result, one has a proliferation of various extensions to objects that make them active, concurrent, distributed, reflective, persistent, and real-time. However, there is no single object-oriented language that encapsulates

---

[4] Real-time here refers to real-time human decision-making, which is typically of the order of a few seconds to a couple of minutes

all the above mentioned features [5]. The primary aim of our work is to abstract the essential aspects of agents and design language constructs for such abstractions. These language constructs will embody the essential aspects of agents (as well as various extensions to objects currently being attempted) within a unified framework. It will have a solid semantic and theoretical basis in the logical formalization of agents. This paper presents an initial attempt in this direction by describing the design of a concurrent agent-oriented language called AgentSpeak. AgentSpeak has sophisticated agent modeling capabilities as found in PRS and appropriate language constructs, influenced by work in OBCP [9, 10, 3]. ¡

2 AgentSpeak: Language Constructs

2.1 Agent Family

An *agent family* is analogous to a class in object-oriented languages. An instance of an agent family is called an *agent*. An agent family contains a *public* area and a *private* area. A part of the database of relations and the services offered by the agent family are public and can be accessed by other agents. The plans that are the means of providing service and the remainder of the database are treated as private to the agent family. In addition, the agent may perform certain services that are private, i.e., satisfying its own desires.

```
agent-family <agent-family-name> '{'
  public:
        database '{'<relation-name>{;<relation-name>}'}'
        services '{'<service-name>{;<service-name>}'}'
  private:
        database '{'<relation-name>{;<relation-name>}'}'
        services '{'<service-name>{;<service-name>}'}'
        plans '{'<plan-name>{;<plan-name>}'}'
'}'
```

Since the plans are not public, other agents in the environment can only request that certain services (i.e., end) be performed, but cannot specify the plans (i.e., means) by which these services are performed. This property is called the *means-end transparency* of agents.

Agent instances, also referred to as agents, are instances of the agent family, i.e., are generated from the agent-family template. A generic function called **create-agent-instance** creates an instance of an agent family. The agent is initialized with a database of relation instances. It is evident that the agent will inherit public/privacy classifications of the family to which it belongs.

```
<agent-instance> := create-agent-instance(<agent-family-name>,
                    <relation-instance>,<relation-instance>,....)
```

---

[5] If such a language were created then whether it is called an agent-oriented language or an object-oriented language is of no significance.

On the creation of an agent instance a unique system generated handle will be created to access the agent instance anywhere in the network. This unique agent handle will have the following form:

```
<agent-qual>.<agent-family-name>.<machine-host>.<creation-time>
```

This implies that no two agents of the same family, created at the same location will have the same name. The qualifier is a tag that distinguishes the handle as one relating to agents. Note that this does not in any way imply that the agents must remain forever in the machine where they were created. All subsequent migration, general-addressing and message passing will be handled by name-server-agents or binder-agents. A similar feature of accessing named processes across anywhere in the network is available in Agent PRocess Interaction Language (APRIL) [13].

2.2   Database Relations

A database definition consists of a set of relations. A relation consists of a relation name followed by a list of fields and their types. For the purposes of this paper we take these types to be the standard types (i.e., integer, real, char, and enumerated type). User defined types will not be considered. Also, if there are not too many relations they can be defined as part of the agent-family definition.

```
relation <relation-name> (<type> <field> {;<type> <field>})
```

A relation instance is a particular instantiation of the above relation. A relation instance consists of the relation name and values of the respective fields. The generic function `create-relation-instance` is used to create a relation instance.

```
<relation-instance> ::=
    create-relation-instance(<relation-name> ::
                field:<field-value>{, field:<field-value>})
```

The `create-relation-instance` function will associate with each relation instance a unique handle, that will serve to identify each relation instance within the agent-space which is generically distributed. The handle will be system generated with the following format.

```
<relation-qual>.<relation-name>.<machine-host>.<creation-time>
```

The latter could also serve as an index of the particular tuple.

Field level comparisons will be permissible within the system; the notation <relation-name>.<field> will be used to denote the value of a particular field.

Relation instances correspond to the beliefs of the Procedural Reasoning System and belief formulas of the formal logic [17]. However, unlike the logical system AgentSpeak does not allow nesting of beliefs.

2.3 Services

An agent is deemed to exist for the purpose of accomplishing its own desires and offer certain service to other agents. Services belonging to the former category are private and those belonging to the latter category are public. A service consists of a service name and a list of service statements. Each service statement is one of three types:

- a service to achieve a certain relational tuple;
- a service to query the existence of particular relational instances;
- a message telling the agent of a particular relational instance;

Services can be defined either globally or within the scope of an agent-family. The scope of the definition suggesting whether the latter is public or private.

```
<service-statement> ::= service <service-name>
                        (<service-type><relation-instance>)


<service-type> ::=achieve | query | told
```

A service could also be pre-instantiated in expectation of a deferred invocation using the `create-service-instance` generic function.

```
<service-instance> := create-service-instance(<service-name>,
                      <service-type>, <relation-instance>)
```

As in the case of agents and relations this creation will result in the generation of a unique handle having the following format.

```
<service-qual>.<service-name>.<machine-host>.<creation-time>
```

Private service instances correspond to internal goals of an agent in PRS and the goal formulas of the formal logic [17]. Public service instances correspond to messages from other agents requesting the testing or achievement of certain formulas in PRS. Unlike the formal logic, AgentSpeak does not allow arbitrary nestings of belief and goal operators.

2.4 Plans

Plans are the means of performing services. A plan is identified by its plan name. It specifies the service name and the abstract situation in which a plan might be applicable. If the plan is applicable the goal statements are performed. After the successful performance of all the goal statements the situation that is to be asserted is specified abstractly.

```
plan <plan-name> '{'
    invoke on <service-statement>
    with context <abs-situation>
    perform
        <goal-statement>{; <goal-statement>}
    finally assert <abs-situation>'}'
```

An abstract situation is a conjunction or disjunction of relations.
A goal statement can be any of the following types:

- an assignment statement;
- a while statement;
- an if-then-else statement;
- a non-deterministic or statement;
- a service statement; or
- a speech-act statement.

An abstract situation, denoted as an `abs-situation` is nothing but either a conjunction or a disjunction of relational instances.

```
<abs-situation> ::= <relation-instance>{ or <abs-situation>}
                                        { and <abs-situation>}


<goal-statement> ::= <assign-stat> | <while-stat> |
                     <if-then-else-stat> |
                     <non-deterministic-or-stat> |
                     <service-statement> |
                     <speech-act-stat>
<assign-stat>       ::= <variable> := <value>
<block>             ::= <goal-statement> {; <goal-statement>}
<while-stat>        ::= while <abs-situation> do <block>
<if-then-else-stat> ::= if <abs-situation>
                        then <block>
                        else <block>
<non-deterministic-or-stat> ::= non-deterministically do '{'
                                <block> {or <block>}'}'
```

The semantics of assignment statements, while statements, if-then-else statements and non-deterministic or statements are taken to be understood. Now we elaborate on the speech act statements.

2.5 Speech Acts

Agents communicate with each other by sending messages. By default, message passing in AgentSpeak is asynchronous. In other words, an agent can send a message whenever it likes; irrespective of the state of the receiving agent. The messages are placed in the receivers mail-box. Synchronous and mixed mode messages are also supported.

In addition to the agent-to-agent message passing as described above, the language also supports agent-to-agent-family message passing [2]. The latter will allow agents to request services on an agent-family basis, without having to specify a particular agent. In this case messages are routed through `message-spaces`, each one of which is linked to a particular agent-family. Message spaces will be scanned by the respective agent processes.

Although communication through message-spaces would be the preferred mode of implementation; either broadcasting or unicasting can also be implemented. In the case of broadcasting it will be necessary for a receive function in the receiving-agent to filter the messages that are due to them. Given the need for an agent to possess a comprehensive list of network addresses, unicasting would not be a preferred solution on account of the absence of location transparency.

We consider three different categories of speech act statements: inform, request while waiting for a reply, and request without waiting for a reply.

```
<speech-act-stat> ::= (<inform-act-stat> |
                       <request-with-wait-stat> |
                       <request-act-stat>)
```

We consider each one of these categories in detail below. Although, we have provided only a small set of basic speech acts, more complex speech acts (similar to that defined by KQML [5]) can be easily defined using this basic set.

Inform Suppose an agent is sending a message with a certain priority to another agent. If the message carries informational content, but no obligation on the part of the receiving agent to do anything we have an *inform* speech act. This type of speech act captures asynchronous communication between agents.

In the case of agent-to-agent-family communication the message is sent to an agent family. If the message is to be received by all agents that are instances of the agent family we use the `inform-all-in-family` speech-act and if the message is to be received by any one agent in the agent family we use the `inform-one-in-family` speech-act.

More formally, the syntax of the inform speech acts are as follows:

```
<inform-act-stat> ::=
   inform(<agent-instance>, <service-instance>, <priority>) |
   inform-all-in-family(<agent-family-name>,
                        <service-instance>, <priority>) |
   inform-one-in-family(<agent-family-name>,
                        <service-instance>, <priority>)
```

In the above definition `priority` is taken to be an integer number. In the case of an inform speech act the only service type allowed is `told` as it is the only service-type that does not oblige the receiving agent to act on the information.

Request with Wait Consider an agent sending a request with a certain priority to another agent and waiting for a reply to be placed in a receiving template. While the sending agent is waiting it is not performing any other activity and thus models synchronous communication between agents.

In the case of agent-to-agent-family communication the request is sent to an agent family. Depending on whether the request is for all agents in the family, or any one agent in the family we have two different speech acts.

More formally, the syntax of the request speech acts with the sending agent waiting for a reply are as follows:

```
<request-with-wait-stat> ::=
  request-with-wait(<agent-inst>, <service-inst>,
    <priority>, <receiver-relation-inst>) |
  request-with-wait-all-in-family(
    <agent-family-name>, <service-inst>, <priority>,
    <receiver-relation-inst>) |
  request-with-wait-one-in-family(
    <agent-family-name>, <service-inst>, <priority>,
    <receiver-relation-inst>)
```

The service types allowed in the above cases are **achieve** and **query**. The `<receiver-relation-inst>` is a `<relation-inst>` that is sent to the receiver.

Request with No Wait Suppose that an agent sends a request to another agent and the reply to the request is not needed by the sending agent immediately. In this situation it will be unnecessary for the sending agent to wait for a reply. In turn when the receiving agent has processed the request it will send a reply that will be placed in a specific template provided by the sending agent. When the sending agent needs the reply it can query the database for the template and get the result. With this mode of communication the receiving template will have to be instantiated with the message, as the sender will need to know this at the time of reply processing.

In the case of agent-to-agent-family communication the request is sent to an agent family. Once again, depending on whether the request is for all agents in the family or any one agent in the family we have two different speech acts:

More formally, the syntax of the request speech acts with the sending agent not waiting for a reply are as follows:

```
<request-act-stat> ::=
 request(<agent-inst>, <service-inst>,
   <priority>, <receiver-relation-inst>) |
 request-all-in-family(<agent-family-name>, <service-inst>,
   <priority>, <receiver-relation-inst>) |
 request-one-in-family(<agent-family-name>, <service-inst>,
   <priority>, <receiver-relation-inst>)
```

The service types allowed in the above cases are once again **achieve** and **query**. The `<receiver-relation-inst>` is a `<relation-inst>` that is sent to the receiver.

2.6 Messages

When a speech act is sent by an agent to another agent or agent family it is given a unique message identifier and the identity of the agent which sent the message. The message syntax is as follows:

```
<message> ::= message(<message-id>, <sending-agent-instance>,
                      <speech-act-stat>)
```

This message is then received by the agent or agent family at the other end where the message is decoded. All speech acts are processed by the receiving agent and appropriate actions are taken.

3   Operational Semantics

AgentSpeak requires that all agent families be defined at compile time. The main program creates instances of agent families by instantiating the public and private databases. Optionally, it can instantiate the agent with a public service instance which is executed as soon as the agent is created. At creation time each agent is associated with a private *mail-box*.

An agent at any point in time can be in any of the following three states: *active* – when it is executing a plan instance; *idle* – when there is no plan instance; or *waiting* – when it is waiting for a message from the external environment or waiting for a certain relation instance to become true.

When a speech act is received by an agent it is placed in the mail box. If the agent is in an *idle* state the agent becomes *active* and responds to the speech act by first selecting plans whose invocation service statement matches the service instance of the speech act.

Such plans are called *relevant plans*. The abstract situation of the context of such relevant plans is then matched with the current database relations of the agent. All relevant plans which have such a match are called *applicable plans*. The invocation bindings and the context bindings obtained during the process of finding relevant plans, and applicable plans, respectively, are used to create *plan instances*. By default [6], the system will select one of these plan instances and start performing the goal statements. Such a selected plan instance is called an *intention*. At any particular instance, there can be many intentions active. Each intention is an independent thread in itself. Thus the agent, as a whole, is multi-threaded.

Unlike object-oriented systems the plan of an agent need not be performed sequentially from the first goal statement to the last goal statement. Any service statement in the performance of the plan results in a service instance which is sent to the agent's mail box. At this stage the agent can process both external service instances or internal service instances. If there is no external service instance of a priority higher than the internal service instance, the internal service

---

[6] One mechanism to override this default is for the user to write meta-level plans for selecting the plan instances.

instance is handled by selecting the applicable plans for that service instance. This process goes on till all the goal statements of the original plan are performed or the plan fails at some stage.

When an agent performs any of the speech acts which requires waiting for a reply from another agent the plan instance and all its parents are suspended resulting in the agent moving to the *waiting* state. If there are other speech acts to be performed in the agent's mail-box, the agent becomes active and a speech act with the highest priority is chosen for processing and is processed. When the reply for a waiting plan instance is received the currently executing plan instance is suspended and the reply is processed. This allows the agent to process the highest priority service and at the same time not remain idle while it is waiting for a reply. The semantics of processing speech acts when an agent is in each of the three states is given in Table 1.

The starting state of R	Highest priority (P1) speech act (S1) in mail box
Idle	Process speech act S1.
Active with speech act S2 with priority P2	if P1 $\leq$ P2 then continue with speech act S2.
Active with speech act S2 with priority P2	if P1 $>$ P2 then suspend S1 and activate S2.
Waiting	Process speech act S1 pending reply.

Table 1. Processing Speech Acts in the Mail Box

4 Example

Having described the syntax and the operational semantics of AgentSpeak, we consider an example in a Computer Integrated Manufacturing (CIM) application [4]. An extract of the AgentSpeak-code for the CIM example is presented in this section.

A small part of the overall production process is to make bolts. A robot picks up a rivet from a stock of rivets and holds it in the lathe. The lathe produces a thread on the rivet to convert it into a bolt. The bolt is then placed into a box of finished bolts.

The robot making the bolts from rivets, called the **bolt-robot**, may be asked by the **door-robot** (frame to door fixer) to deliver the bolts. When this happens the bolt-robot suspends making bolts and delivers the stock of finished bolts to the door-robot. While the bolt-robot R2B is delivering the bolts, the door-robot is fixing the power window unit on the door frame.

Modeling this scenario requires a balance between reactive and proactive behavior. It also requires asynchronous message passing and synchronization of actions. The robots can be modeled as autonomous agents running the language AgentSpeak.

One can define three agent families; `bolt-robots` for making bolts, `lathes` for threading the rivets, and `door-robots` for making doors from the frames.

First consider the description of the `bolt-robots` agent family. The `position` of the robots, the `rivet-box` and `bolt-box` are public. These robots offer two services to the other agents, namely `make-bolts` and `deliver-bolts`. The private database consists of other relations, such as `holding` and `power-status`. The plans that are required to provide the services include `rivets-to-bolts`, `manhattan-move`, `move-straight` etc.

```
agent-family bolt-robots {
 public:
  database {position; rivet-box; bolt-box}
  services {make-bolts; deliver-bolts}
 private:
  database {holding; power-status; self-status}
  services {move; grasp-rivet; choose-lathe; mount-rivet;
           ungrasp-bolt}
  plans {rivets-to-bolts; manhattan-move; move-straight; pick;
        drop; lower-arm; grasp; raise-arm; deliver}
}
```

The `position` of a robot has two fields – its x-coordinate position, `X-pos` and its y-coordinate position, `Y-pos`. The `rivet-box` consists of the `Quantity` field which contains the number of rivets in the box, the `X-pos` and `Y-pos` fields denoting the rivet box's position. The definition of `bolt-box` is similar. The relation `holding` consists of two fields, a boolean `Value` which is `true` or `false` and the `Object` being held. The relation `power-status` consists of the field `Secs-left` that indicates the number of seconds of power left. We use the standard convention that variables start with an upper-case letter and constants start with a lower-case letter.

The services `make-bolts` and `deliver-bolts` achieve a state of the environment where the relation `bolt-box` has changed. The service `make-bolts` changes the quantity of `bolt-box`. The service `deliver-bolts` changes the position of `bolt-box`.

```
relation position (int X-pos; int Y-pos)
relation rivet-box (int Quantity; int X-pos; int Y-pos)
relation bolt-box (int Quantity; int X-pos; int Y-pos)
relation holding (boolean Value; [bolt,rivet] Object)
relation made-thread (boolean Value; identity Lathe-identity)
relation agent-status (identity Agent-instance;
                              [free, busy] Status)
relation power-status (int Secs-left)

service make-bolts (achieve bolt-box)
service deliver-bolts (achieve bolt-box)
```

Consider a plan `rivets-to-bolts` that achieves the goal of making a bolt from a rivet. It is invoked when there is a service request to `make-bolts` by achieving a state of the environment where the quantity of the bolts in the `bolt-box` is increased. Even though the plan is written with the relation name `bolt-box` and its fields at the time of invocation when a plan instance is created the values provided in the service instance will be substituted for these fields.

The context consists of a conjunction of relational instances to make sure that the robot is not holding either a bolt or a rivet. Other constraints, such as, there is at least one rivet in the rivet-box and there is sufficient power for the robot, are checked before the goal statements are to be performed.

The outer while loop ensures that the robot is making bolts until the rivet box is empty. The next statement requires the robot to move by achieving a state where its position is the same as the position of the rivet-box. The move is a private service of the agent and is not available to other agents. There may be many plans for moving and the successful performance of any of one of these plans would be sufficient for the robot to execute the next step of grasping a rivet.

Next the bolt robot sends a message to all agent instances of the lathe agent family, asking for their status. It waits for their replies and then chooses a particular lathe agent that is free. It then requests the position of that lathe agent and moves to that lathe agent. The rivet is mounted and the lathe agent is requested to make a thread on the rivet. Once the job is done the robot moves to where the bolt box is located and then drops it in the bolt box. The loop continues with the robot moving to the rivet box. This will continue until there are no more rivets. The plan for making bolts called `rivet-to-bolts` is given below.

```
plan rivets-to-bolts {
    invoke on make-bolts(achieve,
                         bolt-box(Quantity, X-pos, Y-pos))
    with context
        ((rivet-box.Quantity > 0) and
         (power-status.Secs-left > 300) and
         holding(false, bolt) and
         holding(false, rivet))
    perform
        while (rivet-box.quantity > 0) do {
            move(achieve,
                 position(rivet-box.X-pos, rivet-box.Y-pos));
            grasp-rivet(achieve, holding(true, rivet));
            status-request :=
                create-service-instance(get-lathe-status,
                                         query, self-status(Status));
            request-with-wait-all-in-family(lathe, status-request,
                            1, agent-status(Agent, Status));
            choose-lathe(query, agent-status(Lathe-inst, free));
            position-request :=
```

```
        create-service-instance(get-position,
                        query, position(X-pos, Y-pos));
        request-with-wait(Lathe-inst, position-request,
                        1, position(Lathe-x-pos, Lathe-y-pos));
        move(achieve, position(Lathe-x-pos, Lathe-y-pos));
        mount-rivet(achieve, mounted(rivet, Lathe-inst));
        thread-make-request :=
          create-service-instance(make-thread,
                        achieve, made-thread(true, Lathe-inst));
        request-with-wait(Lathe-inst, thread-make-request,
                2, made-thread);
        move(achieve, position(bolt-box.x-pos, bolt-box.y-pos));
        ungrasp-bolt(achieve, holding(false, bolt)}
   }


   }
```

In the above example the relations `self-status`, `position`, `made-thread` as well as the services `give-lathe-status`, `give-lathe-position` and `make-thread` are public for the lathe-agent. In all cases of message passing note that the agent and service instances will need to instantiate with their respective handles. The mechanics of the latter have not been explored in this paper.

While a bolt robot is performing the above plan, it is possible for the packaging robot to send a higher priority message to deliver bolts. If this happens, by default, the bolt robot will suspend its current intention (i.e., plan instance) of making bolts and instead adopt a plan to deliver bolts. Once this is done it will resume the plan of making bolts. This default can be overridden by the user writing a meta-level plan. In the above case, such a meta-level plan may allow the bolt robot to complete the current iteration of the loop (i.e., finish the bolt which it has started) and then attend to the request.

5   Comparisons and Conclusions

As discussed earlier AgentSpeak abstracts some of the useful concepts of modelling agents that have been used to build multi-agent systems in DAI. In addition, it has language constructs that enable a programmer to program in higher-levels of abstractions than normally found in conventional procedural languages and more recent concurrent object-oriented languages.

The paper draws its inspiration from several sources within the OBCP and DAI areas. The agent structure has been substantially influenced by the object structure of C++ [20] and the message passing mechanics have derived much from those of ABCL [24]. However, the notion of services and plans that can achieve these services (which make AgentSpeak pro-active in its behaviour) is absent in both C++ and ABCL; and the primitives of group communication are absent in ABCL. In fact, The group communication mechanisms were influenced by the tuple-spaces of Linda [2]. However, constructs that enable a proactive modeling of a problem within AgentSpeak, are not found in Linda.

The operational semantics of AgentSpeak is similar to the agent-oriented systems, Procedural Reasoning System (PRS) [8] and its more recent cousin the Distributed Multi-Agent Reasoning System (dMARS). However, unlike AgentSpeak, both of these are agent-oriented architectures and provide a graphical language for writing plans.

Agent-oriented languages such as AGENT0 [19] and PLACA (PLAnning Communicating Agents) [21] are similar in spirit to AgentSpeak. They differ in the definition of the mental state – AgentSpeak considers a mental state to consist of beliefs (or relations), goals (or services), plans, and intentions; AGENT0 considers a mental state to be a list of capabilities, beliefs, and intentions; PLACA has a list of plans, in addition to the components of AGENT0. AGENT0 and PLACA view agent-oriented programming (AOP) as a specialization of object-oriented programming (OOP). However, we view AOP as being an enhancement of OOP. As a result, we have notions such as agent families and agent instances, which are enhancements of the notions of classes and objects.

Our aim of designing an agent-oriented language that is high-level, easy to use, and can be formally specified, executed, and verified, is similar to the goals behind the design of Concurrent Metatem [6]. Both AgentSpeak and Concurrent Metatem have powerful communication primitives; the mental state of AgentSpeak is more complex than that of Concurrent Metatem. Agent behaviours in Concurrent Metatem are specified as temporal logic specifications that are directly executed. Plans in AgentSpeak are based on the plans of PRS that can be translated into a variant of dynamic logic specifications [17, 15]. Hence, the execution of AgentSpeak plans can be viewed as execution of dynamic logic specifications. However, we do not envisage using a theorem prover to execute the plans. The formal relation between an agent program written in AgentSpeak and the execution of corresponding dynamic logic expressions can be shown using techniques similar to that adopted elsewhere [15].

AgentSpeak is still in its design phase. Although, we have provided a foundation and a direction for the language, there are several issues that have to be resolved prior to an implementation. The inheritance mechanism for agents, explicit mechanics of handling multiple-intentions, plan abandonment or interruption, security and integrity of belief-sets within a concurrent execution environment, meta-level programming, reflective capability and mechanics of multi-agent actions being probably the more important ones among them.

The language constructs of AgentSpeak can be implemented as extensions of object-oriented languages, such as C++, or more conventional languages, such as Lisp and Prolog. An interesting possibility is to implement AgentSpeak using the process interaction capabilities of April [13].

Experience has shown that building distributed real-time applications where significant human decision-making is involved, using an agent-oriented architecture, significantly reduces development time [12, 11, 14]. Furthermore, modifications to the system can be made at a fraction of the cost and time compared to building the applications using conventional languages. The success of AgentSpeak will be determined to a large extent on how it can achieve similar reductions in development and maintenance costs, but allow programmers with little or no AI knowledge to achieve such results.

Acknowledgments The authors would like to thank Mike Georgeff for valuable comments on earlier drafts of this paper and the the anonymous reviewers for their useful suggestions. This research was supported by the Cooperative Research Center for Intelligent Decision Systems under the Australian Government's Cooperative Research Centers Program. It has also been supported by the Australian Research Council and the Department of Computer Science at the University of Melbourne.

References

1. M. E. Bratman, D. Israel, and M. E. Pollack. Plans and resource-bounded practical reasoning. *Computational Intelligence*, 4:349–355, 1988.
2. N. Carriero and D. Gelernter. Linda in context. *Communications of the ACM*, 32(4), November 1989.
3. S. A. Dobson. *An approach to Scalable Parallel Programming*. PhD thesis, Dept. of Computer Science, University of York, 1993.
4. E. Dubois, P. Du Bois, and M. Petit. O-o requirements analysis: An agent perspective. In *Lecture notes in Computer Science - 707*, pages 458–481, 1993.
5. T. Finin, J. Weber, G. Wiederhold, M. Genesereth, R. Fritzson, D. McKay, J. McGuire, R. Pelavin, S. Shapiro, and C. Beck. Specification of the kqml agent-communication language: Draft. Technical report, The DARPA Knowledge Sharing Initiative, External Interfaces Working Group, Baltimore, USA, 1993.
6. Michael Fisher. Representing and executing agent-based systems. In *Pre-proceedings of the workshop on Agent Theories, Architectures and Languages. Also appears as Lecture Notes in Computer Science (this Volume)*, Amsterdam, Netherlands, 1994. Springer Verlag.
7. L. Gasser and J. P. Briot. Object-based concurrent programming and distributed artificial intelligence. *Distributed Artificial Intellegence Theory and Practice*, 1992.
8. M. P. Georgeff and A. L. Lansky. Procedural knowledge. In *Proceedings of the IEEE Special Issue on Knowledge Representation*, volume 74, pages 1383–1398, 1986.
9. A. Goscinski. *Distributed Operating Systems - The Logical Design*. Addison Wesley, 1991.
10. C. A. R. Hoare. *Communicating Sequential Processes*. Prentice-Hall, Englewood Cliffs, NJ, 1985.
11. F. F. Ingrand, M. P. Georgeff, and A. S. Rao. An architecture for real-time reasoning and system control. *IEEE Expert*, 7(6), 1992.
12. N. Karppinen, A. Lucas, M. Ljungberg, and P. Repusseau. Artificial Intelligence in Air Traffic Flow Management. Technical Report 16, Australian Artificial Intelligence Institute, Carlton, Australia, 1991.
13. F. G. McCabe and Keith L. Clark. April – agent process interaction language. In *Pre-proceedings of the workshop on Agent Theories, Architectures and Languages*.

Also appears as Lecture Notes in Computer Science (this Volume), Amsterdam, Netherlands, 1994. Springer Verlag.

14. A. Rao, D. Morley, M. Selvestrel, and G. Murray. Representation, selection, and execution of team tactics in air combat modelling. In *Proceedings of the Australian Joint Conference on Artificial Intelligence, AI'92*, 1992.

15. A. S. Rao. Means-end plan recognition: Towards a theory of reactive recognition. In *Proceedings of the Fourth International Conference on Principles of Knowledge Representation and Reasoning (KRR-94)*, Bonn, Germany, 1994.

16. A. S. Rao and M. P. Georgeff. Asymmetry thesis and side-effect problems in linear time and branching time intention logics. In *Proceedings of the Twelfth International Joint Conference on Artificial Intelligence (IJCAI-91)*, Sydney, Australia, 1991.

17. A. S. Rao and M. P. Georgeff. An abstract architecture for rational agents. In C. Rich, W. Swartout, and B. Nebel, editors, *Proceedings of the Third International Conference on Principles of Knowledge Representation and Reasoning*. Morgan Kaufmann Publishers, San Mateo, CA, 1992.

18. A. S. Rao and M. P. Georgeff. A model-theoretic approach to the verification of situated reasoning systems. In *Proceedings of the Thirteenth International Joint Conference on Artificial Intelligence (IJCAI-93)*, Chamberey, France, 1993.

19. Y. Shoham. Agent-oriented programming. *Artificial Intelligence*, 60(1):51–92, 1993.

20. B. Stroustrup. *The C++ Programming Language*. Addison Wesley, 1993.

21. S. R. Thomas. The placa agent programming language. In *Pre-proceedings of the workshop on Agent Theories, Architectures and Languages. Also appears as Lecture Notes in Computer Science (this Volume)*, Amsterdam, Netherlands, 1994. Springer Verlag.

22. M. Wooldridge. This is myworld: The logic of an agent-oriented testbed for dai. In *Pre-proceedings of the workshop on Agent Theories, Architectures and Languages. Also appears as Lecture Notes in Computer Science (this Volume)*, Amsterdam, Netherlands, 1994. Springer Verlag.

23. M. Wooldridge and N. R. Jennings. Agent theories, architectures, and languages: A survey. In *Pre-proceedings of the workshop on Agent Theories, Architectures and Languages. Also appears as Lecture Notes in Computer Science (this Volume)*, Amsterdam, Netherlands, 1994. Springer Verlag.

24. A. Yonezawa and M. Tokoro. Modelling and programming in an object-oriented concurrent language abcl/1. In *Object-oriented Concurrent Programming*, pages 55–89. The MIT press, 1987.

Index

Springer-Verlag
and the Environment

We at Springer-Verlag firmly believe that an international science publisher has a special obligation to the environment, and our corporate policies consistently reflect this conviction.

We also expect our business partners – paper mills, printers, packaging manufacturers, etc. – to commit themselves to using environmentally friendly materials and production processes.

The paper in this book is made from low- or no-chlorine pulp and is acid free, in conformance with international standards for paper permanency.

Lecture Notes in Artificial Intelligence (LNAI)

Lecture Notes in Computer Science